S0-AHE-337

The Faces
of Televisual Media

Teaching, Violence, Selling to Children

LEA's Communication Series
Jennings Bryant/Dolf Zillmann, General Editors

For a complete listing of titles in LEA's Communication Series, contact Lawrence Erlbaum Associates, Inc. at www.erlbaum.com

The Faces of Televisual Media

Teaching, Violence, Selling to Children

Second Edition

CABRINI COLLEGE LIBRARY
610 KING OF PRUSSIA ROAD
RADNOR. PA 19087

Edited by

EDWARD L. PALMER
Davidson College

BRIAN M. YOUNG
University of Exeter

2003

LAWRENCE ERLBAUM ASSOCIATES, PUBLISHERS
Mahwah, New Jersey   London

*50774318

Copyright © 2003 by Lawrence Erlbaum Associates, Inc.
All rights reserved. No part of this book may be reproduced in any form, by photostat, microform, retrieval system, or any other means, without prior written permission of the publisher.

Lawrence Erlbaum Associates, Inc., Publishers
10 Industrial Avenue
Mahwah, NJ 07430

Cover design by Kathryn Houghtaling Lacey

Library of Congress Cataloging-in-Publication Data

The faces of televisual media : teaching, violence, selling to children / edited by Edward L. Palmer and Brian M. Young.—2nd ed.
    p. cm.
    Includes bibliographical references and index.
    ISBN 0-8058-4074-5 (cloth : alk. paper)
    ISBN 0-8058-4075-3 (pbk. : alk. paper)
    1. Television and children. 2. Television programs for children. 3. Television advertising and children 4. Violence on television 5. Television in education   I. Palmer, Edward L.   II. Young, Brian M.

HQ784.T4 F33 2003
302.3'345'083—dc21

2002040756
CIP

Books published by Lawrence Erlbaum Associates are printed on acid-free paper, and their bindings are chosen for strength and durability.

Printed in the United States of America
10   9   8   7   6   5   4   3   2   1

We are honored to dedicate this work to our children:

To Laura and Graham and in memory of Kirsten   —Brian
To Ed, Jenn, and their "significants," Ivy and Mark   —Ed

*And we dedicate this work to all of you who urged us to pursue
and to persevere. Without you and those stirrings,
'twould never have happened.*

—Brian M. Young
— Edward L. Palmer

Contents

PREFACE

In February, 1977, a young, very naïve social psychologist left Davidson, NC, on a Greyhound bus bound—eventually, as it turned out—for Boston. Having corresponded with Gerry Lesser at Harvard, the invitation had been extended to spend a spring sabbatical leave at the Center for Research in Children's Television. As a parent, this naïve traveler had observed that something significant was happening in the family room when his son watched television, but this parent knew full well that—like the tip of an iceberg—there was much about this scene he didn't fathom nor understand. The long day's ride to Harvard was the beginning of a quest for understanding.

After the usual settling-in adjustments to Boston's version of "spring," finding a place to stay, learning the way around Cambridge, and thanking God that he hadn't brought a car, there followed an intense immersion in the work and research of the Center, Gerry's seminar, Center colloquia, and correspondence with key investigators in the field. What seemed readily apparent from the very outset was the degree to which this field and research area was multi-disciplinary. The work and knowledge base sprawled broadly across areas including communication, psychology, business, economics, education, health/nutrition, advertising, and the broadcast industry itself. There seemed both a place and a need for a work that would provide synthesis, and this felt need began germinating. Aimee Dorr, then at Harvard, was quite active in the field, and generously agreed to "sign on" for the challenge of creating—as well as contributing a chapter to—the proposed work. The project had Gerry's blessing and insights—along with his comment that editing a work of this magnitude was "an hellacious undertaking." So began the formative road toward *Children and the Faces of Television: Teaching, Violence, Selling* published in 1980 by Academic Press.

The philosophy and intent of the work was to bring together leading researchers and authorities in each of the three areas—educational/instructional television, television violence, television advertising. With its focus upon children, the goal was to create a framework that would include background and history, current emphases and concerns, content, effects, political landscape, and future perspectives. This framework in each of the areas was designed to facilitate both within-area cohesion as well as comparison across the three areas.

Children and the Faces…was warmly and well-received, and across the years colleagues in the field shared comments about its reference function and its value. As the years moved on the comments continued with an expressed desire to see a current edition. Meanwhile, both Aimee and Ed had entered the relentless halls of academic administration, so the comments lingered unanswered.

Fast forward to the year 2000. Having just bailed out of administration, Ed traded the Greyhound bus for a plane and train ticket to Exeter, UK. Ed and Brian knew of each other and had e-mailed, but had never met. Our academic interests and research areas closely paralleled, and Brian graciously invited Ed to spend his sabbatical at the University of Exeter. In this small historic town in the Southwest of England we worked together and learned together—sharing thoughts and ideas, discussing research articles, exploring common interests. And as we shared, the stirrings of *Children and the Faces*…surfaced once again. We discussed the prospect of revisiting the ground that Ed covered with Aimee in 1980 and putting together a collection of articles written especially for the book that would reflect the state of the art 20 years on.

Chapter 1 outlines in some detail the nature of our formative process. You will notice similarities and changes from the original *Children and the Faces*… While we respected and kept the three-part outline structure with its synthesis and comparative features, we recognized the need to devote an opening chapter to the technological "sea change" that had occurred within the past 20 years. Television now shares time and stage with a vast array of new technologies and cyber developments at children's fingertips. What once was television is now distinctly televisual, and the realities, challenges, and issues accompanying this change truly are monumental.

As the televisual "village" has brought us instant contact with our global neighbors, we recognized the pressing need to broaden our perspective beyond national borders. This revision includes in-depth views from those central to the Western European televisual landscape as well as those knowledgeable about the shape of things present and future in underdeveloped and undeveloped countries. Increasingly, national borders will fade, and this revision takes a first step to move beyond them.

Like the televisual landscape itself, the research community has changed across the past twenty years. Some of our most respected and revered colleagues are no longer with us, and new, fresh, sharply inquiring research minds have emerged on the scene. Only six of the eighteen chapters have veterans from the original work—Valerie Crane with Milton Chen (Ch 4), Aletha Huston with June Lee (Ch 5), Gordon Berry with Joy Keiko Asamen (Ch 6), George Comstock with Erica Scharrer (Ch 9), Rowell Huesmann with Marko Skoric (Ch 11), and Charles Atkin with Stacy Smith (Ch 15). In the teams just cited as well as the remaining chapters, new authors now central to the field have come on board. We find it an exciting blend and a stimulating, informed mix.

We thank all our contributors for their superb contributions. To each and all of you, it has been a true pleasure working with you on this project and being inspired by you along the way. We thank the many who have kept us so beautifully and ably upon the editing and production path at Lawrence Erlbaum Associates. From Day One, Linda Bathgate and Karin Bates were marvelous in working with us and easing us across any bump in the road. And Sara Scudder, as our Senior Book Production Editor, has practiced her craft with unsurpassed expertise and professionalism. To the many at LEA who have worked with our project and made it happen, our sincere and heartfelt thanks.

Jennifer Rushing-Schurr and Ruth M . Bale have provided highly professional and effective subject and author indexing , respectively. We deeply appreciate their efforts and the meaningful contributions they make to the overall work.

We thank, too, our Departmental Assistant, Fern Duncan—who has jumped into the breach at critical moments and pulled us out of red-hot embers. Your gift means far more than you know.

—*Edward L. Palmer*
—*Brian M. Young*

PART

I

Setting the Stage and Context

CHAPTER

1

Introduction

Brian M. Young
University of Exeter

In 1980, *Children and the Faces of Television: Teaching, Violence, Selling* was published by Academic Press. This collection of readings was edited by Ed Palmer and Aimée Dorr, and consisted of 21 chapters equally divided among these three areas. The title and contents reflected the multifunctional nature of this communication medium that has both positive and negative aspects, giving it a potential that can both alarm and enthuse critics, academics, and practitioners. Place this medium with the concept of the child and childhood and you get a heady mix indeed that produces no end of dispute and debate. *Faces* was not on its own, of course, and there were plenty of authors, writers, and polemicists who recognized the interest from both the public and professional audience in reports and writings in this area. But the writers in the 1980 volume never fell victim to pandering to public sentiment, and the level of scholarship and the standing and reputation of the contributors was never in doubt.

EDUCATIONAL ASPECTS OF TELEVISUAL MEDIA

Tarpley

The media landscape has changed, and we need to know those things that are not the same and how they affect and influence children. In chapter 2, Todd Tarpley does just that. Using two prototypical middle-class North American families (the Smiths and the Joneses), Tarpley takes us on a tour of the main new media tech-

3

nologies, with a description of each of them and—most importantly—a look at how families cope with such innovation in radically different ways. The Smiths reflect a positive adaptation to this new media world within their household, whereas the Joneses are dysfunctional and allow the potential of the media to drive them rather than taking charge for the benefit of all the family. The Smiths and Joneses are prototypical, and most families in the developed world will see aspects of each family in their own—and we all recognize how sometimes the sheer power and range of media takes over and at other times we're in charge and utilize these technologies to empower our own families. There are two valuable lessons to be learned here. One is the significant role that families have or can have as mediators of televisual experience between the media sources and the younger members of the family—this theme is now well known in the psychology of media, but it always needs repeating. The second is the active nature of the viewing experience and how media provides a resource that can challenge us. It's up to us whether we use it well or badly and, in our role as parents and educators, it's up to us to teach and tell others how to do so.

Tarpley develops this theme by looking at six primary new technologies: digital television; video on demand, including subscription video on demand; interactive program guides; personal video recorders; interactive and enhanced TV; and the Internet. All of these are described together with the different styles of consuming these media as experienced by the Smiths and the Joneses. The technology of digital transmission means that broadcasters can offer TV with a greater number of channels or a higher-quality delivery, using (expensive) TV sets to receive the enhanced delivery. The solution to this dilemma provides an interesting trade-off for some broadcasters. However, increased upgrading expense for broadcasters also means they will be actively looking at increased revenue streams and a subsequent greater reliance on commercial support. All of these will lead to a change in the parameters of broadcasting. How do our two families cope? Opportunities can be grasped or problems created. Being selective and choosing wisely means the Smiths can choose those programs that have both perceived quality and value for the family; the Joneses, on the other hand, allow the stream to become a flood and binge on TV at the expense of family togetherness.

Video on demand can liberate families from the tyranny of schedules and empower them to control their own family time, but it can also lead to an unremitting diet of poor-quality trash TV in other families. The interactive program guide is another device that makes search more efficient and choice more informed. Families can use it in this way, or it can simply be seen as the couch potato's friend—mindless surfing is made so much easier.

The personal video recorder or PVR (TiVo is probably the best-known brand at the time of writing) is a solid-state device for storing video that makes instant playback a reality and features "smart" software that remembers preferences. Sales have been slow and the business model is changing; although it is sold currently on the basis of both initial outlay and monthly subscription, there is a good possibility that it will evolve as an intrinsic part of televisual functionality along with decoders and satellite or cable connection.[1] PVRs, like other innovations, can be used as a resource that serves the purpose of greater flexibility and freedom to organize media within the household and to customize the flow to suit the needs and wants of different members of the family, including children. Or else (and the Joneses personify this) it merely accentuates and assists viewing behavior that may be undesirable or prove to be dysfunctional, such as obsessive viewing of violent movies.

Interactive and enhanced TV implies some form of control of the screen by the viewer (as in one-click ordering, and purchasing on shopping channels), whereas enhanced TV suggests a synchrony with other similar media activity (e.g., on the Internet). The downside would be the temptation for children to gain instant gratification on shopping channels, which could lead to financial problems within the family, but the positive potential of interactivity encourages viewing as a more social experience.

Finally, we come to the Internet. Much has been written about this medium, and we look at developments and projections in other chapters. The power of the Internet to facilitate is coupled with the dangers, perceived or real, that lie within. These have been discussed extensively in the popular and academic press. The positive features include massive resources of educational material, the ability to share and communicate with like-minded others, and availability of high-quality audio-visual material at the touch of a button. On the negative side are the presence of advertising and commercial communications in an invasive, pervasive, and often unrecognized format; the easy availability of downright dangerous, often obscene, and generally highly mature information to anyone; and the ubiquitous "virtual" people in chat rooms who are not the same as real, live people in everyday social interaction. Tarpley discusses the possible future developments and the ways that different kinds of families might cope.

Moss

In chapter 3, Robin Moss writes from a U.K. perspective on the history of educational television (ETV) for instructing and educating children. He underlines at the beginning what we have heard previously from Todd Tarpley—the importance of mediators in implementing and utilizing new technologies. In this case, the mediators are teachers. Technology is there and it changes things, but in the end it's just a resource and the success and failure of ETV is a measure of the extent to which it is used well. Moss draws on a wide body of cross-cultural evidence to make his case that ETV works best in a society in which both education and television are regarded as important parts of social life. In this way, it is likely that a strong alliance among the main players—teachers, producers, children, and parents—will be

---

[1]Media innovations have a tendency to start as stand-alone devices that eventually migrate "into the box" and are sold as a bundled unit. At the moment I'm writing on a tried and trusty word processor with an external modem and a cable lead to a telephone landline. My portable PC, on the other hand, has an internal modem that could be accessed with a cell phone.

forged, and the economic and political will to fund these enterprises will be found. The history of ETV in North America is, of course, dominated by Children's Television Workshop (CTW) and the radical quality of its methods of production and delivery (with the child as teacher) together with the massive investment in preproduction research as well as evaluation and tracking are well known.

Moss provides a useful summary, but the reader will perhaps be not so familiar with his stories of ETV in Europe, Japan, and the Third World. The reconstruction of Western Europe after 1945 included some sort of state-funded or -supported public service broadcasting system. With the notable exception of Britain, this initial excitement turned to disillusionment by the 1980s, as funding evaporated and commercial interests and principles dominated the public service broadcasts. Britain, on the other hand, had a sound tradition of public service broadcasting that dated back to before World War II and was enshrined in the national institution of the BBC and a tradition of broadcasting to schools first with radio and then TV. Moss describes this history as well as the role of commercial broadcasting with the benefit of personal involvement, and it's an optimistic story with a plea to focus on media education or media literacy skills as children face new challenges of discrimination and judgment in the era of multiple channels and the Internet.

ETV in Japan was strong because the publicly funded national broadcasting service (NHK) had a TV channel devoted entirely to education since 1959 and maintained an almost universal presence in all elementary schools. Japan is more than willing to adopt new technologies, and these have penetrated schools as well. In addition, NHK has always had a strong presence in developing countries and has helped the development of ETV in the developing world. However, Moss paints a much gloomier picture of ETV in the Third World. For example, although at the end of the 1970s millions of dollars of aid had been pumped into transmission and production facilities, there was no comparable investment in reception equipment. Consequently, educational standards were largely unaffected by this investment. Cultural and political factors have unfortunately been neglected in the postcolonial period; both French and British models have been imported, however inappropriate these might be to the indigenous cultural and educational systems.

A public broadcasting system provides a great temptation to aspiring heads of states in newly emergent countries with a fragile hold on democracy. Although there are some countries where ETV has had chronic problems—and Moss does identify parts of South America as quite desperate in this respect—there are parts of the developing world that give grounds for optimism (India is a good example). Thus, what is the recipe for successful ETV in a country? The main participants should recognize the particular value of broadcasts to stimulate the imagination or open a "window on the world," use broadcasts effectively with adequate support material, and acknowledge the effects of such broadcasting with particular groups of students (e.g., those with medium and lesser abilities) and be able to nourish those effects long after viewing.

Crane and Chen

In chapter 4, Valerie Crane and Milton Chen look at the change and development in the content of children's media in the 20 years since *Children and the Faces of Television* was published. They identify four major changes: a dramatic rise in the number of programs available; a greater variety of quality programs that can contribute to educational perspectives; a wider range of providers for these programs; and a greater range of media, such as computers, the Internet, CD-ROMs and DVDs, and VCR appliances. The chapter is structured in three main sections. We are first introduced to a review of changes in the media landscape for children. The theme that emerges here is the value of choice and control. Although practically every statistic comparing the range of home media in the past 20 years shows a greater variety and penetration over time, media consumption overall doesn't seem to have been significantly affected. A useful description of what kids watch and what they visit on various home media outlets is provided, and the presence of multitasking on the Internet—the ability of children to simultaneously do homework, communicate with their friends, and in general switch rapidly from one media task to another—is noted. Crane and Chen flag the possibility that such skilled performance, driven by the demands of the medium with its multiplicity of applications, should encourage researchers to redefine theories and methods of studying children's media behavior. The main change in instructional television (ITV), as identified by Crane and Chen, is the growth and utilization of the VCR and the Internet. If this technology is available and utilized, VCR's can free teachers to plan at their own convenience.[2]

Following the review of media landscape developments, we are then introduced to some of the critical factors that have changed this face of children's media. Here, we have results from a comprehensive survey involving over 60 interviews, each about an hour long, with a wide range of people concerned with media; academics, network or programming researchers, ITV professionals, network heads, programming heads, marketers, Web experts, content experts, and policy or funding professionals were all sampled. The results can be distilled into five major groups of factors. Regulatory influences stemming from "the three-hour rule"—a by-product of the Children's Television Act of 1990—was an issue for discussion but, despite concerns over the commercial broadcast fare, much of children's programming is seen to be improving. The next question centers around issues in funding. Who's investing? Where's it coming from? This issue is discussed in detail. Ideas for development need the kind of vision by which one or more leaders can focus on the future and see the route progress and eventually succeed, and implement it by motivating others and moving forward. Children's cable networks should have an intrinsic advantage here, because they have a well-defined single focus of children, they are usually well-funded, large organizations, and the spur of revenue generation concentrates the mind wonderfully on the child audience (what Crane and Chen call "kidcentric"). The need for research in pursuit of this audience and their needs and wants is developed.

---

[2]This point is also made by Moss in chapter 3.

Finally, and in conclusion, several issues for the future are identified. The challenge of delivering cognitive content remains. Tweens (9- to 14-year-olds) are more difficult to attract and, in general, older child audiences are underserved. There is still the need to focus more on cultural diversity in programming, although there are several examples of good practice cited. The downside of advancing technology is that a wedge has been driven between those who have it and those who don't because their families can't afford computers, cable TV, and so on. To conclude, the authors discuss the danger that, with the emphasis on the benefits of economy of scale provided by the consolidation of media provision, the possible problems of advertising tie-ins (where computers, theme parks, and TV provide the child with heavy brand exposure) could be neglected.

Lee and Huston

Lee and Huston's chapter, chapter 5, looks at the research on the effectiveness of both computer and television technologies in conveying cognitive and prosocial content. Although they are both audiovisual media, the computer is generally seen as the interactive medium and television as the passive one.[3] The authors regard this as an oversimplification, stipulating that television can be and has been analyzed as an active medium in which the child selects and actively processes information. The question is when does this happen, and how it results in more or less active processing. Lee and Huston examine in some detail the factors influencing learning and understanding media content. Although aspects of these, such as formal features and processing demands, will be familiar to the student of television and children, their application to computer-based content is a valuable new approach. The characteristics of children at different developmental levels, and "mindfulness" (related to mental effort, involvement, and depth of processing), are all relevant variables that interact with the medium. Experimental evidence is presented that goes a notable distance toward providing an explanation of how these relevant variables interact. The theme of child-centeredness is underscored here, as it is in other chapters. Information processing, however, does not occur in a cognitive vacuum, and Lee and Huston emphasize the cultural, social, and contextual determinants of children's understanding. Whether a medium is perceived as educational or for entertainment will influence the attributions made and the expectations brought by the child to the learning process. The context of initial learning and the extent to which the child will transfer learning to another context will depend on the different levels of processing that takes place during learning.

Lee and Huston then look at some of the literature from the past 20 years on children's learning from television, and conclude that age-appropriate educational television does have positive effects on children's cognitive and social development. There is no simple line of influence, however, and just looking at and listening to TV is not enough. For example, adult mediation after viewing is likely to help young

---

[3]But see the descriptions of interactive media, including TV, by Todd Tarpley in chapter 2.

children understand the content and effectively extract and recognize the relevance of this material to other situations. Although we now know a lot about how children learn from educational TV, the factors that operate, and how they operate, research on the cognitive outcomes from children's use of educational software at home is less advanced. Most of this research is concentrated in two areas: programming in a school setting and recreational interactive games. Matching its significance in home settings, the role of adult mediation proves important in school as well. There also is evidence that playing video games enhances children's skills and abilities to some extent. For example, although children with poor spatial skills could benefit from video game practice, it did not enhance the spatial skills of those children who were good already. Research indicates that computer technologies have an effect on thought processes that is separate from the content of the information that these technologies transmit. Hence, the authors claim that computer technologies produce "medium effects" by changing users' mode of thought or representation. There is good evidence that frequent viewing of educational TV as a young child leads to success in high school subjects, and that this benefits boys more consistently than girls. Lee and Huston argue that early exposure to ETV initiates a learning trajectory that endures through adolescence. Interest in learning, an enthusiasm for different subjects, and an active search for learning opportunities means that the child is more likely to do well later on.

Asamen and Berry

In chapter 6, Asamen and Berry explore the multicultural worldview of children through the lens of television. Although other agents of socialization, such as family and peers, operate throughout the child's life, television and its relatives also have an important role to play. The idea that one's worldview is shaped and challenged by televisual media is fascinating, and the concept of multiculturalism—with its associated ideas of cultural diversity and pluralism—does justice to the immense variety of cultural groups and even roles that individuals occupy in the 21st century. As this "window on the world" reaches well beyond the child's family and neighborhood, the increasing globalization of media generates forces toward cultural uniformity as well as diversity. The role of culture in child development has always been recognized by many theorists, such as Vygotsky. Even Piaget, with his nativist tendencies, acknowledged the power of culture to influence the child.

The authors do make the important point that television is part of an economic process of production and consumption and, as such, the cultural worldview of the producers often does not reflect the worldview of those they depict. Too often we encounter stereotypes and misrepresentations that send out clear signals to the viewer that "you don't count" or "this is what we think you're like." As Asamen and Berry write, in the year 2000, children were still likely to see "a world overwhelmingly populated by able-bodied, single, heterosexual, White, male adults under 40." Critics might reply that people are free to portray individuals as they wish. Asamen and Berry recognize the dilemma in a society like the United

States, with freedom of expression enshrined in the First Amendment, and their argument is that we have special responsibility to the special audience that children comprise. In addition, their recommendation for multiculturalism is laid out as guidelines that should not unduly constrain the creative freedom of expression that writers, directors, and producers enjoy.

Turning to how children can learn to adopt a multicultural worldview, the authors suggest a proactive role for the parent that would involve both looking at programming that helps the child appreciate human diversity as well as limiting the child's exposure to negative stereotypes. In both cases, the parent would become more aware of ethnicity, gender, and roles in different kinds of programs and be able to discuss them with the children in the family.

There is also a useful section on research issues and questions that need to be pursued. For example, we know little about the mental processes that mediate between viewing and the emerging conception of one's social identity and the identity of others. Television, of course, is only one influence among many socialization agents, and the situation is complex.

Fisch

Shalom Fisch's chapter, chapter 7, looks at the challenges for the future of educational media, much of which is electronic. He draws on examples of existing and projected educational media projects for children to anticipate future challenges, structuring this view by looking in turn at access, design, and use. Unfortunately, one of the main challenges might prove to be simply financial, as budgets for educational media development are dwindling. Access to hardware is still a problem, and this exacerbates the already existing inequality of resources available to different privileged and disadvantaged groups. It's not just investing in "computers for all," because the economics of computer use encourage upgrades and new technological developments mean additional software as well as hardware; an initial outlay requires continual investment in resources. Access should also be taken into account when determining culturally appropriate content. We are a multicultural society (as chapter 6 so appropriately describes), and the needs, wants, and understandings of one cultural grouping are not the same as those of others. For example, simply translating into Spanish or Chinese is not enough, because cultural meanings that are implicit in the dominant English-speaking model need to be reinterpreted and tuned into the other culture as well. This will raise costs, but is essential in an educational context.

Turning to design options, the traditional features of the desktop computer are not really appropriate for children at different levels of development. There is good evidence that a trackball, for example, is a more appropriate control feature than a mouse, but the latter is the industry standard because it is the device of choice of the dominant adult user group. Fisch provides illustrative examples of good practice here, with design that is integrated within the capabilities of the child user and that can be used as extensions of naturally occurring behavior in the child's life, such as free play. Convergent media, such as interactive television, also needs to be designed appropriately. We know already that traditional broadcast TV can elicit viewer participation, so we should ask just what extra benefits interactivity brings to the televisual experience. It can provide individualized feedback that is guided by the viewer's own responses, and offer further choices with supplementary information after viewing. Fisch argues that digital TV can be augmented by other resources such as TiVo (see Tarpley's chapter) and online options, and that the challenge is to provide a medium of communication in which all these functions are integrated.

How do we get people to use these new media? Technology should fit the needs and lifestyles of the audience. Unfortunately, the history of adoption of home computers is one of early adopters setting a trend and others following in the belief that they and their children would be left behind if they didn't. Disillusionment with the product follows. We have then to ask the question of whether consumers actually *want* enhanced TV, and identify the features that are important for them. The setting in which the materials are intended to be used is an important consideration, and we must take into account the demands of the classroom when importing material that was originally designed for the home. In fact, Fisch does not just argue that some material is unsuitable for the classroom; instead, in a positive tone he calls for the educational media to be designed and tailored to the requirements of the context of use, in order to offer an experience that is geared to the advantages of classroom activities.

ENTERTAINMENT ASPECTS OF TELEVISUAL MEDIA

Murray

We now leave the section on educational aspects of the televisual experience and enter the part in which we look at TV programs themselves—the diet of television that families and children watch, which constitutes their staple fare. John Murray's chapter 8 recounts the history of violence concern and research in TV's entertainment programming. He describes the early research in this area, which started almost at the same time on both sides of the Atlantic with the classic works of Himmelweit, Oppenheim, and Vince (1958) and Schramm, Lyle, and Parker (1961). This research set the stage for concern, but it wasn't until the later 1960s that we came closer to understanding how violence on TV might influence children, with the seminal work of Bandura, Ross, and Ross (1963) and Berkowitz (1965). Social learning by watching and imitating does work with filmed content. Various commissions and review panels have reported on what was known at that time about the effects and influence of violence in the media, and Murray traces the development of this right up to Huston et al.'s (1992) report.

Next, Murray analyzes the extensive research history of about 1,000 reports in terms of the research approaches. Correlational research can of course only establish a relation, and in that sense acts as a focus for more detailed unraveling of the processes involved, but by the end of the 20th century we knew that children who watched violent TV showed up as more violent on various behavioral and attitudinal indicators, and as more fearful of a perceived "mean and dangerous world." Again, the evidence for a relationship between violent viewing and subsequent behavior is clearly present. Turning to experimental studies, since Bandura and Berkowitz we can distinguish between the structured laboratory or playroom settings and the more naturalistic locations and quasi-experiments where children and adolescents are given different treatments. There are also the quasi-experimental studies that observed the effects of television when it was introduced to a community and studies are reviewed under these headings.

So, what have we learned? Murray is quite clear about this. The three main classes of effects—aggression, desensitization, and fear—have been established, although we still don't know that much about the processes involved in their production. However, the model presented involves a cycle from viewing TV violence through a script-based set of cognitions to aggressive interpersonal responses. This then leads to more violent viewing, either via a greater identification with TV characters or through social and school-based intermediaries like decreased popularity and lowered academic achievement.

Finally, Murray's own recent research is described. This looks at neurological mediation of viewing violent and nonviolent television. There is evidence, which is provided here, that video violence viewing selectively activates the right hemisphere. This evidence, taken altogether, suggests emotional processing of video violence. This sort of research in which sophisticated brain-scanning techniques are used to confirm various models of human information processing looks like a valuable way forward in the continuing search for theories of mediation that does justice to the complexity of the relationship between viewing violence and being aggressive.

Scharrer and Comstock

In chapter 9, Scharrer and Comstock look at the content of viewing—what do children really watch? They certainly watch a lot from an early age, and their consumption of electronic media can take up 6.5 hours each day on average, with television viewing varying from 2 hours a day for 2- to 4-year-olds, peaking at 3.5 hours for 8- to 13-year-olds, and falling slightly during adolescence. Entertainment predominates, and anything with animation flags the message "for me" to many children. They tend to watch TV as an activity and choose what's on at a given viewing time rather than making appointments to view certain programs. Children will often be found viewing at prime time with other family members. Although children's programming grew dramatically from the middle of 20th century, it now has leveled out and is to be found primarily in dedicated channels such as Nickelodeon. PBS used to carry predominantly educational rather than entertainment programs because of federal funding, but this support has been cut back and consequently there is greater reliance on revenues generated from corporate sponsors. One might have thought that the Children's Television Act of 1990—with its requirement that commercial stations provide a minimum quota of educational programming—would cut into the dominance of entertainment, but Scharrer and Comstock point out there is a way out of this requirement by framing certain programs as "educational" to be in compliance with the Act.

The fictional characters that inhabit media programs are still drawn from a limited stock of stereotypes, and things have not really changed. There are more men than women, and both sexes predominantly occupy gender-stereotypic occupational roles (with a slight recent increase in the number of representations of professional working women). Commercial messages show the same gender role bias and stereotypy, and in video games males are usually aggressive and adventurous whereas female characters are used or portrayed as rewards. Scharrer and Comstock underscore the roles mentioned by Asamen and Berry in chapter 6, and describe them in more detail. There is also evidence that images of beauty are biased in favor of "hopelessly" thin women, and that this can have a deleterious influence on the body image of young women. The elderly are underrepresented, which is surprising given their financial clout and the amount of television they view. There has been much research on the representation of people of Color on TV, and there does not seem to have been much change over the years with both limited and stereotypic roles, although some affluent and successful images have appeared in the last decade or so (e.g., *The Cosby Show* is cited as promoting this trend). People with disabilities tend to occupy a limited range of predictable dramatic roles, such as "dependent and pathetic." There have been a limited number of gay portrayals on TV, although loud criticism from conservative groups has led to some of these being removed from the schedules. Entertainment and sports icons act as aspirational models for many young people and are often used to endorse products in advertising, so we should know what sort of representations are available to children. Unfortunately, there appears to be limited research on this question.

The authors then look at the behaviors that children are likely to encounter on television and, not surprisingly, violence is quite prevalent and extensively documented. Studies have tracked media content over many years. Children's programming contains more violent acts per hour than prime-time programming does, although sitcoms, a popular prime-time staple, contain a lot of verbal aggression. Results have been shown to be quite stable over the years. Cable, especially movies, and video games are particularly violent. Violent behavior can be found in most media for children, including toy commercials. On a more optimistic note, it seems that prosocial messages can be found fairly frequently on children's TV, and there is evidence that viewing this type of program can have some prosocial effect on children.

What are people seen to consume on kids' TV? People snack and "graze," often in fast-food restaurants. In prime-time TV, they drink alcohol and, surprisingly given the decline in smoking in the population, smoking in movies is present in almost 90% of popular movie rentals. TV commercials for food taken together could not be said to constitute a healthy diet, given the almost total absence of fruits and vegetables (a point explored further in Johnson and Young's chapter 16).

Families are portrayed positively on TV, and this is important as soaps, for example, are popular with young people who can identify with other kinds of families and what they do. Although conflict is frequent and problems arise, the family is highly valued and even idealized in television content. Sexual intimacy, although absent from programs for very young children, does appear in programs that teenagers watch; however, there is more talk about sex than sex itself. Programs that emphasize the risks or responsibilities associated with sexual behavior are rare.

Finally, the authors sum up their chapter using several overarching themes. White males have a greater repertoire of roles and appear more frequently in most media used by young people. As well as gender, race, and ethnicity, social class has a similar privilege of selective occurrence. Conflict and risk are endemic to media, and this is recognized by young people as characteristic of the narrative nature of this kind of communication. The resolution of conflict is rapid and effective, and solutions are provided in which "good" frequently prevails. Families are often idealized but certainly valued. On the other hand, many of the themes in televisual media content involve threats to health in many areas, although these threats are rarely recognized within the depiction. Alcohol consumption, pregnancy and sexually transmitted disease, rape myths, sexual aggression, violence, certain styles of food consumption, and socially desirable visions of beauty and body are all there without accompanying messages that, as the authors note, " would convey their ability to become a threat to the physical health and psychological well-being of young people." And it's these last few lines that conclude Scharrer and Comstock's description of "what's on." It is comprehensive and exhaustive, and its length does justice to the end result, which provides an all-inclusive portrayal of media content delivered to our children in the 21st century.

Bryant and Bryant

Bryant and Bryant's chapter 10 looks at the effects of entertainment televisual media on children. Entertainment-based programs are the dominant format of children's TV nowadays. Why? Because entertainment can guarantee profitability by selling airtime to advertisers. Consequently, entertainment is not an end in itself but merely a vehicle for advertising. The quality of the entertainment provided is largely driven by the desire to attract audiences. If the audience consists of children, they have to be attracted and held to the screen. Children, especially young children, are passive victims of their senses and will be grabbed and sustained by the emotional content of what they see. This dominance of intense affective responses will define their enjoyment, because they don't have the cognitive maturity to make a considered evaluation of a TV program. In addition, the worldview that children adopt (see also Asamen & Berry, chapter 6) is based on the formative years of early childhood. The importance of delineating these media-based experiences of early childhood emerges very clearly in the account provided by these authors, who then utilize a model provided by van Evra (1998) to inform our view of how media influences children. It is helpful to the reader to see these accounts of the variables operative between viewing and its consequences (Murray provides another version in chapter 9).

Bryant and Bryant examine both the detrimental and the beneficial effects of viewing. On the detrimental side, it has been claimed that watching television can effectively reduce the time spent on other activities. They review the evidence, and add a cautionary note to the effect that "displacement" itself presumes that one activity is shelved at the expense of another, and that this may not be the case when watching TV accompanies other activities; if displacement occurs, it's often a case of shunting out other time-filling activities; and there is a positive displacement effect by which children may view enriching activities such as ETV. Another effect would be the encouragement of stereotypes, a point discussed in the previous chapter. Fear reactions, because of the intensity of experience that children have and their relative inability to control emotions, means that fear-producing programs need to be considered carefully.

The exposure children might have to explicit sexual material, with the increasing availability of the Internet, is another detrimental effect that the authors of this chapter place on their list. The possible attitudinal influences are undermining values of marriage and stable family life; consolidation of representations of women as objects, who exist to serve men; and cultivation of unsympathetic and callous attitudes toward rape.

Next, the question of violence and the consequences of viewing what is now accepted as a remarkable number of violent episodes are revisited, and the discussion consolidates what Scharrer and Comstock have to say. Theories of transmission from social learning through arousal to desensitization and catharsis are identified, and this section should be taken together with the previous chapter as providing a state-of-the-art account.

Entertainment media is not all bad, however, and Bryant and Bryant identify some beneficial effects that have been relatively neglected compared with the research that has gone into the negative effects of watching. Apart from the well-known prosocial effects of mixing entertainment with education, as in *Sesame Street* and others of that genre, media effects in general (and entertainment is no exception) can increase verbalization in place of aggression, increase creativity and imagination, as well as exert other positive influences on prosocial behavior. Entertainment can provide us with various gratifications such as escape, play opportunities, and stimulation when we are bored, and can be a calming influence when we are stressed. Let's not forget that fun can be good for kids!

Huesmann and Skoric

Chapter 11, by Huesmann and Skoric, looks at the argument for regulating media violence to children. They start in 1972, when the then-Surgeon General sent out very clear signals that the evidence on the causal relationship between televised violence and antisocial behavior had clearly been established, and that action should be taken. And yet, 30 years later, very little has been done either to reduce or to regulate media violence. The authors briefly review the evidence and also present the theories that provide a link between viewing and behaving, although acknowledging the multifactorial nature of the relationship. Severe aggressive and violent behavior seldom occurs unless various predisposing and precipitating factors (e.g., poor childrearing, frustration, and provocation, to name only a few) converge. But we know that exposure to media violence is one such long-term predisposing and short-term precipitating factor. It is refreshing indeed to hear such a clear and unequivocal statement. And is there less violence on TV? No. Citing a recent study, which looks like the most comprehensive ever, the authors find that TV programming targeted at children is more likely to feature violence, and that violent characters in such shows are more likely to receive rewards or praise.

Having made their case that something needs to be done, Huesmann and Skoric identify several important issues that should guide regulation. First, exposure to violence in childhood is formative in that early cognitions are formed and will crystalize and remain there as an internal source of influence in later life; thus, effects are long-lasting. Regulating children's exposure is therefore much more important than regulating adults' exposure. Second, although media violence affects all children to some extent, the presence of other factors, precipitating or predisposing, means that some children are more at risk than others. Children who are unpopular, who watch a lot of TV, who are less intelligent, who are from low socioeconomic-status families, and who watch without parental supervision are more at risk from each of these factors. Thus far, the media have only been described as differing in the extent to which they contain violent episodes. Which particular characteristics will increase risk? The answers from research are: the child identifying with the perpetrator rather than the victim; violence being portrayed as justified; violence being rewarded; and a plot perceived as realistic ("telling about life like it really is"). All of these taken individually constitute a recipe for violent media.

There is a history of regulation of violence in media content, and Huesmann and Skoric take us through it, from the first attempts to introduce movie ratings to today's V-chip technology. The story is predictable, however, with industry attempting, often successfully, to water down and neutralize moves for regulation in the face of compelling evidence. There is also some evidence that "being tough on media violence" is used as a political football by legislators in an opportunistic way when high office beckons, rather than a systematic evaluation of scientific and social policy arguments for and against regulation.

The authors conclude by discussing, in some detail, possible "loci for interventions and regulation." Artists and producers seem more concerned about offending adult viewers, and indeed some believe that violence attracts young audiences. Not that artists are socially inactive, but their repertoire of concerns (e.g., tobacco and landmines) doesn't appear to include violence media shown to kids. Commercial sponsors are a powerful group who are sensitive to public opinion and their brand image, and there is some evidence that violence in shows reduces audiences' memory for commercial messages. Public advocacy groups and parents themselves are also considered and evaluated as groups with influence. Schools have always been seen as a possible locus of regulation, and both media training programs and social cognitive interventions are considered in this regard, although the authors see problems with both approaches. Finally, there are two major obstacles that are endemic to the whole sociopolitical structure of the nation: the economics of violence and constitutional issues concerning regulation. Both of these are examined extensively, and the reader is left with a better understanding of the complexity of intervention as well as an understanding of the research evidence.

Vorderer and Ritterfeld

What's in the future for entertainment media and children? Vorderer and Ritterfeld look at this issue in chapter 12. They too, like Bryant and Bryant, recognize the dominance of the entertainment medium in children's programming. Children's tastes in entertainment differ by age and gender in expected directions; for example, boys prefer more action and violence than girls do, and girls are more interested in programs depicting human relationships. But once these differences are acknowledged, there is a consistent set of preferences, irrespective of cultural background—especially what children see as entertaining. This finding (and cross-cultural research concerning it is cited) is especially fortuitous to producers, who can anticipate a global market with high income from sales of commercial time. These market forces drive a need to find younger, international audiences. Now, parents and teachers may want something more. For example, many products for children (e.g., toys and books) are labeled as age-appropriate for different age bands, whereas the time of broadcast signals the appropriateness of the program. Producers may want to avoid demanding too little of children to avoid the perils of boredom and changing programs and instead provide an experience that is totally consuming, whereas parents want to avoid demanding too much as they are concerned about emotionally or cognitively overloading the child with unsuitable material.

The authors make the interesting distinction between entertainment as a genre or category of media output and the experience of "being entertained" by which the receivers of media will use that resource in different ways. Hence, the news can be experienced as entertainment and soaps as information.[4] The authors remind us by their critique that a variety of experiences may be subsumed under the heading called "entertainment," and that, for example, entertainment and play are closely related. They develop their argument with reference to the qualities of the entertainment experience with one central focus—getting inside the televisual reality, whether we describe the process as immersion, absorption, or engagement. Having established their theoretical position on the nature of entertainment, they move to the child's experience. Their model involves both the formal features of the program (e.g., special effects and music) that arouse attention as well as its narrative features that encourage an investment in "entertainment." The social psychological function is also important, in that one is referencing one's own behaviors relative to both personal and social identities, real and anticipated. All of these are relevant for children.

Vorderer and Ritterfeld present us with many thought-provoking insights when discussing new technologies. For example, the pleasure of not knowing how things

---

[4]I see this interpretation based on reception theory as a more European way of approaching media theory, but as that may not do justice to the wide range of different models in North America it must be speculative and relegated to a footnote.

might end and anticipating what might happen is essential to suspense, which is an ingredient of entertainment. Using interactive media, on the other hand, means empowerment by the user but a loss of the essential element of being at the mercy of the narrative! It is these insights and others in this chapter that, for me, provide much food for thought and the possibility of a fresh research agenda for the new era of interactive media.

ADVERTISING AND TELEVISUAL MEDIA

Now that we've reached the last section, on the commercial and selling nature of the televisual media, I must declare a certain interest. I've been involved in this area for some years now, and have contributed to one chapter here and written another. I feel the need to separate description from comment, because my main role in this introductory chapter is to act as a go-between for you, the reader, and the writer of each chapter. I hope to summarize accurately and succinctly on your behalf. If I do pass comment in this section, I make sure you know when I start and when I finish and what's mine and what's a summary of the other authors' contributions. These chapters can be read separately, as each of them covers a separate aspect of the issue such as history, effects, policy, and so on. Thus, in that sense, they stand alone. They were written independently, based on preliminary outlines submitted to us, so we were able to see if there was any overlap. It is also important to read them together, because as a group they provide a vision of the sort of concerns and consensus about the challenges that face us today as certain themes emerge and reemerge.

Johnson and Young

The first chapter in this section, chapter 13, was written by Melissa Johnson and myself. The order of priority and contribution is just that, and not the linguistic accident that Melissa's surname began with *J* and mine with *Y*! We wanted to look at the history of advertising to children, bring it up to date, and identify some of the major concerns that have emerged in this area. It is perhaps inevitable that the presence of well-crafted commercial communications in the home, coming from outside into that refuge from the world of commerce and marketing and designed to seduce and sell, would cause concern to parents. We spell out the history of the affair among advertising, concerned parents, and the various parties, unraveling the complex tangle of change and response to change. The story is driven by the economic needs of advertising and the relationship among profit, responsibility, and governmental response to expressed concerns by parental groups.

The absent guest, unfortunately, is the child who is used as a political football in much of this and, as in other areas of children and media interaction, the political decisions are as much if not more influenced by the desire for political success and reputation. They are rarely based on evidence from research on children and their understanding and use of advertising. One of the pivotal arguments used by Action for Children's Television (ACT) in the 1970s was that, because children do not understand advertising, advertising to children should be removed from children's programming. The questions of "when children actually do understand advertising" and "how much do they understand at different ages" became important. The advertisers and their representatives were unwilling to effectively ban such advertising, and a self-regulatory resolution emerged in which advertising to children was limited and certain techniques were excluded. Food advertising—cereal advertising in particular—to children came under fire in the 1970s for promoting the wrong kinds of food to children when they needed a different sort of diet to that portrayed on TV. Indeed, this is another theme that still resonates today. By the mid-1970s, "bumpers" that effectively separated advertising spots from the rest of the program were mandatory, and that went some way to assisting the young child who has difficulty identifying ads as being different from programs. In 1978, the Federal Trade Commission (FTC)—supported by a research report—proposed a ban on all advertising to children, but this proposal was violently opposed by commercial interests. The history since that time has been one of swings toward deregulation and a tendency to swing back slightly toward imposing greater regulation and, as mentioned earlier, the regulatory balance seems to reflect the political ethos prevalent at the time.

Johnson and I describe and discuss other concerns that have emerged in the last 30 years or so that are still on the agenda in many cases; for example, gender stereotyping in commercials, and children putting pressure on parents for advertised goods and services. We then go on a tour of some of the empirical evidence concerning the child's understanding of aspects of advertising, together with a guide to what developmental theorists have said about the various issues (there is more on this in subsequent chapters in this section). At the end, we revisit the question of food advertising, and address some more recent issues such as the emergence of advertising in schools and the rise of Internet use and associated problems, including advertising to children.

Kunkel and McIlrath

Kunkel and McIrath's chapter 14 looks at the content in advertising messages to children. The evidence that very young children are exposed to advertising messages and commercial matter from about 1 or 2 years of age by watching TV is not in doubt, and we know that young children have a limited ability to understand commercial messages. Estimations of the number of ads that children are exposed to have grown since the 1970s, and now the average viewer (covering adults as well as children) is exposed to about 60,000 such messages each year. The history of attempts to regulate the amount of TV advertising to children was reviewed in the previous chapter and, since the enactment of Children's Television Act of 1990, between 10.5 minutes an hour during weekend programs and 12 minutes an hour during weekday shows has been the maximum permitted. The authors have detected a worrying trend in which the format of TV commercials stylistically emulates the format of public service announcements (PSAs) occurring during advertising breaks.

   Content analyses of the product categories advertised on TV to children since 1980 show little change, and the categories of toys, cereals, candies, and fast-food restaurants are still relevant today. This pattern is annually affected by bursts of pre-Christmas toy marketing, which temporarily displaces candy/snacks and cereals. The preponderance of foods—which, taken together, would not constitute a healthy diet—has already been noted in chapter 13 and is again mentioned here. The persuasive themes and appeals used in advertising to children associate the brand with fun and happiness. Sensory characteristics such as taste/flavor/smell are used to sell food products to children.

   Kunkel and McIrath also look at gender and ethnic representation in advertising, and cite recent research suggesting that boys and girls are equally represented and that there is also a change in the direction of equality of ethnic representation. Self-regulation of the advertising industry is through the Children's Advertising Review Unit (CARU) and their guidelines are intended to "encourage truthful and accurate advertising sensitive to the special nature of children." In a study co-authored by Kunkel and Gantz (1993), just 4% of 10,000 commercials directed at children were found to present violations of CARU standards. Kunkel and McIlrath describe prohibited techniques used in advertising to children, such as host selling and the program-length commercial, and discuss the requirement for ads to be seen as separate from programs via the use of "bumpers."

   Looking into the future, they anticipate issues on the horizon such as advertising in schools and Internet advertising. In the latter, blurring of the boundaries between commercial and noncommercial content is fast becoming common, and the Web site simply becomes a "branded environment." They conclude by emphasizing the important role of future research in monitoring new sites for commercial messages to children—sites made possible with new technology.

Smith and Atkin

In chapter 15, Smith and Atkin review the empirical research on the impact of advertising on children. They have structured their chapter into four sections. Three are general: the child's understanding of advertising, intended influences, and unintended consequences. The final section focuses on one issue—alcohol advertising and its effect on older children and youth. The child's ability to distinguish commercials from programs would be the first stage in understanding that the two are different, and empirical evidence depends on the methodology used. Interview techniques produce later-age norms than other methods do. The conclusion is that the majority of 4- to 5-year-olds are capable of making the distinction. The next question is concerned with the child's understanding of persuasive intent. It would appear that several abilities are required before this is achieved, including, for example, the ability to take or adopt the role of the other, because this would then predict that children could see that advertisements are communications created from the views and values of "the advertiser." The understanding is certainly age related, although the norms published are again sensitive to methodologies used. There appears to be a consensus that at the age of 7 or 8 years an understanding of selling intent emerges, and children as young as age 5 or 6 years think that "some information" is provided. Certain parts of the message, however—such as disclaimers (e.g., "part of a balanced breakfast" for cereal products)—are used in advertising to children but not all children understand what is being said.

Turning now to intended effects, the authors provide evidence that effective recognition of a range of brand logos (both adult- and child-directed) can occur in 3- to 6-year-olds, and that older children are able to recall brand names after one exposure. Interestingly, the evidence from adults that commercials embedded in violent programs are less well remembered (because of the impairment effect of negative mood states) has also been found in boys. Exposure to advertising can certainly influence a range of affective and motivational states, such as preference, liking, and desire for advertised goods and services in the short term. Long-term effects are more difficult to assess, but self-report measures provide indirect evidence that TV commercials to children are working. If wants are induced by advertising, then do children ask parents for these products? There is research on product purchase requests by children using a variety of methodologies, and according to Smith and Atkin the results are quite consistent. Heavy viewers of television advertising make more purchase influence attempts than light viewers do, but there are also age and gender differences. Older children are more discriminating in their requests, and boys are more forceful and determined in their requests. Results from research on the role advertising plays in consumption patterns shows no consensus on short-term effects (and more research is needed here), but self-report data show a correlation between viewing ads and consumption. Many food promotions to children offer premiums as a persuasive appeal to buy that brand and, although self-report data from mothers and children seem to suggest that's the reason the brand was bought, within-supermarket observations show that less than 10% of children identify the premium as the primary reason for desiring that brand. There is evidence that another technique, celebrity endorsement, increases preference for products.

Smith and Atkin then turn to the unintended effects of advertising. To summarize their conclusions: There is evidence that purchase requests can result in parent–child conflict, but the proportions are below 50% and seem to center around a fourth or a fifth of all respondents. A similar percentage of children report disappointment in the wake of denied purchase requests, and fewer children report experiencing unhappiness. The authors also address the question of the role of food advertising in children's eating habits and dietary beliefs and preferences. There is evidence for relationships between watching TV and eating habits, food choice, and caloric intake. TV exposure may contribute to obesity by reducing energy expenditure and increasing food consumption, with the amount of TV viewed by nonobese children being the most powerful predictor of risk for the development of obesity in adolescence. My own opinion would be that, given the complex multifactorial models needed to account for the role of advertising in children's food-related behaviors and the increase in recent research and recent public concern in this area, there is an urgent need for more research and analyses in the field. Does watching

TV advertising contribute to children developing materialistic attitudes and values? This is another issue that needs further investigation, and there is little research here. Another issue (which emerges in other parts of media) is whether exposure to attractive and thin actors/role models contributes to negative self-perceptions, especially with young adolescent women. Smith and Atkin cite a valuable finding: The motive consumers have in evaluating models in ads will affect their own feelings of self-worth. Thus, an aspirational social comparison ("I can be like that") will enhance self-worth, whereas self-evaluative strategies ("she's much prettier than I am") will have a more negative effect.

Finally, Smith and Atkin provide us with a sustained account of research on alcohol advertising on older children and adolescents. They conclude that not only exposure to alcohol advertising contributes to teen drinking in society, but also that parental mediation and teaching critical viewing may help to lessen negative effects of such advertising.

Young

My own chapter is an attempt to locate the issue of children and advertising in the context of issues and politics surrounding the research. I'm tempted to say "clouding" the research, because there is no getting away from the fact that claims and counterclaims are made, and that evidence is used as a resource by both sides in the debate. My first attempt to make sense of this issue almost 20 years ago was to look at the myths and metaphors that were used and implied in popular and polemical writing on the subject, and it soon became clear that there were two kinds of young people involved in the debate. They were very different. One was sweet, innocent, and in need of protection—the stuff of our dreams for the future. This was the child. The other was existential and exciting, streetwise and savvy, energetic and alive. These people were also our dreams, but for the older ones among us they were what we were and what we also saw in our children and grandchildren. This was the kid. Both are images of children and childhood—real, small, younger people are both. I came up with a relationship that I called "the advertiser as seducer and the child as innocent," which, I believe, has certainly provided if not a lens on which to focus research then at least a fog or mist through which we perceive heroes and villains. There is another world, of course—the brightly lit world of kids with needs and wants and desires who are capable and competent and young consumers. Advertisers can empower them and offer them freedom and choice. This is also a myth, and it would be dangerous to adopt either. Hence, the truth is in between, and as scientists and practitioners all the contributors to this book have given evidence that we have the responsibility to sift through, evaluate, and make up our own minds.

Calvert

The last chapter in this section is chapter 17, by Sandra Calvert, on the future ways of selling to children. She immediately identifies one of the strengths of new technology, which is the ability to deal with larger and larger amounts of data using smaller and smaller appliances. But here lies a danger, in that the act of purchase and indeed all these acts of consumption can constitute a dossier of information that allows businesses to tailor advertising practices to the individual, not just the group. Young children—who, as we've seen from previous chapters, don't understand the intent behind advertising until about 8 years of age—are at risk here. Calvert looks first at "children as a market." Apart from the traditional role that television plays as a vehicle for advertising, the Internet is identified as an important means of directing advertisements toward children. As we know from Kunkel and McIlrath's chapter, the same four categories of product have always been advertised on TV to children, but there is now the possibility that the less-regulated environment of the Internet will lead to more types of products being directed at children, even though these can't be advertised to minors on TV. Selling to kids using interactive media involves a branding strategy in which the child's favorite character is placed within a "branded environment" (see, again, Kunkel & McIrath, chap. 14). Although parental permission is required, the adolescent and older child can start up digital wallets at certain sites and accumulate capital (without parents' knowledge) by bartering or "selling" information about oneself and one's family. Cell phone technology and DTV technologies will all encourage convergence, in which previously distinct media platforms merge together (see Tarpley, chap. 2).

Another issue that's on the horizon is generated partly as a response to the new TiVo technology that has already been referred to by Tarpley. Spot ads can be easily zapped and marketers will increasingly want to pay to have their product appear within the boundaries of the program rather than as a separate entity. The development of technology that involves one-to-one relationships between advertiser and customer becomes easier, as convergent media can easily track your route as you leave electronic footprints. Such relationship marketing can be used with children. Other tricks of the Internet trade that can confuse and entrap kids are spamming, by which e-mails are sent to purchased e-mail lists of users; "mousetrapping," when one can't leave a site as new windows are launched at each click to depart; and innocuous or misleading URLs that actually are sexually explicit sites. The picture that Calvert paints of the new technology makes TV look positively benign.

Calvert then guides us through the future child's use of this media at different ages. Finally, there is a section on social policy directions that raises up flags concerning challenges that new technologies pose. The separation principle, and the debate about "bumpers" already mentioned, will be seriously challenged by branded environments. Convergence means that all media is as one, and legislation that is specific to TV, for example, becomes irrelevant from the viewpoint of those of us who are concerned about children, because the child in the convergent media age can just as easily slip from one platform and use another, like the Internet. Host selling will reach dizzy new heights, with intelligent humanlike characters developed to create personal relationships with individual children and adolescents, cultivating familiarity, affection, and trust. Legislative response has focused on privacy issues with children, but as yet little has been done to make children and their parents aware of, for example, cookies that enable commercial targeting to get very personal.

REALITIES AND CHALLENGES IN THE TELEVISUAL LANDSCAPE

Palmer

I hope that this chapter has whetted your appetite and given you information on what to expect in this volume. Perhaps you see chapter 17 as providing a utopian or maybe a dystopian vision of the future of media. However, that media future will be there arriving soon, and it's up to all of us to be informed about and aware of what to expect for this generation and future generations of children.

The last chapter in this book is written by my friend and colleague, Ed Palmer. My own first chapter was written as an extended summary of what to expect and sticks closely to the format of the extended preçis in order to whet the reader's appetite, and he or she can consume more detailed information and consider arguments in the chapters to come. Ed's approach assumes that the reader has already digested most of the previous content and now wants a synoptic summary that draws together the material in the book and presents it thematically.

The themes that emerge are structured around the three faces of television media. Televisual media has an informational and educational face. Ed Palmer begins by developing the realities of this, including new changes in programming, the presence of corporate conglomerates and commercial influence in the area, group perceptions and the role models, and developing effects. These realities naturally lead to a set of challenges that face us. These are described fully. So, for example, the presence of new technologies suggests a new raft of regulatory issues, such as regulation of access to Internet sites. Finally, what is the research agenda in this area? These are identified for the reader under headings such as technologically based and culturally based innovations.

The realities of the second face of entertainment are then described and many of them are shared with the previous informational and educational aspect. But not all of these change, and the author notes that the staple of program content and plot continues to be the juxtaposition of good and evil. Child-based effects of entertainment are discussed as is the basic need for the child to be entertained and how institutional responses are mediated by children. Challenges and research questions are also elaborated in this section.

Finally, what are the themes that emerge when we look at the changing realities of advertising and commercial intervention? There is still discussion and debate on this issue as there was in the 1980s and research, public concerns, and political intervention rarely, if ever, coincide. The "shop window" that TV advertising to children presents has also not changed much, and the categories of goods and services that are promoted are much the same. Gender frequency of characters in commercials has changed, however. New concerns have emerged, such as the ubiquitous presence of advertising ins schools. Challenges are there and research is still needed.

The child market is growing and marketing techniques become ever more sophisticated using new technologies. The extent to which children understand and cope with such an onslaught means that research will always be needed.

REFERENCES

Bandura, A., Ross, D., & Ross, S. A. (1963). Imitation of film-mediated aggressive models. *Journal of Abnormal and Social Psychology, 66*(1), 3–11.

Berkowitz, L. (1965). Some aspects of observed aggression. *Journal of Personality and Social Psychology, 2,* 359–365.

Himmelweit, H. T., Oppenheim, A. N., & Vince, P. (1958). *Television and the child: An empirical study of the effects of television on the young.* London: Oxford University Press.

Huston, A. C., Donnerstein, E., Fairchild, H., Feshbach, N. D., Katz, P. A., Murray, J. P., Rubinstein, E. A., Wilcox, B., & Zuckerman, D. (1992). *Big world, small screen: The role of television in American society.* Lincoln: University of Nebraska Press.

Kunkel, D., & Gantz, W. (1993). Assessing compliance with industry self-regulation of television advertising to children. *Journal of Applied Communication Research, 21,* 148–162.

Schramm, W. L., Lyle, J., & Parker, E. (1961). *Television in the lives of our children.* Stanford, CA: Stanford University Press.

van Evra, J. (1998). *Television and child development* (2nd ed.). Mahwah, NJ: Lawrence Erlbaum Associates.

2

The Future of Televisual Media

Todd Tarpley
Vice President
Interactive Media
Bravo Network

THE SMITHS AND THE JONESES

The Smiths and the Joneses are two hypothetical families living in upper-middle-class, suburban America. They own wide-screen television sets with superlative picture and sound quality. They receive 175 television channels, plus have access to over 500 additional individual movies and programs that are available 24 hours a day at the touch of a button. They can pause and rewind any program, even live programs, and they can skip past commercials. Without leaving the sofa, they can send and receive e-mail, order pizza, and play along with their favorite game show. They have instant access to the Internet via a high-speed cable modem, from which they can find information about almost any topic or person, see pictures of almost any subject, and converse with almost anyone, almost anywhere in the world.

Throughout this chapter, these two hypothetical families will serve to illustrate—often at opposite extremes—how the coming abundance of new media options may have very different impacts on the way people consume media and interact with others. It may also impact the cognitive, social, emotional, and physical development of children in both positive and negative ways.

The primary new technologies are:

- Digital television (more channels, higher quality).

- Video on demand (VOD) and subscription video on demand (SVOD).
- Interactive program guides (IPGs).
- Personal video recorders (PVRs).
- Interactive and enhanced TV.
- The Internet.

An overview of each new technology and its implications for children follows.

DIGITAL TELEVISION

Digital television is a new transmission standard that uses the broadcast spectrum more efficiently. It offers better image and sound quality, more channels (four channels in the same amount of spectrum currently used by a single channel), and additional text data.

All commercial broadcast stations in the United States were required by law to migrate to digital signals by May 2002, and all noncommercial stations by 2003. As of early 2002, less than one quarter of the country's 1,600 stations had made the transition to digital. About one third of stations were likely to miss the deadline, primarily due to economic conditions (Albiniak, 2001). Cable operators are also in the process of upgrading their traditional analog signals to digital, similarly allowing for increased channel capacity. Satellite TV services such as The Dish Network and DirecTV already transmit digital signals. In short, there is a sweeping migration from analog to digital, and it impacts every form of television transmission.

There currently is debate over how to make best use of this new channel space: more channels versus higher quality. High-definition TV (HDTV) represents the latter option. It offers a screen that is one third wider than traditional television screens. Movies can thus be seen in their original wide-screen format, and sporting events, for example, can encompass more action on screen. HDTV offers improved picture and sound quality, and requires a special television set. There is relatively little HDTV programming being produced now, and only about 1% of TV owners currently have purchased an HDTV set, which costs in the range of $1,500 (Shiver, 2001).

Some broadcasters, including many PBS stations, have proposed multicasting four choices of programming during the day, and switching to HDTV for prime time (Cringely, 1998). In other words, a single PBS channel would be replaced by four PBS channels during the day; viewers might have a choice among children's programming, do-it-yourself shows, adult education, or popular documentaries. During the evenings, the PBS station would again broadcast only a single channel—but in HDTV format.

Ninety-five percent of public broadcasters say they plan to carry at least one educational multicast service ("Cable's 1st Amendment," 2001). Many commercial broadcasters will simply convert their current analog signal to digital.

For cable and satellite subscribers, additional channel capacity created by digital transmission similarly means more channels—often hundreds of channels. Many networks that are not currently available to analog cable subscribers are available on digital service, often for an additional fee. Educational and children-oriented networks primarily available only to digital cable and satellite subscribers include Toon Disney, Noggin, National Geographic Channel, Biography Channel, Discovery Kids, and PBS Kids, to name only a few.

Implications of Digital TV

More viewing options may lead to increased viewing time. Subscribers to digital cable watch 3–4 more hours per week than do analog cable subscribers (Cable & Telecommunications Association for Marketing, 2001).

Digital broadcast TV may bring more viewing options to lower-income households who cannot currently afford cable. However, this depends ultimately on the cost of the digital tuner required to convert traditional analog signals to digital.

Finally, greater interactivity potential may lead to increased intrusion of commerce. Broadcasters must pay for upgrading their stations to digital, at a cost of $1.5–$10 million per station (Grotticelli & Prikios, 2001). They will be looking for new revenue streams to offset this expense. Instant commerce may prove tempting or misleading to kids.

> With regard to our hypothetical families, having access to 14 channels of educational and children's programming has allowed the Smiths to maximize the value of the 2 hours a day they allot to media consumption. The kids choose from a multitude of age-appropriate programming on Nickelodeon, Noggin, Discovery Kids, Disney Channel, and eight PBS stations during the day. The whole family occasionally watches one of several specialized History or Discovery Channels in the evenings.

> The Joneses, on the other hand, have increased their daily media consumption to almost 10 hours a day. With multiple TVs in the household and many more programming options, family members now spend more time alone watching their individual programs: Mom watches one of twenty-five different movie channels in the living room, Dad has his choice of nine news and financial news channels in the den, and the kids watch one of multiple MTV or HBO channels in their own bedrooms. There is always at least one TV on in the household. The result is that the family spends less time together—and more time watching television.

VIDEO ON DEMAND AND SUBSCRIPTION VIDEO ON DEMAND

Most cable and satellite TV subscribers now have access to pay-per-view feature films and sporting events. However, the offerings have generally been limited to a few movie titles each month, each with limited start times.

The next phase of pay-per-view, called video-on-demand (VOD), offers much greater selection and versatility. VOD offers access to hundreds or even thousands of movies and programs, with no preset start time. Additionally, many homes will be equipped with the capability to pause and rewind VOD programs while they are airing. If a child needs attending to, for example, the program can simply be paused and continued later. In this way, the functionality replicates the convenience of video rentals at the touch of a button.

Subscription VOD (SVOD) is one iteration of VOD currently being rolled out in various cable systems across the country. Rather than offering individual programs, SVOD offers access to a group of programs for a set period of time, for a fixed price. For example, a consumer might subscribe to pro wrestling on demand for an additional $5 a month, which would provide the ability to watch a monthly selection of wrestling programs, at any time, as often as desired, being able to pause and rewind. In some cases, SVOD may be offered free of charge to those who subscribe to premium services like HBO or Showtime (Kerver, 2001). By 2005, over 31 million U.S. homes will have digital cable with video-on-demand services (Forrester Research, 2001).

Implications of VOD/SVOD

By presenting more ways for viewers to access an array of programming, VOD and SVOD offer more viewer choice and control over television. Viewers can schedule their TV time around family priorities, rather than vice versa. The danger is that more programming options may lead to greater intrusion of media into family life, rather than less. In addition, those who are willing to pay for these new services may increase their media consumption in order to justify the additional expense—to feel they are "getting their money's worth."

> The Smiths have access at any time of the day or night to a library of kids' programming, which they can stop, pause, fast forward, or rewind; they pay an additional $5 a month for this service and utilize it judiciously.

> The Joneses also pay $5 a month for an SVOD service: unlimited on-demand access to over a dozen pro wrestling events each month. The Jones kids often pause and replay the wrestling moves in slow motion, over and over, in order to imitate the moves on each other and friends. As a result of the increased media usage by the Jones kids, the family spends less time together.

INTERACTIVE PROGRAM GUIDES

Interactive program guides (IPGs) are similar to a scrolling TV listings channel, except that they offer the viewer greater control. The viewer can quickly navigate through the various listings with the remote control, getting more information on programs of interest. In this way, IPGs are more convenient than printed TV listings or scrolling listings channels.

Eighty-two percent of those with IPGs say they use TV newspaper listings less now than before they had an IPG, and more than half (53%) say they channel surf less, reinforcing the convenience of this new service (Statistical Research, 2001).

In some cases, IPGs have parental lockout controls that restrict certain channels or programs from being previewed or viewed. This is useful in homes where parents want to closely monitor their family's viewing—a need that may grow given the increased number of channels to monitor. IPGs are already available to more than one in three U.S. households; by 2004 they will reach more than half of all U.S. homes (Forrester Research, 2000).

Implications of IPGs

By providing faster and more detailed access to program information, IPGs offer the viewer more control over the viewing experience. They also offer parents an additional method for monitoring the viewing habits of their children, via the parental lockout feature.

> Whenever the Smiths want to find out what programs are on, they access the IPG and use the remote control to quickly navigate through the offerings on various channels. This takes much less time than tuning to the TV listings channel and waiting for all the listings to scroll. It also gives them more detailed information about each program and allows them to plan their viewing more efficiently. The Smiths now spend much less time simply "surfing" the various channels, and as a result the quality of their television viewing has increased.
>
> The Jones family still "surfs" channels with the remote control, as most viewers do. There are many more channels than in the past, which increases the amount of time spent surfing and often results in watching programs they have little interest in watching but are simply "there."

PERSONAL VIDEO RECORDERS

Personal video recorders (PVRs) first emerged in the late 1990s under brand names like TiVo, the current market leader. Like traditional VCRs, PVRs record programs for future playback by the viewer. However, they have the added benefits of operating continuously in real time, and being capable of "learning" their owners' viewing preferences. Continuous operation means that the viewer can pause or rewind any television program while it is airing. A viewer can take a bathroom break, replay a controversial sports play, put the children to bed, or turn off the television completely, then return to the program later—even fast-forwarding past the commercials when the program is viewed later. Remembering viewer preferences means that a PVR will automatically record a movie starring Mary Kate and Ashley Olsen, for example, for a viewer who has recently watched other programs featuring the duo.

The PVR landscape is changing rapidly, and the business model is far from proven. It requires a monthly subscription fee from consumers—typically in the $10 range—in addition to an initial outlay of $200 to $400 for the receiver, which consumers have been reluctant to embrace. It also currently requires an additional box alongside the cable or satellite set-top box. Despite visibility in the press, only half a million PVRs had been sold by 2001 (Flynn, 2001). Analysts predict that PVR functionality will eventually become a component of the cable or satellite set-top box rather than a separate device, thus adding to the benefits of cable or satellite service while alleviating the need for an additional box atop the television set. It is estimated that by 2006, 42 million homes will have access to PVR functionality—either as a separate service or as part of their cable or satellite service ("Before you Buy," 2001).

Implications of PVRs

One of the troubling implications of PVRs for the television industry is that they threaten television's traditional advertising model. Most television networks (with the exception of PBS, HBO, and other commercial-free networks) rely on advertising as their predominant means of revenue. Their success depends on the willingness of viewers to sit through frequent commercial interruptions. However, 69% of PVR users say they always or often fast-forward through commercials (Next-Research, 2001). The prospect of 42 million homes bypassing a network's commercials is an issue with which networks—and PVR service operators—are now wrestling. Less viewing of commercials may be a short-term benefit for viewers, but it may ultimately lead to greater intrusion of commercial messages within the programming itself, as networks struggle to incorporate the new behavior into their economic models.

PVRs provide more viewer control over the programming: greater selection, greater scheduling flexibility, and greater control of the actual viewing experience. Less reliance on network scheduling means that parents can schedule children's viewing around particular programs rather than times, which potentially raises quality of TV time and avoids conflicts with family activities. The downside is that improved access to programming may lead to increased consumption of television, which in turn further diminishes the amount of time devoted to nontelevision activities.

> The Smiths especially enjoy their PVR. Instead of having to be in front of the TV at 8 P.M. every Tuesday for their favorite program, the show is automatically recorded every week. Last week, the Smith children stayed outside to play soccer with the neighborhood kids rather than come inside to watch TV, knowing they could watch the show at a more convenient time. And the previous week the whole family was able to attend a school function on Tuesday evening without objections from the kids.

> The Jones kids use their PVR to automatically record violent and adult-oriented movies. Having access to so many more programs has been a contributing factor in their increased media consumption. Last week, the kids missed all three nights of soccer practice in order to stay home and watch martial arts movies that their PVR had recorded. The amount of time the Jones children spend on homework and communicating with friends and other family members has also decreased.

INTERACTIVE AND ENHANCED TELEVISION

Interactive television (ITV) originally referred to any television device or application in which the viewer could influence or interact with the program. In the 1970s, for example, an ITV trial in Columbus, Ohio, called QUBE allowed viewers to influence a football game by voting on which play to relay to the quarterback (Wangberg, 1999). ITV gained notoriety in the early 1990s with the ambitious launch of Time Warner's Full Service Network in Orlando. Time Warner spent more than $100 million in 2 years but ultimately failed to find a viable business model from ITV (Krantz, 1997).

With the rise of the Internet in the mid-1990s, TV networks began experimenting with the notion of providing enhanced or synchronous information on their Web sites. Because this type of interactivity utilized two "screens" rather than one (i.e., the television screen and the computer screen, side by side in a room), it didn't precisely fit the term "interactive television." It did, however, enhance television programming with interactivity, thus spawning a new term, "enhanced television" (ETV).

Although the acronyms ITV and ETV are often used interchangeably, ITV typically refers to interactivity that occurs on a single screen (including, depending on one's definition, VOD, IPGs, and PVRs). ETV generally refers to a TV program that has a synchronous or related interactive component on the Internet, whether or not the interactivity occurs on the TV screen or on a separate computer screen. The acronym ETV has gained prominence over the past few years because it specifically refers to enhanced content, whereas the acronym ITV has become so widely used to describe so many different things that it no longer has a common meaning.

Enhanced television is available to any household with both a TV and an Internet connection—over half of U.S. homes (Niemeyer, 2002). ETV can include additional data or information about the program, live viewer polls whose results are then posted or reported as part of the television program, synchronized game play, or live chat. *Slimetime Live* on Nickelodeon offers kids the opportunity to vote online for which on-air personality gets "slimed." Nick's *BubbleCast* is an online trivia game in which kids answer questions about the program while it is airing. ABC's enhanced version of *Who Wants to Be a Millionaire* was played over 19 million times, and over a million people registered to play the ETV version of an MTV game show called *Web Riot* (Niemeyer, 2002).

Early interactive trials were important in that they demonstrated what was possible. Although some of the early interactive applications, such as the ability to influence the outcome of a movie or television program, were innovative, current ITV applications must have a viable business model to survive. The failure to find viable business models for most ITV applications is a primary reason why ITV has been slow to catch on despite years of experimentation.

One such promising application is one-click ordering of merchandise via the TV remote control. Viewers can purchase music, clothing, jewelry, travel, and even order pizza without dialing a phone number or leaving their chairs. Networks such as Home Shopping Network and ShopNBC hope to increase their sales by making purchases as simple as touching a button; advertisers are likewise experimenting with interactive commercials. ITV shopping is anticipated to generate over $4 billion annually by 2005 (Jupiter Media Metrix, 2001a).

Implications of ITV/ETV

ITV and ETV provide interactivity to traditionally passive television programming, the result being greater intrusion of media into kids' lives. Interactive chatting with friends while watching TV may provide a social benefit.

Early ITV trials were driven by experimentation, but current and future deployment will be driven by economics. This may lead to a greater intrusion of interactive commerce and commercial messages into television viewing. In addition, the educational enhancements promised by early interactive experiments may not materialize to the extent imagined.

> The Smith kids vote online for which Nickelodeon program they wish to see next, and sometimes answer trivia questions online about the show they are watching. They occasionally chat with friends using a corner of the TV screen while they watch the program. In this way, their television viewing has become a more interactive and social experience.

> The Jones kids are obsessed with playing the live, synchronized version of their favorite MTV game show, often forgoing homework or interaction with family or friends. Via their remote control, they frequently make impulse purchases of merchandise featured on TV, which has led to significant credit card bills for their parents.

THE INTERNET

The future of televisual media is tightly bound to the future of the Internet. More than 17 million teens, or 73% of all the 23.8 million U.S. kids aged 12–17, go online each month. This compares to only 42% of adults who surf the Web each month. Three quarters of teens use instant messaging and more than half download music online (Lake, 2001). Six in ten online youths aged 9–17 say they prefer going online to watching TV (America Online/Roper Starch, 2000b). By 2005, 70% of US family households will have children online at home (Cyber Dialogue, 2000). By 2010, according to a Disney Online executive, the first encounter most kids will have with Mickey Mouse won't be in a book, on TV, or even at Disney World—it will be on the Web (Horovitz, 2001).

The Internet: Cognitive Development

The positive influence of computers on children's cognitive and social development is well documented (Clements, 1994). Many parents and educators regard the Internet as an important educational tool: Internet connections in school buildings are nearly universal at 94%, with 82% of classrooms online ("Technology Counts," 2001). Sixty percent of adult online users believe the Internet's greatest impact on society will be on education (America Online/Roper Starch, 2000a). Educational information abounds on the Internet. Online dictionaries and encyclopedias, study guides on virtually any subject and grade level, and even sites specifically devoted to homework help are free and easily accessible.

Although the Internet is thus seen as a potentially positive influence on children's educational development, there are concerns about the optimal amount of time spent online, how that time might otherwise be spent, and what impact increased simultaneous usage of multiple media may have.

The more electronic media there are in the home, the more time children spend with them. Kids with TVs and VCRs spend on average 3.7 hours a day with media, whereas kids with TV, VCR, computers, and video games spent an average 4.8 hours a day with media (Annenberg Public Policy Center, 1999). The American Academy of Pediatrics recommends limiting screen time to 1½ hours a day (American Academy of Pediatrics, 1999).

The Internet has increased the amount of multitasking or simultaneous usage of multiple media. At least one fourth of the U.S. population sometimes uses the Internet while watching TV; teens are most likely to follow this trend (Stump, 2000).

The Internet: Social, Behavioral, and Emotional Development

The Internet is a social activity among children and teens. Communicating with others via e-mail, chat, and instant messages is the most popular online activity among kids 9–17 (America Online/Roper Starch, 2000b). Kids' online social circles are growing: 64% now have instant messaging contact lists, and they have increased from an average 24 names in 1999 to 35 in 2000 (America Online/Roper Starch, 2000b). Chat room conversations, especially among older kids and teens, frequently revolve around meeting members of the opposite gender and forming online relationships (Campbell, 1998). Because of the anonymity provided by the Internet, kids may be more forward in their conversations, as per this excerpt from an online chat, allegedly between preteens:

> "Hi. Do ya remember me?"
>
> "Yep!!! Do you wanna be online boy+girl friend if you are single?"
>
> "Sure! I'd love to."
>
> "Great!!!!!! Cool!!!!!!!"

Chat rooms may allow healthy experimentation with relationships and identity within the safety of an anonymous environment, and e-mail may sustain online dialogues and relationships. However, online social interaction may come at the expense of face-to-face interaction. Asked what they would be doing if not online, over half of online youths surveyed said they would be spending time with friends (70%) and/or family (58%; America Online/Roper Starch, 2000b). During people's first and second years online, greater use of the Internet is associated with declines in the size of participants' social networks, declines in communication within the family and, for teenagers, declines in social support (Kraut et al., 1998). Declines in psychological and social well-being are smaller, and in some cases reversed, with subsequent Internet use.

The unfiltered nature of the Internet allows children relatively easy access to a great deal of content that is less accessible via other media. By typing a few keywords, it is easy to find hard-core pornography, racist and anti-Semitic sites, and graphic violence including crime-scene and morgue photos. Seven of ten online teens aged 15–17 say they have accidentally stumbled across pornography online, 23% "very" or "somewhat" often (Kaiser Family Foundation, 2001). One glaring example: The Web site Whitehouse.com contains pornography; the actual White House site is Whitehouse.gov.

About 6% of parents use filtering software that blocks kids' access to undesirable content ("Digital Chaperones," 2001). This type of software ranges in price from $39 to $80; America Online (AOL) comes with parental controls that filter content. Early versions of filtering software were largely ineffective. They have improved, but in trials most failed to block at least one in five objectionable sites ("Digital Chaperones," 2001). In some cases, filters blocked harmless sites that contained words such as *adult* or *sex*, that were used in an inoffensive context. In short, filtering software is no substitute for parental supervision.

The Internet: Physical Health & Safety

The Internet, because of its anonymity, is often a predatory environment. As indicated earlier, chat is a popular online activity among kids, and conversations are frequently relationship oriented, occasionally sexual. Chat rooms are open to anyone, and there is often no requirement for proof of age or identity. Seventy percent of parents say they are concerned about unsafe chat environments (Jupiter Communications, 1998). Several recent high-profile cases have involved girls lured by older men into meeting them in person, sometimes with dire consequences. In 1999, a high-ranking executive of a Disney-owned Web site was arrested for soliciting sex with a minor he met online in a "dad&daughtersex" chat room (Dube, 2000). A veteran police officer and the chief resident of a children's hospital were arrested on similar charges in separate incidents (Florin & Feijoo, 2001; Hackney, 2000).

The Children's Online Privacy Protection Act of 1998 (COPPA) was enacted to protect the privacy of children using the Internet. COPPA requires sites to prominently post their policies with respect to the collection, use, and disclosure of children's personal information. Sites must also obtain "verifiable parental consent" before collecting, using, or disclosing personal information from children. The law went into effect in April 2000.

Many sites heavily visited by children have responded in additional ways. Nick.com and PBS.org provide "bumper pages" when visitors link to another site, informing them that they are leaving the site and instructing them not to give out information online before checking with their parents. CartoonNetwork.com has eliminated open chats. Its message boards now include pull-down menus with approved lists of phrases (Salfino, 2001).

Another threat to children's health and physical safety is the relatively easy access to dangerous information online, including information about bomb making and the ability to purchase weapons. *The Washington Post* has described discussions among 14-year-olds about "which propellants are best to use, which Web sites have the best recipes and whether tin or aluminum soda cans make better bomb casings" (Shen, 1998, p. D1). A recent search instantly turned up a martial arts site proclaiming: "Check out our weapons and self-defense supplies. We carry an incredible variety of swords, knives, nunchakus, throwing weapons, wooden and foam-covered training weapons...." All were available for immediate purchase online, with a disclaimer placing the responsibility for compliance with laws on the buyer. No proof of age was required.

The potential effects of the Internet on children's health and safety are not all negative. The confidentiality of the Internet may play a key role in providing young people with information on sensitive health issues such as HIV, birth control, and sexually transmitted diseases. Seventy-five percent of online youth aged 15–24 have used the Internet to find health information; among those, 4 out of 10 say they have changed their personal behavior because of information they found online (Kaiser Family Foundation, 2001).

The Future of the Internet

Looking ahead to the next 5 or so years, the Internet will likely become:

- *More ubiquitous:* In the future, almost everyone will have Internet access and use it regularly. Being Internet-savvy will be a prerequisite for any white-collar employment, college admission, and even high school. Those at risk of exclusion include the poorer segments of society, who cannot afford a computer or Internet access in the home, and who are about half as likely to have access in the classroom ("Technology Counts," 2001).
- *More portable:* In the future, Internet access will not be tied to a stationary computer. Detachable, wireless monitors and keyboards will allow users to carry their computer "monitor" from room to room; they will be able to access a recipe in the kitchen, play along with a TV game show in the living room, and send an e-mail from the bathroom. Handheld devices like Palm Pilots and cell phones will be (indeed, some already are) equipped with wireless Internet access, allowing constant communication via voice or e-mail, and constant access to information.
- *More TV-like:* Internet access via high-speed broadband connection will increase from 15% of online households to over 40% of households by 2006 (Jupiter Media Metrix, 2001b). This will result in faster access speed and download speed, which in turn will allow Web sites to feature richer graphics; CD-ROM-quality interactive games; and more audio, video, and animation attributes. Improved software that allows for more complex applications to be delivered with less bandwidth add to the potential for a more TV-like environment online.
- *More commercial:* As the Internet has matured, so have its business models. In the future, more sites will require subscription fees to gain access to their content. The free sites that remain will feature more intrusive advertising that pops up and fills the user's screen before the content can be accessed, and more frequent requests for users' e-mail addresses, which will fill users' mailboxes with yet more junk e-mail.

Implications of the Internet

The Smiths use the Internet to access news, sports scores, and local weather forecasts, as well as to keep in touch with family and friends. The computer is in the family room, where all family members can access it and its use can be more carefully monitored.

The Smith kids use the Internet to do research for homework assignments, play games, and communicate with friends. They frequently exchange e-mails and even photos with their grandparents and other family members who are separated geographically. An e-mail exchange with their grandfather, who requested their help in finding genealogical information online, sparked an interest by the kids in the Smith family's history. They now communicate with their grandfather regularly about new family information they have found online.

The Smith kids have signed up for two e-mail newsletters, one from NationalGeographic.com, which keeps them up to date on breaking news and offers a photo of the month for their screensaver, and one called Creative Writing for Teens, which offers monthly advice, tips, and encouragement for young authors.

Mr. and Mrs. Jones seldom use the Internet and spend little time monitoring their kids' online activities. In an effort to protect their children from exposure to inappropriate material online, Mr. and Mrs. Jones installed content-blocking software on the family computer. However, their son Bobby quickly uninstalled it; his parents have not checked on it since and assume it is still there.

Because Mr. and Mrs. Jones seldom use the computer, it is relegated to the basement so that it does not take up space in more highly trafficked areas of the house. While Bobby and his sister Cindy occasionally use the Internet for research and help with homework assignments, most frequently it is used by Bobby to participate in the Adult Sex Chat Club, compare the specifications of various automatic weapons, and learn how to make homemade bombs from ordinary household materials. He has signed up for three newsletters devoted to pro wrestling, Satanism, and the Ku Klux Klan. He has also joined the online message board discussion group of a foreign terrorist organization.

Cindy Jones uses the Internet to exchange personal e-mail with men she has met in various chat rooms over the past year. She has freely offered to strangers online such personal information as her name, address, and phone number. In the past 2 months, she has begun receiving phone calls from two different men she met online. Although she is growing nervous about the wisdom of having developed personal relationships with these men, she relishes the attention and excitement of a forbidden encounter.

Needless to say, the experiences of these hypothetical families tend toward the extremes. The simple point they make is that the Internet—and all media—can potentially help or hinder the cognitive, social, behavioral, emotional, and physical health of children. How these new technologies impact the real lives of families is, in large part, determined by the actions of the families themselves.

FINAL THOUGHTS

New technologies have the potential to offer parents and families more choice and control over media; but more choice can also lead to less control. A quote from Fred Rogers, TV's beloved "Mister Rogers," sums up the potential of new, interactive technologies: "Imagine how much more meaningful any [type of] television can be when children have a caring person sitting right there beside them ... someone who wants to listen to their questions or comments ... someone who encourages their careful looking and listening and learning! That's what I call 'interactive'" (Rogers, 1998).

REFERENCES

Albiniak, P. (2001, August 20). Stations "waiver" on DTV. *Broadcasting & Cable*, p. 6.

America Online/Roper Starch. (2000a). *America Online/Roper Starch worldwide adult cyberstudy 2000*. Vienna, VA: America Online.

America Online/Roper Starch. (2000b). *America Online/Roper Starch youth cyberstudy 2000*. Vienna, VA: America Online.

American Academy of Pediatrics. (1999). *Understanding the impact of media on children and teens* [Brochure]. Elk Grove Village, IL: Author.

Annenberg Public Policy Center. (1999). *Media in the home 1999: The fourth annual survey of parents and children*. Philadelphia: University of Pennsylvania, Annenberg Public Policy Center.

Before you buy that PVR, read this first. (2001, June 1). *Cable World*, p. 91.

Cable & Telecommunications Association for Marketing. (2001). Impact of digital features on household TV/PC viewing decisions. Alexandria, VA: Author.

Cable's 1st amendment: Sachs warns broadcasters on digital must-carry. (2001, April 19). *CableFAX Daily*, p. 1.

Campbell, T. (1998, May). The psychology of kids' chat. *PreText Magazine*. Retrieved 1/31/02 from http://www.pretext.com/may98/features/story2.html

Clements, D. H. (1994). The uniqueness of the computer as a learning tool: Insights from research and practice. In J. L. Wright & D. D. Shade (Eds.), *Young children: Active learners in a technological age* (pp. 31–50). Washington, DC: NAEYC.

Cringely, R. (1998). *Digital TV; A Cringely crash course*. Retrieved 1/31/02 from http://www.pbs.org/opb/crashcourse

Cyber Dialogue. (2000). *The Internet Consumer: Industry brief, year 2000* (2) [Analyst report]. New York: Author.

Digital chaperones for kids. (2001, March). *Consumer Reports*. Retrieved 1/31/02 from http://www.consumerreports.org /Special/ConsumerInterest/Reports/ 0103fil0.html

Dube, J. (2000, March 17). Former high-tech exec guilty of sex crime. ABC News. Retrieved 1/31/02 from http://abcnews.go.com/sections/tech/DailyNews/naughton000317.html

Florin, H., & Feijoo, K. (2001, December 30). Officer facing sex charges kills himself, police confirm. *The Miami Herald* (local section), p. 1B.

Flynn, L. J. (2001, November 5). Networks see threat in new video recorder. *The New York Times*, p. C4.

Forrester Research. (2000, July). *Smart television* [Analyst report]. Boston: Author.

Forrester Research. (2001, March). *Movie distribution's new era* [Analyst report]. Boston: Author.

Grotticelli, M., & Prikios, K. A. (2001, August 20). DTV dog days. *Broadcasting & Cable*, p. 26.

Hackney, S. (2000, September 30). Doctor charged as sex prowler. *Detroit Free Press*, p. 1A.

Horovitz, B. (2001, June 5). Marketers call on kids to design web sites. *USA Today*, p. 1B.

Jupiter Communications. (1998). *Kids; evolving revenue models for the 2–12 market* [Analyst report]. New York: Jupiter Strategic Planning Services.

Jupiter Media Metrix. (2001a). *iTV revenues: Positioning for incremental and diversified revenue streams* [Analyst report]. New York: Author.

Jupiter Media Metrix. (2001b). *Jupiter internet shopping model* [Analyst report]. New York: Author.

Kaiser Family Foundation. (2001). Generation Rx.com; how young people use the Internet for health information. Menlo Park, CA: Author.

Kerver, T. (2001, November 12). What's next for cable. *Cablevision*, p. 16.

Krantz, M. (1997, November). Marriage of convenience: Interactive television. *Time Digital* (features section), p. 60.

Kraut, R., Patterson, M., Lundmark, V., Kiesler, S., Mukopadhyay, T., & Scherlis, W. (1998). Internet paradox: A social technology that reduces social involvement and psychological well-being? *American Psychology, 53*(9), 1017–1031.

Lake, D. (2001, July 23). Teens turn on, tune in, log off. *The Industry Standard.com*. Retrieved 1/31/02 from Lexis-Nexis.

NextResearch. (2001). *The PVR monitor*. Atlanta, GA: Author.

Niemeyer, B. (2002, January 29). Is there really a two-screen market? *Niemeyer Review* [E-mail newsletter]. Retrieved 1/31/02 from http://www.centrimedia.com/archives/2002_01_29_Intel_Provider_Group.html

Rogers, F. (1998, November). *Digital TV: A letter from Mister Rogers*. Retrieved 1/31/02 from http://www.pbs.org/opb/crashcourse/hdtv/fredrogers.html

Salfino, C. S. (2001, March 19). Great expectations; Younger set demands strong complementary on-line experience. *Broadcasting & Cable*, p. 54.

Shen, F. (1998, April 4). Easy-to-make pipe bombs becoming toys for teens. *Washington Post*, p. D1.

Shiver, J. (2001, July 30). Broadcasters seek to delay digital TV. *Los Angeles Times* (Home ed.), p. 1.

Statistical Research, Inc. (2001). *How people use interactive television*. Westfield, NJ: Author.

Stump, M. (2000, October 16). TV, PC co-exist more, inspiring programmers. *Multichannel News*, p. 61.

Technology counts 2001; the new divides. (2001, May 10). *Education Week*. Bethesda, MD: Editorial Projects in Education, Inc.

Wangberg, L. (1999, June 22). Stay tuned to TV. *USA Today* (bonus section), p. 6E.

Instructional/Educational Televisual Media

3

A Short History of the Window on the World

Robin Moss
*Former Head of Education, Independent Broadcasting Authority
and Independent Television Commission, U.K.*

Viewed globally, the history of using television for the instruction and education of children (educational television, or ETV), is as brief and spectacular as a theme-park ride. The early years, from the 1950s on, saw experiments and developments in many countries, often initially condemned by critics, later welcomed by educators and politicians with extravagant praise and high hopes. During the late 1960s, there was a period of disappointment as experiences proved the expectations of television's educational powers unrealistic. The following decade saw the emergence of several outstandingly successful systems, some of which continue to offer valued services to the education of children, but the 1980s was generally a decade of decline in funding and support for ETV in many countries, a decline that led to large-scale change in the 1990s, as new technologies challenged one another for attention and resources.

There are illuminating parallels between the shape and pace of the development of educational television in different societies, as well as significant differences. It is well worth considering how and why television worked well for teachers and children in some countries, but less well, or even not at all, elsewhere. Certain key features recur in the most adaptable and reliable systems. Those features are highly relevant to the effective utilization of more recently developed technologies, notably online education, by schools. They confirm once more what any teacher knows well—that technology alone does not drive learning revolutions.

Of course, that is not to deny that technology has played a major role in the history of ETV. At the outset of its emergence in schools, in the 1950s and 1960s, television was only available in monochrome; recording was expensive and complex, and external scenes were shot on 16mm film. Receivers were clumsy, unreliable, valve-driven boxes, delivering images and sound of quality that no 21st-century child would accept. By the late 1970s, with color television receivers universally available in homes in the developed world, and ETV programs being produced to high standards at high cost, teachers and children were familiar with the idea of television playing an educative role. Finally, as technical performance of video recorders (VCRs) rose and prices fell, schools and parents found educational uses for that device. In most parts of the developed world it was not until the 1980s that ETV reached its full educational potential. In the Third World, ETV faced innumerable technical problems throughout the whole 1950–2000 period, in addition to the domination of broadcasting by unregulated political and commercial forces, and a chronic lack of resources and skilled staff.

ETV has worked best in societies where both education and television are regarded as important parts of social life. The publication of major research reports on the social impact of television in the lives of children had an important influence on the development of ETV. The first of these, *Television and the Child*, was published in Britain in 1958. Known as "The Nuffield Report," it studied children in homes with and without television, and even in homes before and after the advent of the box in the corner (Himmelweit, Oppenheim, & Vince, 1958). Its findings challenged popular prejudices: "It is not true that most children become heavily addicted to television; it is not true that children view almost continuously; it is not true that television makes children do badly at school; it is not true that in general television causes listlessness, loss of sleep, bad dreams or lack of concentration; it is not true that television causes eyestrain; it is not true that working class children view more that middle class children" (quoted in Langham, 1990, p. 52). The American research report *Television in the Lives of Our Children*, published in 1961, reinforced these findings, underlining the need to consider not what television does to children but "what children do with television" (Schramm, Lyle, & Parker, 1961, p. 169).

Within this broad history, television offered a different teaching face in North America, in Europe, in Japan, and in the Third World. To a great extent, those differences naturally reflected deep differences among societies and educational systems. Nevertheless, comparisons help us to identify some common features in effective use of television for education. The most striking achievements of ETV were based on secure funding for competitive program ideas modified by formative research, and strong alliances among teachers, producers, children, and parents. By the late 1980s, there were imaginative and respected services in action worldwide, apparently capable of contributing to the resolution of almost any educational need. Since then, political excitement about the new "learning revolution" has robbed educational television services of funding and support, ironically making transition to the online era more problematic.

ETV IN NORTH AMERICA

In the United States, television in the service of children's education developed from the 1952 Federal Communications Commission (FCC) reservation of 242 channels for education. Ford Foundation funding later established National Educational Television (NET), to procure and distribute programs and to encourage production. Until the late 1960s, most schoolteachers did not see television as a significant educational force, whereas, for children, "compared to commercial television, interest in ETV was minimal" (O'Bryan, 1980, p. 10). Much of the output at that time "was piecemeal, and production quality low and inconsistent" (O'Bryan, 1980, p. 11).

The creation of the Corporation for Public Broadcasting (CPB) led directly to the formation of Children's Television Workshop (CTW) in 1968, and the launch of *Sesame Street* a year later. The move was in response, as generally for any major ETV initiatives in any country, to a perceived national need. In the United States, continued concern about low attainment in basic skills was allied to concern about the antisocial attitudes of poor, urban, multiethnic youth. Lavishly funded, supported from the first by high-quality research to shape and reshape its output, and sustained by strong educational and political support, CTW proved that educational broadcasts could compete with commercially produced television for children's attention and interest and that they could teach.

During the 1970s, educational television worldwide was influenced by *Sesame Street*. Unlike most ETV programs in other cultures, *Sesame Street* was designed to speak directly to the child, acting as the teacher. Its running time (60 minutes) was three or four times the length of the typical ETV program elsewhere, which was intended to introduce or illustrate a teacher's work with a class. Yet its outstandingly entertaining style and its inventive teaching ideas were very influential. *Sesame Street* showed that ETV could compete head on with popular children's output, and that research had a practical value in making ETV more competitive. From the outset, CTW's heavy investment in research was a key element in its undoubted success in enhancing basic literacy and numeracy as well as civics, at a critical moment in the history of urban America. As O'Bryan noted, "The CTW approach included the marshaling of special consultants to advise in-house staff on target audience characteristics and on the latest teaching technologies. Teams of researchers were hired to test scripts and to conduct field research on experimental segments and pilot programs. Thus formative research in ETV was born" (O'Bryan, 1980, p. 13). Its influence on the morale of those using television worldwide, even in university settings, and on the design of distance-learning projects and outreach adult-learning schemes, is hard to overstate.

Rarely have educational television programs been so carefully prepared and tested prior to use. In addition, intense and continuing summative research programs were undertaken by the Educational Testing Service (ETS), an independent research organization, to examine the effectiveness of *Sesame Street* and of the second major CTW project, *The Electric Company*. The overall findings dovetailed well with later studies in many other settings: "Evaluations demonstrated that children could learn intellectual skills from television productions designed to be both entertaining and instructional. Television was an effective teacher for disadvantaged children and for children as young as three. Home viewing was effective for teaching pre-academic skills to young children.… In all cases, learning from the televised series was enhanced when supplementary learning materials and/or an interested adult were available" (Watkins, Huston-Stein, & Wright, 1980, p. 56). These broad findings were replicated in other parts of the world, even when the scope and aims of the ETV programs were very different from those of CTW.

In the 1970s, public demand for more and better children's television in the United States led to the creation of the Public Broadcasting Services (PBS), which continued to oversee public television licensees in the United States and to create and distribute a wide range of television materials, as well as playing a pioneering role in the 1990s development of online resources for education. To cite just one example of many, at the start of the 21st century, the North Virginia cable station WHRO was using its ETV experience (and staff) to play a lead role in providing interactive links with NASA scientists, or with bases in Antarctica, for the benefit of schools nationwide, offering access to data and teleconferences via digital television and personal computer networks.

Political attitudes toward PBS blew hot and cold over time, forcing cable stations to seek increased proportions of their revenue from sponsorship and donations. From the 1990s onward, all but the largest organizations led a precarious existence. As national excitement over the educational potential of computers and online resources grew, observers noted that the achievements and strengths of ETV were being forgotten; it was as if ETV had gone out of vogue. Jon Baggaley, Professor of Educational Technology at Canada's largest distance-education university, described the North American scene in 2001 like this: "It is as if the passion for on-line methods requires to be consummated by sacrificially destroying the means to produce its component parts. Of course, closing down educational television facilities kills the means to produce the quality video materials that the new technology has looked forward to carrying" (Baggaley, 2001, p. 4).

Trashing the ETV experience also meant forgetting the lessons of its history and repeating them. In 1998, Professor Larry Cuban of Stanford University reviewed the history of technology revolutions in classrooms. He concluded that the development of computer-enhanced instruction (CEI), as a technology with more promising prospects for classroom use than discredited computer-aided instruction (CAI), "faced the familiar conundrum of school reform … requiring teachers to play a far larger role in interactions between students and machines" than originally anticipated and claimed for CAI (Kirkpatrick & Cuban, 1998, p. 7).

ETV IN EUROPE

The constitutions of most Western European states reconstructed after 1945 included some form of state or state-supported public service broadcasting system, generally with limited independence from political controls. These organizations shared in the worldwide excitement about the potential of ETV in the 1960s and 1970s, and set up operations to provide educational services for children, albeit with varying degrees of success. The effectiveness of such ETV services depended on how far they could draw on legal or fiscal support. When they reviewed their output at meetings of the European Broadcasting Union or other international bodies, most public broadcasters in Europe looked with envy on their cousins in the United States or Britain.

From the early 1980s, the public service broadcasting monopoly that had prevailed in European countries (apart from the United Kingdom) began to be overwhelmed by a wave of deregulation, following a key Council of Europe Declaration on the Freedom of Expression and Information in 1982. Italy led the way in 1980, followed by France and Germany in 1984 and smaller countries thereafter. The new commercial broadcasters, soon in action in every European country, were governed "by very few regulations concerning their programming, and, financed from advertising revenue, aimed to reach broad population strata" (Smudits, 1996, p. 98). The weak public service broadcasting organizations continued to be financed by licence fees, but were also required to earn advertising revenue. This put them into competition with commercial rivals, sometimes from neighboring states, or from satellite sources. They tended to lose the contest, and although protected by law to maintain their cultural remit, their ability and will to provide effective ETV services was much reduced by the end of the decade. By and large, "the principles of the commercial broadcasters were imposed on the public service broadcasters" (Smudits, 1996, p. 99), or their ETV work became marginalized.

Britain was exempt from these 1980s changes. No other European country had developed such strong and well-funded public service broadcasting systems, for a variety of historical and cultural reasons. Social traditions meant smaller television audiences in the countries of Southern Europe than in Northern Europe and therefore less public and private support for, and indeed popular interest in, ETV. British educational broadcasters had unique strengths to withstand the challenges of new broadcasters and new technologies. Above all, their relationship with the teaching profession was based on mutual trust built up over many years.

Another key strength lay in the public-service tradition of the British Broadcasting Corporation (BBC). Formed by Royal Charter in the 1920s, the BBC always had a Board of Governors that reported to Parliament rather than to the government of the day, and the BBC's independence and authority had been enhanced by its record in World War II, when its news and comments were trusted and admired in both Britain and occupied Europe. Revenues were ensured from the first by the legal requirement for owners of radio receivers to purchase an annual license. Radio broadcasts to schools began as early as 1925 and were influenced by the views of a powerful committee of educators—the Schools Broadcasting Council (SBC)—and by research into teacher attitudes. In the United Kingdom, when the BBC's ETV service for schools opened in 1957, it could build on a firm financial footing, a secure legal base, and long experience of educational broadcasting.

In 1954, commercial television was established in Britain as a public service like the BBC, "to inform, educate and entertain" (BBC Royal Charter and successive

Broadcasting Acts, 1954–1990). Initially, commercial broadcast licensees were appointed and regulated by a powerful independent body, the Independent Broadcasting Authority (IBA) and, from 1993 on, by its successor, the Independent Television Commission (ITC), reporting directly to Parliament. In spring 1957, commercially funded Independent Television (ITV) actually beat the BBC to the punch with the first national ETV service for Schools in the British Commonwealth. This healthy competition continued for the rest of the 20th century, under the close scrutiny of the IBA and ITC. The regulators had their own group of educational advisers, the Schools Advisory Committee (SAC), chaired by figures of national repute and drawing its membership from teachers encouraged to influence the details of programming output as well as overall policy. Teachers of children of every age, following the curricula devised for all quarters of the country, were offered an enormous range of television stimuli for their work, supported by print and other materials of the highest quality, edited by teams of professional education officers. These arrangements, together with research and liaison functions, were protected by successive Acts of Parliament, even in the Broadcasting Act of 1990, passed by an unsympathetic right-wing government. Other countries could have legislated, as did the United Kingdom, to require ETV and other cultural contributions from commercial broadcasting licensees, as a condition of their tendering for their lucrative advertising revenues, but few did so.

In research terms, there was never a European equivalent to CTW for formative research influence on ETV program making. The most consistent contributor to increased understanding of quality in ETV was undoubtedly the regulator of British commercial broadcasting, the Independent Broadcasting Authority. The impact of the IBA Educational Fellowship scheme between 1970 and 1980 is hard to exaggerate, beginning with the ground-breaking Kemelfield study *The Evaluation of Schools Broadcasts: Piloting a New Approach* (1971). This researcher worked closely with the producers of a program as it was being developed, and later looked in great detail at children's reactions to the program. The resulting study not only gave useful feedback to the producers, but also enhanced general insights into improving the effectiveness of ETV. In the classroom. Kemelfield's approach, together with the ongoing work of the Institute of Educational Technology at the new (1969) Open University, had lasting influence on research methodology in ETV and in distance education, both in Britain and in other countries.

When invited to assess the general standard of schools television in 1995, UK teachers still gave a ringing endorsement of its quality, as they had done in many previous surveys. Although there was a decline in use among secondary teachers, these teachers' respect for the standard of the services had risen from 64% rating them "good" or "very good" in 1990 to 75% in 1995. Primary teachers also increased their approval for the services' standards, with the 78% who had rated them as "good" or "very good" in 1990 rising to 83% by 1995. A further survey in 1997 showed clearly that a continuing fall in secondary school use was regretted by teachers, who felt pressured by curriculum and other demands into withdrawing from ETV.

A remarkable British experiment, the Television Literacy Project, showed how viewers could be helped to learn from television. The skills developed in the Television Literacy Project's courses proved transferable into skills in reading, understanding, and judgment. "The need to view effectively is fundamental to an active participation in modern society, given people's reliance on television. Learning from television is not simply acquired by watching, but it can be taught" (Kelley & Gunter, 1993, p. 1).

The Television Literacy Project course ran over 6 weeks. About half of it was spent on practical television work (mainly recording each other in interviews and discussions); the rest was spent on discussion and analysis of broadcasts with specially trained teachers. Before the course, all pupils were given a standard test of reading ability, and a range of television tests, to establish a "viewing score" (i.e., the ability to remember, understand, and learn from television broadcasts). After the course, the television tests were taken again by all 386 pupils involved. The results showed very highly significant improvements in the viewing scores for those undertaking the course, and one of the preparatory studies suggested that these improvements were not only significant but lasted over time.

In the 21st century, the enormous range of choices available to children accessing television channels, or indeed Internet sites, poses unfamiliar and alarming challenges to their powers of discrimination and judgment. Screen-filtering devices, however sophisticated, offer only negative protection for the young. In Britain, as elsewhere, little attention has been devoted to developing media education or media literacy skills. The loss of the experience and influence of the ETV systems as part of the rush to establish new technologies can only be described as folly: As George Santayana warned us a century ago, "Progress, far from consisting in change, depends on retentiveness. Those who cannot remember the past are condemned to fulfil it" (Santayana, 1905, chap. xii).

ETV IN JAPAN

Japan's deep tradition of disciplined respect for the teacher and enthusiasm for education led to the publicly funded national broadcasting service (NHK) in 1959 devoting its new second television channel entirely to education. Programs for schools attracted remarkable teacher support. By 1964, the year of the Tokyo Olympics, more than 90% of Japanese elementary schools—for 6- to 12-year-olds—had television sets, and three quarters of them (over 15,000) were using NHK programs. The proportion of elementary schools using NHK output peaked at 97.9% in 1986, but continued above 90% for the remainder of the 20th century (Kodaira & Takahashi, 2001). In addition, as computers and Internet access spread into elementary classrooms in the 1990s, teachers purchased and used additional video materials from NHK as well as from commercial sources, with around 80% of schools reporting such activity in the last 5 years of the 20th century.

At the secondary (high school) levels, NHK saw a steady decline in the utilization of ETV programs from the peak year of 1984, as the video products of rival

commercial publishers and the increasing number of PCs in high schools competed for attention. This phenomenon, a relative decline in secondary school
use of ETV programs compared to consistently higher rates of use in primary
schools, was observed in other developed countries, too, as specialist senior
teachers responded to demands to raise the skills and performance levels of
graduating students.

The history of NHK's contribution to education extended far beyond Japan. Over
the 40 years from 1960 to 2000, more than 1,300 experts in ETV were sent to 77 developing countries to assist with technical and production training, and more than 2,500
trainees from 131 territories received training in Japan. Asia and Latin America had
particularly strong support. In addition, since 1965, NHK has hosted the Japan Prize
Contest, a competition open to educational broadcasting organizations worldwide,
with typical entries of over 150 programs from over 40 countries (NHK, 2001). The
closing assembly of this extraordinary festival has traditionally been honored by the
presence of the Crown Prince. With some awards reserved for developing countries,
the Japan Prize has helped to raise standards and morale in ETV systems everywhere
and has deepened international understanding at many levels.

ETV IN THE THIRD WORLD

From the first, television's "window on the world" offered views in both directions,
opening up educational opportunity to the young in the developing world, as well
as offering schoolchildren in more prosperous countries insights and understanding from across the planet. The history of the view from the poorer side of the window has not been a happy one. Despite substantial expenditure on hardware and
training, initial attempts to establish ETV systems in Third World countries almost
all failed to deliver their promise. The reasons were manifold, and their analysis carries useful lessons for education everywhere, as well as for future attempts to har-
ness technology to change. As in so many other fields, the Third World experience
of aid to support ETV was bedeviled by error. Incredibly, a famous survey of 91 territories showed that at the end of the 1970s, millions of dollars of aid initially invested in transmission and production facilities had little or no influence on
educational standards, because there had been no comparable investment in reception equipment (Katz & Wedell, 1978, p. 13).

ETV in the Third World was also negatively affected in many areas by
postcolonial influences, as well as the familiar commercial aspirations of suppliers
from more advanced countries. Postcolonial influences shaped ETV structures in
Africa, for example, with Francophonic Africa adopting French traditions and former British territories establishing ETV on lines derived from the BBC model, however inappropriate such arrangements were to indigenous culture and educational
structures. In many countries, the temptation for heads of state to take over the
"public" broadcasting system, openly or covertly, proved too great to resist. Naturally, education and training attracted the attention of politicians, inhibiting the
growth of healthy ETV systems.

Liberalization of broadcasting in Africa in the 1980s encouraged the emergence of a much greater variety of administrative and funding arrangements: "Despite their limitations, the new private radio and television stations in Africa portend great hopes for democracy, media freedom, social mobilisation and subtle challenge to the monopoly of state-controlled broadcasting" (Okigbo, 1996, p. 152). This is another reminder that *publicly funded* is not a synonym for *public service*, as some North American and most European broadcasters assume. In addition, it is important to recall that radio, no longer a significant contributor to educational broadcasting in developed countries, remains the dominant broadcasting technology for sub-Saharan Africa and for much of Asia, and has played a key role in education and training.

In Latin America, state-owned media have generally been dominated by political machines. Commercial broadcasting, modeled roughly on United States principles of free competition, has attracted the major audiences. There has been little or no regulation of ownership or standards: ETV has suffered accordingly. So poor was the tradition that a senior Peruvian broadcaster at a 1996 UNESCO meeting described community television stations (whether based on university, regional, or municipal funding) as the only form of recognizable ETV established in the continent, because they alone were "non-profit enterprises without partisan aims" (Roncagliolo, 1996, p. 178). The main reason for the failure of ETV to thrive, or even emerge, in many countries lay, above all else, in the general culture of broadcasting itself. In Brazil, for example, even a decade after the 1984 fall of the military dictatorship, the broadcasting situation was not conducive to genuine ETV operations. A single broadcaster (Globo-TV) attracted 80% of the audience and 80% of the advertising revenue, while also owning cable TV and press interests, advertising agencies, publishing companies, record and video corporations, and most of the telecommunications industry. There was no need for Globo-TV to pretend interest in an effective ETV system. Instead, in 1995 alone, Philip Morris spent $24 million on educating young Brazilians to take up cigarette smoking (Moss, 1996).

Even where ETV systems were established in Third World territories, they faced other chronic problems. Untrained teaching staff found the challenge of the television lesson—although aimed at supporting their teaching—too great to handle. As the delegate from Thailand put it at an international conference as long ago as 1964, "the trouble in our country is that teachers will turn on the sets and go fishing" (Scupham, 1967, p. 179). The resistance of equipment to the challenges of climate improved over time, but the massive endemic problems of societies struggling with poverty, disease, and despair generally proved too great for ETV to surmount, except in the great democracy of India, and in other relatively advanced societies such as Singapore or the Philippines.

India, with its vast population and geographic and cultural variety, played major roles in ETV from the first. In the 1960s, for example, an ambitious national English-teaching scheme to train teachers and give children basic language competence was proposed. Nicknamed "Operation Snowball," it aimed to offer language programs direct to rural communities, and in the process of helping children to speak

English also to train "monitors" as teachers. The scheme melted away before it could develop momentum, but the needs and the ambition to use ETV remained great. During the 1970s and 1980s, Indian experience of using ETV for distance education increased. The United Nations education agency UNESCO, through its ORBICOM agency (www.orbicom.uquam.com), supports the Training and Development Communication Channel (TDCC) of the Indian Space Research Agency. This is an interactive satellite-based (one-way video, two-way audio) network for distance training, education, and teleconferencing. Since 1995, it has been used by both the Indira Gandhi Open University and the All-India Management Association. It is also in use by several Indian state governments for rural development training and wider educational purposes. Indian experts have played key roles in the work of the Asian Broadcasting Union (ABU) and similar agencies that encourage effective use of ETV to help resolve specific educational problems. To combat the threat of international satellite broadcasting to indigenous cultures, ABU and its allies have attempted to strengthen the competitive appeal of national and satellite ETV output by a variety of measures (Goonesekera, 1996).

KEY FEATURES OF EFFECTIVE ETV AND LESSONS FROM HISTORY

The history of ETV over the past half-century is kaleidoscopic, but certain key features have recurred in the more effective and durable systems. For example, by the mid-1970s, the rival British educational television services for schools (Independent Television and BBC) had set up very similar arrangements aimed at maintaining elements that would ensure a flow of ETV output that teachers and children would value and use:

- Policy advice influencing programming priorities and styles, from committees of independent educational experts.
- Production teams with specific expertise in particular subject areas and realistic aspirations to follow careers in ETV as a profession.
- Field forces of professional "education officers" working with schools and classes to feed back evaluations of programs and to devise and edit support material for teachers.
- Support materials for teachers, clearly linked to specific broadcasts and made available at the time of first transmission.
- Evaluation of effectiveness of specific series and wide circulation of generalizable findings.
- Independent research into special areas of concern or interest, contributing to ongoing exploration of educational and ETV topics.
- Regular assessment of overall teacher attitudes to services, equipment availability, and other factors affecting greater use of the service.

These key features were first established by an impressively thorough study (Hayter, 1974) to test the educational advantages, if any, of the planned use of broadcasts, given proper levels of equipment. Teachers in 118 schools maintained careful records of their ETV activities over a full school year and submitted three termly reports, amounting in all to well over 2 million words. Despite the lapse of time, the key findings are still expressed by today's teachers and summarize the best aspects of ETV:

- *Value of broadcasts:* The programs act as a stimulus for children's imagination, opening a window on the world. They offer both evidence not readily available to the teacher and help for the nonspecialist teacher. They often show a novel approach to a familiar topic. They have special value for underprivileged schools. Compared to other resources, television is inexpensive and its programs and support material have been found to be reliable and trustworthy.
- *Effective use of broadcasts:* Teachers recognize that carefully planned preparation and follow-up work are essential. For this reason, support material must be available when the programs are viewed. Recording of broadcasts prior to class viewing is also essential.
- *Effects of using broadcasts:* Television's stimulus to children's ideas is often vivid and may continue long after viewing. It may be especially effective with average and below-average ability pupils. Teachers privately acknowledge that they can gain skills and understanding of a subject from programs and support. School–home links can be simply and effectively fostered by the careful use of ETV (and other) broadcasts.

The continuing value of ETV services to schools, even at a time of national and international excitement over the potential educational impact of information and communications technology, was underlined in a report published in 1993 by the British Office for Standards in Education. This confirmed that the use of broadcasts (radio and television) in primary schools (for children aged 4–11) was well above average: "It provided a stimulus which most teachers used effectively to support and enrich the curriculum. The quality of work in 80% of these lessons was satisfactory or better" (OFSTED, 1993, p. 7).

At the heart of this success is the relationship between the broadcaster, teacher, and child. The British ETV broadcasters, themselves mainly from a teaching background, never lost sight of the educational potential of ETV when used by a sympathetic teacher and viewed by a receptive child, and therefore used their technology in programs designed to take account of teacher attitudes to teaching a subject. The dangers of failing to apply this principle are already interfering with the effectiveness of the current learning revolution. A team of United States educational researchers reported in 1999 on how use of Internet resources and new technologies varies dramatically according to the attitudes and practices of "traditional" and "constructivist" teachers, the former apparently outnumbering the latter by more than two to one (64% to 28%). An even higher proportion of teachers, although recognizing the value and attractions of independent student work and complex thinking (constructivist principles), judge that students themselves also value the traditional elements of good teaching that include direct instruction, skills practice, and directed discussion (Becker, 1999). Educational television at its best has shown unparalleled energy, range, and stimulus. It has plenty of life in it yet, for educational projects in many situations. Its history also offers many lessons for effective application of newer technologies, lessons that will be ignored at peril.

REFERENCES

Baggaley, J. (2001, Autumn). Media divergence! *Screenseen*, pp. 4–6.
Becker, H. J. (1999). Quoted in J. Mckenzie, Beware the shallow waters! *From Now On, 8*(9), 11–16.
Goonesekera, A. (1996). Global satellite broadcasting services: Educational and cultural contributions. In *Public service broadcasting: Cultural and educational dimensions* (pp. 69–90). Paris: UNESCO.
Hayter, C. G. (1974). *Using broadcasts in schools: A study and evaluation.* London: BBC/IBA.
Himmelweit, H. T., Oppenheim, A. N., & Vince, P. (1958). *Television and the child.* Oxford, UK: Oxford University Press.
Katz, E., & Wedell, G. (1978). *Broadcasting in the third world—promise and performance.* London: Macmillan.
Kelley, P., & Gunter, B. (1993). *Helping viewers learn from television: A new approach to increasing the impact of the medium.* Unpublished Report of the Television Literacy Project.
Kemelfield, G. (1971). *The evaluation of schools broadcasts: Piloting a new approach.* London: Independent Broadcasting Authority.
Kirkpatrick, H., & Cuban, L. (1998). Computers make kids smarter—right? *TECHNOS Quarterly for Education and Technology, 7*(2), 1–14.
Kodaira, S. I., & Takahashi, Y. (2001). New developments in media use in schools. *NHK Broadcasting Culture and Research, 17.* Tokyo: NHK.
Langham, J. (1990). *Teachers and television.* London: John Libbey.
Moss, R. (1996). Soaps and cigarettes. *Spectrum, 23,* 18–19.
Nippon Hoso Kyokai (NHK). (2001). *Nippon Hoso Kyokai Annual Report 2001.* Tokyo: Author.
O'Bryan, K. G. (1980). The teaching face: A historical perspective. In E. L. Palmer & A. Dorr (Eds.), *Children and the faces of television* (pp. 5–17). New York: Academic Press.
Office for Standards in Education (OFSTED). (1993). *The use of educational broadcasts in primary schools.* London: OFSTED Inspection Report.
Okigbo, C. (1996). Broadcasting liberalisation: Implications for education and culture in sub-Saharan Africa. *Public service broadcasting—cultural and educational dimensions* (pp. 147–168). Paris: UNESCO.
Roncagliolo, R. (1996). Latin America: Community radio and television as public service broadcasting. In *Public service broadcasting—cultural and educational dimensions* (pp. 169–180). Paris: UNESCO.
Santayana, G. (1905). *Life of reason.* New York: Scribner.
Schramm, W., Lyle, J., & Parker, E. (1961). *Television in the lives of our children.* Stanford, CA: Stanford University Press.
Scupham, J. (1967). *Broadcasting in the community.* London: C. A. Watts.
Smudits, A. (1996). The case of Western Europe. *Public service broadcasting—cultural and educational dimensions* (pp. 93–122). Paris: UNESCO.
Watkins, B. A., Huston-Stein, A., & Wright, J. C. (1980). Effects of planned television programming. In E. L. Palmer & A. Dorr (Eds.), *Children and the faces of television* (pp. 49–70). New York: Academic Press.

4

Content Development of Children's Media

Valerie Crane
Research Communications Ltd.

Milton Chen
George Lucas Educational Foundation

This chapter examines the content development process in children's media and the impressive changes in the landscape over the past 20 years. Within this time frame, four striking changes have occurred:

- A dramatic increase in available programming.
- More diverse types of quality programming from an educational perspective.
- A significantly broader range of program providers.
- Expansion of media choices to include the computer, the Internet, CD-ROMs and DVDs, and the VCR.

Twenty years ago, one could clearly distinguish between animated entertainment fare commonly seen on cable, the broadcast networks, and independent television stations, and the educational fare aired on PBS (the Public Broadcasting Service). Today, the lines between these providers and new players have blurred for a variety of reasons, with interesting consequences. For instance, in the 1980s, instructional television was centrally organized with state agencies carrying schedules that led to taping off the air and then distributing the programs to the schools. That system has largely been dismantled and replaced with a highly decentralized system difficult to describe and measure. Only a few regional networks continue to exist, whereas state agencies, some PBS stations, and school systems now control distribution. Two entities that gained prominence in the last decade—Channel One and Cable in the Classroom—provide an interesting contrast to an otherwise fragmented system.

In this chapter, we begin with a review of the children's media landscape, and then discuss critical factors that have changed the face of children's media. We conclude with a look at the themes that emerged from the collection of interviews conducted for this chapter.

CHILDREN'S MEDIA LANDSCAPE: THE VALUE OF CHOICE AND CONTROL

The most striking shift in children's media over the past 20 years is best understood by examining media consumption in the average American home with children. Media choices and modes of delivery have expanded dramatically.

Media in the Home

Every form of media that existed in 1980 (cable and broadcast) as well as new formats (VCRs, computers, and the Internet) have captured significant market share. Table 4.1 illustrates the proliferation of media competing for children's attention in the home.

An Annenberg Public Policy Center report indicates that cable homes in the Philadelphia market have access to children's programming on "29 different channels that air 1,324 shows (279 unique titles) ... over the course of one week" (Woodard, 1999, p. 3). In a national study, Woodard and Gridina (2000) reported that children exert significant *control* over these choices because these media often reside in the children's own bedrooms, including TVs (57%), video games (39%), cable service (36%), telephone (32%), VCRs (30%), computers (20%), and Internet access (11%).

Despite this increase in choice and control, fragmentation of the marketplace is having some surprising effects on children's media usage. TV still occupies most of children's media time (147 minutes per day), with significantly less time spent on the Internet (14 minutes per day; Woodard & Gridina, 2000). However, the expanding media choices in the home are impacting television negatively. Children's television viewing dropped by 3% from 1990 to 2000 (Alexander, 2001).

Combined with a soft advertising marketplace for children's media in 2001, this decline may well mark the end of a significant era of growth for children's television.

Programming Content: What Is Available?

During the 1990s, through acquisition of channels and consolidation of media companies, the largest companies—Viacom (which owns CBS), AOL/Time Warner (which owns Turner Broadcasting), The Walt Disney Company (which

TABLE 4.1

Media in the Home

Media	The 1980 Home	The 2000 Home
Number of Broadcast networks*	3	8
Number of Cable networks*	28	70+
Percentage of Basic cable penetration**	22.6%	67.9%
DBS penetration†	0	16%
Premium networks†	NA	30%
VCR penetration††	<1%	97%
Computers in home††	<1%	70%
Internet access††	0%	52%
Homes with high-speed Internet access†	0%	5%
Video game equipment††	NA	68%

Source: *Chernin, 1998; **NCTA, 2001; †CTAM, 2001a, 2001b, 2001c; ††specifically in homes with children; Woodard & Gridina, 2000. All other data for total U.S. households.

owns ABC), and News Corp. (which owns Fox broadcasting and cable)—have become the key players in programming for children aged 2–14. However, PBS and other cable networks are also important to the children's television landscape. The program offerings in the fall of 2001 included:

- *Nickelodeon* (owned by Viacom), the first children's cable channel, which airs an older children's block as well as a preschool block branded as "Nick Jr." In the fall of 2001, the latter included *Blue's Clues, Dora the Explorer,* and *Little Bill.* The Nick Jr. shows now also air on CBS Saturday morning and fulfill CBS's educational and informational programming requirements (also referred to as E/I) as mandated by the Federal Communications Commission (FCC). Nickelodeon also targets the "tween" age group of 9- to 14-year-olds with *TEENick* on Sunday nights.
- *Noggin* (owned by Viacom/Nickelodeon in partnership with Sesame Workshop) is an educational network featuring programming from Sesame Workshop, Nickelodeon, and other acquired series such as *Bill Nye,*

The Science Guy. New programming is also already on the schedule of this relatively new network, including *A Walk in Your Shoes, On the Team, Big Kids,* and *Sponk!*. Noggin is designed to be a convergent network and uses its Web site to give its audience direct access to what is featured on the air.

- *PBS* has shifted its focus from 2- to 11-year-olds to that of preschoolers. This programming includes their *Ready to Learn* initiative consisting of 6.5 hours of programming daily on 133 PBS stations. Its lineup includes *Arthur* (from WGBH), *Clifford the Red Dog* (from Scholastic Productions), *Dragon Tales* (from Sesame Workshop), *Between the Lions* (from WGBH), and *Reading Rainbow* (from GPN/Nebraska ETV Network and WNED-TV Buffalo). Other programming on PBS for preschoolers includes *Teletubbies, Barney & Friends,* and *Sesame Street.* WGBH brought *ZOOM* back to PBS with a live, interactive experience for 6- to 11-year-olds.

- *Cartoon Network* (owned by AOL/Time Warner) offers animated fare including younger children's classics such as *Scooby Doo, The Bugs and Daffy Show,* and *Tom and Jerry.* The Cartoon Network creates two original series per year, examples of which include *Dexter's Lab* and the popular *Powerpuff Girls* for the 6- to 11-year-old audience. Cartoon Network has also launched a second channel of classic cartoons, *Boomerang.*

- *Discovery Kids* (owned by Discovery Networks) is a 24-hour digital cable channel as well as a programming block on NBC. Examples of programming on Discovery Kids include *Bingo & Molly* and *Ni Ni's Treehouse* for preschool children, and *Sci-Squad* and *Popular Mechanics for Kids* for older children. The Learning Channel (TLC) airs the *Ready, Set, Learn* preschool programming block on Monday through Friday mornings, commercial free.

- *Disney Channel* (owned by The Walt Disney Company) has a preschool offering, Playhouse Disney, which includes programs such as *Rolie Polie Olie* and *Bear in the Big Blue House.* Their block for 9- to 14-year-olds is called Zoog Disney and includes *Lizzie McGuire* (its highest rated live-action series), other original fare, and reruns of shows such as *Boy Meets World.* Disney Channel has also launched a second channel, *Toon Disney,* comprised of animated fare. ABC Kids programs Disney's One Saturday Morning block on the ABC Television Network. Two Disney Channel series—*Even Stevens* and *Lizzie McGuire*—are in that One Saturday Morning block.

- *Fox Kids* (owned by News Corp.) provides a feed to the Fox affiliates on weekend mornings. Their programming includes the *Power Rangers* and *Digimon.* Fox Kids also offers a science show, *The Magic School Bus* (produced by Scholastic Productions), to fulfill their FCC E/I requirement.

- *HBO Family* (owned by AOL/Time Warner) is a 24/7 children/family network and a relative newcomer. This channel is part of the HBO premium offering, for which parents pay a monthly fee. Their programming blocks include HBO Jam, which builds on classic books such as *Babar, Curious*

George, and *Paddington Bear* for preschool children, and HBO Magnet for older kids, which includes *Crashbox* (a revamp of *Braingames), 30 by 30: Kidflicks* (featuring movies made by kids), and *The Worst Witch.* HBO Family is also interested in developing interactive and convergent experiences for their viewers.

- *WAM! America's Kidz Network,* a commercial-free cable network from the Starz Encore Media Group (owned by Liberty Media), provides 24/7 live-action programming for 8- to 16-year-olds, with dayparts including the morning *Mind Zone,* after-school *OH! Zone,* and weekend *End Zone* (movies). Programming includes *Caught in the Middle,* the first high school reality show; *Get Reel, which* focuses on teen lifestyles; and *The Tribe,* a sci-fi series that helps kids solve problems as they band together to recreate social order in a postapocalyptic world.
- *WB Network,* and *UPN* are further examples of commercial TV networks and channels that offer children's programming, each of which meets the broadcast requirements of E/I programming.

With the exception of *Blue's Clues* on Nickelodeon, most programming is produced by a range of providers, including animation houses (e.g., CINAR, Nelvana), public television stations (e.g., WGBH, WNET), publishers (e.g., Scholastic Productions), and production houses (e.g., Sesame Workshop, BBC, and DIC).

To illustrate the value of a family/children's cable channel, in November 2001 Fox Family was sold (including its domestic and international assets) to Disney/ABC for $5.2 billion. At the time of the sale, the ABC network announced that they would rename the channel ABC Family but repurpose at least some ABC network fare on the channel. Hence, Fox Family became the first significant casualty of cable networks targeted exclusively toward children and family.

Media Usage among Children: What Are They Watching?

Although the historical ratings strength of the broadcast networks (NBC, CBS, ABC, and Fox) continues among adults, top children's ratings in the 2000 season shifted from broadcast to branded cable networks' ratings and share. Nickelodeon (4.0/21), Cartoon Network (1.6/7), and Disney Channel (1.2/6) had 20% increases among kids aged 2–11 across 7 days, whereas the six broadcast networks declined 39%, to 1.7/10. The sole exception was CBS, which increased 157% with the Nick Jr. lineup on Saturday mornings (Freeman, 2001).

Nielsen measures network and program viewership, and is currently the only provider of ratings services to the broadcast and cable industry. Tables 4.2 and 4.3 provide the Nielsen ratings for the 2000–2001 season for the top nine networks on Saturday mornings and weekdays, by different age groups (not including PBS). The "rating" represents the percentage of children in the target age group watching a particular program or network by averaging quarter hours. The "share" is the percentage of children in homes using television in that time slot watching a particular

TABLE 4.2

Top Kids' Networks: Saturday Mornings

Kids 2–11	Rating/Share	Kids 6–11	Rating/Share
1. Nickelodeon	5.0/21	1. Nickelodeon	5.4/23
2. Kids' WB	3.0/13	2. Kids' WB	3.7/16
3. Fox Kids	2.4/10	3. Fox Kids	2.8/12
4. ABC	2.2/10	4. ABC	2.2/10
5. CBS	1.8/9	5. Cartoon Network	1.5/6
5. Cartoon Network	1.8/8	6. UPN	1.4/7
7. Disney Channel	1.5/6	7. CBS	1.0/5
8. UPN	1.3/6	7. Disney Channel	1.0/4
9. NBC	0.6/2	9. NBC	0.6/3

Kids 2–5	Rating/Share	Teens 12–17	Rating/Share
1. Nickelodeon	4.3/18	1. Kids' WB	1.8/14
2. CBS	3.2/15	2. NBC	1.4/9
3. Cartoon Network	2.4/10	3. Fox Kids	1.3/10
4. ABC	2.2/10	4. Nickelodeon	1.2/9
5. Kids' WB	2.1/9	4. ABC	1.2/9
5. Disney Channel	2.1/9	6. UPN	1.0/8
7. Fox Kids	1.7/7	7. Cartoon Network	0.6/4
8. UPN	1.1/5	8. CBS	0.3/2
9. NBC	0.5/2	8. Disney Channel	0.3/2

Source: Freeman (2001), 2000–2001 broadcast season.

TABLE 4.3

Top Kids' Networks: Weekdays

Kids 2–11	Rating/Share	Teens 12–17	Rating/Share
1. Nickelodeon	3.0/20	1. Kids' WB	0.9/6
2. Fox Kids	1.5/8	2. UPN	0.8/15
3. Kids' WB	1.4/8	2. Nickelodeon	0.8/7
4. Cartoon Network	1.3/8	2. Fox Kids	0.8/5
5. UPN	1.1/8	5. Disney Channel	0.6/5
6. Disney Channel	0.8/6	6. Cartoon Network	0.5/4

Source: Freeman (2001), 2000–2001 broadcast season.

program or network. The ratings data show the strength of Nickelodeon and other cable networks against broadcast offerings. When the PBS lineup is factored in, however, the story changes, showing that the top five programs are on PBS.

In conclusion, we find that children now have more choice and control over their viewing than ever before, making for a highly competitive marketplace in which Nickelodeon has surged to the top both weekdays and Saturday morning. PBS continues to be strong with kids aged 2–11; the WB and UPN networks show strength among 2- to 11- and 11- to 17-year-olds; and the three traditional networks of 20 years ago do not figure in the top three choices, even on Saturday morning.

The decline in broadcast ratings has resulted in two major broadcasters essentially pulling out of the children's television business. In the fall of 2001, NBC leased its Saturday morning time slot to Discovery Kids for at least $6 million ("Discovery Eyes," 2001). In the same time frame, Fox pulled its weekday programming block for kids, and then leased its 4-hour Saturday block to 4Kids Entertainment Inc. for the fall of 2002 for $25 million (McClellan & Schlosser, 2002).

The Internet

Since the mid-1990s, the Internet has quickly become an important medium for children interested in entertainment as well as educational content. In the numbers of households with Internet access and in time spent with this new medium, the Internet has become the "mass medium" to gain the swiftest widespread use in history. The Internet is leading to new forms of content and media use among children, causing researchers to redefine theories and methods of studying children's media behavior.

TABLE 4.4

Top Children's Programs Including PBS

Kids 2–5	Network	Rating	Kids 2–11	Network	Rating
1. Clifford M–F	PBS	12.4	1. Arthur M–F	PBS	7.1
2. Arthur M–F	PBS	12.2	2. Clifford M–F	PBS	6.9
3. Dragon Tales M–F	PBS	12.0	3. Dragon Tales M–F	PBS	6.5
4. Barney & Friends M–F	PBS	9.8	4. Rugrats Sat.	Nickelodeon	5.0
5. Caillou M–F	PBS	8.9	4. Rugrats Sun.	Nickelodeon	5.0
6. Dora the Explorer M–F	Nickelodeon	7.6	6. Barney & Friends M–F	PBS	4.7
6. Sesame Street M–F	PBS	7.6	6. Spongebob Sat.	Nickelodeon	4.7
8. Bob the Builder M–F	Nickelodeon	6.9	8. Rugrats Sun.	Nickelodeon	4.5
9. Teletubbies M–F	PBS	6.8	8. Rugrats Sat.	Nickelodeon	4.5

Source: For PBS, NTI Pocketpiece for April 2001. For broadcast, cable, and syndication, Nielsen Galaxy Explorer, April 1–30, 2001, as cited in PBS press release, April 2001.

Many children routinely work on several tasks simultaneously on their computers; for example, surfing the Web or working on a homework assignment while also instant messaging with their friends. Another novel reported use of the Internet involves a related type of "media multitasking," using multiple TV and computer screens simultaneously. These new forms of media behavior are not well documented, but offer intriguing possibilities for both future media design and research.

Children's Access to and Use of the Internet.   In less than a decade, the home computer has become a mass medium, experiencing periods of explosive growth similar to those of home radio ownership from the 1920s to 1940s and TV ownership from the 1950s to 1960s—times when both media achieved penetration rates close to 80% (Paik, 2001). From a 51.9% penetration rate in 1997, Grunwald Associates (2000) reported that 64% of family households had a home computer by the last quarter of 1999.

Beyond access, Grunwald Associates (2000) found that 61% of 9- to 17-year-olds reported using the Internet, with a higher percentage of teenagers online than younger children (71% of 13- to 17-year-olds vs. 48% of 9- to 12-year-olds). In contrast to Internet use in 64% of all homes with children, only 46% of lower-income parents report that their children use the Internet from home. Fortunately, schools overcome economic barriers, with 68% of these lower-income parents reporting that their children use the Internet at school. It is likely that more than 80% of homes soon will have a computer, with Internet access available in at least 70% of them. Faster broadband access, enabling downloading of multimedia over the Internet, has also increased at an impressive rate. With close to 11% penetration by August 2000, broadband households are expected to double within a few years.

The Most Popular Web Content.   Table 4.5 shows the most popular Web sites for children aged 2 to 11 and 6 to 11. One striking finding is the number of popular Web sites linked to TV networks with children's programming (e.g., Cartoon Network, Nickelodeon, Fox Kids, PBS, WB Network). Although there are a number of independent children's Web sites without a network TV partner, these also tend to have a well-known product franchise (e.g., Barbie, Pokemon, American Girl). These data point to the importance of Web sites having a strong TV partner, leveraging a strong "brand" of products and characters as well as the substantial promotion and marketing for Web content afforded by a multihour (in some cases, 24-hour) block of children's programs. Rather than the Web proving to be a medium that is competitive to television, it is evolving into a mutually reinforcing partnership across the TV and Internet platforms.

Given the economic downturn in the media and technology sectors in 2000–2001, it is likely that, as with television, the consolidation of children's Web sites also will continue. Independent children's Web providers have found it increasingly difficult to generate revenue from advertising and product sales to support their content. Even those children's TV channels with strong Web traffic have reduced their financial investments in their Web sites. With falling revenues from banner advertising on children's sites, their media companies increasingly view the Web sites as integral to the core television programming. Although federal agencies and private foundations now view a strong, interactive Web presence as an important part of their funding of children's television programming, the overall level of such funding has also dropped.

School Television

Changes in Technology and Content Providers.   As noted in our introduction, the instructional television (ITV) landscape has changed dramatically since 1980,

TABLE 4.5

Top Web Sites for Kids

Domain	Kids 2–11 Unique Audience (in thousands)	Domain	Kids 6–11 Unique Audience (in thousands)
cartoonnetwork.com	1,056	foxkids.com	376
nick.com	870	postopia.com	254
foxkids.com	421	kiddonet.com	195
postopia.com	260	sikids.com	188
kiddonet.com	198	kidswb.com	148
barbie.com	193	mamamedia.com	131
sikids.com	191	pokemon.com	122
pbskids.org	181	americangirl.com*	70
kidswb.com	157	amandaplease.com*	61
mamamedia.com	134	toomunchfun.com*	59

*These sites have a low sample size. Please use for directional purpose only.
Source: Nielsen/NetRatings Inc. data for June 2001.

perhaps even more so than TV use in the home. Although broadcasting of children's educational programming continues to be a viable distribution channel (albeit with more programming sources and competition from new technologies), school television has been affected in major ways by two major technological advancements: the VCR and the Internet.

During the 1980s, the VCR became a significant technology for increasing the flexibility of use of school television. With the growth of the VCR, teachers increasingly used videocassettes, provided by ITV agencies or self-recorded, to time shift video-based lessons from the time of broadcast to more convenient times for their own curricula. Many ITV agencies have reconfigured broadcasting so that educators could record blocks of programs from a series during a 1- or 2-hour block, sometimes even broadcast overnight for VCR recording.

Since the 1980s, a national system for purchasing and distributing instructional TV has existed, operated by education agencies affiliated with public television and state departments of education. However, national broadcasting of school television has gradually declined, with lower levels of state funding. As well, PBS and other educational stations have been devoting less airtime to instructional TV, relying instead on videocassette distribution and increasing content available via the Internet. Two agencies—the Center for Education Initiatives (CEI) and the National Educational Telecommunications Association (NETA)—continue to conduct an annual review process beginning with a program fair called FirstView to screen, purchase, and distribute ITV and other media for classroom use.

In 2001, 74 agencies purchased program leases and related services from 54 distributors, serving a total of nearly 33 million K–12 students. Programming is distributed via open-air broadcast, cable, instructional television fixed service (ITFS), satellite networks, prerecorded videocassettes, electronic networks, and the Internet. Since 1980, cable and satellite television networks have provided major alternative sources of instructional programming to those of ITV agencies and PBS stations. Two of these best-known providers include:

- *Channel One* (owned by Primedia), a daily, 12-minute hosted news program distributed to over 12,000 middle and high schools, reaching over 350,000 classrooms and more than 8 million teens (36% of all 12- to 17-year-olds; Channel One, 2001). Channel One provides the equipment to the schools so they can receive the programming every day. Schools agree to this daily student viewing. Advertising is sold within the program to fund the project. The original purpose of Channel One was to address the decline in cultural literacy among America's youth by providing a daily news program.
- *Cable in the Classroom,* a service that involved the mobilization of the entire cable industry, including cable operators, who wired 80,000 schools (78% of all U.S. schools) and 42 cable networks that prepared or repackaged programming for in-school use. The Cable in the Classroom initiative serves 43 million children in Grades Kindergarten through 12 who receive 525 hours of instructional programming in an average week (Dirr, 2001). What is most interesting about this initiative is that it is entirely funded by the cable industry with no concomitant revenue stream.

During the past decade, these school television groups have placed a growing emphasis on teacher training and have offered programming and workshops to assist teachers in utilizing instructional TV and related technologies, such as the Internet and CDs. This effort recognizes that the growth of media use in schools relies on well-trained teachers, and that the great majority of teachers have not received such training in their schools of education. A number of these agencies, such as WGBH-Boston and Harvard-Smithsonian Center for Astrophysics, have produced video series on the topic and distributed them to other agencies.

Utilization of School Television.   The Corporation for Public Broadcasting's fourth national survey of school television (1997) showed impressive increases in both availability and use. More than 98% of K–12 teachers reported using television and VCRs for instruction. The dominant medium for TV use has been the videocassette, rather than direct broadcast, through cassettes provided by media centers (79%), school districts (54%), a teacher's own home recording (67%), and other teachers or friends (57%). The most popular series were *Reading Rainbow, The Magic School Bus,* and *Bill Nye, The Science Guy* among elementary teachers; *National Geographic, Bill Nye,* and *NOVA* for middle school teachers; and *NOVA, Biography,* and *National Geographic* among high school teachers.

The study also pointed to increasing use of computers during the 1996–97 school year, which has continued over the past 5 years. These survey results suggested that TV and computer use did not supplant one another, but instead were complementary. For instance, teachers used the Internet to access online teacher guides that could be used to more effectively present video lessons in the classroom.

CRITICAL FACTORS THAT HAVE CHANGED THE FACE OF CHILDREN'S MEDIA

Now that we have a better understanding of the vast nature of the children's media landscape, it is important to examine some of the critical factors that impact what ultimately ends up on the program schedule or a Web site. Given the increasing complexity of the children's programming marketplace, the authors of this chapter chose to interview key television and Internet executives and professionals to examine how decisions are made about what and how content is created.

More than 60 interviews, each approximately 1 hour in length, were conducted with academic, network, or programming researchers; instructional television professionals; network heads; programming heads; marketers; Web experts; content experts; and policy or funding professionals.

The factors that influence the content and distribution of children's television fall into five different areas:

Regulatory influences

Funding sources

Vision and leadership

A focus on children

Teamwork

Regulatory influences: The Feds Step In

One of the most significant shifts in the marketplace since 1980 is the result of the Three-Hour Rule—a by-product of the Children's Television Act of 1990, which mandated that broadcast stations carry a minimum of 3 hours of educational and informational programming for children each week (FCC, 1996). The Three-Hour Rule was not met with enthusiasm by most commercial broadcasters. The children's daypart had already been significantly threatened competitively by children's cable networks (Nickelodeon in particular) that were not subject to the rules.

Local affiliates carrying this programming were already concerned about the declining ratings for children's programming, and the networks were not convinced that programming could be both educational *and* entertaining (i.e., retain children's interest), thus posing a serious threat to revenue. The huge success of *Blue's Clues* would suggest that this assumption is false, at least among preschool children, but the mindset persists today.

According to the Annenberg Public Policy Center (Jordan, 2000), the requirements of the Three-Hour Rule have, for the most part, been met. As mentioned earlier, the networks have either purchased existing educational programming or "multiplexed" programming (through repeat broadcasts) from cable networks they own. It is interesting to note that although the cable networks are not subject to these rules, much of their programming would fit the E/I guidelines. Reasons for that are discussed later in the chapter.

On the negative side, two trends in the business over the past 20 years have been reinforced by the Three-Hour Rule. First, the requirements have been met most often with prosocial programming that features positive role models and prosocial content messages rather than with programming such as *3-2-1 Contact* and *The Magic School Bus*, which had a cognitive focus on science content. This latter type of programming often requires extensive content and audience research, necessitating additional production time and expense. Second, in a review of programming available in the Philadelphia market, Jordan (2000) found that only one in five of the E/I programs were highly educational, a decline from a little over one in three the previous year. Over half of the programs (57%) were rated moderately educational, and almost one in four (23%) were rated minimally educational. This number should certainly improve in the future, because the CBS morning lineup now contains the Nick Jr. offerings that are stronger on socioemotional educational content, and Discovery Kids will be providing programming to NBC.

Despite concerns over the commercial broadcast fare, much of children's programming is seen to be improving: "The indication today is that children's programming in the United States is both expanding and improving, although the expansion is found primarily on cable program channels such as Nickelodeon and Disney, along with a host of other new competitors" (Kunkel & Wilcox, 2001, p. 598).

Funding Sources: Who Is Investing?

A variety of public sector organizations, along with private foundations, continue to fund the children's educational programming that is currently available, particularly children's programs on PBS. Those funding sources include the National Science Foundation (NSF; e.g., *The Magic School Bus* from Scholastic Productions, *Cyberchase* from WNET), the U.S. Department of Education (e.g., *Ready to Learn* on PBS), the Corporation for Public Broadcasting (CPB), and PBS itself. A number of private foundations provide lower levels of funding, such as the Carnegie Corporation of New York and the Pew Charitable Trusts.

These government funders and foundations typically require producers to develop clear educational goals, conduct formative research, and document audience reach and impact. They have increasingly required producers to accompany their production and broadcast plans with specific goals for local community outreach and Web site development to provide program content and training for teachers, parents, and child-care providers.

Although these projects are held accountable for defining their educational goals and plans to achieve them, they are also responsible for reaching a critical mass of child viewers to warrant spending public funds. Therefore, PBS—which carries most of this programming—carefully tracks viewership, removing shows that are declining and replacing them with stronger shows that will achieve higher ratings. The funding from these sources, however, is not limited to PBS; profit-making ventures also receive funding or grants from foundations (e.g., Discovery Kids from the Markle Foundation, Scholastic Productions from the NSF for *The Magic School Bus*). *Bill Nye, The Science Guy* was produced by KCET (funded by NSF) but originally distributed by Disney's syndication arm, Buena Vista, with a dual PBS/commercial schedule.

Commercial television programming, including some of the cable networks, continues to be largely supported by advertising sales. Discussing the 2000 ratings season, Salfino (2001) cited $1.138 billion total ad spending on children's and family entertainment and animation programming. The majority of advertising was spent on animated fare ($860 million), with significantly less on children's and family entertainment ($277 million) and the least on educational programs ($108 million). PBS and HBO Family are venues on which no advertising appears in programming. Early in 2002, the Disney Channel began accepting sponsorships on air.

As fragmentation increases, and ratings decline for children's television, the large media companies with multiple platforms for their product are finding that they can recapture their costs through multiple plays of the same program within a short period of time. Exchange of programs across venues is a relatively new development, with much more to come in the future. And although the rerun factor is a negative among adults, children enjoy watching programs more than once, making this model more feasible. For instance, the Nick Jr. lineup may be seen both on Nickelodeon and CBS, whereas Disney Channel programming is also broadcast on ABC. Cross-venue offerings will help to support the development of quality children's programming. However, overall inventory may decline, thereby decreasing choices for children.

Cable subscription fees offer another revenue stream and are considered important in the overall economics of program development. Some cable networks are able to forego advertising altogether because they can recapture costs through subscription fees to cable and satellite distributors. Disney Channel has relatively high monthly subscription fees (75 cents to $1 per cable household), whereas Nickelodeon draws a lower fee of 30 cents to 50 cents per cable household; advertising accounts for the differences in the revenue models for these two channels.

Public television stations pay fees to PBS, and revenue sharing with producers provides needed support for the continued development of shows. Typically, PBS children's productions require additional support from corporations and foundations, beyond funds provided by PBS or CPB.

Most of the existing children's cable networks are carried on an analog tier, meaning that their subscription fees are guaranteed. However, channel capacity is limited for additional analog channels, pushing new children's networks onto a "digital" tier that becomes possible with the introduction of digital boxes into the home. Despite the challenges of generating revenue to support them, some feel that children's programming is one of the services for which families will pay. Discovery Kids is making such a bet by focusing on its full 24/7 channel for kids, but it also benefits from the NBC Saturday morning platform. HBO Family's funding comes from its premium subscription fees. With its rate structure, HBO is able to avoid both advertising (that pleases parents) and being driven by ratings. This frees them up to serve their own loyal viewers rather than deliver "eyeballs" to advertisers.

Since 1980, a significant shift has occurred in the marketplace, with both public sector projects as well as commercial ventures utilizing licensing and merchandising as an increasingly important funding source for children's television. The licensing of *Sesame Street* characters has been central to the financial model for Sesame Workshop since the 1970s. More recent success stories include *Blue's Clues, Teletubbies,* and *Barney* on the educational side and the commercial live action or animation projects of *Power Rangers, Digimon,* and *Spiderman.*

Despite the impressive results that licensing can sometimes provide, it is a high-risk business. According to some children's television executives interviewed, licensing is a difficult business to predict, so some wait until the second season—when a character has caught on—before launching products in the marketplace. Dependence on a licensing model also requires that programs have a strong charactercentric product. Plush toys appeal to a younger, preschool audience, whereas action toys work better with older children, although this market is also softening and giving way to electronic gaming.

Many children's projects today also generate CD-ROMs and other companion media as a way of driving sales and revenue. Despite the availability of so much programming directly to the home, the trip to the video store continues to generate significant revenue. According to Graves (1999), this $17 billion market is split between rentals and purchase. Four in five home video purchases are made for children (McCormick, 1996). Home video is of particular appeal to children, because they enjoy repeated viewings of the same programs.

Other media have also been a revenue source to children's programmers. Scholastic, a major publisher of children's books, has had success with *The Magic School Bus, Clifford the Big Red Dog, The Babysitters Club,* and *Goosebumps* driving sales of books. *Arthur* on PBS and *Paddington Bear, Curious George,* and *Babar* on HBO Family are also based on strong classic children's book titles that continue to sell well in conjunction with broadcasts.

"Windowing" of programming, or distributing programming in multiple venues, is another financial strategy used to increase the return on investment in children's programming. Windowing has taken several forms. International distribution has been a very successful way for companies to produce programming in the United States and either sell it to distributors abroad or establish a coventure and produce programming in a host country (e.g., *Sesame Street*, Nickelodeon, and others have distributed programming in countries around the world). Programming has also traveled from Great Britain to the United States, including such programs as *Noddy*, *Teletubbies*, and *Thomas the Tank Engine* (titled here as *Shining Time Station*).

However, as with licensing, windowing can also limit the kind of product developed. Many of those interviewed felt that this model would drive the development of animation with simple language, plot, and characters in order to permit crossing cultural barriers. The assumption is that the more idiosyncratic the program is to American culture, the less effective it would be for international distribution.

Twenty years ago, it was commonly accepted that commercial sources for funding were more likely to drive the development of entertainment vehicles, whereas public funding was the sole driver of quality educational programming for children. *Sesame Street* was the first notable exception in supplementing government and foundation funding with revenue from product licensing. Today, the funding source does not limit the kind of programming produced, although the public sector continues to require educational programming for children. The commercial models, however, are just as likely to produce programming of high quality, often with educational goals (albeit often prosocial), and a team dedicated to serving children well. The children's television industry has come of age: Without these commercial funding sources, much of what we see for children would not exist.

Vision and Leadership: Where Ideas Come From

Many of the media professionals we interviewed felt that successful shows begin with a vision, and the vision is more than an idea for a show. A second and related element is leadership—the ability of an individual or group of individuals to operationalize the vision.

Gerry Laybourne brought her own vision to Nickelodeon, a full-time network devoted to children. This focused effort introduced branding to the children's television world. *Branding* is defined as a singular way of thinking about a program or network that focuses on the viewer—or, for the purposes of this discussion, is kidcentric. Nickelodeon's genius was in creating not just one series, but an entire channel for kids, branding the channel itself as a "place for kids."

Although branding grows out of the commercial side of the business, PBS and educational producers, such as Sesame Workshop, also increasingly use its concepts in attempting to brand a larger group of programs and in branding across multiple media. Many of those interviewed believe that if there is no branding or organizational fit, the project will fail. Nickelodeon had a vision and created a culture that respected kids. Its vision is to connect with kids, and to connect kids to their world through entertainment. For HBO, viewers expect cutting-edge programming. Therefore, HBO Family feels it has permission to push the envelope on entertainment with products that are cutting edge with safe boundaries appropriate for kids—"edge-ucational," as HBO executive Dolores Morris called it. For Discovery, Discovery Kids is an obvious alignment with their vision of "Explore Your World." Disney Channel is about kids, family, and wholesome entertainment. Michael Eisner recently captured the spirit of the Disney vision when he described it as "the contagious appeal of innocence." Each of these brands was given "permission" by their viewers to develop programming that fits their basic brand, and many of these venues provide programming that serves children well.

Vision was also central to the birth of Cable in the Classroom. In 1989, several cable executives—including Glenn Jones of Jones Cable, John Malone of TCI, Ted Turner of Turner Broadcasting, and Amos Hostetter, founder of Continental Cablevision (now part of AT&T Broadband)—began a service to schools called Cable in the Classroom (described earlier). The initiative was rooted in a concern about service to the communities that had granted the franchises to a cable company to wire their communities. As cable companies grew and penetration of cable increased to a majority of households in the country, community service was considered on a larger scale.

This initiative was remarkable in several respects. First, it was founded on a vision of social responsibility in the form of advancing education. Although it gave the cable companies and cable networks visibility, the investment far exceeded the financial benefit, suggesting this was clearly not a pure profit-based decision. The second factor that was unusual in this initiative was the mobilization of so many cable companies and networks, all of whom supported the vision. Companies that had competed against each other for franchises, and negotiated against each other for programming contracts, all coalesced behind this important initiative. It was largely the vision, the energy, and the dedication of these cable executives that made this possible.

One of the networks offering Cable in the Classroom programming, ESPN, also benefited from the vision of its leadership. George Bodenheimer was a strong supporter of their product, *ESPN SportsFigures* (a series of videos produced to demonstrate principles of science and math using well-known sports figures), assigning key affiliate marketing and research executives to develop a strategy for this initiative. An in-house production team was assigned to this middle/high school math and physics project, and an external expert was hired to develop the content. Many other networks made the same commitment to similar projects.

During the 1980s, there was much debate concerning the public broadcast system, about whether PBS could serve children of all ages. Many argued that kids had "left" PBS by the time they were in school. After much discussion on the issue, PBS began to focus on preschool children. The "children's initiative" took effect in fall 1991, at which point PBS decided to fill the 7:00 A.M.–6:00 P.M. weekday schedule with children's programs. In prior years this slot had been full of holes, assorted adult programs, and so on. PBS also began funding new production. That fall, they added a weekly strip of *Shining Time Station*. In January 1992, they introduced *Lamb Chop's Play-Along*. In April, *Barney & Friends* debuted. The initiative led to a steady increase in ratings among kids aged 2 to 5, which has made PBS the dominant network among that age group during daytime hours, slightly ahead of Nickelodeon.

In 1994, PBS launched the *Ready to Learn* initiative, affirming its commitment to preschoolers at the expense of programming for the older child. At this writing, there are some new initiatives underway within the PBS system to return to serving children in the older age group of 6 to 14.

Another organization that has a clear vision of its core purpose is the educational division of WGBH, under the leadership of Brigid Sullivan. Although there are a number of educational/informational programs on the commercial networks, the WGBH team is different because they take on core curriculum subjects (e.g., *Behind the Lions*, which teaches reading), push the envelope on convergence (e.g., developing *Time Warp Trio*, which combines TV and the Web by presenting a mystery that kids can solve online), and support teachers by training them in the use of technology.

In summary, vision is an important grounding principle in the development of children's programming in cable, broadcast, and public TV. However, several factors give children's cable networks an advantage over their competitors:

- Their sole focus is on children, making it easier to create a continuous culture that serves children.
- They are large organizations with significant resources that they can dedicate to creating great product that attracts and holds the attention of their audience.
- They have to generate revenue and, therefore, have been forced to consider their target audience in everything they do.

This last point is the focus of the next section.

What Kidcentric Really Means: Who Is Our Audience?

Research is the primary tool for helping networks and producers become kidcentric, and three different kinds of research are conducted at children's networks and programming organizations:

- Foundation or basic research that teaches product developers how children think, explores opportunities for programming, and provides insights into trends that can be important in identifying what kids want and need.
- Formative research on a new product that informs the development of specific shows while in production.
- Summative research on an existing product that reveals the impact of viewing.

Basic Research.   Basic research is most likely to occur in organizations that have an ongoing, in-house research department. Sesame Workshop was among the first to have an in-house research team under the direction of the late Dr. Edward Palmer, and many of today's cable networks have such research teams. Basic research can answer questions regarding what parents feel is needed for their children or what is going on in children's lives that matters to them, so messages can be salient and real to them in the children's own context. This kind of research was seminal at Nickelodeon in the early 1990s, showing that what parents really wanted, especially for their preschool children, was educational programming. Being responsive to the parents, Nickelodeon saw an opportunity to fulfill that need with their Nick Jr. block. HBO Family was formed because HBO found in its research that parents wanted a safe haven for their children—a place that could be part of the HBO family of brands, but focused on children.

Formative Research.   Most of the research in children's programming is conducted in the formative stage, before the program is produced (concept testing), or after it is produced but before it airs (pilot testing). Two organizations have an especially robust process for engaging children in the production process: Sesame Workshop (pioneering formative research with *Sesame Street*) and Nickelodeon. The Sesame Workshop research model is well known and extensively documented, most recently by Fisch and Truglio (2001).

Blue's Clues is similar to the Sesame Workshop model, effectively integrating research into the DNA of the show and the team, but takes it to the next level. *Blue's Clues* began with a strong kidcentric vision: Empower, challenge, and build the self-esteem of preschoolers while making them laugh (quote from Anne Sartemero). This play-to-learn philosophy was central to the show. Given the vision for the show, it is not surprising that children were seen more as partners than as targets. Dr. Alice Wilder, who heads up research for *Blue's Clues,* has been testing three versions of *every* episode of *Blue's Clues* for the past several years. Alice and her research team talk to a total of 100 schoolchildren, aged 3 to 5 years old, for each of the three studies for each episode. The entire content/production team is dedicated to participating in this research, with writers visiting the research sessions to observe not only how children react to the episodes, but also to discover and learn how children think. The research methods include playing a game that simulates the TV show to gain feedback on the best order of clues, examining the effectiveness of content, testing a version of the show in video or animatic form, and testing completed shows. This process, one of the most robust of any children's show, is a source of pride to the *Blue's Clues* team, and is considered to be central to the show's success.

Another project that involved extensive testing with children conducted by an external research company was *The Magic School Bus,* produced by Scholastic Productions. This program was designed for 6- to 8-year-olds, and placed a strong emphasis on hands-on, inquiry-based science. Because the shows were based on the books featuring the character Ms. Frizzle, early testing focused on the ability of the shows to retain the essence of the books. A study on two animatics revealed, however, that several "book" techniques did not work in video form. For example, the child characters from the book were not well defined and were passive learners. Ms. Frizzle shared much of her knowledge in a lecture-based format. The content and production team were very responsive to these findings and focused on creating a group of characters who had distinct personalities, represented different ways of solving science problems, worked together as a group, and were empowered through problem solving to share and discover science on their own. This contributed significantly to children's involvement with the show, and also realized the NSF goals of supporting inquiry-based learning over teacher-oriented lectures.

In-house, in-depth research is not feasible for most projects. Although cable networks are more likely to afford an in-house research staff, the focus of commercial program testing is usually on entertainment value rather than educational goals—whether children engage and will watch the programs.

Formative research extends to the development of new media, such as CDs and Web sites for children. A number of these groups have built on the formative research conducted for television program testing and have incorporated these methods. For instance, Lucas Learning, a commercial company that produced educational CDs and Web content until 2002, uses its own in-house testing facility with a one-way mirror so that researchers can observe and analyze how children use the CD product and understand the content. The research extends to school and day-care center visits and homes, where children and their parents are given test products and asked to keep a log of their usage.

PBS, for their PBS Kids section of their Web site, also includes some formative research in the production process. PBS Web editors work closely with production teams to oversee the development of their Web content, and the editors require that producers include focus groups of children to test early versions of Web content.

Summative Research.   Summative research, which examines the impact of a series, is still performed infrequently, with high cost given as the most common reason for not conducting it. The National Science Foundation now requires summative research, and other organizations such as Sesame Workshop have tried to build summative research, when feasible, into its projects. In-school programs have also conducted impact research (e.g., *ESPN SportsFigures*, as mentioned earlier).

In addition to six formative research studies, summative research also was conducted on *The Magic School Bus*. Forty-six children viewed episodes over a period of weeks, and were interviewed in their homes at the beginning and end of the study. With one measure of impact, each child was shown a poster of a nature scene and cut-outs of all *The Magic School Bus* characters. They were asked to tell a story about what would happen there. Stories were examined for science content, inquiry, and learning. In the previewing condition, 43% told stories that were inquiry driven whereas 70% were able to tell inquiry-based stories in the postviewing condition (Research Communications, Ltd, 1996).

In conclusion, research is a much more accepted practice throughout children's media today than was true in the 1970s. In general, most of those who work in children's television have a deep level of concern about meeting the needs of children, and recognize research as one of the best tools available for achieving that goal. Despite the strides that have been made, however, much of the formative research is focused on entertainment value. Many projects would benefit from more rigorous tests of educational goals. Second, although a solid body of summative work was absent in 1980, there is now enough critical mass of research to suggest that children do benefit from targeted, educational programming (Fisch, in press). Greater emphasis on summative research can not only show us where we have been, but can also show us where production efforts need to go.

Teamwork: The Producer/Content/Research Marriage

In our 1980 chapter, we discussed the importance of the team that is created once the vision is articulated, the money is in place, and the audience is targeted. A sharp contrast to the programming field of then and now is that a number of organizations exist today, with ongoing infrastructures, that did not exist years ago; many of these are cable networks. So whether one show comes and goes, the intellectual capital and best practices learned from each lives on within the organization (e.g., Nickelodeon, Disney Channel, Sesame Workshop, and the other networks described previously).

A careful look at the background of the staff tells us a great deal about the focus of programming. Most network professionals interviewed have advanced degrees in child development or education, and their staff has expertise in children and children's television, often with academic backgrounds. Most felt that such credentials were essential for developing children's programming. Content expertise, on the other hand, is often solicited from experts outside the organization. The commercial broadcast networks utilize outside advisors in child development and content to help them evaluate and develop their E/I offerings. Although the expertise is not in-house, Hill-Scott (2001) showed that the process has been quite intensive at the broadcast networks.

The way the team of experts (child development experts, researchers, and producers) works together is crucial for success. The goals have to be organic and integral to the overall creative execution. Educational goals cannot be forced on top of a show concept. As referenced earlier, *Blue's Clues* is an example of the team approach. With *Arthur*, at WGBH, interpreting the books from their essence required close alignments with the author. A "writer's bible" was created to achieve that.

On *The Magic School Bus*, creation of each episode started with topic selection and the development of "science bibles" on content and the visuals. The team (including one practicing scientist and one science educator) would come up with organizing principles that would guide each show. Meetings with the Advisory Board and experts were held to both select topics for each season and review scripts. This model was robust and effective, but also expensive.

Behind the Lions, a series designed to teach reading, made their content experts (teachers) a primary target for their early work. They engaged teachers in discussions for over a year about phonics versus whole-language approaches to teaching reading, and ended up embracing both. They developed a very detailed curriculum and formats that could be repeated and used throughout the series to give it a consistent look and feel.

Lucas Learning has followed the models of many children's TV producers in incorporating research and content staff into their production processes. For CDs, an average production cycle takes 16 months, using a design document as the central product plan. At least 5 months are spent in upfront content/design planning and definition before production begins. From the beginning, a panel of educational advisors (from a much broader range of backgrounds than just teachers and researchers), help define educational goals and review products at various stages of production. The panel for a product on the physics of racing might include a racecar driver, an engineer, or a children's recreation specialist. Each product team has included a researcher trained in child development and educational product design, in addition to producers, programmers, artists, and others. More than 30 in-house seminars have been held on instructional design and developmental theory. Lucas Learning believes a better product results from engaging in these discussions and considering conflicting points of view.

The Exploratorium in San Francisco—one of the leading science centers in the world—has developed a substantial presence on the Web, including "virtual" examples of many of its on-site exhibits and teacher workshops. Its Web site of more than 13,000 pages attracts more than 11 million users a year, nearly 20 times the annual number of adults and children who come to its museum in person. At exploratorium.org, users can see an online version of a cow's eye dissection, a popular exhibit on the floor of the museum, or solar eclipses from around the world (originally done as live Webcasts). This latter example indicates one instance of the convergence of TV and the Internet, and how the Internet is moving toward providing a TV-like experience for its users.

In summary, regulatory influences have changed over the last 2 decades, with the Three-Hour Rule requiring broadcasters to include 3 hours of educational programming for 2- to 17-year-olds on a weekly basis. According to those monitoring broadcasters' performance, most seem to be in compliance with the rule. In an even more impressive accomplishment than compliance, other people had a vision to create kidcentric cable networks. In fact, cable is fast becoming the dominant provider of children's television.

The economics of children's television have become big business, and broadcasters' share of the pie has diminished considerably against the stronger cable brands. Some of this is a function of the focus in cable on creating a kidcentric culture with significant support for research that keeps the producers in touch with this complicated, ever-changing audience. The cable networks are often driven by vision and supported by full-time staff with significant academic grounding in child development. Although the research to date has helped organizations focus on the needs of parents and their children, only one cable network—Noggin—has focused its attention on education as its primary goal. Certainly more programming could be produced to serve the educational needs of children, especially in taking new creative approaches to presenting, for instance, history, culture, or the news. Still, who would have predicted 20 years ago that children would be so well served by profit-making ventures that voluntarily take financial risks, invest, and reap rewards? These success stories are examples of doing good *and* doing well.

THE CHALLENGES AHEAD: WHERE ARE WE GOING?

Although the previous discussion tells a positive story about how far children's television has come, some basic issues remain.

The Development of Cognitive Content Has Decreased Over Time

The good news is that programming has indeed improved. But much of the focus in broadcast, cable, and even on PBS is on socioemotional rather than cognitive content. When "education" was mandated, many programmers took the easier, prosocial route. Most people would agree that cognitive content is more difficult to program. In our interviews, media professionals expressed a need for programming in many content areas, including music, media literacy, how money works, how society works, and history. *Behind the Lions* is an impressive experiment in the teaching of literacy, countering the prosocial trend. Hopefully, others will follow.

Older Child Audiences Are Underserved

Another trend in children's media has been the development of content at the preschool level; this trend is particularly evident on PBS. This strategy makes sense, because the preschooler has more discretionary time to view television. Older children (6- to 8-year-olds) have been targeted as a possible next target for PBS, as have tweens (9- to 14-year-olds), who are harder to reach, harder to please, and divide their time across media. Given the limitations associated with preschoolers getting on the Internet, and the older child's engagement there, interactive and cross-platform initiatives almost demand that media companies pay more attention to the older audience. Disney Channel and Nickelodeon already have initiatives underway. Disney Channel is performing particularly well with the tween audience of 9- to 14-year-olds in prime time; in the 2001 season, it was #1 and leading all basic cable networks in prime time with the tween demographic. Much of the WB programming (owned by AOL/Time Warner) targets the older tween/teen demographic with its entertainment fare, but they focus on entertainment programming.

Cultural Diversity Is Still Limited on Children's Television

Heintz-Knowles (2000) conducted a content analysis of entertainment programming that featured regular child characters up to 18 years of age. She concluded that there were inadequate role models for children of all ethnic groups that "could leave children from these groups without significant role models, and could lead children of all ethnic groups to form a skewed vision of their community and their place in it" (p. 4).

Paul (2001) pointed out that Gen Y (7- to 24-year-olds) are more accepting of both ethnic and household/family diversity than are older generations. Taking advantage of this trend, cultural diversity has been the focus of several programmers:

- *Sagwa, the Chinese Siamese Cat* by author Amy Tan is a new animated series being produced by Sesame Workshop for kids aged 5 to 8 that airs on PBS. Set in ancient China, the show features real kids discussing their cultural heritage, festivals, foods, neighborhoods, and music.
- *The Proud Family* on Disney Channel is an animated comedy that targets the tween audience by following a 14-year-old African American girl and her family.
- *The Famous Jett Jackson* was developed by JP Kids for Disney Channel to address concerns about TV not reflecting what families are today. This series features a 15-year-old African American boy whose parents are divorced but cooperating in the parenting of their son.
- *The Brothers Garcia* is a live-action sitcom on Nickelodeon about a nuclear Latino family.
- *A Walk in Your Shoes,* developed by Noggin, is a series about children from different backgrounds who trade places, such as an American girl and Indian girl who live with each other's families and reflect on their experiences in these foreign cultures.

Although these are admirable starts, more cross-cultural programming is warranted. Television that does not mirror the world as children see it may account for the decline in children's viewing that has been noted. This places enormous pressure on media professionals to keep pace with each generation as they form their own views of our world.

As Technologies Progress, Some Will Be Left Behind

There is still a "ghetto" being created among households with children that cannot afford cable television, computers, and Internet access. Although costs associated with these technologies continue to decline, and there are efforts (e.g., community technology centers) to attempt to provide community-based access, the rapid pace of technology means that new "digital divides" will be created as older ones diminish. Perhaps, in the future, cable operators, other media providers, or government and private funders will have to address this issue.

Fairness in Advertising and Control of Information May Be Under Siege With So Few Media Companies Controlling the Information We Get

Although the consolidation of media companies has had some advantages in creating economies of scale to provide programming to children, there are potential downsides. For instance, at AOL/Time Warner, is it likely that the front page of AOL will promote a particular star when a new Warner music release, new series on the WB, or Warner Brothers movie (e.g., *Harry Potter and the Sorcerer's Stone*) is coming to market? On ABC/Disney venues, is it also likely that children will be exposed to advertising for a trip to Disney World or other ABC/Disney products? The

Viacom/CBS consolidation will likely impact what advertising children see on Nickelodeon. Although the magazine industry historically has had a set of guidelines separating advertising and editorial, such universal guidelines do not exist in the television media. Standards, to the extent that they do exist, are formed by each individual organization. It may be necessary, but not in the best interests of our children, to leave these decisions to companies that control so much share of mind.

Some policymakers and opinion leaders are questioning whether children will be adequately and fairly served by dominant commercial enterprises in this new age of digital media. Although a number of quality children's programs and related digital content have been produced by commercial production companies and networks, a significant policy question remains: Will reliance on commercial interests—seeking to maximize audience and profits—be sufficient to realize the full potential of new media and distribution channels?

Judging from the decades of experience with children's TV (where federal grants funded some of the most innovative series, such as *Sesame Street, The Electric Company, The Magic School Bus,* and *Bill Nye, The Science Guy*), such funding may provide a needed source of experimentation and risk taking to supplement funding from private foundations and corporations. Grossman and Minow (2001) launched an initiative suggesting that the auction of the telecommunications spectrum should fund new digital educational content for children. Whether the political will and financial resources exist for such a bold initiative remains uncertain.

SUMMARY

This chapter has identified several significant trends in the children's television marketplace over the past 20 years. Alternative distribution systems—including increased satellite and cable distribution—have multiplied children's television venues, and the Internet has expanded their "screen" choices well beyond television. Programming has also greatly expanded to eight broadcast networks and numerous cable networks offering part- or full-time children's programming, and the economic models for funding children's television have expanded and become more complex. In addition to advertising and public funding sources, monies generated by subscription fees, licensing, merchandising, and windowing of product have all contributed to children's television becoming big business.

Regulations have entered the mix, providing broadcasters with a mandate for educational/informational programming, and the broadcasters are fulfilling their obligations. However, the model for that fulfillment is changing at this writing. The consolidation of the industry has changed the way television is delivered to the home, and cross-platform and cross-media initiatives are common.

Television—a place for narrative and storytelling—has been described as a "lean back" media experience, where viewers are willing to allow a TV program to unfold over time. The Web—a place for connectivity—has been described as a "lean in" media experience, where information-seeking users are actively searching for specific information or communities to meet their needs. Some people believe that the

Internet is currently more of a text-driven experience whereas television is picture-driven, and that these two groups do not bridge the gap easily from one media to the other. Interactive content may require a new brand of professional who marries these two worlds more effectively.

The branding of networks has created a cadre of sophisticated content providers and marketers who understand children and work to create a product that serves children well. The consolidation of large media companies does, however, pose a threat if the "power" of these companies is not monitored and a system of checks and balances is not put in place.

Despite significant progress in the availability of quality programming for children, challenges yet to be met include cognitive content, diversity, and product for older children. Not all needs can be met with current business models. With signs of a soft advertising marketplace in 2001 extending into 2002 and perhaps beyond, major declines in weekday program viewing for broadcast networks (Freeman, 2001), increasing reluctance among local broadcast stations to carry children's weekday programming, and unknown economic models for new media, we may be reaching the end of a significant growth period for children's television.

But there is more to celebrate than to criticize in the accomplishments of the past 2 decades. There is a significant community of media professionals who take seriously their mandate to serve children. This community of professionals is much larger, more sophisticated, and more knowledgeable than were those who came before them. Children are being served in unexpected ways (the plethora of programming) from unexpected sources (profit makers abound). Just as technology expanded the number of channels serving children over the past 20 years, we can expect technology to continue to provide new channels, platforms, and devices for children's multimedia content. The hopes for better serving the child audience lie in the leadership, vision, and creativity of this growing group of individuals dedicated to children.

REFERENCES

Alexander, A. (2001). Broadcast networks and the children's television business. In D. G. Singer & J. L. Singer (Eds.), *Handbook of children and the media* (pp. 495–505). Thousand Oaks, CA: Sage.

Channel One. (2001). *Channel One report on distribution and usage.* New York: Author.

Chernin, P. (1998, June). *From chaos to control.* Keynote speech presented at CTAM Conference, Chicago, IL.

Corporation for Public Broadcasting. (1997). *Summary report: Study of school uses of television and video, 1996–1997 school year.* Washington, DC: Author.

CTAM. (2001a, January/February). Does anybody really know what "broadband" is? *Pulse,* pp. 00–00. Alexandria, VA: Author.

CTAM. (2001b, March). Games people play. *Pulse,* pp. 00–00. Alexandria, VA: Author

CTAM. (2001c, July). Tracking consumer profiles in a high tech world. *Pulse,* pp. 00–00. Alexandria, VA: Author

Dirr, P. J. (2001). Cable television: Gateway to educational resources. In D. G. Singer & J. L. Singer (Eds.), *Handbook of children and the media* (pp. 533–546). Thousand Oaks, CA: Sage.

Discovery eyes NBC's Saturday morning lineup. (2001, December). *Electronic Media,* p. 1.

Federal Communications Commission (FCC). (1996). *Policies and rules concerning children's television programming: Revision of programming policies for television broadcast stations* (MM Docket No. 93-48). Washington, DC: Author.

Fisch, S. M. (in press). Vast wasteland or vast opportunity?: Effects of educational television on children's academic knowledge, skills, and attitudes. In J. Bryant, & J. A. Bryant (Eds.), *Media effects* (2nd ed., pp. 00–00). Mahwah, NJ: Lawrence Erlbaum Associates.

Fisch, S. M., & Truglio, R. T. (Eds.). (2001). *"G" is for growing: Thirty years of research on Sesame Street.* Mahwah, NJ: Lawrence Erlbaum Associates.

Freeman, M. (2001, March). Broadcast makes a play for young viewers. *Electronic Media*, p. 17.

Graves, T. (1999, May 20). Movies and home entertainment. *Standard & Poor's Industry Surveys, 166*(20), 1–31.

Grossman, L. K., & Minow, N. N. (2001). *A digital gift to the nation: Fulfilling the promise of the digital and Internet Age.* New York: Century Foundation Press.

Grunwald Associates. (2000). *Children, families and the Internet.* Burlingame, CA: Author.

Heintz-Knowles, K. (2000). *The reflection on the screen: Television's image of children.* Retrieved May 2001 from www.childrennow.org/media/mc95/content_study.html

Hill-Scott, K. (2001). Industry standards and practices: Compliance with the Children's Television Act. In D. G. Singer & J. L. Singer (Eds.), *Handbook of children and the media* (pp. 605–620). Thousand Oaks, CA: Sage.

Jordan, A. B. (2000). *Is the three-hour rule living up to its potential?: An analysis of educational television for children in the 1999/2000 broadcast season.* Philadelphia: University of Pennsylvania, Annenberg Public Policy Center.

Kunkel, D., & Wilcox, B. (2001). Children and media policy. In D. G. Singer & J. L. Singer (Eds.), *Handbook of children and the media* (pp. 589–604). Thousand Oaks, CA: Sage.

McClellan, S., & Schlosser, J. (2002, January). 4Kids' win–win deal. *Broadcasting & Cable*, p. 17.

McCormick, M. (1996, December 28). News-filled year in children's media: Disney dominates audio and video. *Billboard, 108*(52), pp. 57–59

NCTA. (2001). *Cable & telecommunications developments* (vol. 25). Washington, DC: Author.

Paik, H. (2001). The history of children's use of electronic media. In D. G. Singer & J. L. Singer (Eds.), *Handbook of children and the media* (pp. 7–28). Thousand Oaks, CA: Sage.

Paul, P. (2001, September). Getting inside Gen Y. *American Demographics*, pp. 42–49.

PBS. (2001). *Top rated children's programs: April 2001* [Press release].

Research Communications Ltd. (1996). *The Magic School Bus summative research study.* Dedham, MA: Author.

Salfino, C. S. (2001, March). Special report: Tykes, tweens and teens. *Broadcasting & Cable*, pp. 16–22.

Woodard, E. H. (1999). *The 1999 state of children's television report: Programming for children over broadcast and cable television* (Report No. 28). Philadelphia: University of Pennsylvania, Annenberg Public Policy Center.

Woodard, E. H., & Gridina, N. (2000). *Media in the home. The fifth annual survey of parents and children.* Philadelphia: University of Pennsylvania, Annenberg Public Policy Center.

Educational Televisual Media Effects

June H. Lee
Aletha C. Huston
University of Texas at Austin

For many years, television has dominated the children's media landscape. In the last decade, however, computer-based technologies have been vying for, and winning, considerable portions of children's leisure time. Although television remains ubiquitous in American homes, children of all ages have readily adopted computers both at home and in school. Ninety-eight percent of American households with children own at least one television; 70% own at least one computer; 68% own video games; and 52% have online access (Woodard & Gridina, 2000). Children between the ages of 2 and 17 spend an average of 4½ hours a day in front of screens, watching television, playing video games, and using the computer (Woodard & Gridina, 2000).

With so much of leisure occupied by screen time, much theoretical and popular speculation abounds as to how these electronic media affect children's development. Researchers have documented that children learn a variety of educational and social lessons, both intended and unintended, from television. Less is known about how and what children learn from interactive technologies, including computer software, video games, and the Internet.

In addition to reviewing research on the effectiveness of television and computer technologies in conveying cognitive and prosocial content, this chapter draws parallels between research on television and computer technologies. It offers a framework on how program, child, and contextual factors influence learning from these media, and how subsequent transfer of learning might occur. It also examines the enduring effects of educational media use, and the processes that may underlie them.

RESEARCH ON TELEVISION AND COMPUTER TECHNOLOGIES: PARALLELS AND DIVERGENCES

Television and computers utilize the same symbol systems. That is, they use the same audio-visual modes of presenting information. Where they differ is in their processing attributes. Computer technology is most usefully distinguished from other media by what it allows users to do with information (Kozma, 1991). By enabling children to search, manipulate, and otherwise interact with material presented, computers afford children the opportunity to engage in activities seldom possible with other media.

Researchers have suggested that various facets of interactivity may accelerate children's cognitive development. By allowing children to organize information, provide structure to the activity, adjust aspects of the material to suit their needs and abilities, and receive feedback, computer activities may encourage processing that will enhance children's learning and increase their metacognitive abilities by prompting them to think about their cognitive strategies (Calvert, 1999; Krendl & Lieberman, 1988; Papert, 1980). Computer software (especially games) is also intrinsically motivating to the user because it presents challenges, offers specific goals with uncertain outcomes, and appeals to the user's fantasy (Malone, 1981).

Research on television and computer technologies share many issues in common, including a focus on their potential educational and prosocial impact (Chen, 1984). Compared with television, opinions about computer technologies as an educational tool have been more optimistic. Perceptions of computer technologies have taken on a different hue compared with those of television: Television has been largely portrayed as a passive medium, whereas computer technologies have been portrayed as being interactive and engaging. With television, the child is often described as a passive viewer (Healy, 1990; Singer, 1980); whereas with computer technologies, the child is depicted as an active user. The negative influences of television are a source of concern among parents, but they are often less concerned about video and computer games (Woodard & Gridina, 2000). Certainly, many criticisms that have been levied against television—such as the absence of viewer control, the lack of interactivity, and the difficulty in conveying cumulative content (Huston & Wright, 1998)—are largely irrelevant with computer technologies.

Because of its interactive capabilities, computer use is typically regarded as educational and scholarly. The underlying assumption is that interactivity necessarily entails active involvement and requires cognitive engagement on the child's part, and is therefore inherently beneficial to learning. Interactivity, however, is often discussed as if it were unidimensional, with little consideration for its degree or quality. Analyses of interactivity have yielded different conceptions stemming from the fields of communication, sociology, and computer science, resulting in some confusion in arriving at a comprehensive definition (Vorderer, 2001). Discussions of interactivity have underscored new technologies' capacity to respond to users, but current theoretical models in the media literature do not yet accommodate the potential of users interacting with content (Vorderer, 2001). The notion of interactivity, seen as so central to computer technologies, remains ill defined, and its effects are ill understood. The educational possibilities of computers are often portrayed in broad strokes, and this oversimplifies how children learn from media.

Much of what research has uncovered on how children learn from television (Anderson & Lorch, 1983; Huston & Wright, 1983, 1989; Rice, Huston, & Wright, 1983) can potentially inform our understanding of how children learn from computers. Researchers have shown that what appears to be a passive activity actually involves active processing. Rather than a child whose attention is captured indiscriminately by salient production features (e.g., fast pacing, sound and visual effects), a more accurate view is one of the child as an active processor who selectively attends to program features that may aid his or her comprehension, and who works to decode and understand television content (Anderson & Lorch, 1983; Huston & Wright, 1983, 1989).

Children's engagement, effort, and means of processing can differ across moments and across programs (Huston & Wright, 1989). In investigating the educational impact of media, then, the important question is not whether the medium results in active or passive processing, but rather when and how it results in more or less active processing (Huston & Wright, 1989). Learning from media occurs as a result of a confluence of factors. A framework for understanding this process must address factors that influence initial learning, as well as those that facilitate the transfer of knowledge to new situations.

FACTORS INFLUENCING LEARNING

Children cannot apply material presented in a program if they have not understood it (Fisch, 2001). Comprehension of content in both television and computer technologies is influenced by the interplay among program characteristics, the child's processing, and the context of learning.

Program Characteristics

Formal Features

Formal features are the "package" of auditory and visual representations that characterize media presentations (Huston & Wright, 1983). They consist of macro-level features like action and pace; and micro-level features such as cuts, zooms, dialogue, and music. Formal features act as a syntax through which certain aspects of content are conveyed, and they affect the intake of information (Calvert, 1999).

Television. Although, in theory, formal features may be considered separate from content, the two are often closely associated. Saturday morning cartoons, for instance, contain features that are perceptually salient, such as rapid action and pace, sound and visual effects, and rapid cuts. Educational programming uses these effects to a lesser extent, and tends to contain long zooms, singing, children's voices, and moderate levels of physical activity (Huston et al., 1981; Huston & Wright,

1994). Children use such production conventions to infer a program's potential comprehensibility, attention-worthiness, and congruence with their needs and goals for viewing (Huston & Wright, 1983). With increased experience with the medium, usually as a function of age, children come to an implicit recognition of these features and use them as hints to effectively deploy attention and form accurate expectations about the nature of the content (Huston & Wright, 1989). Thus, informed use of formal features can highlight central content and guide children toward a better understanding of the message (Bickham, Wright, & Huston, 2001).

Computer Technologies. Formal features in computer technologies have yet to be documented, and their effects on children's attention and comprehension are not well understood. The graphics, animation, light, sound, music, and other visual and audio effects in computer programs (Malone, 1981) parallel the perceptually salient features in television. These features can be combined and used in a variety of ways: as decoration, to enhance the fantasy aspect of a game, as a reward, or as a more effective representation system than words or numbers to convey information (Malone, 1981). These perceptual attributes may serve functions that are similar to those of formal features in television. They can arouse and maintain what Malone called *sensory curiosity,* which contributes to the motivating qualities of a computer game or program. Whether these features are informative to the young user, however, remains to be investigated, as does the relation between attention and comprehension in computer use. Unlike television viewing, where viewers often divide their attention among other ongoing activities, computer activities usually require sustained attention. Research on the implications of such attention for processing, as well as the role of interactivity in attention and comprehension, remains to be conducted.

Demands on Processing

Television. Children have limited cognitive resources to devote to processing an educational program (Fisch, 2000, 2001). Thus, their ability to understand educational content depends in part on the demands that a program exerts on their mental resources. These demands are twofold: The child must comprehend both the educational content and the narrative in which that content is embedded. The extent to which educational content and narrative are integral or tangential to each other further affects the demands of processing (Fisch, 2000, 2001). When content and narrative are tangential to each other, the mental resources available for processing will be primarily dedicated to processing the narrative (a principle called "narrative dominance") and fewer resources will be available to process educational content. When narrative and content are integrated, the two complement each other and jointly enhance comprehension (Fisch, 2001). A program will be easier to understand if processing demands of the narrative and educational content are small, or when narrative and content are well integrated (Fisch, 2000, 2001).

Demands on processing are reduced by other program characteristics, such as the presence of advance organizers or previews. Previews can generate interest in a story, offer information important for understanding its progression, and provide a structural overview that can help children integrate its content (Calvert, Huston, & Wright, 1987; Neuman, Burden, & Holden, 1990). By activating prior knowledge and encouraging prediction and inference, previews can potentially elicit higher levels of cognitive processing in children (Neuman et al., 1990).

Computer Technologies.   Unlike television, content in computer programs is not necessarily embedded in a narrative. Some popular games such as Tetris have no narrative, whereas others such as Mario Brothers are embedded in what might be called a weak narrative. We suggest that the key program characteristic relevant to processing is the interactivity afforded by the program. For our purposes, interactivity may be thought of as the extent to which content may be selected and modified by the user. The essence of interactivity is responsiveness (Rafaeli, 1988); that is, the extent to which responses presented by the user can be responded to.

The type and level of interactivity afforded by the program can affect the extent to which children can learn from it, and they differ across and within computing activities. Studies of adults' learning from computer-based instruction suggested that learning increased with increased levels of interactivity (Kritch, Bostow, & Dedrick, 1995), but an activity or program that offers superficial interactivity (e.g., the ability to start or stop a program) may not have much bearing on a child's learning. With computer programs (including games), form may partly determine the kinds of processing involved. For example, sensorimotor games that elicit little more than quick motor responses will likely involve shallow and fragmented processing, whereas strategy games that require deliberate planning and considered responses will likely entail more deep processing.

Child Characteristics

Clearly, learning is not a function of the medium alone. Rather than effects *of* technology, the key issue in discussing educational media is effects *with* technology (Salomon, 1990). The child affects the encounter with the medium and vice versa. A child watching television, for instance, can be active or passive along several dimensions; there is nothing inherent in television as a medium that fosters intellectual passivity (Huston & Wright, 1989). We propose that the same can be said of a child using a computer. How children process a program depends on their developmental stage as well as their attitudes in approaching information.

Developmental Stage

Research with television has revealed the depth of processing to be dependent in part on television form and in part on the child's developmental stage (Huston & Wright, 1983). Children learn the relations between television form and content over time. At different points in the child's development, features of television programs may play different roles (Bickham et al., 2001). A young, inexperienced viewer may initially engage in an exploration of the stimulus and react primarily to sensory and perceptual cues in the program. Exploration turns into systematic search as the child makes the connections between form and content, focuses on informative aspects of content, and seeks out specific information relevant to his or her goals and needs (Huston & Wright, 1989). This premise has received modest support. Small age differences were found in attention to salient television features. Younger children attended more to magazine-format programs containing high pace rather than low pace, whereas older children responded to continuity in the plot rather than pace (Wright et al., 1984); and younger children attended more to perceptually salient features than did older children (Calvert, Huston, Watkins, & Wright, 1982).

This shift in focus from program features to content marks the progress from stimulus-driven processing to schema-driven processing. Schemas are cognitive structures that are used to anticipate and organize events, and they make it possible for children to process information more thoughtfully by helping them select relevant or important aspects of content (Huston & Wright, 1997). Schema-driven processing denotes goal-directed, internally driven attention that is top-down and guided by anticipatory plans or representations (Salomon, 1983b). It is active in the sense that it is directed by the child (Huston & Wright, 1989). Stimulus-driven processing, on the other hand, is a bottom-up process characterized by responses to salient stimuli and events as they occur, and tends to be fragmented and steered by external influences (Huston & Wright, 1989).

Some evidence suggests that young children depend on program features during computer use much as they might during television viewing. In a computer presentation, younger children relied more on action (an index for perceptual salience) to remember objects and produce their names, whereas older children produced object names and recalled objects well regardless of action (Calvert, 1994). Consistent with the exploration-search model, children's use of perceptually salient features as a guide to information processing undergoes a decline with development. In both television and computer presentations, perceptually salient features appear to direct younger children's information processing, whereas older children process the informative aspects of the presentation rather than the action.

Mindfulness

The depth of processing and comprehension can vary among learners for reasons other than their developmental stage. Many of the outcomes of learning depend on how the child chooses to or tends to process information (Salomon, 1983a; Salomon & Gardner, 1986). Learning is strongly influenced by the amount of invested mental effort (AIME) expended in information processing. AIME is an integral part of mindfulness, which entails effortful, deliberate processing, and elaboration of the material learned. It is, in turn, affected by learners' beliefs and attitudes about the source of the information. Children expend less effort in processing information when they believe that the material encountered will call for little investment of mental effort (Salomon, 1983a, 1983b).

Culturally shared views and attributions exist regarding different media, and they shape the kinds of experiences children experience (or expect to encounter) with media (Salomon, 1983b). Whether a medium is used primarily for educational or entertainment purposes can color children's attributions about it. For instance, adults and children perceive television as entertainment, but consider print important for academic and educational purposes (Salomon, 1984). Children regard television as relatively undemanding and believe themselves to be efficacious in handling it with little effort. They regarded material presented on television to be shallower than that presented in print, reported investing less mental effort in processing televised information than print information, and obtained higher achievement scores when learning from print than from television (Salomon, 1984). These children attributed their success in understanding print to their ability and effort, whereas they attributed failure with print to its difficulty. They ascribed their success in understanding televised material to television's ease, but chose lack of effort to explain their failure with the medium.

Studies of Dutch children suggest, however, that attributions and actual mental effort may not always coincide. Children who saw a televised story performed better than those who read a comparable story in print (Beentjes & van der Voort, 1991). In one study (Beentjes & van der Voort, 1993), children's mental effort during the televised or printed presentation was measured by their reaction times to a secondary task (more rapid response indicated low involvement in the primary task) and reports of mental effort at the end of the presentation. When children were reading, they showed more rapid reaction times (i.e., *less* mental effort) than when they viewed television, but their reports of mental effort after the presentations were higher for reading than for television. Children who viewed television had better recall and inference about the content, especially when tested 2 or 3 weeks later. Thus, the way children perceive a medium is associated with their perceived investment of mental effort in processing its material, but the relations among perceptions, actual mental effort, and learning are complex (Salomon, 1983b).

Children appear to hold similar attitudes toward television and computers. They use both television and computers primarily as entertainment media (Roberts, Foehr, Rideout, & Brodie, 1999), and the most frequent activity performed on a computer at home is game playing (Kafai & Sutton, 1999; Roberts et al., 1999). Little is known about children's perceptions of computer technologies, their relations to mindfulness in processing, and their effects on learning. Children may consider both television and computers as entertainment media, but one might expect more variability in children's perceptions of computer technologies than of television.

When one sees a child performing activities on a computer, one cannot assume that this seeming control is actually mindfully experienced (Chanowitz & Langer, 1980). Different individuals can interact with the same program in different ways. Although researchers have yet to fully understand the qualitative differences in children's computer interaction, such distinctions have been observed in both adults and children. Researchers have found marked differences in adults' navigation through a hypertext document (Lawless & Brown, 1997; Lawless & Kulikowich, 1996). Three navigational profiles emerged: knowledge seekers, feature explorers, and apathetic users (Lawless & Kulikowich, 1996). Knowledge seekers were those who sought information that would directly enhance their understanding of a subject and who were strategic and systematic in searching for information (Lawless & Brown, 1997). Feature explorers spent a long time interacting with computer effects such as quick-time movies, sound effects, and graphics. They seemed more interested in understanding how the program worked than in gathering information contained in the program (Lawless & Brown, 1997; Lawless & Kulikowich, 1996). Apathetic users typified those who did not appear interested in gathering information or exploring features of the computer program, and who engaged in minimal interaction with the program. The same program can therefore be experienced more or less mindfully, depending on the user's inclination.

Analyses of 10- and 11-year-old children's interactions with an educational software program (Luckin, 2001) uncovered distinct profiles in interaction that could be classified along the dimensions of busy-quiet (i.e., number of actions taken), exploration-consolidation (i.e., the extent to which the child's action led him or her to experience more complex or abstract information), and hopper-persister (i.e., the extent to which the child switched from one type of action to another). There was some evidence that children of different abilities exhibited different interaction profiles, and the profiles were predictive of learning gains. For instance, busy-exploration-hoppers demonstrated above-average gains, whereas busy-consolidation-hoppers performed below average. Children also varied in the effectiveness of their collaboration (the number of instances and level of help features used) with the software. Those who used lots of deep support were children of average to high ability and who showed above-average learning gains. Gains were modest to below average for children who used lots of shallow support, little deep support, or little shallow support. Almost half the children belonged to these latter groups, suggesting that children often did not use help functions available to them and did not assume more challenging activities on their own (Luckin, 2001). Providing them with the means to do so was thus not a sufficient condition for learning.

Television researchers have long emphasized the importance of considering what a child brings to the medium as well as what the medium brings to the child (Anderson & Lorch, 1983). Passivity and interactivity lie in the children using the media rather than the media themselves (Chen, 1984). A child actively collaborates with the medium to construct knowledge (Kozma, 1991), and given that computer technologies allow the child interaction and control, child characteristics might have a stronger bearing in learning from computers than from television. As interactions become open ended and user directed, outcomes from computer learning might be more diverse than those for television (Salomon & Gardner, 1986).

The Context of Use

Children's use of media does not occur in a vacuum, yet much research has ignored the importance of context in shaping children's learning from educational media. Studies have indicated that the effects of educational television are likely to be larger when adults are involved in viewing. Children whose mothers were instructed to coview *Sesame Street* learned more from the program than did those whose mothers were not so instructed (Salomon, 1977).

Computer use is often a solitary activity (Roberts et al., 1999). Among 7th to 12th graders, 55% to 65% reported playing interactive games alone, and over 60% reported visiting websites and chat rooms alone (Roberts et al., 1999). Evidence suggests that the presence of others during computer activities may produce stronger effects. Children who played an educational software game cooperatively (i.e., playing as a team against the computer) arrived at more correct answers than did those who played it competitively (Strommen, 1993). The children in the cooperative condition used effective strategies that led to successful outcomes more often than did those in the competitive condition. Other indirect evidence suggests that teamwork during programming tasks may increase learners' mindfulness, which in turn enhances learning and transfer (Clements & Gullo, 1984). The information sharing, explanation of decisions, and exploration of alternatives that are likely to occur when others are present (Salomon & Globerson, 1987) may help children to consider the information more carefully and be better able to extract the messages or strategies that underlie a program.

THE TRANSFER OF LEARNING

Researchers have differentiated among many types of transfer. Particularly relevant to children's learning from media are what Salomon and Perkins (1987, 1989) called *low-* versus *high-road transfer*. Different mechanisms are responsible for each kind of transfer; the nature of the material transferred is also different. Low-road transfer hinges on extensive, varied practice and occurs when a well-learned behavior is activated in a new context (Salomon & Perkins, 1989). High-road transfer involves the intentional mindful abstraction or re-representation of material in one context that allows generalization and application to a new context (Salomon & Perkins, 1989). In discussing children's learning from educational media, one is typically interested in high-road transfer.

Just as mindfulness was important in initial learning, it continues to be vital in the process of transfer. Even with initial comprehension of educational content, children do not necessarily apply the material learned when the opportunity arises ⸱ (Fisch, 2001). Mindful involvement and abstraction are prerequisites for transfer (Salomon & Globerson, 1987). Abstraction entails the representation of material learned on a more abstract and general level. These qualities, attributes, or patterns in the information are extracted and represented internally in a decontextualized, symbolic manner that allows application in other occasions (Salomon & Perkins,

1989). Representing solutions to mathematical problems in the form of a general formula is an example of high-road transfer.

Mindful involvement and abstraction during learning, however, are not sufficient conditions for successful transfer. Transfer requires the learner to be mindful not only during learning but also when faced with the new problem. The learner must perceive the new situation as a variation of an already familiar one, and apply material learned to the new situation (Salomon & Globerson, 1987). Mindful approach to the new problem allows the abstractions that are available to become accessible. Without it, transfer will not take place even if the knowledge or skill has already been mastered (Salomon & Globerson, 1987). Thus, in the transfer situation, the child must appraise the similarities between the learning and transfer situations, recognize the relevance of the educational content to the current situation, and choose it from among other material stored in memory (Fisch, 2001).

Given the complex processes involved in learning and applying educational content to new situations, we next examine whether the educational potential of television and computer technologies is realized, such that they have an impact on children's cognitive and social development.

LEARNING FROM TELEVISION

The past 3 decades of research on children's learning from television have uncovered strong support that age-appropriate educational television has positive effects on children's cognitive and social development.

Cognitive Effects of Viewing

Sesame Street was among the first children's programs to address a detailed, substantive educational curriculum. It pioneered the use of research to inform production, enhance the effectiveness of the show's educational curriculum, and document measurable outcomes of viewing (Palmer & Fisch, 2001). The show has set the standard for children's educational programming, and its impact on children's development has been significant and enduring.

The first large-scale summative evaluation of *Sesame Street* was conducted by the Educational Testing Service (Ball & Bogatz, 1970; Bogatz & Ball, 1971). Children were randomly assigned to a condition in which parents were encouraged to have their children watch *Sesame Street*, or to a control group whose parents were not informed about the program. Children who watched *Sesame Street* improved more on seven academic skill areas emphasized by the program than did nonviewers. These findings, however, were challenged by other researchers, who argued that parental encouragement was confounded with viewing, and the rehearsal and reinforcement that possibly accompanied parental coviewing might have increased the effects of the show. Thus, the gains from viewing could not be attributed solely to the program itself (Cook et al., 1975).

Subsequent assessments of *Sesame Street* have confirmed its positive educational impact. In a longitudinal study following children for 2 years, preschoolers learned vocabulary from *Sesame Street* while viewing at home (Rice, Huston, Truglio, & Wright, 1990). *Sesame Street* viewing contributed to preschoolers' vocabulary development independent of parent education, family size, child gender, and parental attitudes toward television. Positive effects did not occur for other kinds of viewing, namely general-audience and child noninformative programs.

In a nationally representative sample from the 1993 National Household Education Survey (NHES), there were similar positive relations of viewing to school readiness skills (Zill, 2001). Viewing *Sesame Street* or PBS children's programs at least once a week was a significant predictor of scores on emergent literacy and numeracy (e.g., telling connected stories, recognizing letters, counting to 20, writing, and drawing), even after controlling for family background characteristics. These positive effects were stronger for children from low-income families than for those from higher-income families. First- and second-graders who watched *Sesame Street* prior to attending school were also better readers than were nonviewers.

Since the initial evaluation by ETS (Ball & Bogatz, 1970; Bogatz & Ball, 1971), no large-scale evaluations of the effects of *Sesame Street* and other educational children's programs have been performed until The Early Window Study (Wright et al., 2001). The study was a 3-year longitudinal assessment of the relations of early television viewing to school readiness in two cohorts of children (182 children, ages 2–5 and 4–7) from low- to moderate-income families. Children's viewing information was gathered from oral 24-hour time-use diaries, and all programs reported were classified according to their intended audience and content, resulting in four categories of programs: child-audience, informative or educational programs; child-audience, noninformative cartoons; child-audience, other programs; and general-audience programs. Characteristics of the home environment and the child's initial language ability, known to affect the relationship between viewing and achievement, were statistically controlled. Path analyses revealed that children who were frequent viewers of child-audience informative programs when they were 2 and 3 years old performed better on tests of reading, math, vocabulary, and school readiness than did infrequent viewers.

With regard to *Sesame Street* specifically, viewing at age 2 positively predicted reading, math, vocabulary, and school readiness at age 3 (Wright, Huston, Scantlin, & Kotler, 2001). These early viewers continued to have an advantage over infrequent viewers at age 5. Viewing between ages 3 and 4 was also positively related to school readiness and reading skills at age 5.

Viewing child-audience cartoons and general-audience programs had effects that were the opposite to those of educational programs: Frequent viewers of child-audience cartoons had lower scores in subsequent literacy tests compared with infrequent viewers; frequent viewing of general-audience programming negatively predicted vocabulary scores among the younger cohort, and negatively predicted letter and number skills among the older cohort (Wright et al., 2001).

Prosocial Effects of Viewing

Although prosocial and educational programs have become prevalent since the passage of the 1991 Children's Television Act, which requires stations to meet the educational and informational needs of children through their programming, the most extensive research on the effects of prosocial television was conducted in the 1970s and 1980s. The evidence suggests that shows designed to teach positive social lessons can have some impact but, more important, their effects are augmented when viewing is accompanied by relevant activities that reinforce the behaviors modeled in the programs (Mares & Woodard, 2001).

Positive social and affective messages are at the heart of *Mister Rogers' Neighborhood.* In the first of a series of studies, researchers examined its associations with positive behavior. The effects of viewing *Mister Rogers' Neighborhood,* the cartoons *Batman* and *Superman,* and a neutral film on preschoolers' prosocial and aggressive behaviors during free play were observed (Friedrich & Stein, 1973). Children who watched *Mister Rogers' Neighborhood* were more able to obey rules, persist on task, and tolerate delays than were children in the other groups. Children from low socioeconomic backgrounds also showed more prosocial interactions, and these effects persisted for 2 weeks thereafter. Socioeconomic status, however, moderated these outcomes: Children from lower socioeconomic backgrounds benefited from the program, whereas those from higher socioeconomic backgrounds did not.

Other investigations have failed to find such direct effects. Some studies indicated that children might model prosocial behavior in situations similar to those presented in the program *Sesame Street,* but such behaviors did not generalize to free play (Fisch, Truglio, & Cole, 2000). Other studies failed to find positive behavioral effects after *Sesame Street* viewing (Silverman & Sprafkin, 1980).

The findings are more consistent when adults were involved in children's viewing. Researchers compared the effectiveness of verbal labeling and role playing in helping kindergarteners comprehend and enact the lessons presented in *Mister Rogers' Neighborhood* (Friedrich & Stein, 1975). Consistent with the previous study (Friedrich & Stein, 1973), children who watched *Mister Rogers' Neighborhood* scored higher on prosocial measures than did those in the control condition. Lessons from the program generalized to another situation, as evidenced by increased helping behavior among the children. Those who watched the program also received one of four types of postviewing training: verbal labeling, role playing, verbal labeling and role playing, and an irrelevant activity. Effects of the program were stronger when viewing was followed by training in the skills related to prosocial behavior.

A further study with *Mister Rogers' Neighborhood* was conducted with children from urban, low-income areas (Friedrich-Cofer, Huston-Stein, Kipnis, Susman, & Clewett, 1979). Children in Head Start programs were assigned to one of four conditions: prosocial television only (i.e., *Mister Rogers' Neighborhood*); prosocial television and related play materials; prosocial television, related play materials, and teacher training in verbal labeling and role playing; and neutral films. Children saw 20 shows over 8 weeks, and were assessed on their social, imaginative, and self-regulatory behavior. No differences in these measures emerged between children in the prosocial TV-only group and those in the control group, contradicting the findings from the researchers' earlier studies (Friedrich & Stein, 1973, 1975). Compared to children in the other groups, those who were exposed to the program and the play materials showed high levels of positive social interactions with peers and adults, of imaginative play, assertiveness, as well as aggression. Those who received both play materials and teacher involvement also had high levels of the same prosocial behaviors, but without a corresponding increase in aggression. The authors suggested that teacher involvement helped these children to discriminate between socially acceptable and unacceptable behaviors.

More recent investigations of the popular children's program *Barney and Friends* revealed similar results. In a national study of children of lower socioeconomic backgrounds, children showed the largest gains in learning the cognitive and social content conveyed in the show when viewing was complemented with follow-up lessons (Singer & Singer, 1998). Children who viewed *Barney* alone only had a small advantage over the nonviewing control group. In fact, those who had the benefit of follow-up lessons scored almost twice as high on the posttest measures of learning than did those who only viewed the program.

Taken together, these studies highlight the potential benefit in viewing prosocial television programs and the importance of adult mediation in helping children crystallize the lessons presented. Prosocial television programs had some positive impact, but effects were magnified when viewing was followed by activities that overtly reinforced the positive behaviors shown in the program. To refer to our framework for learning, these activities likely helped the young viewers understand the content, extract its messages, and recognize its relevance to other situations.

A recent study, however, did not find postviewing activities to influence children's prosocial behavior. Significant positive effects were found when prosocial segments in *Sesame Street* were consolidated into a video presentation and shown to preschoolers, who viewed in small groups in a day-care setting (Zielinska & Chambers, 1995). Children who watched the prosocial video showed higher levels of prosocial behavior during free play than did those who viewed a cognitive video, regardless of whether they participated in individual or cooperative activities afterward. This finding is consistent with theories about mindfulness, which posit that the presence of others during learning could spur learners to approach material more mindfully (Salomon & Perkins, 1987).

Cognitive Versus Prosocial Effects

Educational television seems to exert a stronger, more consistent effect on cognition than on social behavior. These differences might be attributable in part to differences in program format. Magazine formats are often thought to be effective in teaching children cognitive material, whereas narrative formats seem suitable for teaching children prosocial lessons (Calvert, 1999). According to our framework for transfer, however, the narrative format works against learning compared with the magazine format. The presence of a strong narrative requires more of the child's mental resources for processing. Fewer resources are available to extract the educational message embedded in the narrative (Fisch, 2000). In contrast, the magazine format allows numerous examples of the same behavior to be presented (Zielinska & Chambers, 1995). The magazine format, where the content can be less tied to the narrative, allows the educational content to be delivered multiple times in different contexts, and may be the format that facilitates optimal transfer (Fisch, 2001).

In order to benefit from educational television, the child must recognize the relevance of the educational content and apply it in an appropriate situation (Fisch, 2001). This might be more difficult with social content than with cognitive content. Social situations are fraught with complexities and ambiguities, and the child might have more difficulty choosing the prosocial response from among a vast repertoire of behaviors. With cognitive content, the appropriate material might be more readily apparent because there are fairly limited alternatives from which to choose. As a medium, then, television does not necessarily convey some content better than others. Success in learning and application requires that content, the child, and the contexts of learning and application be examined.

LEARNING FROM COMPUTER TECHNOLOGIES

Computer technologies, by virtue of their interactivity, have been proposed to have significant impact on children's behaviors and cognition. Participating in a virtual reality game had stronger effects on physiological arousal and aggressive thoughts than did mere observation (Calvert & Tan, 1996). Compared with viewing, enacting behaviors through interactivity might magnify effects across content areas.

Cognitive Effects

While research on the cognitive effects of television has centered on children's in-home viewing of educational programs, relatively little is known about the children's use of educational software at home and its relations to cognitive outcomes. Research on computer technologies has focused on two domains of computer use: programming learned in a school setting, and recreational interactive games. The kind of computing activity appears to affect the mechanisms of transfer and the nature of the skills transferred. Existing evidence suggests that programming involves high-road transfer, whereas interactive game play involves low-road transfer.

Programming

Theorists have proposed that computer programming can have powerful effects on children's cognition (e.g., Papert, 1980). The cognitive skills that might be learned from programming include mathematical and geometric concepts, planning, problem solving, formal reasoning, and reflectivity (Salomon & Perkins, 1987). The literature, however, seems to offer little support for the transfer of these skills unless the child receives substantial adult guidance.

Pea, Kurland, and Hawkins (1985) believed that LOGO programming had the potential to teach children planning and thinking skills, but found disappointing results in two studies with fourth and sixth graders. The first study involved a far transfer task. The researchers expected the students to use planning skills learned in programming to help with plan making during a task that seemed dissimilar to programming. After a 4-month period of LOGO instruction, programmers and nonprogrammers did not differ on the quality of their plans, the types of planning decisions, or flexibility in decision making. Despite a considerable 30 hours of programming instruction, these students did not show any transfer of programming skills to another task. The authors suggested that the findings might be attributable to the overcontextualization of programming skills. Students' programming knowledge may have been too entrenched in the context in which it was learned. It did not generalize, especially in a transfer task that did not share much surface similarity with programming.

In their second study, Pea and colleagues constructed a near transfer task that more closely resembled programming. The task involved instructing a robot in a computer program to carry out chores using specific commands. The students also had the benefit of feedback from the computer program, and more guidance from their teachers in their learning. The researchers hypothesized that compared with nonprogrammers, programmers should: be able to accomplish the task with fewer plans, make better use of feedback, spend more time considering alternative plans early in the task, and try to improve their plan through successive revisions rather than embarking on a new plan each time. Contrary to these predictions, programmers and nonprogrammers were not different on any of the previously mentioned measures. These findings were especially remarkable, given that the transfer task was designed to resemble programming.

The authors speculated that transfer did not occur because the students did not thoroughly master programming despite the time devoted to learning it. Further, programming may not have held any functional significance for the students outside of the learning context. Even though programming has the potential to cultivate many useful cognitive practices, it does not ensure that transferable learning will emerge. In this case, transfer seemed to have failed due to a lack of mastery and a failure to recognize the relevance of programming skills to the new context.

Other researchers have found more encouraging evidence of far transfer from programming. Clements and Gullo (1984) compared the effects of LOGO programming with those of computer-based instruction (CAI) on first graders' cognitive style (i.e., reflectivity and divergent thinking), metacognitive ability (i.e., monitoring one's thinking and recognizing when one does not understand), cognitive development, and ability to describe instructions. Pre- and posttest scores were compared for the two groups after 3 months of instruction. The LOGO group improved on overall divergent thinking as well as its components, fluency, and originality, whereas the CAI group did not. Children in the LOGO group might have been better at producing creative ideas than the CAI group because LOGO facilitated divergent thinking. Compared with the CAI group, children in the LOGO group made fewer mistakes and were less impulsive in their decision making, perhaps reflecting the thoughtful planning, deliberation, and analysis of errors involved in programming. In contrast, children in the CAI treatment remained unaffected because its instructional programs rewarded quick responses. The LOGO group also surpassed the CAI group on both metacognition measures (i.e., monitoring one's thinking and realizing when one does not understand), presumably because LOGO entails the awareness of explicit problems and solutions. The LOGO group was better able to describe instructions than was the CAI group, perhaps because LOGO requires children to visualize graphic displays and encode them into verbal directions from the turtle's (an arrow-shaped icon) perspective. The LOGO and CAI groups performed equally well on operational competence (i.e., classification and seriation) and general cognitive ability. The researchers concluded that programming can improve problem-solving ability and cognitive style, but it does not appear to affect cognitive ability.

Why was the cognitive potential for programming realized in some instances and not others? Clements and Gullo (1984) demonstrated significant effects with very young children, whereas Pea and colleagues did not, even with older children. These differences could be attributed to the different measures of transfer used in these studies, but another explanation could lie in the context of learning. The small-group learning in the Clements and Gullo study might have increased the students' mental effort expended in processing information, thus enhancing both learning and transfer (Salomon & Globerson, 1987). The instructors' involvement could have helped students reflect on and abstract from their programming. By re-representing patterns of thinking at a higher level, these students could be engaged by situations outside of programming (Salomon & Perkins, 1987).

As with television viewing, adult mediation is important, particularly with a task as complex as programming. Programming is most promising as a means of fostering thinking and problem-solving skills when students and teachers engage in an exchange of ideas, where discussions and examples of thinking skills can be shared and learned from, and when links between the realms of school and life can be made (Salomon & Perkins, 1987). Thus, engaging in programming itself does not necessarily affect cognition; at least, not without instruction designed to produce such consequences (Salomon & Perkins, 1987).

Interactive Games

Most children do not have the opportunity to learn programming. Most of children's computer use occurs at home and is devoted to playing games (Kafai & Sutton, 1999; Roberts et al., 1999). Although most interactive games do not contain explicitly designed educational content, they utilize dynamic visual-spatial representation and may offer informal education in spatial and representational skills (Greenfield, 1996). Studies have offered support for this premise.

Spatial Skills.   Subrahmanyam and Greenfield (1996) examined the effects of video game play on girls' and boys' spatial skills. The experimental treatment group played the video game *Marble Madness,* which entails the use of spatial skills of guiding and intercepting objects, and judging the speed and distance of moving objects. The control group played with a word game not involving spatial skills. Children's dynamic spatial skills (i.e., skills pertaining to objects in motion) were measured pre- and posttest. The video game group improved on the spatial tests, whereas the control group did not. Boys and girls in the video game group improved their spatial skills to the same extent. Children with poor initial spatial skills benefited from video game practice, whereas those who already possessed strong spatial skills did not benefit from the treatment, although strong spatial skills facilitated the mastery of the video game. Computer games can also teach mental rotation. Children who played computer games performed better in mental rotation tests than did those in a control group, regardless of age or gender (McClurg & Chaillé, 1987).

These studies tested spatial skills that were similar to those used in game play, and are examples of low-road transfer, wherein extensive practice underlined the mechanisms of transfer (Subrahmanyam & Greenfield, 1996). Low-road transfer tends to be narrow, and limited to situations in which skills activated in a new context are similar to ones learned.

Video game practice may not generalize to tasks that were less clearly related to game use. In a study of adults' performance on a mental paper-folding test, the experimental group played an action game *The Empire Strikes Back,* which offers a two-dimensional representation of three-dimensional space by presenting the player the perspective of a starship. The control group received only a pretest (Greenfield, Brannon, & Lohr, 1996). The experimental group did not improve its mental paper-folding test scores more than the control group did. In this instance, the transfer task was more dissimilar to the video game treatment than in the earlier studies reviewed, thus hampering low-road transfer. The authors also pointed out that many participants, particularly women, did not master the game. Because mastery is a prerequisite for transfer (Salomon & Perkins, 1987, 1989), the failure in transfer might have been a result of the failure of the experimental treatment itself (Greenfield, Brannon, et al., 1996).

Although the spatial skills developed through game play may not transfer across broad contexts, they may be useful for developing a basis for visual skills that prepare children for the deeper conceptual aspects of other computer technologies (Subrahmanyam & Greenfield, 1996).

Iconic Skills   Another skill inherent in playing interactive action games is that of iconic representation—the ability to "read" images. Researchers found that adult participants who played a computer memory game improved on tests of inductive generalization compared to those who did not play and those who played a noncomputerized version of the game (Greenfield, Camaioni, et al., 1996). Participants' skill in decoding and encoding the iconic representation in the computer medium was central to the amount of transfer that occurred during the posttest. That participants in the computer group improved more than did those who played the noncomputerized game indicates that the medium of presentation affected learning (Greenfield, Camaioni, et al., 1996). The test of induction was also a test of participants' ability to decode information from animated computer graphics, and their experience with the computer resulted in a more iconic representation of information (Greenfield, Camaioni, et al., 1996).

This finding suggests that computer technologies may have an effect on cognition that is separate from their content. Television research has shown that content, not the medium, is most important in determining outcomes of viewing (e.g., Anderson, Huston, Schmitt, Linebarger, & Wright, 2001; Wright et al., 2001). The same will also likely be true of computer technologies. In addition, however, they may produce "medium effects" by changing users' mode of thought or representation.

Prosocial Effects of Interactive Games

Research on interactive games has focused on the negative influences of violent video games (e.g., Dietz, 1998; Funk, Germann, & Buchman, 1997; Kinder, 1996), rather than prosocial content and its potential positive effects on children's behavior. Behaviors that can be fostered through interactive games can be well suited to prosocial content, wherein positive behavior can be rehearsed and reinforced. Unfortunately, there are few examples of games that combine the engaging features of computer technology with prosocial content (Calvert, 1999).

Existing evidence indicates that prosocial games do not affect prosocial behavior, whereas action or violent games inhibit it. In a study examining the effects of playing a prosocial game versus an aggressive game on children's donating and helping behavior, researchers found that playing the prosocial game did not increase these positive behaviors. Playing the aggressive game, on the other hand, tended to suppress them (Chambers & Acsione, 1987). The authors suggested that the brief 10-minute exposure might have been insufficient to generate effects. Moreover, the theme of the game (rescue) did not correspond to the transfer task (donating and helping). This difference might have made transfer difficult by making the connection between the learning and application contexts more remote.

Others have found negative effects of action or aggressive games on prosocial behavior. In a survey of seventh and eighth graders in the Netherlands, researchers found that boys' preferences for aggressive games were negatively correlated with positive behavior (Wiegman & van Schie, 1998). Another study found that playing the action game *Space Invaders* resulted in a reduction in children's prosocial verbal interactions from the pretreatment levels (Silvern & Williamson, 1987).

As with television viewing, these failures of transfer of prosocial material may have occurred because of inadequate understanding of the content, the absence of abstraction, or the difficulty in selecting appropriate prosocial responses among competing behaviors in the child's repertoire.

THE ENDURING EFFECTS OF EDUCATIONAL MEDIA

Young children who were frequent viewers of educational television were more proficient in preacademic skills and were more ready for school than were infrequent viewers (Ball & Bogatz, 1970; Bogatz & Ball, 1971; Rice et al., 1990; Wright et al., 2001). Do these positive effects of using educational media use endure beyond the initial years of viewing? Evidence indicates that they do. In the Recontact Study (Anderson et al., 2001), researchers surveyed 570 adolescents, whose media use and family characteristics were examined in detail when they were 5 years old. Their viewing diets and total time spent viewing television in preschool and adolescence were used to predict diverse outcomes, including academic achievement, leisure reading, achievement motivation, creativity, extracurricular activities, aggression, health behavior, and self-image. Viewing diet was classified into three content categories: informative, violent, and all other programming.

Boys who viewed more child informative programs as preschoolers received better grades in English, math, and science in high school than did infrequent viewers. Among girls, the relation between viewing and grades was positive, but it was not statistically significant. Compared with infrequent viewers, teens who had watched more child informative programs as preschoolers had higher average competence beliefs and higher competence beliefs in math and science. Among boys, heavier viewers placed more value in high school subjects and in math and science than did lighter viewers. For both boys and girls, heavier viewers of child informative programs also read more books outside those required for school than did lighter viewers. Neither of the other categories of viewing (i.e., violent and "other") positively predicted these outcomes. Educational viewing also had long-term relations to social behavior. Boys who watched child informative programs frequently had lower levels of aggressive attitudes as teens than did those who watched infrequently.

Educational programs seem to benefit boys more consistently than girls. The authors suggested that boys might benefit more from academic and prosocial content in educational programs because they tend to have more behavior and academic problems and be less prepared for school compared with girls. The educational content runs counter to socializing influences, and therefore exerts strong effects for boys but not for girls.

Computer technologies are a relatively new phenomenon in children's lives, and will likely become an increasingly important part of most children's leisure and educational pursuits. Their long-term effects on children's development remain to be discovered.

Explaining Long-Term Effects

What processes translate preschool educational viewing into adolescent academic success? Clearly, the processes for direct transfer do not apply: The specific knowledge in preschool programs does not help high school students academically. Furthermore, viewing educational programs in preschool does not appear to lead to continued viewing of informative programs in adolescence, where it has concurrent effects on achievement, although such a process might play a small role in influencing achievement (Anderson et al., 2001).

Instead, the researchers proposed that early educational viewing could have initiated a trajectory of learning in the formative years of schooling. Viewers of educational programs master preacademic skills, develop an interest and motivation in learning, and seek opportunities for learning. These predispositions become magnified over time and lead these children toward a path of efficacy and achievement that endures into adolescence (Anderson et al., 2001). This is transfer of a different kind. Others have called it *preparation for future learning* (Bransford & Schwartz, 1999). It is transfer not of specific skills, but of positive dispositions toward learning, which prime children for future learning and motivate them to seek out resources for learning and alternative ideas (Bransford & Schwartz, 1999). Beyond concurrent effects on academic skills, early experience with educational media can shape a child's development beyond the preschool years.

CONCLUSION

Research on television and computer technologies share much in common. The same framework can be applied to explain how children learn from television and computers, but there may be some important differences in the explanatory frameworks for these two types of media. Although computer technologies hold the promise of enriching children's learning, we know very little about how children perceive and use these potentials. Researchers' goal of uncovering the effects of these media on children's development has to be taken further, to understanding why such outcomes are obtained and the exact qualities of the medium that account for them, and to uncover how children interact with the medium and its diverse effects (Salomon & Gardner, 1986).

The characteristics that children bring to the medium may become even more important in their learning from computers, given that users are allowed a degree of direct control over their interactions with the medium. The content of television is critical to its potential as a learning resource, but, for computers, the nature of the medium itself may also affect the types and complexity of processing that are stimulated in the user. In the long run, do the results of interactivity relate more to children's perceptions of it, or to its actual presence (Rafaeli, 1988)? With computer technologies, will the medium become the message (Calvert, 1999)? If interactivity enhances the medium's effects, would those effects be magnified or diminished over time?

A complete view of how children learn from media must integrate factors pertaining to the medium, the message, the child, and the context. This may also be particularly true of interactive media.

REFERENCES

Anderson, D. R., Huston, A. C., Schmitt, K. L., Linebarger, D. L., & Wright, J. C. (2001). Early childhood television viewing and adolescent behavior: The Recontact Study. *Monographs of the Society for Research in Child Development, 66* (1, Serial No. 264).

Anderson, D. R., & Lorch, E. R. (1983). Looking at television: Action or reaction? In J. Bryant & D. R. Anderson (Eds.), *Children's understanding of television: Research on attention and comprehension* (pp. 1–33). New York: Academic Press.

Ball, S., & Bogatz, G. A. (1970). *The first year of Sesame Street: An evaluation.* Princeton, NJ: Educational Testing Service.

Beentjes, J. W. J., & van der Voort, T. H. A. (1991). Children's written accounts of televised and printed stories. *Educational Technology Research and Development, 39,* 15–26

Beentjes, J. W. J., & van der Voort, T. H. A. (1993). Television viewing versus reading: Mental effort, retention, and inferential learning. *Communication Education, 42,* 191–205.

Bickham, D. S., Wright, J. C., & Huston, A. C. (2001). Attention, comprehension, and the educational influences of television. In D. G. Singer & J. L. Singer (Eds.), *Handbook of children and the media* (pp. 101–119). Thousand Oaks, CA: Sage.

Bogatz, G. A., & Ball, S. (1971). *The second year of "Sesame Street": A continuing evaluation.* Princeton, NJ: Educational Testing Service.

Bransford, J. D., & Schwartz, D. L. (1999). Rethinking transfer: A simple proposal with multiple applications. *Review of Research in Education, 24,* 61–100.

Calvert, S. (1994). Developmental differences in children's production and recall of information as a function of computer presentational features. *Journal of Educational Computing Research, 10,* 139–151.

Calvert, S. (1999). *Children's journeys through the information age.* Boston: McGraw-Hill.

Calvert, S., Huston, A. C., Watkins, B. A., & Wright, J. C. (1982). The relation between selective attention to television forms and children's comprehension of content. *Child Development, 53,* 601–610.

Calvert, S., Huston, A. C., & Wright, J. C. (1987). Effects of televised preplay formats on children's attention and story comprehension. *Journal of Applied Developmental Psychology, 8,* 329–342.

Calvert, S., & Tan, S. L. (1996). Impact of virtual reality on young adults' physiological arousal and aggressive thoughts: Interaction versus observation. In P. M. Greenfield & R. R. Cocking (Eds.), *Interacting with video* (pp. 67–81). Norwood, NJ: Ablex.

Chambers, J. H., & Ascione, F. R. (1987). The effects of prosocial and aggressive videogames on children's donating and helping. *Journal of Genetic Psychology, 148,* 499–505.

Chanowitz, B., & Langer, E. (1980). Knowing more (or less) than you can show: Understanding control though the mindlessness-mindfulness distinction. In J. Gerber & M. E. P. Seligman (Eds.), *Human helplessness: Theory and applications* (pp. 97–129). New York: Academic Press.

Chen, M. (1984). Computers in the lives of our children: Looking back on a generation of television research. In R. Rice (Ed.), *The new media: Communication, research, and technology* (pp. 269–286). Beverly Hills, CA: Sage.

Clements, D. H., & Gullo, D. F. (1984). Effects of computer programming on young children's cognition. *Journal of Educational Psychology, 76,* 1051–1058.

Cook, T. D., Appleton, H., Connor, R. F., Shaffer, A., Tamkin, G., & Weber. S. J. (1975). *"Sesame Street" revisited.* New York: Russell Sage.

Dietz, T. L. (1998). An examination of violence and gender role portrayals in video games: Implications for gender socialization and aggressive behavior. *Sex Roles, 38,* 425–443.

Fisch, S. M. (2000). A capacity model of children's comprehension of educational content on television. *Media Psychology, 2,* 63–91.

Fisch, S. M. (2001, April). *Transfer of learning from educational television: When and why does it occur?* Paper presented at the biennial meeting of the Society for Research in Child Development, Minneapolis, MN.

Fisch, S. M., Truglio, R. T., & Cole, C. F. (2000). The impact of *Sesame Street* on preschool children: A review and synthesis of 30 years' research. *Media Psychology, 1,* 165–190.

Friedrich, L., & Stein, A. H. (1973). Aggressive and prosocial television programs and the natural behavior of preschool children. *Monographs of the Society for Research in Child Development, 38* (4, Serial No. 151).

Friedrich, L., & Stein, A. H. (1975). Prosocial television and young children: The effects of verbal labeling and role playing on learning and behavior. *Child Development, 46,* 27–38.

Friedrich-Cofer, L. K., Huston-Stein, A., Kipnis, D. M., Susman, E. J., & Clewett, A. S. (1979). Environmental enhancement of prosocial television content: Effect on interpersonal behavior, imaginative play, and self-regulation in a natural setting. *Developmental Psychology, 15,* 637–646.

Funk, J. B., Germann, J. N., & Buchman, D. D. (1997). Children and electronic games in the United States. *Trends in Communication, 2,* 111–126.

Greenfield, P. M. (1996). Video games as cultural artifacts. In P. M. Greenfield & R. R. Cocking (Eds.), *Interacting with video* (pp. 85–94). Norwood, NJ: Ablex.

Greenfield, P. M., Brannon, C., & Lohr, D. (1996). Two-dimensional movement through three-dimensional space: The role of video game expertise. In P. M. Greenfield & R. R. Cocking (Eds.), *Interacting with video* (pp.169–185). Norwood, NJ: Ablex.

Greenfield, P. M., Camaioni, L., Ercolani, P., Weiss, L., Laubler, B. A., & Perucchini, P. (1996). Cognitive socialization by computer games in two cultures: Inductive discovery or mastery of an iconic code? In P. M. Greenfield & R. R. Cocking (Eds.), *Interacting with video* (pp. 141–167). Norwood, NJ: Ablex.

Healy, J. (1990). *Endangered minds: Why our children don't think.* New York: Simon & Schuster.

Huston, A. C., & Wright, J. C. (1983). Children's processing of television: The informative functions of formal features. In J. Bryant & D. R. Anderson (Eds.), *Children's understanding of television: Research on attention and comprehension* (pp. 35–68). New York: Academic Press.

Huston, A.C., & Wright, J. C. (1989). The forms of television and the child viewer. In G. A. Comstock (Ed.), *Public communication and behavior* (vol. 2, pp. 103–158). New York: Academic Press.

Huston, A. C., & Wright, J. C. (1994). Educating children with television: The forms of the medium. In D. Zillmann, J. Bryant, & A. C. Huston (Eds.), *Media, children, and the family: Social scientific, psychodynamic, and clinical perspectives* (pp. 73–84). Hillsdale, NJ: Lawrence Erlbaum Associates.

Huston, A. C., & Wright, J. C. (1997). Mass media and children's development. In W. Damon (Series Ed.) & I. E. Sigel & K. A. Renninger (Vol. Eds.), *Handbook of child psychology: Vol. 4. Child psychology in practice* (4th ed., pp. 999–1058). New York: Wiley.

Huston, A. C., & Wright, J. C. (1998). Television and the informational and educational needs of children. *Annals of the American Academy of Political and Social Science, 557,* 9–33.

Huston, A. C., Wright, J. C., Wartella, E., Rice, M. L., Watkins, B. A., Campbell, T., & Potts, R. (1981). Communicating more than content: Formal features of children's television programs. *Journal of Communication, 31,* 32–48.

Kafai, Y. B., & Sutton, S. (1999). Elementary school students' computer and internet use at home: Current trends and issues. *Journal of Educational Computing Research, 21,* 345–362.

Kinder, M. (1996). Contextualizing video game violence: From *Teenage Mutant Ninja Turtles 1* to *Mortal Komat 2.* In P. M. Greenfield & R. R. Cocking (Eds.), *Interacting with video* (pp. 25–37). Norwood, NJ: Ablex.

Kozma, R. B. (1991). Learning with media. *Review of Educational Research, 61,* 179–211.

Krendl, K. A., & Lieberman, D. A. (1988). Computers and learning: A review of recent research. *Journal of Educational Computing Research, 4,* 367–389.

Kritch, J. A., Bostow, D. E., & Dedrick, R. F. (1995). Level of interactivity of videodisc instruction on college students' recall of AIDS information. *Journal of Applied Behavior Analysis, 28,* 85–86.

Lawless, K. A., & Brown, S. W. (1997). Multimedia learning environments: Issues of learner control and navigation. *Instructional Science, 25,* 117–131.

Lawless, K. A., & Kulikowich, J. M. (1996). Understanding hypertext navigation though cluster analysis. *Journal of Educational Computing Research, 14,* 385–399.

Luckin, R. (2001). Designing children's software to ensure productive interactivity through collaboration in the Zone of Proximal Development (ZPD). *Information Technology in Childhood Education Annual, 13,* 57–85.

Malone, T. W. (1981). Toward a theory of intrinsically motivating instruction. *Cognitive Science, 4,* 333–369.

Mares, M. L., & Woodard, E. H. (2001). Prosocial effects on children's social interactions. In D. G. Singer & J. L. Singer (Eds.), *Handbook of children and the media* (pp. 183–205). Thousand Oaks, CA: Sage.

McClurg, P. A., & Chaillé, C. (1987). Computer games: Environments for developing spatial cognition? *Journal of Educational Computing Research, 3,* 95–111.

Neuman, S. B., Burden, D., & Holden, E. (1990). Enhancing children's comprehension of a televised story through previewing. *Journal of Educational Research, 83,* 258–265.

Palmer, E. L., & Fisch, S. M. (2001). The beginnings of *Sesame Street* research. In S. M. Fisch & R. T. Truglio (Eds.), *"G" is for growing: Thirty years of research on children and Sesame Street* (pp. 3–23). Mahwah, NJ: Lawrence Erlbaum Associates.

Papert, S. (1980). *Mindstorms: Children, computers, and powerful ideas.* New York: Basic Books.

Pea, R. D., Kurland, D. M., & Hawkins, J. (1985). LOGO and the development of thinking skills. In M. Chen & W. Paisley (Eds.), *Children and microcomputers: Research on the newest medium* (pp. 193–212). Beverly Hills, CA: Sage.

Rafaeli, S. (1988). Interactivity: From new media to communication. In R. P. Hawkins, J. M. Wiemann, & S. Pingree (Eds.), *Advancing communication science: Merging mass media and interpersonal processes* (pp. 110–134). Newbury Park, CA: Sage.

Rice, M. L., Huston, A. C., Truglio, R., & Wright, J. (1990). Words from "Sesame Street": Learning vocabulary while viewing. *Developmental Psychology, 26,* 421–428.

Rice, M. L., Huston, A. C., & Wright, J. C. (1983). The forms of television: Effects on children's attention, comprehension, and social behavior. In M. Meyer (Ed.), *Children and the formal features of television: Approaches and findings of experimental and informative research* (pp. 21–55). New York: K. G. Saur.

Roberts, D. F., Foehr, U. G., Rideout, V. J., & Brodie, M. (1999). *Kids and media @ the new millennium.* Menlo Park, CA: Kaiser Family Foundation.

Salomon, G. (1977). Effects of encouraging Israeli mothers to co-observe *Sesame Street* with their five-year-olds. *Child Development, 48,* 1146–1151.

Salomon, G. (1983a). The differential investment of mental effort in learning from different sources. *Educational Psychologist, 18,* 42–50.

Salomon, G. (1983b). Television watching and mental effort: A social psychological view. In J. Bryant & D. R. Anderson (Eds.), *Children's understanding of television: Research on attention and comprehension* (pp. 181–198). New York: Academic Press.

Salomon, G. (1984). Television is "easy" and print is "tough"; The differential investment of mental effort in learning as a function of perceptions and attributions. *Journal of Educational Psychology, 76,* 647–658.

Salomon, G. (1990). Cognitive effects with and of computer technology. *Communication Research, 17,* 26–44.

Salomon, G., & Gardner, H. (1986). The computer as educator: Lessons from television research. *Educational Researcher, 15,* 13–19.

Salomon, G., & Globerson, T. (1987). Skill may not be enough: The role of mindfulness in learning and transfer. *International Journal of Educational Research, 11,* 623–634.

Salomon, G., & Perkins, D. N. (1987). Transfer of cognitive skills from programming: When and how? *Journal of Educational Computing Research, 3,* 149–169.

Salomon, G., & Perkins, D. N. (1989). Rocky roads to transfer: Rethinking mechanisms of a neglected phenomenon. *Educational Psychologist, 24,* 113–142.

Silverman, L. T., & Sprafkin, J. N. (1980). The effects of *Sesame Street's* prosocial spots on cooperative play between young children. *Journal of Broadcasting, 24,* 135–147.

Silvern, S. B., & Williamson, P. A. (1987). The effects of video game play on young children's aggression, fantasy, and prosocial behavior. *Journal of Applied Developmental Psychology, 8,* 453–462.

Singer, J. L. (1980). The power and limitations of television: A cognitive-affective analysis. In P. Tannenbaum (Ed.), *The entertainment function of television* (pp. 31–65). Hillsdale, NJ: Lawrence Erlbaum Associates.

Singer, J. L., & Singer, D. G. (1998). *Barney and Friends* as entertainment and education. In J. K. Asamen & G. Berry (Eds.), *Research paradigms, television, and social behavior* (pp. 305–367). Thousand Oaks, CA: Sage.

Strommen, E. F. (1993). "Does yours eat leaves?" Cooperative learning in an educational software task. *Journal of Computing in Childhood Education, 4,* 45–56.

Subrahmanyam, K., & Greenfield, P. M. (1996). Effect of video game practice on spatial skills in girls and boys. In P. M. Greenfield & R. R. Cocking (Eds.), *Interacting with video* (pp. 95–114). Norwood, NJ: Ablex.

Vorderer, P. (2001). Interactive entertainment and beyond. In D. Zillman & P. Vorderer (Eds.), *Media entertainment: The psychology of its appeal* (pp. 21–36). Mahwah, NJ: Lawrence Erlbaum Associates.

Wiegman, O., & van Schie, E. G. M. (1998). Video game playing and its relations with aggressive and prosocial behavior. *British Journal of Social Psychology, 37,* 367–378.

Woodard, E. H., & Gridina, N. (2000). *Media in the home 2000: The fifth annual survey of parents and children.* Philadelphia: University of Pennsylvania, The Annenberg Public Policy Center.

Wright, J. C., Huston, A. C., Murphy, K. C., St. Peters, M., Piñon, M., Scantlin, R., & Kotler, J. (2001). The relations of early television viewing to school readiness and vocabulary of children from low-income families: The Early Window Project. *Child Development, 72,* 1347–1366.

Wright, J. C., Huston, A. C., Ross, R. P., Calvert, S. L., Rolandelli, D., Weeks, L. A., Raeissi, P., & Potts, R. (1984). Pace and continuity of television programs: Effects on children's attention and comprehension. *Developmental Psychology, 20,* 653–666.

Wright, J. C., Huston, A. C., Scantlin, R., & Kotler, J. (2001). The Early Window Project: *Sesame Street* prepares children for school. In S. M. Fisch & R. T. Truglio (Eds.), *"G" is for growing: Thirty years of research on children and Sesame Street* (pp. 97–114). Mahwah, NJ: Lawrence Erlbaum Associates.

Zielinska, I. E., & Chambers, B. (1995). Using group viewing of television to teach preschool children social skills. *Journal of Educational Television, 21,* 85–99.

Zill, N. (2001). Does *Sesame Street* enhance school readiness?: Evidence from a national survey of children. In S. M. Fisch & R. T. Truglio (Eds.), *"G" is for growing: Thirty years of research on children and Sesame Street* (pp. 115–130). Mahwah, NJ: Lawrence Erlbaum Associates.

6

The Multicultural Worldview of Children Through the Lens of Television

Joy Keiko Asamen
Pepperdine University

Gordon L. Berry
University of California, Los Angeles

MULTICULTURAL AND WORLDVIEW PERSPECTIVES IN A MULTIMEDIA SOCIETY

Since the 1960s, there has been a revival of interest by social scientists, educators, and policymakers to consider ways of developing programs and learning experiences for children that would enhance their ability to function in an ever-changing multicultural world. Clearly, some of the attempts to create cross-cultural models, whether for the schools or the broader society, have not always met with philosophical and programmatic consensus. The same lack of methodological agreement has been true for the research paradigms that have emerged to evaluate the effectiveness of the cross-cultural beliefs and worldviews held or learned by children. Whatever the direction or philosophical base related to cross-cultural programs and educational curricula, few people would deny the importance of having developing children learn from an early age the values inherent in the respect, civility, and dignity that should be given to a person who is of a different ethnicity/race, religion, gender, and age from themselves.

Social scientists have always been aware that attitudes about ourselves and others were formulated early by the family, religious organizations, the school, the community, and peer relationships. The experiences with these institutions provide the framework for our early social beliefs, cross-cultural understandings, and general worldview. The children and youth of today, however, not only have these institutions to shape their view of the world, but also the media of television, the computer, and a vast array of other multimedia devices that communicate images and offer portrayals that assist them in formulating their attitudes, beliefs, and values. This means that television and its electronic relatives not only entertain and inform, but their content and messages become a part of the child's inner circle of primary and secondary socializers—the types of socializing influences that, when coupled with other media, drive a child's worldview.

This chapter, using the worldview construct as a frame of reference, explores the role that the medium of television and selected other media might play in the development of multicultural beliefs and attitudes in children. Within this framework, the chapter provides a context for understanding the principles relevant to the development of multicultural beliefs and attitudes, the impact of television as a communicator of cross-cultural beliefs and attitudes, criteria for judging televised programming for multicultural content, the role of the home and school in teaching children to be wise cross-cultural consumers of television, and the cross-cultural research paradigms that will inform the issues surrounding television content and multicultural understandings in children.

Cross-cultural and multicultural concepts, although finding their way into some of the more recent literature and social debate, have been at the core of human thought from its early beginnings. Morris Jackson (1995) noted that these terms, in one form or another, were recognized in ancient Mediterranean civilizations from the new kingdom of pharaonic Egypt through the collapse of the Roman Empire. Although this chapter's discussion tends to use *cross-cultural* and *multicultural* interchangeably, the latter term is most appropriate because its scope implies more cultural balance and inclusiveness related to within-group differences and between-group differences. That is to say, an advantage of the term *multicultural* is that it implies a wide range of multiple groups without grading, comparing, or ranking them as better or worse than one another, and without denying the very distinct and complementary or even contradictory perspectives that each group brings with it (Pedersen, 1991).

Trying to place the meaning of multiculturalism into some context is difficult. It is difficult because at its roots are the ideas of culture with all of their historical concepts and present-day complexities, and because of the need to move the definition of multiculturalism away from the political debates, slogans, and superficial meanings into a scholarly and theoretical framework for quantitative and qualitative analysis. For example, culture can be seen as the totality of manners, customs, and values of a given society. In this type of concept, culture implies the sum total of ways of living developed by a people to meet their biological and psychological needs (Ibrahim, 1991). Multiculturalism attempts to explain the behavior of people both in terms of those culturally learned perspectives that are unique to a particular culture, and in the search for common-ground universals that are shared across cultures (Pedersen, 1991). Pedersen further stated that "the multicultural perspective seeks to provide a conceptual framework that recognizes the complex diversity of a plural society while, at the same time, suggesting bridges of shared concern that bind culturally different persons to one another" (p. 7).

The linking of shared concerns among culturally different groups introduces the elements of cultural diversity and cultural pluralism into the meanings inherent in a definition of multiculturalism. Grant (1995) noted that cultural diversity relates to the awareness, acceptance, and affirmation of cultural and ethnic differences, as well as an appreciation of human differences. Similarly, to endorse cultural pluralism, within the multicultural context of this chapter, is to understand and appreciate the differences that exist among the citizens of this country (the United States). Equally important, it is to see these differences as a positive force in the continuing development of a society that professes a wholesome respect for the intrinsic worth of every individual (American Association of Colleges of Teacher Education, 1973; Berry & Asamen, 2001). The combinations of these early and recent positions related to the multicultural constructs of culture, cultural diversity, and cultural pluralism are still important today, but no less complex. These constructs remain important because at their core are the notions that in an ever-increasingly culturally diverse nation, no group can live in a vacuum or function with a culturally encapsulated worldview. The country's vast communication system and the changing multicultural landscape mean that each group must exist as a part of an interrelated whole.

The interrelatedness of a country can be seen in the most recent census reports, in which large numbers of people used multiple categories to describe their racial/ethnic group. Equally important, our demographic future tends to suggest that sometime in the middle of the 21st century, the United States will become what is called a "minority-majority society" (Chisman, 1998)—that is, a society in which the various minority groups of Color will constitute a majority (Berry & Asamen, 2001; Chisman 1998). Thus, an ever-changing multicultural country will challenge its citizens and those major agents of socialization to move beyond some of their ethnocentric views of the world in order to understand the concept of cultural diversity and multiculturalism within a climate of unity.

The Developing Child and the Worldview Construct

The culturally encapsulated person may, of course, attempt to evade the reality of the changing nature of our multicultural and multimedia society through ethnocentric beliefs. Such individuals, according to Baruth and Manning (1991), maintain a type of cultural "cocoon" by believing their internalized value assumptions are best for society. Similarly, the worldview assumptions of people can play a role in the way in which they see themselves, the way they feel about others, and their general views about cultural diversity. Sue (1981) pointed out that a worldview relates to how a person perceives his or her relationship to the world (i.e., nature, institutions, other people, and things). Not only are worldviews composed of our attitudes, values, opinions, and concepts, but they also may affect how an individual thinks, makes decisions, behaves, and defines events (Sue, 1981). The attitudes and behaviors held by an individual help to shape the personality constructs that are used to influence a worldview. These personal constructs determine what and how a person will perceive, learn, remember, think, and act in regard to elements that are encompassed by the constructs (Axelson, 1993). Thus, the worldview becomes, for the individual, a construct that directly affects and mediates his or her belief systems, assumptions, modes of problem solving, and conflict resolution (Ibrahim, 1991).

Clearly, children growing and developing in the 21st century, which is partly defined by its multimedia and communications resources, face a special challenge as they are bombarded by values and belief systems that assist in forming their worldviews. The medium of television is one of the major teachers associated with what children learn and how they learn it. This teaching and learning process is especially important when it comes to a child's understanding of the multicultural world in which he or she lives. As Palmer, Smith, and Strawser (1993) stated, "As the world's children catch a glimpse of one another through their television window, perceptions form, stereotypes develop, and expectations abound. No longer will these young be simply children. They will be television portrayals of different children, and this difference can make all the difference in their world of perception, valuing, and interaction" (p. 143). These researchers suggested that television has the ability to create two worlds for children: one White, the other non-White (Palmer et al., 1993). It follows, then, "that television also creates different worldviews for different children" (p. 149).

TELEVISION AS A COMMUNICATOR OF MULTICULTURAL BELIEFS AND ATTITUDES TO CHILDREN

For a child, television "provides a 'window to the world' beyond the immediate culture of the child's family and neighborhood" (Asamen, 1993, p. 308). Through this lens, children learn what others outside their social network assume about them, others, and society in general. Out of this viewing experience, the development of children's cognitions, attitudes, and values about themselves and others is influenced. Thomas (1999), in addressing cultural influences for 25 different theories of human development, referred to communication media as one of the "purveyors of culture" that may interact with biological and other environmental factors, such as "parents, teachers, religious leaders, peers" to influence how children grow and mature from birth to young adulthood (p. 193). Rapidly joining the ranks of television as a prominent socializer are other electronic technologies that have become a mainstay in a child's daily existence (e.g., Internet access).

Cognition—the mental processes (i.e., analysis, synthesis, evaluation, and recall) and the attitudes, values, and beliefs these processes produce (Thomas, 1999)—is unequivocally tied to the environment (i.e., culture) in which the child exists. Theorists of mental processes such as Vygotsky, D'Andrade, Gardner, Jackson, and Jung, acknowledged the prominent role played by culture in how and what we think (Thomas, 1999). Even Piaget, who initially disregarded the salience of environmental influences for a predominately genetics-based cognitive maturation process, began to recognize that these environmental influences could not be ignored. As aptly stated by Thomas (1999), "theories of human development are useful for identifying how different cultures influence the destinies of children and youth" (p. 1).

Learning (or the process of knowledge and behavior acquisition), like cognition, is also heavily influenced by the environment (Thomas, 1999). The acquisition of knowledge occurs through the exchanges one has with various socializing agents on a day-to-day basis. In a contemporary context, these agents of socialization include television and other electronic media. The cognitive maturation of the child influences how much and to what a child attends as well as how completely or distortedly he or she understands what is viewed, so that "Children, particularly preschoolers and younger children, may miss some of what is good about television and be more vulnerable to the influence of what is not" (Doubleday & Droege, 1993, p. 35). Furthermore, the potential risk is that young viewers "are likely to 'fill in' their incomplete representations with stereotypes and familiar scripts taken from their more limited general knowledge of television and the world" (Doubleday & Droege, 1993, p. 35).

So what do children learn about themselves and others from television and its electronic relatives? The answer: just about everything. Children receive messages about who they are and who they are not (Huntemann & Morgan, 2001), what commodities to purchase or what foods to eat (Greenfield et al., 1993; Horgen, Choate, & Brownell, 2001; Kunkel, 2001), and what acts are "good versus bad" or make you popular or unpopular (Bushman & Huesmann, 2001; Malamuth & Impett, 2001; Mares & Woodard, 2001; Rosenkoetter, 2001; Strasburger, 2001). The potential influence television has on the multicultural development of children includes issues of ethnicity and race, class, gender, disabilities, and age, among others (Allen, 2001; Berry & Asamen, 1993, 2001; Geiogamah & Pavel, 1993; Graves, 1993; Hamamoto, 1993; Kovaric, 1993; Makas, 1993; Signorielli, 2001; Subervi-Vélez & Colsant, 1993).

Television has been viewed as a source of vicarious socialization by some researchers (Berry, 1998; Comstock, 1993). This ubiquitous medium—like one's family and faith, the school and community, and peer relations—has become one of the established institutions of socialization and plays a prominent role in the development of a child's worldview. Television programming of diverse populations is still dominated by writers and directors who do not share the worldview of the persons they depict. Images of people of Color and other diverse groups are often based on stereotypes rooted in the constrained experience of those persons who create the programming, or worse yet, caricatures. When children are exposed to a steady diet of these stereotypic messages and images, their understanding of themselves and the world around them is conceptualized accordingly: "The more time viewers spend with television, the more likely their conceptions about the world and its people will reflect what they see on television" (Signorielli, 2001, p. 344). Not only are culturally diverse groups misrepresented, but frequently there is an absence of any representation or visibility in this medium. This absence of a multicultural perspective can have a negative impact on developing children. Huntemann and Morgan (2001) noted, "Children and adolescents who do not see characters like themselves on television are learning a fundamental lesson about their group's importance in society. Daily, they are being sent a loud and clear message that they do not count for very much in society" (p. 316).

The underrepresentation and misrepresentation of diverse populations in television programming may result in a child attributing undesirable traits to a class of people, categorizing a person as belonging to this class, and, finally, attributing the undesirable traits to the person without considering whether the characterization has merit. This process describes how a person develops prejudicial attitudes (Thomas, 1999). Children who do not have access to competing views or who are denied access to diverse life experiences are particularly vulnerable to incorporating prejudiced thinking into their schema about others.

The current state of television programming may not only influence how a child perceives others, but the limited depictions of diverse groups may also have some bearing on a child's perception of self and how he or she relates to persons outside their immediate social network (Palmer et al., 1993). To quantify the influence of television among African Americans, Allen (2001) empirically tested the antecedents involved in the development of an African American racial belief system. In testing his model, the preliminary findings regarding electronic media indicate that majority-based electronic media tended to negatively influence Black self-concept, whereas viewing more Black-oriented electronic media was associated with less of a sense of a Black identity. Allen pointed out that little of Black television is owned by African Americans, and, as a consequence, little of what is televised is independent of non-Black influence, perhaps accounting, in part, for the findings. In addition, Black-oriented and majority-based electronic media may not pursue content themes that foster a strong Black self-concept. Such discussion is speculative at this point but, nonetheless, the influence of media on one's sense of personhood is evident from Allen's research.

It is clear that television is a major player in the socialization of children. Given the prominence of this medium, it is imperative that those individuals who are responsible for television programming decisions make choices in a manner that provides visibility as well as an accurate portrayal of social reality for the diverse groups represented in their audiences.

MULTICULTURAL PORTRAYALS: IDENTIFYING GUIDELINES FOR TELEVISED CONTENT

Whatever else television is or does, three of its goals are to entertain and to inform within the framework of the third goal—being a business. Indeed, there is nothing inherently wrong with these goals for a medium dedicated to various forms of communication. At the same time, because of the power of television to assist in defining social reality, it is important that this medium does not provide images that would distort the multicultural worldview of the developing child. Ploghoft and Anderson (1982) pointed out that television affects the way we think, value things, and behave. Even when it is not intentionally designed to teach, television carries messages about social interactions and about the nature and value of groups in society that can influence attitudes, values, and actions among its viewers (Huston et al., 1992).

Preschool children and those in the lower grades look at a great deal of television that is labeled "programming for children." At the same time, a large audience of boys and girls watch prime-time programs that fall within what was once referred to as the "family hour." Katharine Heintz-Knowles and colleagues (2001) from Children Now conducted research on the 2000 television season. From this research project, it is possible to look at the nature of the multicultural experiences that the children and youth might have encountered from shows on any of the six major television networks (ABC, CBS, FOX, NBC, UPN, and the WB). According to the research from Children Now, a nonpartisan and independent organization, in the 2000 television season the children were most likely to see the following in terms of race/ethnicity:

- More diversity if he/she stays up late, but less diversity in hours when he/she is most likely to be watching.
- More diversity in dramas, but less diversity in the sitcoms that he/she is more likely to be viewing.
- Fewer Latinos than last year, dropping from 3 percent of the total prime time population to 2 per cent, and mostly occupying secondary and tertiary character roles.
- Five Native American characters out of a total prime time population of 2251.
- A world overwhelmingly populated by able-bodied, single, heterosexual, white, male adults under 40 (Heintz-Knowles et al., 2001, p. 2).

It will come as no surprise that selected findings related to the role of women in the 2000 season raised questions of gender, identity, and equity because multicultural portrayals, or the lack of them, frequently show a correlation with other cross-cultural issues in society. For example, there were a total of 88 programs studied in this Children Now research project, with some 2,251 characters. Adult characters tended to engage in a wide range of professional careers in this study, but with race and gender differences influencing the occupations they held. Of the top five occupations shown for the various racial groups, only people of Color filled the positions of domestic worker, homemaker, nurse/physician's assistant, and unskilled laborer. White characters were more likely than African American characters to be shown in professional business occupations, and African Americans were more likely to be shown in law enforcement-related occupations (Heintz-Knowles et al., 2001).

Multicultural images shown on a creative medium and with clear First Amendment rights should not be infringed on in a cavalier manner. However, television and its programs, in any given season, can be judged based on their age-appropriateness and reviewed for their multicultural content and social learning attributes. We can establish criteria and standards for children and youth because they represent a special audience for whom adults have a special responsibility. Based on the premise of this special responsibility to children and to offer content areas that can be subjected to evaluation, we have updated some of the early work of Berry (1988) and identified a set of guidelines related to multicultural portrayals. These multicultural portrayals are constructed into a form that is not prescriptive or designed to retard the creative process. Rather, the cross-cultural areas are presented as a point of departure for considering racial/ethnic elements of content in programs for children and those scheduled for prime time. Although the focus of these criteria for guidelines relates to people of Color, it is clear that they are applicable to women in general, religious groups, the physically challenged, the elderly, gays and lesbians, and a variety of others who have been disenfranchised at some level by society. The guidelines are as follows:

1. Program content portrays various ethnic groups evenly in society, including depictions of historical, cultural, and current events.
2. Program content portrays various ethnic groups evenly in their contributions to the arts and sciences.
3. Program content shows a diversity of professional and vocational roles and careers among various ethnic groups.
4. Program content does not define or limit occupational aspirations in terms of ethnicity.
5. Program content portrays various ethnic groups throughout the range of socioeconomic conditions and lifestyle situations.
6. Program content portrays both traditional and nontraditional activities performed by character, regardless of ethnicity.
7. Program content portrays active, creative, and problem-solving roles proportionally among various ethnic groups.
8. Program content uses dialogue between various characters that is free of stereotypic language, demeaning labels, and/or race-related retorts.
9. Program content portrays emotional reactions such as fear, anger, aggression, excitement, love, and concern regardless of ethnicity.
10. Program content does not stereotype personality traits based on ethnicity.

Nothing in these guidelines suggests that quotas need to be applied to certain types of portrayals or that human foibles cannot be a part of the experiences of people of Color within the creative process of this medium. There is a need to consider the importance of portraying the lifestyles and cultures of people of Color with more "balance" and in-depth analysis of the richness of the minority experience. The balance and richness are not only important for children of Color, but for every child who is growing and developing in a multi-ethnic society. Moody (1980) made this point a number of years ago:

The child in the affluent suburb or the small midwestern town exists within his own limited reality. His experience with social problems or people of different races, religions, or nationalities is probably somewhat limited. It is precisely because he now relies so heavily on T.V. to define other realities for him that we must examine so carefully what those images are. If they are distorted, inaccurate, or unfair, then television's reality is potentially harmful. (p. 111)

Thus, the images of television can help to establish, for cross-culturally unsophisticated children, what is the norm for a cultural group with whom they have limited contact. Equally important, children of Color may learn to accept character portrayals and images of their ethnic groups as the cultural norm. For both groups, the portrayals of people, places, and things from this image-powerful and ubiquitous medium is made even more psychologically robust when there are not counter-balancing attitudes, ideas, and values coming to them from the family, the schools, and religious institutions.

THE CHILD AS A LEARNER: ENABLING PARENTS, SCHOOLS, AND TELEVISION TO BE MULTICULTURAL TEACHERS

It would be natural for any parent or teacher who is considering using television in the home or classroom as a guide to help children better understand multicultural experiences to have some concerns about it. After all, the research literature is full of such issues as children learning aggressive behavior from television, children spending too much time looking at television, children being negatively influenced by advertising, and a host of other professional and parental concerns.

This natural concern for children, especially those in preschool and the elementary grades, stems from the developmental notions that television program content involves character portrayals, ideas, and attractive models that can affect the child's social learning and other socialization activities. Social learning theory is relevant here because it advances the concept that learning occurs through the identification with, and imitation of, significant others. There is little doubt that television, for some children, offers value-oriented messages and attractive portrayals of role models that are admired, believed, and potentially imitated by them. Thus, the more a child admires and believes in a role model whose behaviors are rewarded or recognized as important, the more he or she might imitate and identify with the person (Bandura, 1977; Berger, 1980; Eggen & Kauchak, 1997).

Given both the positive and negative research directions on television and its effects on children, we would say that a major argument for considering it as part of the curriculum for cross-cultural understanding is that teachers and parents will, at the same time, be able to assist young children to use this medium in a more productive manner. It is this potential to help children to become wise consumers of this very powerful medium that should motivate teachers and parents to learn about its effects, and then teach children its uses as a potential instructional tool for better understanding others.

Program content from network, public, and cable television and all of their electronic cousins can, if properly used, offer the young learner a new set of instructional experiences that was not possible before the advent of these media forms. In short, television provides new ways of communicating information to the child. Television also permits many variations in the teaching and learning process, and its effective use is based on the same fundamental psychological principles that apply to all successful processes of learning. For the classroom teacher and parent, television is potentially another teaching tool that can be used to complement the instructional program, because of its power as a communicator. In an article entitled "Learning in the Age of Television," Neil Postman (1985)—a noted social critic of teaching, television, and schools—stated that "one is entirely justified in saying that the major educational enterprise now being undertaken in the United States is not happening in its classrooms, but in front of the television set, and under the jurisdiction not of school administrators and teachers but of network executives and entertainers" (p. 17). Although Postman, even during this early period, saw no conspiracy in this process of where much of the teaching and learning was taking place, he did see the medium as a new type of curriculum for educating children.

A major cautionary implication of the learning influences of the "television curriculum" for the classroom teacher and parent is that the curricular activities, unlike those of the school, can be limited in terms of professionally created objectives, follow no traditional pattern of curricular scope and sequence, and they may not include those values that the broader society wants its children to learn about themselves and other cultural groups. The learning experiences of the school are planned and supervised by a teacher, administrator, or other professionally assigned personnel. In contrast, the "curriculum" of television can have significantly different goals.

Different goals between commercial television and the school or home need not mean that professional educators and parents cannot utilize the medium within their instructional programs. What it does mean is that classroom teachers and parents must utilize the medium with a full understanding that the act of television viewing by the child does involve many of the same cognitive processes associated with learning (i.e., retention, recall, attention, decoding, and comprehension). Similarly, television as a medium of entertainment and information can and frequently does require, especially of young children, active cognitive and affective processing in order for them to understand the content and formal features of selected programs. Wright and Huston (1984) highlighted this mental activity concept by pointing out that selecting central content from incidental content, sequencing and temporally integrating events, inferring conditions and events not shown, and understanding the motives and feelings of characters all require a child to draw on his or her world and television knowledge. Part of what a child uses to understand and learn from television is its formal features, which include such things as action, pace, visual techniques, and verbal and nonverbal auditory events (Huston & Wright, 1983). These formal features are not the same as content, according to these researchers, but it could be stated that there is a strong interrelationship between the two factors because the formal features are the mechanisms that young children use to make the content have meaning. Although not focusing directly on formal features, Pedzdek (1985) did support the notion of the learning activity that a child engages in while watching television by suggesting that there is a need to conceptualize the viewing behavior of children as a series of information-processing stages: We perceive information, attend to it, encode it, retain it in memory, and later retrieve it from memory.

Suggesting that there are selected characteristics associated with television viewing that involve some of the same processes that children engage in during their general learning activities is not to argue that there is a one-to-one relationship between the two. Rather, the point to be made is that television, like other forms of learning and under the right conditions, can also be an active as well as a passive process. However, like other forms of learning activities, the developmental stage and readiness of children to learn are as important in their understanding of the special attributes and features of television as they are with the subjects in their classroom curriculum.

If teachers and parents are to capitalize on the positive uses of television in the classroom and the home, they cannot approach their planning in a piecemeal or haphazard manner. The process of teachers using television effectively can only be accomplished through a systematic approach that does the following: establishes clear goals and objectives for using television in the classroom and home; develops a plan that fully integrates television into the teaching and learning activities; ensures that the children are properly prepared with critical television-viewing skills so that they can understand the content, special features, and unique attributes of the medium; and creates a plan for formal or informal evaluation of the effectiveness of using television in the classroom. For parents, it is suggested that they: limit the child's exposure, especially to negative stereotypes that are subtle in some programs and ads; look closely at the characters and the messages that a television program sends concerning ethnicity, gender, and roles; evaluate the programs and discuss them with children; and search for programs that help the child appreciate human diversity (Chen, 1994).

Visually Literate Students and the Reform Movement

It does appear that the present educational reform movement has not fully appreciated the fact that television sets are available in 98% of all American homes and manage to occupy a great deal of a child's time. Taken alone, television is not a villain. After all, it is only a box full of electronics. Our problem with television today is that our schools, parents, and our children do not use it wisely, educators do not teach about its influence, and professional communicators who make the decisions as to the nature of its content do not challenge children enough with quality cross-cultural content. It is, therefore, worth stating again that television properly used in the home and classroom can be a medium for entertainment *and* cross-cultural information. As Greenfield (1984) stated: "Television and the new electronic media, if used wisely, have great potential for learning and development. They give children different mental skills from those developed by reading and writing. Television is a better medium than the printed word, for conveying certain types of information, and it makes learning available to groups of children who do not do well in traditional school situations and even to people who cannot read" (p. 2).

Teachers and parents can help children become wise television viewers by introducing into their school and home activities those skills that will prepare the learner to be visually literate through critical viewing skills. As Brown (2001) noted, "Critical viewing skills is one major component of media literacy, referring to understanding of and competence with television, including its aesthetic, social, cultural, psychological, educational, economic, and regulatory aspects" (p. 681).

Television is such a powerful force in our society that to merely identify some of its visual and auditory attributes does not do justice to the complexity of helping children understand it in a critical fashion. The truly critical television viewers should be able to: make and defend judgments about what they see; determine which programs are effective and satisfying and recognize which programs are unconvincing and empty; understand the relationships linking television to society, and explore and expand those relationships; approach the medium with balanced perspectives that help them to understand what works and why; and see beyond what merely works, to an appreciation of programming that sustains, informs, and humanizes (England, 1982). Thus, England set a high standard for anyone who wants to provide a programmatic instructional program for children who are later going to use television material as part of their learning activities. Like all activities planned in the school's curriculum or the home, however, television usage needs to be rooted in a solid foundation and based on the learning readiness of the child.

It is important to note at this point that it is a difficult task to discuss using a complicated medium to help children in the classroom and the home to understand the complex issues inherent in multicultural and cross-cultural content. It is also recognized that the foci of this chapter have been, by design, on television and what is referred to as "groups of Color," with some references to women. At the same time, there was a clear awareness of the need to also help all children to understand the meanings related to the media images and portrayals of ethnic groups, such as Jewish, Polish, Italian, German, Irish, and Arab Americans, as well as other European, Middle Eastern, and Far Eastern Americans. From the media and technology sides, Dorr and Brannon (1992, as cited in Anderson & Ploghoft, 1993) summarized the need to provide education for all children this way, "American children need education about the important influential media and technology in their world of today, about how to use any medium or technology well for everyday life activities, about how to adapt to change and about how to become skilled users of whatever medium or technology may become an important part of the world tomorrow" (p. 101). From the need for children to have some form of multicultural education, Banks (1997) stated, "Multicultural education incorporates the idea that all students—regardless of their gender and social class and ethnic, racial, or cultural characteristics—should have an equal opportunity to learn in school" (p. 3).

RESEARCH ISSUES FROM A WORLDVIEW PERSPECTIVE

What a child incorporates into her or his worldview is unquestionably influenced by the transactions that occur between the child and the varied institutions of socialization that he or she encounters. Television and its electronic kin have clearly established themselves as influential socializing agents. The mental processes that are stimulated by television viewing experiences produce cognitions, beliefs, and values of self and others. This schema, in turn, shapes the social behaviors and actions of the child.

Despite the gains we have made in our understanding of the powerful influence television has on the multicultural development of children, there are many long-standing and newly emerging questions with which to grapple. For example, Allen (2001) pointed to the need to better understand why Black electronic media do not have a more positive influence on the Black self-concept and identity of African Americans. One would hypothesize, as did Allen, that African Americans who consume a steady diet of Black-oriented electronic media over majority-based electronic media would have their sense of African personhood reinforced by the experience rather than minimized, as was revealed in his research. So how do we explain what Allen found? Equally important, how do we craft a study to further our understanding of the process that explains this puzzling occurrence? How do we capture the interplay between the cultural world of those who view the medium with the cultural world of those who produce television programming?

The Allen (2001) study serves as an example of how little we know about the mental processes that explain how television viewing influences one's conceptions of self and others. We do know that television has an effect on the viewer, but how does this effect materialize? We know that a child's worldview is influenced by what he or she views, but which of the mental processes appear more relevant, or how do these processes interrelate in explaining how this schema comes about? Two people with the same viewing experience may walk away with a different mental set of what they witnessed. Thus, how do we capture this relativistic quality of a child's worldview development? How do we, as investigators, craft studies that provide answers for questions of process as well as function? Children make sense of what they view filtered through a number of different lens (i.e., through the eyes of their parents; peers; and religious, educational, and social institutions) besides that of television and other electronic media. This influences what they think and believe about the world, and makes research with children necessarily complicated.

To further our understanding of the influence television has on the worldview development of children, methods of study that allow investigators to pursue both questions of function and process are essential. The relativistic nature of a child's worldview requires that any research that is conducted not only be scientifically valid but contextually relevant. One way to take both these needs into consideration is to engage in what Tashakkori and Teddlie (1998) referred to as "mixed method" and "mixed model" studies.

A mixed method study integrates quantitative and qualitative research paradigms in studying a particular phenomenon (Tashakkori & Teddlie, 1998). For example, in a sequential mixed method study, the first study conducted may have
been designed using a qualitative method so that hypotheses can be generated
about the phenomenon under investigation. The second study may actually test the
hypotheses generated from the first study using a quantitative method. In contrast,
a mixed model study mixes quantitative and qualitative methods into the steps of
the research process (Tashakkori & Teddlie, 1998). For example, an experiment
that tests the efficacy of a visual literacy education program may collect data that are
both quantitative and qualitative, analyze these data using statistical and content
analyses, and, finally, triangulate the results of both sets of analyses to come up with
conclusions. Still another example of the number of other possible mixes is to conduct the experiment, which is more typical of a quantitative method of study, and to
assess efficacy by content analyzing data acquired from a semi-structured interview, the qualitative component.

To guide our investigatory efforts, Berry and Asamen (2001) suggested that media researchers consider three philosophical dimensions in the conceptualization
and design of research studies: etic and emic, reality and relativity, and objective
and relational. The etic-emic dimension is concerned with what is typical (etic) versus what is unique (emic), and endeavoring to consider both of these perspectives
in formulating the research plan. As an example, are the families that are portrayed
on television really typical of the diverse groups who compose the viewing audience? Is what is typical to the 13-year-old Latino child who has been raised by a
grandparent since infancy the same as what is typical for a 10-year-old African
American boy who resides with both of his parents or the 6-year-old girl from
China who was adopted by a U.S. family? How do these children process the television portrayals of families given their unique family experiences?

The other two dimensions, reality-relativity and objective-relational, are tied to
the etic-emic discussion. The former dimension wrestles with whether we share in
"one reality" or instead coexist in a society that is comprised of multiple realities.
Would not the Latino child, African American boy, and Chinese girl operate from
different realities concerning the typicality of a family? In other words, how a family is
defined by a child is relative to the uniqueness of one's life experiences. The question,
then, becomes: How do these children negotiate the incongruence that exists between
the television version of family and their own reality as to what a family is? If an inves-
tigator relied strictly on behavioral measures (objective) to understand the child's
way of processing this incongruence without endeavoring to become more inti-
mately acquainted with how these children developed their thoughts (relational), the
findings that result from the investigation may provide a limited, and perhaps even a
distorted, understanding of how television influences the child's worldview.

As investigators, each of us brings to the research enterprise our own views of
what is important in designing research studies and how best to approach our work.
Our predilections are a compilation of our education and training, academic experiences, and simply what we feel competent and comfortable in doing. We are not

arguing in favor of any particular type of research paradigm, mono-method or mixed method. The point being made in this discussion is that to further our understanding of television and other electronic media and their influence on the development of children within a multicultural context will require studying the issues using diverse methods of investigation.

CONCLUSION

There is no questioning that children learn about themselves and others from the images and messages communicated through television and related electronic media. This chapter endeavored to provide a diverse audience of readers who are concerned about children and what they learn about multiculturalism from television with suggestions for making the experience a constructive one. There is no denying that television is a normal part of just about any child's life in the 21st Century. The global presence of this medium makes it an influential purveyor of cultures to children in all parts of the world.

Television is not all bad or all good, but, like any experience, we must first learn how to make the best of it. In other words, we need to educate ourselves on the productive use of this medium. In this chapter, recommendations were offered for righting the underrepresentation and misrepresentation in television programming of people of Color and other diverse groups. Suggestions were proposed to parents and educators on ways to capitalize on the positive uses of television, and, finally, thoughts were shared with other social scientists on ways to further our understanding of television's influence on the development of a child's worldview.

REFERENCES

Allen, R. L. (2001). *The concept of self: A study of Black identity and self-esteem.* Detroit, MI: Wayne State University Press.

American Association of Colleges of Teacher Education. (1973). No model American: A statement on the multicultural education. *Journal of Teacher Education, 14,* 264.

Anderson, J. A., & Ploghoft, M. E. (1993). Children and media in media education. In G. L. Berry & J. K. Asamen (Eds.), *Children and television, images in a changing sociocultural world* (pp. 89–102). Newbury Park, CA: Sage.

Asamen, J. K. (1993). Epilogue: What children learn form television and how they learn it. In G. L. Berry & J. K. Asamen (Eds.), *Children and television, images in a changing sociocultural world* (pp. 308–310). Newbury Park, CA: Sage.

Axelson, J. A. (1993). *Counseling and development in a multicultural society.* Pacific Grove, CA: Brooks-Cole.

Bandura, A. (1977). *Social learning theory.* Englewood Cliffs, NJ: Prentice-Hall.

Banks, J. A. (1997). Multicultural education: Issues and perspectives. In J. A. Banks (Ed.), *Multicultural education: Characteristics and goals* (pp. 3–31). Boston: Allyn & Bacon.

Baruth, L. G., & Manning, M. L. (1991). *Multicultural counseling and psychotherapy: A lifespan perspective.* New York: Merrill.

Berger, S. (1980). *The developing person.* New York: Worth.

Berry, G. L. (1988). Multicultural role portrayals on television as a social psychological issue. In S. Oskamp (Ed.), *Television as a social issue* (pp. 118–129). Newbury Park, CA: Sage.

Berry, G. L. (1998). Black family life on television and the socialization of the African American child: Images of marginality. *Journal of Comparative Family Studies, 19*(2), 233–242.

Berry, G. L., & Asamen, J. K. (Eds.). (1993). *Children and television, images in a changing sociocultural world.* Newbury Park, CA: Sage.

Berry, G. L., & Asamen, J. K. (2001). Television, children, and multicultural awareness. In D. G. Singer & J. L. Singer (Eds.), *Handbook of children and the media* (pp. 359–373). Thousand Oaks, CA: Sage.

Brown, J. A. (2001). Media literacy and critical television viewing in education. In D. G. Singer & J. L. Singer (Eds.), *Handbook of children and the media* (pp. 681–697). Thousand Oaks, CA: Sage.

Bushman, B. J., & Huesmann, L. R. (2001). Effects of televised violence on aggression. In D. G. Singer & J. L. Singer (Eds.), *Handbook of children and the media* (pp. 223–254). Thousand Oaks, CA: Sage.

Chen, M. (1994). *The smart parent's guide to kids' TV.* San Francisco: KQED.

Chisman, F. P. (1998). Delivering on diversity: Serving the media needs and interests of minorities in the twenty-first century. In A. K. Garmer (Ed.), *Investing in diversity: Advancing opportunities for minorities and the media* (pp. 1–30). Washington, DC: Aspen Institute.

Comstock, G. (1993). The medium and the society: The role of television in American life. In G. L. Berry & J. K. Asamen (Eds.), *Children and television, images in a changing sociocultural world* (pp. 117–131). Newbury Park, CA: Sage.

Doubleday, C. N., & Droege, K. L. (1993). Cognitive developmental influences on children's understanding of television. In G. L. Berry & J. K. Asamen (Eds.), *Children and television, images in a changing sociocultural world* (pp. 23–37). Newbury Park, CA: Sage.

Eggen, P., & Kauchak, D. (1997). *Educational psychology: Windows on classrooms.* Upper Saddle River, NJ: Prentice-Hall.

England, D. (1982). Television in the classroom: A critical view and six proposals. *Television and Children, 5*(3), 15–21.

Geiogamah, H., & Pavel, D. M. (1993). Developing television for American Indian and Alaska Native children in the late 20th century. In G. L. Berry & J. K. Asamen (Eds.), *Children and television, images in a changing sociocultural world* (pp. 191–204). Newbury Park, CA: Sage.

Grant, C. A. (1995). Praising diversity in school: Social and individual implications. In C. A. Grant (Ed.), *An anthology of multicultural voices* (pp. 3–16). Needham Heights, MA: Allyn & Bacon.

Graves, S. B. (1993). Television, the portrayal of African Americans, and the development of children's attitudes. In G. L. Berry & J. K. Asamen (Eds.), *Children and television, images in a changing sociocultural world* (pp. 179–190). Newbury Park, CA: Sage.

Greenfield, P. (1984). *Mind and media: The effects of television, video games, and computers.* Cambridge, MA: Harvard University Press.

Greenfield, P. M., Yut, E., Chung, M., Land, D., Kreider, H., Pantoja, M., & Horsley, K. (1993). The program-length commercial: A study of the effects of television/toy tie-ins on imaginative play. . In G. L. Berry & J. K. Asamen (Eds.), *Children and television, images in a changing sociocultural world* (pp. 53–72). Newbury Park, CA: Sage.

Hamamoto, D. Y. (1993). They're so cute when they're young: The Asian-American child on television. In G. L. Berry & J. K. Asamen (Eds.), *Children and television, images in a changing sociocultural world* (pp. 205–214). Newbury Park, CA: Sage.

Heintz-Knowles, K. E., Parker, M. A., Miller, P., Glaubke, C., Thai-Binah, S., & Sorah-Reyes, T. (2001). *Fall colors 2000–01: Prime time diversity report.* San Francisco: Children Now.

Horgen, K. B., Choate, M., & Brownell, K. D. (2001). Television food advertising: Targeting children in a toxic environment. In D. G. Singer & J. L. Singer (Eds.), *Handbook of children and the media* (pp. 447–461). Thousand Oaks, CA: Sage.

Huntemann, N., & Morgan, M. (2001). Mass media and identity development. In D. G. Singer & J. L. Singer (Eds.), *Handbook of children and the media* (pp. 309–322). Thousand Oaks, CA: Sage.

Huston, A. C., Donnerstein, E., Fairchild, H., Feshbach, N. D., Katz, P. A., Murray, J. P., Rubinstein, E. A., Wilcox, B., & Zimmerman, D. (1992). *Big world, small screen: The role of television in American society.* Lincoln: University of Nebraska Press.

Huston, A., & Wright, J. C. (1983). Children's processing of television: The informative functions of formal features. In J. Bryant & D. R. Anderson (Eds.), *Children's understanding of television: Research on attention and comprehension* (pp. 35–68). New York: Academic Press.

Ibrahim, F. A. (1991). Contribution of cultural worldview to generic counseling and development. *Journal of Counseling and Development, 70,* 13–19.

Jackson, M. L. (1995). Multicultural counseling: historical perspectives. In J. G. Ponterotto, J. M. Casas, L. A. Suzuki, & C. M. Alexander (Eds.), *Handbook of multicultural counseling* (pp. 3–16). Thousand Oaks, CA: Sage.

Kovaric, P. M. (1993). Television, the portrayal of the elderly, and children's attitudes. In G. L. Berry & J. K. Asamen (Eds.), *Children and television, images in a changing sociocultural world* (pp. 243–254). Newbury Park, CA: Sage.

Kunkel, D. (2001). Children and television advertising. In D. G. Singer & J. L. Singer (Eds.), *Handbook of children and the media* (pp. 375–393). Thousand Oaks, CA: Sage.

Makas, E. (1993). Changing channels: The portrayal of people with disabilities on television. In G. L. Berry & J. K. Asamen (Eds.), *Children and television, images in a changing sociocultural world* (pp. 255–268). Newbury Park, CA: Sage.

Malamuth, N. M., & Impett, E. A. (2001). Research on sex in the media: What do we know about effects on children and adolescents? In D. G. Singer & J. L. Singer (Eds.), *Handbook of children and the media* (pp. 269–287). Thousand Oaks, CA: Sage.

Mares, M., & Woodard, E. H. (2001). Prosocial effects on children's social interactions. In D. G. Singer & J. L. Singer (Eds.), *Handbook of children and the media* (pp. 183–205). Thousand Oaks, CA: Sage.

Moody, K. (1980). *Growing up on television: The TV effect.* New York: Times Books.

Palmer, E. L., Smith, K. T., & Strawser, K. S. (1993). Rubik's tube: Developing a child's television worldview. In G. L. Berry & J. K. Asamen (Eds.), *Children and television: Images in a changing sociocultural world* (pp. 143–154). Newbury Park, CA. Sage.

Pedersen, P. B. (1991). Introduction to the special issue on multiculturalism as a fourth force in counseling. *Journal of Counseling and Development, 70,* 4.

Pedzdek, K. (1985). Is watching TV passive, uncreative or additive? Debunking some myths. *Television and Families, 8,* 41–46.

Ploghoft, M. E., & Anderson, J. A. (1982). *Teaching critical television viewing skills: An integrated approach.* Springfield, IL: Charles Thomas.

Postman, N. (1985). Learning in an age of television. *Education Week, 4,* 17–24.

Rosenkoetter, L. I. (2001). Television and morality. In D. G. Singer & J. L. Singer (Eds.), *Handbook of children and the media* (pp. 463–473). Thousand Oaks, CA: Sage.

Signorielli, N. (2001). Television's gender role images and contribution to stereotyping: Past, present, future. In D. G. Singer & J. L. Singer (Eds.), *Handbook of children and the media* (pp. 341–358). Thousand Oaks, CA: Sage.

Strasburger, V. C. (2001). Children, adolescents, drugs, and the media. In D. G. Singer & J. L. Singer (Eds.), *Handbook of children and the media* (pp. 415–445). Thousand Oaks, CA: Sage.

Subervi-Vélez, F. A., & Colsant, S. (1993). The television worlds of Latino children. In G. L. Berry & J. K. Asamen (Eds.), *Children and television, images in a changing sociocultural world* (pp. 215–228). Newbury Park, CA: Sage.

Sue, D. W. (1981). *Counseling the culturally different: Theory and practice.* New York: Wiley.

Tashakkori, A., & Teddlie, C. (1998). *Mixed methodology, combining qualitative and quantitative approaches.* Thousand Oaks, CA: Sage.

Thomas, R. M. (1999). *Human development theories, windows on culture.* Thousand Oaks, CA: Sage Publications.

Wright, J. C., & Huston, A. C. (1984). The potentials of television for young viewers. In J. M. Murray & G. Salomon (Eds.), *The future of children's television* (pp. 65–80). Boys Town, NE: Boys Town and The John and Mary R. Markle Foundation.

7

Challenges for the Future of Educational Media[1]

Shalom M. Fisch
MediaKidz Research & Consulting

It is no secret that electronic media—be it television, video games, computers, or other technology—have come to play major roles in the lives of America's children. Estimates of the amount of time children spend viewing television vary widely (from 11 to 28 hours per week), but numerous studies indicate that American children spend more time watching television than in any other activity except sleeping (e.g., Anderson, Field, Collins, Lorch, & Nathan, 1985; Huston, Watkins, & Kunkel, 1989; Huston, Wright, Rice, Kerkman, & St. Peters, 1987). VCR penetration has been estimated at 93% of American households (Lin, 2001), and cable television is present in 60% to 70% of American homes (Wills, 1995).

Other forms of electronic media, although not quite as ubiquitous as television, have also achieved tremendous reach. Two thirds of American families own a video game system such as Nintendo or Sega (Stanger & Gridina, 1999), with more than 75% of children reporting that they play video games "sometimes" and nearly 25% playing every day (Cesarone, 1998). Data from the U.S. Census Bureau show that, in the year 2000, 65% of children aged 3 to 17 lived in households with computers, and nearly 90% of 6- to 17-year-olds had used computers at either home or school (Newburger, 2001).

[1]With the future of educational media as mercurial as it is, I gratefully acknowledge the invaluable contributions of Paul Marcum in helping me to understand the latest generations of technology and the business considerations that surround them. I am also grateful to Allison Druin and the members of the Human–Computer Interaction Lab at the University of Maryland for their helpful comments on an earlier version of this chapter.

125

In addition to this vast proliferation of electronic media, the very nature of these media is also changing at a meteoric pace. New developments seem to arise on an almost daily basis: high-speed broadband access, digital and interactive television, handheld wireless devices for communication and gaming, nonstandard input devices embedded within toys or clothing (e.g., miniaturized computers built into glasses, or jogging suits with built-in sensors to track heartbeat and respiration; Mann, 1997), and so on. It is predicted that, in the near future, global positioning software will allow advertisements for local businesses to be beamed directly to the cell phones of passing pedestrians, and that homeowners will be able to swipe barcodes on their computerized refrigerators to order milk online when they are running low. Indeed, the technology responsible for these innovations already exists (e.g., Bruinius, 1999).

In such a world, it is not difficult to imagine using new technologies in other ways as well, to provide children with educational activities, individualized instruction, and personalized feedback both inside and outside the classroom. From an educational perspective, each new technological advancement carries the potential to provide a broad audience of children with educational content and activities in new and innovative ways. However, although these technological media hold vast potential, they pose vast challenges as well. The mere availability of new or faster technology does not guarantee that the technology will (or, indeed, can) be applied effectively to educational ends. For technology to be used to its greatest benefit, it must be designed and made available in ways that take the needs, habits, and developmental levels of the target audience into account.

This chapter draws on concrete examples of existing and projected educational media products for children, to explore some of the challenges that are likely to face producers and users in developing new generations of educational media. Naturally, with technologies and business models changing so rapidly, it is impossible to know which of the new media will emerge as dominant vehicles for educational content in the future. As a result, the focus here is on three classes of issues that apply across a variety of media: *access* (in terms of not only the physical availability of hardware, but also the need for material to be usable by a diverse audience of users), *design* (regarding both hardware and software), and *use* (concerning the nature and constraints of the real-life settings in which the end product will be used). Each class of issues is discussed in turn.

Before proceeding, it is worth noting a caveat that should be borne in mind throughout this discussion. In recent years, fiscal realities have resulted in dwindling budgets for the development of new media products for children, be they CD-ROMs, online content, or television series. With reductions in budget come reduced resources for developing and actualizing the educational curricula that underlie educational media, as well as reduced funding for the formative research that can be vital in tailoring such media to the needs, abilities, and interests of their target audiences. (For a discussion of the role of formative research in the production of educational media, see, e.g., Druin, 1999; Fisch & Bernstein, 2001; or Flagg, 1990). Thus, in many ways, the greatest challenge for the future of educational media may simply be to survive, as the creators of such media struggle to find adaptive means of maintaining educational viability in the face of reduced resources. A detailed discussion of business models and financial issues is well beyond the scope of this chapter. Instead, the focus here is on issues of design and implementation, with the assumption that resource issues can and will be resolved, because, otherwise, no viable educational media can exist at all.

ACCESS

Challenge 1: Providing Access to Hardware

Perhaps the most basic challenge in the successful implementation of educational media is simply ensuring that it is physically available to those who need it most. Much has been written about the "digital divide"—that is, the overrepresentation of computer technology among Whites and those of higher socioeconomic status (SES), as compared to the concomitant lack of access among minorities and lower-SES populations (e.g., Cakim, 1999; National Center for Educational Statistics, 1998). Researchers such as Wright (2001) have argued that educational media may have their greatest positive impact among poor and minority children, whose environments typically do not provide the same range of enrichments as those of higher-SES children. Ironically, however, the disproportionate lack of hardware among these populations may serve instead to widen the educational gap between demographic groups.

Concerns over such issues have led to a variety of governmental and private programs aimed at placing computers and Internet access in schools and libraries that serve low-SES and minority populations. Indeed, these efforts seem to have begun to bear fruit; as noted earlier, data from the U.S. Census indicate that nearly 90% of 6- to 17-year-olds had used computers at either home or school in the year 2000.

At first glance, then, one might imagine that the problem has been greatly mitigated, if not completely solved. However, this is by no means the case. The same Census Bureau data also showed the digital divide to be far from fully bridged. Home access to computers continued to be much more prevalent among Whites (77%) than among either African Americans (43%) or Latinos (37%). Even more pronounced differences were found as a function of SES: 94% of school-age children in households with incomes of $75,000 or more had access to computers at home, as opposed to only 35% of those with family incomes below $25,000 (Newburger, 2001).

Moreover, even in the context of school, where access was found to be more widely available, the high rates of school access among underserved populations must be interpreted with caution. The Census Bureau data did not reflect the number of computers present within each school, nor were data available on the average age of each school's computers. Thus, computers may be available in schools, but with new generations of hardware and software being produced so rapidly, we have no way of knowing whether (and for how long) those computers will be able to run the latest versions of software that are being produced. Indeed, research concerning similar efforts in the United Kingdom showed that the number of computers per school more than doubled between 1999 and 2001; however, the limited bandwidth of their connections meant that, on average, only six of the children in a given school could use Web sites with significant streaming at the same time (British Educational Suppliers Association, 2001).

It is also worth noting that much of the discussion over the digital divide has centered on traditional desktop computers, laptops, and Internet access. Less has been documented about the access of traditionally underserved populations to other emerging technologies that carry potential educational applications, such as wireless palmtop devices or enhanced, interactive television (e.g., WebTV). Given that platform devices for new media typically debut with significant price tags attached, it seems safe to assume that the same patterns of "trickle-down" penetration that have been found for computers and the Internet (or, several decades ago, for television) are likely to recur with each new medium that emerges as well. Just as poor and minority children are seen as disadvantaged by their relative lack of access to computer-based educational materials today, this same pattern of "catch up" is likely to continue as new generations of media unfold.

Thus, although we should recognize the fact that efforts to date in providing schools and other educational institutions with computers have produced highly worthwhile accomplishments, we also must conceive of the problems as complex and multifaceted. We will not truly bridge this gap until we are able to provide more than a handful of computers per school—perhaps even as many as one per student—and expand efforts to include forms of technology beyond traditional desktop and laptop computers. In addition, such efforts must be undertaken on an ongoing basis, to ensure that equipment is upgraded periodically; only then can it continue to be maximally useful.

Challenge 2: Making Content Accessible

Although discussions of access frequently focus on the presence of hardware, such issues are not the only considerations in making educational media accessible across demographic groups. It is important to consider the accessibility of the material that is delivered through those media as well. For the sake of illustration, imagine trying to use an educational CD-ROM, only to discover that its onscreen text and audio are in a foreign language that you do not understand. Or imagine that, even though the material is written in English, it has been created by a 13th-century Talmudic scholar for an audience of other 13th-century Talmudic scholars; as a result, it assumes a shared cultural context and background that you do not have. A lack of necessary linguistic or cultural knowledge creates barriers that can interfere with, or even negate, the educational impact of the material.

Even when materials are developed for domestic American use rather than international audiences, the diversity of the population of the United States makes the need for linguistic and cultural relevance crucial. For example, the Latino population has emerged as the largest minority in the United States, growing from 3.9% to

11.4% of the total U.S. population between 1960 and 2000. The present size of the Latino American community is estimated at approximately 31 million people, comprising one of the largest Spanish-speaking populations in the world (Larmer, 1999; U.S. Census Bureau, 2000; Valdes, 2000). Many of these people are not native English speakers, yet relatively few American-produced educational television programs, CD-ROMs, or Web sites are available in Spanish. Indeed, it is even more difficult to find materials for American speakers of Chinese, Russian, or other languages. Machine translation is available for some material on the Web, which can help to some degree, but such translations tend to be far from perfect.

Indeed, even if perfect translation into multiple languages were available, it would provide only a partial solution to the underlying issues. Verbatim translations may lack the cultural relevance that can affect interest, appeal, and impact. Betancourt (1997) illustrated this point with a hypothetical example of bilingual nutrition materials designed to encourage well-balanced diets among children; the impact of such a project would be likely to be greatly impaired among Latino children if the materials were translated from English into Spanish but continued to refer only to foods typical of a healthy Anglo diet without referencing familiar foods of the Latino community.

Because the ultimate value of straight translation is limited by these sorts of issues, a more effective (although also more demanding) approach is known as *versioning*. This process results in the creation not of verbatim translations of preexisting English-language materials, but of parallel sets of materials that convey equivalent content and key messages in ways that are culturally and linguistically relevant to the ethnic groups being targeted. In some cases, too, the educational content itself may be modified for particular audiences. For example, efforts in support of video-based *Sesame Street* outreach projects on asthma and lead poisoning revealed that many Latino parents use home remedies to treat their children's illnesses, and that some of these remedies actually pose potential health risks of their own. This knowledge led to the inclusion of issues regarding home remedies in the Spanish-language materials produced for both of these projects—issues that had not been covered in the English-language versions of the materials (Yotive & Fisch, 2001).

Here, too, financial and commercial considerations necessarily intrude. Clearly, it is considerably more costly to produce multiple versions of a product than to produce just one version in a single language. Moreover, the smaller the subgroup being served by a particular version or translation, the more difficult it is to compensate for the additional cost via sales. It is precisely these sorts of issues that often have prevented materials from being made available in multiple versions or languages. However, the current scarcity of multicultural and multilingual materials makes it all the more important to try to create materials for these underserved audiences whenever possible.

DESIGN

Challenge 3: Making Hardware Usable

As a number of researchers have observed, one of the limitations of using traditional desktop computers as vehicles for educational games is that the physical use of desktop computers does not map easily onto children's naturalistic play behaviors (e.g., Association for Computing Machinery, 1993). To use a desktop computer, a user typically must sit upright in front of the machine for an extended period of time; little physical activity is involved, and it is generally easiest for only one user to control the activity at a time. The mismatch between children's natural play and the demands of the medium certainly has not prevented children from using computers, but it seems likely that many children would be more inclined to take advantage of the technology—and do so more often—if the alignment were closer.

In addition to the global match or mismatch between play patterns and the physical use of hardware, it is also important to consider the level of physical development and fine-motor coordination of the user. No matter how wonderful a piece of educational software might be, children (particularly younger children) can benefit from it only if their manual dexterity is sufficient to operate the hardware that controls it. In the early and mid-1990s, a series of three research studies at the Children's Television Workshop (now "Sesame Workshop") was conducted to inform the development of *Sesame Street* interactive materials by investigating preschool children's ability to operate several different input devices: keyboard arrow keys, touch screen, light pen, joystick, trackball, and mouse (Revelle, Strommen, & Medoff, 2001). Taken together, these studies found that the devices that were used most easily by young children were the touch screen, light pen, and trackball (although only the trackball was included in all three studies); the input device that proved most difficult was the keyboard arrow keys.

The superiority of the trackball was attributed to three primary factors. First, the movement of the cursor was consistent with the movement of the child's hand when using the trackball, unlike keyboard arrow keys. Second, the cursor stopped moving when the child's hand stopped moving, unlike a joystick. Third, because the housing of the trackball remained stationary, it avoided the issue of the child's having to keep it in the proper orientation, unlike a mouse.

Yet, although the trackball may have been easier for young children to use than a mouse, the reality of the situation is that the mouse became the industry standard for home computers and, thus, for a great deal of educational software. This has not, of course, made it impossible for young children to use computers; many use them frequently. However, it does mean that when young children use a piece of educational software, they face not only the challenge of learning how to use the software, but also the challenge of using the mouse correctly within the constraints of their limited manual dexterity.

Broadly speaking, attempts to overcome these sorts of issues have taken one of two forms. Some have adopted existing technology as their starting point, and built features into software to compensate for the limitations inherent in hardware such as desktop computers. Conversely, others have taken children's play as their starting point and designed novel types of hardware to fit those patterns of play.

Examples of the former approach can be found in numerous existing pieces of well-designed educational software for young children. Such applications incorporate features such as "hot spots" (i.e., clickable parts of the screen) that are large enough and set far enough apart for children to click easily on the options they desire, despite potential difficulties in using a mouse (Hanna, Risden, Czerwinski, & Alexander, 1999; Strommen & Revelle, 1990).

Ironically, the growth of handheld video games (e.g., GameBoy) and wireless mobile devices (e.g., cellular and PCS phones, personal digital assistants or PDAs) presents avenues for overcoming some of the difficulties surrounding children's use of desktop computers while, at the same time, exacerbating others. Handheld games have been highly popular for several years, and the use of wireless devices for gaming is growing; it is estimated that 120 million people are already playing wireless, noneducational games ("Wireless Game Users ...," 2001). On the one hand, the lightweight portability of such devices can free children from having to sit still in a designated place in order to engage in an activity. On the other hand, however, the small buttons or keys on a palmtop computer or cell phone may be too small for a child to use easily in controlling actions on the screen. (Recall also that keyboard arrow keys proved to be the most difficult input device for young children in the studies cited earlier.) Similarly, the font sizes used on small screens may be difficult for early readers to read, and the necessarily small size of hot spots may not be large enough for children to hit accurately. In this regard, it is noteworthy that in Britain, where more than one half of all 7- to 16-year-olds own cell phones and 91% of them use their phones to send short text messages, teenagers send far more text messages than do younger children; 50% of 14- to 16-year-olds send at least five messages per day, as opposed to only 14% of 7- to 10-year-olds (Strong, 2000). Although we cannot be certain how much of this age difference is due to hardware and software issues such as those discussed previously, it seems likely that they are at least contributing factors. Thus, exploring such technologies as potential platforms for educational materials for young children (as opposed to entertainment and communication for older audiences) will entail a fair amount of formative research and prototype testing to identify ways to capitalize on the strengths of these media while minimizing the impact of their weaknesses.

An alternate approach to overcoming the mismatch between hardware demands and children's natural behavior is to bring educational technology more in line with traditional forms of play, rather than fitting children's play to the constraints of existing technology. These sorts of efforts have led to the creation of what has been termed *physical multimedia* or *tangible interfaces*—interfaces that are controlled by the user's interactions with devices such as dolls, games, floor mats, or even entire rooms (e.g., Druin & Solomon, 1996). In the commercial arena, these sorts of devices are typified by products such as Microsoft's Actimates dolls: plush dolls of familiar television characters, such as Barney or the Teletubbies, that are programmed to play games, offer children puzzles, and even interact with online Web sites when the right part of the doll is pressed (Strommen & Alexander, 1999). Other examples include programmable LEGO bricks that allow children to build working robots (e.g., Resnick, 1993; Shwe, 2001) and playsets in which children move small toys on a board to cause outcomes on a computer screen (Shwe, 2001). By embedding technology within these familiar kinds of toys, such products can guide children's play in directions that encourage cognitive growth while allowing children to control the experience through behaviors that more closely resemble traditional play.

Challenge 4: Designing Convergent Media Effectively

Elsewhere, I have reviewed design features that contribute to the effectiveness of educational media, and shown that many of these features are equally applicable across television, interactive media, and print, whereas others are unique to a specific medium (Fisch, in press-a). Rather than repeat that discussion here, let us instead look to the future of educational media and consider issues that are just beginning to become apparent as media move toward convergence in the form of *enhanced television* (a subcategory of *digital television* that is also referred to as *interactive television;* e.g., Ducey, 1999).

As compared to traditional broadcast television, enhanced television holds the potential to extend the impact of educational television programs by coupling them with simultaneous data streams that can be accessed during viewing, all through the same television receiver device. These data streams can carry supplemental information for further learning, or interactive games and activities in which viewers can engage.

In fact, a sizable body of research literature has demonstrated that, even in the absence of interactivity, children's viewing of traditional (i.e., noninteractive) educational television programs can result in significant, long-lasting increases in their knowledge and attitudes regarding subjects such as literacy, mathematics, and science, among others (for a review, see Fisch, 2002, in press-b). Indeed, although some have labeled broadcast television as a passive medium, even traditional educational television programs can succeed in eliciting viewer participation during viewing (Anderson et al., 2000; Fisch & McCann, 1993).

Given that such effects have already been found for traditional broadcast television, one might ask what increased benefit would be provided by adding an interactive layer to the experience via enhanced television. One benefit is that enhanced television provides the opportunity not only for participative experiences during viewing, but also for individualized feedback—something that is not possible through traditional broadcast television. Another is that it allows viewers the option of extending the experience after they have finished watching the television program; viewers can choose either to watch the television program without further elaboration or to pursue topics further via supplementary information, games and activities, and/or links to outside Web sites.

At the time of this writing, this technology is very much still in its infancy. Although various producers and broadcasters have begun to experiment with possible formats for enhanced television experiences, none of these experiments have yet led to uncovering "the" approach that will prove most effective.

One such experiment within the domain of educational media was a prototype demo of an enhanced version of *Sesame Street* that was jointly produced by Sesame Workshop and WebTV. The brief prototype was comprised of two *Ses-*

ame Street television segments, one about the letter *Z* and the other about the number 6. While the segments ran on a television set attached to a WebTV box, viewers could also use a special remote control or wireless keyboard to click away from the program and play an interactive game (hosted by Elmo) that involved the same letter or number. The prototype was produced for research purposes, rather than broadcast, and was tested for usability with families of 3- to 5-year-old children (Mickel, 1998).

Data from this research pointed to several challenges and implications for the production of enhanced television. Perhaps most significantly, data from the study suggested that the design of the prototype had inadvertently set the television program and interactive game in an "either-or" relationship. Use of the games occurred in real time while the television program continued to run. As a result, because users had to click away from one experience to engage in the other, playing the games meant missing part of the television program (which potentially included moments that were key to comprehending its educational content) and, conversely, watching the program uninterrupted meant not playing the games.

How can this difficulty be avoided, or at least minimized? One answer may come from digital video recorders such as Tivo or Replay TV. Unlike videocassette recorders, the buffers in these devices make it possible for users to time-shift television programs by continuing to record the program "live" even as they watch a portion of the same program that aired several minutes earlier. Combining enhanced television with such technology could allow viewers to watch part of an educational television program, switch over to play a game, and then return to the television program—not in real time, but from the precise point at which they stopped. Whether or not enhanced television is augmented by such technology, however, it is clear that for such material to be maximally effective it should be designed in ways that allow the television and interactive components to complement, rather than compete with, each other.

Indeed, this point can be taken even one step further: Questions of balancing television and interactive content are only relevant if we conceive of enhanced television as the sum of its disparate parts (i.e., a television component and separate, concurrent online component). This sort of model has been assumed in many of the existing prototypes for enhanced television, in which interactive layers have been laid on top of broadcast television programs that were produced without the assumption of an interactive component. In this way, "enhanced television" truly is seen as an enhancement of television, with interactive content serving as an "add on" to a fairly standard broadcast television program. Perhaps it is natural, at this early stage of the development of the medium, for producers to approach enhanced television in this way, particularly in light of the fact that so many of the groups experimenting with enhanced television are television broadcasters and production companies. A significant challenge, as enhanced television evolves and matures, will be to find ways to actualize its potential to grow into a new medium of its own, one that represents a seamless convergence of broadcast television and online, rather than simply a pairing of the two.

USE

Challenge 5: Getting People to Use It

Even if educational media are well designed and made accessible to users, that still does not guarantee that they will be used. For media products to be used in the real world, they must be designed in ways that are not only appealing and educationally valid, but also well suited to the needs and interests of their audiences. In other words, technology must fit the needs and lifestyle of the audience, because the audience is unlikely to change its lifestyle to fit the technology.

Indeed, such issues have likely contributed to the boom and bust that occurred following the popularization of home computers in the 1980s and, subsequently, the parallel trend found for the Internet in the 1990s. In both cases, large numbers of consumers flocked to these new media with the assumption that they—and their children—would be left behind if they didn't. Afterward, they discovered that, in fact, they did not need these media to nearly the degree that they had anticipated, and use leveled out. In many cases, the applications that continued to be seen as essential by consumers were those that provided efficient solutions to needs that would have existed even in the absence of computers (e.g., word processors, spreadsheets, e-mail, online information resources), whereas applications that spoke less to pressing needs became less widely used. Similarly, although sales of early interactive plush toys such as Actimates Barney were high, sales of later, similar toys declined; presumably, consumers felt the need for only so many expensive, interactive stuffed animals.

In looking toward the future, then, we must ask whether each emerging technology—be it computers built into eyeglasses or clothing, electronic coupons beamed to users' cell phones, or barcode scanners on consumers' refrigerators—will pass the test of meeting users' needs. For example, once enhanced television becomes a reality, will consumers *want* to use it? On the one hand, this new medium holds the potential to extend the television experience by placing a wealth of information and activities at users' fingertips. On the other hand, however, it is by no means certain that viewers will want to take advantage of it. Past research has found that one of viewers' primary reasons for watching television is relaxation (e.g., Greenberg, 1974), which raises questions as to whether viewers will want to engage actively while viewing, as opposed to simply sitting back and watching the television program. The key to the success of enhanced television very well may lie in a two-step process. The first step will be to identify the types of enhancements that the majority of users want and need. The second will be to find ways to make those convergent enhancements available to users who are motivated to use them without requiring their use by those who would rather just watch television or surf the Web instead.

Challenge 6: Considering the Setting

In considering users' wants and needs, it is important to recognize that they are likely to differ somewhat as a function of the setting in which the materials are intended to be used. Materials that are well suited to one setting may be less suited to another. For example, when school-based outreach materials were created around the television program *Square One TV* (a series about mathematics, aimed at 8- to 12-year-olds), the video component of the project could not be produced by simply copying the same programs that had been produced for home viewing onto videotape for the classroom. The original format of *Square One TV* had been very successful in the context of broadcast television for home viewing, but for the school-outreach videotapes to be usable in the classroom, the material had to be substantially reedited to meet the constraints of that setting. Research with teachers showed that the half-hour length of the programs was more time than they could afford to spend on a video in the classroom. In addition, to be useful in classroom instruction, the material in the videotapes had to be organized more thematically by mathematical topic than they had been in the original broadcast television series. Thus, material from *Square One TV* was reedited into a series of 15-minute videotapes, each of which was organized thematically by topic, for use in schools (Yotive, 1995).

Analogous concerns emerge for interactive technology. For example, an educational CD-ROM game that has been designed for home use by a single child may not lend itself well to classroom use by a group of children. In addition, to be used effectively (or, often, at all) in the classroom, teachers need to know what topics are covered in the CD-ROM, and how to easily access the specific topic that fits with that day's lesson—and all with a minimum of advance preparation time required.

One interesting, although noneducational, example of designing interactive media to fit the constraints of the setting can be found in Disney's interactive theme park ride, *Pirates of the Caribbean: Battle for the Buccaneer's Gold*. In this ride, a group of approximately six users stand on the mock deck of a ship, surrounded by floor-to-ceiling computer screens that show a three-dimensional (3-D) ocean scene and a fleet of oncoming pirate ships. Users turn a real steering wheel to "steer" the ship through the virtual landscape and mock cannons to defend themselves against the virtual pirates. The design of the ride was informed by an understanding of the ways in which people visit theme parks and the expectations that they bring to the experience. Because people generally visit theme parks in small groups, the ride was designed as a small-group, rather than individual, experience. Because they expect theme park experiences to go beyond what they can get elsewhere (e.g., in a video game), as much emphasis was placed on the real aspects of the experience as on the virtual: a motion base in the deck caused it to move appropriately in reaction to onscreen events such as the hit of a cannonball, 3-D surround sound provided localized sound that seemed to come from individual objects on the screen, and so on. And because of the importance of social interaction to a theme park experience, users shared video and audio displays, as well as input devices (i.e., the cannons) as they had to run back and forth among the various cannons to deal with virtual threats on all sides (Schell & Shochet, 2001).

Although *Battle for the Buccaneer Gold* is not an educational application, the parallels to the design of educational media are clear. The basic concept of the game (i.e., battling pirate ships while gathering gold) could have been implemented in a variety of settings with a variety of platforms, but the same certainly cannot be said of its interface. The interface was uniquely suited to the nature and requirements of its theme park setting; it would not have been appropriate, for example, for home use. In the same way, to be most effective, educational media must be tailored to the settings of their use; media produced for home use should be designed differently than media for schools, which in turn should be designed differently than media intended for museums.

CONCLUSION

Electronic media present tremendous opportunities for reaching large numbers of children with substantive and motivating educational materials. The vast reach of mass media holds the potential to bring such resources, not only to those children who already have access to informal educational enrichments and experiences, but also to those who otherwise would not.

Yet, the simple existence of educational media is not enough. To actualize the potential of such media and reap its benefits, media products must be made accessible to children, designed in ways that make its hardware and software usable, and tailored to the needs of the audience and the constraints of the settings in which they are intended to be used. Doing so entails meeting a variety of challenges in design and implementation, including:

- Providing hardware to low-income and minority children so that the technology is physically accessible.
- Creating and versioning media products in ways that are linguistically and culturally appropriate to a broad and diverse audience.
- Building hardware in ways that make it easily usable by a child audience and that map onto children's natural patterns of play.
- Designing convergent media such that its components complement, rather than compete with, each other.
- Encouraging use by tailoring educational media to meet existing needs of the target audience, to fit their lifestyles, and to accommodate the nature and constraints of the settings in which they will be used.

To meet these challenges, it often may be best if the creators of educational media do not take a given electronic medium as the starting point. Instead, a more fruitful approach may be to begin from the other end—that is, with the target audience and a consideration of its needs, interests, and characteristic patterns of behavior. From this perspective, a key question becomes, not how to employ a given electronic medium, but whether media should be used at all. Some needs may not lend themselves to technological solutions. If it seems that a given need can be addressed via media, however, the next step is to select the medium that may be best suited to it. Only then would one take on the question of how best to apply this medium to the topic of interest.

Realistically, such an approach is not likely to be feasible for many producers of educational media. Most producers do not have the capability to work in every medium, and many are only equipped to work in a single medium or a small, discrete set of media. For these producers, a more workable approach may be, once again, to begin with the needs of the audience, but then to choose to pursue only those topics that fit well with the media in which they have particular expertise.

Still, under either approach, the primary point of departure and ongoing focus remains the target audience. As new technologies appear, it is tempting to want to apply them as broadly as possible. However, not every technology is suitable to every audience, every setting, or every area of need.

As noted in the introduction to this chapter, the meteoric speed with which technologies are appearing and changing makes it difficult to predict which ones will emerge as dominant media in the coming years. No matter which media endure over time, however, there is likely to be much less change in the audience and their needs. Placing the audience at the heart of the process may provide our best opportunity for creating effective educational media in the future, no matter what those media may prove to be.

REFERENCES

Anderson, D. R., Bryant, J., Wilder, A., Santomero, A., Williams, M., & Crawley, A. M. (2000). Researching *Blue's Clues:* Viewing behavior and impact. *Media Psychology, 2,* 179–194.

Anderson, D. R., Field, D. E., Collins, P. A., Lorch, E. P., & Nathan, J. G. (1985). Estimates of young children's time with television: A methodological comparison of parent reports with time-lapse video home observation. *Child Development, 56,* 1345–1357.

Association for Computing Machinery. (1993). Computer augmented environments: Back to the real world [Special issue]. *Communications of the ACM, 36,* 7.

Betancourt, J. (1997). Translating and versioning: What is the difference, and what difference does it make? In S. M. Fisch (Chair), *Translating and versioning: Issues in creating media-based materials in English and Spanish.* Symposium presented at the annual meeting of the American Educational Association, Chicago, IL.

British Educational Suppliers Association (2001). *Information and communication technology in UK state schools.* London: Author.

Bruinius, H. (1999, August). Get 'em in their underwear. *New Media,* pp. 28–34.

Cakim, I. (1999, April 12). Analyst insight: Old racial issues in a new medium. *Industry Standard,* p. 46.

Cesarone, B. (1998). Video games: Research, ratings, recommendations. *ERIC Clearinghouse on Elementary and Early Childhood Education.* Champaign: University of Illinois.

Druin, A. (Ed.). (1999). *The design of children's technology.* San Francisco: Morgan Kaufman.

Druin, A., & Solomon, C. (1996). *Designing multimedia environments for children.* New York: Wiley.

Ducey, R.V. (1999). *Internet + DTV broadcasting = UN-TV.* Washington, DC: National Association of Broadcasters. Retrieved November, 2001, from www.nab.org/Research/Reports/DTV-Internet.asp

Fisch, S. M. (in press-a). Characteristics of effective materials for informal education: A cross-media comparison of television, magazines, and interactive media. In M. Rabinowitz, F. C. Blumberg, & E. Everson (Eds.), *The impact of media and technology on instruction.* Mahwah, NJ: Lawrence Erlbaum Associates.

Fisch, S. M. (in press-b). *Children's learning from educational television: Sesame Street and beyond.* Mahwah, NJ: Lawrence Erlbaum Associates.

Fisch, S. M. (2002). Vast wasteland or vast opportunity?: Effects of educational television on children's academic knowledge, skills, and attitudes. In J. Bryant & D. Zillman (Eds.), *Media effects: Advances in theory and practice* (2nd ed., pp. 397–426). Mahwah, NJ: Lawrence Erlbaum Associates.

Fisch, S. M., & Bernstein, L. (2001). Formative research revealed: Methodological and process issues in formative research. In S. M. Fisch,& R. T. Truglio (Eds.), *"G" is for growing: Thirty years of research on children and Sesame Street* (pp. 39–60). Mahwah, NJ: Lawrence Erlbaum Associates.

Fisch, S. M., & McCann, S. K. (1993). Making broadcast television participative: Eliciting mathematical behavior through *Square One TV*. *Educational Technology Research and Development, 41*(3), 103–109.

Flagg, B. N. (Ed.). (1990). *Formative evaluation for educational technology*. Hillsdale, NJ: Lawrence Erlbaum Associates.

Greenberg, B. S. (1974). Gratifications of television viewing and their correlates for British children. In J. G. Blumler & E. Katz (Eds.), *The uses of mass communication* (pp. 71–92). Newbury Park, CA: Sage.

Hanna, L., Risden, K., Czerwinski, M., & Alexander, K. J. (1999). The role of usability research in designing children's computer products. In A. Druin (Ed.), *The design of children's technology* (pp. 3–26). San Francisco: Morgan Kaufman.

Huston, A. C., Watkins, B. A., & Kunkel, D. (1989). Public policy and children's television. *American Psychologist, 44*, 424–433.

Huston, A. C., Wright, J. C., Rice, M. L., Kerkman, D., & St. Peters, M. (1987, April). *The development of television viewing patterns in early childhood: A longitudinal investigation*. Paper presented at the Society for Research in Child Development, Baltimore, MD.

Larmer, B. (1999, July 12). Society. *Newsweek*, pp. 48–51.

Lin, C. A. (2001). The VCR, home video culture, and new video technologies. In J. Bryant & J. A. Bryant (Eds.), *Television and the American family* (2nd ed., pp. 91–107). Mahwah, NJ: Lawrence Erlbaum Associates.

Mann, S. (1997). Wearable computing: A first step toward personal imaging. *IEEE Computer, 30*(2), 25–32.

Mickel, N. (1998). *Usability testing report for children's testing: Sesame Street interactive-TV demo*. Unpublished research report. Palo Alto, CA: WebTV.

National Center for Educational Statistics. (1998). *Issue brief: Internet access in public schools*. Washington, DC: U.S. Department of Education.

Newburger, E.C. (2001). *Home computers and Internet use in the United States: August 2000*. Washington, DC: U.S. Department of Commerce, U.S. Census Bureau.

Resnick, M. (1993). Behavior construction kits. *Communications of the ACM, 36*(7), 64–71.

Revelle, G. L., Strommen, E. F., & Medoff, L. (2001). Interactive technologies research at the Children's Television Workshop. In S. M. Fisch & R. T. Truglio (Eds.), *"G" is for growing: Thirty years of research on Sesame Street* (pp. 215–230). Mahwah, NJ: Lawrence Erlbaum Associates.

Schell, J., & Shochet, J. (2001, July 6). Designing interactive theme park rides: Lessons from Disney's *Battle for the Buccaneer Gold*. *Inside Gamasutra*. Retrieved July, 2001, from www.gamasutra.com/features/20010706/schell_pfv.htm

Shwe, H. (2001, April). Smart toys: Bringing LEGO bricks to life. In H. Shwe (Chair), *How technology is changing children's play*. Symposium presented at the biennial meeting of the Society for Research in Child Development, Minneapolis, MN.

Stanger, J. D., & Gridina, N. (1999). *Media in the home, 1999: The fourth annual survey of parents and children*. Philadelphia, PA: Annenberg Public Policy Center, University of Pennsylvania.

Strommen, E. F., & Alexander, K. J. (1999, April). *Learning from television with interactive toy characters as learning companions*. Poster session presented at the biennial meeting of the Society for Research in Child Development.

Strommen, E. F., & Revelle, G. L. (1990). Research in interactive technologies at the Children's Television Workshop. *Educational Technology Research and Development, 38*(4), 65–80.

Strong, C. (2000). *M-kids: Mobile phone usage among kids aged 7–16*. London: NOP Research Group.

U.S. Census Bureau. (2000). U.S. population estimates [On-line]. Retrieved June, 2000, from www.census.gov

Valdes, M. I. (2000). *Marketing to American Latinos: A guide to in-culture approach*. Ithaca, NY: Paramount Market Publishing.

Wills, G. (1995, July). Discussion on *Meet the Press* [Television broadcast]. Washington, DC: NBC News.

Wireless game users to increase to 124 million by 2006. (2001, September 10). *Inside Gamasutra*. Retrieved September, 2001, from www.gamasutra.com

Wright, J. (2001, April). Demographic influences on long-term effects of television: A theoretical approach. In S. M. Fisch (Chair), *Theoretical approaches to the long-term effects of television on children*. Symposium presented at the biennial meeting of the Society for Research in Child Development, Minneapolis, MN.

Yotive, W. M. (1995, December). *Square One Math Talk: Using Technology to Help Teachers Implement the NCTM Standards*. Paper presented at the 27th annual conference of the National Staff Development Council, Chicago, IL.

Yotive, W. M., & Fisch, S. M. (2001). The role of *Sesame Street*-based materials in child care settings. In S. M. Fisch & R. T. Truglio (Eds.), *"G" is for growing: Thirty years of research on children and Sesame Street* (pp. 181–196). Mahwah, NJ: Lawrence Erlbaum Associates.

Entertainment Televisual Media

8

The Violent Face of Television: Research and Discussion

John P. Murray
Kansas State University

The violent face of television has been presented to audiences from the first broadcasts of this medium. Television broadcasting in the United States began in the early 1940s, with full development following World War II. Although extensive broadcast schedules did not begin until the late 1940s, and violence was not as graphic as it would become in later years, the first public concerns about violence were evident in the 1950s. The early Congressional hearings (United States Congress, 1952, 1955) set the stage for similar expressions of public concern that continued through the 20th century and still continue in the 21st century (United States Congress, 1990, 2001). What have we learned from all of this research and discussion on the "violent face of television," and what can be done to mitigate the harmful influences?

EARLY RESEARCH AND SOCIAL CONCERNS

The early studies of television's influence began almost simultaneously in England and in the United States and Canada in the mid-1950s. In England, a group of researchers at the London School of Economics and Political Science, under the direction of Hilde Himmelweit, a reader in social psychology, began the first study of children's television viewing patterns while TV was still relatively new (only 3 million TV sets were installed in the 15 million households in England). This study was proposed by the Audience Research Department of the British Broadcasting Corporation (BBC), but was conducted by independent researchers. The research began in 1955 and was published in a 1958 report, *Television and the Child: An Empirical Study of the Effect of Television on the Young* (Himmelweit, Oppenheim, & Vince, 1958). The American and Canadian study was conducted by Wilbur Schramm and his colleagues in communications at Stanford University. This project began in 1957 and was published in a 1961 report, *Television in the Lives of Our Children* (Schramm, Lyle, & Parker, 1961).

The British and American/Canadian surveys provided a very important benchmark for understanding the broad and general effects of television on children. For example, Himmelweit et al. noted, "We have found a number of instances where viewers and controls differed in their outlook; differences which did not exist before television came on the scene. There was a small but consistent influence of television on the way children thought generally about jobs, job values, success, and social surroundings" (pp. 17–18). With regard to aggression, these correlational studies were less specific, as Himmelweit and her colleagues discussed: "We did not find that the viewers were any more aggressive or maladjusted than the controls; television is unlikely to cause aggressive behaviour, although it could precipitate it in those few children who are emotionally disturbed. On the other hand, there was little support for the view that programmes of violence are beneficial; we found that they aroused aggression as often as they discharged it" (p. 20). In the case of the Schramm et al. study, their conclusions about television violence included the observation that those Canadian and American children who had high exposure to television and low exposure to print were more aggressive than those with the reverse pattern. Thus, the early correlational studies or surveys identified some areas of concern about television violence and set the stage for more focused investigations. Finally, it should be noted that these 1950s studies of viewers and nonviewers took place when television was new in the United States, Canada, and England. Later studies—in the 1970s—would revisit these issues and this research strategy when television was being introduced into isolated communities in Australia (Murray & Kippax, 1977, 1978, 1979) and Canada (MacBeth, 1996; Williams, 1986).

Moving beyond these 1950s surveys, there was another set of studies that emerged in the early 1960s—not surveys or correlational studies, but experimental studies that were addressed to cause-and-effect relationships in the TV violence/aggressive behavior equation. These initial experiments were conducted by Albert Bandura, at Stanford University, who studied preschool-age children, and Leonard Berkowitz, at the University of Wisconsin, who worked with college-age youth. In both instances, the studies were experimental in design, which meant that subjects were randomly assigned to various viewing experiences and, therefore, the results of this manipulated viewing could be used to address the issue of causal relationships between viewing and behavior. The early Bandura studies, such as *Transmission of Aggression Through Imitation of Aggressive Models* (Bandura, Ross, & Ross, 1961) or *Imitation of Film-Mediated Aggressive Models* (Bandura, Ross, & Ross, 1963), were set within a social learning paradigm and were designed to identify the processes governing the ways that children learn by observing and imitating the behavior of others. In this context, therefore, the studies used stimulus films (videotape was not generally available) back projected on a simulated television screen, and the behavior of the children was observed and recorded in a playroom setting, immediately following the viewing period. Despite the structured nature of these studies, Bandura's research was central to the debate about the influence of media violence. Moreover, the work of Berkowitz and his colleagues, such as *Effects of Film Violence on Inhibitions Against Subsequent Aggression* (Berkowitz & Rawlings, 1963) or *Film Violence and the Cue Properties of Available Targets* (Berkowitz & Geen, 1966), studied the simulated aggressive behavior of youth and young adults following the viewing of segments of violent films (i.e., the Kirk Douglas boxing film *The Champion*).The demonstration of increased willingness to use aggression against others following viewing further fueled the debate about the influence of media violence.

Concern about the influence of TV violence began as early as the start of this new medium. As mentioned previously, the first Congressional hearings were held in the early 1950s (United States Congress, 1952, 1955). At these early hearings, developmental psychologist Eleanor Maccoby (1954) and sociologist Paul Lazarsfeld (1955) presented testimony that relied on some early studies of violence in films, such as the 1930s report *Boys, Movies, and City Streets* (Cressey & Thrasher, 1933), to outline a necessary program of research on the issue of TV violence and its effects on children.

As the 1960s progressed, concern in the United States about violence in the streets and the assassinations of President John F. Kennedy, Martin Luther King, Jr., and Robert Kennedy stimulated continuing interest in media violence. In response, from the 1960s through the 1990s, several major government commissions and scientific and professional review committees were established to summarize the research evidence and public policy issues regarding the role of television violence in salving or savaging young viewers.

The five principal commissions and review panels—National Commission on the Causes and Prevention of Violence (Baker & Ball, 1969), Surgeon General's Scientific Advisory Committee on Television and Social Behavior (1972; Murray, 1973), National Institute of Mental Health (1982) Television and Behavior Project, Group for the Advancement of Psychiatry (1982) Child and Television Drama Review, and the American Psychological Association Task Force on Television and Society (Huston et al., 1992)—have been central to setting the agenda for research and public discussion.

In 1982, the National Institute of Mental Health (NIMH) published a 10-year followup of the 1972 Surgeon General's study. The two-volume report (National Institute of Mental Health, 1982; Pearl, Bouthilet, & Lazar, 1982), collectively titled *Television and Behavior: Ten Years of Scientific Progress and Implications for the Eighties,* provided a reminder of the breadth and depth of knowledge that had accumulated on the issue of TV violence. In this regard, the NIMH staff and consultants concluded:

> After 10 more years of research, the consensus among most of the research community is that violence on television does lead to aggressive behavior by children and teenagers who watch the programs. This conclusion is based on laboratory experiments and on field studies. Not all children become aggressive, of course, but the cor-

relations between violence and aggression are positive. In magnitude, television violence is as strongly correlated with aggressive behavior as any other behavioral variable that has been measured. (p. 10)

In 1986, the American Psychological Association (APA) empaneled a Task Force on Television and Society to review the research and professional concerns about the impact of television on children and adults. The nine psychologists assigned to this committee undertook reviews of relevant research, conducted interviews with television industry and public policy professionals, and discussed concerns with representatives of government regulatory agencies and public interest organizations. The final report, entitled *Big World, Small Screen: The Role of Television in American Society* (Huston et al., 1992), included the following observation about television violence: "American television has been violent for many years. Over the past 20 years, the rate of violence on prime time evening television has remained at about 5 to 6 incidents per hour, whereas the rate on children's Saturday morning programs is typically 20 to 25 acts per hour. There is clear evidence that television violence can cause aggressive behavior and can cultivate values favoring the use of aggression to resolve conflicts" (p. 136).

The extent of concern—both social and scientific—is demonstrated by the fact that over the past half-century, about 1,000 reports have been published on the issue of TV violence (Murray, 1980, 1993, 1998, 2000; Pecora, Murray, & Wartella, 2003). Of course, only a small percentage of these thousands of pages represent original studies or research reports, but there is an extensive body of research on the impact of TV violence. Nevertheless, the research history is best described in terms of the nature of the research approaches: correlational and experimental, and their variants cross-lagged panel studies and field studies.

CORRELATIONAL RESEARCH

The demonstration of a relationship between viewing and aggressive behavior is a logical precursor to studies of the causal role that TV violence may play in promoting aggressive behavior. In this regard, the early surveys of the impact of television on children, conducted by Himmelweit et al. (1958) and Schramm et al. (1961)—discussed in an earlier section—addressed some of these concerns about violence. However, later research was more focused in studying the correlations between TV violence viewing and aggression.

In typical correlational studies, such as those conducted for the Surgeon General's research program (Dominick & Greenberg, 1972; McLeod, Atkin, & Chaffee, 1972a, 1972b; Robinson & Bachman, 1972), the researchers found consistent patterns of significant correlations between the number of hours of television viewed or the frequency of viewing violent programs and various measures of aggressive attitudes or behavior. Also, in another study, Atkin, Greenberg, Korzenny and McDermott (1979) found that heavy viewers of TV violence were more likely to choose physical and verbal aggressive responses to solve hypothetical interpersonal conflict situations (i.e., 45% of the heavy-violence viewers chose physical/verbal aggressive responses vs. 21% of the low-violence viewers) . Similarly, a further study in this genre (Walker & Morley, 1991) found that adolescents who reported enjoying TV violence were more likely to hold attitudes and values favorable to behaving aggressively in conflict situations.

In another approach, a large database—the Cultural Indicators Project—has been used to explore the relationship between television portrayals and the viewer's fearful conception of the world. In a series of studies begun in the 1960s, George Gerbner and his colleagues at the University of Pennsylvania (Gerbner, 1970; Gerbner, Gross, Morgan, & Signorielli, 1994) tracked public perceptions of society in relation to the respondent's extent of television viewing. Of relevance to the violence issue, these researchers identified differences in the risk-of-victimization perceptions, described as the "mean world syndrome" effect, of light versus heavy viewers. The heavy viewers (usually watching 5 or more hours per day) are much more fearful of the world around them than are light viewers (watching about 2 or fewer hours per day). When questioned about their perceptions of risk, heavy viewers are much more likely to overestimate (i.e., greater than the FBI crime reports for their locale would suggest) the chance that they will be the victim of crime in the ensuing 6 months, have taken greater precautions by changing the security of their homes or restricting their travels at night, and are generally more fearful of the world. As Gerbner et al. (1994) noted: "We have found that long-term exposure to television, in which frequent violence is virtually inescapable, tends to cultivate the image of a relatively mean and dangerous world ... in which greater protection is needed, most people cannot be trusted," and "most people are just looking out for themselves" (p. 30).

SPECIAL-CASE CORRELATIONAL RESEARCH

Studies such as the early surveys clearly demonstrate that violence viewing and aggressive behavior are related, but they do not address the issue of cause and effect. And yet, there are some special-case correlational studies in which "intimations of causation" can be derived from the fact that these studies were conducted over several time periods. There have been three major "panel" studies: a study funded by CBS (Belson 1978), one funded by NBC (Milavsky, Kessler, Stipp, & Rubens, 1982), and the third funded by the Surgeon General's Committee and NIMH (Huesmann & Eron, 1986; Huesmann, Eron, Lefkowitz, & Walder, 1984; Lefkowitz, Eron, Walder, & Huesmann, 1972).

The CBS study (Belson, 1978) was conducted in England with 1,565 youths who were a representative sample of 13- to 17-year-old males living in London. The boys were interviewed on several occasions concerning the extent of their exposure to a selection of violent television programs broadcast during the period 1959 through 1971. The level and type of violence in these programs were rated by members of the BBC viewing panel. Thus, it was possible to obtain, for each boy, a measure of both the magnitude and type of exposure to televised violence (e.g., realistic, fictional, etc.). Furthermore, each boy's level of violent behavior was determined by his report of how often he had been involved in any of 53 categories of violence over the previous 6 months. The degree of seriousness of the acts reported by the boys ranged from only slightly violent aggravation, such as taunting, to more serious and very violent behavior, such as: "I tried to force a girl to have sexual intercourse with me," "I bashed a boy's head against a wall," "I burned a boy on the chest with a cigarette while my mates held him down," and "I threatened to kill my father." Approximately 50% of the 1,565 boys were not involved in any violent acts during the 6-month period. However, of those who were involved in violence, 188 (12%) were involved in 10 or more acts during the 6-month period. When Belson compared the behavior of boys who had higher exposure to televised violence to those who had lower exposure (and had been matched on a wide variety of possible contributing factors), he found that the high-violence viewers were more involved in serious interpersonal violence.

The NBC study (Milavsky et al., 1982) was conducted over a 3-year period from May 1970 to December 1973 in two cities, Fort Worth and Minneapolis. Interviews were conducted with samples of second- to sixth-grade boys and girls and a special sample of teenage boys. In the elementary school sample, the information on television viewing and measures of aggression were collected in six time periods over the 3 years. The aggression measure consisted of peer ratings of aggressive behavior based on the work of Eron and his colleagues (Eron, Walder, & Lefkowitz, 1971). In the teenage sample there were only five waves of interviews over the 3 years, and the aggression measures were self-report rather than peer-reported aggression. In summarizing the results of this study, the authors concluded: "On the basis of the analyses we carried out to test for such a causal connection there is no evidence that television exposure has a consistently significant effect on subsequent aggressive behavior in the [elementary school] sample of boys" (Milavsky et al., 1982, p. 482). Similar null findings were reported for the elementary school girls and the teenage boys. However, reanalyses of these data by Kenny (1984) and Cook and his associates (Cook, Kendzierski, & Thomas, 1983) concluded that there are small but clear causal effects in the NBC data and that these effects become stronger when analyzed over longer time periods through successive waves of interviews.

Finally, one of the longest panel studies, 22 years in duration, was the work of Leonard Eron and his colleagues (Eron, 1963; Eron, 1982; Huesmann et al., 1984; Husemann & Eron, 1986; Lefkowitz, Eron, Walder, & Huesmann, 1972). In the initial studies, conducted for the Surgeon General's investigation of TV violence (Lefkowitz et al., 1972), the researchers were able to document the long-term effects of violence viewing by studying children over a 10-year period from age 8 to age 18. At these two time periods, the youngsters were interviewed about their program preferences and information was collected from peer ratings of aggressive behavior. The violence levels of their preferred TV programs and other media and measures of aggression across these two time periods suggested the possibility that early television violence viewing was one factor in producing later aggressive behavior. In particular, the findings for 211 boys followed in this longitudinal study demonstrated that TV violence at age 8 was significantly related to aggression at age 8 ($r = .21$) and the 8-year-old's violent TV preferences were significantly related to aggression at age 18 ($r = .31$), but TV violence preferences at age 18 were not related to aggressive behavior at the earlier time period of age 8 ($r = .01$). When other possible variables, such as parenting practices and discipline style, were controlled, it was still clear that early media violence could be part of the cause of later aggressive behavior. Furthermore, in a follow-up study, when these young men were now age 30 (Huesmann et al., 1984), the authors found a significant correlation ($r = .41$) between TV violence levels at age 8 and serious interpersonal criminal behavior (e.g., assault, murder, child abuse, spouse abuse, rape) at age 30.

Thus, it seems clear that a correlation between television violence and aggression can be established from diverse studies. As well, some special cases of longitudinal correlational studies (described as cross-lagged/panel studies) can lead to intimations of causation. However, the issue of causation is best assessed in experimental designs that allow for random assignment of subjects to various treatment conditions or, in the case of field studies, take advantage of naturally occurring variations in television viewing experiences.

EXPERIMENTAL STUDIES

The potential role of television violence in the causation of aggressive behavior was, as noted earlier, among the first topics investigated by social scientists. The studies by Bandura (e.g., Bandura, Ross, & Ross, 1961, 1963) and Berkowitz (e.g., Berkowitz & Rawlings, 1963) set the stage for later experimental studies in which causal influences of TV violence could be assessed by randomly assigning subjects to various viewing conditions. These later studies employed both the structured, laboratory-based settings as well as more naturalistic settings in schools and communities.

One of the earlier studies in this genre (Liebert & Baron, 1972) assessed the effects of viewing segments of a violent television program, *The Untouchables*, on the aggressive behavior of 5- to 9-year-old boys and girls. In this study, the children viewed either *The Untouchables* or a neutral but active track race. Following viewing, the child was placed in a playroom setting in which he or she could help or hurt another child who was ostensibly playing a game in another room. The subject could help the other child by pressing a button that would make the game easier to play and allow the other child to win more points. Similarly, the child could hurt the other child by pressing a button that would make the game very difficult to play and hence the child would lose points. The results indicated that youngsters who had viewed the violent program manifested a greater willingness to hurt the other child than did youngsters who had watched the neutral program. Moreover, an elaboration of this study by Paul Ekman and colleagues (Ekman et al., 1972) included the recording of the facial expressions of these children while they were watching the television violence. In this instance, the children whose facial expressions indicated interest or pleasure while watching TV violence were more willing to hurt the other child than were the youngsters whose facial expressions indicated disinterest or displeasure while watching TV violence. Thus, this set of studies identified some potential moderating variables in the violence viewing/aggressive behavior equation.

Other early experiments by researchers using physiological measures of arousal (e.g., GSR, heart rate, respiration changes) while the subject watched violent cartoons (Cline, Croft, & Courrier, 1973; Osborn & Endsley, 1971) found that children are emotionally responsive even to cartoon violence. Similarly, other studies (Ellis & Sekyra, 1972; Hapkiewitz & Roden, 1971; Lovaas, 1961; Mussen & Rutherford, 1961; Ross, 1972) found that exposure to even one violent cartoon leads to increased aggression in the structured playroom settings. Furthermore, studies by Drabman and his colleagues (Drabman & Thomas, 1974; Thomas, Horton, Lippincott, & Drabman, 1977) showed that children who view violent television programs become desensitized to violence and are more willing to tolerate aggressive behavior in others. Moreover, later studies with emotionally disturbed children (Gadow & Sprafkin, 1993; Grimes, Vernberg, & Cathers, 1997) found that these youngsters may be more vulnerable to the influence of TV violence. For example, Grimes et al. (1997) found that 8- to 12-year-olds who were diagnosed as having either attention deficit hyperactivity disorder, oppositional defiant disorder, or conduct disorder, manifested less emotional concern for victims and were more willing to accept the TV violence as justified than did a matched group of children who did not have these disorders.

All of the studies described here were conducted in fairly structured laboratory or playroom settings where the display of aggression or emotional arousal or desensitization were relatively contiguous to the viewing of TV violence. Questions remain about what might happen in more naturalistic settings or field studies of violence viewing and aggressive behavior. One early study that assessed these issues in was the work of Aletha (Stein) Huston and Lynette (Friedrich) Cofer (Friedrich & Stein, 1975; Stein & Friedrich, 1972), in which they assessed the impact on the behavior of preschoolers in their normal child-care settings of viewing aggressive versus prosocial television programs. In this study, the preschoolers were assigned to view a diet of either Batman and Superman cartoons, or Mister Rogers' Neighborhood, or neutral programming that contained neither aggressive nor prosocial material (i.e., special travel stories for preschoolers). The "diet" consisted of 12 half-hour episodes that were viewed 1 half-hour per day, 3 days per week, for 4 weeks. The researchers observed the children in the classroom and on the playground for 3 weeks prior to the start of the viewing period, to establish a baseline for the amount of aggression or prosocial behavior, and continued to observe the children during the 4 weeks of viewing and for an additional 2 weeks. The results were that children who were initially more aggressive and had viewed the diet of Batman and Superman cartoons were more active in the classroom and on the playground, played more roughly with toys, and got into more aggressive encounters. Conversely, youngsters from lower-income families who had viewed the Mister Rogers diet increased their prosocial helping behavior. One suggestion from this early field study is that viewing aggressive program content can lead to changes in aggressive behavior, whereas the opposite is also true for prosocial programming. Moreover, these changes were demonstrated in a relatively short viewing period (12 half-hours) and in the context of other viewing that took place outside of the classroom setting.

Other field studies have used restricted populations such as boys in detention centers or secure residential settings. In one such study, conducted for NBC, Feshbach and Singer (1971) presented preadolescent and adolescent males in a security facility with a diet of aggressive or nonaggressive television programs over a 6-week period and measured their daily aggressive behavior. They found that the youngsters who watched the nonaggressive programs were more aggressive than the other group. However, this study was criticized on methodological grounds relating to the selection of subjects and the assignment of viewing conditions (Liebert, Sobel, & Davidson, 1972) and a subsequent replication (Wells, 1973) failed to duplicate the findings. Moreover, a later study conducted by Berkowitz and his colleagues (Parke, Berkowitz, Leyens, West, & Sebastian, 1977), using aggressive or nonaggressive films presented to adolescent males living in minimum-security institutions, did demonstrate increases in both verbal and physical interpersonal aggression among the teens viewing the aggressive diet.

Another approach to field studies involved the assessment of the effects of naturally occurring differences in the television exposure available to children in communities with or without television or communities with differing television content. In one set of studies (Murray & Kippax, 1977, 1978), the researchers were able to study the introduction of television in a rural community in Australia, in contrast to two similar communities that had differing experiences with television. In a second set of studies (Macbeth, 1996; Williams, 1986), the research team studied the introduction of television in a rural Canadian community, in contrast to two similar communities with differing television experience. In general, the results of both the Australian and Canadian studies converge in showing that the introduction of television had a major influence on restructuring the social lives of children in these rural communities. In this regard, both studies found that television displaced other media use and involvement in various social activities—a finding not dissimilar to the earlier studies of children in England (Himmelweit et al., 1958) or the United States and Canada (Schramm et al., 1961). However, with regard to the effects of TV violence, these newer field studies provided stronger evidence of negative influence, in differing but complementary ways. Murray and Kippax (Murray, 1980) found changes in perceptions of the seriousness and prevalence of crime among children in the town exposed to higher levels of television violence, whereas Williams/(aka Macbeth) (Joy, Kimball, & Zabrack, 1986) found increases in aggression among children following the introduction of television in the town.

WHAT HAVE WE LEARNED?

Research conducted over the past 50 years leads to the conclusion that televised violence does affect viewers' attitudes, values, and behavior (Hearold, 1986; Murray, 1994; Paik & Comstock, 1994). In general, there seem to be three main classes of effects: aggression, desensitization, and fear:

- *Aggression:* Viewing televised violence can lead to increases in aggressive behavior and/or changes in attitudes and values favoring the use of aggression to solve conflicts.

- *Desensitization:* Extensive viewing of violence may lead to decreased sensitivity to violence and a greater willingness to tolerate increasing levels of violence in society.
- *Fear:* Extensive exposure to television violence may produce the "mean world syndrome" in which viewers overestimate their risk of victimization.

Although the body of research on the effects of viewing television violence is extensive and fairly coherent in demonstrating systematic patterns of influence, we know surprisingly little about the processes involved in the production of these effects. Although we know that viewing televised violence can lead to increases in aggressive behavior or fearfulness and changed attitudes and values about the role of violence in society, it would be helpful to know more about how these changes occur in viewers. In this regard, Fig. 8.1, drawn from the work of Eron and Huesmann (Donnerstein, Slaby, & Eron, 1994), is a model of the long-term effects of mass media violence.

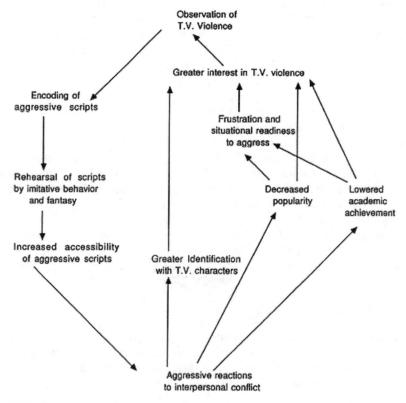

FIG. 8.1.   Model of the long-term effects of viewing media violence (Donnerstein, Slaby & Eron, 1994). Copyright 1994, American Psychological Association, reprinted with permission.

It can be seen that the relationships outlined in Fig. 8.1 involve a description of the encoding of the aggressive behavior observed in television or film and some *hypothesized* but *unspecified* storage and cognitive rehearsal of the observed behavior. This storage and rehearsal then allows the TV violence to serve as a guide for future behavior in contexts that might elicit aggression. Our continuing research is addressed to elucidating the left side of Fig. 8.1.

To set the context for the continuing research—within the broad framework of a social learning paradigm—we know that changes in behavior and thoughts can result from observing models in the world around us, be they parents, peers, or other role models, (e.g., those provided by mass media). The processes involved in "modeling" or imitation and vicarious learning of overt behavior were addressed in social learning theories in the 1960s (Bandura, 1962, 1965, 1969; Berkowitz 1962, 1965), but we need to expand our understanding of the neurological processes that might govern the translation of the observed models into thoughts and actions.

As a start in this new direction, both Bandura (2002) and Berkowitz (1984) provided some theoretical foundations for the translation of communication "events" into thoughts and actions. Bandura's "social-cognitive" approach and Berkowitz's outline of a "cognitive-neoassociation" analysis posit a role for emotional arousal as an affective tag that may facilitate lasting influences. As Bandura (2002) noted: "People are easily aroused by the emotional expressions of others. Vicarious arousal operates mainly through an intervening self-arousal process.... That is, seeing others react emotionally to instigating conditions activates emotion-arousing thoughts and imagery in observers" (p. 136). With regard to aggression, we know that viewing television violence can be emotionally arousing (e.g.,Cline et al., 1973; Osborn & Endsley, 1971; Zillmann, 1971, 1982), but we lack direct measures of cortical arousal or activation patterns in relation to viewing of violence.

The pursuit of neurological patterns of cortical arousal in viewing of violence would likely start with the amygdala, because it has a well-established role in the control of physiological responses to emotionally arousing or threatening stimuli (Damasio, 1994, 1999; Kosslyn & Koenig, 1995; LeDoux, 1996; LeDoux & Hirst, 1986; Ornstein, 1997; Panksepp, 1998; Steward, 2000). Indeed, a National Research Council (1993) report from the Panel on the Understanding and Control of Violent Behavior concluded:

> All human behavior, including aggression and violence, is the outcome of complex processes in the brain. Violent behaviors may result from relatively permanent conditions or from temporary states.... Biological research on aggressive and violent behavior has given particular attention to the following in recent years: ... (2) functioning of steroid hormones such as testosterone and glucocorticoids, especially their action on steroid receptors in the brain; ... (6) neurophysiological (i.e., brain wave) abnormalities, particularly in the temporal lobe of the brain; (7) brain dysfunctions that interfere with language processing or cognition.... (pp. 115–116)

Thus, one suggestion for further research on the impact of media violence is to assess some of the neurological correlates of viewing televised violence. In particular, the use of videotaped violent scenes can serve as the ideal stimulus for assessing activation patterns in response to violence.

It is very likely that the amygdala will be involved in processing violence, but the projections to the cortex are not clear. However, developing hypotheses about viewing of violence and related brain activation needs to start with research on physiological arousal (e.g., Osborn & Endsley, 1971; Zillmann, 1982; Zillmann & Bryant, 1994) and link this to cortical arousal. In this regard, the work of Paul Ekman and Richard Davidson (Davidson, Ekman, Saron, Senulis, & Friesen, 1990; Ekman & Davidson, 1993, 1994; Ekman, Davidson, & Friesen, 1990) using EEG recordings while subjects viewed gruesome films (a leg amputation) indicated asymmetries in activation patterns in the anterior regions of the left and right hemispheres. In particular, positive affect (indexed by facial expression) has been found to be associated with left-sided anterior activation, whereas negative affect is associated with right-sided activation (Davidson & Tomarken, 1989; Ornstein, 1997).

In our pilot study (Liotti et al., in press; Murray et al., 2001; Murray, 2001), we found that both violent and nonviolent viewing activated regions implicated in aspects of visual and auditory processing. In contrast, however, viewing TV violence selectively recruited right precuneus, right posterior cingulate, right amygdala, bilateral hippocampus and parahippocampus, bilateral pulvinar, right inferior parietal and prefrontal, and right premotor cortex. Thus, viewing TV violence appears to activate brain areas involved in arousal/attention, detection of threat, episodic memory encoding and retrieval, and motor programming. These findings are displayed in Fig. 8.2 through a graphic summary of these data. It can be seen that the regions of interest (ROI) of the composite activations of 8 children, combined in adjusted Talairach space (Talairach & Tournoux, 1988), include the amygdala, hippocampus, and posterior cingulate because these areas are likely indicators of the perception of threat and possible long-term memory storage of the threat event (particularly, these patterns are similar to the memory storage of traumatic events by posttraumatic stress disorder patients These activation patterns are important because they demonstrate that viewing video violence selectively activates the right hemisphere, and some bilateral areas, that collectively suggest significant emotional processing of video violence.

Our continuing research is designed to address these questions about violence viewing in a more robust study that employs a larger and more differentiated sample of children who have had differing experiences with violence (e.g., children who are identified as high or low in aggressive tendencies, and children who have been victims of abuse). We will continue to use the methods and procedures that were demonstrated to be effective in the pilot study—we will conjoin measures of physiological arousal (e.g., GSR, heart rate) with neuroimaging techniques (e.g., functional magnetic resonance imaging—fMRI) to track the emotional and neurological processes involved in viewing televised violence—and we will explore the responses of this larger and more specialized group of children. We anticipate that experience with violence as victims (abused children) would lead to heightened arousal and indications of threat. On the other hand, children who are more

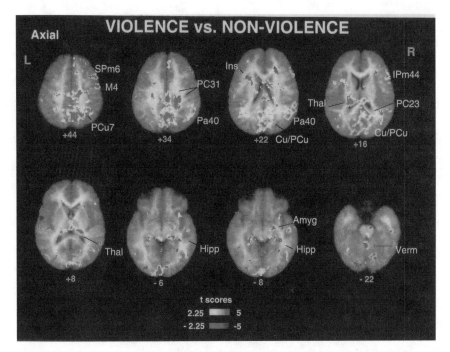

FIG. 8.2. Composite (in Talairach space) of the brains of 8 children viewing violence.

aggressive and have had more experience with violence as aggressors may manifest less threat and less arousal in response to the violent scenes.

CONCLUSION

What we have learned from this broad and diverse compilation of research, conducted over the past 50 years, is the realization that we are all affected by the violence that we encounter on television and in other media. Moreover, our society must come to terms with the effects of media violence, and we must begin to develop ways to mitigate the influences of media mayhem.

One of the ways that we can limit the effects of television violence is to provide youngsters (and their parents) with "inoculations" or insightful experiences that will help them to understand the workings of the industry and the role of violence in entertainment programming. Although this is an additional role for community education, the development of a curriculum on "critical viewing skills" has been undertaken by many organizations. For example, groups as diverse as MediaScope (1994, 1996), the George Lucas Educational Foundation (1999), and the Center for Media Literacy (1995) have provided outstanding educational programs for use in schools and community settings.

REFERENCES

Atkin, C. K., Greenberg, B. S., Korzenny, F., & McDermott, S. (1979). Selective exposure to televised violence. *Journal of Broadcasting, 23*(1), 5–13.

Baker, R. K., & Ball, S. J. (1969). *Mass media and violence: A staff report to the National Commission on the Causes and Prevention of Violence.* Washington, DC: United States Government Printing Office.

Bandura, A. (1962). Social learning through imitation. In M. R. Jones (Ed.). *Nebraska symposium on motivation* (pp. 00–00). Lincoln: University of Nebraska Press.

Bandura, A. (1965). Vicarious processes: A case of no-trial learning. In L. Berkowitz (Ed.), *Advances in experimental social psychology* (vol. 2, pp. 00–00). New York: Academic Press.

Bandura, A. (1969). Social-learning theory of identificatory processes. In D. A. Goslin (Ed.), *Handbook of socialization theory and research* (pp. 00–00). Chicago: Rand McNally.

Bandura, A. (2002). *Social cognitive theory of mass communication.* In J. Bryant & D. Zillmann (Eds.), *Media effects: Advances in theory and research* (pp. 121–153). Hillsdale, NJ: Lawrence Erlbaum Associates.

Bandura, A., Ross, D., & Ross, S. A. (1961). Transmission of aggression through imitation of aggressive models. *Journal of Abnormal and Social Psychology, 63*(3), 575–582.

Bandura, A., Ross, D., & Ross, S. H. (1963). Imitation of film-mediated aggressive models. *Journal of Abnormal and Social Psychology, 66*(1), 3–11.

Belson, W. (1978). *Television violence and the adolescent boy.* Farnborough, UK: Saxon House, Teakfield Limited.

Berkowitz, L. (1962). *Aggression: A social psychological analysis.* New York: McGraw-Hill.

Berkowitz, L. (1965). Some aspects of observed aggression. *Journal of Personality and Social Psychology, 2,* 359–365.

Berkowitz, L. (1984). Some effects of thoughts on anti- and prosocial influences of media events: A cognitive-neoassociation analysis. *Psychological Bulletin, 95,* 110–427.

Berkowitz, L., & Geen, R. G. (1966). Film violence and the cue properties of available targets. *Journal of Personality and Social Psychology, 3*(5), 525–530.

Berkowitz, L., & Rawlings, E. (1963). Effects of film violence on inhibitions against subsequent aggression. *Journal of Abnormal and Social Psychology, 66*(5), 405–412.

Center for Media Literacy. (1995). *Beyond blame: Challenging violence in the media.* Los Angeles: Author.

Cline, V. B., Croft, R. G., & Courrier, S. (1973). Desensitization of children to television violence. *Journal of Personality and Social Psychology, 27,* 360–365.

Cook, T. D., Kendzierski, D. A., & Thomas, S. A. (1983). The implicit assumptions of television research: An analysis of the 1982 NIMH report on "Television and Behavior." *Public Opinion Quarterly, 47*(2), 161–201.

Cressey, P. G., & Thrasher, F. M. (1933). *Boys, movies, and city streets.* New York: Macmillan.

Damasio, A. R. (1994). *Descartes' error: Emotion, reason, and the human brain.* New York: Putnam.

Damasio, A. R. (1999). *The feeling of what happens: Body and emotion in the making of consciousness.* New York: Harcourt Brace.

Davidson, R. J., Ekman, P., Saron, C., Senulis, J., & Friesen, W. V. (1990). Emotional expression and brain physiology I: Approach/withdrawal and cerebral asymmetry. *Journal of Personality and Social Psychology, 58,* 330–341.

Davidson, R. J., & Tomarken, A. J. (1989). Laterality and emotion: An electrophysiological approach. In F. Boller & J. Grafman (Eds.), *Handbook of neuropsychology* (pp. 419–441). Amsterdam: Elsevier.

Dominick, J. R., & Greenberg, B. S. (1972). Attitudes toward violence: The interaction of television exposure, family attitudes, and social class. In G. A. Comstock & E. A. Rubinstein (Eds.), *Television and social behavior, vol. 3, television and adolescent aggressiveness* (pp. 314–335). Washington, D.: United States Government Printing Office.

Donnerstein, E., Slaby, R., & Eron, L. D. (1994). Mass media violence. In L. D. Eron, J. H. Gentry, & P. Schlegel (Eds.), *Reason to hope: A psychosocial perspective on violence and youth* (pp. 219–250). Washington, DC: American Psychological Association.

Drabman, R. S., & Thomas, M. H. (1974). Does media violence increase children's toleration of real-life aggression? *Developmental Psychology, 10,* 418–421.

Ekman, P., & Davidson, R. J. (1993). Voluntary smiling changes regional brain activity. *Psychological Science, 4*(5), 342–345.

Ekman, P., & Davidson, R. J. (1994). *The nature of emotion: Fundamental questions.* New York: Oxford University Press.

Ekman, P., Davidson, R. J., & Friesen, W. V. (1990). The Duchenne smile: Emotional expression and brain physiology II. *Journal of Personality and Social Psychology, 58,* 342–353.

Ekman, P., Liebert, R. M., Friesen, W., Harrison, R., Zlatchin, C., Malmstrom, E. V., & Baron, R. A. (1972). Facial expressions of emotion as predictors of subsequent aggression. In G. A. Comstock, E. A. Rubinstein, & J. P. Murray (Eds.), *Television and social behavior, vol. 5, television's effects: Further explorations* (pp. 22–58). Washington, DC: United States Government Printing Office.

Ellis, G. T., & Sekyra, F. (1972). The effect of aggressive cartoons on behavior of first grade children. *Journal of Psychology, 81,* 37–43.

Eron, L. (1963). Relationship of TV viewing habits and aggressive behavior in children. *Journal of Abnormal and Social Psychology, 67,* 193–196.

Eron, L. (1982). Parent child interaction, television violence and aggression of children. *American Psychologist, 27,* 197–211.

Eron, L. D., Walder, L. O., & Lefkowitz, M. M. (1971). *Learning of aggression in children.* Boston: Little, Brown.

Feshbach, S., & Singer, R. D. (1971). *Television and aggression: An experimental field study.* San Francisco: Jossey-Bass.

Friedrich, L. K., & Stein, A. H. (1975). Aggressive and prosocial television programs and the natural behavior of preschool children. *Monographs of the Society for Research in Child Development, 38*(4, Serial No. 151).

Gadow, K. D., & Sprafkin, J. (1993). Television violence and children with emotional and behavioral disorders. *Journal of Emotional and Behavioral Disorders, 1*(1), 54–63.

George Lucas Educational Foundation (1999). *Learn & live.* San Rafael, CA: Author.

Gerbner, G. (1970). Cultural indicators: The case of violence in television drama. *Annals of the American Academy of Political and Social Science, 388,* 69–81.

Gerbner, G., Gross, L., Morgan, M., & Signorielli, N. (1994). Growing up with television: The cultivation perspective. In J. Bryant, & D. Zillmann (Eds.), *Media effects: Advances in theory and research* (pp. 17–41). Hillsdale, NJ: Lawrence Erlbaum Associates.

Grimes, T., Vernberg, E., & Cathers, T. (1997). Emotionally disturbed children's reactions to violent media segments. *Journal of Health Communication, 2*(3), 157–168.

Group for the Advancement of Psychiatry. (1982). *The child and television drama: The psychosocial impact of cumulative viewing.* New York: Mental Health Materials Center.

Hapkiewitz, W. G., & Roden, A. H. (1971). The effect of aggressive cartoons on children's interpersonal play. *Child Development, 42,* 1583–1585.

Hearold, S. (1986). A synthesis of 1043 effects of television on social behavior. In G. Comstock (Ed.), *Public communication and behavior* (vol. 1, pp. 65–133). New York: Academic Press.

Himmelweit, H. T., Oppenheim, A. N., & Vince, P. (1958). *Television and the child: An empirical study of the effects of television on the young.* London: Oxford University Press.

Huesmann, L. R., & Eron, L. D. (Eds.). (1986). *Television and the aggressive child: A cross-national comparison.* Hillsdale, NJ: Lawrence Erlbaum Associates.

Huesmann, L. R., Eron, L. D., Lefkowitz, M. M., & Walder, L. O. (1984). Stability of aggression over time and generations. *Developmental Psychology, 20,* 1120–1134.

Huston, A. C., Donnerstein, E., Fairchild, H., Feshbach, N. D., Katz, P. A., Murray, J. P., Rubinstein, E. A., Wilcox, B., & Zuckerman, D. (1992). *Big world, small screen: The role of television in American society.* Lincoln: University of Nebraska Press.

Joy, L. A., Kimball, M., & Zabrack, M. L. (1986). Television exposure and children's aggressive be-
   havior. In T. M. Williams (Ed.), *The impact of television: A natural experiment involving three
   towns* (pp. 303–360). New York: Academic Press.
Kenny, D. A. (1984). The NBC study and television violence. *Journal of Communication, 34*(1),
   176–182.
Kosslyn, S. M., & Koenig, O. (1995). *Wet mind: The new cognitive neuroscience*. New York: Free Press.
Lazarsfeld, P. F. (1955). Why is so little known about the effects of television and what can be done?
   Public Opinion Quarterly, 19, 243–251.
LeDoux, J. (1996). *The emotional brain: The mysterious underpinnings of emotional life*. New York: Si-
   mon & Schuster.
LeDoux, J. E., & Hirst, W. (Eds.). (1986). *Mind and brain: Dialogues in cognitive neuroscience*. New
   York: Cambridge University Press.
Lefkowitz, M., Eron, L., Walder, L., & Huesmann, L. R. (1972). Television violence and child aggres-
   sion: A follow up study. In G. A. Comstock & E. A. Rubinstein (Eds.), *Television and social behav-
   ior, vol. 3, television and adolescent aggressiveness* (pp. 35–148). Washington, DC: United States
   Government Printing Office.
Liebert, R. M., & Baron, R. A. (1972). Short term effects of television aggression on children's aggressive behavior. In J. P. Murray, E. A. Rubinstein, & G. A. Comstock (Eds.), *Television and
   social behavior, vol. 2, television and social learning* (pp. 181–201). Washington, DC: United
   States Government Printing Office.
Liebert, R. M., Sobel, M. D., & Davidson, E. S. (1972). Catharsis of aggression among institutional-
   ized boys: Fact or artifact? In G. A. Comstock, E. A. Rubinstein, & J. P. Murray (Eds.), *Television
   and social behavior, vol. 5, television's effects: Further explorations* (pp. 181–201). Washington, DC:
   United States Government Printing Office.
Liotti, M., Murray, J. P., Ingmundson, P., Mayberg, H. S., Pu, Y., Zamarripa, F., Liu, Y., Woldorff, M.
   G., Gao, J.-H., & Fox, P. T. (in press). Children's brain activations while viewing televised vio-
   lence revealed by fMRI. *Human Brain Mapping.*
Lovaas, O. I. (1961). Effect of exposure to symbolic aggression on aggressive behavior. *Child Develop-
   ment, 32,* 37–44.
MacBeth, T. M. (1996). *Tuning in to young viewers: Social science perspectives on television*. Thousand
   Oaks, CA: Sage.
Maccoby, E. E. (1954). Why do children watch television? *Public Opinion Quarterly, 18,* 239–244.
McLeod, J. M., Atkin, C. K., & Chaffee, S. H. (1972a). Adolescents, parents, and television use: Ado-
   lescent self-report measures from Maryland and Wisconsin samples. In G. A. Comstock & E. A.
   Rubinstein (Eds.), *Television and social behavior, vol. 3, television and adolescent aggressiveness* (pp.
   173–238). Washington, DC: United States Government Printing Office.
McLeod, J. M., Atkin, C. K., & Chaffee, S. H. (1972b). Adolescents, parents and television use:
   Self-report and other measures from the Wisconsin sample. In G. A. Comstock & E. A.
   Rubinstein (Eds.), *Television and social behavior, vol. 3, television and adolescent aggressiveness* (pp.
   239–313). Washington, DC: United States Government Printing Office.
MediaScope. (1994). *The kids are watching* [Video]. Los Angeles: Author.
MediaScope. (1996). *National television violence study—executive summary, 1994–95*. Thousand
   Oaks, CA: Sage.
Milavsky, J. R., Kessler, R. C., Stipp, H. H., & Rubens, W. S. (1982). *Television and aggression: A panel
   study*. New York: Academic Press.
Murray, J. P. (1973). Television and violence: Implications of the Surgeon General's research pro-
   gram. *American Psychologist, 28*(6), 472–478.
Murray, J. P. (1980). *Television and youth: 25 years of research and controversy*. Boys Town, NE: The
   Boys Town Center for the Study of Youth Development.
Murray, J. P. (1993). The developing child in a multimedia society. In G. L. Berry & J. K. Asamen
   (Eds.), *Children and television: Images in a changing sociocultural world* (pp. 9–22). Newbury Park,
   CA: Sage.
Murray, J. P. (1994). The impact of televised violence. *Hofstra Law Review, 22*(4), 809–825.

Murray, J. P. (1998). Studying television violence: A research agenda for the 21st Century. In J. K. Asamen & G. L. Berry (Eds.), *Research paradigms, television, and social behavior* (pp. 369–410). Thousand Oaks, CA: Sage.

Murray, J. P. (2000). Media effects. In A. E. Kazdin (Ed.), *Encyclopedia of psychology* (vol. 5, pp. 153–155). New York: Oxford University Press.

Murray, J. P. (2001). TV violence and brainmapping in children. *Psychiatric Times, 17*(10), 70–71.

Murray, J. P., & Kippax, S. (1977). Television diffusion and social behavior in three communities: A field experiment. *Australian Journal of Psychology, 29*(1), 31–43.

Murray, J. P., & Kippax, S. (1978). Children's social behavior in three towns with differing television experience. *Journal of Communication, 28*(1), 19–29.

Murray, J. P., & Kippax, S. (1979). From the early window to the late night show: International trends in the study of television's impact on children and adults. In L. Berkowitz (Ed.), *Advances in experimental social psychology* (vol. 12, pp. 253–320). New York: Academic Press.

Murray, J. P., Liotti, M., Ingmundson, P., Mayberg, H. S., Pu, Y., Zamarripa, F., Liu, Y., Woldorff, M., Gao, J.-H., & Fox, P. T. (2001, April). *Children's brain response to TV violence: Functional magnetic resonance imaging (fMRI) of video viewing in 8–13-year-old boys and girls.* Paper presented at the biennial meeting of the Society for Research in Child Development, Minneapolis.

Mussen, P., & Rutherford, E. (1961). Effects of aggressive cartoons on children's aggressive play. *Journal of Abnormal and Social Psychology, 62*(2), 461–464.

National Institute of Mental Health. (1982). *Television and behavior: Ten years of scientific progress and implications for the eighties, vol. 1, summary report.* Washington, DC: United States Government Printing Office.

National Research Council. (1993). *Understanding and preventing violence.* Washington, DC: National Academy Press.

Ornstein, R. (1997). *The right mind: Making sense of the hemispheres.* New York: Harcourt Brace.

Osborn, D. K., & Endsley, R. C. (1971). Emotional reactions of young children to TV violence. *Child Development, 42*(1), 321–331.

Paik, H., & Comstock, G. (1994). The effects of television violence on antisocial behavior: A meta-analysis. *Communication Research, 21*(4), 516–546.

Panksepp, J. (1998). *Affective neuroscience: The foundations of human and animal emotions.* New York: Oxford University Press.

Parke, R. D., Berkowitz, L., Leyens, J. P., West, S. & Sebastian, R. J. (1977). Some effects of violent and nonviolent movies on the behavior of juvenile delinquents. In L. Berkowitz (Ed.), *Advances in experimental psychology* (vol. 10, pp. 135–172). New York: Academic Press.

Pearl, D., Bouthilet, L., & Lazar, J. (Eds.). (1982). *Television and behavior: Ten years of scientific progress and implications for the eighties, vol. 2, technical reviews.* Washington, DC: United States Government Printing Office.

Pecora, N., Murray, J. P., & Wartella, E. (2003). *Children and television: 50 years of research.* Hillsdale, NJ: Lawrence Erlbaum Associates.

Robinson, J. P., & Bachman, J. G. (1972). Television viewing habits and aggression. In G. A. Comstock & E. A. Rubinstein (Eds.), *Television and social behavior, vol. 3, television and adolescent aggressiveness* (pp. 372–382). Washington, DC: United States Government Printing Office.

Ross, L. B. (1972). *The effect of aggressive cartoons on the group play of children.* Unpublished doctoral dissertation, Miami University, Oxford, OH..

Schramm, W., Lyle, J., & Parker, E. B. (1961). *Television in the lives of our children.* Palo Alto, CA: Stanford University Press.

Stein, A. H., & Friedrich, L. K., with Vondracek, F. (1972). Television content and young children's behavior. In J. P. Murray, E. A. Rubinstein, & G. A. Comstock (Eds.), *Television and social behavior, vol. 2, television and social learning* (pp. 202–317). Washington, DC: United States Government Printing Office.

Steward, O. (2000). *Functional neuroscience.* New York: Springer.

Surgeon General's Scientific Advisory Committee on Television and Social Behavior. (1972). *Television and growing up: The impact of televised violence.* Washington, DC: United States Government Printing Office.

Talairach, J., & Tournoux, P. (1988). *Co-planar stereotaxic atlas of the human brain*. New York: Thieme Medical.

Thomas, M. H., Horton, R. W., Lippincott, E. C., & Drabman, R. S. (1977). Desensitization to portrayals of real life aggression as a function of television violence. *Journal of Personality and Social Psychology, 35*(6), 450–458.

United States Congress, House Committee on Interstate and Foreign Commerce. (1952). *Investigation of radio and television programs, hearings and report, 82nd Congress, 2nd session, June 3–December 5, 1952*. Washington, DC: United States Government Printing Office.

United States Congress, Senate Committee of the Judiciary, Subcommittee to Investigate Juvenile Delinquency. (1955). *Juvenile delinquency (television programs), hearings, 83rd Congress, 2nd session, June 5–October 20, 1954*. Washington, DC: United States Government Printing Office.

United States Congress. (1990). *Children Television Act (CTA) of 1990, as adopted by the Federal Communications Commission (FCC)*. FCC Adopts New Children's TV Rules, Docket Number, MM-93-48, 1996.

United States Congress, United States Senate. (2001). *Children's Protection Act of 2001 (SR4I5)*, January 22, 2001, 107th Congress, 1st Session. Washington, DC: United States Government Printing Office.

Walker, K. B., & Morley, D. D. (1991). Attitudes and parental factors as intervening variables in the television violence-aggression relation. *Communication Research, 8*(2), 41–47.

Wells, W. D. (1973). *Television and aggression: Replication of an experimental field study*. Unpublished manuscript, Graduate School of Business, University of Chicago.

Williams, T. M. (Ed.). (1986). *The impact of television: A natural experiment in three communities*. New York: Academic Press.

Zillmann, D. (1971). Excitation transfer in communication-mediated aggressive behavior. *Journal of Experimental Social Psychology, 7*, 419–434.

Zillmann, D. (1982). Television viewing and arousal. In D. Pearl, L. Bouthilet, & J. Lazar (Eds.), *Television and behavior: Ten years of scientific progress and implications for the eighties, vol. 2, technical reviews* (pp. 53–67). Washington, DC: United States Government Printing Office.

Zillmann, D., & Bryant, J. (1994). Entertainment as media effect. In J. Bryant & D. Zillmann (Eds.), *Media effects: Advances in theory and research* (pp. 437–461). Hillsdale, NJ: Lawrence Erlbaum Associates.

9

Entertainment Televisual Media: Content Patterns and Themes

Erica Scharrer
University of Massachusetts, Amherst

George Comstock
Syracuse University

Children are particular fans of television, watching an average of approximately 3 hours per day (Comstock & Scharrer, 1999, 2001). Television viewing begins early in the United States and continues rather steadily through childhood and adolescence (Comstock & Scharrer, 2001). Two- to 4-year-olds view an average of 2 hours, 8- to 13-year olds watch 3½ hours, and adolescents view 2¾ hours per day (Roberts, Foehr, Rideout, & Brodie, 1999). When other media—including taped television programs, videotaped rentals, movies, video games, print media, radio, CDs and tapes, and the computer—are added to the equation, the daily exposure rate for children aged 2 to 18 rises to 6½ hours per day (Roberts, Foehr, et al., 1999).

With time spent with the media occupying such an immense proportion of children's daily lives, parents, educators, and media scholars alike have posed the central question: To what messages and patterns in content are young people exposed when they watch television or use other media? In this chapter, we examine the major themes and patterns of content present in contemporary televisual media favored by young audiences. We then identify the stability of some types of content over time as well as point to new and novel patterns brought about by the rapidly changing televisual environment.

We start by discussing three overarching themes, the domination of entertainment-oriented programming, the popularity but limited role of children's programming, and the minor role that educational programming plays. We next turn to consistent staples in content in programming viewed by children in terms of people present on the screen and behaviors portrayed. Finally, we identify five broad themes that underlie much of the content in televisual media used by young people, including the dominance of the White male, the introduction of conflict, the solution of conflict with speedy resolutions, the idealized role of the family, and the presence of health threats.

PROGRAMMING

Entertainment Predominates

The vast majority of television programming viewed by children ages 8 to 13 and a substantial proportion of programming viewed by 2- to 7-year-olds is entertainment based (Roberts, Foehr, et al., 1999). Younger children often prefer cartoons, and for decades this genre has dominated such child-friendly time slots as weekend mornings and after-school blocks (Comstock, 1991; Comstock & Scharrer, 2001). Animation, for instance, signals to a child that the content is designed with him or her in mind, and is an effective device for drawing a young audience. As children enter early adolescence, sitcoms and action adventure programs become their preferred genres (Comstock, 1991; Roberts, Foehr, et al., 1999). Thus, programs listed as favorites or reported as frequently viewed by children are typically rather light-hearted and whimsical fare, often with comedy at the center.

Regardless of the stated preferences of young audiences, however, child viewers—like their adult counterparts—are often rather indifferent to the content they view (Comstock, 1991; Comstock & Scharrer, 2001). Rather, children tend to first decide to view television and then select from those available the programs they find most appealing, rather than making "appointments" to view favorite programs at specific times (Barwise & Ehrenberg, 1988; Comstock & Scharrer, 1999; Rubin, 1983, 1984). Children are also often present in large numbers in the audience for general audience programming, such as during prime time, in addition to in time slots and during programs specifically designated for young viewers (Comstock, 1991). Thus, because the vast majority of the television programming schedule, across time slots and channel types, is entertainment based, patterns in the behavior of young audiences result in their viewing entertainment programs most frequently.

Historically, critics such as Peggy Charren, head of the now-defunct Action for Children's Television, have pointed to the role of advertising in children's television in creating and maintaining this entertainment-oriented model (Comstock & Scharrer, 1999). With advertising fees financially supporting programming, program creators are inclined to offer programs they presume will bring the largest or most demographically attractive audience. Conventional wisdom in the television industry suggests that this is entertainment television. Thus, programs like cartoons and family-based sitcoms abound as options from which children can choose to view. Some critics argue for the elimination of advertising in children's television programming altogether, in the hope that removing this economic orientation will eliminate the need to deliver the largest possible audience to advertisers and, subsequently, pave the way for more educational and cultural programming (Pecora, 1998).

Children's Programming

Programming specifically designed for and targeted toward children is, indeed, popular with young audiences. In a nationally representative sample of over 3,000 children, 84% of 2- to 7-year-olds, 49% of 8- to 13-year-olds, and 16% of 14- to 18-year-olds reported that they had watched entertainment content created specifically for children, such as cartoons, the previous day (Roberts, Foehr, et al., 1999). Thus, quite understandably, preference for children's programs is profound in very young children, still strong but balanced out by other programming interests in middle childhood, and drops considerably as children enter adolescence.

The number of children's programs on the three original broadcast networks increased dramatically over the medium's first 3 decades before decreasing somewhat as entire cable networks exclusively or primarily catering to child audiences emerged. Pecora (1998) tracked offerings beginning with the 1948–49 season on ABC, CBS, and NBC, and found sporadic growth in number of children's programs, from a low of 10 in 1948–49 to a high of 67 in 1979–1980 to recent levels in the high 50s. On cable, The Disney Channel (a premium channel mostly funded by subscriber fees) and Nickelodeon (a basic channel funded by both fees and advertising) are examples of stations that primarily target a child audience. Both use a similar programming formula: "morning hours for the preschool audience, an afterschool block for older children, and family entertainment in the evening hours" (Pecora, 1998, p. 85). The Disney Channel offers mostly Disney productions featuring Disney characters, such as *Little Mermaid, Pooh Corner,* and *Disney's House of Mouse,* with many opportunities for merchandise tie-ins. Nickelodeon, one of many of mega-conglomerate Viacom's media holdings, began commercial free for its first 4 years but subsequently included advertising in its programming. Nickelodeon features entertainment-oriented programs popular with somewhat older children, such as *Rugrats,* as well as socially or academically educational programs, such as preschool favorites *Blues Clues, Bob the Builder,* and *Dora the Explorer.*

However, it is important to remember that such programs do not always constitute the majority of what children of all ages watch. On the contrary, all but some very young children are more frequently in the audience for general audience programming, such as during prime time on the networks or in weekend daytime on cable channels, than they are in the audience for children's programming per se (Comstock, 1991). This phenomenon is explained not only by changing tastes as children grow, but also by the simple fact that children's programs are somewhat limited in number and in placement in the programming schedule. Therefore, when tuning in at other times of day and due to differences in what appeals to pre-

schoolers compared to middle or high school students, young people quite frequently join older audiences in watching general audience programs.

Educational Programming

PBS has historically been the most consistent and successful purveyor of educational programs for children, offering such long-lasting and celebrated fare as *Sesame Street* and *Mister Rogers' Neighborhood.* Social scientific research has
demonstrated the educational value of *Sesame Street,* associating viewing the program with language learning, school readiness, and better grades (Comstock &
Scharrer, 1999; Huston, Wright, Rice, Kerkman, & St. Peters, 1990; Rice, Huston,
Truglio, & Wright, 1990; Wright & Huston, 1995; Zill, Davies, & Daly, 1994). The
relative ability of PBS to deemphasize market concerns and rely more heavily on
funding from the federal government long allowed public television stations to
dedicate programming that was concerned, first and foremost, with helping children learn, and only secondarily with entertaining them. More recently, however,
decreases in federal funding have necessitated a greater emphasis on revenues generated from underwriting by corporate sponsors as well as by public contributions.
Although contemporary PBS programs still have an educational focus, there is frequently a commercial element as well, often through the creation and marketing of
videotapes, books, clothing, lunch boxes, backpacks, and other products that bear
the images of popular PBS characters. Consequently, recent PBS program lineups
have included a litany of programs with multiple product tie-ins, such as *Barney
and Friends* and *Lamb Chop's Play-Along* (Pecora, 1998), and the "sponsorship"
messages between programs on PBS look increasingly similar to the advertising
messages on commercial television.

In the Children's Television Act of 1990, Congress decreed that commercial stations must provide educational programming for children (later set at 3 hours per
week) in order to have their licenses renewed. Whether the act has actually stimulated greater availability of educational children's television programs, however,
has been and continues to be hotly debated. Many critics suggest that rather than seriously address the principle underlying the act by increasing the number and attractiveness of educational program options for children, some network executives
have merely attempted to make the case that existing programs are educational
(Kunkel, 1998). According to many critics, what ensued was a shameful attempt to
frame a program like *Yogi Bear* or *America's Funniest Home Videos* as educational in
order to be in compliance with the Congressional ruling (Kunkel, 1998; Kunkel &
Canepa, 1994; Kunkel & Goette, 1997). In 1996, the Federal Communication Commission (FCC; the entity put in charge of defining "educational programming" for
the act by Congress) established clearer and more stringent standards, including
the presence of education as a "significant purpose" of the program and the identification in program guides of the program as educational. Critics hope this latter element will create a public accountability that will minimize the presentation of
preexisting entertainment programs as "educational" (Kunkel, 1998).

PEOPLE

The potential for children and teenagers to learn social roles, attitudes, and behaviors from characters they encounter in the mass media (Bandura, 1986; Comstock, 1991; Comstock & Scharrer, 1999) underscores the importance of studying the people, primarily the fictional characters, who populate media programs. Next we describe the primary characteristics of those people as they exist in stable patterns across programs, genres, and dayparts in television as well as across types of televisual media. What emerges is only striking and surprising in terms of the longevity and perseverance of the dominant representations in media content according to gender, beauty and body image, age, race and ethnicity, persons with disabilities, and sexual orientation and relationships.

Gender

Studies of gender roles on television reveal a long history of unequal representations of men and women. There have been some limited and isolated pockets of improvements in portrayals over the years but, generally, narrow and limited "role-appropriate" attitudes and behaviors pervade. Entertainment-based media specifically designed for children, in both programs and advertising, often contain gender stereotypes similar to those found in general audience programming. Results are consistent over time and across national boundaries.

Men consistently outnumber women on television (Davis, 1990; Greenberg & Collette, 1997; Lauzen & Dozier, 1999; Signorielli, 1985, 1989, 1993; Signorielli & Bacue, 1999). Among the most recent of these analyses, the Signorielli and Bacue (1999) study examined selections of prime-time network broadcast weeks between 1967 and 1998, and found women represented 24% of characters in 1967, 43% in 1996, and 38% in 1998. Thus, despite some general improvement over time in numbers of female characters, growth has been slow and sporadic, and women on television are still underrepresented compared to their numbers in real life.

Analyses documenting content patterns in television programs over time have consistently shown limited occupational roles, with an emphasis on nonprofessional jobs for women, gender-stereotyped jobs for both men and women, or gender-specific activities performed at the workplace (e.g., Signorielli, 1984, 1993; Vande Berg & Streckfuss, 1992). The most recent analyses of content show some improvement in the variation of occupational roles held by women, with a significant increase in professional roles (e.g., Signorielli, 2001). Yet, this change is accompanied by a strict divide between marriage and family situations (in which women are often not working outside the home) and the single, working woman portrayal, thereby providing limited models for success at combining these elements of many modern women's lives (Signorielli, 2001).

In advertising images as well as in the stories told in television dramas and situation comedies, household tasks are assigned according to gender in traditional ways. Women are almost solely in charge of caring for children, nursing family members to health, cleaning, and cooking (Craig, 1992; Kaufman, 1999). Men are presented as uninvolved fathers, as inept (Scharrer, 2001) or infrequent (Bartsch, Burnett, Diller, & Rankin-Williams, 2000) "househusbands," but often as very effective handymen. In general, children viewing general audience television programming are presented with a world in which women and men are confined to rather rigid roles, and challenges to those roles are infrequent and often unsuccessful.

Research regarding general audience programming and its portrayal of gender was summarized in a meta-analysis combining eight studies of gender representations on television (Herrett-Skjellum & Allen, 1996). Based on their meta-analysis, the authors concluded that "males are seen more often on television, appear more often in major roles, exhibit dominant behaviors and attitudes, and are represented outside the home in jobs of authority" (Herrett-Skjellum & Allen, 1996, p. 171). Furthermore, international research reveals similar patterns in several gender role stereotypes (men as voiceovers, women shown via visuals, men as having authority and autonomy, women as dependent, women in the home and men outdoors) in television programs in countries such as the United Kingdom, Italy, Portugal, Australia, Hong Kong, and Indonesia (Furnham & Mak, 1999).

In children's media, entertainment-based programming contains more of the same messages about gender. One analysis of characters in children's television programs on Saturday morning during the 1995–96 season shows male characters outnumbering female characters by three to one, and a dearth of female heroes (Calvert, Stolkin, & Lee, 1997). Barner (1999) analyzed 33 episodes of 11 programs airing in the Buffalo, New York market that were identified as meeting the requirements for the mandatory 3-hour block of the "social/emotional needs" aspect of educational programming (rather than the "intellectual/cognitive" aspect). He determined that even in this sample of ostensibly exemplary educational programs, gender stereotypes were pervasive, with female characters significantly more likely to show deference, dependence, and nurturing, and male characters more likely to show activity, dominance, and aggression.

Gender roles in commercials parallel those in programs. In the 1970s, for example, a sample of Saturday morning television commercials found 80% of the characters to be male (McArthur & Eisen, 1976). More recently, commercials during child-friendly time slots were determined to still overrepresent boys and convey stereotypical gender roles (Browne, 1998; Larson, 2001; Smith, 1994; Thompson & Zerbinos, 1997). Furnham, Abramsky, and Gunter (1997) found that boys and adult men in children's television commercials were more likely to be central characters and were presented as more authoritative in both American and British commercial television. Browne (1998) determined that in both U.S. and Australian television commercials aimed at children, boy characters were presented as being more active, aggressive, and knowledgeable, and exhibited more nonverbal dominance and control, than girl characters.

Finally, in video games (another televisual medium that is increasing in reach and popularity and is used some 20 minutes a day by 2- to 18-year-olds; Roberts, Foehr, et al., 1999), gender role stereotypes and unequal representations also prevail. In an analysis of 82 popular video games, 61 were determined to be targeted toward boys, 18 toward boys and girls, and only three toward girls alone (Oldenburg, 1994). Characteristics of video games and video game characters are often severely gender stereotyped, with male characters used for aggression and adventure and female characters used as rewards (Calvert, 1999; Gailey, 1993).

Beauty and Body Image

Television portrayals consistently show women as being much younger than men (Gerbner, Gross, Morgan, & Signorielli, 1980; Lauzen & Dozier, 1999; Lin, 1997; Signorielli & Bacue, 1999) and also as more likely to be blonde (Davis, 1990). The ideal image of women as presented in the media is extremely thin, with very few exceptions (e.g., Fouts & Burggraf, 1999; Harrison, 2000), and a frequent emphasis in conversations and interactions with other characters is about a woman's physical appearance and attractiveness (Signorielli, 2001). One study found only 5% of female television characters could be described as "heavy" compared to 69% described as "thin" (Silverstein, Perdue, Peterson, & Kelly, 1986). For males, a muscular ideal has become increasingly the norm in media representations (Mishkind, Rodin, Silberstein, & Striegel-Moore, 1986), although there is more variation in the ways in which the male body is portrayed in televisual media compared to the female body.

Fouts and Burggraf (1999) performed a content analysis of 28 prime-time situation comedies, the preferred genre of 10- to 16-year-old females, which is a group at risk for body image disturbances. They found female characters who were below average weight were overrepresented compared to the general population, and those characters also received a greater number of favorable comments from male characters regarding their appearance. Female characters that were dieting tended to punish themselves verbally for their body weight and shape. Ogletree and colleagues (Ogletree, Williams, Raffeld, Mason, & Fricke, 1990) found that 86% of all commercial messages on television dedicated to enhancing one's appearance were targeted toward young women.

Narrow depictions of beauty in the media—which few, if any, typical young persons can attain—can lead to body dissatisfaction, diminished self-esteem, unhealthy relationships with food and exercise, and, in extreme cases, eating disorders such as anorexia or bulimia (Fouts & Burggraf, 1999; Harrison, 2000). Children and teenagers, primarily females but increasingly males as well, are especially vulnerable to body image disturbances. One source of information that is often quite compelling for young people who are considering and occasionally trying to live up to standards of beauty is, of course, the media. In children's television, as in general audience programming, portrayals of women and girls almost never stray from the singular thin attractive ideal. In music television, displays of the ultrathin bodies of ever-younger female performers (Signorielli, McLeod, & Healy, 1994) combine with depictions of muscle-bound or thin male performers to provide restricted images of a beauty ideal.

In video games, scantily clad, buxom, yet hopelessly thin female characters are only rarely primary characters who set out on an adventure but are more often secondary or even minor characters such as "damsels in distress" in need of rescue or trophy-carrying objects used to reward male characters (Calvert, 1999; Gailey, 1993). For example, Dietz (1998) examined a sample of 33 popular Nintendo and Sega Genesis video games and determined that a full 41% contained no female characters, 28% had women portrayed as sex objects, and 21% contained violence directed toward women.

Age

The distribution of ages of television characters is quite different from that of the general population. Television overrepresents young adults, and underrepresents both the elderly and children in programs and commercials and male teenagers in commercials (Comstock & Scharrer, 1999). The latter is presumably because fewer products are deemed relevant to male teenagers compared to their female counterparts, who are frequently wooed with advertisements for health and beauty products. Children (Heintz, Delwiche, Lisosky, & Shively, 1996) and the elderly (Al-Deen, 1997) have rarely been seen on television programs at any point in time, especially as main characters.

The elderly are surprisingly neglected in terms of representation, considering the size of their ranks in the general population, their growing collective financial clout, and the long-standing finding that they watch more television than do younger audiences (Comstock & Scharrer, 1999). Older characters are exceptionally rare on television, especially in starring rather than minor or supporting roles. A survey conducted by the child advocacy group Children Now in 2000 of over 2,000 prime-time television characters on broadcast and cable found that just 3% were 70 or older, 13% were between the ages of 50 and 69, and 31% was over 40 (Children Now, 2001). Older female characters have been even more infrequent than older male characters (Children Now, 2001; Comstock & Scharrer, 1999). Kovaric (1993) reviewed existing content analyses of the elderly on television, most conducted in the 1970s, and found some examples of largely favorable and occasionally prominent roles (e.g., *Matlock; The Golden Girls; Murder, She Wrote*), but determined they have been only sporadically available to children and adult audiences viewing television.

The work of Anderson and colleagues (Anderson & Lorch, 1983; Schmitt, Anderson, & Collins, 1999) suggests that children will look at television more frequently when child, nonhuman, or animated characters appear, thus pointing to the importance of portrayals of young people on television in determining what young viewers will learn from watching. Peterson (1998) studied the primary roles that children take on when they appear in television commercials, performing a content analysis of over 5,000 commercials appearing on broadcast and cable stations during randomly selected dates in 1994. Results determined that children were frequently shown eating or drinking (in 15.5% of the commercials in the sample), engaging in athletic activity (14.6%), visiting with friends (12.9%), performing personal care tasks (11.8%), or participating in family activities (10.6%). In only 6.5% of the sample commercials were children shown engaging in scholastic activities. Depictions varied by the product featured in the commercial, so that, for instance, in toy commercials children were shown playing over 28% of the time.

Finally, another genre in which the presence of young people in media content has been studied is in television news. Research suggests television news overrepresents crime committed by youth compared to its occurrence in crime statistics in the general population (Dorfman & Schiraldi, 2001). Critics have noted that this may influence the ways in which youth, in general, are perceived by members of other population segments and may contribute to a sense of distrust or fear.

Race and Ethnicity

A long-standing and unwavering conclusion based on decades of research is that there has been and continues to be a severe lack of representation of people of color on television (Comstock & Scharrer, 1999). In the historical literature, Head (1954) and Smythe (1954) conducted two of the first scientific analyses of content on television and determined that four out of five television characters were European Americans. The majority of the remaining characters were African Americans, and other racial and ethnic groups were virtually nonexistent. The most striking aspect of this early research is how little has changed on the television screen since the early 1950s. New seasons historically brought little alteration in television's demography, according to Greenberg and Collette's (1997) examination of over 1,700 new characters added to the broadcast network lineups from 1966 to 1992.

Research points consistently to a limited number of roles on television for African Americans, especially lead roles (Northcott, Seggar, & Hinton, 1975), and even fewer roles for other racial and ethnic minorities (Gebner et al., 1980; Gerbner & Gross, 1976; Greenberg, 1980a; Seggar & Wheeler, 1973). Asian Americans, Latinos, and Native Americans are especially underrepresented compared to population figures (Atkin, 1992). Native Americans and Asian Americans have typically constituted a mere 1% of the television character population (Steenland, 1990), whereas Latinos have been documented at 1.5% to 3% (Gerbner & Signorielli, 1979; Greenberg & Baptista-Fernandez, 1980). Mastro and Greenberg's (2000) recent analysis of 64 prime-time television programs from a 1-week sample from the fall 1996 lineup on ABC, CBS, NBC, and FOX showed more of the same pattern. Eighty percent of all main and minor characters were Caucasian or European American, 16% were African American, 3% Latino, 1% Asian American, and none were Native American. Variations occurred by program type: Over three fourths of all Latino roles were in crime dramas, whereas African American roles were split between sitcoms and crime dramas.

Not only are members of racial and ethnic minority groups not frequently seen on television, but when they do appear, they are often in unfavorable and unflattering stereotypes and roles. Depictions of Latinos in the media have advanced stereotypical characterizations as criminals, lovers, police officers, and being undereducated rather than holding other occupational roles or characteristics (Berg, 1990; Greenberg &

Baptista-Fernandez, 1980). Portrayals of African Americans, some argue, have gotten less unidimensional over time, beginning with similar stereotypes regarding crime and poverty in earlier programs but, with the success of sitcoms such as *The Cosby Show*, evolving toward more affluent and successful depictions (Atkin, 1992; Cummings, 1988). Although portrayals of Asian Americans are few and far between, stereotypes regarding roles as shopkeepers, martial arts experts, or "overachievers" nonetheless emerge in media depictions (Hamamoto, 1993).

In children's media, specifically, research regarding race is less prevalent but what exists supports the same major patterns. Greenberg and Brand (1993) taped a Saturday morning block of children's programming on ABC, CBS, and NBC, as well as a weekday morning block on PBS. They examined the 10-plus hours of programming and over 100 commercials that aired, looking at the ethnic and racial diversity of characters. On the commercial networks, out of 20 programs just three had regularly appearing characters from racial minority groups, only one featured a Latino character, and none had Asian American or Native American characters. Interestingly, all characters of color were male. There was substantially more racial diversity in the sample of commercials and PBS programs. Other studies have found that children's television programs contain few interracial interactions among characters, and African American characters are particularly infrequent in cartoons (Barcus, 1983; Williams & Condry, 1989). Geiogamah and Pavel (1993) traced the history of the limited appearances of Native American characters and themes in television history, and concluded that they are "fleeting, insubstantial, or infrequent," are fraught with stereotypes, and often employ non-Native actors in Native roles (p. 192). Finally, Dietz (1998) determined that most video game characters in a sample of 33 Nintendo and Sega Genesis games were Caucasian.

Many Latino children in the United States may also choose programs from Spanish-language television, in which networks such as Univision and Telemundo offer cartoons dubbed into Spanish, such as *Super Mario Brothers*, *Bugs Bunny*, and *Daffy Duck* (Subervi-Velez & Colsant, 1993). These networks also broadcast children's programs created in Mexico, such as *T.V.O.*, that feature musical numbers, games, and contests, as well as the occasional Spanish-language children's program made especially for U.S. child audiences, such as Univision's *Pepe Plata*. Subervi-Velez and Colsant (1993) pointed out that these programs provide more opportunities for Latino children to see Latino child and adult characters onscreen.

Disabilities

Research on people with disabilities on television is scant. Makas' (1981) content analysis of 168 hours of randomly selected network television programming in afternoon and prime-time slots from the 1980–1981 season found 40 instances of portrayals of people with disabilities. By the 1983 season, the number of such portrayals found in 90.5 hours of programming had risen to 71 (Turow & Coe, 1985).

Research finds that when characters with disabilities are present, the disability tends to be emphasized in the plot (Makas, 1981), thus sending the apparent message that the presence of a disability completely consumes one's life. Television characters with disabilities are also more likely to be White, somewhat young, unmarried, and male compared to other television characters, in both U.S. programs (Zola, 1985) and U.K. programs (Cumberbatch & Negrine, 1992). Disabilities that involve communication processes are rare, whereas those that involve motor skills and disfigurement are overrepresented compared to their occurrence in the general population (Cumberbatch & Negrine, 1992), the former presumably due to the difficulty of acting with communicative disabilities and the latter for their dramatic effect. Finally, a number of stereotypes exist in media portrayals of the disabled, including the sinister or evil character, the "dependent or pathetic" character, and the "courageous and inspirational" character (Cumberbatch & Negrine, 1992; Makas, 1981). Although other television programs have been applauded for their inclusion of well-rounded characters with disabilities (e.g., "Corky" on *Life Goes On*, "Benny" on *LA Law*, Dr. Carrie Weaver on *ER*), PBS' *Sesame Street* is perhaps most frequently praised for its quantity and quality of depictions of people with disabilities (Makas, 1993).

Sexual Orientation and Relationships

The overwhelming majority of relationships presented on television are heterosexual, thus positioning heterosexuality as the norm and homosexuality, at best, at the margins. Kielwasser and Wolf (1992) determined that recurring adolescent characters on network television are "always heterosexual and the adolescent audience is addressed as if it were composed exclusively of heterosexual viewers" (p. 350). Despite some noteworthy changes in the decade since this analysis, television programs with younger characters designed to attract younger audience members contain very few examples of gay, lesbian, or bisexual characters.

In general, media messages that imply by the sheer absence of alternatives that being gay or lesbian is "abnormal," when considered in conjunction with other messages from one's family and other social environments, can contribute to gay, lesbian, and bisexual teenagers engaging in many "at-risk" behaviors (Nichols, 1999). Conversely, and importantly, research has also determined that when homosexual characters are present on television, gay, lesbian, and bisexual viewers gain a sense of support. For instance, interviews with gay men in Western Australia have revealed that images of gay men on television were important in raising their self-esteem and helping to shape their identities (McKee, 2000). Such representations may also be instructive for heterosexual audience members. Newman (1989), for example, determined that exposure to media depictions of same-sex relationships, in addition to other factors such as gender role attitudes and parental attitudes, were found to predict research subjects' attitudes toward lesbians.

Over the years, there have been a limited number of examples of portrayals of gay or lesbian television characters, and they have met with varying responses from segments of the audience as well as the television industry. The depiction of same-sex relationships on television became headline news when the character played by Ellen DeGeneres on the ABC sitcom *Ellen* came out in the 1997 season to an audience of 42 million (Justin, 1999), thereby making her the first openly gay lead character in prime-time television ("ABC Cancels," 1998). Prominent conservative clergymen loudly criticized the program, and major advertisers (including JC Penney and Chrysler) pulled their ads (Hubert, 1999). The show was canceled 1 year later after ratings dropped. More recently, the critically acclaimed program *Will & Grace* has consistently received high audience ratings. The program features a gay man as a lead character (Will, played by Eric McCormack) and another as a supporting character, and has progressed from rare depictions of Will's love life to more recent inclusion of his dating experiences (Justin, 1999). In the 1999–2000 television season, according to the Gay and Lesbian Alliance Against Defamation (GLAAD), there were 27 gay characters, comprising 2% of all television characters. The figure shows considerable growth compared to past seasons but still falls short of the estimate of the gay and lesbian presence in the general population, 10% (Justin, 1999). Finally, GLAAD points to the need for more and more well-rounded representations of same-sex relationships in the media, including more lesbians, fewer jokes about sexual orientation made on sitcoms, and more examples of adolescent gays and lesbians that can provide crucial role models for young audience members (Justin, 1999).

Icons

Finally, we turn to a category of people who star in the media content favored by young people, entertainment and sports icons. Children and teenagers have unique relationships with media celebrities in that they may look up to these figures and have a higher likelihood of viewing them as models for behavior or guides for possible future successes than do adults. In fact, in a survey of 137 African American youth, Austin and Freeman (1997) found that perceptions of the attractiveness of media depictions led to an increased identification with and imitation of celebrities. The youth in the sample reported being influenced by celebrities they viewed in the media on such topics as their social attitudes and goals.

Surprisingly, although the Amateur Athletic Foundation of Los Angeles (1999) determined that one in every three children and teenagers from 8 to 17 years of age uses some sports media each day, research on youth, sports, and media is scant. In the data collected from a very large, randomly selected national sample by Roberts and colleagues (Roberts, Foehr, et al., 1999), sports media exposure was substantial among older and modest among younger children and varied significantly by gender. Respondents were asked to cite the types of programs they had seen on television the previous day. Of the 2- to 7-year-olds in the sample, 6% of boys and 2% of girls listed sports media as being among the previous day's viewing. Of the 8- to 18-year-olds, 27% of boys and 7% of girls reported such exposure.

Media practices and routines lead to the creation (and the occasional destruction) of sports icons. Lines (2000) observed that it is common practice for the media to focus on particular individuals in sports, advancing them as "stars"; additionally, talk shows, news coverage, and other nongame-based sports media content often position these stars as either "ideal role models" or "questionable idols" for young people. Lines collected quantitative and qualitative data from 25 young people in the United Kingdom, asking them to report on their experiences with specified sports media. Most individuals reported attachment to either teams or players and admitted to emulating specific elements of sports stars' performances, personalities, and lifestyles. However, the sample of British youth also described a rather discerning attitude toward sports stars that suggests the notion of complete and utter idolatry is not an accurate description of young people's views of such stars. Lines explained, "They saw sports stars as real people, rarely placed on a pedestal of perfection. They did not ... idolize sports stars to the extent that they could not detect flaws in their character or behavior" (p. 677).

Advertisers are well aware of the esteem in which young people hold certain celebrities. They have used such figures to endorse their products to young audiences since broadcasting began on radio (Scharrer, in press), and continue to do so through contemporary television commercials (Adler et al., 1980; Ross et al., 1984). Sports and entertainment figures from Michael Jordan to Britney Spears and from Bart Simpson to Fred Flintstone have been used effectively by advertisers to peddle products to children and teens. The use of such icons as endorsers triggers a sense of relevance to young people in the audience, creates an instant recognition that is attention getting, and can result in the transference of positive feelings about the celebrity to positive feelings about the product. Lines (2000) underscored the ability of sports-related events in general to draw an audience of adolescents as consumers, noting "the images of media sport with its glamour, show-biz appeal and proliferation of stars provide an obvious market for such marketing" (p. 670).

BEHAVIOR

Not only are the characteristics of the people who populate media content important to viewers, but so are their actions. The behavior of media characters demonstrates norms and repercussions for the defiance of norms in social relationships. Observations of the actions of media characters are related to one's own life and considered when making decisions about one's own behavior (Bandura, 1986; Comstock, 1991; Comstock & Scharrer, 1999). Children and young audience members are especially likely to learn from the behavior of media characters in light of the fact that they are engaging in a developmental process in which they "try on" specific thoughts, attitudes, values, and behavior themselves to determine which work in which situations (Comstock, 1993). Next, we review the existing literature regarding the behavior of characters introduced to audiences via televisual media, paying particular attention to patterns in the major types of behavior that emerge from analysis, including violence, prosocial behaviors, consumption, interactions among family members, and sexually intimate behaviors.

Violence

Children are exposed to staggering amounts of violence on television. By the time a child in the United States finishes elementary school, she or he will have witnessed over 8,000 murders and 100,000 other acts of violence on television (Huston et al., 1992). These numbers grow considerably in the presence of VCRs and cable television in the home (Bushman & Huesmann, 2001). Times during which children are often present in the audience, including Saturday mornings, weekday late afternoons, and early evenings, are when television is at its most violent (Comstock, 1991; Hamilton, 1998).

Violence has been the most thoroughly examined aspect of television entertainment. This is largely due to persisting concerns over its effects, especially for children and teenagers who are sometimes perceived as being more susceptible to the influence of media exposure on the learning of aggression, desensitization, and fear or pessimism about violence in society (National Television Violence Study, 1998). From the decades of content analysis research examining media violence, we extract a select number of key efforts to document the presence and types of violent and antisocial messages, and give particular attention to content marketed to young audiences.

Gerbner and colleagues were in the vanguard in the analysis of violent media content, contributing regular "violence profile" tallies over the past 30 years, allowing for a rare longitudinal perspective (Gerbner, Morgan, & Signorielli, 1994). They have examined television violence, defined as "the overt expression of physical force against self or other, compelling action against one's will on pain of being hurt of killed, or actually hurting or killing" (Signorielli, Gerbner, & Morgan, 1995, p. 280) in prime-time and weekend entertainment, beginning with the 1967–68 season. The data of Gerbner and colleagues reveal a persisting pattern: Children's programming, as measured by rate of violent acts per hour, invariably has been much more violent than general audience prime-time programming. Saturday morning children's programming, dominated by cartoons, has been found to contain between 17.9 and 32 acts of violence per hour and involve 8 out of 10 characters in violence. Child characters are more often victims rather than perpetrators, with 13 to 16 child victims for every 10 child perpetrators (Gerbner et al., 1994).

The Gerbner data also determine that the rate of violence on television has been quite stable in the long term. Sporadic peaks and valleys in amount of violence on television occur from season to season, explained in part by fluctuations in public and political concern or changing popularity of a violence-saturated genre, but the pattern over decades is one of relative stability. Recent years have represented a "valley," a slight decrease in numbers of violent acts, presumably due to the political pressure put on the industry to curb violent content. The same pressure contributed to the passing of the Telecommunications Act of 1996, mandating the inclusion of a V-chip in new television sets that would read labels reporting violent and sexual content that also appear in the corner of the screen (Comstock & Scharrer, 1999). However, the longitudinal data suggest such "valleys" are typically short-lived.

Analyses by Greenberg (1980b) and Potter and Vaughan (1997) spanned almost 2 decades, used the same methods, and tabulated verbal as well as physical aggression and pro- as well as antisocial behavior. These two studies further supported the stable presence of violence on television. Furthermore, these analyses revealed that the inclusion of verbal aggression, defined as diminishing or hurtful statements, in the study of television content consistently more than doubles the rate of instances of violence. When physical and verbal aggression are used as measures, the amount of violence in most types of general audience programs is quite similar, including situation comedies. Because sitcoms become favorites of older children, these data further the argument that television content popular with children of all ages is fraught with violence and aggression.

Recent data were gathered in the late 1990s to study violence in cable and broadcast entertainment programming via the National Television Violence Study, led by a team of researchers from the University of California at Santa Barbara (National Television Violence Study, 1996, 1997,1998). The definition of violence employed was "any overt depiction of a credible threat of physical force or the actual use of such force intended to physically harm an animated being or group of beings" (National Television Violence Study, 1998, p. 20). The researchers recorded over 10,000 hours of programming and examined the frequency of violent incidents (including a perpetrator, act, and target) per scene (connected incidents) and per program, and applied the social scientific research concerning the effects of viewing violence to determine which characteristics of violent depictions to record. This latter strategy allowed the researchers to develop a list of ways in which violence can be depicted that make it more likely for viewers to learn aggression, become desensitized, or turn fearful or pessimistic about society.

Results found that cable, particularly the movie channels, is a source of greater violent programming than is broadcast. Cartoons were once again identified for their frequency of violent acts. Television content contains substantial portrayals of violence in ways that might encourage negative outcomes—with infrequent and unrealistic consequences, justification for violence and/or the presence of appealing rewards, appealing characters (e.g., "good guys") as perpetrators, humor that makes light of violence, and the exciting display of weapons that could be perceived as tantalizing. Furthermore, despite occurring in a period of heightened public and political scrutiny of violence in the entertainment industry, there were no significant changes in the portrayal of violence on television over the 3 years of the study. Overall, in the sample in the third year of analysis, 61% of all programs contained violence and only 3% had an antiviolence theme. In children's television specifically, long-term negative consequences were more rare, violence was combined with humor more often, and unrealistically low levels of harm were portrayed more frequently compared to portrayals in other genres (National Television Violence Study, 1998). Similarly, Potts and Henderson (1991) discovered in a sample of 57 children's television programs that 15.2 injuries occurred per hour, with about half caused by direct assaults from other characters and 76% involving impact, often either with objects or other characters.

Violence is also a pervasive theme in video games. Funk's (1993) survey of 357 seventh and eighth graders found fantasy violence games listed as the most favored type (32% of the sample), with human violence games listed as the favorite of 17% of the sample. A later survey of 900 children in fourth through ninth grade, undertaken by Buchman and Funk (1996), found that 50% of the young respondents listed fantasy violence games as their favorite, with boys more likely than girls to choose human violence games as favorites. Dietz (1998) performed a content analysis of popular Nintendo and Sega Genesis video games and discerned that 80% have violence or aggression as a central theme. Furthermore, the nature of video game violence has changed over time, becoming increasingly realistic, graphic, and featuring human rather than inanimate characters (Provenzo, 1991; Subrahmanyam, Kraut, Greenfield, & Gross, 2001).

Other studies have examined the link between children's programming and the advertising and marketing of toys and other products. Eaton and Dominick (1991) sampled 16 hours of network and syndicated children's cartoons and noted that those cartoons with a toy merchandising link—defined according to expenditures on advertising of toys and retail sales of toys—were more likely to contain violence (including shootings, verbal aggression, and assault) than were those without such a link. Larson (2001) analyzed a sample of 595 commercials in programming that appealed directly to children, and concluded that violence and aggression occurred in considerable amounts. Anderson (1997) studied the presence of violence in commercials that aired during "family friendly" programming, the 1996 Major League Baseball playoffs. He determined that during 15 televised games, 6.8% or 104 of 1,528 commercials that aired contained violence, 69 had a violent act, 90 a violent threat, and 27 a violent outcome. Promotional messages for other television programs and movie trailers comprised the vast majority of these commercials. The year 2000 also saw harsh criticism of the media industry for marketing violent entertainment content to children after the release of the findings of a Federal Trade Commission study in which evidence of such marketing was found in the movie, music, and electronic game industries (Federal Trade Commission, 2000).

Prosocial

Television, especially children's television, mainly deals with morality in absolute, black-and-white terms. Thus, not surprisingly, in addition to antisocial messages, prosocial messages also appear fairly frequently on screen. Such themes range from examples of how to solve problems effectively to how to share and how to be responsible to how to care for the environment and how to be helpful to others to how to celebrate cultural difference, and so on. In short, prosocial content is about contributing positively to the social world.

Substantial quantities of verbal and physical prosocial behavior have consistently been recorded in television programming, although at a somewhat lower rate than (Potter & Ware, 1987) and often in conjunction with antisocial behavior (Greenberg, Atkin, Edison, & Korzenny, 1980; Liss & Reinhardt, 1980). Potter and Ware (1987), in a 1985 prime-time sample of ABC, CBS, and NBC programs, analyzed both antisocial and prosocial acts and found that females appeared somewhat more often as perpetrators and as receivers of prosocial rather than antisocial acts. Mares and Woodard (2001) argued that the positioning of prosocial strategies used in response to antisocial plot elements, common in adult and children's programs alike, is counterproductive, with the possible effect of reinforcing aggression as a acceptable and normative means to solve problems.

Other researchers have examined prosocial content in children's programming specifically. Woodard (1999), in a composite-week sample of children's programming in a large market in the 1998–99 season, noted that half of all such shows contained at least one "social lesson," although most occurred in programming for preschool children rather than older children. Seventy-two percent of PBS programs contained a social message, compared to 59% on Disney or HBO. Analysis that is not restricted to educationally defined children's programming shows lower levels of prosocial content. Mares and Woodard (2001), for instance, reported that of the top 20 programs viewed by children aged 2 to 17, only 4 contained prosocial lessons (*Disney's One Saturday Morning, 7th Heaven, Boy Meets World,* and *Hey Arnold!*). Therefore, there are a limited number of prosocial messages in programs for all but the very youngest of television audiences.

An early meta-analysis (Hearold, 1986) summarized existing studies on the effects associated with the viewing of prosocial television, using a rather broad definition that included such outcomes as effects of television on imagination, on purchasing books or using the library, and on information regarding safety. This meta-analysis discerned that positive effects of viewing were stronger and lasted longer than negative effects of viewing. A more recent meta-analysis (Mares & Woodard, in press) updated this research, employing a stricter definition in which prosocial outcomes were defined as encompassing "friendly interaction, aggression reduction, altruism, and stereotype reduction" (Mares & Woodard, 2001, p. 185) and assessing 34 studies using over 5,000 children as subjects. The Mares and Woodard meta-analysis found a weak to moderate effect of the viewing of such content on children, with altruistic depictions having the strongest effects.

Home education computer games are gaining popularity in the modern media environment and may modestly expand children's opportunities to encounter prosocial content. Unlike console-based video games like Nintendo or Sega Genesis that are frequent sources of violent content (see earlier discussion), games that are played on the computers of young people are often educational in nature (Roberts, Foehr, et al., 1999). Children's games played on the computer often feature such tasks as matching, identifying patterns, and helping characters solve problems. However, as in television content, this type of educational and/or prosocial content in computer games is typically available for and popular with only very young audiences, such as preschoolers and elementary school children (Subrahmanyam et al., 2001).

Consumption

Critics have long been concerned about the messages sent to children via television programs and advertising regarding consumption, ranging from the consumption of foods to alcoholic beverages and cigarettes to any and all consumer products. Such media depictions have the potential to effect important consequences on young audience members' health and well being. Research attention in this area has centered around three topics: the nutritional qualities of foods in commercials directed toward children, messages containing appealing portrayals of the consumption of alcohol or cigarettes, and the emphasis in media messages on the acquisition of possessions.

Food products are commonly marketed to children on television, and commercials have been found to both contain little accurate information about nutritional quality and include a multitude of largely nonnutrient-rich items. Between half and two thirds of all commercials aired during children's television are for food-related products in both the United States (Kotz & Story, 1994; Taras & Gage, 1995) and the United Kingdom (Lewis & Hill, 1998; National Food Alliance, 1995). Breakfast cereals and confectionery products or snacks are the most common types of foods advertised, and studies have shown the vast majority (between 80% and 100%) of these commercials tend to be for foods high in fat, sugar, or salt (Lewis & Hill, 1998).

In an analysis of over 800 commercials airing during 91 hours of children's television in the United Kingdom, Lewis and Hill (1998) determined that food product commercials also used many form features designed to appeal to young audiences, including animation, stories, humor, and the modeling of fun and happy mood states. Hill and Radimer (1997) analyzed 239 food commercials that aired during 27 hours of children's programming in Australia. They noted that the most common food categories in the commercials were fast food (25%), and chocolate (22%). Only 8% of the commercials featured fruit, 1% promoted vegetables, and none were for meat.

Story and Faulkner (1990) analyzed program (11 top-rated sitcoms and dramas of 1988) and commercial content in the United States during prime time for messages related to food and eating. In prime-time programs, references to food occurred nearly five times per half-hour of programming, and 60% of all references were for low-nutrient beverages (e.g., coffee, alcohol, and soft drinks) or sweets. Healthy foods were scarcely seen, with fruits and vegetables eaten as snacks in between meals less than 10% of the time and shown as part of a meal only three to four times in the sample. Of the 261 commercials analyzed, 35% were for food, with fast-food restaurants being the most frequent type. Only three commercials advertised fruits; none advertised vegetables. Finally, Byrd-Bredbenner and Grasso (2000) conducted a content analysis of 700 commercials shown during 17.5 hours of prime-time programs that, according to Nielsen data, were heavily viewed by 2- to 11-year-olds. Information about the nutrition of food and beverages was found to be rare, and when it was included, the researchers determined it was misleading or inaccurate nearly half of the time. Instead, most commercials emphasized the taste of food products over their nutritional value.

Researchers have also examined the presence of messages about alcoholic beverages and cigarette smoking in media to which children are exposed, due to their potential effect on children's attitudes and behavior. Research estimates show that children are exposed to 1,000 to 2,000 beer and wine commercials on prime-time television per year (Strasburger, 1997). Commercials for alcohol often employ techniques that are effective in appealing to young people, including celebrity endorsers, contemporary and popular music, attractive young models, humor, and animated or live-action "mascots" such as frogs, dogs, and lizards (Strasburger, 2001). Story and Faulkner (1990) noted that just over one in four beverages consumed on prime-time television were alcoholic beverages, and one third of all meal depictions were accompanied by alcohol. Six instances of drinking occurred per hour in prime-time television in 1991, compared with ten per hour in 1984 and five per hour in 1976, and alcohol portrayals were often described as "glamorous" (Grube, 1993). One drinking scene occurs every 22 minutes (and one smoking scene every 57 minutes) on American television programming in general, with MTV containing such a message every 14 minutes and prime-time television every 27 minutes (Gerbner & Ozyegin, 1997). Sports programming contains over twice as many commercials for alcoholic beverages as does prime-time programming (Grube, 1995; Madden & Grube, 1994).

In a study of prime-time programming in the fall of 1992, Hazan and Glantz (1995) found that about one fourth (24%) of all programs contained scenes in which characters were smoking, and only 8% of those included an antismoking message. On MTV, DuRant and colleagues (DuRant et al., 1997) determined that one fourth of all videos contained instances of tobacco use. Gerbner and Ozyegin (1997) ascertained that depictions of young and middle-aged female smokers are on the rise, and promotional messages for upcoming movies are frequent sources of appealing smoking portrayals. Finally, in movies (perennial favorites for teens), studies have found that smoking occurs at a rate that is up to three times greater than that found in the general population (Hazan, Lipton, & Glantz, 1994), and is present in almost 90% of popular movie rentals from 1996 and 1997 (Roberts, Henriksen, & Christenson, 1999).

Finally, many critics have lamented the pervasive consumerism that is directed toward children in a modern, media-saturated world. Not only do characters consume food and beverages on television, but they also consume a multitude of other commercial goods at a steady pace. Such emphasis on consumerism led Cheung and Chan (1996) to conclude that the most pervasive message on television is consumerism, apparent in the central place afforded to expensive goods including cars, homes, clothes, and equipment for sports or hobbies.

Indeed, commercial messages are relentless and inescapable in modern society. Not only are commercial messages in the mass media, they are also on toys, backpacks, clothing, billboards, transit stops, and in ballparks as well as in schools. A full 40% of U.S. teenagers in middle and high schools see commercial messages during the school day via Channel One, featuring 10 minutes of news and 2 minutes of commercials (Coeyman, 1995). Furthermore, Richards, Wartella, Morton, and Thompson (1998) discovered that commercial messages are also present in school gyms, on school buses, on school athletic uniforms, and in school cafeterias and food and soft-drink vending machines. What emerges is an unmistakable picture of a consumer culture in which—for all audiences, young and old—the acquisition of goods is a central value.

Families

Interactions between family members and implicit messages about what constitutes "family" is also a major theme in media programming popular with children and teenagers (Weiss & Wilson, 1996). Since television programming began, situation comedies, soap operas, dramas, and some cartoons have often centered around a domestic unit, ranging from "traditional" definitions of family to variations on the theme. In fact, over 200 fictional families had been introduced to viewers via "family series" on television between the late 1940s and early 1980s (Glennon & Butsch, 1982).

The structure of families on television has undergone some changes over time. In the 1970s, families on television were approximately equally split among married couples with and without children, single parents, and other combinations of relatives; divorce caught up to the death of a spouse as a reason for single parenthood; and relatives outside of the nuclear family were infrequently seen (Greenberg, Buerkel-Rothfuss, Neuendorf, & Atkin, 1980). In the early 1980s, a shift back toward a "conventional" family configuration was noted, with over two thirds of all prime-time families from 1979 to 1985 consisting of couples with or without children (Skill, Robinson, & Wallace, 1987). A longitudinal content analysis determined that 63% of all long-lasting family television series from 1947 to 1990 featured a "conventional" family, 29% single-parent families (17% headed by males, 12% by females), 12% working class, 6% African American, and in 17% there was a female employed outside the home (Moore, 1992). Over the 4 decades examined, Moore (1992) documented increasing portrayals of nonconventional families over time and an increase in female characters working outside the home, whereas the proportions of working-class and African American families remained remarkably consistent.

Other researchers have examined interactions between and among family members on the screen. Parent/child conflicts, adolescent foolishness or emotional tribulations (Cantor, 1990; Weiss & Wilson, 1996), sibling conflicts (Larson, 1991), and male/female conflicts (Rowe, 1995; Scharrer, 2001) are frequent sources of temporary tension on television programs. However, "affiliative" communication frequently prevails, and problems are solved quickly and completely, by talking it out, making compromises, and supporting one another (Cantor, 1990; Kubey & Donovan, 2001; Larson, 1989; Skill & Wallace, 1990). Olson and Douglas (1997) examined 10 popular domestic comedies for their gender role interactions and noted that more recent programs displayed more exhibits of dominance among characters and less family stability, although conflicts were still typically resolved. The overall conclusion on examining portrayals of families in television and televisual media over time is that although conflict is frequent and problems arise, the family, however one defines it, is clearly valued and even idealized (Comstock & Scharrer, 1999).

Sexual Intimacy

The depiction of sexual imagery and sexual intimacy in media consumed by children is a topic that triggers and fuels the concern of parents and caregivers. Although the favored programs of very young children—preschool educational programs and cartoons—are relatively devoid of explicit sexual messages, the sitcoms and other prime-time programs most popular with the vast majority of all children have an abundant number of sexual themes. Other sources of sexual messages in the media to which many children are exposed are video games and commercials.

Kunkel, Cope, and Colvin (1996) studied the sexual messages in a sample of 128 programs broadcast during the so-called "family hour," the first hour of prime time, (8:00 P.M.–9:00 P.M. for most of the United States). Sixty-one percent of such programs contained some form of sexual behavior (from passionate kisses to implied intercourse), 12% depicted or strongly implied sexual intercourse, and 59% featured talk about sex. Cope (1998) examined three episodes each of the favored programs of 12- to 17-year-olds, arriving on a sample of 95 shows. She found that 67% of programs contained talk about sex, 62% contained instances of sexual behavior (occurring at a rate of 2.2 per hour), and 13% depicted or strongly implied intercourse. A recent study (Kunkel, Cope-Farrar, Biely, Farinola, & Donnerstein, 2001) looked at sexual messages around the clock on television, using a series of composite-week samples encompassing over 900 programs aired between 7:00 A.M. and 11:00 P.M. on the four major broadcast networks, a WB affiliate, three basic cable stations (Lifetime, TNT and USA), PBS, and HBO. The researchers found that 4.1 scenes per hour and over two thirds (68%) of all programs contained sexual messages. The number of teenagers depicted in sexual situations increased between the 1997–98 season and the 1999–2000 season, from 3% to 5%. All of these studies discovered that talk about sex was more common than sexual behavior, and all determined that program elements emphasizing risks or responsibilities associated with sexual behavior were rare (6% of all programs in the Kunkel, Cope, & Colvin study, and 9% in the Cope study).

Existing research also extends this topic beyond general television programming to other media messages, including those found in commercials, movies, music television, and video games. Lin (1998) provided a rare study of sexual appeals in prime-time television commercials on ABC, CBS, and NBC, coding the 500-plus male and female models that appeared. Results showed that female models were more likely to be depicted in a state of undress and were more likely to be rated as physically attractive and sexy than were male models. Yet, in the sample overall, only about 8% of the models engaged in "sexually oriented conduct," about 3% demonstrated physical sexual innuendo, and less than 1% displayed verbal innuendo. Thus, sexuality was largely confined to appearances. In music television, research has determined that 60% of all videos in one sample (Baxter, De Reimer, Landini, Leslie, & Singletary, 1985) and 76% of concept videos (those that tell a story rather than featuring the band members performing the song) in another sample (Sherman & Dominick, 1986) contained sexual content. With the proliferation of cable and satellite subscriptions and the consistent popularity of movie rentals, children and teenagers are also sometimes able to view R-rated films (Donnerstein & Smith, 2001). Greenberg and colleagues (Greenberg et al., 1993) studied a sample of popular R-rated films and found, on average, 17.5 sexual acts and 9.8 scenes of nudity per film.

Finally, sexual content in media used by children also contains messages about gender. Commercials emphasize the sexuality of women (Lin, 1998). In music television, research has discerned that female characters engage in more implied sexual behavior and are the targets of more sexual overtures than male characters (Sommers-Flanagan, Sommers-Flanagan, & Davis, 1993). In video game content, Dietz's (1998) analysis of 33 Nintendo and Sega Genesis games determined that the overwhelming way in which female characters were presented was in a manner emphasizing their sexuality, with most having large breasts and thin bodies and being scantily clad. Dietz found over one fourth of the games in the sample (28%) depicted women as sex objects, and 21% contained violence directed at women. In short, depictions of sexual intimacy are common in media popular with children and teenagers, and advance potentially harmful representations of gender as well as a lack of information about consequences or context for sexual relationships.

OVERARCHING THEMES

The content of media to which children attend has been outlined in terms of programming, people, and behaviors. These three large categories encompass many of the patterns in media content that have been the subject of study in social scientific research as well as the topic of conversation and sometimes concern in the general public. Yet, the manner in which they have been outlined in this chapter, although necessary for systematic organization and discussion, mistakenly implies that the categories are discrete and mutually exclusive. To challenge this overly simplistic interpretation, we end with a discussion of the ways in which the topics described here can be extended into other areas and can be viewed as overlapping with one another, making connections between and among types of content. The result is the emergence of five overarching themes in content that are pervasive, complex, and multidimensional. They are the dominance of White males and those from the middle and upper class, the presence of risk and conflict, the depiction of problems with speedy and effective resolutions, the importance of the family, and the inclusion of behaviors and activities that pose a risk to health and well-being (Comstock & Scharrer, 1999).

Dominance of the White Male and Middle and Upper Classes

Across a wide sweep of television programming viewed by audiences young and old, White males appear in greater numbers and in a wider range of roles, most with higher status, compared to females or characters from racial minority groups. Likewise, in specific types of television programming popular with young audiences (e.g., cartoons, music television, and sitcoms), the White male dominates when measured both by quantity and quality of representations. The same pattern holds in the study of other televisual media content used regularly by young people, including commercials, video games, and movies viewed on VCR or DVD systems. Although some studies have documented sporadic and limited progress in the portrayal of women and people of color, depictions conveying inequality continue to be the norm in the aggregate.

In addition to privileging characters by gender and race or ethnicity, the media also tend to privilege characters according to social class. The occupations of the vast majority of television characters suggest a middle-class to upper-class existence, as seen in the prevalence of television doctors, lawyers, executives, and other professionals (Gerbner, Gross, Signorielli, & Morgan, 1986; Greenberg & Collette, 1997). In the domestic, family-oriented sitcom (a major staple in programming over time), the working-class family—especially the role of the sitcom father—is replete with "dysfunction," social and occupational failure, and other negative situations and outcomes (Scharrer, 2001). From commercials to sitcoms to dramas to movies, working-class characters are either absent or tend to be unfavorably portrayed.

Risk and Conflict

Television, in addition to other entertainment-based media, is essentially a storyteller (Gerbner et al., 1986), and the producers of television's stories use storytelling techniques that have been in place since ancient Greek plays were enacted on stage. At the heart of the classic storytelling tradition are the introduction of conflict and/or the dramatic portrayal of risks to one's physical or psychological well-being (Baldwin & Lewis, 1972; Comstock & Scharrer, 1999). Television sitcoms use this formula in introducing tense situations or verbal arguments among characters that create situations of misunderstandings, and sometimes biting exchanges that are often humorous to the audience. Television dramas may contain severe conflicts, including those that we labeled as "violence" earlier in this chapter, in depicting crime in our nation's cities, or less severe but still substantial conflicts in the trials of the modern family, the contemporary young adult, or the current employee. Television commercials also employ elements of conflict between competing products or brands as well as depictions of social and personal risks if one decides on the "wrong" product or brand.

Young people in the audience are well aware of the presence of conflict and risk as a major theme in the media. Potter (1988) found that middle and high school students listed conflict between good and evil as, by far, the most frequent television theme. This is most likely due to the examples of conflict and risk in general audience programming outlined previously, as well as the overwhelming tendency for children's media, specifically, to advance the theme. Cartoons are perhaps the most obvious example of the use of conflict between "good" and "evil" as a major storytelling mechanism, yet educational television for young people also introduces ways in which interpersonal conflicts can be resolved effectively. Video games and movies popular with young audiences also feature conflict in a central role.

Effectiveness of Remedies

Not only are conflicts and risks addressed frequently, they are also often resolved quickly and effectively in stories told in the media. Sitcoms are known for neatly tying up loose ends and solving all problems in 22 minutes (Larson, 1991). The serial nature of dramas suggests that with the exception of the occasional "to be continued" episode, even the more severe conflicts arising in these programs are typically resolved in one episode. In crime dramas, either fictional or reality based, police officers solve crimes at a miraculous rate of 70% to 90%, vastly outscoring the "clearance rate" of crime statistics in the real world (Dominick, 1973; Estep & MacDonald, 1983; Oliver, 1994). In medical series, illnesses are typically alleviated and treatment is largely effective (Turow, 1989). In commercials, problems are solved promptly and decisively by the product or service advertised (Comstock, Chaffee, Katzman, McCombs, & Roberts, 1978). In an analysis of over 200 subplots in prime-time fictional programs, Selnow (1986) discovered that approximately 95% introduced a problem and concluded with a resolution. Although audiences accustomed to the exaggerative qualities of entertainment media are likely to be skeptical of the realism of such speedy remedies, their pervasive presence is nonetheless striking.

In children's media, specifically, resolutions and remedies for conflicts and risks are also readily apparent. For example, the good versus evil narrative that characterizes cartoons ultimately results in the triumph of the forces of good as "bad guys" are dispatched by the heroes (Potter, 1988). The same narrative is apparent in video game content (Dietz, 1998); in this case, success in ridding the world of wrongdoers is dependent on the skill of the video game user. In movie content, the action adventure genre (a favorite among young people) frequently features the same plot formula, the sometimes protracted struggle between "good guys" and "bad guys," with the heroes winning in the end. Even in educational programming that delivers social and cultural messages, examples of peaceful conflict resolution abound. Thus, the presentation of problems or conflicts and the solution of those encounters constitute an underlying theme in televisual media content consumed by audiences of all ages.

Importance of Family

The structure of the family as presented on television has been defined in a variety of ways since as early as the 1950s (Skill & Robinson, 1994). Yet, regardless of how one defines it, the family is often idealized in televised depictions. The family is frequently at the center of many long-standing traditional genres in television content, including sitcoms, dramas, soap operas, and even talk shows. Commercials also frequently feature interactions among family members, most warm and loving in nature, from images of mothers caring for sick children to families visiting a fast-food restaurant to parents driving children to soccer practice in minivans. Educational programs with live-action (e.g., the adults on *Sesame Street*) or animated characters (e.g., *Arthur, Maurice Sendak's Little Bear*) also often demonstrate loving and supportive family environments, and cartoon families such as *The Jetsons* and *The Flintstones* have had a steady presence on children's programming schedules over time.

Traditionally, sitcom families have generally been presented quite favorably, with supportive parents, ultimately compliant children, and the fair and competent resolution of the temporary difficulties that arise (Skill & Wallace, 1990; Weiss &

Wilson, 1996). A slight increase in hostility among sitcom family members has been recorded in recent analyses (Douglas, 1996; Douglas & Olson, 1996). *The Simpsons, Malcolm in the Middle,* and *Everybody Loves Raymond* are good examples of sitcoms in which interactions are occasionally rather biting or somewhat rancorous in nature. Yet, even in these cases there is an underlying level of loyalty and mutual support in the family. Therefore, the overall message in televisual media content—across genres and in programming and advertising alike—is that family is important and should be valued.

Threats to Health

Finally, many of the themes in televisual media content, especially those attended to by children and teenagers, involve threats to health. For example, problematic behaviors abound on television, from heavy alcohol consumption to sexual behaviors shown without context or consequence to aggression and violence that is celebrated in plots and through exciting and appealing production techniques. Other problematic behaviors include the consumption of foods and beverages with little nutritional quality, and the advancement of an ultrathin body as a beauty ideal. Ironically, although we've dubbed this section "threats to health," the health risks that are associated with these behaviors are often absent or deemphasized in media depictions.

As described previously, alcohol consumption is often presented in a fun-loving manner in commercials, as a requisite activity at social gatherings, or as a way to handle problems in movies and television programs such as soap operas or dramas. Likewise, the failure to address risks of pregnancy or disease in sexual messages in the media, the sheer number of such messages in content targeted toward the young, and the advancement of rape myths (Brinson, 1992) and the acceptance of sexual aggression (Check & Malamuth, 1983) may also pose a threat to health. Regardless of whether it is presented with a sexual element, violence is alarmingly prevalent in children's televisual media and is often presented in a way that paints it in a positive light, thereby encouraging imitative behaviors or permissive or even calloused attitudes (National Television Violence Study, 1996, 1997, 1998). Commercials targeted to children as well as television programs in general contain many fun-loving and visually appealing messages peddling foods and beverages of limited nutritional quality. Consumption of such foods—including fast food, soft drinks, sugary cereals, and sweet or salty snacks—may also present a health threat. Finally, in televisual media content across the board—from commercials to television programs to movies and video games—there is also the pervasive advancement of Hollywood and Madison Avenue's narrow definition of beauty, an image that has grown thinner and thinner over time. The overwhelming presence of such a limited range of female body sizes and shapes in different types of televisual media can work together to threaten the health and well-being of girls and young women in the audience. These problematic behaviors combine to form our final underlying theme in the messages that children receive time and time again in their televisual environment. They are perhaps most striking in terms of the absence of accompanying messages that would convey their ability to become a threat to the physical health and psychological well-being of young people.

REFERENCES

ABC cancels gay sitcom "Ellen" after ratings fall. (1998, April 24). *Los Angeles Times,* p. A6.

Adler, R. P., Lesser, G. S., Meringoff, L. K., Robertson, T. S., Rossiter, J. R., & Ward, S. (1980). *The effect of television advertising on children: Review and recommendations.* Lexington, MA: Lexington Books.

Al-Deen, H. S. N. (Ed.). (1997). *Cross-cultural communication and aging in the United States.* Mahwah, NJ: Lawrence Erlbaum Associates.

Amateur Athletic Foundation of Los Angeles. (August, 1999). *Children and sports media.* Los Angeles: Amateur Athletic Foundation of Los Angeles. retrieved July 30, 2002, from www.aafla.org/9arr/ResearchReports/kidsTV2.pdf

Anderson, C. (1997). Violence in television commercials during nonviolent programming: The 1996 Major League Baseball playoffs. *Journal of the American Medical Association, 278*(13), 1045–1046.

Anderson, D. R., & Lorch, E. P. (1983). Looking at television: Action or reaction? In J. Bryant & D. Anderson (Eds.), *Children's understanding of television: Research on attention and comprehension* (pp. 1–34). New York: Academic Press.

Atkin, D. (1992). An analysis of television series with minority lead characters. *Critical Studies in Mass Communication, 9,* 337–349.

Austin, E. W., & Freeman, C. (1997). Effects of media, parents, and peers on African American adolescents' efficacy toward media and the future. *The Howard Journal of Communications, 8,* 275–290.

Baldwin, T. F., & Lewis, C. (1972). Violence on television: The industry looks at itself. In G. A. Comstock & E. A. Rubinstein (Eds.), *Television and social behavior, Media content and control* (Vol. 1, pp. 290–373). Washington, DC: U.S. Government Printing Office.

Bandura, A. (1986). *Social foundations of thought and action: A social cognitive theory.* Englewood Cliffs, NJ: Prentice-Hall.

Barcus, F. E. (1983). *Images of life on children's television.* New York: Praeger.

Barner, M. B. (1999). Sex-role stereotyping in FCC-mandated children's educational television. *Journal of Broadcasting & Electronic Media, 43*(4), 551–564.

Bartsch, R. A., Burnett, T., Diller, T. R., & Rankin-Williams, E. (2000). Gender representation in television commercials: Updating an update. *Sex Roles, 43*(9/10), 735–743.

Barwise, T. P., & Ehrenberg, A. S. C. (1988). *Television and its audience.* Newbury Park, CA: Sage.

Baxter, R. L., De Reimer, C., Landini, A., Leslie, L., & Singletary, M. W. (1985). A content analysis of music videos. *Journal of Broadcasting & Electronic Media, 29,* 333–340.

Berg, C. (1990). Stereotyping in films in general and of the Hispanic in particular. *The Howard Journal of Communications, 2,* 286–300.

Brinson, S. L. (1992). The use and opposition of rape myths in prime-time television dramas. *Sex Roles, 27*(7/8), 359–375.

Browne, B. A. (1998). Gender stereotypes in advertising on children's television in the 1990s: A cross-national analysis. *Journal of Advertising, 27*(1), 83–97.

Buchman, D. D., & Funk, J. B. (1996). Video and computer games in the '90s: Children's time commitment and game preference. *Children Today, 24*(1), 12–16.

Bushman, B. J., & Huesmann, L. R. (2001). Effects of televised violence on aggression. In D. G. Singer and J. L. Singer (Eds.), *Handbook of children and the media* (pp. 223–254). Thousand Oaks, CA: Sage.

Byrd-Bredbenner, C., & Grasso, D. (2000). What is television trying to make children swallow?: Content analysis of the nutrition information in prime-time advertisements. *Journal of Nutrition Education, 32*(4), 187–195.

Calvert, S. (1999). *Children's journeys through the information age.* Boston: McGraw-Hill College.

Calvert, S. L., Stolkin, A., & Lee, J. (1997, April). *Gender and ethnic portrayals in children's Saturday morning television programs.* Poster presented at the biennial meeting of the Society for Research in Child Development, Washington, D.C.

Cantor, M. G. (1990). Prime-time fathers: A study in continuity and change. *Critical Studies in Mass Communication, 7,* 275–285.

Check, J. V. P., & Malamuth, N. M. (1983). Sex-role stereotyping and reactions to depictions of stranger versus acquaintance rape. *Journal of Personality and Social Psychology, 45,* 344–356.

Cheung, C. K., & Chan, C. F. (1996). Television viewing and mean world value in Hong Kong adolescents. *Social Behavior and Personality, 24*(4), 351–364.

Children Now. (2001). *The local TV news media's depiction of children.* Oakland, CA: Children Now. Retrieved November 8, 2002, from www.childrennow.org/newsroom/news-01/pr-10-23-01.cfm

Coeyman, M. (1995, July 20). Follow the customer: New media ventures may help marketers target a market. *Restaurant Business,* p. 36.

Comstock, G. (1991). *Television and the American child.* San Diego: Academic Press.

Comstock, G. (1993). The medium and the society: The role of television in American life. In G. L. Berry & J. K. Asamen (Eds.), *Children and television: Images in a changing sociocultural world* (pp. 117–131). Newbury Park, CA: Sage.

Comstock, G., Chaffee, S., Katzman, N., McCombs, M., & Roberts, D. (1978). *Television and human behavior.* New York: Columbia University Press.

Comstock, G., & Scharrer, E. (1999). *Television: What's on, who's watching, and what it means.* San Diego: Academic Press.

Comstock, G., & Scharrer, E. (2001). Use of television and other film-related media. In D. G. Singer & J. L. Singer (Eds.), *Handbook of children and the media* (pp. 47–72). Thousand Oaks, CA: Sage.

Cope, K. M. (1998). *Sexually-related talk and behavior in the shows most frequently viewed by adolescents.* Unpublished master's thesis, University of California, Santa Barbara.

Craig, R. S. (1992). The effect of television day part on gender portrayals in television commercials: A content analysis. *Sex Roles, 26,* 197–211.

Cumberbatch, G., & Negrine, R. (1992). *Images of disability on television.* London: Routledge.

Cummings, M. (1988). The changing image of the Black family on television. *Journal of Popular Culture, 22,* 75–86.

Davis, D. M. (1990). Portrayals of women in prime time network television: Some demographic characteristics. *Sex Roles, 23,* 325–332.

Dietz, T. L. (1998). An examination of violence and gender role portrayals in video games: Implications for gender socialization and aggressive behavior. *Sex Roles, 38*(5/6), 425–442.

Dominick, J. R. (1973). Crime and law enforcement in the mass media. In C. Winick (Ed.), *Deviance and the mass media* (pp. 105–131). Beverly Hills, CA: Sage.

Donnerstein, E., & Smith, S. (2001). Sex in the media: Theory, influences, and solutions. In D. G. Singer & J. L. Singer (Eds.), *Handbook of children and the media* (pp. 289–307). Thousand Oaks, CA: Sage.

Dorfman, L., & Schiraldi, V. (2001). *Off balance: Youth, race and crime in the news.* Retrieved July 30, 2002, from www.buildingblocksforyouth.org

Douglas, W. (1996). The fall from grace? The modern family on television. *Communication Research, 23*(6), 675–702.

Douglas, W., & Olson, B. M. (1996). Subversion of the American family? An examination of children and parents in television families. *Communication Research, 23*(1), 73–99.

DuRant, R. H., Rome, E. S., Rich, M., Allred, E., Emans, S. J., & Woods, E. R. (1997). Tobacco and alcohol use behaviors portrayed in music videos: A content analysis. *American Journal of Public Health, 87,* 1131–1545.

Eaton, B. C., & Dominick, J. R. (1991). Product-related programming and children's TV: A content analysis. *Journalism Quarterly, 68*(1/2), 67–75.

Estep, R., & MacDonald, P. T. (1983). How prime-time crime evolved on TV, 1976–1981. *Journalism Quarterly, 60*(2), 293–300.

Federal Trade Commission. (2000, Sept. 13). *Marketing violent entertainment to children: A review of self-regulation and industry practices in the motion picture, music recording, and electronic game industries.* Prepared statement before the Committee on Commerce, Science, and Transportation, United States Senate. Downloaded July 30, 2002, from www.ftc.gov/os/2000/09/violencerpttest.htm

Fouts, G., & Burggraf, K. (1999). Television situation comedies: Female body images and verbal reinforcements. *Sex Roles, 40*(5/6), 473–481.

Funk, J. (1993). Reevaluating the impact of video games. *Clinical Pediatrics, 32*(1), 86–90.

Furnham, A., Abramsky, S., & Gunter, B. (1997). A cross-cultural content analysis of children's television advertisements. *Sex Roles, 37*(1/2), 91–99.

Furnham, A.; & Mak, T. (1999). Sex-role stereotyping in television commercials: A review and comparison of fourteen studies done on five continents over 25 years. *Sex Roles, 41*(5/6), 413–437.

Gailey, C. W. (1993). Mediated messages: Gender, class, and cosmos in home video games. *Journal of Popular Culture, 27*(1), 81–97.

Geiogamah, H., & Pavel, D. M. (1993). Developing television for American Indian and Alaska Native children in the late 20th century. In G. L. Berry & J. K. Asamen (Eds.), *Children and television: Images in a changing sociocultural world* (pp. 191–204). Newbury Park, CA: Sage.

Gerbner, G., & Gross, L. (1976). Living with television: The violence profile. *Journal of Communication, 26*, 171–180.

Gerbner, G., Gross, L., Morgan, M., & Signorielli, N. (1980). The "mainstreaming" of America. *Journal of Communication, 30*(3), 10–29.

Gerbner, G., Gross, L., Signorielli, N., & Morgan, M. (1986). *Television's mean world: Violence profile no. 14-15.* Unpublished manuscript, The Annenberg School of Communication, University of Pennsylvania, Philadelphia.

Gerbner, G., Morgan, M., & Signorielli, N. (1994). *Television violence profile no. 16.* Unpublished manuscript, The Annenberg School of Communication, University of Pennsylvania, Philadelphia.

Gerbner, G., & Ozyegin, N. (1997, March 20). *Alcohol, tobacco, and illicit drugs in entertainment television, commercials, news, "reality shows," movies, and music channels* (Report from the Robert Wood Johnson Foundation). Princeton, NJ: Robert Wood Johnson Foundation.

Gerbner, G., & Signorielli, N. (1979). *Women and minorities in television drama, 1969–1978.* Philadelphia: Annenberg School of Communication, University of Pennsylvania.

Glennon, L. M., & Butsch, R. (1982). The family as portrayed on television, 1946–1978. In D. Pearl (Ed.), *Television and behavior: Technical reviews (vol 2).* Washington, DC: U.S. Department of Health and Human Services.

Greenberg, B. S. (1980a). Three seasons of television characters: A demographic analysis. *Journal of Broadcasting, 24*, 49–60.

Greenberg, B. S. (1980b). *Life on television: Content analysis of U.S. TV drama.* Norwood, NJ: Ablex.

Greenberg, B. S., Atkin, C. K., Edison, N. G., & Korzenny, F. (1980). Antisocial and prosocial behaviors on television. In B. S. Greenberg, (Ed.), *Life on television: Content analysis of U.S. TV drama.* Norwood, NJ: Ablex.

Greenberg, B. S., & Baptista-Fernandez, P. (1980). Hispanic Americans: The new minority on television. In B.S. Greenberg (Ed.), *Life on television: Content analysis of U.S. TV drama* (pp. 3–12). Norwood, NJ: Ablex.

Greenberg, B. S., & Brand, J. (1994). Minorities and the mass media: 1970s to 1990s. In J. Bryant & D. Zillmann (Eds.), *Media effects: Advances in theory and research* (pp. 273–314). Mahwah, NJ: Lawrence Erlbaum Associates.

Greenberg, B. S., Buerkel-Rothfuss, N., Neuendorf, K., & Atkin, C. (1980). Three seasons of television family role interactions in commercial television. In B. S. Greenberg (Ed.), *Life on television: Content analysis of U.S. TV drama* (pp. 161–172). Norwood, NJ: Ablex.

Greenberg, B. S., & Collette, L. (1997). The changing faces on TV: A demographic analysis of network television's new seasons, 1966–1992. *Journal of Broadcasting & Electronic Media, 41*(1), 1–13.

Greenberg, B. S., Edison, N. G., Korzenny, F., Fernandez-Collado, C., & Atkin, C. K. (1980). Antisocial and prosocial behaviors on television. In B.S. Greenberg (Ed.), *Life on television: Content analysis of U.S. TV drama* (pp. 99–128). Norwood, NJ: Ablex.

Greenberg, B. S., Siemicki, M., Dorfman, S., Heeter, C., Stanley, C., Soderman, A., & Linsangan, R. (1993). Sex content in R-rated films viewed by adolescents. In B. S. Greenberg, J. D. Brown, & N. Buerkel-Rothfuss (Eds.), *Media, sex, and the adolescent* (pp. 29–44). Cresskill, NJ: Hampton Press.

Grube, J. W. (1993). Alcohol portrayals and alcohol advertising on television: Content and effects on children and adolescents. *Alcohol Health & Research World, 17*(1), 61–66.

Grube, J. W. (1995). Television alcohol portrayals, alcohol advertising, and alcohol expectances among children and adolescents. In S. E. Martin (Ed.), *The effects of the mass media on use and abuse of alcohol* (pp. 105–121). Bethesda, MD: National Institute on Alcohol Abuse and Alcoholism.

Hamamoto, D. Y. (1993). They're so cute when they're young: The Asian-American child on television. In G. L. Berry & J. K. Asamen (Eds.), *Children and television: Images in a changing sociocultural world* (pp. 205–214). Newbury Park, CA: Sage.

Hamilton, J. (1998). *Channeling violence: The economic market for violent television programming.* Princeton, NJ: Princeton University Press.

Harrison, K. (2000). The body electric: Thin-ideal media and eating disorders in adolescents. *Journal of Communication, 50*(3), 119–143.

Hazan, A. R., & Glantz, S. A. (1995). Current trends in tobacco use on prime-time fictional television. *American Journal of Public Health, 85,* 116–117.

Hazan, A. R., Lipton, H. L., & Glantz, S. A. (1994). Popular films do not reflect current tobacco use. *American Journal of Public Health, 84,* 998–1000.

Head, S. W. (1954). Content analysis of television drama programs. *Quarterly Journal of Film, Radio and Television, 9*(2), 175–194.

Hearold, S. (1986). A synthesis of 1043 effects of television on social behavior. In G. Comstock (Ed.), *Public communication and behavior* (vol. 1, pp. 65–133). New York: Academic Press.

Heintz, K. E., Delwiche, A., Lisosky, J., & Shively, A. (1996, May). *The reflection on the screen: Television's image of children.* Paper presented at the annual meeting of the International Communication Association, Chicago.

Herrett-Skjellum, J., & Allen, M. (1996). Television programming and sex stereotyping: A meta-analysis. *Communication Yearbook, 19,* 157–185.

Hill, J. M., & Radimer, K. L. (1997). A content analysis of food advertisements in television for Australian children. *Australian Journal of Nutrition and Dietetics, 54*(4), 174–181.

Hubert, S. J. (1999). What's wrong with this picture? The politics of Ellen's coming out party. *Journal of Popular Culture, 3,* 31–37.

Huston, A., Donnerstein, E., Fairchild, H., Feshbach, N. D., Katz, P. A., Murray, J. P., Rubinstein, E. A., Wilcox, B. L., & Zuckerman, D. (1992). *Big world, small screen: The role of television in American society.* Lincoln: University of Nebraska Press.

Huston, A., Wright, J. C., Rice, M. L., Kerkman, D., & St. Peters, M. (1990). Development of television viewing patterns in early childhood: A longitudinal investigation. *Developmental Psychology, 26*(3), 409–420.

Justin, N. (1999, Nov. 7). Gays of our lives. *Minneapolis Star Tribune,* p. 1F.

Kaufman, G. (1999). The portrayal of men's family roles in television commercials. *Sex Roles, 41*(5/6), 439–458.

Kielwasser, A. P., & Wolf, M. A. (1992). Mainstream television, adolescent homosexuality, and significant silence. *Critical Studies in Mass Communication, 9*(4), 350–374.

Kotz, K., & Story, M. (1994). Food advertisements during children's Saturday morning television programming: Are they consistent with dietary recommendations? *Journal of the American Dietary Association, 94,* 1296–1300.

Kovaric, P. M. (1993). Television, the portrayal of the elderly, and children's attitudes. In G. L. Berry & J. K. Asamen (Eds.), *Children and television: Images in a changing sociocultural world* (pp. 243–254). Newbury Park, CA: Sage.

Kubey, R., & Donovan, B. W. (2001). Media and the family. In D. G. Singer & J. L. Singer (Eds.), *Handbook of children and the media* (pp. 323–339). Thousand Oaks, CA: Sage.

Kunkel, D. (1998). Policy battles over defining children's educational television. *The Annals of the American Academy of Political and Social Science, 557,* 39–54.

Kunkel, D., & Canepa, J. (1994). Broadcasters' license renewal claims regarding children's educational programming. *Journal of Broadcasting & Electronic Media, 38,* 397–416.

Kunkel, D., Cope, K. M., & Colvin, C. (1996). *Sexual messages on family hour television: Content and context.* Menlo Park, CA: Kaiser Family Foundation.

Kunkel, D., Cope-Farrar, K. M., Biely, E., Farinola, W. J. M., & Donnerstein, E. (2001, May). *Sex on TV: Comparing content trends from 1997–98 to 1999–00.* Paper presented at the annual meeting of the International Communication Association, Washington, DC.

Kunkel, D., & Goette, U. (1997). Broadcasters' response to the Children's Television Act. *Communication Law and Policy, 2,* 289–308.

Larson, M. S. (1989). Interaction between siblings in primetime television families. *Journal of Broadcasting & Electronic Media, 33*(3), 305–315.

Larson, M. S. (1991). Sibling interactions in 1950s versus 1960s sitcoms: A comparison. *Journalism Quarterly, 68,* 381–387.

Larson, M. S. (2001). Interactions, activities and gender in children's television commercials: A content analysis. *Journal of Broadcasting & Electronic Media, 45*(1), 41–56.

Lauzen, M. M., & Dozier, D. M. (1999). Making a difference in prime time: Women on screen and behind the scenes in the 1995–96 television season. *Journal of Broadcasting & Electronic Media, 43*(1), 1–19.

Lewis, M. K., & Hill, A. J. (1998). Food advertising on British children's television: A content analysis and experimental study with nine-year-olds. *International Journal of Obesity, 22*, 206–214.

Lin, C. A. (1997). Beefcake versus cheesecake in the 1990s: Sexist portrayals of both genders in television commercials. *The Howard Journal of Communication, 8*(3), 237–249.

Lin, C. A. (1998). Uses of sex appeals in prime-time television commercials. *Sex Roles, 38*(5/6), 461–475.

Lines, G. (2000). Media sport audiences: Young people and the Summer of Sport '96: Revisiting frameworks for analysis. *Media, Culture & Society, 22*(5), 669–681.

Liss, M. B., & Reinhardt, L. C. (1980). Aggression on prosocial television programs. *Psychological Reports, 46*, 1065–1066.

Madden, P. A., & Grube, J. W. (1994). The frequency and nature of alcohol and tobacco advertising in televised sports, 1990 through 1992. *American Journal of Public Health, 84*, 297–299.

Makas, E. (1981). *Guess who's coming to prime time.* Unpublished manuscript.

Makas, E. (1993). Changing channels: The portrayal of people with disabilities on television. In G. L. Berry & J. K. Asamen (Eds.), *Children and television: Images in a changing sociocultural world* (pp. 255–268). Newbury Park, CA: Sage.

Mares, M. L., & Woodard, E. H. (2001). Prosocial effects on children's social interactions. In D. G. Singer & J. L. Singer (Eds.), *Handbook of children and the media* (pp. 183–205). Thousand Oaks, CA: Sage.

Mares, M. L., & Woodard, E. H. (in press). Positive effects of television on children's social interactions: A meta-analysis. In R. Carveth & J. Bryant (Eds.), *Meta-analyses of media effects* (pp. 00–00). Hillsdale, NJ: Lawrence Erlbaum Associates.

Mastro, D. E., & Greenberg, B. S. (2000). The portrayal of racial minorities on prime time television. *Journal of Broadcasting & Electronic Media, 44*(4), 690–703.

McArthur, L. Z., & Eisen, S. V. (1976). Television and sex-role stereotyping. *Journal of Applied Social Psychology, 6*, 329–351.

McKee, A. (2000). Images of gay men in the media and the development of self esteem. *Australian Journal of Communication, 27*(2), 81–98.

Mishkind, M. E., Rodin, J., Silberstein, L. R., & Striegel-Moore, R. H. (1986). The embodiment of masculinity. *American Behavioral Scientist, 29*, 545–562.

Moore, M. L. (1992). The family as portrayed on prime-time television, 1947–1990: Structure and characteristics. *Sex Roles, 26*, 41–60.

National Food Alliance. (1995). *Easy to swallow, hard to stomach.* London: Author.

National Television Violence Study. (1996). *National television violence study: Executive summary, 1994–1995.* Studio City, CA: Mediascope.

National Television Violence Study. (1997). *National television violence study* (vol. II). Santa Barbara, CA: Center for Communication and Social Policy, University of California.

National Television Violence Study. (1998). *National television violence study* (vol. III). Santa Barbara, CA: Center for Communication and Social Policy, University of California.

Newman, B. S. (1989). The relative importance of gender role attitudes to male and female attitudes toward lesbians. *Sex Roles, 21*(7/8), 451–466.

Nichols, S. L. (1999). Gay, lesbian, and bisexual youth: Understanding diversity and promoting tolerance in schools. *The Elementary School Journal, 99*(5), 505–524.

Northcott, H. C., Seggar, J. F., & Hinton, J. L. (1975). Trends in TV portrayal of Blacks and women. *Journalism Quarterly, 52*, 741–744.

Ogletree, S. M., Williams, S. W., Raffeld, P., Mason, B., & Fricke, K. (1990). Female attractiveness and eating disorders: Do children's television commercials play a role? *Sex Roles, 22*, 791–797.

Oldenburg, D. (1994, Nov. 24). The electronic gender gap. *The Washington Post*, p. D5.

Oliver, M. B. (1994). Portrayals of crime, race, and aggression in "reality-based" police shows: A content analysis. *Journal of Broadcasting & Electronic Media, 38*(2), 179–192.

Olson, B., & Douglas, W. (1997). The family on television: Evaluation of gender roles in situation comedy. *Sex Roles, 36*(5/6), 409–427.

Pecora, N. O. (1998). *The business of children's entertainment.* New York: Guilford.

Peterson, R. T. (1998). The portrayal of children's activities in television commercials: A content analysis. *Journal of Business Ethics, 17,* 1541–1549.

Potter, W. J. (1988). Three strategies for elaborating the cultivation hypothesis. *Journalism Quarterly, 65*(4), 930–939.

Potter, W. J., & Vaughan, M. (1997). Anti-social behavior in television entertainment: Trends and profiles. *Communication Research Reports, 14*(1), 116–124.

Potter, W. J., & Ware, W. (1987). Traits of perpetrators and receivers of antisocial and prosocial acts on television. *Journalism Quarterly, 21*(3), 382–391.

Potts, R., & Henderson, J. (1991). The dangerous world of television: A content analysis of physical injuries in children's television programming. *Children's Environments Quarterly, 8*(3/4), 7–14.

Provenzo, E. F., Jr. (1991). *Video kids: Making sense of Nintendo.* Cambridge, MA: Harvard University Press.

Rice, M. L., Huston, A. C., Truglio, R., & Wright, J. C. (1990). Words from "Sesame Street": Learning vocabulary while viewing. *Developmental Psychology, 26*(3), 421–428.

Richards, J. I., Wartella, E. A., Morton, C., & Thompson, L. (1998). The growing commercialization of schools: Issues and practices. *Annals of the American Academy of Political and Social Science, 557,* 148–163.

Roberts, D. F., Foehr, U. G., Rideout, V. J., & Brodie, M. (1999). *Kids and media at the new millennium* (Kaiser Family Foundation Report). Menlo Park, CA: Kaiser Family Foundation.

Roberts, D. F., Henriksen, L., & Christenson, P.G. (1999). *Substance use in popular movies and music.* Washington, DC: Office of National Drug Control Policy.

Ross, R. P., Campbell, T., Wright, J. C., Huston, A. C., Rice, M. L., & Turk, P. (1984). When celebrities talk, children listen: An experimental analysis of children's responses to TV ads with celebrity endorsement. *Journal of Applied Developmental Psychology, 5*(4), 185–202.

Rowe, K. (1995). *The unruly woman: Gender and the genres of laughter.* Austin: University of Texas Press.

Rubin, A. M. (1983). Television uses and gratifications: The interactions of viewing patterns and motivations. *Journal of Broadcasting, 27*(1), 37–51.

Rubin, A. M. (1984). Ritualized and instrumental television viewing. *Journal of Communication, 34*(3), 67–77.

Scharrer, E. (2001). From wise to foolish: The portrayal of the sitcom father, 1950s–1990s. *Journal of Broadcasting & Electronic Media, 45*(1), 23–40.

Scharrer, E. (in press). Children's programs. In C. Sterling (Ed.), *Encyclopedia of radio. Chicago:* Fitzroy Dearborn.

Schmitt, K. L., Anderson, D. R., & Collins, P. A. (1999). Form and content: Looking at the visual features of television. *Developmental Psychology, 35*(4), 1156–1167.

Seggar, J. F., & Wheeler, P. (1973). World of work on TV: Ethnic and sex representation in TV drama. *Journal of Broadcasting, 17,* 201–214.

Selnow, G. W. (1986). Solving problems on prime-time television. *Journal of Communication, 36*(2), 63–72.

Sherman, B. L., & Dominick, J. R. (1986). Violence and sex in music videos: TV and rock 'n' roll. *Journal of Communication, 36,* 79–93.

Signorielli, N. (1984). The demography of the television world. In G. Melischek, E. Rosengren, & J. Stappers (Eds.), *Cultural indicators: An international symposium* (pp. 137–157). Vienna, Austria: Osterreichischen Akademie der Wissenschaften.

Signorielli, N. (1985). *Role portrayal on television: An annotated bibliography of studies relating to women, minorities, aging, sexual behavior, health, and handicaps.* Westport, CT: Greenwood.

Signorielli, N. (1989). Television and conceptions about sex roles: Maintaining conventionality and the status quo. *Sex Roles, 21,* 341–360.

Signorielli, N. (1993). Television and adolescents' perceptions about work. *Youth & Society, 24,* 314–341.

Signorielli, N. (2001). Television's gender role images and contribution to stereotyping: Past, present, future. In D. G. Singer & J. L. Singer (Eds.), *Handbook of children and the media* (pp. 341–358). Thousand Oaks, CA: Sage.

Signorielli, N., & Bacue, A. (1999). Recognition and respect: A content analysis of prime-time television characters across three decades. *Sex Roles, 40*(7/8), 527–544.

Signorielli, N., Gerbner, G., & Morgan, M. (1995). Violence on television: The cultural indicators project. *Journal of Broadcasting & Electronic Media, 39*(2), 278–283.

Signorielli, N., McLeod, D., & Healy, E. (1994). Gender stereotypes in MTV commercials: The beat goes on. *Journal of Broadcasting & Electronic Media, 38*(1), 91–101.

Silverstein, B., Perdue, L., Peterson, B., & Kelly, L. (1986). The role of mass media in promoting a thin standard of bodily attractiveness for women. *Sex Roles, 14*, 519–532.

Skill, T., & Robinson, J. D. (1994). Four decades of families on television: A demographic profile, 1950–1989. *Journal of Broadcasting & Electronic Media, 38*(4), 449–464.

Skill, T., Robinson, J. D., & Wallace, S. P. (1987). Portrayal of families on prime-time TV: Structure, type and frequency. *Journalism Quarterly, 64*, 360–367, 398.

Skill, T., & Wallace, S. P. (1990). Family interactions on primetime television: A descriptive analysis of assertive power interactions. *Journal of Broadcasting & Electronic Media, 34*(3), 243–262.

Smith, L. (1994). A content analysis of gender differences in children's advertising. *Journal of Broadcasting & Electronic Media, 38*(3), 323–337.

Smythe, D. W. (1954). Reality as presented by television. *Public Opinion Quarterly, 18*(2), 143–156.

Sommers-Flanagan, R., Sommers-Flanagan, J., & Davis, B. (1993). What's happening on music television? A gender role content analysis. *Sex Roles, 28*, 745–753.

Steenland, S. (1990). *What's wrong with this picture: The status of women on screen and behind the scenes in entertainment TV*. Washington, DC: National Commission on Wider Opportunities for Women.

Story, M., & Faulkner, P. (1990). The prime time diet: A content analysis of eating behavior and food messages in television program content and commercials. *American Journal of Public Health, 80*(6), 738–740.

Strasburger, V. C. (1997). "Sex, drugs, rock 'n' roll": Are the media responsible for adolescent behavior? *Adolescent Medicine: State of the Art Reviews, 8*(3), 403–414.

Strasburger, V. C. (2001). Children, adolescents, drugs, and the media. In D. G. Singer & J. L. Singer (Eds.), *Handbook of children and the media* (pp. 415–446). Thousand Oaks, CA: Sage.

Subervi-Velez, F.A., & Colsant, S. (1993). The television worlds of Latino children. In G. L. Berry & J. K. Asamen (Eds.), *Children and television: Images in a changing sociocultural world* (pp. 215–228). Newbury Park, CA: Sage.

Subrahmanyam, K., Kraut, R., Greenfield, P., & Gross, E. (2001). New forms of electronic media: The impact of interactive games and the Internet on cognition, socialization, and behavior. In D. G. Singer & J. L. Singer (Eds.), *Handbook of children and the media* (pp. 73–99). Thousand Oaks, CA: Sage.

Taras, H. L., & Gage, M. (1995). Advertised foods on children's television. *Archives of Pediatric Adolescent Medicine, 149*, 649–652.

Thompson, T. L., & Zerbinos, E. (1997). Television cartoons: Do children notice it's a boy's world? *Sex Roles, 37*(5/6), 415–432.

Turow, J. (1989). *Playing doctor: Television, storytelling, and medical power*. New York: Oxford University Press.

Turow, J., & Coe, L. (1985). Curing television's ills: The portrayal of health care. *Journal of Communication, 35*(4), 36–51.

Vande Berg, L. R., & Streckfuss, D. (1992). Prime-time television's portrayal of women and the world of work: A demographic profile. *Journal of Broadcasting & Electronic Media, 36*(2), 195–208.

Weiss, A. J., & Wilson, B. J. (1996). Emotional portrayals in family television series that are popular among children. *Journal of Broadcasting & Electronic Media, 40*(1), 1–29.

Williams, M. E., & Condry, J. C. (1989, April). *Living color: Minority portrayals and cross-racial interactions on television*. Paper presented at the 1989 biennial meeting of the Society for Research in Child Development, Kansas City, MO.

Woodard, E. H. (1999). *The 1999 state of children's television report: Programming for children over broadcast and cable television* (Report No. 28). Philadelphia: University of Pennsylvania, Annenberg Public Policy Center.

Wright, J. C., & Huston, A. C. (1995). *Effects of educational TV viewing of lower income preschoolers on academic skills, school readiness, and school adjustment one to three years later* (Technical Report). Lawrence: University of Kansas.

Zill, N., Davies, E., & Daly, M. (1994). *Viewing of Sesame Street by preschool children in the United States and its relationship to school readiness* (Report prepared for the Children's Television Workshop). Rockville, MD: Westat, Inc.

Zola, I. K. (1985). Depictions of disability—metaphor, message, and medium in the media: A research and political agenda. *Social Science Journal, 22*(4), 5–17.

10

Effects of Entertainment Televisual Media on Children

J. Alison Bryant
University of Southern California

Jennings Bryant
University of Alabama

A detached observer would undoubtedly determine that the dominant function of modern televisual media is entertainment. "In fact, entertainment offerings obtrusively dominate media content and are bound to do so in the near future" (Zillmann & Vorderer, 2000, p. vii). Such content seems designed to exact chills and thrills, to elicit laughter and tears, and, in general, to provide a panoply of emotional experiences that serve as immediate gratification of the seemingly insatiable hedonic needs and wants of modern media consumers.

If entertainment is the goal of modern televisual fare, why are so many parents, teachers, and other critics concerned that children who consume such programming will suffer detrimental social and psychological effects? Indeed, if the real purpose of modern commercial fare were to create high levels of audience enjoyment, negative effects might not be such a major issue. However, in reality, if we focus on the dominant televisual medium—television—then creating a satisfying entertainment experience for audiences is barely a secondary goal of the executives in charge of this vast institution. The clearly dominant primary goal is to garner the attention of as many viewers as possible for television content that really matters—those increasingly omnipresent commercials. In other words, the primary objective of the commercial television system is profitability. Entertainment reactions are a functionally necessary by-product if one is to keep the eyes and ears of children on the TV set and guarantee ample advertising exposure for significant profitability. Entertainment really is the means to an end, not the goal.

Although the distinction between entertainment as a means rather than an end may be subtle, it is important nevertheless. If your primary goal is audience attention to commercial messages, entertainment programs become *vehicles* for advertising. Moreover, commercial potential is best served through audience maximization; that is, by attracting the largest possible audience of desirable young viewers. How much those droves of viewers really like what they are watching is of little importance, unless enjoyment affects processing of or responses to advertising messages.

The heavy reliance on Nielsen ratings and shares as the primary performance indicators of television is tangible evidence of the preeminence of this drive for potential exposure to advertising in commercial television (e.g., Beville, 1988; Webster, Phalen, & Lichty, 2000). Nielsen ratings are measures of *exposure* that are designed to serve the advertising industry; they are not in any real sense ratings of the entertainment value of programs. Over the years, calls have been issued for major overhauls to the existing system of audience assessment, and various consumer groups have asked the major audience assessment firms (e.g., Nielsen, Arbitron) and television's primary federal regulators (e.g., Federal Communications Commission, Federal Trade Commission) to incorporate some measures of the quality of the entertainment experience; but no matter how enthusiastic or well reasoned such calls have been, they have gone unheeded. This disregard for the quality of the entertainment experience provides yet another clear indication that the commercial media industries really care about potential exposure to advertising messages, not audience gratifications from entertainment.

The end result of this drive toward numbers is that media producers, distributors, and exhibitors consistently favor content that they believe will attract the largest possible audience (e.g., Brown, Steele, & Walsh-Childers, 2002; Goldstein, 1998; Gunter, 2002). This is the primary reason for media's overreliance on violence, sexual titillation and voyeurism, and other sensationalistic fare. Because such programming content is deemed necessary to attract a sufficiently large number of consumers to underwrite the costs of producing the programming—much less the costs of producing and placing the commercials, as well as making a profit—such controversial content saturates the contemporary television landscape. As Dorr (1986) commented about the nature of television programming children watch, "Some of it is decidedly aggressive, sexist, ageist, racist, consumption-oriented, sexy, inane, or moronic. Little of what children watch is truly uplifting, visionary, educational, or informative" (p. 82). Of course, not all televisual content that children watch is so negative or potentially detrimental. The Children's Television Act of 1990 and the Telecommunications Act of 1996 have ushered in some excellent curriculum-based children's programming, and some adult fare is also meritorious. The point is that the economic motive of the televisual industries, in combination with a hide-bound management tradition, yields a particular bias to programming traditions.

This hypercapitalistic programming context, which provides the intellectual infrastructure of most modern televisual media, is a primary reason why critics are perennially concerned about harmful side effects of watching television, playing video games, surfing the Internet, and the like. Other subsidiary reasons are introduced and discussed in this chapter in the discussion of various categories of media effects.

INTENTIONAL VERSUS UNINTENTIONAL EFFECTS

A slightly different perspective on the notion that undesirable media effects are by-products of reckless campaigns for large audiences is the classic notion of *intentional* versus *unintentional* media effects; that is, whether the effects were planned for or accidental. Although it is hard to say this without dripping irony, from the perspective of administrative research, "which yield[s] data to marketing or policy decision makers so that they can predict the impact of media campaigns" (Perse 2001, p. 14), only beneficial media effects are intentional. For example, actions such as presenting a highly successful flexible-thinking curriculum via *Blue's Clues*, facilitating 30 years of children's cognitive growth via *Sesame Street*, or sensitizing the audience to the need for regular breast examinations via *All in the Family* are intentional. All other sorts of effects tend to fall into the category of detrimental effects and are unintentional in the sense that they are the "innocent" by-products of creating programming that is alluring to those fickle audiences who so cherish heavy doses of gratuitous sex and violence.

DEVELOPMENTAL CONSIDERATIONS

Up to this point, everything we have said applies to adult audiences as well as it does to child consumers of electronic media. However, because of their developmental immaturity and resultant vulnerabilities, children are a special audience for television as well as special users of video games and the Internet. As Clifford, Gunter, and McAleer (1995) indicated: "Although children are known to be eager learners from any and all media, it is held that they lack the skills and abilities to 'read' the adult television messages being given out because of their limited knowledge of the physical and social world, and because of the presence of only embryonic learning and processing mechanisms" (p. viii).

In order to fully understand the issues of media effects on children, developmental characteristics must be considered. Fortunately, such differences have been delineated and examined in a number of places (e.g., Clifford et al., 1995; Dorr, 1986; Singer & Singer, 2001; Van Evra, 1998); therefore, we briefly focus on only one developmental issue that typically has been underrepresented in discussions of media effects on children: emotional development. We include this discussion not only because the area typically is given short shrift, but also because emotional reactions are an essential portion of media entertainment as well as of media effects. As Zillmann (2002) argued: "One of the foremost objectives of entertainment is to provide 'emotional roller-coaster rides,' and there can be little doubt that the entertainment media manage to manipulate and toy with our emotions, often creating affective intensities that rival and often equal those of distress during actual personal challenges or elation from meeting them successfully" (pp. 25–26).

According to Greenfield (2000), "Emotions are the building blocks of consciousness" (p. 21). Children are more "passive victims of their senses" (p. 52) than adults, and therefore they more readily tap into their emotions when watching televisual material. Because of a lack of previous experiences and limited cognitive schemata, children are not able to interpret present circumstances in a sophisticated manner, but instead rely on their senses in the here and now. They "feel" both positive and negative emotions more intensely than do adults, because they have fewer filters with which to dull them. Greenfield offered two examples of this type of unfiltered emotion. First, children laugh an average of 300 times a day, compared to an average adult's 50 times. Second, children are much more likely to be intensely fearful of a person under a white sheet, whom they perceive to be a "ghost," than are adults, who recognize this as an amusing child's interpretation of what a ghost would look like and "laugh it off." The point is, both positive and negative emotions are amplified in the mind of a child. Because children, especially young children, do not have the cognitive maturity necessary for evaluating television programming, video games, or Internet content on the basis of their social or intellectual merits, the children's enjoyment is based largely on their immediate, affective responses to what they are watching or playing.

Adults interpret what they watch on television or on other screens in complex ways due to their individualized reference frameworks, which are based on personal experiences, formal education, and, presumably, on a wide variety of socialization experiences. If they watch a violent police drama on television, they are able to derive the moral manifestation of the storyline of good versus evil, due to their experiences over many years in a society that is constantly playing out this narrative in homes, schools, churches, and workplaces. Younger children, on the other hand, do not have these complex frameworks on which to rely; instead, they comprehend the program by relying on more primitive, purely emotional and sensory mechanisms. This combination of enhanced emotional reactivity and limited experiential response repertoires creates a situation that virtually begs for detrimental media effects to occur.

To further complicate matters, it is what we see, experience, understand, and ultimately learn in early childhood that most deeply affects the worldview from which we begin to develop our more mature, adult reference framework (Greenfield, 2000). To dramatize the potential of different worldviews that have been developed to a large extent based on the emotion-biased reception processes of early childhood, imagine two children entering late childhood. Because of their different family lives and the different media content they have consumed, among other factors, one child has a worldview that other people are essentially good and can be trusted; the other has acquired a worldview that others are out to get you and are not to be trusted—a *weltanschauung* derived in part from an accumulation of life experience with people who have mistreated him or her, as well as from exposure to media content laden with sex, violence, injustice, insurrection, hostility, and the like. Assuming highly similar experiences throughout their late childhood years, the two children's interpretations of and responses to these later experiences undoubtedly will be vastly different because of the divergent emotional development of their formative years—unless, of course, some critical intervention or mediation processes occur. If we assume a cultivation perspective (e.g., Gerbner, Gross, Morgan, Signorielli, & Shanahan, 2002) on entertainment effects, and if we utilize cultivation terminology, we might hypothesize that one of our children would experience a "mean world," whereas the other would experience a kind one. Such are the potential long-term ramifications of these emotional experiences of early childhood.

EXPLICATING DEVELOPMENTAL CONSIDERATIONS IN MEDIA EFFECTS MODELS

If we examine a rudimentary model of media effects, the prominent and diverse roles and functions of developmental differences become apparent. An archetypal stimulus-organism-response (S-O-R) model of media effects can be derived from Van Evra's (1998) "summary chart of variables involved in children's television viewing experience" (p. xiv). In Van Evra's own words, "If we are to evaluate television's actual impact on development, then it is essential to study not only the types of content children are viewing, and the amount of viewing they do, but also differences in their developmental level and background variables to see how they influence the child's viewing experience and mitigate television's impact" (p. xiii). It should be noted that Van Evra was presenting a typology, not a media effects model; but the simple elegance of the schema makes it ideal for our purposes; therefore, we present the information as an informal, generic model of media effects.

Van Evra's (1998) model begins with *television input* and separates this content into programming categories (e.g., violent, prosocial) and by so-called formal features (e.g., pace, cuts). It would be equally feasible to differentiate between reality versus fantasy programming; in fact, such distinctions have been applied very productively over the years. The point is that the nature of the television (or video game, or Internet) content children consume is hypothesized to have significant effects on their development. Considerable research has supported such formulations (e.g., Bryant & Zillmann, 2002; Singer & Singer, 2001).

The second unit of Van Evra's (1998) model is labeled *mediating variables,* which include organismic variables (e.g., age, gender), ecological variables (e.g., viewing alone versus with parents), and functional variables (e.g., viewing for entertainment versus information). Utilizing such mediating variables, we can, for example, hypothesize that older, more intelligent children who watch television for educational purposes in the presence of interacting parents would undergo very different media effects than would younger, less intelligent children who watch television for entertainment and view alone. Substantial research has supported these and analogous hypotheses (e.g., Bryant & Bryant, 2001; Singer & Singer, 2001).

A third category of variables in Van Evra's (1998) model is called *viewing activity* and includes factors like amount of viewing, cognitive processing mechanisms, and

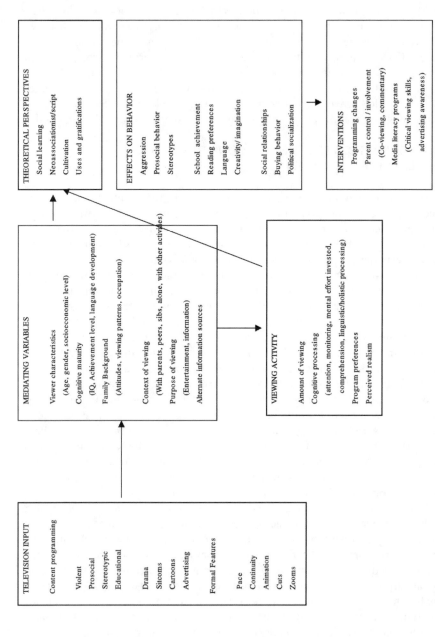

FIG. 10.1. Summary chart of variables involved in children's television viewing experience (from Van Evra, 1998, p. xiv).

the like. These variables have received considerable attention over the years (e.g., Bryant & Anderson, 1983; Bryant & Zillmann, 1991; Singer & Singer, 2001) and have been found to be critical determinants of media effects, especially for children.

The next entry in Van Evra's (1998) media uses and effects model is called *theoretical perspectives*. In a very short list (social learning, neo-associationist, cultivation, uses and gratifications), she indicated a few of many different theories of media effects that have been offered to explain how and why media effects occur. Numerous other theories could have been listed, offering quite different explanatory mechanisms (e.g., Bryant & Thompson, 2002; Perse, 2001). Obviously, if this were a formal theoretical model, mechanisms derived from one or more of these theories would be incorporated into the model as logical operators.

The section of the Van Evra's (1998) model labeled *effects on behavior* provides a sort of typology of media effects on children based on behavioral consequences (e.g., aggression, creativity). Some of these categories (e.g., aggression, buying behavior) have received considerable research attention with children; others (e.g., stereotyping, social relationships) have been the subject of considerable attention by way of content analyses but still warrant additional attention in terms of research ascertaining cause and effects; and for other areas (e.g., creativity, language), the surface has barely been scratched in terms of examining media effects systematically.

The final section of this model is labeled *interventions*, and presents a few of the numerous mediation strategies that have been examined during the past 30 years. Considerable research has been expended in testing the effectiveness and efficiency of such intervention models, especially during the past decade (e.g., Austin, 2001; Bousch, 2001; Buerkel-Rothfuss & Buerkel, 2001). Some intervention strategies have been found to be quite effective with children; others have essentially been found to be a waste of time and effort.

DETRIMENTAL EFFECTS OF ENTERTAINMENT MEDIA

We now review a number of categories of effects of entertainment televisual media on children, beginning with detrimental effects, and then examining beneficial effects. Among the potentially detrimental effects examined are displacement, stereotyping, fear and fright reactions, sexual attitudes and behaviors, and violence and aggression.

Displacement Effects

Perse (2001) discussed media effects as being either *content dependent* or *content irrelevant*: "Displacement effects are a commonly identified content-irrelevant effect" (p. 20), in that these effects occur from devoting time to media use, not because of any particular content of the televisual media being utilized. In other words, "the medium is the message" (McLuhan, 1964). Valkenburg (2001) "argued that children spend a considerable portion of their free time watching television, at the expense of other leisure activities" (p. 125), and "television's reductive effect is not the result of television viewing itself but the fact that television viewing displaces the time for other, more beneficial activities" (p. 125). With increasing amounts of children's time devoted to video games and using the Internet, more generalized displacement effects of televisual media have become of considerable concern to caregivers.

When television was a new medium of communication, displacement effects were often discussed and examined. Concerns for how this powerful new medium might reshape the lives of children were commonplace. For example, classic large-scale investigations—by Himmelweit, Oppenheim, and Vince (1958) in England; by Schramm, Lyle, and Parker (1961) in North American; and by Furu (1962) in Japan—addressed issues such as whether television viewing was associated with later bedtimes, less time spent on homework, less recreational and educational reading, and a variety of other displacement issues. These early studies often presented mixed findings depending on a variety of factors. Some early studies were able to compare the activities of children in homes that had television sets with the behavior of children who lived in households that had not yet adopted television. Two such investigations found that watching television was associated with a decrease in time spent in general play (Maccoby, 1951; Schramm et al., 1961).

In order to help untangle the mixed results of some of the earlier investigations into displacement effects, Williams (1986) focused considerable attention on conceptualization of the issue, prior to testing displacement hypotheses empirically in a classic longitudinal field investigation. Williams reasoned, "Conceptualization of the effects of television by simply distinguishing between content and displacement would, however, be overly simplistic. In particular, the displacement hypothesis requires considerable refinement. We must ask not only *whether* displacement occurs but more specifically *for whom* and *what* is displaced. In some circumstances the effect may be positive, in others, negative" (p. 10).

The study in which displacement issues were addressed was a naturalistic, longitudinal field investigation of life in three Canadian communities, one of which received television signals for the first time during the course of the investigation. That community (Notel) received no television reception during Phase 1 of the investigation, but they did receive one channel (CBC) during Phase 2, conducted 2 years after the initial phase. A second community (Unitel) received one channel (CBC) during Phase 1 and two channels (both CBC) during Phase 2. A third community (Multitel) received the same four channels (CBC, ABC, CBS, and NBC) during both Phases 1 and 2 of the investigation.

The findings of this naturalistic investigation into displacement effects (Williams & Handford, 1986) were complex. For example, it was found that television does displace some leisure activities of children directly, such as active participation in sports. Other activities that were engaged in singularly prior to the adoption of television, such as reading, were frequently time shared with television viewing once a set was introduced into the household. Williams and Handford also went beyond their findings and hypothesized that television might be expected to enhance, rather than replace, other leisure activities: "It seems likely that television could stimulate participation in other leisure activities. Viewers might see an activity portrayed as enjoyable and as a result, try it themselves" (p. 188). This investigation clearly threw down the gauntlet for additional research on displacement effects, and in recent years, the challenge has been accepted.

In a review of the research on television usage and the displacement of creative play, van der Voort and Valkenburg (1994) noted different effects depending on what sort of programming the child watched. Highly violent programs were found to reduce imaginative play, neutral programs seemed to have no effects, and, in some cases, viewing educational television enhanced creative play.

Another commonly examined displacement effect is that of the reduction in reading because of watching television, playing video games, or surfing the Internet. In a review of research on children, television, and reading, Beentjes and van der Voort (1988) determined that the majority of the studies supported displacement effects of television on reading, especially among children who were heavy television viewers. In addition to the obvious time encroachment rationale, two other reasons cited for television's displacement of reading were its effects on children's ability to concentrate while reading, and children's overall attitudes toward reading and books (Koolstra & van der Voort, 1996).

In recent years, with the U.S. Surgeon General's highly publicized reports on the poor state of children's physical health, considerable attention has been directed toward examinations of how electronic media usage can affect physical activity. Gortmaker et al. (1996) examined the literature on obesity and leisure and concluded that the odds of being overweight were 4.6 times greater for youth who watched more than 5 hours of television per day than they were for children who watched between 0 and 2 hours per day. Crespo et al. (2001) examined results from the Third National Health and Nutrition Examination Survey, which covered the period 1988–1994, and reported findings very similar to those from Gortmaker et al. The prevalence of obesity was found to be lowest among children watching 1 or fewer hours of television per day, and highest among those watching 4 or more hours of television per day. Robinson (1999) reviewed extant survey research and concluded that reducing television, videotape, and video game usage would be a major population-based approach to preventing childhood obesity. Later, Robinson (2001) argued that television viewing causes obesity by one or more of three mechanisms: displacement of physical activity, increased caloric consumption while watching or via direct effects of advertising food products, and/or reduced resting metabolism.

In concluding our discussion of displacement effects, several cautionary notes offered by Perse (2001), which highlight conceptual issues and problems with displacement hypotheses as applied to television effects, appear germane:

- Displacement appears to assume that time is spent on only one activity at a time, whereas research documents that television viewing is often a secondary activity to other tasks—that is, it often accompanies rather than displaces activities.
- The activities television displaces are not necessarily better than television viewing. In fact, many are "time fillers."

- Some displacement effects of television may include viewing educational programs on television, which may be more enriching than the activities they replace.

Stereotyping

Whereas displacement effects occur because of the potential of entertainment media to attract a scarce resource—children's attention—away from other, less attractive alternatives, the locus of the potentially detrimental effects of stereotyping are quite different. Stereotyping—or the use of overly simplistic, overly narrow representations of a particular group without consideration of group members' true diversity—occurs in entertainment televisual media for a variety of reasons. One reason is ignorance and laziness. Writers, producers, and directors may not have had primary experience with anyone of the ethnicity of the character they are being asked to present in a program, so they rely on prevailing "pop culture" representations without undertaking any research to find out how accurate their images are. An even more common reason for relying on stereotypes is because they serve as dramatic shortcuts. In short-form television programs or video games, creators rarely have enough time to develop a character in full-blown form. In fact, true character development is extremely rare in popular electronic media fare. Therefore, in order to present a hero, villain, agent of justice, or whomever efficiently and parsimoniously, writers and directors rely on commonly held stereotypes to present easily understood and identified character types. Essentially, stereotyping is a cost-effective way of taking shortcuts in drama, and it is an all-too-common practice.

Unfortunately, media stereotyping can also have very detrimental effects. Much of what children learn about the world outside of their immediate family and community comes from the media, especially television. In other words, televisual media are potent agents of socialization, and they cause children to classify the world around them, to some extent, in the terms and categories provided by television's reality. Portrayals that are biased, overly narrow, or lack diversity in depictions of one or another gender or ethnic group can affect the way in which children create the *scripts* they use to deal with "real life" (Durkin, 1985; Harris, 1999; Perse, 2001; Van Evra, 1998). Although research has been conducted on several categories of stereotypes portrayed on television—racial, gender, age, sexuality, disability, occupation, and so on—in this discussion we focus primarily on the effects of racial and gender stereotypes in entertainment programming.

For the most part, educational programming for children has been sensitive to issues of stereotyping since it became a major force in programming in the late 1960s, generally portraying both minorities and interracial relationships positively (Dohrmann, 1975). From early public broadcasting programs, such as *Sesame Street* and *The Electric Company*, to more recent programming, such as *Gullah Gullah Island* and *Dora the Explorer* on Nickelodeon, considerable care has been taken to provide balanced and diverse representations of minorities as well as to portray minorities in significant roles. Children's entertainment programming has been an entirely different story, largely for the reasons delineated previously. Research over the past 30 years consistently has found that minorities are underrepresented and misportrayed in children's entertainment fare (Barcus, 1975, 1983; Barcus & Wolkin, 1977; Greenberg & Brand, 1993; Greenberg, Mastro, & Brand, 2002).

Another form of stereotyping that children are routinely exposed to via entertainment television programming is gender stereotyping. Although some improvement has been made during the past 3 decades in this regard, television is still infused with stereotypes of both men and women. In general, women on television are portrayed less often (e.g., in the late 1990s, men still outnumbered women in television land 2:1) and in roles of lesser status or importance (Greenberg & Collette, 1997; Heintz-Knowles, 2001; Liebert & Sprafkin, 1988; Signorielli, 2001; Signorielli & Bacue, 1999). In addition, although progress has been made since Cheney (1983) found only five major occupations for half of all women on television (model, nurse, maid, secretary, and entertainer), considerable room for improvement remains (Signorielli, 2001; Signorielli & Bacue, 1999; Van Evra, 1998).

The genre of television programming in which the greatest strides have been made in terms of gender stereotyping, in both sheer numbers and roles and relationships, is children's programming. Nickelodeon has been a major factor in this movement, with programming such as *The Secret World of Alex Mack, The Mystery Files of Shelby Woo,* and *Clarrisa Explains It All.* In addition, preschool programming has also included more and stronger female leads, such as *Blue's Clues* (the animated dog Blue is female), *Allegra's Window, Dora the Explorer,* and *Madeline.*

So what do children learn from stereotypes on television, especially when they watch prime-time entertainment programming? Social learning theory (e.g., Bandura, 1977), social cognitive theory (e.g., Bandura, 2002), and cultivation theory (e.g., Gerbner et al., 2002) suggest that children would learn stereotypical attitudes and would perform associated behaviors from viewing a steady stream of stereotyped roles. In most cases, this is what the research has shown. For example, children learn and reinforce their attitudes toward gender stereotyping through television viewing, with heavier television viewers holding more traditional gender role stereotypes than do light viewers (e.g., Huston, Greer, Wright, Welch, & Ross, 1984; Lemar, 1977; O'Bryant & Corder-Bolz, 1978). Meta-analyses of this body of literature conclude that television has a significant overall effect on holding gender-role stereotypes on all age groups ($r = .10$); however, among children under 6, the relationship is more pronounced ($r = .16$), and for children under 3, the relationship is most pronounced ($r = .30$; Herrett-Skjellum & Allen, 1996).

Much of how children interpret stereotypes in entertainment programming is dependent on the "connections" they make with characters on television. For example, young children tend to choose their favorite character based on race (Eastman & Liss, 1980), and African American students prefer shows featuring African American characters (Dates, 1980; Dates & Stroman, 2001). According to several studies, however, African Americans tend to identify with high-status, powerful, and socially adept characters, especially African American characters. When no racially similar character is available, however, African American children will identify with the most positive White character (Jhally & Lewis, 1992).

What are the effects of making connections between child audiences and potentially stereotyped characters? In reality, only a relatively few studies have empirically investigated such effects. A summary of their findings is presented in Greenberg et al. (2002): "The findings indicate that televised portrayals of racial/ethnic minorities influence majority group members' real-world perceptions about minority groups as well as minority group members' evaluations of self" (p. 343). Obviously, with children, *caveat emptor* cannot be the order of the day. Marked improvements in eradicating potentially harmful stereotypes are essential if the televisual media's storytelling is not to leave harmful and potentially indelible impressions on the psyches of young viewers.

Fear and Fright Reactions

The use of fear to arouse and entertain is not unique to modern societies. Cultural anthropologists have traced frightening stories to prerecorded history (Kluckhorn, 1960; Levin, 1960), and many features of these frightening narratives that became part of oral traditions apparently are similar to today's horror films (e.g., Weaver & Tamborini, 1996). The key to understanding how fear in television programming affects children is to recall that children are less able to control their emotions, plus they more intensely feel their emotional reactions to frightening fare than do adults (Greenfield, 2000). Add to those phenomena the fact that a fright reaction to something seen on television is an "immediate emotional response" (Cantor, 1994, 2002), and the implications of fear-based television and Internet programming and video games becomes obvious. Some researchers, Derdeyn and Turley (1994) for example, have gone so far as to say that exposure to frightening programming can lead to impairment of a child's psychological development. Others have bemoaned the loss of security deemed necessary for normal emotional development, because of the intrusion of horror into the everyday lives of children through televisual fare: "When the worst fears of a child can be confirmed in reality, the child loses his own best means of dealing with external danger…. None of us can imagine what it is like to be a child today, to be helpless against the most extreme dangers and to be confronted in his own living room, in his classroom, with the full knowledge of the real dangers that exist in our world" (Fraiberg, 1987, p. 578).

It is also important to recognize that children do not necessarily avoid programming that frightens them; perhaps they are motivated by needs for mastery or novelty. In fact, children may watch programming specifically intended to incite fright reactions. *Tales from the Crypt*, adapted from a popular 1950s comic series, and Nickelodeon's *Are You Afraid of the Dark?* are two examples of fear-based programming that have been extremely popular with young people.

In some ways, television programming that includes fear as an element of entertainment is "safer" than its film counterpart, due to broadcast restrictions that require horrific depictions to be less graphic than is typical in movies (although households with premium cable channels or satellite services can now bypass many of these regulatory controls). On the other hand, children have far greater access to television than to many other media, and parents tend to underestimate the amount of frightening material on television (Cantor, 1994, 2002; Cantor & Reilly, 1982). For example, children who watch the nightly news may have fright reactions to portrayals of real-life shootings, car chases, robberies, bloody accidents, and the like. A survey of parents of children in kindergarten through 6th grade found that 37% of their children had been frightened or troubled by a news story on television (Cantor & Nathanson, 1996).

Children's reactions to scary programming vary according to their developmental level. Cantor (1994) highlighted three generalizations about children's cognitive development and its consequences for fright reactions:

- "The relative importance of the immediately perceptible components of a fear-inducing media stimulus decreases as a child's age increases" (p. 231).
- "As children mature, they become more responsive to realistic, and less responsive to fantastic dangers depicted in the media" (p. 233).
- "As children mature, they become frightened by media depictions involving increasingly abstract concepts" (p. 233).

In additional to developmental considerations in children's reactions to frightening fare, gender also is a key variable. Results of research on gender differences in fright reactions have fallen along stereotypical lines, in that girls have been found to be more emotional (Fabes & Martin, 1991) and more easily frightened (Birnbaum & Croll, 1984) than boys. These stereotypes apparently play out in adolescent social viewing of scary entertainment fare, in that boys have been found to enjoy frightening media fare more in the company of a frightened female than when accompanied by an unexpressive female (Zillmann, Weaver, Mundorf, & Aust, 1986).

Some interesting research has revealed an additional dimension of fright reactions to media fare. Although fright reactions may be an immediate emotional experience, their impression and impact can be extremely durable. Not only are some fright reactions lasting, they can be quite intense (e.g., Blumler, 1933; Cantor, 1998; Eisenberg, 1936; Hess & Goldman, 1962; Wilson, Hoffner, & Cantor, 1987). Using recollective self-reports or autobiographical memory techniques, Harrison and Cantor (1999) and Hoekstra, Harris, and Helmick (1999) found that college undergraduates still had enduring fright reactions to mass-media portrayals that they had experienced in childhood. Moreover, more than a quarter of the undergraduates in one investigation (Harrison & Cantor, 1999) still experienced anxiety when recalling their initial frightening exposure to media fare. Such durable reactions reinforce the importance of a more complete understanding of children's fright reactions.

Sexual Attitudes and Behavior

According to a 1998 *Time*/CNN national poll, 29% of American teenagers indicated that television was their primary source of information about sex, whereas only 7% cited parents and 3% cited sex-education classes as primary sources (Harris, 1999; Harris & Scott, 2002; Stodghill, 1998).[1] Given the way that television presents human sexuality, that finding is very frightening.

Gunter (2002) recently articulated the nature of many people's concerns about media sex and young people:

> The concern about the exposure of young people to sex in the media has two main aspects. First, there is a worry that very young children may be upset by seeing explicit sexual scenes that they lack the maturity to interpret. Second, exposure to media content that places emphasis on sexual themes among teenagers is believed to encourage early onset of sexual behavior and contributes, in turn, to the growth in unwanted teenage pregnancies and sexually transmitted diseases. (p. 5)

The nature of sexual content in the media (e.g., sex is presented or alluded to frequently; fictional media characters and live media "personalities" are preoccupied with sex; media role models often behave irresponsibly about sexual behaviors) adds dramatically to the nature of public concern about young people's exposure to sexual content via the media.

Harris and Scott (2002) pointed to the multiple standards in televisual media as an increasingly complex issue: Broadcast television still assumes (or is required by regulators to assume) a relatively protective stance about sexual themes, because of concerns about television being a public medium and providing a safe-haven for children; premium cable or satellite programming is permitted more license regarding the explicitness of sexuality depicted; and sexual content on the Internet is essentially unregulated, unless caregivers select some content-filtering device to safeguard their children's exposure to explicit sexuality. With the widespread adoption of Internet services in homes, and with Internet connections in children's bedrooms increasing at a dramatic rate (the vast majority of which do not utilize content filters), all a child has to do is keystroke "hot sex" or any number of other such terms into the search engine of a favorite portal, and literally scores of sites featuring every possible permutation and combination of sexual behavior pop up on the computer screen, readily available to children at any developmental level. Even if the child does not use Mom or Dad's credit card number to explore the site more fully, the amount and explicitness of the preview material provided free of charge boggles the mind of any caregiver who wants to prevent the loss of innocence of childhood. Internet access provides a degree of exposure to explicit sexual content never before imagined.

What kind of social and psychological effects might children's exposure to explicit sexual materials be expected to have? Because of concerns for children as research participants, we really have no direct evidence for youngsters. However, if

---

[1]Sutton, Brown, Wilson, and Klein (2002) conducted survey research with adolescents that presented contrary findings. They noted that media provide teenagers with a "noisy sexual maelstrom," but concluded, "Our survey data reveal that today's adolescents most frequently turn to a comparatively quiet and previously unheralded source for responsible sexual information: school" (p. 27).

we assume that findings with adolescents and young adults hold for children (and from what we have learned about emotionality in childhood, we should expect such effects to be magnified for children), here are just a few of the findings that might be expected:

- Because depictions of sex in the media often take place outside of supposedly durable, legal relationships like marriage, regular exposure to such content might be expected to undermine the values of marriage and having a stable family (e.g., Gunter, 2002; Zillmann & Bryant, 1982, 1984).
- "Feminists claim that depictions of sexual behavior in the mainstream media have tended to show women as sex objects and sexual subordinates to men" (Gunter, 2002, p. 6); therefore, repeated exposure to such images may create images of women as promiscuous, hypersexual creatures whose primary function is to serve men (Zillmann & Bryant, 1984).
- Rape and rape victims are commonly alluded to if not depicted on television and in films. Some evidence suggests that repeated viewing of such materials by young adults leads to more callous attitudes about rape, less sympathy for a rape victim, and more sympathy for those accused of rape (Gunter, 2002; Linz, Donnerstein, & Penrod, 1988).

These points present only the tip of the proverbial iceberg of the findings about the long-term consequences of children's early exposure to sexual content as commonly presented in mass culture fare.

Sutton et al. (2002) presented what may well be the most important point about the effects of the sexual content of television on children and adolescents—that it serves as sex education: "*Dawson's Creek* may not sell itself as educational television, but it is. As in its trend setting predecessors, *Melrose Place* and *Beverly Hills, 90210*, beautiful adolescents are locked in an elaborate waltz of ever-changing intimate relationships, spiced with sex that rarely has dire consequences" (p. 43). What kind of lessons are today's televisual media providing for children? What are the long-term societal consequences of these lessons? The latter question poses monumental challenges to today's and tomorrow's social scientists.

Media Violence

Over the years, far and away the most active area of media-effects inquiry has concerned media violence and children. Literally scores of books and thousands of scholarly and popular press articles have been devoted to this topic. Obviously, doing the topic justice in the space available to us is impossible without painting with an extremely broad brush.

Expressions of concern about the effects of media violence on children are usually introduced with a veritable catechism of statistics. We like the way Harris (1999, p. 189) introduced the topic with a question-and-answer session:

Q: How many murders has the average child seen on TV by the time he or she finishes elementary school?

A: Eight thousand, plus 100,000 other acts of violence.

Q: How many murders were in the film *Die Hard*?

A: 264.

Q: How many hours per week do eighth graders spend playing video games?

A: Boys spend 4.2 hours and girls 2 hours, mostly at home.

Q: What percentage of video games have violence as a major theme?

A: 85%.

Whichever of the plethora of statistics one utilizes, the conclusion has to be the same: Children's televisual world is a very violent place.

Not only is this televisual world violent, but children are big-time consumers of this violence. Anyone who was previously unaware of children's commitment to televisual media undoubtedly was shocked by the widely publicized Kaiser Family Foundation report entitled *Kids & Media @ the New Millennium* (Roberts, Foehr, Rideout, & Brodie, 1999). Their conclusion: "What may be surprising, however, is just how much exposure children report: only 5% report an hour or less of daily media exposure, and over 30% report 7 hours or more.... the average child in our sample consumes 6 hours and 32 minutes of media per day" (p. 18). Given these levels of exposure, and given the amount of violence in everyday, ordinary media fare, it is safe to say the media violence permeates the daily lives of American children.

What effects does this steady diet of symbolic violence have on children? Abundant research has addressed this question from a variety of perspectives, and several theories have been advanced both to generate hypotheses and to clarify findings. In terms of theoretical mechanisms, the most prominent theories of the effects of media violence on human aggression fall into the general categories of social learning, priming, arousal, cultivation, desensitization, and catharsis (Sparks & Sparks, 2002). To provide a capsule version of each:

- *Social learning* posits that media characters who act aggressively serve as models for viewers whose likelihood of imitating the aggression observed is facilitated if the character is rewarded, and inhibited if the character is punished (e.g., Bandura, 1965, 1977, 2002).
- *Priming* rationales argue that media violence provides stimuli that prime more general aggressive thoughts or thoughts of prior aggressive accounts, which, in turn, can activate motor processes that increase the like-

lihood of aggressive behaviors or increase the likelihood that ambiguous stimuli are interpreted as aggressive (e.g., Jo & Berkowitz, 1994; Roskos-Ewoldsen, Roskos-Ewoldsen, & Carpentier, 2002).

- *Arousal* theories note that media violence has arousal-inducing properties for many viewers; this violence-instigated arousal can subsequently transfer into a viewer's emotional state of anger, thereby intensifying aggressive behaviors (e.g., Zillmann, 1991, 2002).
- *Cultivation* argues that regular, prolonged viewing of television's world of hyperviolence ultimately shifts viewers' perceptions of reality toward television's "mean world" (Gerbner et al., 2002).
- *Desensitization* rationales focus on habituation mechanisms and posit, "with repeated exposure to media violence, a psychological saturation of emotional adjustment takes place such that initial levels of tension, anxiety, or disgust diminish or weaken" (Sparks & Sparks, 2002, p. 280), thereby enhancing the likelihood of increased aggression.
- *Catharsis* harkens to philosophical notions from Aristotle, who thought that vicarious participation with violent protagonists in drama permitted audience members to purge their feelings of violence and hostility, thereby reducing subsequent aggression (e.g., Feshbach, 1955).

What does the research say? Reviewing individual studies is impossible here, so we rely instead on the findings of an excellent synthesis of the research literature on the effects of media violence on children. After studying cross-sectional and longitudinal studies as well as a number of meta-analyses, Bushman and Huesmann (2001) concluded, "In summary, the scientific data lead to the same inescapable conclusion: TV violence increases aggression.... The bottom line is that, on average, TV violence is making our children behave more aggressively in childhood, and the aggressive habits they learn from TV in childhood carry over into adolescence and even young adulthood" (pp. 233–234). Recent research summaries of the impact of violent video games on aggressive behavior reached highly similar conclusions about the effects of this medium (Dill & Dill, 1998).

As the adoption of emerging televisual technologies becomes more complete, it is highly likely that subsequent research syntheses on their effects will report similar results, because it appears that media violence will be prevalent in new media (although obviously we should not pass final judgment prematurely). Sparks and Sparks (2002) put it well: "As the video technology changes rapidly to permit more realistic depictions of violence and online contests between virtual strangers, researchers will undoubtedly take up the new gauntlet and begin to study the effects of media violence in this new, high-tech arena" (p. 280).

BENEFICIAL EFFECTS OF ENTERTAINMENT MEDIA

It is likely that entertainment media have as many beneficial effects as they do detrimental ones. However, social scientists have spent little time and effort exploring

beneficial effects, relative to the time they have spent examining antisocial consequences of media exposure. Moreover, most examinations of beneficial effects have
focused on educational media rather than on entertainment fare. Nevertheless, a
couple of research bailiwicks that examine beneficial effects of entertainment media are briefly profiled here: prosocial effects, and entertainment effects per se.

Prosocial Effects

We know a great deal about the antisocial content of televisual media because Congress, consumer groups, and scholars all seem interested in counting such incidents. However, accurate indications of prosocial content are less common. When
they do occur—for example, in a meta-analysis of prosocial effects of television on
children's social interactions, conducted by Mares and Woodard (in press)—the
prosocial effects of educational programming "swamps" that of entertainment
programming. When all of television is considered, it appears that the frequencies
of prosocial and antisocial messages are virtually equal (e.g., Greenberg, Atkin, Edison, & Korzenny, 1980; Mares & Woodard, in press; Mares & Woodard, 2001).

Of course, much children's fare liberally mixes learning with fun, and hybrid
"edutainment" programs have had demonstrable success in teaching prosocial lessons, as a review of 30 years of research on the venerable *Sesame Street* has shown
(Fisch & Truglio, 2001). In more recent years, children's commercial cable networks
have entered the prosocial marketplace with entertainment programming that has
mixed motives and has included an educational curriculum as infrastructure. There,
too, programs like the widely successful *Blue's Clues* have demonstrated that children
can learn positive lessons while they laugh and sing (e.g., Anderson et al., 2000).

Van Evra (1998) provided an excellent summary of areas of prosocial behavior
in which television has been found to be successful. She included the following in
her categories in which prosocial media effects have been empirically established:

- Increased generosity, cooperation, adherence to rules, delay of gratifica-
  tion, friendliness, and decreased fear (e.g., Rushton, 1988).
- Increased verbalization in place of aggression (e.g., Potts, Huston, &
  Wright, 1986).
- Increased in creativity and imagination (e.g., Valkenburg, 2001).
- Greatly enhanced effects under conditions of adult coviewing (e.g., Singer
  & Singer, 1976).

Entertainment Effects

Often overlooked as a category of media effects is assessment of one of the intended
effects of entertainment media messages—entertainment. Two rather substantial
research traditions—uses and gratifications (e.g., Rubin, 2002) and entertainment
theory (e.g., Bryant & Miron, 2002)—have clearly demonstrated the beneficial effects of media fare for a wide variety of media users, including children.

Uses-and-gratifications research was spawned by the functionalist tradition of media research. Precursor investigations in functional analysis proposed several specific entertainment functions of media, such as providing parasocial relationships with media personalities (e.g., Horton & Wohl, 1956), escape from unpleasant life experiences (e.g., Pearlin, 1959), reduction of anxiety (e.g., Mendelsohn, 1963), and providing opportunities for play (e.g., Stephenson, 1967). Subsequent research, more directly within the purview of uses and gratifications, suggested how media met consumers' cognitive and affective personal and social needs, and developed connections between particular types of media content and sets of needs that could be met by consuming such fare (Rubin, 2002).

Entertainment theory (e.g., Bryant & Miron, 2002; Zillmann & Bryant, 1994) has provided complementary evidence. For example, this tradition has demonstrated that people select media fare that stimulates them when they are bored and calms them when they are stressed; that individuals, even children (Masters, Ford, & Arend, 1983), can use television, music, video games, and Internet content in psychologically valid ways to manage their own moods—a phenomenon referred to as "mood management" (Zillmann, 1988); and that individuals often systematically use media fare to provide comfort and help avoid discomfort.

With the advent of newer forms of mediated communication, in which the end user is both producer and consumer and assumes considerable agency over media content through interactivity and other means of selectivity and control, the potential for productive entertainment research is almost unlimited. In many regards, understanding children's entertainment needs—and creating media content to address these needs beneficially—while at the same time avoiding unwanted detrimental social and psychological effects, is almost certain to be one of the new frontiers in media-effects inquiry. The best is yet to be.

REFERENCES

Anderson, D. R., Bryant, J., Wilder, A., Santomero, A., Williams, M., & Crawley, A. M. (2000). Researching *Blue's Clues*: Viewing behavior and impact. *Media Psychology, 2,* 179–194.

Austin, E. W. (2001). Effects of family communication on children's interpretation of television. In J. Bryant & J. A. Bryant (Eds.), *Television and the American family* (2nd ed., pp. 377–395). Mahwah, NJ: Lawrence Erlbaum Associates.

Bandura, A. (1965). Influence of models' reinforcement contingencies on the acquisition of imitative responses. *Journal of Personality & Social Psychology, 1,* 589–595.

Bandura, A. (1977). *Social learning theory.* Englewood Cliffs, NJ: Prentice-Hall.

Bandura, A. (2002). Social cognitive theory of mass communication. In J. Bryant & D. Zillmann (Eds.), *Media effects: Advances in theory and research* (2nd ed., pp. 121–153). Mahwah, NJ: Lawrence Erlbaum Associates.

Barcus, F. E. (1975). *Weekend children's television.* Newtonville, MA: Action for Children's Television.

Barcus, F. E. (1983). *Images of life on children's television.* New York: Praeger.

Barcus, F. E., & Wolkin, R. (1977). *Children's television: An analysis of programming and advertising.* New York: Praeger.

Beetjes, J. W. J., & Van der Voort, T. H. A. (1988). Television's impact on children's reading skills: A review of research. *Reading Research, Quarterly, 23,* 389–413.

Beville, H. M., Jr. (1988). *Audience ratings: Radio, television, cable* (Rev. ed.). Hillsdale, NJ: Lawrence Erlbaum Associates.

Birnbaum, D. W., & Croll, W. L. (1984). The etiology of children's stereotypes about sex differences in emotionality. *Sex Roles, 10,* 677–691.

Blumler, H. (1933). *Movies and conduct.* New York: Macmillan.

Bousch, D. M. (2001). Mediating advertising effects. In J. Bryant & J. A. Bryant (Eds.), *Television and the American family* (2nd ed., pp. 397–412). Mahwah, NJ: Lawrence Erlbaum Associates.

Brown, J. D., Steele, J. R., & Walsh-Childers, K. (2002). *Sexual teens, sexual media: Investigating media's influence on adolescent sexuality.* Mahwah, NJ: Lawrence Erlbaum Associates.

Bryant, J., & Anderson, D. R. (Eds.). (1983). *Children's understanding of television: Research on attention and comprehension.* New York: Academic Press.

Bryant, J., & Bryant, J. A. (Eds.). (2001). *Television and the American family* (2nd ed.). Mahwah, NJ: Lawrence Erlbaum Associates.

Bryant, J., & Miron, D. (2002). Entertainment as media effect. In J. Bryant & D. Zillmann (Eds.), *Media effects: Advances in theory and research* (2nd ed., pp. 549–582). Mahwah, NJ: Lawrence Erlbaum Associates.

Bryant, J., & Thompson, S. (2002). *Fundamentals of media effects.* New York: McGraw-Hill.

Bryant, J., & Zillmann, D. (Eds.). (1991). *Responding to the screen: Reception and reaction processes.* Hillsdale, NJ: Lawrence Erlbaum Associates.

Bryant, J., & Zillmann, D. (Eds.). (2002). *Media effects: Advances in theory and research* (2nd ed.). Mahwah, NJ: Lawrence Erlbaum Associates.

Buerkel-Rothfuss, N. L, & Buerkel, R. A. (2001). Family mediation. In J. Bryant & J. A. Bryant (Eds.), *Television and the American family* (2nd ed., pp. 355–376). Mahwah, NJ: Lawrence Erlbaum Associates.

Bushman, B. J., & Huesmann, L. R. (2001). Effects of televised violence on aggression. In D. G. Singer & J. L. Singer (Eds.), *Handbook of children and the media* (pp. 223–254). Thousand Oaks, CA: Sage.

Cantor, J. (1994). Fright reactions to mass media. In J. Bryant & D. Zillmann (Eds.), *Media effects: Advances in theory and research* (pp. 213–245). Hillsdale, NJ: Lawrence Erlbaum Associates.

Cantor, J. (1998). *"Mommy, I'm scared": How TV and movies frighten children and what we can do to protect them.* San Diego: Harvest/Harcourt.

Cantor, J. (2002). Fright reactions to mass media. In J. Bryant & D. Zillmann (Eds.), *Media effects: Advances in theory and research* (pp. 287–306). Mahwah, NJ: Lawrence Erlbaum Associates.

Cantor, J., & Nathanson, A. I. (1996). Children's fright reactions to television news. *Journal of Communication, 46*(4), 139–152.

Cantor, J., & Reilly, S. (1982). Adolescents' fright reactions to television and films. *Journal of Communication, 32*(1), 87–99.

Cheney, G. A. (1983). *Television in American society.* New York: F. Watts.

Clifford, B. R., Gunter, B., & McAleer, J. (1995). *Television and children: Program evaluation, comprehension, and impact.* Hillsdale, NJ: Lawrence Erlbaum Associates.

Crespo, C. J., Smit, E., Troiano, R. P., Bartlett, S. J., Macera, C. A., & Andersen, R. E. (2001). Television watching, energy intake, and obesity in U.S. children—Results from the Third National Health and Nutrition Examination Survey, 1988–1994. *Archives of Pediatrics & Adolescent medicine, 155,* 360–365.

Dates, J. (1980). Race, racial attitudes and adolescent perceptions of black television characters. *Journal of Broadcasting, 24,* 549–560.

Dates, J., & Stroman, C. A. (2001). Portrayals of families of color on television. In J. Bryant & J. A. Bryant (Eds.), *Television and the American family* (2nd ed., 207–228). Mahwah, NJ: Lawrence Erlbaum Associates.

Derdeyn, A. P., & Turley, J. M. (1994). Television, films, and the emotional life of children. In D. Zillmann, J. Bryant, & A. C. Huston (Eds.), *Media, children, and the family: Social scientific, psychodynamic, and clinical perspectives* (pp. 131–138). Hillsdale, NJ: Lawrence Erlbaum Associates.

Dill, K. E., & Dill, J. C. (1998). Video game violence: A review of the empirical literature. *Aggression and Violent Behavior, 3,* 407–428.

Dohrmann, R. (1975). A gender profile of children's educational TV. *Journal of Communication, 25*(4), 56–65.

Dorr, A. (1986). *Television and children: A special medium for a special audience.* Beverly Hills, CA: Sage.

Durkin, K. (1985). *Television, sex roles and children: A social developmental psychological account.* Philadelphia: Open University Press.

Eastman, H., & Liss, M. (1980). Ethnicity and children's preferences. *Journalism Quarterly, 57,* 277–280.

Eisenberg, A. L. (1936). *Children and radio programs.* New York: Columbia University Press.

Fabes, R. A., & Martin, C. L. (1991). Gender and age stereotypes of emotionality. *Personality and Social Psychology Bulletin, 17,* 532–540.

Feshback, S. (1955). The drive-reducing function of fantasy behavior. *Journal of Abnormal and Social Psychology, 50,* 3–11.

Fisch, S. M., & Truglio, R. T. (2001). *"G" is for growing: Thirty years of research on children and Sesame Street.* Mahwah, NJ: Lawrence Erlbaum Associates.

Fraiberg, S. (1987). The mass media: New schoolhouse for children. In L. Fraiberg (Ed.), *Selected writings of Selma Fraiberg* (pp. 573–587). Columbus: Ohio State University Press.

Furu, T. (1962). *Television and children's life: A before–after study.* Tokyo: Japan Broadcasting Corporation.

Gerbner, G., Gross, L., Morgan, M., Signorielli, N., & Shanahan, J. (2002). Growing up with television: Cultivation processes. In J. Bryant & D. Zillmann (Eds.), *Media effects: Advances in theory and research* (2nd ed., pp. 43–67). Mahwah, NJ: Lawrence Erlbaum Associates.

Goldstein, J. (Ed.). (1998). *Why we watch: The attractions of violent entertainment.* New York: Oxford University Press.

Gortmaker, S. L., Must, A., Sobol, A. M., Peterson, K., Colditz, G. A., & Dietz, W. H. (1996). Television viewing as a cause of increasing obesity among children in the Unites States, 1986–1990. *Archives of Pediatrics & Adolescent Medicine, 150,* 356–362.

Greenberg, B. S., Atkin, C. K., Edison, N. G., & Korzenny, F. (1980). Antisocial and prosocial behaviors on television. In B. S. Greenberg (Ed.), *Life on television: Content analysis of U.S. TV drama.* Norwood, NJ: Ablex.

Greenberg, B. S., & Brand, J. E. (1993). Cultural diversity on Saturday morning television. In G. Berry & J. K. Asamen (Eds.), *Children and television in a changing socio-cultural world* (pp. 132–142). Newbury Park, CA: Sage.

Greenberg, B. S., & Collette, L. (1997). The changing faces on TV: A demographic analysis of network television's new seasons, 1966–1992. *Journal of Broadcasting & Electronic Media, 41,* 1–13.

Greenberg, B. S., Mastro, D., & Brand, J. E. (2002). Minorities and the mass media: Television into the 21st Century. In J. Bryant & D. Zillmann (Eds.), *Media effects: Advances in theory and research* (pp. 333–351). Mahwah, NJ: Lawrence Erlbaum Associates.

Greenfield, S. (2000). *The private life of the brain: Emotions, consciousness, and the secret self.* New York: Wiley.

Gunter, B. (2002). *Media sex: What are the issues?* Mahwah, NJ: Lawrence Erlbaum Associates.

Harris, R. J. (1999). *A cognitive psychology of mass communication* (3rd ed.). Mahwah, NJ: Lawrence Erlbaum Associates.

Harris, R. J., & Scott, C. L. (2002). Effects of sex in the media. In J. Bryant & D. Zillmann (Eds.), *Media effects: Advances in theory and research* (2nd ed., 307–331). Mahwah, NJ: Lawrence Erlbaum Associates.

Harrison, K., & Cantor, J. (1999). Tales from the screen: Enduring fright reactions to scary media. *Media Psychology, 1,* 97–116.

Heintz-Knowles, K. (2001). Balancing acts: Work–family issues on prime-time TV. In J. Bryant & J. A. Bryant (Eds.), *Television and the American family* (2nd ed., pp. 177–206). Mahwah, NJ: Lawrence Erlbaum Associates.

Herrett-Skjellum, J., & Allen, M. (1996). Television programming and sex stereotyping: A meta-analysis. In B. R. Burleson (Ed.), *Communication yearbook* (vol. 19, pp. 157–185). Thousand Oaks, CA: Sage.

Hess, R. D., & Goldman, H. (1962). Parents' view of the effects of television on their children. *Child Development, 33,* 411–426,

Himmelweit, H. T., Oppenheim, A. N., & Vince, P. (1958). *Television and the child.* London: Oxford University Press.

Hoekstra, S. J., Harris, R. J., & Helmick, A. L. (1999). Autobiographical memories about the experience of seeing frightening movies in childhood. *Media Psychology, 1,* 117–140.

Horton, D., & Wohl, R. R. (1956). Mass communication and para-social interaction. *Psychiatry, 19,* 215–229.

Huston, A. C., Greer, D., Wright, J. C., Welch, R., & Ross, R. (1984). Children's comprehension of televised formal features with masculine and feminine connotations. *Developmental Psychology, 20,* 707–716.

Jhally, S., & Lewis, J. (1992). *Enlightened racism: The Cosby Show, audiences, and the myth of the American dream.* Boulder, CO: Westview.

Jo, E., & Berkowitz, L. (1994). A priming effect analysis of media influences: An update. In J. Bryant & D. Zillmann (Eds.), *Media effects: Advances in theory and research* (pp. 43–60). Hillsdale, NJ: Lawrence Erlbaum Associates.

Kluckhorn, C. (1960). Recurrent themes in myths and myth-making. In H. A. Murray (Ed.), *Myth and myth making* (pp. 46–59). New York: George Braziller.

Koolstra, C. M., & van der Voort, T. H. A. (1996). Longitudinal effects of television on children's leisure-time reading. *Human Communication Research, 23,* 4–35.

Lemar, J. (1977). Women and blacks on prime time television. *Journal of Communication, 27*(1), 70–80.

Levin, H. (1960). Some meanings of myth. In H. A. Murray (Ed.), *Myth and myth making* (pp. 103–114). New York: George Braziller.

Liebert, R. M., & Sprafkin, J. (1988). *The early window: Effects of television on children and youth* (3rd ed.). Elmsford, NY: Pergamon Press.

Linz, D., Donnerstein, E., & Penrod, S. (1988). Effects of long-term exposure to violent and sexually degrading depictions of women. *Journal of Personality and Social Psychology, 55,* 758–768.

Maccoby, E. E. (1951). Television: Its impact on school children. *Public Opinion Quarterly, 15,* 421–444.

Mares, M. L., & Woodard, E. H. (2001). Prosocial effects on children's social interactions. In D. G. Singer & J. L. Singer (Eds.), *Handbook of children and the media* (pp. 183–205). Thousand Oaks, CA: Sage.

Mares, M. L., & Woodard, E. H. (in press). Positive effects of television on children's social interactions: A meta-analysis. In R. Carveth & J. Bryant (Eds.), *Meta-analyses of media effects* (pp. 00–99). Mahwah, NJ: Lawrence Erlbaum Associates.

Masters, J. C., Ford, M. E., & Arend, R. A. (1983). Children's strategies for controlling affective responses to aversive social experience. *Motivation and Emotion, 7,* 103–116.

McLuhan, M. (1964). *Understanding media: The extensions of man.* New York: McGraw-Hill.

Mendelsohn, H. (1963). Socio-psychological perspectives on the mass media and public anxiety. *Journalism Quarterly, 40,* 511–516.

O'Bryant, S. L., & Corder-Bolz, C. R. (1978). The effects of television on children's stereotyping of women's work roles. *Journal of Vocational Behavior, 12,* 233–244.

Pearlin, L. I. (1959). Social and personal stress and escape television viewing. *Public Opinion Quarterly, 23,* 255–259.

Perse, E. M. (2001). *Media effects and society.* Mahwah, NJ: Lawrence Erlbaum Associates.

Potts, R., Huston, A. C., & Wright, J. C. (1986). The effects of television form and violent content on boys' attention and social behavior. *Journal of Experimental Child Psychology, 41,* 1–17.

Roberts, D. F., Foehr, U. G., Rideout, V. J., & Brodie, M. (1999). *Kids & media @ the new millennium.* Menlo Park, CA: Henry J. Kaiser Family Foundation.

Robinson, T. N. (1999). Reducing children's television viewing to prevent obesity—A randomized controlled trial. *JAMA—Journal of the American Medical Association, 282,* 1561–1567.

Robinson, T. N. (2001). Television viewing and childhood obesity. *Pediatric Clinics of North America, 48,* 1017–1031.

Roskos-Ewoldsen, D. R., Roskos-Ewoldsen, B., & Carpentier, F. R. D. (2002). Media priming: A synthesis. In J. Bryant & D. Zillmann (Eds.), *Media effects: Advances in theory and research* (2nd ed., pp. 97–120). Mahwah, NJ: Lawrence Erlbaum Associates.

Rubin, A. M. (2002). The uses-and-gratifications perspective of media effects. In J. Bryant & D. Zillmann (Eds.), *Media effects: Advances in theory and research* (2nd ed., pp. 525–548). Mahwah, NJ: Lawrence Erlbaum Associates.

Rushton, J. P. (1988). Television as a socializer. In M. Courage (Ed.), *Readings in developmental psychology* (pp. 437–456). Peterborough, Ontario: Broadview.

Schramm, W., Lyle, J., & Parker, E. B. (1961). *Television in the lives of our children.* Stanford, CA: Stanford University Press.

Signorielli, N. (2001). Television's gender role images and contribution to stereotyping: Past, present, future. In D. G. Singer & J. L. Singer (Eds.), *Handbook of children and the media* (pp. 341–358). Thousand Oaks, CA: Sage.

Signorielli, N., & Bacue, A. (1999). Recognition and respect: A content analysis of prime-time television characters across three decades. *Sex Roles, 40,* 527–544.

Singer, D. G., & Singer, J. L. (Eds.). (2001). *Handbook of children and the media.* Thousand Oaks, CA: Sage.

Singer, J. L., & Singer, D. G. (1976). Can T.V. stimulate imaginative play? *Journal of Communication, 26*(3), 74–80.

Sparks, G. G., & Sparks, C. W. (2002). Effects of media violence. In J. Bryant & D. Zillmann (Eds.), *Media effects: Advances in theory and research* (2nd ed., pp. 269–285). Mahwah, NJ: Lawrence Erlbaum Associates.

Stephenson, W. (1967). *The play theory of mass communication.* Chicago: University of Chicago Press.

Stodghill, R. (1998, June 15). Where'd you learn that? *Time,* pp. 52–59.

Sutton, M. J., Brown, J. D., Wilson, K. M., & Klein, J. D. (2002). Shaking the tree of knowledge for forbidden fruit: Where adolescents learn about sexuality and conception. In J. D. Brown, J. R. Steele, & K. Walsh-Childers (Eds.), *Sexual teens, sexual media: Investigating media's influence on adolescent sexuality* (pp. 25–55). Mahwah, NJ: Lawrence Erlbaum Associates.

Valkenburg, P. M. (2001). Television and the child's developing imagination. In D. G. Singer & J. L. Singer (Eds.), *Handbook of children and the media* (pp. 121–134). Thousand Oaks, CA: Sage.

van der Voort, T. H. A., & Valkenburg, P. M. (1994). Television's impact on fantasy play—A review of research. *Developmental Review, 14,* 27–51.

Van Evra, J. (1998). *Television and child development* (2nd ed.). Mahwah, NJ: Lawrence Erlbaum Associates.

Weaver, J. B., III, & Tamborini, R. (Eds.). (1996). *Horror films: Current research on audience preferences and reactions.* Mahwah, NJ: Lawrence Erlbaum Associates.

Webster, J. G., Phalen, P. F., & Lichty, L. W. (2000). *Ratings analysis: The theory and practice of audience research* (2nd ed.). Mahwah, NJ: Lawrence Erlbaum Associates.

Williams, T. M. (1986). Background and overview. In T. M. Williams (Ed.), *The impact of television: A natural experiment in three communities* (pp. 1–38). Orlando, FL: Academic Press.

Williams, T. M., & Handford, A. G. (1986). Television and other leisure activities. In T. M. Williams (Ed.), *The impact of television: A natural experiment in three communities* (pp. 143–213). Orlando, FL: Academic Press.

Wilson, B. J., Hoffner, C., & Cantor, J. (1987). Children's perceptions of the effectiveness of techniques to reduce fear from mass media. *Journal of Applied Developmental Psychology, 8,* 39–52.

Zillmann, D. (1988). Mood management: Using entertainment to full advantage. In L. Donohew, H. E. Sypher, & E. T. Higgins (Eds.), *Communication, social cognition, and affect* (pp. 147–171). Hillsdale, NJ: Lawrence Erlbaum Associates.

Zillmann, D. (1991). Television viewing and physiological arousal. In J. Bryant & D. Zillmann (Eds.), *Responding to the screen: Reception and reaction processes* (pp. 103–133). Hillsdale, NJ: Lawrence Erlbaum Associates.

Zillmann, D. (2002). Theory of affective dynamics, emotions and moods. In J. Bryant, D. Roskos-Ewoldsen, & J. Cantor (Eds.), *Communication and emotion: Essays in honor of Dolf Zillmann* (pp. 1–35). Mahwah, NJ: Lawrence Erlbaum Associates.

Zillmann, D., & Bryant, J. (1982). Pornography, sexual callousness and the trivialization of rape. *Journal of Communication, 32*(4), 10–21.

Zillmann, D., & Bryant, J. (1984). Effects of massive exposure to pornography. In N. M. Malamuth & E. Donnerstein (Eds.), *Pornography and sexual aggression* (pp. 115–141). Orlando, FL: Academic Press.

Zillmann, D., & Bryant, J. (1994). Entertainment as media effect. In J. Bryant & D. Zillmann (Eds.), *Media effects: Advances in theory and research* (pp. 437–461). Hillsdale, NJ: Lawrence Erlbaum Associates.

Zillmann, D., Weaver, J. B., III, Mundorf, N., & Aust, C. F. (1986). Effects of an opposite-gender companion's affect to horror on distress, delight, and attraction. *Journal of Personality and Social Psychology, 51,* 586–594.

Zillmann, D., & Vorderer, P. (2000). *Media entertainment: The psychology of its appeal.* Mahwah, NJ: Lawrence Erlbaum Associates.

11

Regulating Media Violence: Why, How, and by Whom?

L. Rowell Huesmann
Marko M. Skoric
The University of Michigan

> My professional response today is that the broadcasters should be put on notice.... It is clear to me that the causal relationship between [exposure to] televised violence and antisocial behavior is sufficient to warrant appropriate and immediate remedial action ... *there comes a time when the data are sufficient to justify action. That time has come.*
>
> —Jesse Steinfeld, Surgeon General of the United States, March 21, 1972
> (U.S. Senate Committee on Commerce, 1972, pp. 26–29)

It was 30 years ago when the then Surgeon General of the United States made these statements before Senator John Pastore's Subcommittee on Communications. The statement resonated with many researchers and policymakers who had been, at that time, investigating the effects of media violence for over 20 years. It was stimulated by the release of the Surgeon General's massive five-volume report on television and social behavior (Comstock, Murray, & Rubinstein, 1972) with a summary volume on television violence and aggression (Surgeon General's Scientific Advisory Committee, 1972). This report contained both reviews of prior research and the results of specific projects funded by the Surgeon General's Scientific Advisory Committee. It seemed to be well received by the senators, although, like most research, it was minimized and played down by the network executives who testified at the time. Nevertheless, those executives made seemingly concessionary statements that they would work on the problem. However, the sad fact is that despite what the Surgeon General said at that time, very little has been done in the way of reducing and regulating media violence over the subsequent 30 years. Children are exposed to as much or more violence in the media than ever. Although the case for the effects of media violence has grown stronger, producers are as reluctant as ever to admit that violence could be having any effect on children; and, although it speaks out against media violence, the government seems just about as reluctant as ever to do anything about it. In this chapter, we try to address why that is the case and what could and should have been done up to now and in the future.

MEDIA VIOLENCE STIMULATES AGGRESSION

Let us begin with a brief summary of some important facts about the effects of media violence on children. Over the past 50 years, a body of literature has emerged that strongly supports the conclusion that media violence viewing is one factor contributing to the development of aggression. By *aggression,* we mean serious interpersonal acts intended to harm the other person. By *media violence,* we mean visual portrayals of one person behaving physically aggressively against another. The majority of empirical studies over the past 50 years have focused on the effects of watching violence in television and film dramas (Huesmann, Moise, & Podolski, 1997), although studies on video games and music videos started to appear in the last decade (Anderson & Bushman, 2001; Johnson, Adams, & Ashburn, 1995). In any case, the total number of empirical studies now approaches 400 or more. Many are experimental studies in which cause and effect can be unambiguously determined. These almost uniformly show that watching media violence causes the child viewer to behave more aggressively immediately afterward (e.g. Bjorkqvist, 1985). Many are static observational studies. These almost uniformly show a positive correlation between media violence viewing and aggression (e.g., Belson, 1978; McLeod, Atkin, & Chaffee, 1972). A few are longitudinal studies, and they generally show that early childhood exposure to media violence predicts later childhood and even adult aggression and violence, even when other relevant potential causal factors are controlled (e.g. Huesmann, Moise, Podolski, & Eron, 2003). These studies have been cogently summarized in a number of reviews and meta-analyses (Anderson & Bushman, 2001; Andison, 1977; Paik & Comstock, 1994; Huesmann & Miller, 1994). Taken together, they indicate that exposure to media violence is not only related to childhood aggression; it is one factor stimulating childhood aggression.

A substantial body of psychological theory has developed explaining the processes through which exposure to violence in the mass media could cause both short- and long-term increases in a child's aggressive and violent behavior (Bandura, 1977; Berkowitz, 1993; Eron, 1963; Huesmann, 1988, 1998; Zillmann, 1979). Long-term effects with children are now generally believed to be primarily due to long-term *ob-*

servational learning of cognitions (schemas, beliefs, and biases) supporting aggression (Berkowitz, 1993; Huesmann, 1988, 1998), although habituation of negative emotional responses to violence—which makes violence more palatable (*desensitization*)—may also play a role. Short-term effects with adults and children are recognized as primarily due to *priming* (Huesmann, 1998), *excitation transfer* (Zillmann, 1983), or *observational learning (imitation) of specific behaviors* (Bandura, Ross, & Ross, 1961). Most researchers of aggression agree that severe aggressive and violent behavior seldom occurs unless there is a convergence of multiple predisposing and precipitating factors such as neurophysiological abnormalities, poor childrearing, socioeconomic deprivation, poor peer relations, attitudes and beliefs supporting aggression, drug and alcohol abuse, frustration and provocation, and other factors. The evidence is already substantial that exposure to media violence is one such long-term predisposing and short-term precipitating factor. Exposure to media violence is only one of many factors that contribute to a youth's risk of behaving violently, but it is a significant factor in raising that risk in many children.

TRENDS IN AMOUNT OF MEDIA VIOLENCE

Given these facts, many of which were apparent in 1972, one might wonder whether the amount of violence in the mass media has declined in recent years. Unfortunately, the answer is no. For instance, the Cultural Indicators Projects, in examining images on television since 1967, demonstrated the remarkable stability in violent aspects of TV programming for almost 3 decades, with an average of more than 70% of programs featuring some forms of violence (Signorielli, 1991). Furthermore, it was found that this number has been even higher for children's weekend programming. Researchers have reported that 9 of 10 programs have included violence, at an average rate of 22 violent acts per hour (Gerbner & Signorielli, 1990; Signorielli, 1991). Although these studies produced reliable and robust findings, they suffered from two major limitations. First, Gerbner and colleagues focused on programming from major broadcast networks only; and second, they used an intact week sampling technique that could possibly have distorted the findings (Wilson et al., 2002). These issues have been addressed by the National Television Violence Study (NTVS), led by a group of researchers from the University of California–Santa Barbara who created and content analyzed one of the most comprehensive samples of television programming in the United States. They sampled approximately 2,700 hours of programming each year (1994–1998) across 23 broadcast and cable channels (Wilson et al., 1997, 1998). A major finding of the study (Wilson et al., 2002) was that TV programming targeted to children is significantly more likely to feature violence, with 69% of children's and 57% of nonchildren's programs containing some form of violence. The study also revealed that violent characters in children's shows are more likely to receive rewards or praise for their actions than are similar characters in other types of shows (32% vs. 21%, respectively). Furthermore, children's programs are less likely to portray the serious consequences of violence, like physical harm or pain, than are other nonchildren's shows. Another recent report on the study (Wilson, Colvin, & Smith, 2002) suggested that younger perpetrators of onscreen violence, compared to their older counterparts, are more frequently depicted as attractive, are less likely to be punished, and their violent acts are less likely to result in negative consequences to the victims. Moreover, the study showed that young perpetrators portrayed in such fashion hold prominent positions in children's programming.

WHAT REALLY NEEDS TO BE REGULATED

So far we have summarized the research demonstrating that media violence does indeed stimulate lasting propensities toward aggressive and violent behavior in many youth, and the research demonstrating that TV is still filled with a lot of violence of different types. Let us turn now to the question of what the body of research suggests really needs to be regulated about media violence in order to reduce its potential effects. There are several important empirical facts that help guide our answers to this question.

Children's Exposure Is of Greatest Concern

There are two realities that lead to the conclusion that we need to be much more concerned about children's exposure to media violence than about adults' exposure. First, one of the best-known facts about aggressive and violent behavior is that the origins of serious adult aggression can almost always be found in childhood experiences. There is no more powerful predictor of adult aggression and violence than childhood aggression (Huesmann & Miller, 1994). Whatever contributes to increases in a child's aggression is also increasing the likelihood that that child will behave more aggressively as an adult. Why? Cognitive structures—scripts, world schemas, normative beliefs—are being formed in young children that will determine the child's habitual behaviors and personality for a long time. These cognitions are easily molded in the child through observational learning and conditioning but, once the cognitions have crystallized, they become resistant to change. Thus, on the average, a more aggressive child grows up to be a more aggressive adult.

Second, research indicates that the most lasting effects of exposure to media violence occur with children. In their meta-analysis of 217 key studies, Paik and Comstock (1994) reported that the largest effects of media violence occurred with preschoolers and the smallest effects occurred with adults. Furthermore, longitudinal studies that have examined the same people in young childhood and later in teenage years or adulthood have generally found much stronger correlations between childhood viewing and childhood aggression than between young adult viewing and young adult aggression (Eron, Huesmann, Lefkowitz, & Walder, 1972; Huesmann et al., 2003; Huesmann & Eron, 1986; Milavsky, Kessler, Stipp, & Rubens, 1982). Additionally, some of these longitudinal studies have shown stronger correlations from early childhood exposure to later young adult aggression than from adult violence viewing to adult aggression (Lefkowitz, Eron, Walder, &

Huesmann, 1977). At the same time, experimental studies investigating short-term effects on hostile behavioral responses to provocation or short-term effects on expressed aggressive attitudes and beliefs seem to show effects for young adults that are similar in size to effects on children (Huesmann & Miller, 1994; Malamuth & Donnerstein, 1982; Paik & Comstock, 1994). From a theoretical standpoint, this is not surprising: The short-term processes of priming and excitation transfer increase the expression of aggressive ideas and the use of aggressive scripts in adults as well as in children. It is the encoding of new aggressive scripts, hostile world schemas, and normative beliefs approving of aggression that occurs more readily in childhood, with long-lasting effects (Huesmann, 1998).

The conclusion is that exposure to media violence may increase risk for aggressive behavior in the short run for both adults and children, but that the greatest concern about long term effects should be reserved for children. This leads to the conclusion that regulating children's exposure is much more important than regulating adults' exposure. Media violence has long-term effects on children that pose a public health threat. Effects on adults should not be dismissed as nonexistent, but they tend to be short term. Consequently, regulating only children's exposure could have significant positive social consequences while avoiding at least some of the moral and philosophical issues surrounding regulating adult exposure.

Some Children Are More at Risk

As far as empirical research has shown, media violence affects all children to some extent. The frequently voiced claim that only children who are predisposed to be aggressive are affected does not hold up under scrutiny. Of course, because many different things increase aggressiveness, a child who has many such risk factors is more likely to display aggression in response to media violence. However, that does not mean that media violence affects such a child more. In experimental studies of short-term effects, there is no published evidence that only already-aggressive children are affected. In longitudinal studies, analyses that separate high- and low-aggressive children show that both types of children become more aggressive when they are exposed to high diets of violent TV (Eron et al., 1972). Nevertheless, there are a number of factors that seem to put some children more at risk in one way or another.

High TV Viewers. Children who watch more TV are inevitably exposed to more violence on TV because of the pervasive presence of violence on television. Thus, high viewers are more at risk. There are a wide variety of individual factors that may influence some young children to watch more TV than others.

Unpopular Children. There is some evidence that unpopular children watch more television (Huesmann & Eron, 1986). It may be that television provides rewards for them that they cannot obtain in their social life, or it may be that watching a lot of television removes them from social contacts and makes them less popular.

Less Intelligent Children.   Low IQ and low achievement are even stronger correlates of amount of TV viewing and exposure to TV violence (Huesmann & Eron,
1986). However, as with unpopularity, the direction of the relation is unclear and
probably bidirectional. Spending time watching TV instead of reading and studying undoubtedly contributes to lower achievement, but lower-IQ children may also
turn to watching TV to obtain vicarious rewards and escape the failures they encounter in academic pursuits.

Children from Lower-SES (Socioeconomic) Families.   Children from lower-SES
families on the average tend to view more television and see more television violence
(Anderson, Mead, & Sullivan, 1986; Comstock & Paik, 1991). This added exposure increases the risk that media violence will have a substantial effect on the children. Television also has a more central role in lower-SES households.

Children Without Parental Supervision.   Children in one-parent families watch
more television and television violence (Webster, Pearson, & Webster, 1986). The
less time parents have available, the more time the young child watches TV, often
alone without an adult to comment on or discuss what is being shown. Mediating
comments by adults are one factor that can reduce the effect of media violence on a
child (Nathanson, 1999); hence, lack of the possibility of mediation increases risk.

Do risk factors for viewing explain the relation between viewing and aggression?
A legitimate question about all of these factors that increase the risk of a child being
exposed to media violence is whether these factors "account for" the relation between TV violence viewing and aggression. The simple answer is, "No!" Although
indeed most of these factors are also correlated with aggression, statistical analyses
(see Eron et al., 1972; Huesmann et al., 2003; Huesmann & Eron, 1986) show that
they do not account for the relation between TV violence viewing and aggression.

Some Characteristics of Violent Shows Increase Concern

Independent of the specific child viewer, there are also a number of characteristics
of a violent program that seem to increase the risk of it having an effect on the
viewer. The evolved theory explaining why media violence affects children's aggression suggests that many of these characteristics should be important, and their importance has also been supported by empirical studies. Regulation could be
targeted at these characteristics rather than violence as a whole.

A substantial literature has evolved on what attracts children to specific television shows (see Comstock & Paik, 1991). Visual and auditory form, subject matter,
character, and genre all affect whether children will watch a program, and children
must attend to a program to learn from it. Unfortunately, violent programs tend
naturally to have elements that attract children's attention. Also unfortunately, attention to a program is all that is needed psychologically for the short-term processes of priming and excitation transfer to come into play. However, the
magnitude of the long-term effects of exposure to violence should and does seem to
depend on some more subtle characteristics of the presentation.

Does the Child Identify with the Perpetrator of the Violence?   When observing a violent scene, a child might identify with the victim or the perpetrator. The child is more likely to encode scripts for behaving violently and beliefs supporting violence if that child identifies with the perpetrator (Bandura, 1986). Thus, highly charismatic, heroic, powerful, attractive characters who behave violently (e.g., Indiana Jones and Dirty Harry) are more likely to teach aggression to an observing child.

Is the Violence Portrayed as Justified?   A child is also more likely to encode observed scripts including violent acts if the act is presented as justified (Berkowitz, 1993). Was the aggressor provoked? Does the victim deserve to be attacked? Of course, the typical crime drama or western showing criminals being shot or beaten by avenging citizens or lawmen (e.g., Dustin Hoffman in *Straw Dogs*, Charles Bronson in *Death Wish*, or Spenser Tracy in *Bad Day at Black Rock*) falls perfectly into this category. Retribution themes are common in violent dramas, and they convey the impression that violence is justified.

Is the Violence Rewarded?   In some violent scenes, the perpetrator of violence receives rewards or accolades for what he or she has done. The male hero saves the world by eliminating the terrorists (violently, of course) and is rewarded with adulation and often the attentions of a beautiful woman (e. g., Arnold Schwarzenegger in *True Lies*). Research has shown that impressionable young viewers are more likely to imitate aggressive scripts they observe when the violence in them is rewarded in this manner (Bandura, 1986). Therefore, these scenes are of more concern than even more violent scenes in which the perpetrator meets a disastrous end.

Is the Plot Perceived as Realistic?   Finally, research has shown that children are more likely to be influenced by violent scenes they perceive as "telling about life like it really is" than scenes that seem divorced from reality (Huesmann & Eron, 1986). Of course, the perception of reality is in the beholder as much as in the drama. For example, cartoons may be perceived as very realistic by young children, even though most adults see them as complete fantasy.

SUMMARY OF CONCERNS

Thus far we have concluded that regulation of children's exposure to media violence is most important because media violence affects children more and the effects last longer. In fact, regulation of adults' exposure may not have much societal benefit because the effects on adults are mostly short term. Unfortunately, the evidence indicates that all children are affected, although children who are high TV viewers, are more aggressive, are less intelligent, are from lower-SES families, and have less parental supervision may be more affected. At the same time, the evidence indicates that not all violence is of equal concern. Repeated exposures to very graphic, bloody violence may maximize the emotional desensitization of the child to violence. However, the learning of cognitive scripts, schemas, and beliefs that promote violence is quite probably maximized by exposing a child repeatedly to charismatic heroes, with whom the child identifies, who use justified violence to save the world from "bad guys," and who are rewarded for their actions.

HISTORY OF REGULATION OF VIOLENCE

Given this background, let us now review the history of attempts to regulate exposure to televisual media perceived to be "bad" for the public. Ever since the days of nickelodeons, children have been among the most frequent and devoted moviegoers. In the 1920s, the advent of sound technology coupled with more sophisticated scripting, camera work, and editing techniques brought the movie-viewing experience to a new level and started raising societal alarms about potential impact of motion pictures (particularly "sexy" pictures) on children. Intervention soon ensued by the industry, which addressed the issue (probably for commercial reasons) by introducing matinee screenings of selected movies for children, usually on Saturday mornings and early afternoons (Paik, 2001). However, the American public had to wait for 40 more years to see any further action taken in this respect, although the first congressional hearing on television and juvenile delinquency took place as early as 1954 (Hamilton, 1998b; Signorielli, 1991). Indeed, it was not until 1968 that the Motion Pictures Association of America (MPAA), headed by Jack Valenti, in partnership with National Association of Theatre Owners (NATO) bowed to public pressure and created the first comprehensive movie rating system. The aim of this self-imposed system was to provide "advance cautionary warnings" about movies (Valenti, 2000) and help parents make decisions about whether or not their children should be allowed to watch any particular movie shown in theatres. Ever since the introduction, the MPAA ratings (www.mpaa.org) have classified movies into categories: G (general audiences/all ages admitted), PG (parental guidance suggested), R (restricted), and NC-17 (no one 17 and under admitted; MPAA, 2002). The category of PG-13 (parents strongly cautioned) was added a decade or so after the first four classifications, to further clarify things for parents.

Those first U.S. Senate hearings on media violence in 1954 did have some immediate effects, however. It was during them that violence on television and movies first received serious public and political attention. Writing in *Public Opinion Quarterly* at that time, distinguished researcher Paul Lazarsfeld (1955), who testified at the hearings, reported that there was little scientific knowledge about the effects of televised violence on youth behavior, and it was a social topic that needed to be investigated. Those first hearings started a trend of government hearings interacting with government-sponsored research initiatives on television effects on behavior that continued to the end of the 20th century. Schramm, Lyle, and Parker (1961) published their milestone report *Television in the Lives of Our Children* shortly afterward. This was followed in 1969 by the *Violence and the Media* report of the National Commission on the Causes and Prevention of Violence (Baker & Ball, 1969).

Then, just a few years after the movie ratings were introduced, in 1972 the Surgeon General presented the first comprehensive and well-documented report on television violence and its effects on social behavior. The report was commissioned by the federal government in 1969, when the Surgeon General's Scientific Advisory Committee on Television and Social Behavior was appointed to deal with this issue. Interestingly, in the 12-member committee, academic researchers were outnumbered by representatives of the broadcasting industry by 5 to 3; moreover, some of the most prominent media effects researchers (including Albert Bandura) were vetoed off the committee by the broadcasters (Cooper, 1996; Newton, 1996). This is probably one of the main reasons why the committee's final conclusions about the effects of television violence were perceived by the scientific community as being watered down, and by the general public as confusing (Cooper, 1996; Newton, 1996). Researchers were particularly disappointed and frustrated because scientific evidence for a causal link between TV violence and aggression was indeed very strong. Still, the report did make a difference as the TV networks' behavior came under closer public scrutiny following the report's release. For instance, in 1972 the FCC received about 2,000 complaints regarding violent and sexual content; by 1974 the number of complaints was 25,000 (Cooper, 1996). In addition, the report stimulated the widely publicized Senate Commerce Committee hearings on television violence chaired by Senator Pastore, at which network executives appeared. Although they denied that media violence could be having any effect, they promised to be concerned about it. Perhaps more important, the Surgeon General's report stimulated a number of research studies investigating the effects of televised violence, some of which were included in the 1982 National Institute for Mental Health (NIMH) report.

The 1982 NIMH report has been called "the last great federally funded study of media violence" (Newton, 1996, p. 36), and its major conclusions were more damaging to the television industry than were the conclusions from the previous report by the Surgeon General. Most important, the report claimed that research findings suggested a causal link between television violence and aggressive behavior, an accusation strongly denied by the broadcasting industry (Newton, 1996). The timing of the report's release was also a subject of considerable controversy as it coincided with the start of a new TV season, but the NIMH stressed that the timing coincidence had not been planned, and that the report was to be published then only after someone had leaked it to *The Washington Post* (Cooper, 1996). The ABC network responded to the accusations by producing a study that tried to refute every major conclusion of the report, but largely failed as its study was strongly criticized by the research community and U.S. Surgeon General (Cooper, 1996).

Although there was no immediate congressional or governmental action as a consequence of the NIMH report, it probably signaled the start of an increasing political concern with the issue. By the late 1980s, that concern became apparent in Congress through the actions of Senator Paul Simon in the Senate and Representative Ed Markey in the House. Hearings became more frequent, and the sentiment expressed by more and more members of Congress, reflecting the testimony, became more proregulation. Senator Simon called on the industry to regulate itself, and sponsored legislation adopted in 1990 that granted the industry an antitrust exemption to permit it to cooperate in reducing violence on television. However, the industry did nothing, and over the next few years public consensus for action emerged. Not only did parent and children's television action groups make their opinions felt, but professional health organizations such as the American Psychological Association, the American Medical Association, and the American Academy of Pediatrics weighed in on the side of action. As Kunkel and Wilcox (2001) reported, the industry, "sensing a shift in the political winds, finally agreed to a formal response ... (but it) proved to be 'too little, too late' to avoid further government intervention" (p. 592).

First, the Children's Television Act of 1990 was passed, which limited the amount of advertising in children's programming and mandated broadcasting of some educational programming for young viewers. At the same time, the development of V-chip technology, which would enable viewers to block certain programs that they found objectionable, was announced (Newton, 1996). By the mid-1990s, Representative Markey had introduced legislation mandating both the incorporation of V-chips into new televisions and a ratings system. President Clinton endorsed the proposal and the legislation, which was incorporated into the 1996 Telecom Act with an aim of providing "technology for parents to control the viewing of programming they believe is inappropriate for their children, and for other purposes" (Parental Choice in Television Act of 1995, 104th Congress).

From the perspective of those most concerned about violence, the "fly in the ointment" of this proposal was the need for a rating system. The ratings for each program could be transmitted as part of the coded stream normally used for "closed captioning." However, the act, attempting to skirt constitutional issues, gave the television industry the right to devise its own rating system. The industry, following the approach used for movies, introduced an age-based ratings system despite published evidence that age-based ratings attract children to mature programs (Bushman & Stack, 1996) whereas content-based ratings for violence do not. The new parental guidelines system was unveiled in late 1996, and was quickly implemented by the major broadcast network and cable operators. The new guidelines were modeled on the old MPAA rating system with some minor changes (i.e., children's programming and general audience programming were categorized separately). Thus, programs designed for children were labeled as either TV-Y (all children) or TV-Y7 (directed to older children), whereas programs designed for the entire audience received one of the four labels: TV-G (general audience), TV-PG (parental guidance suggested), TV-14 (parents strongly cautioned), and TV-MA (mature audiences only; TV Parental Guidelines, 2002; http://www.tvguidelines.org). The ratings were strongly criticized by the academics, interest groups, and politicians who supported a system that would provide more information about the content of a program, including levels of violence, sex, and adult language. The system was amended by the industry in late 1997 to include content descriptors: FV for fantasy violence, V for violence, S for sexual situations, L for language, and D for suggestive dialogue; however, the NBC network refused to implement the new ratings (Hamilton, 1998b).

At present, Congress and the FCC, with their general reluctance to directly regulate speech on the basis of content, seem at least partially satisfied with the current voluntary ratings systems for motion pictures and television. Yet, it is impossible to dispute the fact that media violence has been one of the most hotly debated issues on the congressional floor and has been frequently mentioned in presidential candidate speeches. However, an empirical study by Hoerrner (1999)—examining the relationship among social, economic, and political factors and congressional actions regarding television violence—demonstrated that legislators' actions are generally more symbolic than substantive. The author reported that there is no relationship between the amount of violence in the media and related congressional activity in any given year, even when 1- or 2-year delays for legislative action are taken into account. On the contrary, Hoerrner (1999) suggested that the status of media violence as a national issue, coupled with its ability to generate press coverage and boost name recognition for those legislators who are planning to seek higher office, are among the main factors predicting congressional action.

Indeed, although the subject of media violence has been covered extensively in the national press in the last 50 years, the coverage itself has left much to be desired (Anderson & Bushman, 2001). Recent consolidations of the media industry—via mergers, acquisitions, and takeovers—have created media conglomerates that have commercial interests across several different industries, including television, motion pictures, video games, and newspapers. There is little doubt that such market conditions are not very conducive for impartial reporting about the effects of media violence. Bushman and Anderson (2001), on the basis of a content analysis of press reports, concluded that there is a growing disparity between scientific findings and news reports about the effects of media violence. Although research evidence gathered since 1975 has repeatedly demonstrated the existence of a link between media violence and aggression, with the size of this relationship increasing over the years, Bushman and Anderson's analysis shows that news reports have changed from suggesting a weak relationship to a moderate relationship and back to a weak (or even nonexistent) relationship between media violence and aggression.

LOCI FOR INTERVENTIONS AND REGULATION

The previous summary of attempts to regulate violence has focused on governmental actions spurred by public discontent. However, there are other loci for interventions to regulate violence that need to be considered. Furthermore, none of the regulatory attempts so far have addressed the issue that different kinds of violence may have different effects.

One way to categorize the loci for regulatory interventions is whether they are aimed at the producer of the message being transmitted in the media or at the receiver of the message being transmitted. For example, regulation through ratings can be viewed as involving both the transmitter who must provide the ratings (e.g., movie ratings or ratings a V-chip can read) and the receivers who must alter their behaviors on the basis of the ratings. Let us now examine some other potential loci for interventions involving the transmitters of violent messages.

Artists and Producers

Of course, violent content in dramas begins with the artist and producer. Good stories often involve violence, and the argument is compelling that no one is in a better position than the artists and producers to determine how necessary or how gratuitous a violent scene is. The presentation form that an artist selects, the visuals that accompany it, the dialogue, and the implications are all chosen to achieve a particular artistic effect. Artistic license means that the artist should generally retain control over these elements, but compromises are always made to balance taste with effect and to create the emotional reactions the artist and producers want. Compromises are also often made to avoid offending an audience to the extent that its members won't watch the production. In the televisual industry, ratings are the bottom line for economic success, and a production that drives viewers away will be unsuccessful. The producers of movies, television programs, and even electronic games are always balancing the tastes of the targeted audience against artistic desires, often in both directions. Sometimes productions add titillating material to increase ratings. Other times productions avoid politically incorrect material that they fear might stimulate negative reactions. Most major production organizations already have staff that regularly monitor and edit production material, including evaluating sexual and violent material (Potter, 1999), although it is not clear that they distinguish appropriately among different types of violence that might affect children. They appear to be more concerned with not offending adult viewers. The point is that the argument that artists and producers should not consider the issue of the impact of violence in their productions is contradicted by the fact that they already consider the social impact of all sorts of other sensitive content in their productions, ranging from nudity and sexuality to race to religion. Thus, from a regulatory perspective, the problem becomes one of convincing artists and producers that violence has detrimental effects on the audience and such violence might offend a significant segment of the audience.

The majority of artists and producers probably have not yet been convinced either that violence really is detrimental to the audience or that the audience will be sufficiently offended by violence such that they will not watch. In fact, many seem to believe that violence attracts young audiences (Potter, 1999). Consequently, although many artists are social activists on issues ranging from the environment to land mines to tobacco, they do not see violence reduction as a social concern. Of course, there are some who do, but until a more general consensus emerges among artists that violence in the mass media has adverse effects on a substantial part of the audience, it is unrealistic to expect them to regulate violence substantially.

Commercial Sponsors of Television

Another possible powerful source of regulatory influence for violence on commercial television is the "sponsor." Sponsors advertise because they want to sell their products, and, if it becomes apparent that sales will not be helped by the sponsorship because of counteracting negative effects, they will withdraw their sponsorship. Again, the crucial missing link here is that, on average, sponsors have probably not been convinced either that violence is detrimental to a significant part of the audience or that the audience will be offended enough by violence that they will not buy the product. However, research evidence is only recently emerging that may help change sponsors' perspectives on this point. Bushman (1998) showed that violent segments in shows reduce the audience's memory for commercial messages, probably by focusing their attention away from the commercials. Additionally, there is good reason to believe that the association of products with the negative emotions stimulated by viewing violence will cause negative feelings to be "primed" in the future by the sight of the product (Berkowitz, 1993; Huesmann, 1998). When coupled with a growing awareness of public concerns about media violence, these kinds of findings may make sponsors wary of paying for programs containing violence. In fact, the producers of violence seem to be well aware of this possibility and have opposed content-based ratings for fear of losing their sponsors.

Public Advocacy Groups and Professional Organizations

Another potential locus of regulatory efforts directed against the transmission of violent messages could be public pressure groups such as the national Parent Teachers Association or Action for Children's Television, and professional organizations dealing with mental health issues. Many of these groups have played a significant role in swaying sentiment among politicians to do something about violence. Their success in influencing artists, producers, and sponsors is less apparent. Most of these groups, as well as the individual members in the groups, express no doubts about the detrimental effects of media violence. However, these public interest groups are sometimes not as well informed as desirable about the subtleties of the psychological processes involved or about whom the at-risk populations are. Additionally, they may be misinformed about the kinds of violence that is of most concern. This sometimes leads to some misdirected efforts by these groups, which detracts from the impact of all their efforts. When a group takes a questionable stance on one part of an issue, its credibility on all parts suffers.

A related issue is that a large segment of the general public from which many of the advocacy groups draw their members often display "third-person effects" with regard to this issue (Hoffner, Plotkin, Buchanan, & Anderson, 2001). Many people are absolutely convinced that media violence is having a detrimental effect on some children, but not on their own children. Furthermore, many believe that there can't be anything wrong with the kind of media violence they like to watch—only with the media violence they find repulsive. This thinking leads to the kinds of statements that Senator Dole once made in the midst of a presidential race when he stated that there needed to be fewer violent films and more films like *True Lies*, which in fact is a film filled with the kind of violence that many people find most enjoyable.

Parents

Let us turn now to potential loci of regulation that are intended to directly affect the receiver of the violent message. The first of these are the child's parents. Limiting the child's exposure to violence in the media would clearly reduce the risk of media violence affecting the child. This point is often made forcefully by industry spokespeople, and the validity of the point is clear. Parents have a strong influence on the child during the critical early years when television habits are being formed and when television content can affect the child most. Children of parents who watch more television also watch more television themselves (Comstock & Paik, 1991; Huesmann & Eron, 1986). Furthermore, apart from controlling overall viewing, research suggests that parents could also have an impact by interpreting the media content for the child. As described earlier, the less the child identifies with the perpetrator, the less the child perceives the violence as justified or normative, and the less the child perceives the violence on TV as realistic, then the less the violence is likely to have a lasting influence on the child. Parents have a unique opportunity to intervene on these dimensions. Nathanson and Cantor (Nathanson, 1999; Nathanson & Cantor, 2000) in fact showed that even minimal parental mediation of violent messages can reduce the effects of the violent messages.

At the same time, the realities of 21st-century family life must be considered when regulation and intervention strategies involving parents are considered. In the majority of families with young children, both parents are now working. Both parents are under time pressure each day. Consequently, being able to closely supervise a child's television viewing habits is not easy for most parents. In fact, less than 10% of most children's viewing time consists of coviewing by parents and children (Comstock & Paik, 1991). Active mediation requires even more effort by a parent. Furthermore, as children reach the school-age years and media contacts occur more and more at peers' houses and in peer groups, the ability of the parent to monitor exposure and mediate is reduced still further. Unfortunately, those children who are least likely to have their media exposure monitored and mediated by a parent tend to be those who would be most at risk for aggression in any case, such as children with low SES, low IQ, and/or from broken families.

Schools

Partially because of these difficulties with parental regulation, those people interested in regulating children's exposure to media on the reception side have turned more toward schools as a possible locus of regulation. The idea is that the schools would somehow prepare children so that they are not influenced as much by the violent messages they are bound to encounter. Two general approaches have been advocated for use within schools: media literacy training, and social-cognitive training.

Media Literacy Training.   A large number of programs have been developed for media literacy training over the past several decades in both the United States and in many other countries (Brown, 2001). They have ranged from attempts to improve critical thinking about media programs through discussion and learning about production (Dorr, Graves, & Phelps, 1980), to attempting to increase children's cognitive gains from TV by teaching children how it works (Singer & Singer, 1983), to trying to help children think logically about TV and distinguish fantasy from reality (Singer & Singer, 1983). State-sponsored and federally sponsored programs have become common. The most common themes in these programs seem to be that teaching children to think critically about what they see will enable them to learn more of what they should learn from TV, learn less of what they should not learn, and believe less of what they should not believe. Most proponents of media literacy programs believe that such training should reduce the negative impact of media violence on young viewers. However, the theoretical basis for such a belief is rarely specified in such programs and, even where it has been specified, it has rarely been rigorously evaluated for success. Although some elements of many media literacy programs (e.g., teaching that the dramas do not tell about life as it really is) theoretically could be expected to reduce the extent to which aggressive scripts, beliefs, and schemas are learned from watching violence, other elements of media literacy interventions could in fact be expected to promote the learning of aggression from observing dramas (e.g., teaching children to critically analyze and understand scripts of complex adult dramas).

The evaluations of media literacy programs that have been conducted to date generally do not provide an answer to the question of whether they reduce the impact of viewing violence (Brown, 2001). Most evaluations have assessed intermediate outcomes such as the ability of the child viewer to understand the narrative or to learn from it, and skills in media analysis. It is probably fair to say that no study to date has shown that media literacy training, per se, is effective in reducing the tendency of children to acquire aggressive scripts and beliefs from watching media violence.

Social Cognitive Interventions. Social cognitive interventions are those that are intended to reduce the negative effects of media violence on the receiver by changing the receiver's cognitions. Proponents think of this approach to regulating the effects of media violence as similar to regulating diseases by vaccinating children against them. The goal is to instill in children beliefs, schemas, and attributional tendencies that make it less likely that the children will acquire aggressive scripts, schemas, or beliefs from observing other people behaving violently. A very few interventions of this type have been tested separately or as part of larger interventions intended to prevent the development of violent tendencies in children. For example, Huesmann, Eron, Klein, Brice, and Fischer (1983) showed that a counterattitudinal intervention in which children's beliefs about the appropriateness of aggression, the realism of violence on TV, and the dangers of imitating the violence on TV were changed did engender reduced aggression in the treated group 1 year later compared to a control group. This intervention has also been included in two general interventions to prevent the development of aggression in young children, but with less success (Metropolitan Area Child Study Research Group,

2002). Certainly, more successful replications of this and similar approaches need to be conducted before one should count on such interventions as being an important part of a regulatory strategy.

OBSTACLES AND OBJECTIONS TO REGULATION

We have reviewed a variety of approaches to regulating children's exposure to violence in the televisual media, ranging from artists' actions to government action to parents' and schools' actions. All of the regulatory approaches discussed in this chapter have obstacles to their successful utilization. For each type and loci of the regulation, some obstacles are more important than others. In this section we discuss two main obstacles that seem to pose more of a problem: the economics of violence and constitutional issues about regulation.

Economics of Violence

As described earlier in this chapter, about 60% of television programs contain some violence. It is also clear that these programs are watched by many viewers. Although a majority of viewers may well believe that there is too much violence on television, a substantial portion of American viewers watch the violence (Hamilton, 1998). A better understanding of the economics of this situation and its implications for regulation can be obtained if we discuss the arguments about why so many people are exposed to media violence.

One common argument is simply that violence "sells"—that is, that violence per se attracts viewers. Some psychological theories support this view. Researchers know that children are attracted to fast-paced shows, with rapid changes of scenes, rapid changes in music and sound, and suspense or other factors that produce emotional arousal and relief (Comstock & Paik, 1991; Miron, Bryant, & Zillmann, 2001). Also, cognitive justification theory proposed by Huesmann (1982) suggests that viewers who already are more aggressive might prefer to watch violence in order to justify their behavior to themselves. However, there is only very weak longitudinal empirical data indicating that aggressive children indeed turn to watching more violence. Furthermore, although many violent shows have high ratings, the average ratings are higher for prime-time nonviolent shows than for prime-time violent shows.

An alternative, more sophisticated view of the economics of violence was provided by Hamilton's (1998a) market-based model. He argued that there is a subset of viewers who do prefer violent programming, and producers compete for these viewers to varying degrees depending on the relative benefit of attracting them compared to other audiences. If advertisers value these violence-preferring viewers because of their demographics, then the amount of violence offered should also increase. The bottom line is that the amount of violence on TV should be a function of the income generated because of the audience attracted and sponsors' interest in them minus the costs associated with producing the violent program. For example, the highest consumers of media violence are people aged 18 to 34 years, and these people are also one of the most attractive segments of the population to advertisers. Yet, advertising on violent prime-time shows costs less per thousand viewers than does advertising on nonviolent prime-time shows. Additionally, violent shows have higher expected profits from the foreign and residual sales of the program than do nonviolent shows. These all increase the economic value of violent programs to the producers.

One of the most important facts about Hamilton's model (1998a) is that he distinguished between the true costs of producing violence, including the "externalities" (costs to society of having the violence broadcast and having viewers influenced by it), and the costs to the producer alone. One of his major arguments was that violence appears economically attractive to producers because they do not consider the externalities in their profit equation. The public health costs of media violence are such an externality to the producers. So, too, would be whether children watch or don't watch an adult violent show that is being rated only for adult viewing. On the other side of the coin, Hamilton (1998a) argued that the costs to the public of regulating media violence or dealing with the violence engendered by the media are extremely high. For example, the cost and effort required of parents to monitor and mediate what their own child watches is very high and the benefits only accrue to that one child.

CONSTITUTIONAL OBSTACLES

In contrast to many other liberal democracies, the U.S. televisual environment has been shaped since its inception by two major economic and political conditions: the overwhelmingly commercial nature of broadcasting, and the First Amendment protection of free speech. Both of these features have had a crucial impact on the character of television programming, and have also influenced research on the effects of television, regulatory practices, and public debates about the relationship between the media and social behavior. Historically, the broadcast media have not enjoyed the same level of First Amendment protection as the print media have, mainly because of the perceived scarcity of the airwaves, which have been treated as a public good. However, new technological developments and cable television's increasingly ubiquitous reach have made the scarcity argument largely obsolete, which—coupled with the general trend toward deregulation—have produced an environment in which media violence may be even harder to curb.

Given all that, the V-chip seems like a step in the right direction, although its effects are likely to be limited by several factors, especially by the shortcomings of the ratings system and a relatively low adoption rate for the V-chip technology. In addition, concerns about the impact of the V-chip on free speech have been voiced by numerous individuals and organizations, and the technology has been labeled a "digital placebo" (Katz, 1999) and a "Big Brother" (ACLU, 1996). Whereas some have called the technology unconstitutional, others have complained only about certain aspects of the V-chip ratings system. For example, American Civil Liberties Union (ACLU) has not objected to the V-chip technology itself, but it has instead opposed any governmental control over the technology and/or the ratings system and has advocated development of independent private ratings systems and technology (ACLU, 1996). Still, scholars have argued that the V-chip ratings system may be constitutional, but the age-based ratings system may be declared unconstitutional (Spitzer, 1998); furthermore, the Supreme Court suggested in dicta that the V-chip technology may be constitutional (Ryan, 1999). The system can either be defended as being content neutral (i.e., providing information to consumers, similar to warning labels on cigarette packages and disclosure requirements for prescription drugs) or as a content-based regulation, which is narrowly tailored to achieve a compelling governmental interest (Ryan, 1999).

The First Amendment protagonists have treated the free speech guarantee as a proof that the government should not regulate speech at all, thus forgetting that the government is indeed allowed to regulate many forms of speech, including perjury, unlicensed medical advice, criminal solicitation, blackmail, verbal fraud, false advertising, and child pornography (Sunstein, 2001). Furthermore, the Supreme Court has continuously argued that the government may regulate obscene content (Ryan, 1999; Sunstein, 2001), and the FCC has generally followed the Miller test in making decisions about obscenity (*Miller v. California*, 413 U.S. 15, 1973). According to the FCC, material must meet a three-pronged test in order to qualify as obscene: An average person, applying contemporary community standards, must find that the material, taken as a whole, appeals to the prurient interest; the material must depict or describe, in a patently offensive way, sexual conduct specifically defined by applicable law; and the material, taken as a whole, must lack serious literary, artistic, political, or scientific value (http://www.fcc.gov/eb/broadcast /obscind.html). It is quite clear that a similar test for judging violent content does not exist. Still, Saunders (1996) made an interesting argument about obscenity and media violence, suggesting that violence may be considered obscene too, and thus could be subjected to state regulation. He maintained that throughout legal history, obscenity laws failed to distinguish between sex and violence and that in legal contexts the word *obscene* started to be exclusively associated with sex only following an obsession with limiting sexual expression dating from Victorian times. Therefore, Saunders indicated that clear statutory procedures should be established (i.e., describing specific violent acts) in order to classify certain films as legally obscene, acknowledging that contemporary community standards regarding violence should play a decisive role in this process. Although this proposal may seem promising, it is unlikely that this form of regulation would indeed be effective because it would only deal with the most extreme and goriest forms of violence, whereas other forms would remain unchecked. This is particularly true for the types of onscreen violence that are most likely to influence children—that is, when the violent acts are committed by heroic and attractive characters and are portrayed as being justified and rewarded.

Overall, the Constitution does not seem to present insurmountable obstacles to *some* government regulation of *children's* exposure to violence. The courts have upheld some of the FCC's attempts to regulate speech. In general, the courts have cited three "unique attributes" of broadcasting in their defense of regulation: the scarcity of airwaves, the uniquely pervasive presence of broadcasting in the lives of all Americans, and its unique accessibility by children, even by those who are too young to read (see Ryan, 1999). Currently, the federal law prohibits obscene broadcasts at all times (United States Code, 18 U.S.C. § 1464), whereas the FCC's rule restricts broadcasting of indecent material to the period of 10 P.M. to 6 A.M. (Code of Federal Regulations, 47 C.F.R. § 73.3999). In the last few years, the FCC has fined more than two dozen radio broadcasters for violating indecency laws, and complaints against TV broadcasters have also been examined. It should be noted, however, that similar restrictions do not apply to cable-only channels (FCC, 2002; for more information see http://www.fcc.gov/eb/broadcast/obscind.html). Interestingly, there are no federal laws regulating violent content, even though the case for harmfulness of media violence is unarguably stronger than for obscene, indecent, or profane material.

SUMMARY

In this chapter, we began by reviewing the compelling evidence that exposure to media violence needs to be regulated. We presented evidence that regulating children's exposure is much more important than regulating adults' exposure. We also pointed out that many characteristics of the way violence is presented and the kind of violence being presented influence its "toxicity" to children, although most of the public and policymakers appear to be unaware of those factors. We also concluded that all children are at risk, although some children are more at risk than others. We then reviewed the history of governmental attempts to regulate media violence that culminated in the V-chip law and associated ratings. We pointed out that there are a number of other powerful sources that could contribute to regulating the transmission of violence or to mitigating the impact it might have on young viewers, and discussed the pros and cons of each. Finally, we concluded with a discussion of the economic and legal obstacles to successful regulation.

So, what is the regulatory solution that seems best—better parental control, more government control, training children not to be affected by media violence, better rating systems for violence, boycotting sponsors of violence? Some part of all of these may be needed. Each society needs to make decisions based on what is best for it. However, it is time for every society to take this problem seriously and to act on it. The future of our children and society is too precious for us not to act.

REFERENCES

American Civil Liberties Union (ACLU). (1996). *TV ratings scheme is government-coerced censorship; "Don't let big brother take over the remote control."* Retrieved June 12, 2002, from http://www.aclu.org/news/n121996a.html

Anderson, B., Mead, N., & Sullivan, S. (1986). *Television: What do national assessment results tell us?* Princeton, NJ: Educational Testing Service.

Anderson, C. A., & Bushman, B. J. (2001). Effects of violent video games on aggressive behavior, aggressive cognition, aggressive affect, physiological arousal, and prosocial behavior: A meta-analytic review of the scientific literature. *Psychological Science, 12,* 353–359.

Andison, F. S. (1977). TV violence and viewer aggression: A cumulation of study results 1956–1976. *Public Opinion Quarterly, 41,* 314–331.

Baker, R., & Ball, S. (1969). *Mass media and violence: A report to the National Commission on the Causes and Prevention of Violence.* Washington, DC: U.S. Government Printing Office.

Bandura, A. (1977). *Social learning theory.* Englewood Cliffs, NJ: Prentice-Hall.

Bandura, A. (1986). *Social foundations of thought and action: A social-cognitive theory.* Englewood Cliffs, NJ: Prentice-Hall.

Bandura, A., Ross, D., & Ross, S. A. (1961). Transmission of aggression through imitation of aggressive models. *Journal of Abnormal Social Psychology, 63,* 575–582.

Belson, W. (1978). *Television violence and the adolescent boy.* Hampshire, UK: Saxon House.

Berkowitz, L. (1993). *Aggression: Its causes, consequences, and control.* New York: McGraw-Hill.

Bjorkqvist, K. (1985). *Violent films, anxiety and aggression.* Helsinki: Finnish Society of Sciences and Letters.

Brown, J. A. (2001). Media literacy and critical television viewing in education. In D. G. Singer & J. L. Singer (Eds.), *Handbook of children and the media* (pp. 681–697). Thousand Oaks, CA: Sage.

Bushman, B. J. (1998). Priming effects of violent media on the accessibility of aggressive constructs in memory. *Personality and Social Psychology Bulletin, 24,* 537–545.

Bushman, B. J. & Anderson C. A. (2001). Media violence and the American public. *American Psychologist, 56,* 477–489.

Bushman, B. J., & Stack, A. D. (1996). Forbidden fruit versus tainted fruit: Effects of warning labels on attraction to television violence. *Journal of Experiment Psychology: Applied, 2,* 207–226.

Code of Federal Regulations, Title 47, Volume 4. Washington, DC: U.S. Government Printing Office.

Comstock, G. A., & Paik, H. (1991). *Television and the American child.* San Diego, CA: Academic Press.

Comstock, G. A., Murray, J. P., & Rubinstein, E. A. (1972). *Television and social behavior: A technical report to the Surgeon General's Scientific Advisory Committee on television and social behavior.* Rockville, MD: National Institute of Mental Health.

Cooper, C. A. (1996). *Violence on television: Congressional inquiry, public criticism and industry response: A policy analysis.* Lanham, MD: University Press of America.

Dorr, A., Graves, S. B., & Phelps, E. (1980). Television literacy for young children. *Journal of Communication, 30*(3), 71–83.

Eron, L. D. (1963). Relationship of TV viewing habits and aggressive behavior in children. *Journal of Abnormal and Social Psychology, 67*(2), 193–196.

Eron, L. D., Huesmann, L. R., Lefkowitz, M. M., & Walder, L. O. (1972). Does television violence cause aggression? *American Psychologist, 27,* 253–263.

Federal Communications Commission (FCC). (2002). *EB—obscene & indecent broadcasts.* Retrieved June 12, 2002, from http://www.fcc.gov/eb/broadcast/obscind.html

Gerbner, G., & Signorielli, N. (1990). Violence profile, 1967 through 1988–1989: Enduring patterns. Unpublished manuscript, University of Pennsylvania, Annenberg School of Communication.

Hamilton, J. T. (1998a). *Channeling violence: The economic market for violent television programming.* Princeton, NJ: Princeton University Press.

Hamilton, J. T. (1998). Media violence and public policy. In J. T. Hamilton (Ed.), *Television violence and public policy* (pp. 1–12). Ann Arbor: University of Michigan Press.

Hoerrner, K. (1999). Symbolic politics: Congressional interest in television violence from 1950 to 1996. *Journalism of Mass Communication Quarterly, 76,* 684–698.

Hoffner, C., Plotkin, R. S., Buchanan, M., & Anderson, J. D. (2001). The third person effect in perceptions of the influence of television violence. *Journal of Communication, 51*(2), 283–299.

Huesmann, L. R. (1982). Television violence and aggressive behavior. In D. Pearl, L. Bouthilet, & J. Lazar (Eds.), *Television and behavior: Ten years of scientific programs and implications for the 80s* (vol. 2, pp. 126–137). Washington, DC: U.S. Government Printing Office.

Huesmann, L. R. (1988). An information processing model for the development of aggression. *Aggressive Behavior, 14,* 13–24.

Huesmann, L. R. (1998). The role of social information processing and cognitive schemas in the acquisition and maintenance of habitual aggressive behavior. In R. G. Geen & E. Donnerstein (Eds.), *Human aggression: Theories, research, and implications for policy* (pp. 73–109). New York: Academic Press.

Huesmann, L. R., & Eron, L. D. (1986). *Television and the aggressive child: A cross-national comparison.* Hillsdale, NJ: Lawrence Erlbaum Associates.

Huesmann, L. R., Eron, L. D., Klein, R., Brice, P., & Fischer, P. (1983). Mitigating the imitation of aggressive behaviors by children's attitudes about media violence. *Journal of Personality and Social Psychology, 44*, 899–910.

Huesmann, L. R., & Miller, L. S. (1994). Long-term effects of repeated exposure to media violence in childhood. In L. R. Huesmann (Ed.), *Aggressive behavior: Current perspectives* (pp. 153–186). New York: Plenum.

Huesmann, L. R., Moise, J. F., & Podolski, C. P. (1997). The effects of media violence on the development of antisocial behavior. In D. Stoff, J. Breiling, & J. Maser (Eds.), *Handbook of antisocial behavior* (pp. 181–193). New York: Wiley.

Huesmann, L. R., Moise, J., Podolski, C. & Eron, L. (2003). Longitudinal relations between childhood exposure to media violence and adult aggression and violence. *Developmental Psychology, 39*(2), 201-221.

Johnson, J. D., Adams, M. S., & Ashburn, L. (1995). Differential gender effects of exposure to rap music on African American adolescents acceptance of teen dating violence. *Sex Roles, 33*(7/8), 597–605.

Katz, J. (1999). Are V-chips and content ratings necessary? No. In A. Alexander & H. Hanson (Eds.), *Taking sides: Clashing views on controversial issues in mass media and society* (pp. 236–296). Guilford, CT: Dushkin/McGraw-Hill.

Kunkel, D., & Wilcox, B. (2001). Children and media policy. In D. G. Singer & J. L. Singer (Eds.), *Handbook of children and the media* (pp. 589–604). Thousand Oaks, CA: Sage.

Lazarsfeld, P. F. (1955). Why is so little known about the effects of television on children and what can be done? *Public Opinion Quarterly, 19*, 243–251.

Lefkowitz, M. M., Eron, L. D., Walder, L. O., & Huesmann, L. R. (1977). *Growing up to be violent: A longitudinal study of the development of aggression.* New York: Pergamon.

Malamuth, N. M., & Donnerstein, E. (1982). The effects of aggressive and pornographic mass media stimuli. In L. Berkowitz (Ed.), *Advances in experimental social psychology* (vol. 15, pp. 103–136). New York: Academic Press.

McLeod, J. M., Atkin, C. K., & Chaffee, S. H. (1972). Adolescents, parents and television use: Adolescent self-report measures from Maryland and Wisconsin samples. In G. A. Comstock & E. A. Rubinstein (Eds.), *Television and social behavior: A technical report to the Surgeon General's Scientific Advisory Committee on television and social behavior. Vol. 3. Television and adolescent aggressiveness* (DHEW Publication No. HSM 72-9058; pp. 173–238). Rockville, MD: National Institute of Mental Health.

Metropolitan Area Child Study Research Group. [In alphabetical order: Eron, L. D., Guerra, N. G., Henry, D., Huesmann, L. R., Tolan, P., & VanAcker, R.]. (2002). A cognitive/ecological approach to preventing aggression in urban settings: Initial outcomes for high-risk children. *Journal of Consulting and Clinical Psychology, 70*, 179–194.

Milavsky, J. R., Kessler, R., Stipp, H., & Rubens, W. S. (1982). *Television and aggression: A panel study.* New York: Academic Press.

Miller v. California, 413 U.S. 15 (1973).

Miron, D., Bryant, J., & Zillmann, D. (2001). Creating vigilance for better learning from television. In D. Singer & J. Singer (Eds.), *Handbook of children and the media* (pp. 153–182). Thousand Oaks, CA: Sage.

Motion Picture Association of America (MPAA). (2002). *Movie ratings.* Retrieved June 12, 2002, from http://www.mpaa.org

Nathanson, A. I. (1999). Identifying and explaining the relationship between parent mediation and children's aggression. *Communication Research, 26*(2), 124–143.

Nathanson, A. I., & Cantor, J. (2000). Reducing the aggression-promoting effect of violent cartoons by increasing children's fictional involvement with the victim: A study of active mediation. *Journal of Broadcasting and Electronic Media, 44*(1), 125–142.

Newton, D. E. (1996). *Violence and the media: A reference handbook.* Santa Barbara, CA: ABC-CLIO.

Paik, H. (2001). The history of children's use of electronic media. In D. G. Singer & J. L. Singer (Eds.), *Handbook of children and the media* (pp. 7–28). Thousand Oaks, CA: Academic Press.

Paik, H., & Comstock, G. A. (1994). The effects of television violence on antisocial behavior: A meta-analysis. *Communication Research, 21*, 516–546.

Parental Choice in Television Act of 1955, 104th Congress.

Potter, W. J. (1999). *On media violence*. Thousand Oaks, CA: Sage.

Ryan, A. M. (1999). Don't touch that V-chip: A constitutional defense of the television program ratings provisions of the Telecommunications Act of 1996. *Georgetown Law Journal, 87*, 823–848.

Saunders, K. W. (1996). *Violence as obscenity: Limiting the media's First Amendment protection*. Durham, NC: Duke University Press.

Schramm, W., Lyle, J., & Parker, E. (1961). *Television in the lives of our children*. Stanford, CA: Stanford University Press.

Signorielli, N. (1991). *A sourcebook on children and television*. Westport, CT: Greenwood.

Singer, J. L., & Singer, D. G. (1983). Psychologists look at television: Cognitive, developmental, personality, and social policy implications. *American Psychologist, 38*, 826–834.

Spitzer, M. L. (1998). A first look at the constitutionality of the V-chip rating system. In J. T. Hamilton (Ed), *Television violence and public policy* (pp. 335–383). Ann Arbor: University of Michigan Press.

Sunstein, C. (2001). *Republic.com*. Princeton, NJ: Princeton University Press.

Surgeon General's Scientific Advisory Committee on Television and Social Behavior (1972). *Television and growing up: The impact of televised violence*. Washington, DC: U.S. Government Printing Office.

TV Parental Guidelines. (2002). *Understanding the TV ratings*. Retrieved June 12, 2002, from http://www.tvguidelines.org/default.asp

United States Code, Title 18, Section 1464 (Broadcasting Obscene Language). Washington, DC: U.S. Government Printing Office.

U.S. Senate Committee on Commerce. (1972). Serial No. 92–52.

Valenti, J. (2000). *A response to the FTC report offered by Jack Valenti, president & chief executive officer, Motion Picture Association of America, on behalf of The Walt Disney Company, Dreamworks SKG, Metro-Goldwyn-Mayer Studios, Paramount Pictures, Sony Pictures Entertainment, Twentieth Century Fox Film Corporation, Universal Studios, Warner Bros*. Retrieved June 12, 2002, from http://www.mpaa.org/jack/2000/00_09_26.htm

Webster, J. G., Pearson, J. C., & Webster, D. B. (1986). Children's television viewing as affected by contextual variables in the home. *Communication Research Reports, 3*, 1–8.

Wilson, B., Colvin, C., & Smith, S. (2002). Engaging in violence on American television: A comparison of child, teen and adult perpetrators. *Journal of Communication, 52*, 36–60.

Wilson, B. J., Kunkel, D., Linz, D., Potter, J., Donnerstein, E., Smith, S. L., Blumenthal, E., & Gray, T. (1997). Violence in television programming overall: University of California, Santa Barbara study. In M. Seawall (Ed.), *National television violence study* (vol. 1, pp. 3–184). Thousand Oaks, CA: Sage.

Wilson, B. J., Kunkel, D., Linz, D., Potter, J., Donnerstein, E., Smith, S. L., Blumenthal, E., & Berry, M. (1998). Violence in television programming overall: University of California, Santa Barbara study. In M. Seawall (Ed.), *National television violence study* (vol. 2, pp. 3–204). Thousand Oaks, CA: Sage.

Wilson, B., Smith, S., Potter, W. J., Kunkel, D., Linz, D., Colvin, C., & Donnerstein, E. (2002). Violence in children's television programming: Assessing the risks. *Journal of Communication, 52*(1), 5–35.

Zillmann, D. (1979). *Hostility and aggression*. Hillsdale, NJ: Lawrence Erlbaum Associates.

Zillmann, D. (1983). Transfer of excitation in emotional behavior. In J. T. Cacioppo & R. E. Petty (Eds.), *Social psychophysiology: A sourcebook* (pp. 215–240). New York: Guilford.

12

Children's Future Programming and Media Use Between Entertainment and Education

Peter Vorderer
Ute Ritterfeld
University of Southern California

FUTURE PROGRAMMING AND USE OF ENTERTAINMENT MEDIA: WHAT IS THERE TO EXPECT?

Televisual media, there is no doubt, has tremendously changed over the comparatively short period of the past 10 years (Bryant & Bryant, 2001). Although less than 1% of U.S. families have no television set (Kaiser Family Foundation, 1998), and more than 85% of American homes receive cable television (Labaton, 1999), traditional television is currently merging with other forms of media. Looking at the domestic screen, we now see devices that are connected to and sometimes fused with video recorders, personal computers, the Internet, computer games, and so on. There is WebTV, DirecTV, and interactive television. The televisi on screen is about to be transformed into the site of a multimedia culture, and this primarily technological development has significantly increased the already wide array of programming as much as it has opened new possibilities of using it. More individualized programming is possible now, and the opportunities to fulfill specific needs of precisely defined subaudiences are myriad.

In respect to traditional television and other forms of televisual media, the programming as much as the use of the media has always been dominated by *entertain-*

ment purposes (Zillmann & Bryant, 1994; Zillmann & Vorderer, 2000a), and it does so today maybe more than ever before (Vorderer, 2001). This brings up the question of where all of this will lead to, particularly in respect to children and teenagers, who have been regarded as the most vulnerable part of the audience (Walker & Bellamy, 2001) and who are described to be fond of entertainment programming and use just as much of it as adults do (Beentjes, Koolstra, Marseille, & van der Voort, 2001). Will they—and will we—see more or less entertainment on televisual media? What about other popular media for children, like audiotapes? Will educational programs exist or, perhaps, even dominate prime-time TV and/or the emerging market of games? Could this lead to a reduction of programs that have purely entertaining contents without any educational value? Or will purely educational programs even be able to compete with entertainment?

Regarding children's future programming and media use, one has to keep in mind that the socializing institution of the family, as well as the culture of childhood and youth, have also changed over recent years, both in the United States and in Western Europe (Bryant & Bryant, 2001; Livingstone & Bovill, 2001). Today, only 38% of U.S. homes have children, and two married parents with kids can now be found in only about 25% of households. This alone leads to expectations about the various functions of media for children might have changed altogether. Where particularly television once was the homes' entertainer and educator, it may have become a pseudo caregiver in many households, particularly to preschool children (Bryant, Bryant, Mullikin, McCollum, & Love, 2001).

Despite all the technological and social developments, the relationship between children and television is still of utmost importance, not only but particularly in the United States. On average, American children watch 2 to 3 hours of broadcast or cable television on a weekday, plus about 1 hour of videotapes, and a bit more than that on the weekend (Kaiser Family Foundation, 1998). Compared to this, children in Western Europe tend to watch less, but still would miss television more than any other medium if they had to do without it. Hence, television remains to be the most important and pervasive medium in European, just as in American, homes (Beentjes et al., 2001; d'Haenens, 2001).

Nevertheless, "technology forecasting has long been known as a 'dangerous' profession" (Lin, 2001, p. 218), and this is also true when it comes to predicting programming and media use. This is because those people and institutions who are directly involved or affected by the respective developments have different interests and presumably also different estimations: Whereas children, producers, and advertisers may be united in claiming more and better entertainment in all sorts of media, parents and teachers in particular are often concerned about the potentially negative impact of such programs on their children and students, and therefore arrogate for less entertainment and more education through media.

Children, Producers, and Advertisers Want More Entertainment

From what we know on the basis of many empirical studies that have been carried out in North America and Western Europe, more than anything else children primarily expect to be entertained when using the various media (Beentjes et al., 2001). This holds true for traditional television and for any other form of televisual media, as much as for new media (for the example of Germany, cf. Feierabend & Klingler, 1999; Fritzsche, 2000). That is, kids expose themselves to television, movies, books, comics, audiotapes, and computer games not primarily because they are interested in learning by using a certain program, but simply because they're fun. This is not to say that these media cannot also provide their users with opportunities for learning, but apparently the wish to learn is not the main motive of children turning to use these programs.

Exactly what kind of media and what kind of entertainment program children prefer depends more than anything else on the children's age, gender, and socioeconomic status (SES). By first or second grade, for example, American kids start preferring situation comedies (Huston, Wright, Marquis, & Green, 1999); at the end of elementary school, they appear to be more interested in dramatic programs (Cantor & Nathanson, 1996); and in the middle of their teens, their favorites are adult entertainment programs, like comedies (Hawkins, Reynolds, & Pingree, 1991). As far as gender is concerned, the findings are somewhat inconsistent when it comes to explain the differences in viewing times of boys and girls. However, there is clear evidence that boys tend to prefer more action and violence than girls do (e.g., van der Voort, 1986), whereas girls are more attracted by family shows, particularly programs that portray relationships and sexual content (e.g., Greenberg, Linsangan, & Soderman, 1993). Looking at age and gender at the same time, as a more recent study that interviewed and surveyed some 11,000 6- to 16-year-olds in Europe did, it becomes clear, for example, that "girls' preference for soaps peaks between the ages of 9 to 13," and that "interest in sport increases with age only in the case of boys; girls' comparative lack of interest in this topic remains stable" (Garitaonandia, Juaristi, & Oleaga, 2001, p. 150). The same study also pointed to the importance that SES still has on the preference for entertainment media and their contents (as an overview, cf. Livingstone & Bovill, 2001). Most striking in this respect is that reading books continues to be associated with a higher SES more than using other forms of media (Beentjes et al., 2001).

The influence of the children's cultural background on their media use and preferences in different European countries is, however, rather weak: "Once age and gender are taken into account, similarities in tastes among children and teenagers from different countries greatly outnumber differences" (Garitaonandia et al., 2001, p. 155). And even when European and U.S. children are compared, as in a study by Valkenburg and Janssen (1999), both groups show only little differences in what they value about entertainment programming, which is comprehensibility and action, humor, compellingness, innocuousness, realism, violence, and romance. Valkenburg and Janssen's results even suggested "that there are certain elements in children's entertainment programs that universally attract children, irrespective of their cultural background" (Valkenburg & Janssen, 1999, p. 16). These data support the assumption that children's media use is even cross-culturally driven by their seeking of entertainment, because "The media that fulfill entertaining or emotional functions are the media that are used most frequently, because these two motives for using media are by far the strongest in determining media choices" (Beentjes et al., 2001, p. 89).

Children's interest matches perfectly with the producers' and programmers' interest to sell content to a preferably large audience. Because of the described children's preference for entertainment, the ratings for such programs have always been higher than those for educational programs, and this is—simply speaking—why producers prefer entertainment to education. From a producer's perspective, what is even better than a large audience within the United States is an international audience, so that the program may be sold worldwide. Based on the size of their audience, producers, distributors, and programmers may sell time slots for commercials within their programs to the advertisement industry and thereby generate the largest portion of their profit. The higher their ratings are (i.e., the larger the premature audience), the higher the prices are for the time slots. Naturally, the advertisement industry's interests are also met, simply because they seek a large and often global audience in order to sell their products more easily worldwide.

What can producers and advertisers do to improve their success? There are basically two ways to accomplish this. First, they may produce and invest in better entertainment programs (i.e., programs that are more entertaining and more appealing to children). Second, they may try to enlarge their audience. Improving the quality of the program by being more entertaining isn't as easy as it may sound. In order to be able to do this, one must understand what makes a program entertaining in the first place (this is discussed in more detail later in the chapter). The second way—to increase the size of the audience—seems to be easier to manage. However, it is not possible to instantly increase the number of child viewers or to extend the time of childhood and adolescence arbitrarily. What is possible, however, is to address more and more younger children and thereby shift the age boundary downward to include children that haven't, as yet, been using specific media or specific programs. This is exactly what we have seen in the United States over the last 20 years or so, and more recently in European countries. The British production Teletubbies, for example, is meant to address an audience of 1- and 2-year-olds, displaying a new focus for the entertainment and advertisement industries. More generally speaking, programs that may be appreciated—to some extent even understood by toddlers and kindergarten children—create an additional audience that hasn't existed before. Simultaneously, media devices have been produced in such a way that even preschool children have no problems in handling them. A very good example of this are audiotape players, which are capable of satisfying preschool children's desire to entertain themselves by managing these devices independently from their parents and caretakers.

To sum up, providing more entertainment for more and younger children is not only in the interests of the young audience, but also in the interests of the industry. The estimation should therefore be that children's future programming and media use may be characterized by entertainment more than ever before. This, however, generates a new concern, namely that specific media, and even more important, certain programs, may not be appropriate for children of a specific age. More precisely, the concern exists that a program, because it is produced to attract an older audience, does not fit a younger audience's cognitive and emotional capacities or abilities and would therefore be overwhelming and disturbing to the children's well-being or to psychological development. This, however, is not so much a concern vocalized by the industry but instead is one of parents and teachers.

Parents and Teachers Are Concerned About Too Much Entertainment

Based on the observation that, since the late 1970s, there has been more violence and more explicit sexual content on American television (Huston, Wartella, & Donnerstein, 1998; Huston & Wright, 1997), parents in the United States have increasingly worried about the potential effects of this programming on their children's well-being and further development. The Kaiser Family Foundation (1999) found that 60% of parents reported a "great deal" of concern about the violence, and 66% felt the same in respect to the sexual content, in television programs. In contrast to European and in particular to German parents, who worry more about the sheer time children spend with television, the concern of American parents is primarily directed toward specific contents (Brown & Hayes, 2001). Of course, both forms of problematic programming (violence and sex) are considered to be strongly related to entertainment, so one might conclude that parents would favor less entertainment for their children.

The reason for this can be found in the conviction of most parents and teachers that children are more vulnerable than other media users, that they might easily be affected by what they see on the screen (Walker & Bellamy, 2001), and that media use, particularly that of computers and of computer games, has a tremendous impact on the process of socialization (Krotz & Hasebrink, 2001). One of the most feared, publicly discussed, and thoroughly investigated potential effects have been the so-called "fright and fear" reactions of children, primarily in respect to television or film (cf., Cantor, 1994; Cantor & Mares, 2001). More recently, the question also emerged whether televisual media provide stereotypes about ethnic minorities, and research has started to address the question in how far those stereotypic images influence the children's and teenagers' conceptions of these minorities (Cortes, 2000).

No matter what the concern is about, the viewers' and users' age is of central importance here, because both the audience's motivation to use the media as well as its experience with the content depends on how old the children are. The younger and more premature the audience is, the more defenseless it may be: From a psychological point of view this suspicion has been backed up by social cognitive theory (cf. Bandura, 2001), with its assumption that characters in entertainment programs work as models for an audience that, under certain conditions, is ready not only to acquire but also to perform the same kind of behavior. The already described attempt to extend the size of the premature audience by addressing smaller children through particular features of the program that are meant to appeal to toddlers and preschool children has only added a new concern to the already existing precautionary attitude of parents and teachers (i.e., the concern of age related *inappropri-*

ateness of a program for a specific child). Usually, books, audiotapes, and computer games are labeled with recommendations to best fit the interests and needs of children of a specific age group. With television, this labeling often determines the time frame for its appropriate broadcasting. With those media (contents) that are meant to be bought (audiotapes, computer games, books, etc.), the labeling is supposed to help parents (and caretakers, teachers, etc.) select a specific offering because it is meant to suit their children's interests best. All of this underlines the assumption that specific media contents may or may not fit the child's cognitive and/or emotional state of development (i.e., that in the case that it does not fit, it will either demand too much or too little, given the capabilities and capacities of a specific child). Although demanding too little may be a major concern for producers, distributors, and advertisers (see the earlier discussion), because it could lead to boredom on the users' side and thereby to less appreciation, demanding too much is certainly more of a concern for parents (and other caretakers), because it could lead to a state of short- or even long-term disturbance.

This is consistent with a current perspective in developmental psychology, which regards development as a transition resulting from coeffective influences both from the individual and the environment (Montada, 1998). Depending on the specific area of development that is at stake, either the individual or the environmental part might be of more importance. The cooperating modus has been labeled *transactionalism* (Oerter, 1998) and described as a process in which both sides may influence each other. In the case of media use, it is not only the program that influences the user but also the program that will be modified through the fact that is has been used. Of course, the latter type of influence takes place only over a certain period of time, and it is this consideration of long-term processes that is most prototypical for this theoretical perspective (in contrast, e.g., to an interactionist perspective). Whenever the conditions and prerequisites on the subject's side meet the specific features and characteristics on the environmental side, a perfect fit (Ritterfeld, 2000) in the sense of appropriateness is given, and this fit is optimal for development. Given that both sides continuously change over time, this moment of fit is necessarily temporary, and hence development implies and requires a consistent flow of moments of fit. Therefore, developmental problems have been considered problems of appropriateness (Brandtstädter, 1985).

If one applies this perspective to children's media consumption, the distinction can be made between a type of exposure that has no fostering impact on human development and another type of exposure that actually is a hindrance to human development. Such negative effects are conceivable in all domains of individual development (i.e., cognitive, socioemotional, language related, etc.). But how do media contents fit? According to the concept of developmental tasks (Havighurst, 1948), a fit is made when media contents and programs help children to cope with a current task (cf., Boehnke, Hoffmann, Münch, & Güffens, 1997). If, for example, a child is learning numbers up to 20, a specific episode of *Sesame Street* might be a fit because it is also dealing with these numbers. If however, this episode focuses on numbers up to 10 or on numbers from 100 to 200, it will be less useful. Apparently, the public debate points to and focuses on the fact that those programs that are less useful may be emotionally overwhelming and thereby harm the children's well-being.

ENTERTAINMENT FOR CHILDREN

What Is Media Entertainment?

From an everyday point of view, entertainment is seen as a feature of the media offer itself. According to this view, some media contents—like TV shows, films, soap operas, sitcoms, and so on—are entertaining, whereas others—like news, documentary, and learning programs—are not. In so being, they are capable of determining what the media users do with them, what they think and feel, what they experience or miss; in short, whether the users are entertained or not. But as much as we have to admit that media users do in fact often watch a news program with more concentration, feeling earnest and less amused, and that they often relate to the characters of a talk show in a primarily affective way and less in order to learn from them, it is also true that viewers do not necessarily have to do so and, in fact, they sometimes don't. In other words: It's the users who decide whether they want to entertain themselves or to learn from a program, be it the news or the utterances of a talk show guest. In this perspective, entertainment is a *reception phenomenon;* it is an experience that may be described in psychological terms by referring to what the user goes through during his or her exposure to the program.

By the same token, entertaining does not necessarily oppose, nor even hinder, information processing, although our everyday point of view may again presuppose this. Viewers often watch entertainment genres, like daily talk shows or films, in order to also reflect on their own life circumstances (Bente & Fromm, 1997) or to learn from them (Trepte, Zapfe, & Sudhoff, 2001). At the same time, onlookers of news programs develop affective dispositions toward people on the screen and feel amusement and enjoyment when these characters encounter good or bad fortunes (Zillmann, Taylor, & Lewis, 1998, 1999). For example, watching a sport event on TV certainly offers both information and entertainment, and provides a specific combination of these two experiential dimensions (cf. Bryant & Raney, 2000). The dichotomy of entertainment and information is not even plausible: Media users who feel entertained are more interested, more attentive, and therefore more eager to select, follow, and process the information given by a program than are those users who are not (Vorderer, Ritterfeld, & Klimmt, 2001). Instead of being in opposition to successful information processing, entertainment appears more and more to be a crucial condition for it.

Based on these two notions—of entertainment as a reception phenomenon and of entertainment as not being in contradiction with information processing—Bosshart and Macconi (1998) systematized six different dimensions that are often implied when the entertainment experiences of media users are described. According to them, for media users

Entertainment means:

- psychological relaxation—It is restful, refreshing, light, distracting;

- change and diversion—It offers variety and diversity;

- stimulation—It is dynamic, interesting, exciting, thrilling;

- fun—It is merry, amusing, funny;

- atmosphere—It is beautiful, good, pleasant, comfortable;

- joy—It is happy, cheerful. (Bosshart & Macconi, 1998, p. 4)

Apparently, entertainment experiences are described as being primarily pleasant and joyful. Zillmann and Bryant (1994) agreed when they defined it "as any activity designed to delight and, to a smaller degree, enlighten through the exhibition of fortunes and misfortunes of others, but also through the display of special skills by others and/or self" (p. 438). Defining entertainment as a primarily pleasant experience helps us to understand why so many media users seek entertainment so often and so intensively. Based on this understanding, the explanation of entertainment seeking behavior may easily be found in the audience's desire to have a good time. Bosshart and Macconi (1998) continued their dimensional analysis and subdivide pleasure into four subcategories:

1. pleasure of the senses, as in the use of physical abilities, or in the experience of motor and sensory activity;

2. pleasure of the (ego-) emotions, as in evoking and experiencing emotions, or in mood-management;

3. pleasure of personal wit and knowledge, as in the use of cognitive or intellectual powers or competence in being able to use one's wit;

4. and pleasures of the (socio-)emotions, such as the ability to feel an emotion with and for others, to identify with others. (Bosshart & Macconi, 1998, p. 5)

This differentiation helps to systematize the research that has been conducted over the last few years on various aspects of entertainment. Without a doubt, most of the empirical and psychological work in this area has focused on the last-mentioned dimension (4); that is, on the analysis of feelings and emotions that occur in the context of the relation between media users and people who appear in the media. Primarily within communication research, the concepts of "parasocial interactions" and "parasocial relations," as explicated by Horton and Wohl (1956) and Horton and Strauss (1957), have repeatedly been applied to the audiences' attitude toward people featured in diverse media offers and programs, such as news anchors (Rubin, Perse, & Powell, 1985), characters of TV serials and soap operas (Rubin & Perse, 1987; Vorderer, 1996a; Vorderer & Knobloch, 1996), or, in general, the viewers' favorites on TV (Gleich, 1997). Exposure to these contents has been deemed as entertaining, and the description of this particular experience, from a parasocial interaction point of view, helps to explain why media users select and watch these programs (cf., as an overview, Gleich, 1997; Vorderer, 1998).

From a more psychological point of view, Zillmann (1991, 1994, 1996) and his collaborators (e.g., Zillmann & Bryant, 1994; Zillmann & Cantor, 1977) studied entertainment as being, above all, a process in which the media user becomes involved during exposure in a particular way. Zillmann conceptualized viewers, readers, listeners—generally, all media users—as witnesses to events that characters in a narrative undergo. Essentially, in his model is the assumption that these witnesses morally evaluate what they witness and therefore either applaud or condemn the characters' actions and intentions. Approval of these actions leads to dispositions of liking and caring, and the character becomes the hero or heroine. Condemnation, however, generates dispositions of dislike and resentment, such that the characters are consequently seen as evil-type villains. As a further consequence of this, affective dispositions toward liked characters trigger the media users' hopes for positive outcomes, and, conversely, their fear of negative dénouements. Similarly, a disapprobation of the characters' behavior causes a dislike and fear of outcomes that are positive for an antagonist. The audiences' emotionality—their hopes and fears toward the ongoing and outcome of narratives together with the relief they experience in the end when the good forces triumph—is what Zillmann identified as crucial for any entertainment experience within the media. This affective disposition theory has been tested, proofed, and applied to many different genres and audiences (cf., as an overview, Zillmann & Vorderer, 2000b), so that today it may be identified as the strongest theory on entertainment available.

Complementary to this, Vorderer (2001) proposed that the entertaining use of the media and its offers could be considered play. According to Oerter (1999), play is a particular form of an action that is characterized by three major aspects:

- It is intrinsically motivated and highly attractive.
- It implies a change in perceived reality, because players construct an additional reality while they are playing.
- It is frequently repeated.

Based on the background of observing children at play, Oerter (2000) pointed out that play experiences show two more conspicuous features that should also be considered here: Children's games may be suspenseful and sometimes even lead to disappointment, as is the case when a player loses, and games are often played on an intellectual level that is not appropriate to the cognitive capacities and competences of the child (Oerter, 2000). Based on explanations given by Freud, Piaget, and Wygotski, Oerter described children's playing in more general terms as a form of coping with one's own life (i.e., an activity that helps children to compensate for their problems, desires, and socialization pressure). Looking more closely at the various forms of playing, it becomes clear that early games of make believe express the children's wish for control, power, and to overcome their inability to influence their environment, all of which help children to come to terms with their own identity and individuation. This perspective clearly regards playing as a form of transforming reality in a way that serves the psychological needs of children.

The analogy is evident: Not only has the use of the media already been conceptualized as action, rather than as behavior or pure response (Vorderer, 1993), it has also been shown to be motivated more by internal than external causes. This means that the use of the media is to be regarded as an activity that is serving not extrinsic but instead intrinsic purposes, and this is particularly true when it is entertainment for which viewers, listeners, and readers are looking. The changes in perceived reality while using the media are also well known. Many theoretical considerations have described in detail, addressing how media users change their sense of reality by taking on the reality provided by the media while temporarily ignoring the physical and social reality in which they are actually living and of which the media is a part. Various theorists have labeled this sense of nonmediation with different terms; for example, as *identification* (Oatley, 1994), *involvement* (Vorderer, 1993), *immersion* (Biocca & Levy, 1995), *absorption* (Wild, Kuiken, & Schopflocher, 1995), or *presence* (Lombard & Ditton, 1997). No doubt, all these constructs focus on different aspects of this particular experience, but what they all have in common is their attempt to describe and explain what media users are going through in terms of their sense of reality.

The third characteristic of play—that of repetition—is another typical feature of entertainment, because most media users develop entertainment preferences and return to them in a more or less regular way. As far as the two additional characteristics of playing—that is, their potential to disappoint the player, and the low intellectual level on which they are often played—are concerned, they have striking similarities to the less pleasant aspects of entertainment (e.g., to feelings of sadness while watching a movie; Vorderer, in press). In addition to this, the empirical research that has been conducted on the mental effort required when watching TV should also be mentioned because it confirms this analogy. Salomon (1979, 1984) demonstrated that watching TV is not necessarily easy but it is usually *regarded* as being less demanding than reading. Due to this *expectation,* viewers consequently invest less mental effort into this activity than they would for reading a book (cf., as an overview, Weidenmann, 1989).

What Is Children's Media Entertainment?

Are there any relevant differences when it comes to children's entertainment in contrast to that of adults? Yes and no: Surely, children are attached to protagonists in the way that affective disposition theory describes adults to be. Children also feel the same kind of pleasure when witnessing the preferred ongoing of a movie as adults do, although they might show it more openly. Children often empathize with their heroes and heroines and disapprove the villains' behavior, as can easily be seen when considering their exposure to theatrical plays or fairy tales. But what also has repeatedly been found in studies on children's media use is their specific emphasis on formal aspects of the program. For example, children tend to prefer music as a part of the narrative on audiotapes (Vorderer, Klimmt, & Liebetruth, 2002), they particularly like special effects and animation in movies and computer games, they prefer female and warm voices over male and cold ones in TV and radio programs (Groebel, 1994a, 1994b), and so on. It seems as though their desire for formal characteristics is similar to the well-known and thoroughly investigated aesthetic preferences of adults that usually contribute to their selection of contents. However, with adults we wouldn't regard these dimensions of their experience as being a part of entertainment, because we are used to dichotomizing entertainment and art (Gabler, 1998), function and form (Bourdieu, 1987), the useful and the beautiful. But there is no doubt that these formally aesthetic dimensions play a role when adults have to choose among a variety of programs, and thus we assume it is the same for children.

We regard these formal characteristics as important for children's entertainment experiences, just like their affective dispositions toward the characters. More precisely, we believe that the children's interest is first triggered by these formal characteristics, as they instantly draw the children's involuntary attention (Anderson & Collins, 1988) and subsequently lead to the development of affective dispositions. In order to elucidate these various influences, we have proposed a process model of children's entertainment experience while listening to audiotapes (Vorderer et al., 2001), but it may be applied to other forms of media as well. Central to this model is the notion of attention (cf., for an overview, Underwood, 1993). Attention is crucial both in respect to the selection of specific stimuli as well as in respect to the allocation of limited cognitive resources. We assume a particular experience of media use to be more entertaining if the program has more entertainment potential to offer and children allocate more attention to this potential (see Fig. 12.1.). Only when attention is drawn to this potential can children process and enjoy the program, so that attention and entertainment influence each other. Only through this more thorough processing of information is learning possible and fostered. Necessary, however, is a fit between the complexity of the information given and the capacities of the child (i.e., that the program does not demand too much in comparison to what the child may be able to perform).

In addition to this short-term process model, we have also proposed, for consideration, various selections of media contents and programs on a larger time scale (see Fig. 12.2). Many children select specific programs repeatedly, in some cases very often, which is particularly true for audiotapes but also applies to entertainment programming in general. As should be visualized in this model, the entertainment experience elucidates the further selection of a particular content, and the ongoing media exposure helps to keep up the process of learning.

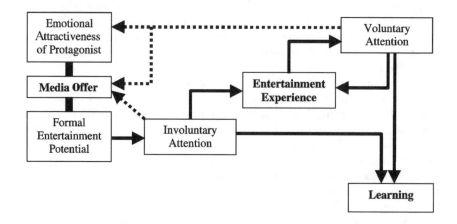

FIG. 12.1.   Model of the relation among attention, entertainment experience, and learning (cf. Vorderer, Ritterfeld, & Klimmt, 2001).

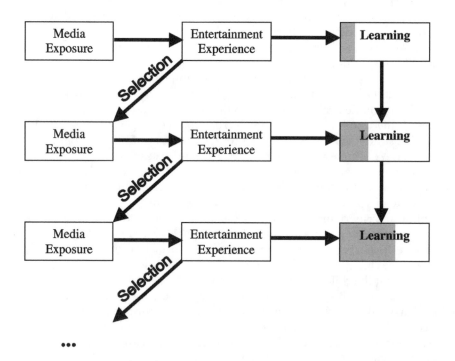

FIG. 12.2.   Model of the relation between entertainment experience and learning, from a behavioral perspective (cf. Vorderer, Ritterfeld, & Klimmt, 2001).

Why Do Children Often Use What Is Not Appropriate for Them but Only Like What They Understand? The Social Psychological Function of Entertainment

No matter whether we deal with children's or adults' entertainment, there is a "third dimension" to people's experience that remains neglected, quite regularly, by communication research—its social psychological function. This function has to do with benefits that result only indirectly from a performed behavior. For example, when people entertain themselves, they might gain what they were seeking (e.g., pleasure, relief, distraction, etc.). But in addition to this direct gratification, other benefits are also possible, such as a certain impression one makes on others (being "cool" because one is capable of braving a horror movie), or even an improvement in of one's own self-understanding, based on the fact that a certain behavior (e.g., the selection of the horror movie) has been performed. We have shown elsewhere (Ritterfeld & Vorderer, 1993) how important this "self-serving" function might be in the context of selecting and reading books. Additionally, Trepte (2002) could empirically demonstrate how much the decision to participate in a daily talk show on TV is influenced by the viewers' and guests' intention to complete (in the sense of self-completion theory; Wicklund & Gollwitzer, 1982) their own selves.

A similar function may be applied to children's selection of and exposure to entertainment programs. Such an application is not only possible, but necessary, if one seeks to explain why kids often choose and watch entertainment shows that are not appropriate for them, a behavior they tend to display more and more often (Feierabend & Simon, 2001; Garitaonandia et al., 2001). Children appear to do this *although* the comprehensibility of these shows is of utmost importance for their experience of entertainment (Nikken, van der Voort, & Bochove, 1996). Thus, if they wish to select adults' programs regularly, they need to understand and comprehend them at least partially, and the programs' aesthetic quality must at least to some extent be appealing to the children. This, however, would imply that a premature audience would never be overwhelmed by the content to which it is exposed, and that the previously mentioned inappropriateness or misfit between a program and the children's cognitive or emotional capacities is simply not possible.

This contradiction may be solved if one takes three additional aspects into account: the specificity of any particular audience, the situation in which the selection of a particular program takes place, and the social dimension of media use. As far as the specificity of a premature audience is concerned, we have already learned from existing studies that any specific group of media users (in our case, an audience that is defined by a certain developmental state) perceives and processes distinct features of a program, such that children and their parents might watch the same TV show but still use a different input from that program for their information processing, entertainment, and learning (cf. Cantor, 1998). Second, many studies on children's media use neglect the ecological situation in which the selection of the program takes place. Although implying that children select their own program, we have to be aware that this is usually only true in the case of audiotapes, which may be run by the children themselves and without much parental concern, and for those children who have access to or own their own TV set. As big as the number of premature TV set owners might already appear (Walker & Bellamy, 2001), at least children without access to their own TV set often have to watch what their caretakers have selected. Third, the selection of a program by a child may also serve to boost his or her identity by demonstrating (to others and to oneself) how mature and grownup one is, given that he or she has already been exposed to a specific content. These three aspects may often lead to inappropriate selection of various contents; that is, to the selection of programs that do not fit with the developmental state a child is in, and consequently to the already-mentioned problems of demanding too much or too little of a child through media.

ENTERTAINMENT AND INTERACTIVITY: WILL TECHNOLOGICAL DEVELOPMENTS ALTER CHILDREN'S ENTERTAINMENT EXPERIENCES?

Interactive Entertainment: Same Old Story?

With the possibility of digitizing and compressing data and, as a consequence of this, the tremendously growing capacity to generate and transmit information, much has changed in our media environment over the last 2 decades. With television, for example, there is now more content in more programs on more channels than ever before, and this amount will grow further in the years to come. In addition to this, there will also be more specialization and diversification of programs; that is, the emergence of special-interest contents for any type of audience, including children of all ages, with different sorts of interests, and on various developmental stages. The merging of broadcasting, entertainment, and telecommunications to what has been called "new media" will also move on, providing children and other audiences with new ways of using the media. Some of these new ways—like interactive TV, computer games, and the Internet—already offer their users not only the opportunity to select specific content and respond to it, but also to modify the content that is presented to them. Of course, all of this applies particularly to entertainment programs, which have already been described as "killer application" for the new media (Biocca & Levy, 1995; Bryant & Love, 1996; Mundorf & Westin, 1996). The question, however, is whether we are capable of explaining what entertainment means for its users, now that the audience is able to interact with the media and its content—whether we know what "interactive entertainment" (Vorderer, 2000) means, just as whether we know what "noninteractive entertainment" means. The problem is apparent: Affective disposition theory is a very useful tool that helps to understand entertainment, but it necessarily implies a role for the media user that he or she is about to overcome (Vorderer, 2001, in press).

As we have seen, the predictability of storylines, plots, narrative structures, and the like is of utmost importance for the explanation of entertainment. Put more precisely, the limited predictability of what will happen next is crucial to the enjoyment of the user. For example, a story can only be suspenseful when the viewer can anticipate what will happen and has preferences for what should happen. If the audience knows for sure what will happen, their preferences cannot be in conflict with their expectations and, therefore, suspense will not emerge (cf., Vorderer & Knobloch, 2000). Does this imply that an interactive movie can never be suspenseful? Or that an interactive video game cannot be as involving as a noninteractive one? Obviously not. Research in this area shows how fascinating these games are, particularly to adolescents (Fritz, 1995; Klimmt, 2001).

But how is it possible that interactivity does not prevent involvement, suspense, and enjoyment, whereas noninteractivity (i.e., the fact that a passive viewer is surrendered to what happens on the screen) seems to be an important prerequisite for the emotional participation of the viewer? The solution lies in the more complex structure within which interactive media use takes place. Watching traditional TV remains an activity with few obligations and few consequences (Vorderer, 1992). However, with interactive TV, video games, and/or entertainment through the Internet, the situation changes. Whatever the users do and however they deal with the media, if they can use them interactively (i.e., if they can select and modify), their abilities are put to the test. Being interactive with TV, a video game, the Internet, and so on affords knowledge, skills, and competence. Whereas a traditional TV viewer can hardly fail, an interactive user may fail easily (Vorderer, 1999). What does that mean for the users within an interactive situation? They have to concentrate on what to do; they must coordinate their attention on what can be observed and their decisions about how to influence the ongoing developments. These users are monitoring their success and failure, and may internally attribute them to the user's own potentials. All of this is of personal relevance to the user. It provides him or her with personal information, on which self-esteem, well-being, and so on may be grounded. As Grodal (2000) put it, the users' control is not absolute, but relative to their skills. The more their use of the media pushes the users to their optimal mental level and motor capacity, the higher is their experience of involvement, immersion, or flow (Csikszentmihalyi, 1991; Turkle, 1995). Whatever the users do, it has an impact on the story or game, but also on their picture of themselves. Users of interactive media seem to be captivated by two roles at the same time: the role of a witness, and the role of a participant or player. As a player, they compete with three entities: the expectations that are set by the game, potential enemies, and themselves (i.e., their last performance on that game).

In this respect, new theorizing is indeed necessary. What we need are models and theories that help us to describe and explain the ways in which these two processes influence each other. We certainly know what influences witnesses of depicted events, what makes them feel and why (Zillmann, 1996). We also know how people feel in achievement situations where they can potentially succeed or fail. What we cannot account for yet, however, are situations such as those of interacting with new media, where these two situations merge.

Interactive Entertainment for Children

Thus far, the discussion has demonstrated that in addition to the experience of "traditional entertainment" where pleasure results from witnessing the fortunes and misfortunes of others (Zillmann & Bryant, 1986), interactive entertainment has yet another crucial component that is closely connected to the achievement a user reaches and performs. Affective dispositions toward a character in an interactive movie or a computer game are also necessary to develop hopes and fears in respect to the outcome or ongoing of the narrative. But how well a user is doing—particularly in comparison with the expectations of the game, with other players, or with oneself—is just as necessary in order to feel entertained. How do children perform in these situations? How do they respond to the achievement dimension in computer games, to quiz shows on TV, or the demands of using the Internet? Unfortunately, there is very little research on interactive entertainment in general, and as good as no research at all with children using interactive media. However, what we already know points to the importance of feeling self-efficacious and having control of the unfolding events.

Interactive media, as has been shown, is not only capable of registering the user's input but also able to give him or her feedback. The media's (i.e., the computer's) state depends on this input. It may be that it performs by simply writing letters, providing new pictures, or actually connecting to another program, but each "activity" results directly from the user's action. This may be felt by the user as a high level of self-efficacy (Bandura, 1977; Jerusalem & Schwarzer, 1986; Klimmt, in press): Because of the contingency between a given input and a computer's response, the impact can be identified and felt by the user far more easily than is the case with actions in daily life. This experience of self-efficacy and control over the immediate environment is known to be a very good predictor of pleasure (cf., in general, Krampen, 1986; with respect to interactive TV, Knobloch, 2000; in respect to computer applications, Weidenmann, 1996). Hence, children can be expected to enjoy situations of self-efficacy and control as they are provided by interactive media use just as much as adults, if not even more: Childhood and adolescence have often been described as developmental phases that are characterized by a particularly limited amount of control and power that children often have on their environment. It appears to be no coincidence that many of the children's media heroes and heroines are highly comparable to the children themselves when it comes to age, social background, and skills, so that the users may feel close to the heroes and heroines. However, the heroes usually also possess an additional feature (be it their exceptional cleverness, or—as is the case with Harry Potter—their unknown family background that allows them to use magic) that helps them to overcome the well-known situation of powerlessness and provides the premature media users with the possibility of "wishful identification" (Hoffner, 1996).

We have attempted to show what children, parents, teachers, and media producers might expect from the future of programming and media use, as well as what their concerns may look like. We have argued that entertainment for children as well as for adults can be described as a form of play, part of which is witnessing the fortunes and misfortunes of others. We regard this as a process, in which the voluntary and involuntary allocation of attention plays the prominent role of opening a door to information processing, where content consequently becomes generally important, and where entertainment does not necessarily hinder or even contradict learning. The future, however, might hold more emphasis on the use of interactive entertainment media, which will increase the possibility of experiencing self-efficacy and control through the use of the media (i.e., media-induced states of mind that have already been attracting users). To return to our starting point and to the concerns of parents and teachers about the shortcomings of entertaining media, it can now be assumed that their concerns will manifest themselves in the expectation that interactive entertainment will be even more harmful. The backup argument for this speculation could be that these media's potential to attract premature audiences may be even stronger, and that their impact on children (i.e., in particular their power to waste children's time instead of using it for learning) may become even more unresistible.

Given our understanding of entertainment, our perception of actual developments, and our knowledge about children's media use and their ways of dealing with entertainment, the question remains as to whether these apprehensions hold true (i.e., whether entertainment contradicts learning). The implicit understanding within the public is clear (entertainment, at the very least, is a hindrance to learning), and remains as a contradiction to our theoretical understanding (entertainment may foster learning). Fortunately, two developments took place over the last few years that lets us consider children's future programming and media use rather optimistically. First, "an explosion of high quality, educational (and even curriculum-based) television programs for children, especially for preschoolers, has occurred" (Bryant et al., 2001, p. 424), which is due to the fact that (a) children have been recognized as a diverse and economically important group, and (b) the number of programs available has increased so tremendously. This shows that from the industry's perspective, entertainment and learning do not have to be in conflict. Second, there are now the first longitudinal experimental studies on the impact of regularly watching these programs on preschool children's thinking, problem solving, and prosocial behavior (Bryant & Maxwell, 1997). The results of these studies are very clear and very positive: "Regular viewing of this ... program contributed substantially to preschooler's problem-solving abilities and flexible-thinking skills" (Bryant, et al., 1999, p. 35). This shows that entertainment and learning may not only be combined, but also that even from a communication perspective and those of media scholars, parents, and teachers, such a combination is highly welcome. On the background of these prospects, our hope is that children's future programming and media use will integrate what children like and what is helpful for them.

REFERENCES

Anderson, D. R., & Collins, P. (1988). *The impact of children's education: Television's influence on cognitive development.* Washington, DC: U.S. Department of Education.

Bandura, A. (1977). Self-efficacy: Toward a unifying theory of behavioral change. *Psychological Review, 84*(2), 191–215.

Bandura, A. (2001). Social cognitive theory of mass communication. *Media Psychology, 3*(3), 265–299.

Beentjes, J. W. J., Koolstra, C. M., Marseille, N., & van der Voort, T. H. A. (2001). Children's use of different media: For how long and why? In S. Livingstone & M. Bovill (Eds.), *Children and their changing media environment. A European comparative study* (pp. 85–111). Mahwah, NJ: Lawrence Erlbaum Associates.

Bente, G., & Fromm, B. (1997). *Affektfernsehen. Motive, Angebotsweisen und Wirkungen* [Affect TV. Motives, programs, and effects]. Opladen: Leske + Budrich.

Biocca, F., & Levy, M. (1995). Communication applications of virtual reality. In F. Biocca & M. Levy (Eds.), *Communication in the age of virtual reality* (pp. 127–157). Hillsdale, NJ: Lawrence Erlbaum Associates.

Boehnke, K., Hoffmann, D., Münch, T., & Güffens, F. (1997). Radiohören als Entwicklungschance? Zum Umgang ostdeutscher Jugendlicher mit einem alltäglichen Medium [Listening to radio as a chance for development? How East German adolescents use a daily life medium]. *Zeitschrift für Pädagogik, 37,* 53–70.

Bosshart, L., & Macconi, I. (1998). Defining "entertainment." *Communication Research Trends, 18*(3), 3–6.

Bourdieu, P. (1987). *Die feinen Unterschiede. Kritik der gesellschaftlichen Urteilskraft.* [Fine distinctions. A critique of the societal power of judgments]. Frankfurt: Suhrkamp.

Brandtstädter, J. (1985). Entwicklungsberatung unter dem Aspekt der Lebensspanne: Zum Aufbau eines entwicklungspsychologischen Anwendungskonzeptes [Developmental counseling from a life span perspective: Elaborating the use of a practical concept in developmental psychology]. In J. Brandtstädter & H. Gräser (Eds.), *Entwicklungsberatung unter dem Aspekt der Lebensspanne* [Developmental counseling from a life span perspective] (pp. 1–15). Göttingen: Hogrefe.

Brown, D., & Hayes, T. (2001). Family attitudes toward television. In J. Bryant & J. A. Bryant (Eds.), *Television and the American family* (2nd ed., pp. 111–135). Mahwah, NJ: Lawrence Erlbaum Associates.

Bryant, J., & Bryant, J. A. (Eds.). (2001). *Television and the American family* (2nd ed.). Mahwah, NJ: Lawrence Erlbaum Associates.

Bryant, J. A., Bryant, J., Mullikin, L., McCollum, J. F., & Love, C. C. (2001). Curriculum-based preschool television programming and the American family: Historical development, impact of public policy, and social and educational effects. In J. Bryant & J. A. Bryant (Eds.), *Television and the American family* (2nd ed., pp. 415–433). Mahwah, NJ: Lawrence Erlbaum Associates.

Bryant, J., & Love, C. (1996). Entertainment as the driver of new information technology. In R. R. Dholakia, N. Mundorf, & N. Dholakia (Eds.), *New infotainment technologies in the home* (pp. 91–114). Mahwah, NJ: Lawrence Erlbaum Associates.

Bryant, J., & Maxwell, M. (1997). *Executive summary: Longitudinal assessment of the effects of viewing Allegra's Window and Gullah Gullah Island.* Tuscaloosa, AL: Institute for Communication Research.

Bryant, J., Mullikin, L., Maxwell, M., Mundorf, N., Mundorf, J., Wilson, B., Smith, S., McCollum, J., & Owens, J. W. (1999). *Effects of two years' viewing of Blue's Clues.* Tuscaloosa, AL: Institute for Communication Research.

Bryant, J., & Raney, A. A. (2000). Sports on the screen. In D. Zillmann & P. Vorderer (Eds.), *Media entertainment. The psychology of its appeal* (pp. 153–174). Mahwah, NJ: Lawrence Erlbaum Associates.

Cantor, J. (1994). Fright reactions to mass media. In J. Bryant & D. Zillmann (Eds.), *Media effects: Advances in theory and research* (pp. 213–245). Hillsdale, NJ: Lawrence Erlbaum Associates.

Cantor, J. (1998). *"Mommy, I'm scared": How TV and movies frighten children and what we can do to protect them.* San Diego, CA: Harcourt Brace.

Cantor, J., & Mares, M.-L. (2001). Effects of television on child and family emotional well-being. In J. Bryant & J. A. Bryant (Eds.), *Television and the American family* (2nd ed., pp. 317–332). Mahwah, NJ: Lawrence Erlbaum Associates.

Cantor, J., & Nathanson, A. (1996). Children's fright reactions to television news. *Journal of Communication, 46*(4), 139–152.

Cortes, C. E. (2000). *The children are watching: How the media teach about diversity.* New York: Teachers College Press.

Csikszentmihalyi, M. (1991). *Flow: The psychology of optimal experience.* New York: HarperCollins.

d'Haenens, L. (2001). Old and new media: Access and ownership in the home. In S. Livingstone & M. Bovill (Eds.), *Children and their changing media environment. A European comparative study* (pp. 53–84). Mahwah, NJ: Lawrence Erlbaum Associates.

Feierabend, S., & Klingler, W. (1999). Kinder und Medien 1999 [Children and media 1999]. *Media Perspektiven, 10,* 610–625.

Feierabend, S., & Simon, E. (2001). Was Kinder sehen [What children watch]. *Media Perspektiven, 4,* 176–188.

Fritz, J. (1995). *Warum Computerspiele faszinieren. Empirische Annäherungen an Nutzung und Wirkung von Bildschirmspielen.* [Why computer games are fascinating. An empirical approach to study the usage and effects of video games] Weinheim: Juventa.

Fritzsche, Y. (2000). Modernes Leben: Gewandelt, vernetzt und verkabelt [Modern living: Changing, interconnected, and wired]. Deutsche Shell (Ed.), *Jugend 2000* (vol. 1, pp. 181–219). Opladen: Leske + Budrich.

Gabler, N. (1998). *Life the movie. How entertainment conquered reality.* New York: Knopf.

Garitaonandia, C., Juaristi, P., & Oleaga, J. A. (2001). Media genres and content preferences. In S. Livingstone & M. Bovill (Eds.), *Children and their changing media environment. A European comparative study* (pp. 141–157). Mahwah, NJ: Lawrence Erlbaum Associates.

Gleich, U. (1997). *Parasoziale Interaktionen und Beziehungen von Fernsehzuschauern mit Personen auf dem Bildschirm: Ein theoretischer und empirischer Beitrag zum Konzept des aktiven Rezipienten* [Parasocial interactions and relationships of TV viewers with people on the screen: A theoretical and empirical contribution to the concept of the active viewer]. Landau: Verlag Empirische Pädagogik.

Greenberg, B. S., Linsangan, R., & Soderman, A. (1993). Adolescents' reactions to television sex. In B. S. Greenberg, J. D. Brown, & N. L. Buerkel-Rothfuss (Eds.), *Media, sex and the adolescent* (pp. 196–224). CressKill, NJ: Hampton.

Grodal, T. (2000). Video games and the pleasures of control. In D. Zillmann & P. Vorderer (Eds.), *Media entertainment. The psychology of its appeal* (pp. 197–213). Mahwah, NJ: Lawrence Erlbaum Associates.

Groebel, J. (1994a). Kinder und Medien: Nutzung, Vorlieben, Wirkungen [Children and media: Usage, preferences, and effects]. *Media Perspektiven, 1,* 21–27.

Groebel, J. (1994b). Aufmerksamkeit und Informationsaufnahme beim Medienkonsum von Kindern [Attention and information processing of children while using media]. In Deutsches Jugendinstitut (Ed*.), Handbuch Medienerziehung im Kindergarten. Teil 1: Pädagogische Grundlagen* [Handbook media education in preschool and kindergarten. Part 1: Educational foundations] (pp. 203–209). Opladen: Leske & Budrich.

Havighurst, R. J. (1948). *Developmental tasks and education.* New York: McKay.

Hawkins, R. P., Reynolds, N., & Pingree, S. (1991). In search of television viewing styles. *Journal of Broadcasting and Electronic Media, 35*(3), 375–383.

Hoffner, C. (1996). Children's wishful identification and parasocial interaction with favorite television characters. *Journal of Broadcasting and Electronic Media, 40,* 389–402.

Horton, D., & Strauss, A. (1957). Interaction in audience-participation shows. *The American Journal of Sociology, 62*(6), 579–587.

Horton, D., & Wohl, R. R. (1956). Mass communication and para-social interaction: Observation on intimacy at a distance. *Psychiatry, 19,* 185–206.

Huston, A. C., Wartella, E., & Donnerstein, E. (1998). *Measuring the effects of sexual content in the media: A report to the Kaiser Family Foundation.* Menlo Park, CA: Kaiser Family Foundation.

Huston, A. C., & Wright, J. C. (1997). Mass media and children's development. In I. E. Sigel & K. A. Renninger (Eds.), *Handbook of child psychology. Vol. 4: Child psychology in practice* (pp. 999–1058). New York: Wiley.

Huston, A. C., Wright, J. C., Marquis, J., & Green, S. (1999). How young children spend their time: Television and other activities. *Developmental Psychology, 35,* 912–925.

Jerusalem, M., & Schwarzer, R. (1986). Selbstwirksamkeit [Self-efficacy]. In R. Schwarzer (Ed.), *Skalen zur Befindlichkeit und Persönlichkeit* [Measures of well-being and personality] (pp. 15–28). Berlin: Institut für Psychologie, Freie Universität Berlin.

Kaiser Family Foundation (Ed.). (1998). *Parents, children and the television ratings system: Two Kaiser Family Foundation Surveys.* Menlo Park, CA: Kaiser Family Foundation.

Kaiser Family Foundation (Ed.). (1999). *Parents and the V-chip. A Kaiser Family Foundation Survey.* Menlo Park, CA: Kaiser Family Foundation.

Klimmt, C. (2001). Computer-spiel: Interaktive Unterhaltungsangebote als Synthese aus Medium und Spielzeug [Computer games: Entertaining products as synthesis of media and toys]. *Zeitschrift für Medienpsychologie, 13*(1), 22–32.

Klimmt, C. (in press). Computer- und Videospiele [Computer and video games]. In P. Vorderer, R. Mangold, & G. Bente (Eds.), *Lehrbuch der Medienpsychologie* [Textbook media psychology]. Göttingen: Hogrefe.

Knobloch, S. (2000). *Schicksal spielen: Interaktive Unterhaltung aus persönlichkeitspsychologischer und handlungstheoretischer Sicht* [Playing fate: Interactive entertainment from the psychological perspective of personality and action theory]. München: Reinhard Fischer.

Krampen, G. (1986). Zur Spezifität von Kontrollüberzeugungen für Problemlösen in verschiedenen Realitätsbereichen [On the specificity of control believes in problem-solving under varying circumstances]. *Schweizerische Zeitschrift für Psychologie und ihre Anwendungen, 45*(1–2), 67–85.

Krotz, F., & Hasebrink, U. (2001). Who are the new media users? In S. Livingstone & M. Bovill (Eds.), *Children and their changing media environment. A European comparative study* (pp. 245–262). Mahwah, NJ: Lawrence Erlbaum Associates.

Labaton, S. (1999, March 8). Cable rates rising as industry nears end of regulation. *New York Times*, pp. A1, A12.

Lin, C. A. (2001). The VCR, home video culture, and new video technologies. In J. Bryant & J. A. Bryant (Eds.), *Television and the American family* (2nd ed., pp. 91–107). Mahwah, NJ: Lawrence Erlbaum Associates.

Livingstone, S., & Bovill, M. (Eds.). (2001). *Children and their changing media environment. A European comparative study*. Mahwah, NJ: Lawrence Erlbaum Associates.

Lombard, M., & Ditton, T. (1997). At the heart of it all: The concept of presence. *Journal of Computer Mediated Communication, 3*(2). Retrieved May 5, 2000, from http://209.130.1.169/jcmc/vol3/issue2/lombard.html

Montada, L. (1998). Fragen, Konzepte, Perspektiven [Questions, concepts, and perspectives]. In R. Oerter & L. Montada (Eds.), *Entwicklungspsychologie* [Developmental psychology] (pp. 1–83). Weinheim: Psychologie Verlags Union.

Mundorf, N., & Westin, S. (1996). Adoption of information technology: Contributing factors. In R. R. Dholakia, N. Mundorf, & N. Dholakia (Eds.), *New infotainment technologies in the home* (pp. 157–172). Mahwah, NJ: Lawrence Erlbaum Associates.

Nikken, P., van der Voort, T. H. A., & Bochove, E. (1996). Maternal quality standards for children's television programs. *Journal of Educational Media, 22*, 41–54.

Oatley, K. (1994). A taxonomy of the emotions of literary response and a theory of identification in fictional narrative. *Poetics, 23*, 53–74.

Oerter, R. (1998). Kultur, Ökologie und Entwicklung [Culture, ecology, and development]. In R. Oerter & L. Montada (Eds.), *Entwicklungspsychologie* [Developmental psychology] (pp. 84–127). Weinheim: Psychologie Verlags Union.

Oerter, R. (1999). *Psychologie des Spiels. Ein handlungstheoretischer Ansatz* [Psychology of playing. An action theory approach]. Weinheim: Beltz.

Oerter, R. (2000). Spiel als Lebensbewältigung [Playing as coping with life]. In S. Hoppe-Graff & R. Oerter (Eds.), *Spielen und Fernsehen. Über die Zusammenhänge von Spiel und Medien in der Welt des Kindes* [Playing and watching TV. On the interdependencies of play and media in a child's world] (pp. 47–58). Weinheim: Juventa Verlag.

Ritterfeld, U. (2000). Welchen und wieviel Input braucht das Kind? [What kind of and how much input a child requires?] In H. Grimm (Ed.), *Sprachentwicklung. Enzyklopädie der Psychologie* [Language acquisition. Encyclopedia of psychology] (Vol. C3/3, pp. 403–432). Göttingen: Hogrefe.

Ritterfeld, U., & Vorderer, P. (1993). Literatur als identitätsstiftendes Moment? Zum Einfluss sozialer Kontexte auf den Leser [Building identity through literature? On the impact of social contexts on reader]. *Siegener Periodicum zur Internationalen Empirischen Literaturwissenschaft, 2*, 217–229.

Rubin, A. M., & Perse, E. M. (1987). Audience activity and soap opera involvement. A uses and effects investigation. *Human Communication Research, 14*(2), 246–268.

Rubin, A. M., Perse, E. M., & Powell, R. A. (1985). Loneliness, parasocial interaction, and local television news viewing. *Human Communication Research, 12*(2), 155–180.

Salomon, G. (1979). *Interaction of media, cognition, and learning.* San Francisco: Jossey-Bass.

Salomon, G. (1984). Television is "easy" and print is "tough": The differential investment of mental effort in learning as a function of perceptions and attributions. *Journal of Educational Psychology, 76,* 647–658.

Trepte, S. (2002). *Der private Fernsehauftritt als Selbstverwirklichung. Die Option des Auftritts als Rezeptionsphänomen und zur Konstruktion des Selbst* [Being on stage in TV as self-realization]. München: Reinhard Fischer.

Trepte, S., Zapfe, S., & Sudhoff, W. (2001). Orientierung und Problembewältigung durch TV-Talkshows: Empirische Ergebnisse und Erklärungsansätze [Orientation and problem-solving through TV shows: Empirical results and explanatory attempts]. *Zeitschrift für Medienpsychologie, 13*(2), 73–84.

Turkle, S. (1995). *Life on the screen: Identity in the age of the Internet.* New York: Simon & Schuster.

Underwood, G. (Ed). (1993). *The psychology of attention.* Aldershot: Elgar.

Valkenburg, P. M., & Janssen, S. C. (1999). What do children value in entertainment programs? A cross-cultural investigation. *Journal of Communication, 49*(2), 3–21.

van der Voort, T. H. A. (1986). *Television violence: A child's eye view.* Amsterdam: North Holland.

Vorderer, P. (1992). *Fernsehen als Handlung. Eine motivationspsychologische Analyse der Fernsehfilmrezeption.* Berlin: Edition Sigma.

Vorderer, P. (1993). Audience involvement and program loyalty. *Poetics. Journal of Empirical Research on Literature, Media and the Arts, 22,* 89–98.

Vorderer, P. (1996). Picard, Brinkmann, Derrick und Co. als Freunde der Zuschauer. Eine explorative Studie über parasoziale Beziehungen zu Serienfiguren [Picard, Brinkmann, Derrick, and Co. An exploratory study on parasocial relationships to soap figures]. In P. Vorderer (Ed.), *Fernsehen als "Beziehungskiste." Parasoziale Beziehungen und Interaktionen mit TV-Personen* [TV as a way to establish social relationships: Parasocial relations and interactions with TV protagonists] (pp. 153–171). Opladen: Westdeutscher Verlag.

Vorderer, P. (1998). Unterhaltung durch Fernsehen: Welche Rolle spielen parasoziale Beziehungen zwischen Zuschauern und Fernsehakteuren? [Entertainment through TV: What role do parasocial relations between TV users and TV protagonists play?] In G. Roters, W. Klingler, & O. Zöllner (Eds.), *Fernsehforschung in Deutschland. Themen, Akteure, Methoden* [Research on television in Germany. Issues, people, methods] (pp. 689–708). Baden-Baden: Nomos.

Vorderer, P. (1999). Psychologie der Medienrezeption [Psychology of media usage]. In G. Roters, W. Klingler, & M. Gerhards (Eds.), *Mediensozialisation und Medienverantwortung* [Media socialization and media responsibility] (pp. 37–46). Baden-Baden: Nomos.

Vorderer, P. (2000). Interactive entertainment and beyond. In D. Zillmann & P. Vorderer (Eds.), *Media entertainment: The psychology of its appeal* (pp. 21–36). Mahwah, NJ: Lawrence Erlbaum Associates.

Vorderer, P. (2001). It's all entertainment—sure. But what exactly is entertainment? Communication research, media psychology, and the explanation of entertainment experiences. *Poetics. Journal of Empirical Research on Literature, Media and the Arts, 29,* 247–261.

Vorderer, P. (in press). Entertainment theory. In J. Bryant, D. Roskos-Ewoldsen, & J. Cantor (Eds.), *Communication and emotion: Essays in honor of Dolf Zillmann.* Mahwah, NJ: Lawrence Erlbaum Associates.

Vorderer, P., Klimmt, C., & Liebetruth, D. (2002). Spaß, Spannung, Spiel. Eine Beobachtungsstudie zum Unterhaltungserleben drei- bis vierjähriger Kinder während der Rezeption formal unterschiedlich unterhaltsamer Varianten eines Hörspiels [Fun, suspense, play. An observational study on the entertainment experiences of 3- to 4-year- old children while listening to formally different audio tales]. In P. Rössler, V. Gehrau, & S. Kubisch (Eds.), *Empirische Perspektiven der Rezeptionsforschung—der Prozess der Rezeption* [Empirical perspectives on the study of media usage—the process of use] (pp. 117–132). München: Fischer.

Vorderer, P., & Knobloch, S. (1996). Parasoziale Beziehungen zu Serienfiguren: Ergänzung oder Ersatz? [Parasocial relations to soap protagonists: Completion or supplement?]. *Medienpsychologie, (8)*3, 201–216.

Vorderer, P., & Knobloch, S. (2000). Conflict and suspense in drama. In D. Zillmann & P. Vorderer (Eds.), *Media entertainment: The psychology of its appeal* (pp. 59–72). Mahwah, NJ: Lawrence Erlbaum Associates.

Vorderer, P., Ritterfeld, U., & Klimmt, C. (2001). Spaß am Hören—Hörspielkassetten als sprachförderliche Unterhaltungsangebote für Vorschulkinder [Enjoy to listen. Using audio tapes to foster language acquisition in preschoolers]. *Medien und Kommunikationswissenschaft, 49*(4), 462–479.

Walker, J. R., & Bellamy, R. V., Jr. (2001). Remote control devices and family viewing. In J. Bryant & J. A. Bryant (Eds.), *Television and the American family* (2nd ed., pp. 75–89). Mahwah, NJ: Lawrence Erlbaum Associates.

Weidenmann, B. (1989). Der mentale Aufwand beim Fernsehen [Mental efforts while watching TV]. In J. Groebel & P. Winterhoff-Spurk (Eds.), *Empirische Medienpsychologie* [Empirical media psychology] (pp. 134–149). München: Psychologie Verlags Union.

Weidenmann, B. (1996). Instruktionsmedien [Instructional media]. In F. E. Weinert (Ed.), *Psychologie des Lernens und der Instruktion. Enzyklopädie der Psychologie* [Psychology of learning and instruction. Encyclopedia of psychology] (vol. D1/2, pp. 319–368). Göttingen: Hogrefe.

Wicklund, R. A., & Gollwitzer, P. M. (1982). *Symbolic self-completion.* Hillsdale, NJ: Lawrence Erlbaum Associates.

Wild, T. C., Kuiken, D., & Schopflocher, D. (1995). The role of absorption in experiential involvement. *Journal of Personality and Social Psychology, 69*(3), 569–579.

Zillmann, D. (1991). Empathy: Affect from bearing witness to the emotions of others. In J. Bryant & D. Zillmann (Eds.), *Responding to the screen: Reception and reaction processes* (pp. 135–167). Hillsdale, NJ: Lawrence Erlbaum Associates.

Zillmann, D. (1994). Mechanisms of emotional involvement with drama. *Poetics, 23,* 33–51.

Zillmann, D. (1996). The psychology of suspense in dramatic exposition. In P. Vorderer, H. J. Wulff, & M. Friedrichsen (Eds.), *Suspense: Conceptualizations, theoretical analyses, and empirical explorations* (pp. 199–231). Mahwah, NJ: Lawrence Erlbaum Associates.

Zillmann, D., & Bryant, J. (1986). Exploring the entertainment experience. In J. Bryant & D. Zillmann (Eds.), *Perspectives on media effects* (pp. 303–324). Hillsdale, NJ: Lawrence Erlbaum Associates.

Zillmann, D., & Bryant, J. (1994). Entertainment as media effect. In J. Bryant & D. Zillmann (Eds.), *Media effects: Advances in theory and research* (pp. 437–461). Hillsdale, NJ: Lawrence Erlbaum Associates.

Zillmann, D., & Cantor, J. R. (1977). Affective responses to the emotions of a protagonist. *Journal of Experimental Social Psychology, 13,* 155–165.

Zillmann, D., Taylor, K., & Lewis, K. (1998). News as nonfiction theater: How dispositions toward the public cast of characters affect reactions. *Journal of Broadcasting and Electronic Media, 42*(2), 153–169.

Zillmann, D., Taylor, K., & Lewis, K. (1999). Dispositions toward public issues as determinants of reactions to bad and good news. *Medienpsychologie, 11*(4), 231–243, 287.

Zillmann, D., & Vorderer, P. (2000a). Preface. In D. Zillmann & P. Vorderer (Eds.), *Media entertainment. The psychology of its appeal* (pp. vii–xi). Mahwah, NJ: Lawrence Erlbaum Associates.

Zillmann, D., & Vorderer, P. (Eds.). (2000b). *Media entertainment. The psychology of its appeal.* Mahwah, NJ: Lawrence Erlbaum Associates.

PART

IV

Selling Televisual Media

Advertising History of Televisual Media

Melissa D. Johnson
Davidson College

Brian M. Young
University of Exeter

The purpose of this chapter is to describe the history of advertising to children. Most of the story takes place in the United States; developments in, for example, China and India, are not covered. However, there is no reason to believe that the major themes—rapid advances in communication technology, tension and potential conflict between the interests of commerce and the consumer, and the various issues that emerged since the mid-1950s when television became popular—are not found in most of the European countries, although the relationship between public broadcasting and national identity might well be more salient in Europe. But that story remains to be written, and we focus on the United States here. In another chapter, Huesmann and Skoric have written about another central concern that surrounds television—the portrayal and effects of violent behavior—and cite evidence that there is no relationship in time between research findings and public concern, suggesting that concern is orchestrated and adopted by politicians to suit their own ends. There is no reason to believe that advertising to children has never been used as a political tool, and the reader should interpret the evidence with that in mind.

Television took America by storm. Once mass marketing got underway, people rapidly purchased sets, and television quickly became the major source of family entertainment. Parental concern surfaced early as parents worried that their children might be ill prepared to cope with well-crafted commercial messages designed with sophisticated production values (Melody, 1973).

265

Debate has spanned the past 40 years as different constituencies have questioned the potentially adverse effects that commercials could have on children. Now, ads from the Internet and other diverse televisual media platforms vie continuously for children's attention. Advertising to children continues to demonstrate a conflict of interest between media goals and parental concerns. Whether our society values the entertainment or the best interests of children more remains a poignant question.

In the early 1950s, television producers targeted ads to all family members and all ages. In the ensuing years, the average number of American homes having television sets increased from just less than 1 out of every 10 homes in 1950, to 9 out of 10 homes in 1960, to virtually every home in 1970 (Adler, 1980). By the late 1980s, young children (aged 2–5) watched 28 hours of television per week on average, and older children (6–11) watched an average of 27.5 hours (A. C. Nielsen, 1986, as cited in Kunkel & Watkins, 1987). Initially, television networks were interested in satisfying the viewers in order to sell television sets (Melody, 1973). Very few network programs were commercially sponsored, and the primary goal was developing quality programs that people would want to see. One tactic was to include programs that appealed to children so that parents could be more productive and use television as a form of babysitter, entertainer, and educator (Adler, 1980). If someone had the time, the entertainment was waiting.

However, as television ownership became more common and fewer homes did not have a TV set, the networks became more concerned with sustaining themselves financially. This change in focus involved the addition of sponsors to television programs (Melody, 1973). Revlon provided an early blueprint for this approach with *The $64,000 Question* game show, and the marvelous success of this show made Revlon a household name and product line (Palmer, 1988). Other broadcasters quickly followed this sponsorship lead, and shows soon added commercial breaks during the programs themselves. Another variation on the advertising theme was the host program, in which a "host" functioned as a type of salesperson in a 30-minute advertisement (Adler, 1980).

The advertisers first targeted adults instead of children, because adults were more likely to purchase the advertiser's products (Melody, 1973). Because commercial networks' prime time was more lucrative in adult programming than in children's, networks shifted children's shows to the morning and early afternoon hours, when it was less likely that adults would be able to watch television (Melody, 1973). Prime time became exclusively adult time. Occasionally, a family-oriented program would take a prime-time spot, but the commercials remained adult oriented (Adler, 1980).

Most of the networks gave the 4:00 P.M. to 7:00 P.M. time slots to the local stations (Adler, 1980). These stations found it profitable to air movies or cartoons with a host who would help to advertise products to the children. After some time, the networks wanted more money to supplement revenues from prime-time advertisements, and they decided to add cartoons on Saturday mornings, when most adults wouldn't be willing to watch television but many children would. Unlike adult programming, the cartoons were not expensive to create and could be rerun many times (Melody, 1973). Also, by the National Association of Broadcasters' Television Code (1965), the networks could show twice as many advertisements during the cartoons as during prime-time TV (Adler, 1980). The Saturday morning "kidvid ghetto" proved very successful, and by 1970, the three major networks made a combined annual revenue of $66.8 million from this programming (Pearce, 1974). Saturday mornings provided an excellent opportunity for advertisers to promote many products to a large audience of children.

In 1961, the Toy Advertising Guidelines were accepted by the National Association of Broadcasters as an attempt at self-regulation. Because children's advertising was not yet a big issue in society, these regulations were not very strict (Kunkel & Gantz, 1993), but advertising to children remained a concern. However, television advertising to children did become a major issue around the 1970s. In 1968, the first meeting of Action for Children's Television (ACT) was held (Melody, 1973). The founding members were mothers in Massachusetts concerned with the television programs—especially violent ones—offered to their children. ACT quickly realized that their initiatives for violent programs would be fraught with complexity, and the focus of their concern rapidly shifted to the advertisements aimed at children (Cole & Oettinger, 1978).

The group first made an appeal to the broadcasting networks, encouraging them to adopt a "code of ethics" for the treatment of children (Cole & Oettinger, 1978). Overall, ACT wanted quality television viewing for their children (Kunkel & Watkins, 1987). Although children are capable of watching and partially understanding television before they are 2 years old, this does not mean that they understand the intent behind the advertisements (Hollenbeck & Slaby, 1979). It was this vulnerability of children, due to their inability to understand and defend against the persuasive intent of commercials, that concerned the members of ACT. In addition, although older children can demonstrate an apparent understanding of advertising if they are asked about it, they will not necessarily be able to use that understanding when faced with television commercials in other situations because their ability to process information is limited and relies on cues (John, 1999). In fact, the Communications Act of 1934 required that all commercials (at that time, radio commercials) be identifiable to the audiences (Kunkel & Wilcox, 2001). The concern of the mothers was that this rule, still in effect in the 1970s, was not being followed in respect to children. Only one of the three existing networks would consider the idea, but they dragged their heels on any changes (Cole & Oettinger, 1978). In the early 1970s, ACT petitioned the Federal Communications Commission (FCC) to adopt three rules for broadcasters:

1. The elimination of sponsorship and commercials during children's programs.
2. No advertising of any sort during children's programs.
3. The requirement that each station air 14 hours of children's programming per week, with the programming divided into age categories.

The broadcasters and advertisers were vehemently opposed to this proposition, and ACT used this standoff to bring nationwide publicity to the issue of advertising to children (Melody, 1973).

The FCC's major function was to ensure that broadcasters do whatever is in the best interest of the public (Kunkel & Watkins, 1987; Palmer, 1988). A principle of reciprocity operates in that the FCC is giving away public space for a private company's gain, so the company must give something back to the public (Palmer, 1988). The FCC grants licenses to broadcasters to use airwaves, they can deny licensure if broadcasters do not meet their public service responsibilities (Kunkel & Watkins, 1987), and they can enforce rules for all broadcasters. However, cable, Internet, and other forms of media that do not require public airwaves also do not require licenses in order to operate (Kunkel & Wilcox, 2001).

In 1960, the FCC had recognized that children should constitute a special audience (Kunkel & Watkins, 1987). By 1970, public concern over advertising to children had grown dramatically, and to quell this concern the television industry made several attempts at self-regulation during that decade. The National Association of Broadcasters' Television Code limited the amount of commercial time allowed during children's programming to 12 minutes per hour during the week and 9.5 minutes per hour on weekends (Kunkel & Gantz, 1993). This code, and similar regulations by the National Advertising Division (NAD) of the Council of Better Business Bureaus, included prevention of specific types of advertising techniques that were inappropriate for children (Adler, 1980).

Also in the 1970s, formats known variously as "pop-ups," "drop-ins," "snippets," "mortar messages," and "educational additives" were added to children's television. These creative commercial formats were educational, teaching various things like mathematics, social studies, current events, and grammar. These "snippets" carrying educational messages were able to reach all children, especially those whose parents could not afford to purchase educational videos, VCRs, or cable television. These messages helped children learn about other cultures, creating a context for understanding and accepting ethnic diversity (Palmer, 1999). The problem was that both the educational and the marketing groups wanted access to broadcast television due to its ability to reach all socioeconomic and racial groups (Palmer, 1988).

Almost simultaneously, the Council on Children, Media, and Merchandising (CCMM) petitioned the FCC and FTC (Federal Trade Commission) to encourage research on the effects that advertising (most notably cereal ads) was having on children. Preschoolers were being told that heavily sugared cereals were "part of a balanced breakfast" or "part of a good breakfast" when, in reality, the product made no contribution to nutritional balance. Robert Choate, President of CCMM, publicly noted that for many of these products the cereal box cardboard itself had more nutritional value than the cereal (Adler, 1980; Palmer, 1987). Advertisements were being criticized on many fronts.

In October 1971, the FCC's newly created children's division, dealing with broadcasting issues relating to children, began operations (Cole & Oettinger, 1978). In 1973, the National Association of Broadcasters (NAB) prohibited host selling (the selling of products by specific show characters during that character's program) in children's television and decreased the number of minutes per hour allowed for commercials from 16 to 12. In 1974, the Council of Better Business Bureaus formed the Children's Advertising Review Unit (CARU) to evaluate commercials that had received complaints (Adler, 1980). CARU, then as now, depended on the good-faith cooperation of advertisers, who participated on a voluntary basis. CARU also provided a way for advertisers to check their own adherence to regulations (Kunkel, 2001). Among nonprofit organizations, the Center for Science in the Public Interest (CSPI) was created in 1971 to analyze the content of advertisements in relation to nutrition and health, and to improve health consciousness among children. In 1991, the Center for Media Education (CME) was founded to improve the quality of children's media (Horgen, Choate, & Brownell, 2001). Although they are not governmental programs, these organizations have brought media issues to national attention, facilitating governmental change (Horgen et al., 2001).

In 1974, the FCC released the Children's Television Report and Policy Statement (FCC, 1974). It stated that "broadcasters have a special responsibility to children" and that they should have special protection against advertising (FCC, 1974, p. 399). The policy also implemented commercial limitations of 12 minutes per hour during the week and 9.5 minutes per hour on the weekends during children's television shows, the same requirements that the National Association of Broadcasters already held as self-regulation for children's programming (Kunkel & Gantz, 1993). More minutes of advertisements were allowed during weekdays because the audiences were smaller and advertisers needed to make the same profit from the programming (Kunkel & Roberts, 1991). The new policy also required a distinct separation between the programs and commercials. Bumpers—several-second introductions to the commercials and programs, similar to "And now a word from our sponsor"—were implemented. Although host selling was not allowed, by 1988 the practice had reappeared illegally (Kunkel, 1988). A study by Kunkel showed that both younger (aged 4–5 years) and older (aged 7–8 years) children had more difficulty distinguishing between advertisements and programming when host selling occurred. Even standard separation devices did not make children more likely to recognize that an advertisement was occurring in the host-selling situation. Finally, the promotion of products was not allowed during children's programs, although no stringent guidelines were formulated. The FCC preferred self-regulation by the broadcasters (Melody, 1973). In 1979, the National Association of Broadcasters' Television Code Board finally agreed with the FCC and suggested separators between commercials and programs (National Association of Broadcasters, 1979).

In addition, in 1974 the FCC requested that broadcasters air more children's programming. The FCC considered the option of passing minimum programming requirements for children, but instead decided to allow the broadcasters to add the children's programming voluntarily, in the interest of society. Unfortunately, by 1975 no significant changes in programming had occurred (Palmer, 1988).

By the late 1970s, it was apparent that there were still four major concerns relating to children and television advertising: Children were viewing potentially harmful and unhealthy commercials, advertisements were occasionally deceptive to children, advertising to children appealed to their weaknesses, and negative effects on development could occur to children (Adler et al., 1977). Within its role of restricting unfair or deceptive media practices, the FTC in 1978 proposed a ban of all television advertisements to children (FTC, 1978a). In addition, they included an in-depth summary of research supporting their position (FTC, 1978b). The 350-page research report and its proposals were immediately opposed by broadcasters, advertisers, and some of the largest corporations in America (Kunkel, 2001; Palmer, 1987). The corporations worked with Congress to have the FTC Improvements Act of 1980 passed. It removed the FTC's ability to place restrictions on unfair advertising and therefore prevented any further regulations on children's advertising (FTC, 1981). The general conclusion was that a ban on advertising to children would cause a financial termination of children's programming. Congress was able to ignore the large body of research evidence in the interest of perceived overall societal values (Kunkel & Roberts, 1991).

In 1983, the FCC decided against adding minimum programming requirements for children. This led to multiple show cancellations, including highly respected shows like *Captain Kangaroo*. None of the commercial networks maintained any regularly scheduled weekday children's programs (Palmer, 1988).

In 1984, during the Reagan Administration's era of deregulation (Horwitz, 1989), the 1974 Children's Television Report and Policy Statement was repealed by the FCC (Kunkel & Watkins, 1987). The NAB's self-regulation code had already been removed in 1982 (Maddox & Zanot, 1984). Also, during this time program-length commercials were once again allowed (Kunkel, 2001). It was believed that if the industry regulated itself, a good balance of commercials to programs would be discovered by advertisers. Ideally, if there were too many commercials, people would become annoyed, not buy the products, not watch TV, and the industry would suffer. However, this contradicted the evidence that young children were not capable of understanding the persuasive content of commercials and consequently were unable to defend against these communications (Kunkel, 2001). Also, it was presumed that children would view educational material through other media like cable or videotapes if they were not satisfied with commercial broadcasting. However, the extra expense required to access alternative media posed a problem for those of lower economic standing (Kunkel & Watkins, 1987).

In 1990, Congress passed the Children's Television Act, which imposed educational programming requirements and limited commercials to 10.5 minutes per hour on weekends and 12 minutes per hour on weekdays (Kunkel, 2001). These limitations also were extended to cable television. In addition, Congress requested that the FCC consider reinstituting the ban on program-length commercials. The FCC again prohibited the program-length commercials, but revised the definition to "a program associated with a product in which the commercials for that product are aired" (FCC, 1991, as cited in Kunkel, 2001, p. 386). Before, no violation would occur unless traditional commercials were placed in the programs, even if the programs advertised within themselves (Kunkel, 2001). The American Academy of Pediatrics Committee on Communications requested that this guideline restrict all program-length commercials, regardless of inclusion of traditional commercials (American Academy of Pediatrics, Committee on Communications, 1995). Other countries, like Sweden, have banned all advertising aimed at children younger than 12 years old, and Greece has banned all toy commercials before 10:00 P.M. (Strasburger, 2001).

Although much research has been done on the ability of children to understand commercials, the evidence on other issues still needs to be examined. For example, the promotion of gender stereotyping in advertisements is another concern. A study in 1984 by Macklin and Kolbe showed that little change had occurred in terms of the level of gender stereotyping in advertisements to children since the early 1970s. The ads were still dominated by males, the males were more active and aggressive than the females, most voiceovers were done by males, and the background music was more likely to be performed by males. This trend did not change in the 1990s (Browne, 1998). Boys were shown as being more aggressive, active, knowledgeable, instrumental, dominating, and controlling than girls. Even though social norms for males and females have changed over the past few decades, in advertisements the portrayals of males and females are still basically the same. Although it seems that eliminating stereotypes would increase the number of people targeted by advertisements, stereotyped roles are still portrayed.

In 1993, Kunkel and Gantz found that of over 10,000 commercials (604 hours) aimed at children, only 3.7% violated CARU standards. The self-regulation seems to be working fairly well in terms of ensuring adherence to the rules. The USA channel had the most violations, and the broadcast network affiliates had the fewest violations. However, the rules do not ensure that no intentional deception occurs, such as the use of confusing disclaimers (Kunkel, 2001). Disclaimers usually employ adult language and, in 1984, they occurred in one third of all commercials aimed at children (Stern & Harmon, 1984). Liebert, Sprafkin, Liebert, and Rubinstein (1977) studied the effect of disclaimers on children. The results revealed that 6- to 8-year-old children do not understand the disclaimers. Regardless of whether children understand the meaning of disclaimers, advertisers may continue to use them in order to decrease their liability for product deception. Perhaps children would understand commercials better if the disclaimers were part of the advertisements (Stutts & Hunnicutt, 1987).

In the 1990s, it was estimated that children aged 2 to 11 years watched over 3. 5 hours of television per day (A. C. Nielsen Company, 1991) and therefore viewed about 3,000 commercials a week (Condry, Bence, & Scheibe, 1988). Now, at the start of the 21st century, approximately 1 in 4 preschoolers, 1 in 2 older children, and 2 of 3 adolescents have televisions in their bedrooms (Robinson, Saphir, Kramer, Varady, & Haydel, 2001; Stanger, 1998).

The three primary concerns from the 1980s are still relevant: that television will have adverse effects on children, that television does not educate or inform children appropriately, and that television is unfair for children and deceives them (Kunkel

& Watkins, 1987). Another concern is that television advertisements increase the likelihood of parent–child conflict (American Academy of Pediatrics, Committee on Communications, 1995). What are the arguments? Supporters of advertising to children argue that if the products are legal to sell to children then their advertisements should be as well (Murray, 1980). Also, these supporters emphasize the point that children's advertisements provide the finances for children's programming and, without the advertising, children's programming may not exist. Additionally, they mention that children must be exposed to advertisements to learn how to cognitively oppose the ads. Finally, they argue that children can understand advertisements better than people believe (Zuckerman & Gianinno, 1981).

On the other hand, opponents of advertising to children argue that the children are unaware of the persuasive bias of commercials and are left unable to defend against it (Kunkel & Wilcox, 2001). Moreover, opponents maintain that young children simply do not possess the proper verbal skills to demonstrate their understanding of advertisements, and that a nonverbal methodology for assessing understanding is more appropriate than are techniques, such as interviewing, that rely extensively on the subject's being able to understand and answer questions (Donohue, Henke, & Donohue, 1980). Roberts (1982) argued that children respond to the informational content of commercials, but not the persuasive content. A study by Donohue et al. (1980) showed that regardless of verbal or nonverbal methodologies, children develop an understanding of commercials after they develop verbal skills. Until age 4 or 5, most children are unable to distinguish between commercials and programming (Kunkel & Wilcox, 2001). Kunkel (1988) found that only 31% of children could tell that a commercial was not part of the storyline, even though 91% could tell that it was a commercial. Most children are also unable to understand the persuasive intent of television advertising until age 7 or 8 (Kunkel & Wilcox, 2001).

As children get older, they become less accepting of advertisements (Robertson & Rossiter, 1974; Rossiter, 1977; Ward, Wackman, & Wartella, 1977). It is at this point that they understand that commercials are "trying to get people to buy something" (John, 1999, p. 188). Brucks, Armstrong, and Goldberg (1998) found that even 9- to 10-year-olds need more knowledge of the advertising process than simply a skeptical attitude in order to resist the persuasive intent of commercials. Even if children know about persuasive intent and rhetorical techniques used in advertising, they do not use cognitive defenses (understanding of the persuasive intent combined with a distrust of advertisements) to protect themselves from advertisements without the presence of a cue alerting them to the need to use these defenses.

Children must progress from noticing simply the salient, major features of advertisements one at a time to understanding multiple features and abstract features. In fact, although 68.5% of first graders reported liking all ads, only 55.9% of third graders and only 25.3% of fifth graders reported liking all ads (Robertson & Rossiter, 1974). This trend increases with age, ultimately progressing to the comprehension of the perspectives of both the advertisers and the viewers. It is not until the eighth grade that children adhere to their preferences despite the outpouring of advertisements (Brucks et al., 1998). The children must have enough experience with advertisements and the products on the market to compare the actual products with the claims made in the advertisement.

What are some of the psychological theories that inform our understanding of children and advertising? One of the major developmental theorists was Jean Piaget. According to Piaget, there are four major stages in his developmental theory: sensorimotor (until 2 years of age), preoperational (from 2 to 7), concrete operational (7 to 11), and formal operational (11 and older; Piaget, 1952). Beginning in the preoperational phase, children possess the cognitive abilities that provide only a partial understanding of advertising. Preoperational children notice the perceptual attributes of single things at a time, and use that limited aspect to make judgments about reality (Piaget, 1952). For example, a study by Wartella et al. (1979) showed that kindergarteners notice salient features, whether or not they are important in terms of the overall product. Children in the concrete operational stage are able to understand that their perceptions may not correspond to reality. Additionally, they can consider relationships between elements. In the formal operational stage, adults and children are capable of complex and abstract thought (Piaget, 1952). In an analysis related to Piaget's stage theory, a child would not be fully capable of understanding the persuasive intent of advertisements (an abstract idea) until he or she had reached the formal operational stage of development.

John (1999) proposed three developmental stages in consumer socialization: perceptual (aged 3 to 7), analytical (7 to 11), and reflective (11 to 16). In the first stage, children are only aware of the visual features of the advertisements. During the analytical stage, children become more aware of the functioning of the market system, of advertising and its purposes, and can somewhat understand the motives of others in the marketplace (including parents). These children are capable of requesting products by using manipulative methods that consider the viewpoint of a parent. For example, most second graders are capable of understanding the concept of paying for products, whereas most preschoolers are not (John, 1999; Marshall, 1964). In the reflective stage, children develop more sophisticated information-processing skills and understand the concepts of brands and prices better. Before purchasing things, older adolescents check for satisfaction and recommendations from other sources besides advertisements (Moore & Stephens, 1975; Moschis & Moore, 1979). Until that stage, children are not fully capable of understanding advertising in the sense of contextualizing it within society and the economic system.

People have increasingly negative views of television advertisements in general, not just of those aimed at children (Mittal, 1994). Some observers consider this a crisis time in advertising—a trend of increasingly negative public opinion since the 1960s and 1970s (Stewart, 1992). By contrast, commercials were viewed favorably through the 1950s, but negative opinion has steadily grown ever since (Mittal, 1994). In 1968, Bauer and Greyser determined that people do not hold negative views of the economic role of advertising in the economy, but do hold negative views of the social role of advertising. This would suggest that attitudes toward advertising are not unidimensional but instead are multidimensional. Bauer and Greyser also discovered that higher education levels are correlated with more negative views of advertising. Mittal (1994) found that consumers as a group associated advertising with increasing materialism, increasing product costs, the promotion of unethical values, and taking advantage of children. (However, consumers favorably embraced the notion that advertisements make television free.) About two thirds of consumers surveyed stated that they support government regulation of television commercials and even banning television commercials. In addition, the majority of consumers surveyed disagreed with the statement that advertisements build confidence in one's purchases. Of the adults surveyed, one of every three reported indifference to television ads during viewing, two of every five said they ignored the ads, and one in three reported paying attention to ads. Children, however, may be incapable of showing indifference to commercials. Half of the participants agreed with banning all ads aimed at children. Perhaps if advertisers designed their commercials to children with less rhetoric and more factual information, the issue of advertising to children would not be as emotive to consumers.

It is apparent that children and the ideas they develop from watching television advertisements have a major impact on our economy. Although children younger than 12 years old watch television for an average of 3 hours a day, they do not participate in any other form of extracurricular entertainment for more than an hour a day, on average (Roberts, Foehr, Rideout, & Brodie, 1999). Children younger than 14 years spend approximately $20 billion per year and influence adults to spend another $200 billion (McNeal, 1998, as cited in Horgen et al., 2001). The money spent and purchases influenced by children aged 4 to 12 years approximately doubled between 1988 and 1998, as did advertising aimed at these children (McNeal, 1998). Preschool children show definite brand preference (Hite & Hite, 1995), which strengthens through elementary school (Ward et al., 1977); by adolescence, favorite brands are well established and based on the images portrayed by each brand (Achenreiner, 1995). A study of 9-year-olds in Ireland, Norway, Australia, and the United States revealed that television commercials play a major role in sparking the interests of children (Collins, Tonnessen, Barry, & Yeates, 1992). In America, a study by Easterlin and Crimmins (1991) showed that materialistic life goals in high school seniors increased between the early 1970s and through the 1980s. More materialism is shown by adolescents who watch more television (Churchill & Moschis, 1979; Moschis & Moore, 1982).

In 1993, Kunkel and Gantz reviewed over 10,000 advertisements and found strong adherence to the CARU regulations. The two major types of violations that occurred were advertisements for telephone message services that children could call, and the use of premiums in advertisements. CARU assesses 1,500 commercials per month for compliance with guidelines. The problem is that despite the adherence to guidelines, CARU has not evaluated the guidelines themselves to see whether they are truly effective in protecting children (Kunkel & Gantz, 1993). Therefore, having the guidelines and following the guidelines satisfies the public, but may not be helping the children.

In 1996, the FCC implemented a required 3-hour weekly minimum of time that broadcasters must devote to educational children's programming (FCC, 1996).

Advertisers, however, still attempt to influence children during the commercial breaks. In addition, a study by Kuribayashi, Roberts, and Johnson (2001) showed that television stations show an average of 15 minutes of nonprogram content per hour. This is well above the allowed maximum by the Children's Television Act of 1990. Although some stations have been fined, these types of penalties have not prompted consistent changes (Stern, 1995). In 1984, advertisers spent $88 billion on advertisements. In 1992, advertisers spent more than $150 billion (Russell & Lane, 1993). In 1998, advertisers spent $2 billion on advertisements aimed at children, 20 times as much as in 1990; and advertisers' current expenditures top $12 billion per year targeting the youth market (Lauro, 1999; Rice, 2001).

Thus, it is still apparent that television advertising is a major source of influence on children. In 1997, the average child watched 3 hours and 3 minutes of television per day, and the average teenager watched 2 hours and 54 minutes per day (Television Bureau of Advertising, 1998, as cited in Horgen et al., 2001).

Another major issue is the influence of advertisements on children's eating behaviors. Recently, a study in Australia revealed that over 50% of children aged 9–10 think that Ronald McDonald knows the best food for children to eat (Food Commission, 1997, as cited in Horgen et al., 2001). Food and food product advertisements comprise 50% to 60% of all advertisements on television (Kuribayashi et al., 2001). Between 1989 and 1991, a study by Rajecki et al. (1994) showed that the most frequent food ads for children were for dry cereals, toasted products, and canned pasta products. Food advertisements are more frequent during children's programming than during the afternoon hours (Kuribayashi et al., 2001). However, children may see the morning advertisements during the children's programming as well as the afternoon commercials while their parents are watching television. Therefore, they may be exposed to more food and other advertisements than adults or than children who watch only the morning programming. This could increase the impact of the advertisements on the children's eating behaviors (Kuribayashi et al, 2001).

The relationship between food advertising on television and health and well-being is becoming a major issue. We know that there is a relationship between increased obesity and increased television watching (American Association of Pediatrics Committee on Communications, 1995). Between 1976 and 1991, the greatest increase in obesity of 6- to 11-year-olds occurred (Horgen et al., 2001). The number of obese children has doubled in the past 2 decades (Yanovski & Yanovski, 1999). Also, the incidence of type II diabetes has dramatically increased among children and adolescents (Pinhas-Hamiel & Zeitler, 2001). Exposure to television food advertisements is related to more snacking, higher caloric consumption, and decreased nutritional value in the foods eaten (Bolton, 1983). Also, foods high in added sugar are advertised with stereotyped gender roles and the accompanying idealistic and unreal female body images that the actors portray (Lavine, Sweeney, & Wagner, 1999). In these advertising practices, children are receiving mixed messages. From 1973 to 1991, more diet food advertisements were aired, and the incidence of child-based eating disorders paralleled the increase (Wiseman, Gunning, & Gray, 1993).

Of the top 100 advertisement campaigns of the 20th Century, 24 were food advertisements (Klein & Donaton, 1999). The typical child sees 170 McDonald advertisements on television per year (Bell, 1997). In 1997, more advertising money—$1.4 billion—was spent on commercials for food and food products than any other product type (Television Bureau of Advertising, 1998). The group spending the second-highest dollar amount on ads was also food related: restaurants, which spent $1.2 billion. Between 1976 and 1987, the ratio of high-sugar to low-sugar products advertised in commercials increased from 5:1 to 12:1 (Cotugna, 1988). Advertising of food-related products is indeed prevalent in the lives of America's children.

It is difficult however to ascertain just what contribution food-related advertising makes to health-related problems in children and adolescence, notwithstanding the evidence cited here. We do not have such a history of research evidence and explanatory models linking the two together (in contrast to the evidence adduced by Huesmann and Skoric in chapter 11 concerning viewing violence and aggressive behavior). We do know that eating patterns—both dysfunctional and normative—are subject to various sources of influence including culture and socialization. It is to be hoped that an answer to this multifactorial problem will be forthcoming, and more research will be conducted to provide answers.

Another problem with food advertisements is that children do not understand that the foods shown are not representative of entire, balanced meals. Palmer and McDowell (1981) found that only one third of kindergarteners and first graders noticed anything on the table in the commercials other than the food that was advertised. Although disclaimers are intended to clarify misleading information, they are better understood with increasing age. Most preschoolers do not understand the meanings of disclaimers (Stutts & Hunnicutt, 1987).

A study of 8-year-olds showed that they would rather get a treat with Tony the Tiger or Ronald McDonald than with their father, teacher, or grandparent (Dibb, 1994). The use of exciting characters in food commercials also helps to attract kids to the products. In addition, the characters also provide brand-related cues that children remember (Lieber, 1998).

A problem is posed by the dominance of commercial messages that advertise foods that, taken together, do not constitute a healthy diet. Of 52.5 hours of Saturday morning programming studied in 1994, there were 564 food commercials, but only 10 nutrition-related public service announcements (Kotz & Story, 1994). Kuribayashi et al. (2001) found that children's morning programming blocks air more commercials for high-sugar/high-cholesterol foods; and after only one exposure to a product, a child is more likely to have a positive attitude about that product (Gorn & Goldberg, 1977).

Alcohol advertisements pose another child-based issue that could lead to health problems. Knowledge about television beer commercials leads to more positive attitudes about drinking and increased intentions to drink later in life (Grube & Wallack, 1994). America's television-viewing children see almost 2,000 wine and beer advertisements per year (American Association of Pediatrics, Committee on

Communications, 1995). A study by Aitken, Leathar, and Scott (1988) found that alcohol ads become increasingly influential and favorable to children between the ages of 10 and 14. The 14-year-olds notice the abstract qualities emphasized in alcohol advertisements, whereas 10-year-olds focus on the visible images and moralistic aspects of the ads. Teenagers perceive nondrinkers to be less attractive, weaker, and less sociable than drinkers (Aitken, 1978; Davies & Stacey, 1972). Attracted by ad humor, children also mention alcohol commercials as being some of their favorites (Aitken, Leathar, & O'Hagan, 1985).

The people who support the idea of federal regulation of high-fat food advertisements are those people who reported eating the fewest high-fat foods (Jeffrey et al., 1990). The Food, Drug, and Cosmetics Act (FDCA) works in conjunction with the Food and Drug Administration (FDA) to prevent misleading or inaccurate food labeling. At the same time, the FTC prevents false or deceptive advertisements of food or food products (Horgen et al., 2001). If an advertisement does not follow the FTC regulations, a preliminary injunction, a penalty, or a restraining order may be implemented (FTC, 1994). It is possible that if advertisers were required to state the nutritional information of their products during the products' advertisements, it would help the state of nutrition problems encountered in our society (Kuribayashi et al., 2001). A study by Goldberg, Gorn, and Gibson (1978) showed that public service announcements can lead to better nutritional food choices. Unfortunately, we presently do not have an equal number of nutritional public service announcements to balance the effects of the food advertisements. Also, parents should monitor their children while they watch TV, to ensure that they are not exposed to too many unhealthy advertisements (Kuribayashi et al., 2001).

Food advertising to children is only one issue that has emerged recently as a topic of concern. Another such issue is the emergence of advertising in schools. Now, even school environments are overflowing with advertising. There are four basic types of in-school advertising: direct, indirect, product sales, and marketing research. "Channel One" exemplifies the most prominent direct-advertising approach. This 10-minute news program, plus 2 minutes of advertisements, is shown daily to over 8 million middle and high schoolers (Consumers Union, 1995; Mifflin, 1998). Advertisers spend $175,000 per each 30-second spot to reach the 40% of American children who watch Channel One (Coeyman, 1995). Indirect advertising in schools takes several forms, including corporate-sponsored educational materials for the classroom (SEMS), brand-name product examples in textbooks, book covers that feature products, and free samples of candy, snack food, or personal hygiene products (Consumers Union, 1995). The most prominent product sales approach is exemplified by the contracts that soft-drink companies make with entire school districts for the exclusive rights to sell, for example, only Coke products or only Pepsi products. Covering over 150 school systems in 29 states, this trend continues to experience rapid growth nationwide (McKay, 2001;Ward, 2000). In the fourth type of in-school commercialism, market research covers a broad range of ways in which corporations and advertisers tap students' consumer preferences and lifestyles. Methods such as cola taste tests, questionnaires, Internet surveys, and Internet use tracking are commonplace (U.S. GAO Report, 2000). Clearly, industry self-regulation is not preventing children from being exposed to advertisements (Strasburger, 2001). Even in movies and television programs, brand names appear. This is a form of subtle influence on the viewers, because the presence of product placement—unlike spot advertising—is not immediately obvious to the viewer. At this writing, a Task Force on Advertising and Children is extensively examining the broad range of advertising approaches to children, with the intent to formulate a set of recommendations (Palmer et al., 2002).

It has been demonstrated in various studies that teaching advertising behavior curricula during school can improve children's verbal skepticism about the advertisements (Roberts, Christenson, Gibson, Mooser, & Goldberg, 1980). In a study by Robinson et al. (2001), children who received a 6-month intervention program designed to create televisual media ad literacy reported fewer product requests than did children who had not attended the intervention program. Another study showed that school programs to reduce television viewing time can reduce the incidence of child obesity and aggression (Robinson, 1999).

With the advent of the Internet and other kinds of electronic media, a new set of concerns has arisen recently, whereas many existing media entertainment concerns have also carried over. To phrase these concerns as questions: Will children spend less time involved in various social interactions or physical activities, and will these children be unfairly targeted by advertisers? Approximately 14% of America's children are online: some from home and some from school, using the Internet both for entertainment (e.g., games, contests, communications) and for education (e.g., help with homework; Austin & Reed, 1999). These children unwittingly can click an icon and be linked to an advertiser.

According to Roberts et al. (1999), there are two major types of interactive, electronic games: Stand-alone video games like Sega Genesis, Nintendo, and arcade games; and PC games that are either played on the computer or downloaded from the Internet (Subrahmanyam, Kraut, Greenfield, & Gross, 2001). In a study by Roberts et al. (1999), over 60% of married couples with children also have personal computers . However, the higher the parents' education level is, the less time their children spend on the computer (Roberts et al., 1999). Roberts et al. (1999) found that computer ownership is highly correlated with household income and ethnicity.

Preteen girls use the Internet less than younger girls, but preteen boys use the Internet more than younger boys. Overall, boys spend more time on the Internet than girls. Also, overall, as children get older, they spend more time using e-mail and accessing Web sites (Roberts et al., 1999). Chat room use is roughly equivalent to e-mail use (Roberts et al., 1999). A study by Stanger in 1998 showed that if children have a computer, they are more likely to do more homework, watch fewer videos, and read more periodicals.

With children using the Internet so frequently, one must question the content and advertisements on the Web sites being accessed. Concerns include exploitation of the trusting nature of children; their inability to distinguish between entertainment content and advertisements or between a game and an ad online; and children's inability to understand that their personal information may be misused, that characters may intend to get information from them for advertising purposes, and that it is dangerous to communicate with a stranger online (Austin & Reed, 1999).

There is a considerable amount of advertising online, even for adults. The Internet has both subtle icons on Web sites and pop-up advertisements that our children observe, and young televisual media users lack the critical eye of adults (Martin, 1997). In addition, Web sites use words that children do not understand, such as *preferences* and *registration* (Austin & Reed, 1999), and disclaimers usually are not written in language familiar to a child. Some Web sites even give children rewards for revealing personal information (Austin & Reed, 1999). Also, many of the electronic games are themselves advertisements for the action figures of the characters included in the games (Subrahmanyam et al., 2001). The advertisements are commonly mixed with the noncommercial content, making it difficult for children to discern the distinction between the two. For example, a game popular with girls is Barbie Fashion Design (Subrahmanyam et al., 2001). The problem is that the game is basically an advertisement for Barbie dolls and encourages children to want the dolls. Sometimes all a child has to do is click an icon in a game to find that they may purchase a related product. The games are not even separated from the sales (Austin & Reed, 1999). At this writing, the government has not placed specific regulations on this type of advertising (Kunkel & Wilcox, 2001).

Advertisers also use Internet site kids' clubs to obtain personal information about children. They may allow children to play interactive games that show how many products are offered. However, they occasionally obtain information from a club, but do not provide entertainment (Austin & Reed, 1999).

In addition, advertisers use knowledge about personal preferences to direct "one-to-one marketing" approaches to children. Advertisers are able to track the actions of children and tailor specific types of advertisements to them. Therefore, children are being exposed to a considerable number of advertisements, and many of these are specifically of interest to them (Austin & Reed, 1999).

As shown here, most electronic media seem to include some kind of advertising. The difficulty is regulating all Internet advertising, because it spans the entire world (Kunkel & Wilcox, 2001). At this point, children are less likely than parents to order products via the Internet or to search for information on products using the Internet (Subrahmanyam et al., 2001), primarily because they do not have as much money, nor do they have credit cards. However, children are still able to encourage their parents to purchase products and do so with regularity. In addition, viewing so many advertisements may lead children to develop more materialistic views. They may learn to base their self-confidence on possession.

Parents are concerned that children will trust all Internet content, including advertisements (Subrahmanyam et al., 2001). The question of whether some form of prevention or regulation to limit children's exposure to such an extensive amount of advertising together with inappropriate material is a serious issue for discussion. Parents may prefer that their children use the Internet rather than watch television, because advertising on the Internet is less rhetorical and is often limited to brand names. Unfortunately, advertising to children still occurs on the

Internet, and there is no way to predict how much more obtrusive and attractive to children this advertising trend will become in the years ahead. In chapter 14 of this volume, Kunkel and McIlrath speak compellingly about its current prevalence, and in chapter 17, Calvert gives us every reason to believe this growth trend will become all the more prevalent with emerging, smaller, and increasingly sophisticated technological devices.

As with television, the FTC prohibits unfair advertising to children via the Internet. On their Web site (www.ftc.gov), they provide suggestions for consumer protection and recommend self-regulation by advertisers via the Web. In 1997, the FTC discovered that 86 of 120 children's sites studied asked for personally identifiable information from children, including names, mailing and e-mail addresses, and telephone numbers (Bernstein, personal communication, 1997). Only 4% of the sites asked for parental authorization, and only 30% contained privacy policies. After this, the FTC stated a warning that they would legally control Web sites that are unfair to children. The Children's Online Privacy Protection Act (COPPA) requires restriction of access to Web sites with advertisements or material that could be harmful to minors (Austin & Reed, 1999; U.S. Congress, 1998).

The Center for Media Education (CME) has developed guidelines for advertiser self-regulation that protect children from unfair Internet practices (Center for Media Education, 1998):

1. To protect the anonymity and autonomy of children and parents, they should be able to understand the purpose of information collection.
2. The purposes of the information collection should be disclosed in child-friendly language.
3. Parental consent should be obtained if the child's information will be personally identifiable.
4. Data should only be used for stated purposes.
5. Data should be protected.
6. When parents request it, they should be allowed access to a child's information profile (Center for Media Education, 1998).

The Direct Marketing Association (DMA) is another self-regulating organization for advertisers. Representing 3,600 corporate entities across the youth product spectrum, the group suggests online privacy policies explaining the purpose of any information obtained. The DMA guidelines are:

1. The age of the viewer should be a factor in deciding whether or not to collect data.
2. Parents should be able to access a child's information profile if they desire.
3. Data should only be used for appropriate marketing.
4. Explanations of the purpose of data collection should be present.
5. The data should be protected.

The DMA also encourages parents to actively monitor their children's Internet use and to use filters to protect their children from inappropriate Web sites (Yoegel, 1997; CyberSavvy, 2002).

CARU reviews all forms of advertised media (CARU, 1997). As mentioned earlier, CARU is another self-regulatory organization funded by advertisers, and they request voluntary changes by advertisers when they discover violations of their guidelines. Aimed at children younger than age 12, these ad guidelines state that:

1. Children should know they are being asked to purchase something.
2. Children should understand that parental permission is necessary to purchase something.
3. Parents should be able to cancel undesired orders.
4. Parental permission should be required for information collection.
5. The purpose of the collected data should be clearly stated in child-friendly language.
6. Advertisers should ask children to use "screen names."
7. Advertisers should allow children to stop unwanted e-mails (CARU, 1997).

It is apparent that despite concerns about television, the Internet, and other forms of electronic media, they appeal to people of all ages. Hopefully, advertisers will consider the effects on children in their company guidelines and ethics codes (Austin & Reed, 1999). Also, parents should block certain types of Web sites by using filters, and should monitor their children's Internet and television usage. Family members and friends must help to invoke skepticism and develop critical viewing skills in children. Also, it makes sense that because children's viewing of television and use of the Internet are considered to be a problem, advertising literacy curricula should be included on the sources of that problem—television programming and Internet Web sites (Roberts, 1982). It is important and necessary to study the effect of those advertisements on children, who are the future of our nation.

REFERENCES

Achenreiner, G. B. (1995). *Children's reliance on brand name heuristics: A developmental investigation.* Unpublished doctoral dissertation, University of Minnesota, Minneapolis.

Adler, R. P. (1980). Children's television advertising: History of the issue. In E. L. Palmer & A. Dorr (Eds.), *Children and the faces of television* (vol 1, pp. 237–249). New York: Academic Press.

Adler, R. P., Friedlander, B. Z., Lesser, G. S., Meringoff, L., Robertson, T. S., Rossiter, J. R., & Ward, S. (1977). *Research on the effects of television advertising on children.* Washington, DC: U.S. Government Printing Office.

Aitken, P. P. (1978). *Ten- to fourteen-year-olds and alcohol.* Edinburgh: HMSO.

Aitken, P. P., Leathar, D. S., & O'Hagan, F. J. (1985). Children's perceptions of advertisements for cigarettes. *Social Science and Medicine, 21,* 785–797.

Aitken, P. P., Leathar, D. S., & Scott, A. C. (1988). Ten- to sixteen-year-olds' perceptions of advertisements for alcoholic drinks. *Alcohol & Alcoholism, 23,* 491–500.

American Academy of Pediatrics, Committee on Communications. (1995). *Children, adolescents and advertising* (RD9504). Retrieved June 2002 from http://www.aap.org/policy/00656.html

Austin, M. J., & Reed, M. L. (1999). Targeting children online: Internet advertising ethics issues. *The Journal of Consumer Marketing, 16,* 560–602.

Bauer, R. A., & Greyser, S. A. (1968). *Advertising in America; the consumer view.* Boston: Harvard Business School.

Bell, R. (1997, June 19). *Advertising. Judgment: Justice Bell's verdict, section 7.* Retrieved June 2002 from http://www.mcspotlight.org/case/trial/verdict/verdict_jud2b.html

Bolton, R. N. (1983). Modeling the impact of television food advertising on children's diets. *Current Issues and Research in Advertising, 6*(1), 175–199.

Browne, B. A. (1998). Gender stereotypes in advertising on children's television in the 1990s: A cross national analysis. *Journal of Advertising, 27,* 83–96.

Brucks, M., Armstrong, G. M., & Goldberg, M. E. (1998). Children's use of cognitive defenses against television advertising: A cognitive response approach. *The Journal of Consumer Research, 14,* 471–482.

Center for Media Education/Consumer Federation of America. (1998). *Guidelines and policy principles for the collection and tracking of information from children on the Global Information Infernation Infrastructure and Interactive Media.* Retrieved June 2002 from http://tap.epn.org

Children's Advertising Review Unit (CARU). (1997). *Self-regulatory guideline for children's advertising.* Retrieved June 2002 from http://bbb.org

Churchill, G. A., & Moschis, G. P. (1979). Television and interpersonal influences on adolescent consumer learning. *Journal of Consumer Research, 6,* 23–35.

Coeyman, M. (1995, July 20). Follow the customer: New media ventures may help marketers target a market. *Restaurant Business,* p. 36.

Cole, B., & Oettinger, M. (1978). *Reluctant regulators: The FCC and the broadcast audience.* Reading, MA: Addison-Wesley.

Collins, J., Tonnessen, E. S., Barry, A. M., & Yeates, H. (1992). Who's afraid of the big bad box? Children and advertising in four countries. *Educational Media International, 29*(4), 254–260.

Condry, J. C., Bence, P. J., & Scheibe, C. L. (1988). Nonprogram content of children's television. *Journal of Broadcasting and Electronic Media, 32,* 255–270.

Consumers Union (1995). *Captive kids: Commercial pressures on kids at school.* Consumers Union Education Series. Yonkers, NY: Author.

Cotugna, N. (1988). TV ads on Saturday morning children's programming: What's new? *Journal of Nutrition Education, 20,* 125–127.

CyberSavvy (2002). Direct Marketing Association. Retrieved December 2002 from http://www.cybersavvy.org/cybersavvy/children/index.html

Davies, J., & Stacey, B. (1972). *Teenagers and alcohol.* London: HMSO.

Dibb, S. (1994, November). *Advertising witnesses* [Statement of advertising researcher, witness for defense]. Retrieved June 2002 from http://www.mcspotlight.org/cgi-bi/zv/people/witnesses/advertising/dibb_sub.html

Donohue, T. R., Henke, L. L., & Donohue, W. A. (1980). Do kids know what TV commercials intend? *Journal of Advertising Research, 20,* 51–57.

Easterlin, R., & Crimmins, E. (1991). Private materialism, personal self-fulfillment, family life, and public interest: The nature, effects, and causes of recent changes in the values of American youth. *Public Opinion Quarterly, 55,* 499–533.

Federal Communications Commission (FCC). (1974). Children's television programs: Report and policy statement. *Federal Register, 39*(215), 396–409.

Federal Communications Commission (1996). In the matter of policies and rules concerning children's television programming: Report and order. *Federal Communications Commission Record, 11,* 10660–10778.

Federal Trade Commission (FTC). (1978a). Children's advertising: Proposed trade regulation rulemaking and public hearing. *Federal Register, 43*(82), 17967–17972.

Federal Trade Commission (FTC). (1978b). *Staff report on television advertising to children.* Washington, DC: U.S. Government Printing Office.

Federal Trade Commission (FTC). (1981). *In the matter of children's advertising: FTC final staff report and recommendation.* Washington, DC: Author.

Federal Trade Commission (FTC). (1994, May). *Enforcement policy statement on food advertising.* Retrieved June 2002 from http://www.ftc.gov/bcp/policystmt/ad-food.htm

Goldberg, M. E., Gorn, G. J., & Gibson, W. (1978). TV messages for snack and breakfast foods: Do they influence children's preferences? *Journal of Consumer Research, 5,* 73–81.

Gorn, G. J., & Goldberg, M. E. (1977). The impact of television advertising on children from low income families. *Journal of Consumer Research, 4,* 86–88.

Grube, J. W., & Wallack, L. (1994). Television beer advertising and drinking knowledge, beliefs, and intentions among schoolchildren. *American Journal of Public Health, 84,* 254–259.

Hite, C. F., & Hite, R. E. (1995). Reliance on brand by young children. *Journal of the Market Research Society, 37,* 185–193.

Hollenbeck, A. R., & Slaby, R. G. (1979). Infant visual and vocal responses to television. *Child Development, 50,* 41–45.

Horgen, K. B., Choate, M., & Brownell, K. D. (2001). Television food advertising: Targeting children in a toxic environment. In D. G. Singer & J. L. Singer (Eds.), *Handbook of children and the media* (pp. 447–461). London: Sage.

Horowitz, R. (1989). *The irony of regulatory reform: The deregulation of American telecommunications.* New York: Oxford University Press.

Jeffrey, R. W., Forster, J. L., Schmid, T. L., McBride, C. M., Rooney, B. L., & Pirie, P. L. (1990). Community attitudes toward public policies to control alcohol, tobacco, and high-fat food consumption. *American Journal of Preventive Medicine, 6,* 12–19.

John, D. R. (1999). Consumer socialization of children: A retrospective look at twenty-five years of research. *Journal of Consumer Research, 26,* 183–213.

Klein, D., & Donaton, S. (1999). The advertising century: Top 100 advertising campaigns. *Advertising Age.* Retrieved June 2002 from http://adage.com/century/campaigns.html

Kotz, K., & Story, M. (1994, November). Food advertisement during children's Saturday morning television programming: Are they consistent with dietary recommendations? *Journal of the American Dietetic Association,* pp. 1296–1300.

Kunkel, D. (1988). Children and host-selling television commercials. *Communication Research, 15,* 71–92.

Kunkel, D. (2001). Children and television advertising. In D. G. Singer & J. L. Singer (Eds.), *Handbook of children and the media* (pp. 375–393). London: Sage.

Kunkel, D., & Gantz, W. (1993). Assessing compliance with industry self-regulation of television advertising to children. *Journal of Applied Communication Research, 21,* 148–162.

Kunkel, D., & Roberts, D. (1991). Young minds and marketplace values: Issues in children's television advertising. *Journal of Social Issues, 47,* 57–72.

Kunkel, D., & Watkins, B. (1987). Evolution of children's television regulatory policy. *Journal of Broadcasting and Electronic Media, 31,* 367–389.

Kunkel, D., & Wilcox, B. (2001). Children and media policy. In D. G. Singer & J. L. Singer (Eds.), *Handbook of children and the media* (pp. 589–604). London: Sage.

Kuribayashi, A., Roberts, M. C., & Johnson, R. J. (2001). Actual nutrition information of products advertised to children and adults on Saturday. *Children's Health Care, 30,* 309–322.

Lauro, P. W. (1999, November 1). Coaxing the smile that sells: Baby wranglers in demand in marketing for children. *The New York Times,* p. C1.

Lavine, H., Sweeney, D., & Wagner, S. H. (1999). Depicting women as sex objects in television advertising: Effects on body dissatisfaction. *Personality and Social Psychology Bulletin, 25,* 1049–1058.

Lieber, L. (1998). Commercial and character slogan recall by children aged 9 to 11 years. *Center on Alcohol Advertising.* Retrieved June 2002 from http://www.igc.org/trauma/alcohol/ads/budstudy.html

Liebert, D. E., Sprafkin, J. N., Liebert, R. M., & Rubinstein, E. A. (1977). Effects of television commercial disclaimers on the product expectations of children. *Journal of Communication, 27,* 118–124.

Macklin, M. C., & Kolbe, R. H. (1984). Sex role stereotyping in children's advertising: Current and past trends. *Journal of Advertising, 13,* 34–42.

Maddox, L., & Zanot, E. (1984). Suspension of the NAB code and its effect on the regulation of advertising. *Journalism Quarterly, 61,* 125–130, 156.

Marshall, H. R. (1964). The relation of giving children an allowance to children's money knowledge and responsibility and to other practices of parents. *Journal of Genetic Psychology, 104,* 35–51.

Martin, M. (1997). Children's understanding of the intent of advertising: A meta-analysis. *Journal of Public Policy and Marketing, 16*(2), 205–224.

McKay, B. (2001, June 26). Coke finds its exclusive contracts aren't so easily given up. *Wall Street Journal* (Eastern Edition), pp. B1, B4.

McNeal, J. U. (1998). Tapping the three kids' markets. *American Demographics, 20,* 37–41.

Melody, W. (1973). *Children's television.* London: Yale University Press.

Mifflin, L. (1998, December 28). Nielsen to research Channel One's audience. *The New York Times,* p. C6.

Mittal, B. (1994). Public assessment of TV advertising: Faint praise and harsh criticism. *Journal of Advertising Research, 34,* 35–53.

Moore, R. L., & Stephens, L. F. (1975). Some communication and demographic determinants of adolescent consumer learning. *Journal of Consumer Research, 2,* 80–92.

Moschis, G. P., & Moore, R. L. (1979). Decision making among the young: A socialization perspective. *Journal of Consumer Research, 6,* 101–112.

Moschis, G. P., & Moore, R. L. (1982). A longitudinal study of television advertising effects. *Journal of Consumer Research, 9,* 279–286.

Murray, J. (1980). *Television and youths: 25 years of research and controversy.* Boys Town, NE: Boys Town Center for the Study of Youth Development.

National Association of Broadcasters (1965, August). *The television code* (10th ed.). Washington, DC: Author.

National Association of Broadcasters (1979). *The television code* (22nd ed.). Washington, DC: Author.

Nielsen Media Research. (1991). *1991 report on television.* New York: Author.

Palmer, E. L. (1987). *Children in the cradle of television.* Lexington, MA: Lexington Books.

Palmer, E. L. (1988). *Television & America's children: A crisis of neglect.* New York: Oxford University Press.

Palmer, E. L. (1999). Impact of television on children. In L. Kurtz (Ed.), *Encyclopedia of violence, peace, and conflict* (pp. 257–268). San Diego, CA: Academic Press.

Palmer, E., Cantor, J., Dowrick, P., Kunkel, D., Linn, S., & Wilcox, B. (2002). Psychological implications of commercialism in schools: Report of the APA Task Force on Advertising and Children. Unpublished report, American Psychological Association, Washington, DC.

Palmer, E., & McDowell, C. (1981). Children's understanding of nutritional information presented in breakfast cereal commercials. *Journal of Applied Communication Research, 21,* 148–162.

Pearce, W. B. (1974). Trust in interpersonal communication. *Speech Monographs, 41,* 236–244.

Piaget, J. (1952). *The origins of intelligence in children* (M. Cook, Trans.). New York: International University Press.

Pinhas-Hamiel, O., & Zeitler, P. (2001). Type 2 diabetes: Not just for grownups anymore. *Contemporary Pediatrics, 18,* 102–125.

Rajecki, D. W., McTavish, D. G., Rasmussen, J. L., Schreuders, M., Byers, D. C., & Jessup, K. S. (1994). Violence, conflict, trickery, and other story themes in TV ads for food for children. *Journal of Applied Social Psychology, 24,* 1685–1700.

Rice, F. (2001, February 12). Superstars of spending: Marketers clamor for kids. *Advertising Age,* p. s1, s10.

Roberts, D. F. (1982). Children and commercials: Issues, evidence, interventions. *Prevention in Human Services, 2,* 19–35.

Roberts, D. F., Christenson, P. G., Gibson, W., Mooser, L., & Goldberg, M. E. (1980). Developing discriminating consumers. *Journal of Communication, 30*(2), 94–105.

Roberts, D. F., Foehr, U. G., Rideout, V. J., & Brodie, M. (1999). *Kids and media @ the new millennium: A comprehensive national analysis of children's media use.* Menlo Park, CA: Kaiser Family Foundation.

Robertson, T. S., & Rossiter, J. R. (1974). Children and commercial persuasion: An attribution theory analysis. *Journal of Consumer Research, 1,* 13–20.

Robinson, T. N. (1999). Reducing children's television viewing to prevent obesity: A randomized controlled trial. *Journal of the American Medical Association, 282,* 1961–1967.

Robinson, T. N., Saphir, M. N., Kramer, H. C., Varady, A. M. S., & Haydel, K. F. (2001). Effects of reducing television viewing on children's requests for toys: A randomized controlled trial. *Developmental and Behavioral Pediatrics, 22,* 179–184.

Rossiter, J. R. (1977). Reliability of a short test measuring children's attitudes toward TV commercials. *Journal of Consumer Research, 3,* 179–184.

Russell, J. T., & Lane, W. R. (1993). *Kleppner's advertising procedure* (11th ed.). Englewood Cliffs, NJ: Prentice-Hall.

Stanger, J. D. (1998). *Television in the home 1998: The third annual national survey of parents and children.* Philadelphia: University of Pennsylvania, Annenberg Public Policy Center.

Stern, C. (1995, April 3). Kids TV fines set record. *Broadcasting & Cable,* p. 78.

Stern, B., & Harmon, R. (1984). The incidence and characteristics of disclaimers in children's television advertising. *Journal of Advertising, 13*(2), 12–16.

Stewart, D. W. (1992). Speculations on the future of advertising research. *Journal of Advertising, 21,* 1–18.

Strasburger, V. C. (2001). Children and TV advertising: Nowhere to run, nowhere to hide. *Journal of Developmental and Behavioral Pediatrics, 22,* 185–187.

Stutts, M. A., & Hunnicutt, G. G. (1987). Can young children understand disclaimers in television commercials? *Journal of Advertising, 16,* 41–46.

Subrahmanyam, K., Kraut, R., Greenfield, P., & Gross, E. (2001). New forms of electronic media: The impact of interactive games and the Internet on cognition, socialization, and behavior. In D. G. Singer & J. L. Singer (Eds.), *Handbook of children and the media* (pp. 73–99). London: Sage.

Television Bureau of Advertising. (1998). *TV basics.* Retrieved June 2002 from http://www.tvb.org/tvfacts/index.html

United States Congress. (1998). *Children's Online Privacy Protection Act of 1998,* S. 2326. Washington, DC: U.S. Government Printing Office.

U.S. General Accounting Office (2000, September). *Public education: Commercial activities in schools.* Washington, DC: U.S. General Accounting Office.

Ward, C. L. (2000, September 14). New report examines commercialism in U.S. schools. *The New York Times,* p. D1.

Ward, S., Wackman, D. B., & Wartella, E. (1977). *How children learn to buy: The development of consumer information-processing skills.* London: Sage.

Wartella, E., Wackman, D., Ward, S., Shamir, J., & Alexander, A. (1979). The young child as a consumer. In E. Wartella (Ed.), *Children communicating.* Beverly Hills, CA: Sage.

Wiseman, C. V., Gunning, F. M., & Gray, J. J. (1993). Increasing pressure to be thin: 19 years of diet products in television commercials. *Eating Disorders, 1*(1), 52–61.

Yanovski, J. A., & Yanovski, S. Z. (1999). Recent advances in basic obesity research. *Journal of the American Medical Association, 282,* 1504–1506.

Yoegel, R. (1997, November). Reaching youth on the web. *Target Marketing, 20*(11), 38–41.

Zuckerman, P., & Gianinno, L. (1981). Measuring children's response to television advertising. In J. F. Esserman (Ed.), *Television advertising and children: Issues, research, and findings* (pp. 84–93). New York: Child Research Service.

Message Content
in Advertising to Children

Dale Kunkel
Mary McIlrath
University of California, Santa Barbara

Most American children begin viewing television even before they develop the physical ability to walk out the front door of their home. One- and 2-year olds watch television regularly (Barr & Hayne, 1999; Meltzoff, 1988), and more than a quarter (26%) of 2- to 4-year-olds have a television set in their bedroom (Roberts, Foehr, Rideout, & Brodie, 1999). Children aged 2 to 7 years average between 3.0 to 3.5 hours per day of television viewing, with most of that time spent watching commercially supported channels (Comstock & Scharrer, 1999; Roberts et al., 1999). Given that roughly 15% to 20% of all television content is devoted to commercial matter (Comstock & Scharrer, 1999), these data make it clear that children experience significant exposure to television advertising at very young ages. Such exposure raises sensitive issues because of the findings documented elsewhere in this volume (see chaps. 13, 15, & 16) about young children's limited ability to recognize and defend against televised commercial persuasion.

Advertising to children has grown to be an extraordinarily large segment of the commercial media marketplace. Advertisers spend more than $12 billion per year to target the youth market because of its strong contribution to the consumer economy (Lauro, 1999). According to 1998 data, children aged 14 and under spent $24 billion and influenced $190 billion in family purchases that year (McNeal, 1998). As a result, children today encounter significant levels of commercial messages, primarily although not exclusively on television.

Certainly businesses have directed marketing messages to children long before the advent of television. For example, popular children's periodicals in the 1910s and 1920s such as *St. Nicholas Magazine* and *Boys Magazine* included ads directly targeted at youth (Heintz-Knowles & Van Horn, 1993). Yet, because of the reading skills required for comprehending the written word, there is an inherent obstacle that precludes advertisers from targeting younger groups of children via the print media. Television long ago rendered that barrier obsolete. In the 1950s, ads began to target children during such programs as *Howdy Doody, The Mickey Mouse Club,* and *Roy Rogers* (Alexander, Benjamin, Hoerrner, & Roe, 1998). Since the 1960s, television has clearly become the dominant vehicle by which commercial enterprises reach child audiences with their advertising messages.

In this chapter, we examine the nature and extent of advertising messages directed to children, focusing primarily on television content due to its primacy as a vehicle for marketing to youth. We first consider the overall amount of children's advertising exposure, then survey the key elements of the content of advertisements targeting children. We also review the limits and controls that directly impact the content of advertising to children, and finally consider the implications of recent innovations in marketing to children, which include expanding commercialization in the schools and advertising on Web sites.

CHILDREN'S EXPOSURE TO ADVERTISING

Estimates of the number of commercials seen annually by most U.S. children have grown from 20,000 per year in the 1970s (Adler et al., 1977) to 30,000 per year in the 1980s (Condry, Bence, & Scheibe, 1988) to 40,000 per year in the early 1990s (Kunkel & Gantz, 1992). More recently, Comstock and Scharrer (1999) indicated that the average viewer (encompassing both children and adults) is exposed to approximately 60,000 commercials per year, underscoring the consistent escalation in the number of marketing messages conveyed on television.

Our focus in this chapter emphasizes commercials specifically targeted to children. Although a substantial amount of children's viewing after the preschool years includes programs primarily intended for adults (Lyle & Hoffman, 1972; Roberts et al., 1999), the advertising on such programs is generally less salient for youngsters and thus less likely to exert direct influence on child audiences. Indeed, Gorn and Florsheim (1985) demonstrated the reduced level of "purchase influence attempts" by children after watching adult-oriented ads as compared to advertising for child-oriented products. Accordingly, the emphasis here is on commercials designed specifically for children, for it is these ads that are most likely to attract children's attention (Greer, Potts, Wright, & Huston, 1982) and to have the most immediate effects on young viewers (Kunkel, 2001).

Concern about advertising to children first gained public attention about 1970, when a new child advocacy group, Action for Children's Television (ACT), began to champion the cause (Cole & Oettinger, 1978). ACT commissioned Boston University Professor F. Earle Barcus to conduct a series of studies that provided a rich history of the children's advertising environment at the time (Barcus, 1971, 1972, 1975, 1977, 1978). One of Barcus' first discoveries was that the amount of time devoted to commercials in children's shows, averaging as much as 15 to 16 minutes per hour, far exceeded the amount of advertising time in virtually all other types of programming (Barcus, 1971). This evidence, coupled with research demonstrating young children's unique vulnerability to commercial persuasion, led the Federal Communications Commission (FCC) in 1974 to adopt a policy limiting advertising during children's programs on broadcast television to no more than 9:30 minutes per hour on weekends, and 12 minutes per hour on weekdays (FCC, 1974).

Studies have documented a general pattern of compliance with these time limits during the 1970s (Fontes, 1978) and 1980s (Condry et al., 1988). However, in 1984 the FCC deregulated all of its policies limiting the amount of advertising time that could be aired by broadcast television licensees, arguing that marketplace competition would serve as effectively as government regulation to keep excessive commercial practices in check (FCC, 1984). Congress soon reversed the FCC's decision to deregulate advertising to children, adopting statutory limits of 10:30 minutes per hour of commercials during weekend children's programming, and 12 minutes per hour during weekday shows, as part of the Children's Television Act of 1990 (Kunkel, 1991). In a noteworthy development, these time limits were applied for the first time to cable television networks as well as broadcast stations.

There is some evidence that the amount of commercial advertising during children's programs on cable television may be lower than that found on broadcast channels. Kunkel and Gantz (1992) reported that broadcast networks aired the greatest amount of commercials, averaging 10:05 minutes per hour during children's shows, followed closely by independent broadcasters at 9:37 minutes per hour. In contrast, cable channels averaged much less time (6:48 per hour) devoted to commercial messages. These data, however, were gathered in the early 1990s, and the academic community has yet to provide an update on cable's advertising levels, so this finding should be viewed with caution given the significant changes that have occurred in the media environment over the past decade.

Other Nonprogram Content

There are other forms of nonprogram content besides commercial advertising found in breaks during children's shows, including both program promotions and public service announcements (PSAs). Neither of these formats are defined as advertising for purposes of the regulatory limits on advertising to children. Thus, to identify the total volume of persuasive messages presented during children's programming, one must add together the time devoted to traditional advertising messages and the time devoted to these other types of segments.

Early studies examining commercial content reported only the sheer number of program promotional messages rather than the overall time devoted to such segments. Barcus (1978) observed an average of 5 program promotions per hour, whereas Condry et al. (1988) found a mean of 4.4 promos per hour between 1983 and 1987, with both samples of programming drawn primarily from network broadcast channels. In the early 1990s, Kunkel and Gantz (1992) reported that network broadcasters averaged nearly 1 minute per hour (0:58) of program promotions, but that independent broadcasters (2:52/hour) and cable networks (2:53/hour) devoted much more time to these segments. The most recent data available, gathered in 1998, indicate that program promotions during children's shows have increased on the broadcast networks and held relatively stable on cable channels (Gantz & Schwartz, 2000). Across six commercial broadcast networks (ABC, CBS, NBC, Fox, UPN, WB), program promotions averaged 4:05 per hour, compared to 2:25 per hour for cable networks. In this study, a sizable proportion (40%) of all promotions airing during children's shows were for prime-time, adult-oriented programming.

Public service announcements during children's programs occur with some regularity, albeit in small amounts averaging between 30 seconds and 1 minute per hour (Condry et al.,1988; Kunkel & Gantz, 1992). PSAs are found more frequently on Saturday morning children's programs than elsewhere in the television environment (Comstock & Scharrer, 1999), and television industry officials indicate that child and family issues are their top priority in deciding what PSAs to air (Gantz, 2002).

With the changing nature of advertising styles, some product commercials are now designed to resemble PSAs, which raises new challenges for young viewers just learning to successfully categorize the different types of persuasive messages found on television. For example, Fox (1996) described a Pepsi-Cola commercial campaign entitled "It's Like This" that featured a documentary style in which kids talked about their problems in short segments aired in black and white, with each speaker interrupted by a brief color visual of a red, white, and blue Pepsi can. Fewer than half of ninth through twelfth graders who saw such ads thought they were real commercials, instead assuming they were some other form of noncommercial content such as a PSA (Fox, 1996). One ninth grader, for example, responded, "It's not really a commercial, it's just a commercial *sponsored* by Pepsi" (Fox, 1996, p. 3). This blurring of the boundaries between commercial and noncommercial content is an increasing trend that we consider further later in this chapter.

In summary, the average hour of children's programming on broadcast television appears to include approximately 10 minutes of product commercials, 3 to 4 minutes of program promotions, and up to 1 minute of PSAs. Collectively, this means that up to 25% of a child's time spent viewing television may consist of watching messages meant to persuade and to influence subsequent behavior. These figures may be slightly lower for cable, although the evidence for this medium is somewhat dated and in need of reexamination.

PRODUCT TYPES

In an overview of his numerous content studies conducted throughout the 1970s, Barcus (1980) observed that more than 80% of all advertising to children fell within just four product categories: toys, cereals, candies, and fast-food restaurants. The stability of this pattern has been confirmed by subsequent research over the years, as noted in Table 14.1. This table displays the relative distribution of product types in advertising during children's programs as reported by the three largest content studies conducted in this area.

The data appear to have held remarkably stable over time, with the modest exception that toy commercials seem to have surged in the 1980s through the 1990s and to have displaced some of the candy/snack ads that aired previously. This shift likely reflects an increase in toy marketing stimulated by growth in product tie-ins with children's programs, which were first allowed in the mid-1980s following the FCC's deregulation of its previous restriction on program-length commercials (Kline, 1993; Kunkel, 1988b).

Another pattern that has held constant over time is the seasonal variation in product advertising that occurs each year during the pre-Christmas months. During this period, toy commercials gain a much larger share of the market, jumping from their normal rate of about one in every four or five commercials to half or more of all ads in children's programs at Christmastime (Atkin & Heald, 1977; Barcus, 1976; Condry et al., 1988; Kunkel & Gantz, 1994). This increase in toy advertising generally displaces commercials for cereals and candy/snacks, which then reemerge after the holidays in their normal volume.

Most of the foods advertised to children are for highly sugared products, such as presweetened cereals, candy, snacks, cookies, and sodas; few commercials advertise any healthy foods (Barcus, 1980; Kunkel & Gantz, 1992). The propensity of advertising to children to feature unhealthy foods has been linked to a number of negative outcomes, including a lack of understanding of proper diet and nutrition as

TABLE 14.1

Comparison of Product Types Observed in Content Studies of Advertising to Children

Product Type	Barcus (1977)	Condry, Bence, & Scheibe[1] (1988)	Kunkel & Gantz (1992)
toys	18%	30%	34%
cereals	25%	22%	22%
candy/snacks	29%	19%	18%
restaurants/fast foods	10%	10%	6%
Total of ads across these categories	82%	81%	80%

[1]Percentages derived by combining data reported for advertising sampled in 1983, 1985, and 1987.

well as obesity in childhood (Horgen, Choate, & Brownell, 2001; Strasburger, 2001). Similarly, the advertising of toys, particularly at Christmastime, has been associated with increased purchase-influence attempts that trigger parent–child conflict when parents cannot honor all of their child's product requests (Robertson, 1979; Sheikh & Moleski, 1977).

PERSUASIVE THEMES AND APPEALS

Stern and Resnik (1991) reported that roughly half of all commercials targeting adults include salient product information such as price, quality, or availability. In contrast, commercials targeting children rarely provide information about specific product attributes. The most common persuasive strategy employed in advertising to children is to associate the product with fun/happiness (Atkin & Heald, 1977; Barcus, 1980; Kunkel & Gantz, 1992). For example, a commercial featuring Ronald McDonald dancing, singing, and smiling in a McDonald's restaurant without any mention of the food products available there would be categorized as employing a fun/happiness theme.

Barcus (1980) noted that this pattern was also common with cereal advertising, which frequently features spokescharacters (e.g., Tony the Tiger, Cap'n Crunch) in an adventure scenario. In contrast, it is impossible to discern the major grain used in the cereal in most cases unless it is included as part of the product name, such as in Bran Flakes. Interestingly, in the small number of ads aired for healthy food products, the fun/happiness theme still predominates as the primary appeal (47%), whereas a health/nutrition theme is only rarely employed (6%), even when it would arguably be most salient (Kunkel & Gantz, 1992).

Other common themes/appeals are closely tied to particular types of product ads. For example, taste/flavor/smell is by far the most frequent appeal used in commercials for cereals, snacks, and drinks (Kunkel & Gantz, 1992). Commercials for toy products are the most likely to convey information about product performance, although fewer than one in five such ads employ this as their primary theme/appeal (Barcus, 1980; Kunkel & Gantz, 1992).

In addition to themes/appeals, advertising to children typically includes formal features, or production conventions, meant to elicit attention to the screen and thereby increase the impact of the ad (Rice, Huston, & Wright, 1982). For example, commercials attract children's attention by using unusual sound effects, lots of movement and fast pacing of visual cuts, and fantasy or magic that involves appearances/disappearances and mystical flight of people or objects (Barcus, 1977, 1980). Finally, commercials for children often employ creative use of music as well as jingles to help aid in product recall (Macklin, 1988).

DISCLOSURES/DISCLAIMERS

Another common feature of advertising to children is the use of product disclosures and disclaimers such as "batteries not included" or "each part sold separately." The frequency with which such messages appear in advertising to children ranges between one in every three ads (Stern & Harmon, 1984) and one in every two (Kunkel & Gantz, 1992). Studies make it clear that young children do not comprehend the intended meaning of the most widely used disclaimers (Liebert, Sprafkin, Liebert, & Rubinstein, 1977; Stern & Resnik, 1978; Stutts & Hunicutt, 1987). Although fewer than one in four kindergarten through second-grade children could grasp the meaning of "some assembly required" when shown a commercial, the use of child-friendly language such as "you have to put it together" more than doubled the proportion of children who understood the qualifying message (Liebert et al., 1977; Lingsweiler & Wilson, 2002).

The phrase "part of a balanced breakfast" is another frequent disclosure, included in most cereal ads to combat the concern that sugared cereal products hold little nutritional value for children. Consistent with the data on toy disclaimers, Atkin and Gibson (1978) found that fewer than one in three 4- to 7-year-olds had any idea what the term "balanced breakfast" means. Rather than informing young viewers about the importance of a well-rounded nutritious breakfast, this common disclaimer actually leaves many children with the misimpression that cereal alone is sufficient for a meal (Palmer & McDowell, 1981).

Children's understanding of disclosure statements is greatest when both audio and visual formats are employed to convey the qualification message (Liebert et al., 1977; Palmer & McDowell, 1981). However, only about one of every five children's commercials with a disclosure uses this approach (Kunkel & Gantz, 1992). Cereal commercials most commonly employ an audio-only strategy to convey the "balanced breakfast" information, whereas toy ads rely primarily on visual disclosures in textual form. These findings regarding children's interpretation of disclosures and disclaimers in television commercials underscore the importance of considering how children of different ages make sense of advertising messages.

CHARACTER GENDER AND ETHNICITY

As with all television content, advertising can contribute to a child's perceptions about how the different genders behave and how people of different ethnicities may interact. The proportion of male and female characters featured in commercials across television overall is generally considered to be equivalent (Comstock & Scharrer, 1999). In contrast to this pattern of relative balance, several studies of advertising to children found a male bias in the range of 54% to 64% of featured characters (Bretl & Cantor, 1988; Browne, 1998; Macklin & Kolbe, 1984; Riffe, Goldson, Saxton, & Yu, 1989). Recently, however, a broad-based study of roughly 600 children's ads that aired in 1997 and 1998 found almost identical numbers of male and female characters (Larson, 2001), suggesting that gender equality within children's advertising may be improving.

Many children's advertisements target one gender over the other in framing their message. For example, toy ads frequently target either boys or girls because toys are strongly gender linked in the minds of both children and parents (Clark & Higonnet, 1999). When a gender bias exists in advertising to children, boys are consistently the privileged group. This disparity is attributable to the advertising adage that girls will consider using boys' products, whereas boys will not typically associate with girls' items (Smith, 1994). Although male-oriented ads have consistently predominated in advertising to children, the degree of bias has clearly and consistently diminished over time from 84% of all single-gender ads in the 1970s (Doolittle & Pepper, 1975) to 72% to 76% in the 1980s (Macklin & Kolbe, 1984; Riffe et al., 1989) to 67% in the 1990s (Smith, 1994) and to 63% more recently (Larson, 2001).

Some studies have examined the level of activity or passivity of the actors in commercials, and here again boys fare somewhat differently than girls. Verna (1975) noted that the overwhelming majority (87%) of girls in children's advertising were passive, whereas most boys (72%) were active. Similar findings regarding activity levels have been reported for toy advertisements (Welch, Huston-Stein, Wright, & Plehal, 1979), for children's advertising in general (Macklin & Kolbe, 1984), and for Australian as well as U.S.-based children's commercials (Browne, 1998). Aggression is an extreme form of physical activity, and numerous studies have found that advertisements directed at boys are moderately to highly likely to contain aggressive behavior, whereas commercials directed at girls almost never depict aggression (Larson, 2001; Macklin & Kolbe, 1984; Verna, 1975; Welch et al., 1979). Finally, commercials targeted at girls are much more likely to be set in the home than commercials targeted at boys (Larson, 2001; Smith, 1994).

The diversity of ethnic representation in advertising to children was first studied in the 1970s and found to be lacking, with at least 90% of all characters apparently White (Atkin & Heald, 1977; Barcus, 1983; O'Kelly & Bloomquist, 1976). During the 1970s, fewer than one in four commercials depicted any ethnic minority figures (Atkin & Heald, 1977; Doolittle & Pepper, 1975; Winick, Williamson, Chuzmir, & Winick, 1973), and those who were included were more likely to play token roles than to be featured characters. More recent research suggests some change in the direction of equality of ethnic representation, although this topic has not attracted as much research scrutiny as in the past. Riffe et al. (1989) reported that 13% of all prominent human characters in a sample of Saturday morning commercials were non-White, whereas Wulfemeyer and Mueller (1992) found the identical proportion of minority characters in advertising on Channel One, a national news service airing in junior and senior high schools. Another study of Saturday morning commercials noted that a non-white character was observed in almost every commercial pod analyzed (Greenberg & Brand, 1993).

In summary, it appears that television advertising to children continues to reflect many common gender stereotypes, and to present little diversity in terms of the characters featured in the commercials, although there are some modest indications of improvements in the most recent data examining these topics.

POLICIES THAT SHAPE THE CONTENT OF ADVERTISING TO CHILDREN

Both industry self-regulation and formal governmental regulation play a role in shaping certain aspects of the content of television advertising to children. Since the 1980s, the television industry has not maintained industrywide self-regulation of any sort; judgments about the acceptability of both programming and advertising content are rendered at the level of the individual station or network. Self-regulation by the advertising industry is accomplished through the Children's Advertising Review Unit (CARU), a subsidiary of the National Council of Better Business Bureaus. The CARU operation, which is funded by contributions from the advertising industry, relies on the good faith and cooperation of advertisers to accomplish its work. The CARU guidelines are intended to "encourage truthful and accurate advertising sensitive to the special nature of children" (Weisskoff, 1985, p. 12).

Guidelines are established in such areas as product presentations and claims; sales pressure; and safety concerns. Within each area, a range of criteria are included that indicate practices to be either avoided or required. Some of these standards are fairly specific, such as the requirement that "a product should be demonstrated in a way that can be duplicated by the child for whom the product is intended." Others are more vague and general, such as the admonition that "care should be taken not to exploit a child's imagination."

Although many elements of the guidelines are not amenable to any empirical evaluation of compliance, those that are were examined in an independent study of more than 10,000 commercials directed at children (Kunkel & Gantz, 1993). Overall, just 4% were found to present violations of CARU standards. Among the most common violations were ads that placed greater emphasis on a premium than on the advertised product, which occurred most often with fast-food commercials.

Children's advertising content is also shaped to some extent by formal governmental regulation. Certainly the limits on commercial time during children's programs discussed earlier in this chapter play a significant role in constraining the overall amount of advertising to children. In addition, the FCC maintains several policies that restrict several specific advertising practices targeted at children. One such policy is a restriction on host selling during children's programs (FCC, 1974).

Host selling refers to the same character appearing in a program as well as in an ad placed adjacent to the show in which that character is featured. This practice is prohibited because it exacerbates the young child's difficulty in discriminating programs from commercials, which is the first level of defense for children against commercial persuasion (Kunkel, 1988a). For example, Bugs Bunny could not be used to promote a cereal product in a commercial aired during *The Bugs Bunny Show*. In contrast, however, Bart Simpson is allowed to promote Butterfinger candy bars during a commercial interruption in the prime-time program *The Simpsons*, because the show is not considered a children's program. The FCC specifies that a children's program is a show originally produced for and primarily directed to audiences of children aged 12 and under (FCC, 1974). In addition, an ad featuring Bugs Bunny promoting a cereal product may be aired during any other children's program not featuring his character, including the program immediately preceding or following *The Bugs Bunny Show.*

A second FCC policy, known as the program-length commercial restriction, prohibits ads that are closely related to the theme or content of a program from airing adjacent to that same children's show. This policy would prohibit a commercial for a Bugs Bunny costume or playset (regardless of whether or not the Bugs Bunny character appeared in the ad) from airing during a break in *The Bugs Bunny Show.* This policy has been significantly relaxed since its origin in 1969, when it was more broadly applied to restrict any program based primarily on a children's toy product (Kunkel, 1988b, 2001). In one of its earliest applications, it resulted in the program *Hot Wheels,* a cartoon based on the Mattel toy car products of the same name, being removed from the airwaves (Kunkel, 1988b). Under current FCC policy, a Hot Wheels program would be permitted, although no Hot Wheels product ads would be allowed during the show.

Finally, a third FCC policy mandates that program/commercial separation devices must be employed at each commercial break during a children's program. These devices, known as "bumpers" in the television industry, are roughly 5-second segments that say something like "and now a word from our sponsor" before and after each commercial break. As with the host-selling policy, this regulation is intended to assist child viewers in distinguishing between program and commercial content on television. In practice, however, these devices have not proven successful over the years in improving young children's capability at discriminating programming from advertising (Butter, Popovich, Stackhouse, & Garner, 1981; Palmer & McDowell, 1979; Stutts, Vance, & Hudleson, 1981). There is some indication this is primarily because the separators are not perceptually distinct from the adjacent programming content (Kunkel, 2001).

ISSUES ON THE HORIZON

As advertisers have increasingly recognized the economic value of marketing to children, many new and innovative practices have surfaced in an effort to reach child audiences. One key example of this trend is advertising in the schools, which has grown dramatically in recent years (U.S. General Accounting Office, 2000). Among the wide range of marketing strategies employed are presenting commercials on televised newscasts that are mandatory viewing for students (e.g., Channel One), providing corporate-sponsored educational materials for use in the classroom (e.g., food companies provide support materials about nutrition; insurance companies provide support materials about safety); and inserting brand-name product placement pictures in textbooks (e.g., children learn to count by tallying M&Ms).

Another new advertising venue is the Internet, where many Web sites frequented by children include significant commercial matter (Montgomery, 2001; Montgomery & Pasnik, 1996). Advertising in this new medium poses a broad range of interesting questions in terms of how children are affected by types of content quite distinct from the content that is possible on television. With interactivity, children can convey their interests and preferences, which may result in a Web site transmitting more carefully tailored messages in response, potentially increasing the persuasive power of advertising as compared to traditional mass-market commercials that take the same shape for everyone in the audience.

An issue of greater significance for children is the increased blurring of the boundaries between commercial and noncommercial content that is possible on the Internet. Advertising on Web sites includes traditional "billboard" ads, but is hardly limited to them, encompassing "branded environments" provided by companies such as Mattel and Frito-Lay. These sites provide entertaining games and activities embedded within depictions of the company's products, as this excerpt illustrates: "Emblematic of this trend is Mattel's Barbie.com web site.... The site offers a variety of on-line activities designed to appeal to girls, such as sending e-postcards, receiving newsletters, entering contests, and voting for their favorite Barbie" (Montgomery, 2001, p. 641).

For children who are just developing an understanding of the difference between commercial and noncommercial messages, advertising on the Internet may prove to be more effective precisely because it is not so easily recognized as the commercial matter that it actually represents.

Developments in these areas have so far eluded the attention of academic researchers, which in turn has allowed such advertising practices targeting children to grow without much attention from policymakers. These new developments are symptomatic of a culture in which children seem to be surrounded by attempts at commercial persuasion at virtually every turn. Learning to deal with slick, attractive ads for products of dubious value has clearly become an unavoidable part of growing up in America.

CONCLUSION

Children are a particularly sensitive audience for advertising because of their limited ability to recognize the nature and purpose of commercial messages. As a result, young children are more easily persuaded than are older children or adults. This chapter focused on the content of the persuasive messages directed at children by television advertisers. Child audiences today spend, on average, more than 15% of their time with the television set watching product-based commercials.

The commercial advertisements directed to children are limited primarily to four product types: toys, sugared cereals, candy/snacks, and fast-food restaurants. The appeals employed to promote these products offer little information to help evaluate the product, focusing instead on efforts to make the merchandise appear fun and attractive to the child. Product disclosures and disclaimers, which are presented ostensibly to help protect the consumer, are not easily comprehensible to the intended audience in most advertising to children. Additionally, the portrayals of gender and minority figures in advertising to children still seem stereotypical when viewed from an overall perspective, although there are some modest indications that this situation is improving.

Governmental and industry self-regulatory policies restrict a handful of specific advertising practices on television, but these efforts cannot alter the fundamental imbalance that exists between advertisers and child audiences. It is well established that advertising to children is highly effective; it is easy to understand why, given children's limited capability to defend against commercial persuasion. These considerations underscore the importance of tracking the content of advertising directed to children. In today's changing media environment, marketers are finding new contexts and new forms for conveying their message to children. In the future, it will clearly be necessary to look well beyond television in order to identify the full range of commercial content that reaches children.

REFERENCES

Adler, R., Friedlander, B., Lesser, G., Meringoff, L., Robertson, T., Rossiter, J., & Ward, S. (1977). *Research on the effects of television advertising to children: A review of the literature and recommendations for future research.* Washington, DC: U.S. Government Printing Office.

Alexander, A., Benjamin, L., Hoerrner, K., & Roe, D. (1998). We'll be back in a moment: A content analysis of advertisements in children's television in the 1950s. In M. Macklin & L. Carlson (Eds.), *Advertising to children: Concepts and controversies* (pp. 97–116). Thousand Oaks, CA: Sage.

Atkin, C., & Gibson, W. (1978). *Children's nutrition learning from television advertising.* East Lansing: Michigan State University, Dept. of Communication.

Atkin, C., & Heald, G. (1977). The content of children's toy and food commercials. *Journal of Communication, 27*(1), 107–114.

Barcus, F. E. (1971). *Saturday children's television: A report of TV programming and advertising on Boston commercial television.* Newtonville, MA: Action for Children's Television.

Barcus, F. E. (1972). *Network programming and advertising in the Saturday children's hours: A June and November comparison.* Newtonville, MA: Action for Children's Television.

Barcus, F. E. (1975). *Weekend children's television.* Newtonville, MA: Action for Children's Television.

Barcus, F. E. (1976). *Pre-Christmas advertising to children.* Newtonville, MA: Action for Children's Television.

Barcus, F. E. (1977). *Children's television: An analysis of programming and advertising.* New York: Praeger.

Barcus, F. E. (1978). *Commercial children's television on weekends and weekday afternoons.* Newtonville, MA: Action for Children's Television.

Barcus, F. E. (1980). The nature of television advertising to children. In E. Palmer & A Dorr (Eds.), *Children and the faces of television* (pp. 273–285). New York: Academic Press.

Barcus, F. E. (1983). *Images of life on children's television: Sex roles, minorities, and families.* New York: Praeger.

Barr, R., & Hayne, H. (1999). Developmental changes in imitation from television during infancy. *Child Development, 70,* 1067–1081.

Bretl, D. J., & Cantor, J. (1988). The portrayal of men and women in U.S. television commercials: A recent content analysis and trends over 15 years. *Sex Roles, 18*(9/10), 595–609.

Browne, B. A. (1998). Gender stereotypes in advertising on children's television in the 1990s: A cross-national analysis. *Journal of Advertising, 27*(1), 83–96.

Butter, E., Popovich, P., Stackhouse, R., & Garner, R. (1981). Discrimination of television programs and commercials by preschool children. *Journal of Advertising Research, 21*(2), 53–56.

Clark, B. L., & Higonnet, M. R. (Eds.). (1999). *Girls, boys, books, toys: Gender in children's literature and culture.* Baltimore: Johns Hopkins University Press.

Cole, B., & Oettinger, M. (1978). *Reluctant regulators.* Reading, MA: Addison-Wesley.

Comstock, G., & Scharrer, E. (1999). *Television: What's on, who's watching, and what it means.* New York: Academic Press.

Condry, J., Bence, P., & Scheibe, C. (1988). Nonprogram content of children's television. *Journal of Broadcasting & Electronic Media, 32,* 255–270.

Doolittle, J., & Pepper, R. (1975). Children's TV ad content: 1974. *Journal of Broadcasting, 19*, 131–151.

Federal Communications Commission (FCC). (1974). Children's television programs: Report and policy statement. *Federal Register, 39*, 39396–39409.

Federal Communications Commission (FCC). (1984). Revision of programming and commercialization policies, ascertainment requirements, and program log requirements for commercial television stations. *Federal Register, 49*, 33588–33620.

Fontes, B. F. (1978). Non-program material time aired on Saturday morning children's television. In FCC (Ed.), *Television programming for children: A report of the Children's Television Task Force, Vol. 3*. Washington, DC: Federal Communications Commission.

Fox, R. F. (1996). *Harvesting minds: How TV commercials control kids*. Westport, CT: Praeger.

Gantz, W. (2002). *Shouting to be heard: Public service advertising in a new media age*. Menlo Park, CA: Kaiser Family Foundation.

Gantz, W., & Schwartz, N. (2000). Promotion in children's programming. In S. T. Eastman (Ed.), *Research in media promotion* (pp. 163–201). Mahwah, NJ: Lawrence Erlbaum Associates.

Gorn, G., & Florsheim, R. (1985). The effects of commercials for adult products on children. *Journal of Consumer Research, 11*, 962–967.

Greenberg, B. S., & Brand, J. E. (1993). Cultural diversity on Saturday morning television. In G. L. Berry & J. K. Asamen (Eds.), *Children and television: Images in a changing sociocultural world* (pp. 132–142). Newbury Park, CA: Sage.

Greer, D., Potts, R., Wright, J., & Huston, A. (1982). The effects of television commercial form and commercial placement on children's social behavior and attention. *Child Development, 53*, 611–619.

Heintz-Knowles, K., & Van Horn, C. (1993, May). *A brief history of children's print advertising: 1900–1930s*. Paper presented at the annual conference of the International Communication Association, Washington, DC.

Horgen, K., Choate, M., & Brownell, K. (2001). Television food advertising: Targeting children in a toxic environment. In D. G. Singer & J. L. Singer (Eds.), *Handbook of children and the media* (pp. 447–461). Thousand Oaks, CA: Sage.

Kline, S. (1993). *Out of the garden: Toys, TV, and children's culture in the age of marketing*. London: Verso.

Kunkel, D. (1988a). Children and host-selling television commercials. *Communication Research, 15*, 71–92.

Kunkel, D. (1988b). From a raised eyebrow to a turned back: The FCC and children's product-related programming. *Journal of Communication, 38*(4), 90–108.

Kunkel, D. (1991). Crafting media policy: The genesis and implications of the Children's Television Act of 1990. *American Behavioral Scientist, 35*, 181–202.

Kunkel, D. (2001). Children and television advertising. In D. G. Singer & J. L. Singer (Eds.), *Handbook of children and the media* (pp. 375–394). Thousand Oaks, CA: Sage.

Kunkel, D., & Gantz, W. (1992). Children's television advertising in the multi-channel environment. *Journal of Communication, 42*(3), 134–152.

Kunkel, D., & Gantz, W. (1993). Assessing compliance with industry self-regulation of television advertising to children. *Journal of Applied Communication Research, 21*, 148–162.

Kunkel, D., & Gantz, W. (1994, July). *Children's television advertising at Christmas time*. Paper presented to the annual conference of the International Communication Association, Sydney, Australia.

Larson, M. S. (2001). Interactions, activities, and gender in children's television commercials: A content analysis. *Journal of Broadcasting & Electronic Media, 45*(1), 41–56.

Lauro, P. (1999, November 1). Coaxing the smile that sells: Baby wranglers in demand in marketing for children. *The New York Times*, p. C1.

Liebert, D., Sprafkin, J., Liebert, R., & Rubinstein, E. (1977). Effects of television commercial disclaimers on the product expectations of children. *Journal of Communication, 27*(1), 118–124.

Lingsweiler, R., & Wilson, B. (2002, July). *Children's comprehension of modified disclaimers in television advertising*. Paper presented at the annual conference of the International Communication Association, Seoul, South Korea.

Lyle, J., & Hoffman, H. R. (1972). Children's use of television and other media. In E. A. Rubinstein, G. A. Comstock, & J. P. Murray (Eds.), *Television and social behavior. Television in day-to-day life: Patterns of use* (vol. 4, pp. 257–273). Washington, DC: U.S. Government Printing Office.

Macklin, M. C. (1988). The relationship between music in advertising and children's responses: An experimental investigation. In S. Hecker & D. Stewart (Eds.), *Nonverbal communication in advertising* (pp. 225–243). Lexington, MA: Lexington Books.

Macklin, M. C., & Kolbe, R. H. (1984). Sex role stereotyping in children's advertising: Current and past trends. *Journal of Advertising, 13*(2), 34–42.

McNeal, J. (1998). Tapping the three kids' markets. *American Demographics, 20*(4), 36–41.

Meltzoff, A. N. (1988). Imitation of televised models by infants. *Child Development, 59,* 1221–1229.

Montgomery, K. (2001). Digital kids: The new on-line children's consumer culture. In D. G. Singer & J. L. Singer (Eds.), *Handbook of children and the media* (pp. 635–650). Thousand Oaks, CA: Sage.

Montgomery, K., & Pasnik, S. (1996). *Web of deception.* Washington, DC: Center for Media Education.

O'Kelly, C. G., & Bloomquist, L. E. (1976). Women and Blacks on TV. *Journal of Communication, 26*(4), 179–184.

Palmer, E., & McDowell, C. (1979). Program/commercial separators in children's television programming. *Journal of Communication, 29*(3), 197–201.

Palmer, E., & McDowell, C. (1981). Children's understanding of nutritional information presented in breakfast cereal commercials. *Journal of Broadcasting, 25,* 295–301.

Rice, M., Huston, A., & Wright, J. (1982). The forms of television: Effects on children's attention, comprehension, and social behavior. In D. Pearl, E. Bouthilet, & J. Lazar (Eds.), *Television and behavior: Ten years of scientific progress and implications for the eighties* (vol. 2, pp. 24–38). Rockville, MD: National Institute of Mental Health.

Riffe, D., Goldson, H., Saxton, K., & Yu, Y. (1989). Females and minorities in TV ads in 1987 Saturday children's programs. *Journalism Quarterly, 66,* 129–136.

Roberts, D. F., Foehr, U. G., Rideout, V. G., & Brodie, M. (1999). *Kids & media @ the new millennium: A comprehensive national analysis of children's media use.* Menlo Park, CA: Kaiser Family Foundation.

Robertson, T. (1979). Parental mediation of advertising effects. *Journal of Communication, 29*(1), 12–25.

Sheikh, A., & Moleski, M. (1977). Conflict in the family over commercials. *Journal of Communication, 27*(1), 152–157.

Smith, L. J. (1994). A content analysis of gender differences in children's advertising. *Journal of Broadcasting & Electronic Media, 38*(2), 323–337.

Stern, B., & Harmon, R. (1984). The incidence and characteristics of disclaimers in children's television advertising. *Journal of Advertising, 13*(2), 12–16.

Stern, B., & Resnik, A. (1978). Children's understanding of a televised commercial disclaimer. In S. Jain (Ed.), *Research frontiers in marketing: Dialogues and directions* (pp. 332–336). Chicago: American Marketing Association.

Stern, B. L., & Resnik, A. J. (1991, June–July). Information content in television advertising: A replication and extension. *Journal of Advertising Research, 30,* 36–46.

Strasburger, V. (2001). Children and TV advertising: Nowhere to run, nowhere to hide. *Developmental and Behavioral Pediatrics, 22*(3), 185–187.

Stutts, M., & Hunnicutt, G. (1987). Can young children understand disclaimers in television commercials? *Journal of Advertising, 16*(1), 41–46.

Stutts, M., Vance, D., & Hudleson, S. (1981). Program-commercial separators in children's television: Do they help a child tell the difference between Bugs Bunny and the Quik Rabbit. *Journal of Advertising, 10,* 16–25, 48.

U.S. General Accounting Office. (2000). *Public education: Commercial activities in the schools.* Washington, DC: Author.

Verna, M. E. (1975). The female image in children's TV commercials. *Journal of Broadcasting, 19,* 301–309.

Weisskoff, R. (1985). Current trends in children's advertising. *Journal of Advertising Research, 25*(1), 12–14.

Welch, R. L., Huston-Stein, A., Wright, J. C., & Plehal, R. (1979). Subtle sex-role cues in children's commercials. *Journal of Communication, 29*(3), 202–209.

Winick, C., Williamson, L. G., Chuzmir, S. F., & Winick, M. P. (1973). *Children's television commercials: A content analysis.* New York: Praeger.

Wulfemeyer, K. T., & Mueller, B. (1992). Channel One and commercials in classrooms: Advertising content aimed at students. *Journalism Quarterly, 69,* 724–742.

Television Advertising and Children: Examining the Intended and Unintended Effects

Stacy L. Smith
Charles Atkin
Michigan State University

Children are bombarded with advertising messages. Kunkel (2001) has calculated that the typical American child sees well over 40,000 commercials per year on TV, not to mention the vast number of ads they may be exposed to on the Internet, in magazines, or on their own school campuses. These persuasive messages seem to be having a positive impact on youngsters' annual spending. A total of $23.4 billion was spent in 1997 by 4- to 12-year-olds (McNeal, 1999), which is up substantially from $17.1 billion in 1994 and $4.2 billion in 1984. Such expenditures are independent of their direct influence in $188 billion of annual household purchases.

Psychologists, policymakers, and medical practitioners have challenged recently the ethics involved in advertising to children (Clay, 2000). They argue that advertising contributes to such ill effects as childhood obesity and materialism. It has also been asserted that advertising can negatively influence the parent–child relationship. As Dr. Alvin F. Poussaint of the Harvard Medical School stated, "Advertisers ... also push this 'nag factor'—for children to nag their parents to buy them certain things. This sets up a tension and strife between parents and children" (Linnett, 2000, p. 1).

Given these concerns, it becomes important to examine empirical research on the impact of exposure to television advertising on youth—the goal of this chapter. To this end, the chapter is divided up into four major sections. First, we examine children's understanding of advertising. In particular, the research on children's ability to decipher programs from commercials as well as their comprehension of selling intent is reviewed. In the second section, the intended influences of advertising are examined. The research on the effect of exposure to television commercials on children's brand recall, product desires, purchase influence attempts, and consumption rates is explicated. Third, we assess some of the unintended consequences of advertising exposure, such as child unhappiness, poor eating habits, and negative self-perceptions. Fourth, we devote our attention to the impact surrounding one specific type of potentially negative commercial content: alcohol advertising.

Before we begin, a few caveats about this review must be noted. We are only going to review research on television. Although advertising may appear in many other televisual media (e.g., Internet, videos), children still unequivocally spend the most time with broadcast and cable TV programming (Kaiser Family Foundation, 1999). Also, we are only going to review studies involving children. By child, we mean any youngster who is 16 years of age or younger. Such a definition is consistent with public policy surrounding children and television advertising, such as the Children's Television Act of 1990. Finally, the aim of this review is to update Atkin's (1980) chapter from the first edition of *Children and the Faces of Television*. Although some changes have been made to the structure of the original chapter, we use many of the same sections and subsections to guide our review.

COMPREHENSION

Since the early 1970s, a great deal of public concern has surrounded children's understanding of television advertising (Kunkel & Gantz, 1992; Kunkel, 2001). Because of their limited information-processing capabilities and experience, it has been argued that young children may not be able to recognize commercial television messages nor comprehend their persuasive intent. As a result, many people have argued that commercials targeting young children are simply "unfair" (see Kunkel & Roberts, 1991) and may take undue advantage of the young consumer. In this section, we examine the validity of this argument by assessing research on two key aspects of advertising comprehension: the ability to differentiate programs from commercials, and understanding selling intent. Theoretically, most of this research has embraced a Piagetian (Piaget, 1929, 1962) or an information-processing perspective (Roedder, 1981; Siegler, 1991) by examining developmental differences in children's ad comprehension. At the end of the section, the impact of disclaimers on enhancing children's comprehension of misleading commercials is considered.

Distinguishing Programs From Commercials

When do children begin to recognize that commercial messages are independent from program content? The answer to that question is dependent on the type of measure used. Some research has relied on children's attention to commercials and programs to answer this query (Wartella & Ettema, 1974). Ward, Levinson, and

Wackman (1972) had mothers of 5- to 12-year-olds record their child's visual attentiveness to (roughly) a week of television programming. For Saturday morning television, the results showed age-related differences in children's attention to commercial content. Older children (9- to 12-year-olds) paid less "full" attention during commercials than did their younger counterparts (5- to 8-year-olds). These results show that older viewers may be more likely to detect commercials and thus "tune out" such content when it appears on screen (Calvert, 1999, p. 111).

Scholars have also relied on verbal questions in surveys or interviews of children. Much of this research reveals a positive relationship between program/commercial differentiation and age (Robertson & Rossiter, 1974; Ward, Reale, & Levinson, 1972). These studies show that children master the program/commercial distinction somewhere between 6 and 9 years of age. However, a potential criticism of these studies is that many young children have difficulty expressing their answers verbally, and thus such measures may grossly underestimate their abilities to distinguish programs from commercials (Levin, Petros, & Petrella, 1982; Martin, 1997; Zuckerman & Gianinno, 1981).

Still other studies have relied on showing children actual television content and having them identify message types. Blosser and Roberts (1985) showed videotapes of different types of television content to children, and asked them to label the portrayal. Although accuracy increased with age, the findings revealed that a majority of 5- to 6-year-olds in their sample could correctly identify televised depictions of both child- and adult-oriented commercials. Similar findings have been observed with other samples of children in preschool, kindergarten, and 1st grade (Levin et al., 1982; Palmer & McDowell, 1979). Given this evidence, it is probable that most 4- to 5-year-olds are quite capable of distinguishing commercials from the immediately adjacent programming content.

Although many children can make this distinction, the cues that younger and older viewers rely on to make such judgments vary dramatically by age. Younger children (Palmer & McDowell, 1979; Ward, Reale, et al., 1972) are more likely to recognize commercials based on perceptual qualities of the ad, such as its length (e.g., commercials are short). Older children, on the other hand, are more likely to rely on conceptual attributes of programming (e.g., commercials are intended to make money, programs have a theme/moral). These findings are consistent with developmental theory and research documenting age-related shifts in children's perceptual dependence (Bruner, 1966; Hoffner & Cantor, 1985). Indeed, studies show that as they develop, elementary schoolers are less likely to group items based on their perceptual features (e.g., form, color), and are more likely to do so based on conceptual features (Melkman, Tversky, & Baratz, 1981).

Given concern about children's ability to differentiate between television shows and commercials, the Federal Communications Commission in the 1970s began requiring licensees to "clearly separate" advertising from entertainment messages in children's programming (see Kunkel, 2001, p. 385). To this end, broadcasters have utilized "bumpers" or audio/visual material featured before and/or after commercial messages (e.g., "We'll return after these messages").

These audio/visual bumpers are still being used today in children's shows aired on the broadcast networks.

Studies show that these separation devices have not been very effective, however (Butter, Popovich, Stackhouse, & Garner, 1981; Stutts, Vance, & Hudleson, 1981). For example, Palmer and McDowell (1979) assessed the effectiveness of three different separation techniques employed by the broadcast networks (ABC, NBC, CBS) in increasing children's program/commercial discrimination. The results showed that those kindergarten and first-grade children exposed to the control condition (i.e., where no separator was used) distinguished programs from commercials as well as—and sometimes better than—those children in the separators conditions (p. 198). The authors explained these findings by arguing that "buffers appear to create 'bridges' between programs and commercials—retaining attention without prompting discrimination" (p. 200).

The research reviewed here suggests that a majority of young children (4- to 5-year-olds) are capable of making distinctions between programs and commercials. However, level of development or age of the viewer seems to be positively correlated with this ability. If many children can accurately identify commercial versus program content, the next critical issue becomes whether they can comprehend an advertisement's selling intent—which is the focus of the next section of this chapter.

Persuasive Intent

What skills are needed to comprehend the persuasive intent of advertising? Roberts and Maccoby (1985, pp. 570–571) argued that "adult" understanding of television advertising requires the recognition of four key elements: the sender has other interests than the receiver, the sender intends to persuade, persuasive messages are biased, and biased messages require different interpretation than do informational messages. Many of these skills are based on the ability to "role take" or consider the advertiser's intent/perspective when creating and disseminating commercial messages (Kunkel, 2001).

Much theorizing and research has been conducted on children's ability to role take. Although hotly debated, empirical evidence seems to reveal developmental differences in children's cognitive role-taking capabilities (Chandler & Greenspan, 1972; John, 1999; Kurdek, 1977). For example, Kurdek and Rodgon (1975) found developmental increases across elementary-school-aged children in the ability to recognize and understand messages from another child's point of view. Given their increased role-taking abilities, older children should be more likely than younger children to comprehend the persuasive intent of advertising and to realize that the strategies used in such messages may be biased or misleading.

Research reveals that age does influence comprehension of selling intent. In one survey, Ward, Reale, et al. (1972) asked 5- to 12-year-olds, "Why are commercials shown on TV?" The responses were coded as showing low (confused, unaware of selling intent), medium (recognition of selling motive), or high (clear recognition of selling and profit-seeking motives) levels of understanding selling intent. Although few children demonstrated high levels of understanding, a clear trend emerged that comprehension of selling intent increases with age. In Blosser and Roberts' (1985) study, a majority of the children could not articulate selling intent until 8 to 10 years of age. After exposing first and second graders to programs with child-oriented commercials, Christenson (1982) found that youngsters could identify selling intent in 3 out of 15 ads. Among fifth and sixth graders, selling intent was recognized in 14 out of 15 ads. Together, the research seems to suggest that children typically do not understand selling intent until mid elementary school (see also Macklin, 1985).

Despite their inability to grasp selling intent, younger children do perceive that commercials function "informationally" for consumers. For example, Paget, Kritt, and Bergemann (1984) showed kindergarten, third-grade, and sixth-grade children a series of commercials and immediately after asked, "Why did they put this commercial on TV?" Preschoolers were more likely to state that the commercials were assistive or provided information about products and services, whereas older children (third graders) were more likely to say that commercials were intended to persuade. Similar findings have been observed with other samples of elementary-school-aged children (Blatt et al., 1972; Robertson & Rossiter, 1974).

There seem to be two direct consequences associated with children's understanding of persuasive intent. The first is that children's trust in advertising should be altered. As children realize that advertising is misleading, their faith in such messages should decline. Indeed, research reveals that older children are less trusting of advertising than are their younger counterparts (Blatt et al., 1972; Christenson, 1982; Robertson & Rossiter, 1974). The second is that children's affect toward advertising may change. Increased skepticism of advertising should decrease youngsters' liking of ads. Studies show that age is negatively related to positive attitudes or liking of advertising (Blatt et al., 1972; Robertson & Rossiter, 1974).

Disclaimers

To facilitate children's comprehension of the potentially misleading nature of advertising, disclaimers are often used. A recent content analysis revealed that a majority of all ads in children's shows feature at least one disclaimer (Kunkel & Gantz, 1992), with most concentrated in commercials for cereal/breakfast foods (86%) and toys (75%). This study also found that the two most prevalent disclaimers were "parts sold separately," and "part of a balanced breakfast" (p. 146).

However, studies reveal that not all disclaimers are equally effective in helping youngsters comprehend the disingenuous nature of advertising (Atkin & Gibson, 1978; Stern & Resnik, 1978; Stutts & Hunnicutt, 1987). One of the reasons for this is that many standard disclaimers feature language that many children have difficulty comprehending (Palmer & McDowell, 1981). For example, Liebert, Sprafkin, Liebert, and Rubinstein (1977) showed kindergartners and second graders a commercial for a toy with (a) a standard audio disclaimer (e.g., "some assembly required"), (b) a modified audio disclaimer (e.g., "you have to put it together"), or (c) to the same ad with no disclaimer. The results showed that children exposed to the commercial with the modified disclaimer understood the idea that the toy advertised had to be put together significantly more than did those children exposed to commercial with the "standard" disclaimer or those in the control condition.

However, the results from a more recent experiment reveal that comprehension of disclaimers may not only be a function of verbal simplicity (Lingsweiler & Wilson, 2002). A child's level of development, familiarity with disclaimers, and prior experience with different toys/games may independently and interactively facilitate his or her understanding of such disclosure messages. Clearly, more research is needed on all those audio and visual strategies that may foster younger and older children's recognition and understanding of the misleading nature of commercial messages.

In total, the purpose of this section was to review what is known about children's comprehension of advertising. Three major conclusions can be drawn from this research. First, a majority of young children can understand the difference between commercials and programs by 4 to 5 years of age. Second, a developmental progression exists in children's comprehension of the intent of advertising. Preschool- and early elementary-school-aged children perceive that advertising is intended to inform, whereas older children are more likely to perceive that it is intended to sell products. As a result of such knowledge, older children have more negative attitudes and skepticism toward ads than do their younger counterparts. Third, some disclaimers may be effective with children. Simple verbal disclaimers—especially if they are familiar to the child—may facilitate comprehension of the product or service advertised.

INTENDED EFFECTS

There are several intended cognitive, affective, and behavioral effects associated with exposure to advertising. In general, scholars have evoked a variety of different mechanisms to explain and predict the impact of advertising on children's socialization processes, such as classical conditioning, reinforcement theory, social learning and later social cognitive theory (Bandura, 1986), a cultivation perspective (Gerbner, Gross, Morgan, & Signorielli, 1994), and other persuasion approaches (see Reardon, 1991). Next, we address four intended effects of advertising on youth, as well as empirical studies on the effectiveness of two different types of appeals used in ads targeting children.

Brand Recognition and Recall

One of the cognitive goals of advertisers is to get consumers to remember their brand name. Ads directed at children are no different. But does exposure to such advertising—whether intended for younger audiences or not—influence children's brand recognition and recall? Research suggests that it does, despite the fact that some youngsters reduce their attentiveness to television when commercials are featured onscreen (Ward, Levinson, et al., 1972; Zuckerman, Ziegler, & Stevenson, 1978).

Fischer et al. (1991) assessed 3- to 6-year-olds' ability to recognize products associated with children's and adults' brands. The youngsters were asked to match 22 cards featuring logos to 1 of 12 products presented on a game board (p. 3146). Results showed that children had very high recognition memory for products associated with child brand logos, ranging from 92% for the Disney Channel to 25% for Cheerios (p. 3146). All of these recognitions were well above chance. A majority of the children also recognized products (e.g., cars, cigarettes) associated with adult brands such as Chevrolet, Ford, and even Old Joe Camel.

In addition to simple recognition, studies reveal that exposure to ads can influence recall among elementary schoolers. For example, Gorn and Goldberg (1980) found that almost half of the 8- to 10-year-old children in their sample could accurately identify the brand name in a commercial after a single exposure to an ad that was embedded in a kids' show. Assessing children who viewed at least 3 hours of Saturday morning television programming 2 weeks before being interviewed, Hendon, McGann, and Hendon (1978) found that 7- to 13-year-olds could recall details from over half of the cereal brands about which they asked the children. Clearly, these findings suggest that advertising can have a positive influence on memory.

The influence of ads on children's recognition and recall may be affected by a variety of variables. Perhaps the most important viewer variable is age. Research reveals a positive relationship between age and awareness/recognition of brand names (Fischer et al., 1991; Macklin, 1996; Wackman, Wartella, & Ward, 1977; Zuckerman & Gianinno, 1981). Differences have also been observed in the complexity of children's recall of commercials by age (Paget et al., 1984). Younger children are more likely to remember single aspects of commercials, such as a particular image or picture. Older children, on the other hand, are more likely to recall concrete and coherent sequences and messages in ads (Blatt et al., 1972; Ward, Reale, et al., 1972). Such findings are consistent with theory and research demonstrating that children shift from perceptual to conceptual processing of television content with age. It is also possible that older children are more efficient processors of information, and possess encoding and retrieval strategies superior to those of their younger counterparts (Siegler, 1991), thereby facilitating their richer and more complete memory of ads.

There are three content factors of commercials that may also influence children's memory of ads. In a series of experiments, Macklin (1996) found that presenting brand names with prior associated visual cues (e.g., pictures or colors linked with product name) increases preschoolers' memory. Using an associative memory perspective, Macklin argued that related perceptual cues assist children in remembering target information (p. 252). Another content factor that may influence recall is repetition of the ad. At least one study shows that repetition of exposure to multiple ads for a brand can improve children's recall (Gorn & Goldberg, 1980), presumably due to the fact that repeated examples serve as a form of cognitive rehearsal. However, it is also possible that too much repetition can become irritating and thus have little or even negative effects on recall (Ray, Sawyer, & Strong, 1971).

The immediately adjacent program content surrounding the ad can also influence recall. Prasad and Smith (1994) found that boys exposed to an ad after a highly violent program recalled significantly less of the ad copy than did those exposed to an ad after a mildly violent program. These findings are presumably due to the fact that the highly violent program evoked a negative mood state in young viewers, thereby impairing memory performance.

Product Desires

Beside cognitive effects, the impact of advertising on attitudinal outcomes also has been examined. Many studies have assessed whether exposure to advertising contributes to children's preference, liking, or desire for different toys and/or food products. In fact, experiments reveal that exposure to ads can have an immediate impact on children's desires for food, toys, or other products (Atkin, 1975b; Atkin & Gibson, 1978; Goldberg, Gorn, & Gibson, 1978; Goldberg & Gorn, 1978; Gorn & Florsheim, 1985; Heslop & Ryans, 1980; Resnik & Stern, 1977). For example, Kunkel (1988) found that children exposed to commercials for breakfast cereals (either Fruity Pebbles or Smurf Berry Crunch) chose the seen brand as their first cereal preference more often than two other very popular choices combined (p. 84). Borzekowski and Robinson (2001) found that 2- to 6-year-olds exposed to popular children's programs embedded with commercials were more likely to immediately after choose the advertised food items than were those children exposed to the same programs without commercials.

Several surveys and interviews have also examined the relationship between exposure to ads and product desires. One approach has been to ask children to list their favorite foods or toys and then indicate where the children first heard about them. Studies interviewing children and/or their mothers generally show that television is youngsters' most frequently mentioned informational source for toys or foods (Barry & Sheikh, 1977; Donohue, 1975; Frideres, 1973; Robertson & Rossiter, 1976), followed by friends, stores, and catalogues.

A slight variation of this approach has been to assess the impact of advertising on children's product wants and desires during the Christmas season (Caron & Ward, 1975; Rossiter & Robertson, 1974). To illustrate, Buijzen and Valkenburg (2000) not only asked 7- to 12-year-olds to write down their top two Christmas wishes in early December, but also asked children about their patterns of exposure to kids' programs on two different children's networks in the Netherlands (i.e., Kindernet, RTL-4) that routinely feature ads targeting youth. Their results revealed that the most frequently advertised brands during the holiday season were the most frequently mentioned toys on children's wish lists, especially among those heavy viewers of RTL-4—the network airing the most children's commercials (p. 462).

Yet another derivation of this method has been to ask children more directly about the effect of television advertising on their product desires (Ward, Wackman, & Wartella, 1977). Atkin, Reeves, & Gibson (1979) assessed 5- to 12-year-olds' preferences for various food brands. The researchers found a strong positive relationship between exposure to TV commercials and liking of the 12 advertised foods $r = .59$). On average, 66% of heavy viewers said they liked each advertised product, compared with 46% of light viewers. More generally, research reveals a positive relationship between exposure to television and attitudes toward ads (Clancy-Hepburn et al., 1974; Rossiter & Robertson, 1974).

In total, the research reveals that television advertising impacts children's product desires. Furthermore, heavy viewers' product desires seem to be more affected by television commercials than are those of light viewers.

Product Purchase Requests

If exposure to advertising creates a desire for particular toys or foods, then do children make more purchase requests for such items from their parents? Four different methods have been used to answer this question. The first is self-report surveys. In the mid-1970s, Atkin (1975c) asked 3- to 12-year-olds: "Many of the TV commercials are for toys—things like games and dolls and racing cars. After you see these toys on TV, how much do you ask your mother to buy them for you?" A full 83% responded that they asked "a lot" or "sometimes." Atkin repeated the question for breakfast cereals. A third of the children said they asked "a lot" and almost half (45%) indicated they asked "sometimes." Requests reported by the mothers of the children in this study were almost identical.

A handful of surveys have also documented differences between heavy and light viewers in the number of product purchase requests. Querying mothers of 8- to 13-year-olds, Clancy-Hepburn et al. (1974) found a positive correlation between children's purchase influence attempts for food and their exposure to Saturday morning television programming. Atkin (1975c) noted that children who watched the most Saturday morning commercials asked much more often for toys and cereals, with about twice as many heavy viewers as light viewers falling into the "a lot" category. In another study, Atkin (1975d) discovered that heavy viewers of cereal ads made more requests, by a 2:1 margin over light viewers. Almost half of those who watched TV heavily often asked to go to highly advertised fast-food restaurants, compared to one fourth of light viewers. Finally, Donkin, Tilston, Neale, and Gregson (1992) found a very small but positive correlation between 7- to 11-year-olds' exposure to television and number of food requests as reported by parents.

Another method used is the diary study. Isler, Popper, and Ward (1987) had mothers of children from three age groups (3 to 4 years, 5 to 7 years, 9 to 11 years) fill out product request diaries and television viewing logs for 4 weeks. The results revealed that children made an average of 13.5 purchase influence attempts across the time period. A small but positive correlation ($r = .18$, $p < .01$) between TV viewing and purchase requests was observed. Slightly larger correlations were observed between exposure to television and requests for heavily advertised products such as cereals ($r = .24$, $p < .01$) and candy $r = .19$, $p < .05$). Asking mothers of 3- to 10-year-olds in three countries to fill out 2-week diaries, Robertson, Ward, Gatignon, and Klees (1989) also found a positive relationship between exposure to television and product purchase requests.

The third type of method is the projective technique or story completion. Sheikh and Moleski (1977) had first, third, and fifth graders listen to a story featuring a child exposed to a TV show with commercials advertising an appealing food, toy, or article of clothing. When asked if the child in the story felt like asking his or her parents for the product, a full 90% of the children responded affirmatively. However, the children were also asked if the child in the story actually asked his/her parents for the advertised product. Just over half of the children in the sample (57%) said yes. These findings suggest that many elementary-school-aged children may show discretion in the types of requests they make of their parents for different advertised products.

The last type of method is behavioral observation (Galst & White, 1976; Reeves & Atkin, 1979; Stoneman & Brody, 1981). Galst and White (1976) exposed 3- to 5-year-olds to television content with commercials embedded throughout. After exposure, children were escorted individually by their mothers to a grocery store, where trained observers recorded the preschoolers' purchase influence attempts (PIAs). On average, a total of 15 purchase influence attempts were made, roughly one every 2 minutes. In addition, a positive relationship emerged between attention to the ads in the laboratory context and subsequent purchase influence attempts. That is, the more children attended to ads, the more they requested products while shopping with their mothers. Using a similar observational procedure, Stoneman and Brody (1981) exposed 3- to 5- year-olds to either a children's television program with food commercials aimed at young consumers or to the same show with the ads removed. After exposure, the children and their mothers went shopping for a week's worth of groceries. The results revealed that those children exposed to the program with commercials engaged in more total purchase attempts than did those exposed to the program without commercials.

Overall, the results reviewed here are quite consistent. Across different types of methods, studies revealed that exposure to television advertising increases children's purchase influence attempts, with heavy viewers of television more likely to make such product requests than light viewers. Besides repeated exposure, there are two other variables that may moderate the advertising-product request relationship. The first is age. Older children may be more discriminating in their requests, only asking for those products that they know their parents are likely to purchase. In general, studies show that older children make fewer purchase requests than do younger children (Clancy-Hepburn et al., 1974; Robertson et al., 1989; Robertson & Rossiter, 1977). The second is gender. When compared to girls, boys are not only more resistant to their parents' requests but also use more forceful compliance-gaining strategies (cf. Buijzen & Valkenburg, 2000, p. 458). Consistent with this rationale, research reveals that boys have a tendency to be more determined in their requests for products advertised on television than are girls, especially if they are younger (Buijzen & Valkenburg, 2000; Ward & Wackman, 1972).

Consumption Patterns

To date, only a handful of studies have examined children's consumption patterns as a function of exposure to television advertising. At least two experimental studies have found that viewing ads for nonhealthy foods can have an immediate effect on children (Gorn & Goldberg, 1982; Jeffrey, McLellarn, & Fox, 1982). For example, Jeffrey et al. (1982) discovered that when compared to seeing pronutritional or nonfood ads, seeing ads for low-nutrient foods can increase boys' total caloric consumption and intake of low-nutrition foods and drinks. Yet contradictory findings are found in Gorn and Goldberg's (1980) study. The results from these researchers' experiment reveal that neither single nor multiple exposures to an ice cream commercial embedded within a *Flintstones* program increased boys' consumption. Together, the results from these studies suggest that more research on the short-term impact of ads on consumption patterns is warranted.

However, several correlational studies have found a relationship between exposure to television and consumption (Atkin, 1975d; Atkin et al., 1979; Dussere, 1976; Sharaga, 1974). Atkin (1975d) observed that among fourth through seventh graders, those exposed to the most ads for cereals reported eating cereals more regularly. To illustrate, 25% of the heavy viewers of cereal ads reported consuming Sugar Smacks "a lot" in comparison to 13% of light viewers. A moderately strong relationship also was found between exposure to candy advertising and self-reported candy consumption. More recently, Coon, Goldberg, Rogers, and Tucker (2001) noted that watching television during meals among fourth-, fifth-, and sixth-grade children is a significant and positive predictor of pizza, salty snacks, and soda consumption and a negative predictor of fruit and vegetable consumption, even after controlling for parents' level of socioeconomic status (SES) as well as the caregivers' nutritional knowledge, attitudes, and norms.

Persuasive Appeals

Advertisers rely on a variety of appeals to persuade consumers to purchase their products. Two types of appeals are premiums and celebrity endorsers. Premium appeals are present in roughly 10% of ads that appear when children are likely to be in the viewing audience (Kunkel & Gantz, 1992), especially in commercials for fast foods. Self-report and observational studies reveal that such strategies may be persuasive. For example, Burr and Burr (1977) found that mothers of 2- to 10-year-olds were most likely to report purchasing the product for their child when he or she requested the prize premium or said the product appeared on TV. The results from Atkin's (1975c) study also revealed that mothers were most likely to state that the premium was the most frequently mentioned reason for their child's request for a specific cereal. The findings additionally showed that exposure to Saturday morning TV programming increases the likelihood of children's requests for cereal because of the premium, with 70% of those viewing an hour or less making such an appeal, 86% viewing 2 hours, and 90% watching for 3 or more hours.

Children also have been surveyed directly about the reasons for their product choices and desires (Reilly Group Incorporated, 1973). Donohue (1975) asked African American first, second, and third graders which was more important when selecting a cereal, the nature of the cereal or the prize inside (p. 44). Roughly half of the children in the sample indicated the premium, with a majority of the girls stating the premium is more important than the cereal itself. Surveying 5- to 12-year-olds, Atkin et al. (1979) found that heavy viewers were more than twice as likely as light viewers to cite premiums as an important reason for cereal preferences. When unobtrusively observing both children and their mothers in the cereal aisle at the grocery store, Atkin (1978) discovered that only 9% of the 3- to 12-year-old children identified the premium as the primary reason for desiring a particular cereal brand.

A series of experiments examined the impact of exposure to commercials with or without premiums on children's attitudes and behavioral responses to the ads. This set of studies yielded a contradictory set of findings. Two studies showed that exposure to ads with premiums have little or no short-term impact on children's desires or product requests (Heslop & Ryans, 1980; Shimp, Dyer, & Devita, 1976). Yet close examination of these studies reveals that the type of premium (hypothetical vs. actual, targeting boys vs. girls, new premium offer vs. existing premium offer) and product advertised may matter. Using a popular breakfast food, Atkin (1975a) exposed children to a commercial for Kellogg's Pop-Tarts either with or without a premium appeal. Children exposed to the commercial with the appeal showed a greater desire for the product than did those exposed to the nonpremium commercial (83% vs. 72%, respectively). Consistent with the other experiments on premiums, Atkin (1975a) found that the inclusion of a premium in a commercial had no impact on children's intent to ask for the product. Over three fourths of the children in the sample (77%) already intended to request the product.

In addition to premiums, another type of appeal that may be used in ads for children's toys and games is celebrity endorsers. Celebrities may be real-life actors, sports figures, or animated characters that convey expertise about the advertised brand or product. Such endorsers are likely to be attractive because of their physical appearance, humorous personality, or familiarity to young viewers. According to social cognitive theory, attractive characters are more likely to be attended to and emulated than unattractive ones (Bandura, 1986). Thus, attractive celebrity endorsers may have a particularly potent effect on children's product knowledge and desires.

Studies show that celebrity endorsers are perceived as credible sources of information about products (Ross et al., 1984). For instance, Atkin and Gibson (1978) found that 33% of 4- to 7-year-olds thought Fred Flintstone and Barney Rubble knew "very much" about which cereals children should eat. Celebrity endorsers also influence children's product desires. Ross et al. (1984) observed that including a celebrity endorser in a race car commercial increased boys' generic product preference relative to an ad without a celebrity endorser. Furthermore, boys who saw the celebrity endorser more often thought that the presenter had expertise in model race cars than did those who saw the ads without the celebrity endorser (p. 195).

UNINTENDED EFFECTS

A great deal of concern surrounds the ill effects that exposure to advertising may have on children. In the section that follows, we review research documenting five unintended effects of advertising: parent–child conflict, unhappiness, unhealthy eating habits, materialism, and negative self-perception.

Parent–Child Conflict

Policymakers have long been concerned with the impact of advertising on parent–child relationships (Federal Trade Commission, 1978; 1979). One specific concern voiced is that exposure to television advertising increases children's purchase requests and thus puts parents in a position of approval or denial. When such requests are not granted, it may trigger arguments and verbal aggression between caregiver and child (see Buijzen & Valkenburg, 2001). Generally, research supports this concern. Surveys of both children and/or their parents reveal that denying youngsters' purchase requests sometimes results in conflict (Atkin, 1975c, 1975d). For example, Atkin (1975c) discovered that among mothers of preschool- and elementary-school-aged children, roughly half said arguments developed occasionally after denying cereal or toy requests (44% and 53%, respectively). Ward and Wackman (1972) found a small but positive relationship between children's purchase requests and family conflict.

Diary studies reveal a similar set of findings. Isler et al. (1987) asked mothers of 3- to 11-year-olds to report their child's reaction to "refusal-to-buy responses" (p. 36). Roughly a fifth (22%) of the mothers indicated that their child either argued (a little or a lot) or got really angry. Robertson et al. (1989) also found that purchase requests and parent–child conflict were highly associated. Using a projective technique, Sheikh and Moleski (1977, p. 156) asked first, second, and fifth graders what a child in a story would do when his or her parent did not yield to the child's purchase requests. Open-ended responses revealed that 23% of the children spontaneously reported that the story child would engage in an aggressive response (p. 156).

Finally, observational studies in grocery stores also reveal that conflict may ensue when children's requests are not granted. Atkin (1978) observed that roughly a fourth (24%) of the parent–child interactions in the supermarket cereal aisle resulted in conflict. Stoneman and Brody (1981) found that those preschoolers viewing a kids' show with food ads made more subsequent purchase influence attempts, and their parent had to engage in more power assertion techniques (e.g., saying no, physical or verbal "put back"), than did those preschoolers viewing a kids' show without ads.

Unhappiness

Although exposure to television advertising may evoke child unhappiness in several different ways (see Atkin, 1980), we focus on only two here. First, children may experience unhappiness when they perceive their life as less satisfying than the lives of young actors depicted in commercials. To illustrate, Donohue, Meyer, and Henke (1978) exposed 6- to 8-year-old children to two commercials for McDonald's: one featuring a happy family eating lunch at the fast-food chain, and one featuring the McDonald's fantasy cast (e.g., Ronald, Hamburgler, Grimace).

Immediately after exposure to the family-oriented commercial, 75% of the African American children perceived the fictitious family as being significantly happier than their own.

Second, children may experience unhappiness when parents refuse their requests for advertised products. Atkin's (1978) observational study of 3- to 12-year-old children and their parents found that approximately 16% of the interactions in the cereal aisle of supermarkets resulted in youngster unhappiness. Sheikh and Moleski (1977) observed that 33% of children in their sample spontaneously reported that having a purchase request refused by a parent should result in unpleasant feelings, with girls mentioning this more than boys. Similar results were obtained by Goldberg and Gorn (1978). Based on diary reports, Isler et al. (1987) found that over a fourth of children reportedly experience disappointment when their mother refuses their product requests. Consistently, this research revealed that a significant proportion of children seem to be experiencing negative affect or feelings of disappointment when their parent refuses to purchase a product advertised on TV.

Eating Habits

One of the major concerns surrounding children's exposure to television is the development of unhealthy eating habits. Research shows that exposure to television advertising for food products can negatively influence children's perceptions and beliefs about nutrition (Sharaga, 1974). For instance, Donohue (1975) found that a significant number of African American children in his study perceived that drinking Coke and consuming fast food were nutritional strategies to maintain good health (cf. Donohue et al., 1978, p. 35). In another study, Donohue et al. (1978) also found that race affects children's perceptions of nutrition. Over two thirds (68%) of the African American children surveyed perceived McDonalds to be more nutritious than the food at their homes. Only 15% of White children felt the same way (see page 39).

Many of these perceptions and beliefs may be fostered by repeated exposure to television advertising. Indeed, research shows that heavy viewing can substantially alter children's nutritional knowledge. Atkin et al. (1979) observed that heavy viewers of food ads were twice as likely as light viewers to indicate that sugared cereals and candies are highly nutritious. Using multiple controls, Signorielli and Lears' (1992) results showed that exposure to TV is positively associated with inaccurate beliefs about both the components of a nutritious breakfast and that fast-food meals are as nutritious as those prepared at home (p. 254). Signorielli and Staples (1997) found that older elementary schoolers' viewing of television was related positively to indicating that unhealthy foods were healthy, especially among those of minority status. The results from these studies suggest that exposure to television in general and advertising in specific may be teaching and/or reinforcing poor nutritional beliefs in young consumers, especially among minorities and heavy viewers.

In addition to altering perceptions and beliefs, there is also concern that repeated viewing of television advertising may contribute to obesity in childhood and adolescence. To examine this relationship, Dietz and Gortmaker (1985) conducted both cross-sectional and longitudinal studies with 6- to 11-year-olds. Obesity was assessed by way of a triceps skinfold procedure. After taking a variety of variables into account—such as SES, season, region, population density, family size, birth order, and race—the results from their cross-sectional data revealed that television viewing is positively and significantly associated with obesity in children and adolescents. Furthermore, the regression analysis revealed that the frequency of obesity in adolescents increased roughly 2% with each additional hour spent with TV per day (Dietz, 1990, p. 78).

Because the findings were based on correlational data, the direction of the relationship between the two variables is impossible to ascertain. It may be the case that obese children are seeking out more TV viewing. To assess the issue of directionality, Dietz and Gortmaker (1985) longitudinally examined whether early exposure to TV in childhood predicted obesity in adolescence. Controlling for several variables, the results revealed "the amount of TV viewed by non-obese children was the most powerful predictor [of] risk for the development of obesity in adolescence" (Dietz, 1990, p. 78).

Dietz (1990) reasoned that TV exposure may contribute to obesity in children in two ways. First, exposure to television may reduce children's energy expenditure. If children are watching television, they are less likely to be engaging in some other physical activity. In fact, at least one study found that heavy viewing among adolescent males is associated with lower levels of physical fitness (Tucker, 1986). Second, viewing television may increase food consumption. Given that children's shows are saturated with ads for food high in calories and sugar (Kunkel & Gantz, 1992), youngsters may be bombarded with messages encouraging or reminding them to consume such unhealthy options. Consistent with this reasoning, research reveals that exposure to food advertising is positively associated with snacking and caloric intake in 2- to 11-year-olds (Bolton, 1983). More generally, studies have found a positive association between exposure to TV and children's caloric intake, choosing unhealthy food, and having poor eating habits (Signorielli & Lears, 1992; Signorielli & Staples, 1997; Taras, Sallis, Patterson, Nader, & Nelson, 1989).

Materialism

Another potential problem with exposure to TV advertising is that it may contribute to children developing materialistic attitudes and values. In fact, a recent poll conducted by the Center for a New American Dream revealed that 87% of parents of 2- to 17-year-olds said that advertising targeting children makes them materialistic (Spencer, 2001, p. 162). Furthermore, almost half of the parents surveyed indicated that their child would rather go shopping at the mall than hiking with the family.

Summarizing previous research and theorizing, Buijzen and Valkenburg (2001, p. 6) argued that television advertising may contribute to materialism among children "because it is designed to arouse desires for products that would not otherwise be salient. Advertising emphasizes that possessions are important, and that obtaining these possessions will result in many desirable qualities, such as beauty, success, status, and happiness. Advertising communicates the ideology that desirable qualities can be obtained only by material possessions." To date, only a few studies have been conducted on the impact of television advertising on children's materialistic ideals.

In one quasi-experimental study, Greenberg and Brand (1993; Brand & Greenberg, 1994) examined the impact on high school students' materialist attitudes of commercials embedded in a Channel One (a privately produced, in-school news program that prominently features commercials) show. Their materialism scale was composed of items such as "When I watch commercials, I usually want what is shown" and "Most people who have a lot of money are happier than most people who have only a little money." The results from this research revealed that high schoolers exposed to Channel One were more likely to have materialistic attitudes than were those who did not have access to such programming.

A few correlational studies have also examined the TV advertising-materialism link. Atkin (1975d) examined the impact of exposure to television on fourth through seventh graders' materialistic attitudes. He found that repeated viewing of television had a significant effect on materialism. Almost 20% of the heavy viewers and 10% of light viewers were likely to state that "the most important thing is to have lots of money" (c.f. Brand & Greenberg, 1994, p. 20). Among middle and high school students, Churchill and Moschis (1979) also observed a positive relationship between TV exposure and materialistic values, even after controlling for multiple variables.

Examining the impact of viewing TV advertising more directly, Moschis and Churchill (1978) found that motivations for commercial viewing were a significant predictor of materialism. After applying multiple controls, watching TV ads for information about lifestyles associated with certain products was positively related to materialistic attitudes (p. 604). Although these correlational studies are informative, they fail to reveal the directionality between exposure to advertising and materialism.

Addressing this issue, Moschis and Moore (1982) surveyed sixth through twelfth graders twice across 14 months about their materialistic values and attitudes as well as exposure to television commercials. The cross-sectional data at Time 1 revealed a positive relationship between exposure to advertising and materialism. To assess directionality, Moschis and Moore (1982) correlated early exposure to television advertising at Time 1 with materialism score at Time 2, controlling for initial levels of materialism as well as age, gender, race, social class, and peer communication. The overtime analysis was statistically insignificant, except for those children who came from families that rarely discussed consumption issues ($r = .22$, $p < .01$). As Moschis and Moore (1982) stated, "These data suggest that parents mediate television advertising effects by discussing consumption matters with the child" (p. 284).

Self-Perception

Exposure to advertising may also contribute to negative self-perceptions, especially among young adolescent females. That is, many television and magazine ads feature physically attractive and thin models and/or actors. According to social comparison theory (Festinger, 1954), viewing these ads may cause adolescents to compare their physical appearance and weight to the models shown (Martin & Gentry, 1997, p. 2). Such comparison processes may negatively influence youngsters' self-esteem, self-perception, and body image.

Only a couple of experiments have examined the impact of physically attractive models in ads on adolescent females' perceptions. Martin and Kennedy (1993) exposed fourth, eighth, and twelfth graders to magazine ads featuring highly attractive models, moderately attractive models, or no models, and then had the students respond to measures assessing their self-perception and esteem. The results revealed that comparing oneself to models in ads is negatively related to self-esteem and perceptions of physical attractiveness. In general, the girls who were more likely to compare themselves to models already had the lowest self- esteem and self-perception of their own physical attractiveness. Unexpectedly, the exposure to physically attractive models had *no* influence on girls' perceptions of their own physical attractiveness.

In a follow-up study, Martin and Gentry (1997) argued that the type of motive consumers have when evaluating models in ads makes a difference. In particular, a self-evaluative (e.g., "the model is prettier than I am") motive may result in lowering females' self-esteem, self-perception, and even body image, whereas a self-improvement (e.g., "the model can illustrate ways to improve my appearance") or self-enhancement (e.g., "I am prettier than the model on a specific dimension" or "I discount the model's beauty") motive may actually heighten such judgments. To test this idea, fourth-, sixth-, and eighth-grade girls were shown ads that primed these different types of motives. Congruent with predictions, girls' perceptions of their own physical attractiveness were significantly lower after exposure to an ad that induced self-evaluation and were significantly higher after exposure to ads inducing self-improvement or enhancement. Among sixth graders, those who were exposed to ads that induced self-evaluation perceived their bodies more negatively (e.g., body image seen as heavier).

ALCOHOL ADVERTISING

Young people start forming drinking attitudes and experimenting with alcohol during the age range of 10 to 14 years, a stage when they are exposed increasingly to TV commercials for beer and other alcohol products. Adolescent curiosity and uncertainty about drinking-related phenomena, combined with limited opportunity to directly observe drinking in bars and party situations, motivates vicarious observational learning and heightens susceptibility to media-based cultivation. These children's emerging tastes and values increase receptivity to conventional alcohol advertising appeals (e.g., fun, sociability, adventure, masculinity/femininity).

Promotion of alcoholic beverages on television has generated controversy for several decades, based primarily on concerns about the impact of these commercials on children and teenagers. The issue became particularly salient when adolescent drinking rose sharply in the 1970s and teenage drunk driving attracted attention in the 1980s. Advertising practices have been the focal point of several congressional hearings and a Surgeon General's workshop, and have generated widespread debate involving health organizations, public interest groups, advertising agencies, and alcohol producers.

Although beer companies have advertised since the earliest days of TV, liquor commercials were traditionally considered to be too sensitive for television. Due to declining sales, distillers began airing commercials on certain cable channels and local stations in the late 1990s and, when the NBC network finally decided to accept liquor ads in 2001, harsh criticism forced a reversal several months later.

Nevertheless, distillers have recently partnered with brewers to aggressively promote a new form of malt liquor aimed at the youthful segment of the market. These "alcopops" are lightly carbonated, slightly sweetened, fruit-flavored clear malts that are appealing to the tastes of entry-level drinkers. Brand names such as Mike's Hard Lemonade, Smirnoff Ice, and Bacardi Silver quickly gained popularity with teenagers following advertising campaigns that included prominent placements in late-night TV shows frequently viewed by underage audiences.

In a national poll conducted by Atkin and Thorson (2000), almost three fourths of all adult respondents believed that teenagers are susceptible to influence by televised liquor ads, and most perceived that underage audiences are encouraged to experiment with liquor or to drink a greater amount of this product. Half of the adults felt that liquor companies are trying to influence teenagers to drink liquor. By a 2:1 margin, adults disapproved of teenagers seeing liquor ads on TV; by a 5:1 margin, they disapproved of children seeing liquor commercials.

The poll also showed that more than two thirds of adults favor a strict prohibition of these ads in order to protect youthful viewers. Indeed, there is broader public support for prohibiting TV liquor ads than prohibiting sex and violence in youth-oriented programming. If liquor advertising is to be permitted on TV, a large majority of adults support requiring warnings in ads, delaying ads until late evening, restricting content that might appeal to young people, and balancing ads with more public service spots.

Alcohol advertisers have asserted consistently that the main purpose of ads is to retain product loyalty or induce brand switching, rather than to lure new customers (particularly those who are under the legal drinking age). The alcohol industry claims that parents and peers are the primary determinants of adolescent drinking, whereas advertising has no impact on consumption.

On the other hand, social science theory suggests that advertising can positively influence drinking behavior via development and reinforcement of favorable attitudes toward alcohol and drinking practices, mainly as a result of advertising-induced creation of images and beliefs that operate through persuasion processes of conditioning, social cognitive learning, and reasoned action. In addition, ads can disinhibit drinkers through legitimization and rationalization, because viewers form conceptions that drinking is a widespread norm, that alcohol is a harmless substance, and that escape and relief are acceptable reasons for drinking. Simple gains in knowledge from informational content of ads can contribute to consumption during formative years, as viewers learn about new types of alcohol and gain familiarity with conventional drinking practices and appropriate situations for consuming alcohol.

Survey research indicates that young people respond positively to TV alcohol commercials that are ostensibly targeted to adults, and that these ads contribute to drinking intentions and behaviors during adolescence. Pioneering research with teenagers by Atkin, Hocking, and Block (1984) and Strickland (1983) demonstrated that televised beer advertising mildly increases consumption of beer; for example, 52% of teens highly exposed to these commercials had tried each of six brands of beer, compared to 37% of the lightly exposed respondents.

For predrinkers, beer commercials have sizable cognitive effects. Atkin and Block (1984) reported that heavily exposed junior high school students display much greater brand awareness (brand names, slogans, logos, endorsers, and themes), and are more likely to hold favorable stereotypes of the typical beer drinker as fun loving, friendly, happy, and manly. Moreover, frequent viewers of beer ads are more likely to anticipate future consumption. Similarly, Grube and Wallack (1994) found that fifth and sixth graders with high recognition of TV beer commercials are more likely to know beer brands and slogans, to hold positive beliefs about drinking, and to express intentions to drink as an adult.

A focus group study showed that most 10- to 13-year-olds believe that alcohol advertisers are targeting teenage audiences, particularly with ads featuring sexy and young-looking characters, cute animals, extreme sports, upbeat music, fast-paced action, and fun party scenes (Smith, Atkin, & Fediuk, 2001). Grube and Wallack (1994) found that as children move through early adolescence, they become more engaged in alcohol advertisements, particularly ads that portray fun lifestyles, celebrity endorsements, humor, animation, and rock music.

According to Austin and Knaus (2000), children's liking of alcohol ads increases steadily from third to ninth grade. Identification with commercial characters leads to expectancies of positive social benefits of drinking and predisposition to consume alcohol. The researchers concluded that beliefs and desires developing by third grade serve to prime children for future decisions regarding substance use.

A survey of 10- to 17-year-olds showed that liking for beer commercials contributes to current drinking and expected future drinking (Wyllie, Zhang, & Casswell, 1998). Those in the age range of 10 to 13 are most likely to accept the portrayals in beer ads as realistic. Kelly and Edwards (1998) argued that theories underlying self-monitoring and imaginary audience ideation suggest that adolescents are more likely than adults to prefer image-oriented alcohol ads. They found a positive relationship between the preference for image advertising and intention to consume alcohol. Image ads featuring female models are especially appealing to younger boys.

A potentially vulnerable audience segment is young people growing up in families with alcohol problems. A sample of children of alcoholics (aged 11 through 16) were more likely than other respondents to report that the beer ads trigger negative feelings about drinkers they know personally (Atkin, 1996).

Slater et al. (1997) presented a series of beer commercials to adolescents, who wrote down their thoughts and feelings after watching each ad. Positive responses to beer ads were associated with current and planned alcohol use. Male adolescents responded more positively than did females, especially when the ads depicted sports content or were embedded in a sports programming context.

In another study examining reactions to specimen ads, sixth to ninth graders were presented with three beer commercials portraying bar, beach, and party scenes (Atkin, 1996). When asked to estimate how many drinks the various characters in the ads were consuming, almost half of the adolescents said five or more drinks (the definition of "binge" drinking). Smith et al. (2001) reported even higher proportions of adolescents perceiving heavy drinking in two liquor ads.

On the other hand, research indicates that critical viewing skills and parental mediation may limit the influence of alcohol ads by the early teenage years. Slater et al. (1998) presented beer ads to middle school students, and asked the viewers to generate counterarguments. Students most often cited the lack of realistic portrayals of outcomes of alcohol use; the irrelevance of depicted associations between the alcohol product and various recreational and social activities; and the misleading suggestions of social, romantic, or athletic success implied in many ads. Austin, Pinkleton, and Fujioka (2000) found that the relationship between alcohol ad viewing and consumption among ninth graders is partially moderated by parents.

CONCLUSION

The goal of this chapter was to review research on the impact of advertising on children. The research reveals that younger children are uniquely susceptible to advertising content given their inability to differentiate programs from commercials as well as to comprehend selling intent. In addition to comprehension, the cognitive, affective, and behavioral "intended" effects of advertising were explored. Studies show that advertising can influence children's product recall, desires, and patterns of consumption. Some important moderators of these effects may be the child's age, extensiveness of exposure to advertising, ethnicity, and gender. We then turned our attention to the unintended effects of advertising on children and adolescents. The review reveals that more research is needed, especially on the impact of advertising on outcomes such as materialism, self-perception, and unhappiness. Furthermore, scholars should continue to examine those individual, family, and peer-related variables that may reduce the ill effects of exposure to television commercials. The last section dealt with the role of alcohol advertising on older children's and adolescents' thoughts, attitudes, and drinking-related behaviors. Clearly, this body of work reveals that not only can exposure to alcohol ads contribute to teen drinking in society, but also that parental mediation and teaching critical viewing may help to ameliorate negative effects.

REFERENCES

Atkin, C. (1975a). *Effects of television advertising on children—first year experimental evidence* (Technical report). East Lansing: Michigan State University.

Atkin, C. (1975b). *Effects of television advertising on children—second year experimental evidence* (Technical report). East Lansing: Michigan State University.

Atkin, C. (1975c). *Effects of television advertising on children—survey of children's and mothers' responses to television commercials* (Technical report). East Lansing: Michigan State University.

Atkin, C. (1975d). *Effects of television advertising on children—survey of preadolescents' responses to television commercials* (Technical report). East Lansing: Michigan State University.

Atkin, C. (1978). Observation of parent–child interaction in supermarket decision-making. *Journal of Marketing, XX,* 41–45.

Atkin, C. (1980). Effects of television advertising on children. In E. L. Palmer & A. Dorr (Eds.), *Children and the faces of television* (vol 1, pp. 287–306). New York: Academic Press.

Atkin, C. (1996). *Adolescent responses to televised beer advertisements: Children of alcoholics and others.* Washington, DC: Center for Science in the Public Interest.

Atkin, C., & Block, M. (1984). The effects of alcohol advertising. *Advances in Consumer Research, 11,* 688–693.

Atkin, C., & Gibson, W. (1978) *Children's nutrition learning from television advertising.* Unpublished manuscript, Michigan State University, East Lansing.

Atkin C., Hocking, J., & Block, M. (1984). Teenage drinking: Does advertising make a difference? *Journal of Communication, 34,* 157–172.

Atkin, C., Reeves, B., & Gibson, W. (1979). *Effects of television food advertising on children.* Paper presented at the annual meeting of the Association for Education in Journalism, Houston, TX.

Atkin, C., & Thorson, E. (2000). *National opinion poll on liquor commercials and billboards.* Technical Report #1 submitted to Robert Wood Johnson Foundation.

Austin, E., & Knaus, C. (2000). Predicting the potential for risky behavior among those "too young" to drink as the result of appealing advertising. *Journal of Health Communications, 5*(1), 13–27.

Austin, E., Pinkleton, B., & Fujioka, Y. (2000). The role of interpretation processes and parental discussion in the media's effects on adolescents' use of alcohol. *Pediatrics, 105*(2), 343–349.

Bandura, A. (1986). *Social foundations of thought and action.* Englewood Cliffs, NJ: Prentice-Hall.

Barry, T., & Sheikh, A. (1977). Race as a dimension in children's TV advertising: The need for more research. *Journal of Advertising, 6,* 5–10.

Blatt, J., Spencer, L., & Ward, S. (1972). A cognitive development study of children's reactions to television advertising. In E. A Rubinstein, G. A. Comstock, & J. P. Murray (Eds.), *Television and social behavior: Reports and papers* (vol. 4, pp. 452–467). Washington, DC: U.S. Department of Health, Education, and Welfare.

Blosser, B. J., & Roberts, D. F. (1985). Age differences in children's perceptions of message intent: Responses to tv news, commercials, educational spots, and public service announcements. *Communication Research, 12,* 455–484.

Bolton, R. (1983). Modeling the impact of television food advertising on children's diets. *Current Issues and Research in Advertising, 6,* 173–199.

Borzekowski, D. L. G., & Robinson, T. N. (2001). The 30-second effect: An experiment revealing the impact of television commercials on food preferences of preschoolers. *Journal of the American Dietetic Association, 101,* 42–46.

Brand, J. E., & Greenberg, B. S. (1994). Commercials in the classroom: The impact of Channel One advertising. *Journal of Advertising Research, 34,* 18–27.

Bruner, J. S. (1966). On cognitive growth I & II. In J. S. Bruner, R. R. Oliver, & P. M. Greenfield (Eds.), *Studies in cognitive growth* (pp. 1–67). New York: Wiley.

Buijzen, M., & Valkenburg, P. M. (2000). The impact of television advertising on children's Christmas wishes. *Journal of Broadcasting & Electronic Media, 44,* 456–470.

Buijzen, M., & Valkenburg, P. M. (2001, July). *The effects of television advertising on materialism, parent–child conflict, and unhappiness: A meta-analytic review.* Paper presented at the annual conference of the International Communication Association, Seoul, South Korea.

Burr, P., & Burr, R. M. (1977). Product recognition and premium appeal. *Journal of Communication, 27,* 115–117.

Butter, E. J., Popovich, P. M., Stackhouse, R. H., & Garner, R. K. (1981). Discrimination of television programs and commercials by preschool children. *Journal of Advertising Research, 21,* 53–56.

Calvert, S. (1999). *Children's journey through the information age.* Boston, MA: McGraw-Hill.

Caron, A., & Ward, S. (1975). Gift decisions by kids and parents. *Journal of Advertising Research, 15,* 15–20.

Chandler, M. J., & Greenspan, S. (1972). Ersatz egocentrism: A reply to H. Borke. *Developmental Psychology, 7,* 104–106.

Christenson, P. G. (1982). Children's perceptions of TV commercials and products: The effects of PSAs. *Communication Research, 9,* 491–524.

Churchill, G. A., & Moschis, G. P. (1979). Television and interpersonal influences on adolescent consumer learning. *Journal of Consumer Research, 6,* 23–35.

Clancy-Hepburn, K., Hickey, A. A., & Nevill, G. (1974). Children's behavior responses to TV food advertisements. *Journal of Nutrition Education, 6,* 93–96.

Clay, R. A. (2000, September 1). Advertising to children: Is it ethical? *Monitor on Psychology, 31*(8). Retrieved February 22, 2002, from http://www.apa.org/monitor/sep00/advertising.html

Coon, K. A., Goldberg, J., Rogers, B. L., & Tucker, K. L. (2001). Relationships between use of television during meals and children's food consumption patterns. *Pediatrics, 107,* e7.

Dietz, W. H. (1990). You are what you eat—what you eat is what you are. *Journal of Adolescent Health Care, 11,* 76–81.

Dietz, W. H., & Gortmaker, S. L. (1985). Do we fatten our children at the TV set? Television viewing and obesity in children and adolescents. *Pediatrics, 75,* 807–812.

Donkin, A. J. M., Tilston, C. H., Neale, R. J., & Gregson, K. (1992). Children's food preferences: Television advertising vs. nutritional advice. *British Food Journal, 94,* 6–9.

Donohue, T. R. (1975). Effect of commercials on Black children. *Journal of Advertising Research, 15,* 41–47.

Donohue, T. R., Meyer, T. P., & Henke, L. L. (1978). Black and White children's perceptions of TV commercials. *Journal of Marketing, 42,* 34–40.

Dussere, S. (1976). *The effects of television advertising on children's eating habits.* Unpublished doctoral dissertation, University of Massachusetts, Amherst.

Federal Trade Commission (FTC). (1978). *Staff report on television advertising to children.* Washington, DC: U.S. Government Printing Office.

Federal Trade Commission (FTC). (1979). *Presiding officer's order no. 78: Certification to the commission of recommended disputed issues of fact.* Washington, DC: Author.

Festinger, L. (1954). A theory of social comparison processes. *Human Relations, 7,* 117–140.

Fischer, P. M., Schwartz, M. P., Richards, J. W., Goldstein, A. O., & Rojas, T. H. (1991). Brand logo recognition by children aged 3 to 6 years. *Journal of the American Medical Association, 266,* 3145–3148.

Frideres, J. S. (1973). Advertising, buying patterns and children. *Journal of Advertising Research, 13,* 34–36.

Galst, J. P., & White, M. A. (1976). The unhealthy persuader: The reinforcing value of television and children's purchase-influencing attempts at the supermarket. *Child Development, 47,* 1089–1096.

Gerbner, G., Gross, L., Morgan, M., & Signorielli, N. (1994). Growing up with television: The cultivation perspective. In J. Bryant & D. Zillmann (Eds.), *Perspectives on media effects* (pp. 17–40). Hillsdale, NJ: Lawrence Erlbaum Associates.

Goldberg, M. E., & Gorn, G. J. (1978). Some unintended consequences of TV advertising to children. *Journal of Consumer Research, 5,* 22–29.

Goldberg, M. E., Gorn, G. J., & Gibson, W. (1978). TV messages for snack and breakfast foods: Do they influence children's preferences? *Journal of Consumer Research, 5,* 73–81.

Gorn, G. J., & Florsheim, R. (1985). The effects of commercials for adult products on children. *Journal of Consumer Research, 11,* 962–967.

Gorn, G. J., & Goldberg, M. E. (1980). Children's response to repetitive television commercials. *Journal of Consumer Research, 6,* 421–424.

Gorn, G. J., & Goldberg, M. E. (1982). Behavioral evidence of the effects of televised food messages on children. *Journal of Consumer Research, 9,* 200–205.

Greenberg, B. S., & Brand, J. E. (1993). Television news and advertising in schools: The "Channel One" controversy. *Journal of Communication, 43,* 143–151.

Grube, J., & Wallack, L. (1994). Television beer advertising and drinking knowledge, beliefs, and intentions among school children. *Journal of Public Health, 84,* 254–259.

Hendon, D. W., McGann, A. F., & Hendon, B. L. (1978). Children's age, intelligence and sex as variables mediating reactions to TV commercials: Repetition and content complexity implications for advertising. *Journal of Advertising, 17,* 4–12.

Heslop, L. A., & Ryans, A. B. (1980). A second look at children and the advertising of premiums. *Journal of Consumer Research, 6*, 414–420.

Hoffner, C., & Cantor, J. (1985). Developmental differences in responses to a television character's appearance and behavior. *Developmental Psychology, 21*, 1065–1074.

Howard, J. A., Hulbert, J. M., & Lehmann, D. (1977). An exploratory analysis of the effect of television advertising on children. A working paper described in R. P. Adler, B. Z. Friedlander, G. S. Lesser, L. Meringoff, T. S. Robertson, J. R. Rossiter, & S. Ward (Eds.), *Research on the effects of television advertising on children*. Washington, DC: United States Government Printing Office. (Revised ed., Lexington, MA: Lexington Books, 1980).

Isler, L., Popper, E. T., & Ward, S. (1987). Children's purchase requests and parental responses: Results from a diary study. *Journal of Advertising Research, 27(5)*, 28–31, 33–39.

Jeffrey, D. B., McLellarn, R. W., & Fox, D. T. (1982). The development of children's eating habits: The role of television commercials. *Health Education Quarterly, 9*, 78–93.

John, D. R. (1999). Consumer socialization of children: A retrospective look at twenty five years of research. *Journal of Consumer Research, 26(3)*, 183–213.

Kaiser Family Foundation. (1999). *Kids and media @ the new millennium*. Menlo Park, CA: Author.

Kelly, K. & Edwards, R. (1998). Image advertisements for alcohol products: Is their appeal associated with adolescents' intention to consume alcohol? *Adolescence, 33(129)*, 169–184, 199.

Kunkel, D. (1988). Children and host-selling television commercials. *Communication Research, 15*, 71–92.

Kunkel, D. (2001). Children and television advertising. In D. G. Singer & J. L. Singer (Eds.), *Handbook of children and the media* (pp. 375–394). Thousand Oaks, CA: Sage.

Kunkel, D., & Gantz, W. (1992). Children's television advertising in the multi-channel environment. *Journal of Communication, 42(3)*, 134–142.

Kunkel, D., & Roberts, D. (1991). Young minds and marketplace values: Issues in children's television advertising. *Journal of Social Issues, 47*, 57–72.

Kurdek, L. A. (1977). Structural components and intellectual correlates of cognitive perspective taking in first- through fourth-grade children. *Child Development, 48*, 1503–1511.

Kurdek, L. A., & Rodgon, M. M. (1975). Perceptual, cognitive, and affective perspective taking in Kindergarten through sixth-grade children. *Developmental Psychology, 11*, 643–650.

Levin, S. R., Petros, T. V., & Petrella, F. W. (1982). Preschoolers' awareness of television advertising. *Child Development, 53*, 933–937.

Liebert, D. E., Sprafkin, J. N., Liebert, R. M., & Rubinstein, E. A. (1977). Effects of television commercial disclaimers on the product expectations of children. *Journal of Communication, XX*, 118–124.

Lingsweiler, R., & Wilson, B. J. (2002, July). *Children's comprehension of modified disclaimers in television advertising*. Paper presented at the annual conference of the International Communication Association, Mass Communication division in Seoul, Korea.

Linnett, R. (2000). Psychologists protest kids' ads. *Advertising Age, 71*, 4, 69.

Macklin, M. C. (1985). Do young children understand the selling intent of commercials? *The Journal of Consumer Affairs, 19*, 293–304.

Macklin, M. C. (1996). Preschoolers' learning of brand names from visual cues. *Journal of Consumer Research, 23*, 251–261.

Martin, M. C. (1997). Children's understanding of the intent of advertising: A meta-analysis. *Journal of Public Policy and Marketing, 16*, 205–216.

Martin, M. C., & Gentry, J. W. (1997). Stuck in the model trap: The effects of beautiful models in ads on female preadolescents and adolescents. *Journal of Advertising, 26*, 19–33.

Martin, M. C., & Kennedy, P. F. (1993). Advertising and social comparison: Consequences for female preadolescents and adolescents. *Psychology & Marketing, 10 (6)*, 913–950.

McNeal, J. U. (1999). *The kids' market: Myths and realities*. Ithaca, NY: Paramount Market Publishing.

Melkman, R., Tversky, B., & Baratz, D. (1981). Developmental trends in the use of perceptual and conceptual attributes in grouping, clustering, and retrieval. *Journal of Experimental Child Psychology, 31*, 470–486.

Moschis, G. P., & Churchill, G. A. (1978). Consumer socialization: A theoretical and empirical analysis. *Journal of Marketing Research, 14*, 599–609.

Moschis, G. P., & Moore, R. L. (1982). A longitudinal study of television advertising effects. *Journal of Consumer Research, 9*, 279–286.

Paget, K. F., Kritt, D., & Bergemann, L. (1984). Understanding strategic interactions in television commercials: A developmental study. *Journal of Applied Developmental Psychology, 5*, 145–161.

Palmer, E. L., & McDowell, C. N. (1979). Program/commercial separators in children's television programming. *Journal of Communication, 29,* 197–201.

Palmer, E. L., & McDowell, C. N. (1981). Children's understanding of nutritional information presented in breakfast cereal commercials. *Journal of Broadcasting, 25,* 295–301.

Piaget, J. (1929). *The child's conception of the world.* London: Routledge & Kegan Paul.

Piaget, J. (1962). *Plays, dreams, and imitation in childhood.* New York: Norton.

Prasad, V. K., & Smith, L. J. (1994). Television commercials in violent programming: An experimental evaluation of their effects on children. *Journal of the Academy of Marketing Science, 22,* 340–351.

Ray, M. E., Sawyer, A., & Strong, E. (1971). Frequence effects revisited. *Journal of Advertising Research, 11,* 14–20.

Reardon, K. K. (1991). *Persuasion in practice.* Thousand Oaks, CA: Sage.

Reeves, B., & Atkin, C. (1979, August). *The effects of televised advertising on mother–child interactions at the grocery store.* Paper presented at the annual meeting of the Association of Education in Journalism, Houston, TX.

Reilly Group Incorporated. (1973). Assumption by the child of the role of the consumer. *The Child, 1* (entire volume).

Resnik, A., & Stern, B. (1977). Children's television advertising and brand choice: A laboratory experiment. *Journal of Advertising, 6,* 11–17.

Roberts, D. F., & Maccoby, N. (1985). Effects of mass communication. In G. Lindzey & E. Anderson (Eds.), *The handbook of social psychology* (vol. 3, pp. 539–598). New York: Random House.

Robertson, T. S., & Rossiter, J. R. (1974). Children and commercial persuasion: An attribution theory analysis. *Journal of Consumer Research, 1,* 13–20.

Robertson, T. S., & Rossiter, J. R. (1976). Short-run advertising effects on children: A field study. *Journal of Marketing Research, 13,* 68–70.

Robertson, T. S., & Rossiter, J. R. (1977). Children's responsiveness to commercials. *Journal of Communication, 27,* 101–106.

Robertson, T. S., Ward, S., Gatignon, H., & Klees, D. M. (1989). Advertising and children: A cross cultural study. *Communication Research, 16,* 459–485.

Roedder, D. L. (1981). Age differences in children's responses to television advertising: An information-processing approach. *Journal of Consumer Research, 8,* 144–153.

Ross, R. P., Campbell, T., Wright, J. C., Huston, A. C., Rice, M. L., & Turk, P. (1984). When celebrities talk, children listen: An experimental analysis of children's responses to TV ads with celebrity endorsers. *Journal of Applied Developmental Psychology, 5,* 185–202.

Rossiter, J. R., & Robertson, T. S. (1974). Children's tv commercials: Testing the defenses. *Journal of Communication, 24,* 137–144.

Sharaga, S. (1974) *The effect of television advertising on children's nutrition attitudes, nutrition knowledge, and eating habits.* Unpublished doctoral dissertation, Cornell University, Ithaca, NY.

Sheikh, A. A., & Moleski, L. M. (1977). Conflict in the family over commercials. *Journal of Communication, 27,* 152–157.

Shimp, T. A., Dyer, R. F., & Devita, S. F. (1976). An experimental test of the harmful effects of premium-oriented commercials on children. *Journal of Consumer Research, 3,* 1–11.

Siegler, R. S. (1991). *Children's thinking* (2nd ed.). Englewood Cliffs, NJ: Prentice-Hall.

Signorielli, N., & Lears, M. (1992). Television and children's conceptions of nutrition: Unhealthy messages. *Health Communication, 4,* 245–257.

Signorielli, N., & Staples, J. (1997). Television and children's conceptions of nutrition. *Health Communication, 9,* 289–301.

Slater, M., Rouner, D., Domenech-Rodriguez, M., Beauvais, F., Murphy, K., & Estes, E. (1998). How adolescents counterargue television beer advertisements: Implications for education efforts. *Journal of Health Education, 29*(2), 100–105.

Slater, M., Rouner, D., Domenech-Rodriguez, M., Beauvais, F., Murphy, K., & Van Leuven, J. (1997). Adolescent responses to TV beer ads and sports content/context: Gender and ethnic differences. *Journalism and Mass Communications Quarterly, 74*(1), 108–122.

Smith, S., Atkin, C., & Fediuk, T. (2001). Youth reactions to televised liquor commercials. *Journal of Alcohol and Drug Education, 47,* 1.

Spencer, P. (2001, November). I want that. *Woman's Day,* p. 162.

Stern, B., & Resnik, A. J. (1978). Children's understanding of a televised commercial disclaimer. In S. C. Jain (Ed.), *Research frontiers in marketing: Dialogues and directions* (pp. 332–336). Chicago, IL: American Marketing Association.

Stoneman, Z., & Brody, G. H. (1981). The indirect impact of child-oriented advertisements on mother–child interactions. *Journal of Applied Developmental Psychology, 2,* 369–376.

Strickland, D. (1983). Advertising exposure, alcohol consumption and misuse of alcohol. In M. Grant, M. Plant, & A. Williams (Eds.), *Economics and alcohol: Consumption and controls* (pp. 201–222). New York: Gardner Press.

Stutts, M. A., & Hunnicutt, G. G. (1987). Can young children understand disclaimers in television commercials? *Journal of Advertising, 16,* 41–46.

Stutts, M. A., Vance, D., & Hudleson, S. (1981). Program–commercial separators in children's television: Do they help a child tell the difference between *Bugs Bunny* and the *Quik Rabbit? Journal of Advertising, 10,* 16–25, 48.

Taras, H. L., Sallis, J. F., Patterson, T. L., Nader, P. R., & Nelson, J. (1989). Television's influence on children's diet and physical activity. *Developmental and Behavioral Pediatrics, 10,* 176–180.

Tucker, L. A. (1986). The relationship of television viewing to physical fitness and obesity. *Adolescence, 21,* 797–806.

Wackman, D., Wartella, E., & Ward, S. (1977). Learning to be consumers: The role of the family. *Journal of Communication, 27,* 138–151.

Ward, S., Levinson, D., & Wackman, D. (1972). Children's attention to television advertising. In E. A Rubinstein, G. A. Comstock, & J. P. Murray (Eds.), *Television and social behavior: Reports and papers* (vol. 4, pp. 491–515). Washington, DC: U.S. Department of Health, Education, and Welfare.

Ward, S., Reale, G., & Levinson, D. (1972). Children's perceptions, explanations, and judgments of television advertising: A further exploration. In E. A Rubinstein, G. A. Comstock, & J. P. Murray (Eds.), *Television and social behavior: Reports and papers* (vol. 4, pp. 468–490). Washington, DC: U.S. Department of Health, Education, and Welfare.

Ward, S., & Wackman, D. B. (1972). Children's purchase influence attempts and parental yielding. *Journal of Marketing Research, 9,* 316–319.

Ward, S., Wackman, D. B., & Wartella, E. (1977). *How children learn to buy: The development of consumer information-processing skills.* Beverly Hills, CA: Sage.

Wartella, E., & Ettema, J. (1974). A cognitive developmental study of children's attention to television commercials. *Communication Research, 1,* 46–64.

Wyllie, A., Zhang, J. F., & Casswell, S. (1998). Responses to televised alcohol advertisements associated with drinking behavior of 10–17-year-olds. *Addiction, 93*(3), 361–371.

Zuckerman, P., & Gianinno, L. (1981). Measuring children's response to television advertising. In J. F. Esserman (Ed.), *Television advertising and children: Issues, research, and findings* (pp. 84–93). New York: Child Research Service.

Zuckerman, P., Ziegler, M., & Stevenson, H. W. (1978). Children's viewing of television and recognition memory of commercials. *Child Development, 49,* 96–104.

16

Issues and Politics of Televisual Advertising and Children

Brian M. Young
University of Exeter

Children and commercial communications: issues and politics

In all cultures and at all times in history, children have been nurtured, cared for, and brought up to take their rightful place as adult members of society. Although the history of childhood is tainted by abuse, individually and collectively, against children, the general principle remains that we as a people take care of our offspring. One of the purposes of this chapter is to look at the concerns and anxieties that people in the 21st century feel about just one aspect that appears to threaten the well-being of the younger members of their culture—the real or imagined threat posed by the presence of commercial communications. What are the problems? Is it unfair to subvert the developing rationality of children with sophisticated marketing techniques? Should children be protected from the wilder excesses of the commercial and material world? If parents won't do this, who will? Should the state step in? In this chapter, we see that some of these concerns are well founded and others are based on false assumptions about the role of advertising, marketing, and promotion in general. Here you can find the evidence and the arguments, but the decision is yours. These are your children and this is their future. I hope that this chapter makes you think but also helps you make up your mind. The debate is not just a cool evaluation of alternative arguments and a winnowing of contradictory findings; it's inextricably tied up with politics, values, attitudes, and ultimately visions of what children are like and what they deserve.

Where shall we start? Twenty years ago, when the first version of this book emerged, the world of media was relatively simple by today's standards, with TV advertising to children dominating the discussions in the popular and academic literature. Advertising in magazines and on billboards was relegated to a minor issue as far as advertising to children was concerned, and the focus of concern was on television advertising and its effects on children and younger people in general. There was some worry about whether media representations in ads would cultivate an unattainable and undesirable body image concept in young and impressionable pubescent girls, and this concern has not gone away. There are still anxieties expressed that commercial communications convey images of food, for example, that encourage poor diet (Lewis & Hill, 1998), as well as arguments that body images of models will precipitate eating disorders such as anorexia nervosa or bulimic conditions.

However, the media landscape has changed beyond all recognition. Although these changes are documented extensively elsewhere in this book, we can perhaps summarize them by saying this: More choice is available to the child, who is very much in charge. In 1981, interactive media was nonexistent, and the only interaction children had was with primitive video games. Choice for kids then was being able to select from a range of three to four broadcast channels at most, and to "negotiate" within the family for a time for viewing after school and on Saturday mornings. ("Negotiate" is in quotes because most families had one TV and it is well known that the member of the family in charge of the remote control is rarely the child and usually a parent—often Dad.) Broadcasting with a "diet" that tried to satisfy all the wants and needs of a demographically defined population was the dominant model. For example, Melody (1973) argued that Saturday morning children's television had attempted to satisfy the different interests and wants of cohorts of children of various ages by organizing programming that appealed to the youngest children early in the morning and programs for older children later in the morning. The aim was to build a continuous audience flow designed so that switching to the other networks was minimized.

Note that the reason for structuring the "kidvid ghetto" (Melody & Ehrlich, 1974) was not concern for the interests of children in different age bands. The market was specialized, and one of the principles of selling in a specialized market is to seek a relatively high response rate from a smaller, selected audience. The concept of *demographic purity* is often mentioned in the literature with this meaning. The goal of the marketing strategy is that only a certain type of audience watches a particular program and the associated advertisements as the impact of the advertisement would be wasted on other, nontarget groups. Demographic purity was the aim of Saturday morning programming, by which different age groups of children were selectively attracted at different times in the morning. This strategy was designed to promote brands of interest to different groups of children. It is not surprising that an effects model of influence was still used by media researchers as a popular way of conceptualizing the role of media in the child's life. The image of many millions of children passively viewing a restricted range of televisual content was not an inaccurate picture of what was happening in homes across the nation.

Things have changed, and in the early 21st century the average household in Europe or the United States or in many cities in Asia has many access points to enter the world of communications. Consider a household with children. They will have more than one TV set. There will be a telephone with a landline, and possibly a dedicated line for Internet use. Mobile phone use by children is increasing: In the United Kingdom, whereas only 22% of children aged 9 and 10 years use mobile phones, this figure has increased to over 60% for 11- to 12-year-olds (Jones, 2002). However, there are cross-national differences, and many countries in Europe (where the geography is more conducive to cell phone coverage than in the United States) have remarkable figures for mobile phone ownership. Powell and Wicken (2002) compared survey data in the United States and the United Kingdom, and whereas only 44% of 12- to 17-year-olds in the United States owned or used mobile phones, the equivalent figure for the United Kingdom was 75%. Many urban households in Europe and many more in the United States have cable feeds for hundreds of TV channels, or have installed satellite dishes that can receive various bundles of TV transmissions at different subscription rates. A computer with Internet capabilities and storage devices that include CD-ROM and DVD is available in many homes. The television receiver will no doubt be linked to a video recorder (VCR) and possibly a DVD player. There are other forms of storage like TiVo, a solid-state store that affords instant playback and smart memory to prompt the user to record frequently viewed program categories at the touch of a button. There is a growth in digital television, with an associated interactive capability and choice of camera angle at sporting events. What used to be known as "MTV" is now a generic category for many branded channels, some with interactive capability such as viewer voting onscreen for the most popular music videos. Children use the Internet frequently. A 6-year study on Internet use by children (79% from the United States) showed that a quarter of children in 2001 could be classified as heavy users, "spending ten hours or more online each week—up from an average of just 19% for the previous four years" (Clarke, 2002; p. 45).

Hence, it would appear that children of the new media age have a wide variety of media from which to choose. It can be argued that the child is an active consumer of media (and other goods and services) from an early age and displays a wide variety of associated skills, from setting the controls on a VCR to sending text messages using an abbreviated message code on a mobile phone. Nevertheless, anxieties and concerns about children and media have shown no signs of disappearing. Additionally, as new media have emerged, concerns have grown, ranging from worries about pornography and advertising on the Internet to violence in video games and marketing in schools. Why should this be so?

I have argued elsewhere (Young, 1990) that advertising to children is an activity that produces concern and anxieties in adults, and that the reason behind these worries may be misplaced. This does *not* mean that marketing and promoting goods and services to younger people is a benign activity, harmless to both society in general and children in particular. We have to look at the evidence carefully, and I intend to develop this side of the argument later in the chapter. But if we look at the issue of why advertising to children has been a recurrent anxiety for many decades now, we see that some of the emotional energy discharged is targeted at myths and misunderstandings of both the nature of children and childhood, and the nature of promotional communications. It is only by cutting through the rhetoric that we will be in a better position to make a more dispassionate judgment on this vexed question.

There are many reasons why people should feel uncomfortable with the general idea that marketing and commercial promotion are legitimate activities. To a certain extent, advertisers are their own enemy. For example, I have on my desk a glossy color brochure inviting me to attend an "Annual Kids Marketing Summit" in London entitled *Tapping Into the Hearts & Minds of Toddlers, Tweens & Teens*. Inside I am told about "winning the hearts and minds of 3–13s" and "penetrating the kid lifestyle...." Although the intended readers of this kind of message are advertising practitioners who know from experience that so-called kids are fickle and that new brands fail more often than succeed, the language used reflects a particular way of thinking about marketing to children. Children are seen as passive recipients who are targeted and probed and seduced into purchase. In fact, children are far from passive and marketing is not a black art in which psychologists are priests of darkness. However, in order to establish just why advertising to children is seen in a negative light, it is necessary to look at several themes. I review these in light of changes in the media landscape over the last 20 years.

ADVERTISING

Pollay (1986) reviewed much of the popular writing from the United States by cultural critics on advertising, but these criticisms were predominantly based on advertising and promotional activity before the radical media changes described earlier in this chapter. One set of criticisms was based on the persuasive and pervasive nature of advertising. Advertising is everywhere, cultivating particular attitudes to problems or creating problems where none previously existed. This way of thinking about advertising can be considered as originating from a root metaphor. Root metaphors deeply influence our thinking. They can be specified as principles that guide thought and that can be found in sayings, vivid images, metaphors, and idioms in language. They frame the problems we are dealing with and constrain the ways we think about them (see Lakoff & Johnson, 1980). I have argued (Young, 1990) that the root metaphor that guided this thinking about advertising can be described as "advertising as dry rot." If society is conceived as an old building, then advertising can creep in undetected and influence the very fabric of society, corrupting the basic moral and spiritual values the culture holds dear. Advertising should now be seen in popular imagination as more insidious rather than less, just because it appears in less recognizable forms. For example, one of the issues in the academic literature of the 1970s was the extent to which advertising was flagged as visibly separate from the program context. It was argued that physical signals that were recognizable as such should be used to separate program from advertisement (see, e.g., Palmer & McDowell, 1979), especially when the audience was comprised of children, because they might not be able to recognize the difference.

Advertising at the beginning of the 21st century can be found everywhere in its different forms. Web-based advertising, for example, is not immediately recognizable but is present in banners on Web sites. Little is known about how children understand this form of promotional activity (but see Henke, 1999). Promotional activity such as sponsorship and branding in the context of sporting events, or the use of product placement in popular films, is commonplace. The development of computer technology such as that used in TiVo (see previous discussion) will threaten the existence of spot advertising on TV, because the economics of such advertising depend on being able to guarantee purchasers that an end audience of demographically defined households, based on audience research, is assured. Zapping and replay on demand confounds this data. In addition, marketing activity has developed into so-called "viral marketing" where fashions are socially engineered by the tactical cultivation of youthful opinion leaders. Viral marketing has been aptly described as spreading a message through electronic word of mouth and is a recent development in marketing to children and young people (Procter & Richards, 2002). Agencies are encouraged to be ironic or postmodern in their approach to creative solutions for campaigns that are directed at an ever-more cynical and cool population of "tweens." The landscape looks less recognizable as conventional advertising than it did 20 years ago, and one would predict more anxiety about the presence of advertising now.

The origins of the anxieties that people feel about advertising and marketing to children can be found, in my opinion, in three main sites. One is concerned with the preconceptions and assumptions that are brought to bear about the nature of commercial activity in general and advertising and marketing in particular, and a similar set of visions of what children and childhood are really like. Put the two together and a nightmare scenario emerges, as we see later in this chapter. The second is concerned with the vehicle that carries commercial communications—whether it is the Internet, mobile phones, video game consoles, or television. And, finally, there is the issue of the location of such activity, whether it is the home, the school, or the mall. Let's look at these in turn.

ADVERTISING AND CHILDREN

Advertising is one aspect of the general social arrangements in any culture that surround the economic activities of commerce and trade, and can be seen as its communicative function. Commercial communications have a positive role to play inasmuch as information is transmitted from trader or manufacturer to consumer or retailer, as well as between and within commercial organizations. This flow can have a facilitative effect like any other communication network, because all participants have access to information and can make decisions more effectively and rapidly. Taken with the spur of competition, it can be argued that advertising "lubricates" the economy. Although advertising as oil is an image that advertisers and businesspeople are keen to promote, it is not one that is shared by commentators on advertising, who tend to be more critical in their comments. For example,

Leiss, Kline, and Jhally (1997) suggested that the messages in advertising tap into our most serious concerns, like interpersonal and family relationships, the use of affluence, our sense of happiness and contentment, and so on. Unnikrishnan and Bajpai (1996) argued that young consumers will also believe that advertising tells us our way of life will change for the better if we buy, use, and own certain products. Jhally (1987) underscored this theme by warning of "commodity fetishism" by which people worship commodities as a result of advertising, and that advertising creates false expectations that make consumption a habit or way of life. Thus, a picture of advertising in the popular imagination emerges in which it is seen as a major source of influence on our ways of thinking, feeling, and acting on the material world. There is also an unease that this influence is beyond our control and that it cultivates images that are detrimental to our well-being. Whether this is actually true is irrelevant to the argument that focuses on why people in general are concerned about advertising and, in particular, advertising directed at children. Although "the consumer as victim" is only one of the images of the consumer that has emerged in the discourse surrounding advertising and consumption (see Gabriel & Lang, 1995), it is a representation that is enduring.

There are other concerns about advertising that are very central to the argument about advertising to children. Advertising carries information, but this information is not just a factual representation of what's in the product or the brand. Exactly what lies beyond factual information is difficult to establish, but it would appear that the other factors can be subsumed under the general head of information that is designed to influence us emotionally. The cold presentation of facts about a brand is better processed by some sort of calculus of costs and benefits (i.e., in a rational way, perhaps, bounded by "satisficing"; Simon, 1978), because of constraints imposed by time or circumstances or the sheer number of criteria to consider. Beyond that there are various ways of emotionally communicating the various selling propositions about a brand. First, it has always been generally accepted that some legitimate exaggeration about the brand is acceptable. This puffery is characteristic of the advertising genre and involves presentation so that food always looks perfect, clothes are immaculate, and so on. But there is more to advertising than that. It uses rhetoric, both visual and verbal (Forceville, 1996), that is carefully designed to evoke emotions about the brand. In a sense, it is no different than the imagery that poets use to invoke complex feelings in a reader or the verbal skills of a lawyer who attempts to convince a jury of his or her client's innocence. Many people will see poetry as a legitimate use of rhetoric, and it would be difficult to argue that children should not be exposed to poetry because they are too young. However, the use of rhetoric in the court and in advertising might be seen as an activity to which it's dangerous to expose children. Why? Because of truth. In poetry, truth is in the words and the emotions themselves, but in advertising and court, rhetoric gets in the way of truth. Children, then, are too young for advertising just because they can't counterargue and, in general, stand outside the flow of communication and critically evaluate it. This inability to erect cognitive defenses against advertising suggests that advertising should be banned for children or at least children younger than a certain age.

There is another aspect of advertising that should be considered—the promotional aspect. Advertising, quite simply, provides biased information, so that the case that is made for the product is the best case that can be made. In this respect, advertising is similar to advocacy in court (where the case for the client is paramount) or self-promotion (e.g., presenting oneself at interview). My contention would be that the factual information that is there for consumer evaluation, together with rhetorical and promotional affect-based communicative forms, produce a heady cocktail in the marketing mix in general and in advertising in particular. Reason and emotion sit together awkwardly at the best of times (in Anglo-Saxon cultures in particular), and their presence in the same message called advertising means that advertising will tend to be demonized.

I mentioned earlier that the language used in marketing to kids can be insensitive at best and offensive at worst, and in that sense marketers to children are their own worst enemy. But there is another theme that appeared to emerge when I looked through the various invitations and promotions for commercial conferences on advertising to children: The words *children* or *child* are rarely if ever used. Instead, these little people were *kids*. *Kids* and *children* are not the same, and the connotations are very different. Children go to school and wash regularly. They are dutiful and eat their vegetables. They are born pure and need to be protected from the sinful adult world. Kids, on the other hand, are junior anarchists! They make a lot of noise, don't ever sit still, and play tricks with grownups as their victims. *Bart Simpson* is a kid. Kidhood (as opposed to childhood) is a wild and free time, and kids have license to do what they want until responsibility comes along. They're imps, and of all the images of childhood, the imp and the innocent are the main ones. Kids become tweenies. Kids are streetwise, hang out in malls, and love the right stuff. Marketers love kids. It seems, then, that advertisers and marketers appropriate an image or a social construction of children and childhood that best suits their ends. Kids, the robust self-contained and self-maintained streetwise creation, will be comfortable in the world of commerce, goods, and services. But will the child? Certainly not! Children need protection from the strange mix of reason and emotion—of hard sell and subterfuge—that is advertising in the public imagination. It is no accident that Vance Packard, in his notorious book *The Hidden Persuaders* (Packard, 1962), entitled one of his chapters "The Psycho-seduction of Children." The anxieties caused by advertising to children are based on an implied relationship in which advertising is seen as the seducer and the child is viewed as an innocent.

It's not just the world of advertising that is seen as dangerous for children but good for kids—the world of commerce and industry is often viewed as malevolent, and there are historical grounds for assuming this was driven by changes in the economy and consequent constructions of childhood. Kessen (1979) argued that the changes from a rural to an industrial economy in the United States in the 19th century resulted in far-reaching changes in the way people viewed the family and childhood. Because many West European societies have also gone through this rapid period of change, and because many third-world societies are now also going in this direction, Kessen's claims must be taken seriously. The world of commerce and industry was centered round the town. This was where men worked—this was where wheeling and dealing, haggling, arguing, buying and selling, and negotiation in smoke-filled saloons occurred. The world of commerce and industry was rough, tough, sinful, and self-interested. In contrast, the world of the home—where men returned with a "Hi honey, I'm home"—was romanticized and transformed into an idealized world of domestic bliss and motherly values. Childhood was sentimentalized. Children were to be protected from the decadence of downtown, and to be a child was to be innocent and pure. This vision of home as a sanctuary was, of course, not solely a result of large-scale changes in patterns of work in the United States. Home in a frontier setting was a refuge, a place that needed to be protected from marauders, real or imagined. Home was where childhood and motherhood existed and thrived.

There are two aspects of advertising to children that are especially relevant in the context of new technology: the vehicle that carries advertising and the context in which advertising is found. I next look at these in turn.

Although advertising has a history that goes back several centuries, it was only in the 20th century that its audiovisual potential was realized with first radio and film advertising and then television advertising. In the United Kingdom, television was seen in a positive light when it was introduced, and until 1955 all television broadcast was regulated by the state, under the control of the BBC. The BBC had long stood for respectability and firm moral righteousness and, at that time, memories of the World War II and the fight against Nazism were very much alive. Television did not carry advertising. The BBC's reputation and the absence of advertising or even any hint of commercial activity meant that television was safely corralled from the imagined perils of the commercial world. Consequently, TV was seen as a window on the world and as a new hearth that would bring the family closer. Indeed, as Seiter (1993) argued, this image was also common at that time in the United States, where TV was seen as promoting family harmony and togetherness in the media. This image did not last long. I would argue that a contributory factor was the introduction of advertising, with all the connotations of the adult world of commerce. The window on the world image—in which the family extends its horizons and gains a wider, more informed vision of the workings of the external world—can only exist if the medium (television) is essentially seen as benign, credible, and trustworthy. Given a state broadcasting system and a respectful and trusting population (as Britain was in the 1950s), then one can adopt this stance. Advertising (and I have argued that advertising has a special privilege as a medium in terms of being perceived as threatening and dangerous to children) is a contributory factor to a change from seeing television as a way of extending one's vision of the world to imagining television as a conduit that allows all sorts of uncontrolled information into the household. The benevolent image of television as a positive vision of all the best that's out there has been replaced by a more scary and malign image of multichannel TV pumping programs that are heavily laced with promotional communications and that are potentially subversive to family life into the sanctity of the home. Television is delivered by satellite and by cable as well as the traditional broadcast route, and there are hundreds of channels carrying commercials, programs that are sponsored, and channels that are devoted to shopping.

Promotional information in the form of television spot advertising is not the only carrier of information that invades the sanctity of the home. Indeed, even 30 years ago radio carried advertising, the mail carrier brought direct mail shots, and newspapers and magazines carried advertising. In most of these examples, however, the ad was clearly identified as separate from the content of either the paper or the TV or radio program. The presence of ads on mobile phones (Jones, 2002), in the context of the Internet, in video games, at sponsored sports—all suggest a blurring of the demarcation lines between advertising and the context in which it occurs. This tendency would suggest public anxiety with advertising to children could increase rather than decrease.

In summary, the nature of advertising to children and the vehicle that carries this advertising will influence the anxiety that people feel about advertising and promoting goods and services to children. I have suggested that the home is perceived as a sacred place that deserves to be protected from the onslaught of commercial communications and, more recently, a similar concern has been voiced about the extent to which commercial sponsorship has invaded schools. Geuens, De Pelsmacker, and Mast (2002) observed that in-school marketing is common in the United Kingdom, extensively practiced in Finland, but banned in Denmark (Atherton & Wells, 1998), so there is no pan-European consistency here. The use of the term *sacred* here may strike some readers as excessive, but there are good anthropological grounds for arguing a case that the child is not just a slippery concept and there are special reasons for invoking the sacred-profane distinction.

Although the distinction is recognized in anthropology and will be familiar to many readers through the work of the well-known sociologist Emile Durkheim (1915), it was the publication of a much-cited paper in the late 1980s (Belk, Wallendorf, & Sherry, 1989) that marked the extension of the idea into consumer behavior. Here it was argued that religion was now secularized and aspects of the secular, consumption in particular, were made sacred. This neat reversal could be observed in certain everyday patterns of behavior such as shopping, creating a home, and collecting. Belk et al.'s interpretation of the distinction is wide ranging and also psychologically valuable, and can be applied in the context of children and advertising. Before doing so, however, I describe the terms and how they can be applied to human behavior and experience.

Many behaviors in everyday life can be characterized as ritual. For example, we have set ways of approaching and behaving toward religious objects, whether they are the texts of the Koran, the sign of the cross in Christian religions, or how to circle round a stupa in Nepal. *Sacred* and *profane* are terms borrowed and extended from their original meaning, and can be understood as the elevated or special versus the ordinary. They are complementary terms in that one can only be defined and understood relative to the other. Although Belk et al. identified 12 properties of the sacred, there is no reason to suppose all 12 would have to be present in order for a case for sanctification to be made. For example, the events of September 2001 in New York and Washington are often referred to in a standard way as "9/11" or "September 11" and the New York site of this tragedy is known as "Ground Zero." Proposals for a memorial of remembrance and the presence of pilgrims bear witness to the need to sanctify, although the presence of ecstasy and flow (in Belk et al.'s list) are obviously absent in their literal sense but present in many as intense grief.

Belk et al. took us on a tour of some of the sacred sites of contemporary culture, including shopping malls, department stores, and, of course, the home. Sanctity can be achieved in other domains, such as kinds of time, objects (e.g., the automobile), symbols, and experiences (e.g., eating). The school, in my contention, is a good candidate for elevation. Schools are places where children are educated, and although the rituals are less obvious now than a generation ago they are still intrinsic to the process in a transformed way. Children may not sit in rows and teachers no longer wear cap and gown (as they used to in the United Kingdom), but there are still expectations for group behavior and rituals such as graduation, sorority and fraternity initiations, and so on. In addition, the history of schooling in many cultures overlaps with the history of monastic life and scholarship. One of the characteristics of the sacred is the expectation that certain behaviors are inappropriate or even taboo. These prescribed behaviors are learned as culturally appropriate patterns and can change over time. Funerals can be formal and solemn in England, where people wear black, or noisy and emotional in China, with participants dressed in white. Religious services might have been formal, serious, and solemn 50 years ago, but now are often informal with laughter, praise, and music. I would contend that schools are places where information is critically presented and both sides of any argument get a hearing. Education is evidence based and rhetoric is kept firmly in its place in the literature and poetry classes. The peculiar mix of reason and emotion that characterizes advertising is then seen as inappropriate in the setting of school. Cook (2000) argued that the literature on marketing research in the 20th century represented and construed the child in certain ways. In particular, by the 1930s, it was recognized that children develop through stages and that marketing was an activity that should be tailored to the child's perspectives and preferences. It is interesting to note how even at that time and in the 1950s books on marketing to kids were available, based on developmental psychology (Gilbert, 1957; Grumbine, 1938). This set the stage for the evolution of an image of children as competent and knowledgeable young people—an image far removed from the gullible innocents seduced by the wiles and guiles of advertisers. By the 1960s and 1970s, according to Cook, the pioneering work of McNeal (1964) and Wells (1965) established the child[1] as a "little consumer" with preexisting consumer desires. Finally, in the last couple of decades of the 20th century, the precocious ("growing older younger") and knowledgeable vision of an autonomous child emerged in the marketing literature (see, e.g., Acuff, 1997). This was and is one powerful kid, *par excellence*, who is capable of influencing household decisions, is actively knowledgeable about products, and is quite capable of making purchase decisions as an autonomous consumer.

I am not supporting that the "child" or the "kid" is the right or correct vision of what younger people are like, and I would suggest that if we take the idea of childhood

---

[1]Lest it be thought I'm abandoning the distinction between "kid" and "child" as separate concepts in the discourse surrounding "small people" in the commercial world, I'm using "child" here as a term of convenience!

as a social construction seriously then there is no correct version of childhood, and society gets the childhood and children it defines, uses, and deserves. All that one is left with is, perhaps, a politically correct vision of childhood (perhaps with expressions like "younger people" or even "people of youth"?). And even this vision is cast in the image of the autonomous kid as it recognizes respect and an equal status with other groups. There is a way out, and that is to find out what psychologists know about child development and the strengths and limitations of the growing person. Because unlike ethnic and racial categories of people there is some biology and growth in child development, and the developmental psychologist might just be able to make claims about truth and not merely be a source of so-called "expert" or "quasi-expert" knowledge that has equal status with lay perceptions.

ADVERTISING LITERACY

So where can we take this slippery idea of the child faced with the world of advertising? The main argument in this section is that there is a set of competencies and skills that, taken together, constitute being able to understand this peculiar medium of communication called advertising. There is no one skill that suddenly emerges and then the child understands and has effectively become an adult viewer. One can argue, however, that there are several occasions—from about 5 or 6 years of age until 12 years of age—when claims can be made that the child now understands major aspects of advertising and this understanding is cumulative. Although one's literacy with advertising and promotional material in general develops through adolescence and adulthood,[2] there is a case, and I shall put it, that by about 8 years of age children have a good-enough understanding such that they cannot be considered as a special audience requiring special regulation.

Let's start at the beginning, at the point when the marketers become interested in reaching subjects—the toddler years. According to the various norms (Berndt, 1997), children in the United States are able to walk well about 13 months, run by 16 months, and pedal a tricycle at 24 months. They also go into supermarkets, either walking or running with Mom or sitting in the cart. They certainly watch TV. Hence, they are quite capable of seeing brands in promotional contexts and requesting brands by gestures and early language forms such as "gimme dat" or "want dat." Of course, they are not economic actors at this stage, and the market for toddlers is a market for families. However, they do recognize brands and commercial symbols such as logos (McNeal, 1987). According to Derscheid, Kwon, and Fang (1996), this recognition generates preferences that can, for some 2-year-olds, become an obsession: "Parents may often wonder why their two-year-old insists on wearing the same outfit everyday. Often this outfit has a particular symbol that the child really enjoys" (p. 1172). Derscheid's own research concluded that preschool children's recognition of symbols was related to the frequency of media exposure,

---

[2]One could argue that a complete understanding is only reached when one has read and understood all the extensive writings on "decoding" or "reading" advertising by semioticians, linguists, and assorted obscure theorists!

especially TV and books, an argument that Ellen Seiter (1993) had put forward previously. More recently, Dammler and Middelmann-Motz (2002) reported that 81% of 3- to 6-year-olds remember having seen the Coca-Cola logo and 69% remember the McDonald's "yellow M".

But do they understand what advertising is all about? Although the research that surrounds the child's understanding of advertising intent often produces results that are contradictory and sensitive to methodology, there is a clear consensus here. Children younger than 5 years of age simply see advertising as entertainment, although they might put forward other reasons it is on TV, such as "so we can go to the bathroom" or "gives us a break." In my 1990 review (Young, 1990), it was very clear that the occasional research article reporting that children could understand the selling intent of advertising (e.g., Donohue, Henke, & Donohue, 1980) could be criticized as having serious methodological flaws and that the overwhelming trend was that children thought advertising was there for fun. And this is in line with a well-established finding by Piaget, that children interpret reality at this age as being what is experienced through the senses. In other words, children are not yet capable of inferring beyond the realm of their senses. The advertising they see makes them laugh and smile and feel good—that's why it's there. This theory can also explain why children sometimes provide structural explanations of the difference between advertising and programming ("ads are short but programs are long") because they are referring to *spot* advertising where there is a very obvious, perceptually based, concrete difference between advertising and programs. However, as I argued earlier, spot advertising is dying with new technology and advertising is now with us in forms that are not obviously perceptually different from programming. In order to know the difference between advertising and programming, the child must be capable of diagnosing the intent behind advertising and establish some rules for "reading" advertising that are different from those employed with other televisual genres.

There is some evidence that some 5- to 6-year-olds can understand one aspect of the genre called television spot advertising. Advertising is promotional. By this I mean that it only communicates the best about a brand. In this sense it is similar to other forms of promotion in everyday life, such as self-promotion or the promotion of one's family or team or immediate social group. There is an identifiable genre of communication that has the quality we can call "interested" (May, 1981)—that means the communicator has a particular goal to achieve and the communication will be designed with the interests of the communicator in mind. Many communications are interested in that sense, and it could be argued that in today's electronic world—with the constant ebb and flow of institutional communications and interpersonal e-mails, texts, and face-to-face communications—the dominant mode is an interested one. We're all pushing to promote, to advocate, to get our own way. May's small paper (which deserves a wider audience) has a resonance at the beginning of the 21st century. The last refuge of disinterested communication is the school or the academy—maybe that is why it is seen as sacred and why we want to maintain it as a commercial-free zone.

Young (2000) wanted to measure the child's understanding of promotional communication, by giving children examples of television commercials that broke the promotional rule and then asking them if these rule-breakers would make suitable TV commercials. Seven TV commercials were chosen from a pool of TV ads that had been made over a 20-year span. Each commercial had a structure that Berger (1974) called the "pain-pill-pleasure" narrative. This narrative starts with a problem that gives the actor some pain or discomfort. Maybe it's washing that's not whiter than white, or a cough that keeps one awake, or a face that feels dry and chapped in cold weather. The brand is brought into the narrative, and the final part of the ad shows the pleasure and absence of pain that consuming the brand brings. We presented to each child a video of each of the seven commercials, but the last part (the pleasure bit) was missing. Afterward, we showed each child three alternative pictures simultaneously. One was a still from the actual ending showing the actor smiling broadly with the branded product in view; the second was a control with the actor's face changed to make it look neutral and no brand in sight; and the third was a shot from the missing ending that displaced the brand, but the images had been changed so that the ending was funny and amusing but the brand was shown in a negative way. For example, in an ad for face cream, the third type of picture showed the actor's face covered in spots, and in another ad for cough candies, the actor was shown being violently sick! We then asked each child to choose the picture that "would be the best one to use if the ad's shown on TV."

We tested 133 children, aged from 4 and 5 years to 8 and 9 years. It was found that the majority of the 4- to 5-year-olds chose the funny ending that broke the promotional rule; this result confirms what we know about younger children's understanding of advertising. After that age, however, the majority of children demonstrated a growing awareness that it was *not* appropriate to choose an ending that provided a negative portrayal of the brand and, by the age of 7 or 8, many were capable of justifying their choice by claiming that "you wouldn't be able to sell any stuff if you said bad things about it."

Thus, somewhere between 5 and 6 years, through the years of middle childhood, until adolescence, children experience a change and growth in advertising literacy that needs to be charted. There is some evidence (see Young, 1990) that between 5 and 6 and 8 and 9 years of age the child begins to understand that advertising is not just promotional as described earlier, but is also assistive (provides information), commercial (relates to buying and selling), and persuasive (tries to get you to buy)—although there is some conceptual and methodological confusion in the literature. Some recent papers have informed the debate.

Bulmer (2001) conducted focus groups with 5- to 8-year-old children in New Zealand. Although the classic focus group is based on a vision of talk and discussion as a spontaneous process within a group of participants, where themes emerge naturally without intervention, from the paper's description the groups used by Bulmer appeared to be more directive, with the facilitator asking questions. Results were presented in tables, by percentage of occurrence. Bulmer concluded that 5- to 6-year-olds found television advertising to be informative and entertaining. They were aware of the fact that TV commercials "told you about things to buy" and what was "new in the shops," but there was no reference to the persuasive function of advertising until about 7 years of age, when comments like "gets you to buy things" predominated. Bulmer certainly claimed a sophisticated level of understanding with her 8-year-old groups: "By eight years of age almost all children seemed to have some concept of the multi-stage process of supply chains and believe that profit is the desired result of most advertising. There were elaborate explanations of the commercial motivations of advertisers. These children also understood that advertising devices are used to enhance persuasion and motivates desires and buying behaviour" (p. 11). Hence, for example, she cited the following response as typical of 8-year-old explanations: "Getting people to come to your shop and get them to give you so much money to buy groceries and stuff, and get so rich that you can buy anything you want" (p. 11).

Although the previous quote is slightly ambiguous about which one of the parties to the transaction will "get so rich," the fact that children of this age can take into account the actual and anticipated consequences of economic transactions based on the results of promotional activity demonstrates a telling sophistication in New Zealand children. It is important, however, to take focus group data as indicative of the capabilities of *some* children, and not as providing normative data.

Pine and Nash (2002) presented evidence that young children (ranging from 3.8 years to 6.5 years) who watched more commercial television requested a greater number of items from Father Christmas (Santa Claus) and also requested more branded items. Pine and Nash additionally took a sample from Sweden, where advertising to children is not permitted, and found that the Swedish children asked for significantly fewer items. As well, logs were kept of what was advertised on commercial television in the United Kingdom during the research period, but TV viewing data by the child was assessed by self-report or parent's report. However, it is difficult to draw conclusions from studies that attempt to correlate viewing patterns with subsequent behavior and it would certainly be inappropriate to draw conclusions about the effects of Sweden's lack of TV advertising to children on the Swedish children's lower interest in the world of goods and services. There is no way of knowing, for example, the extent to which parental mediation or cultural mediation affects the process of requesting gifts from Father Christmas. For example, children who watch a lot of commercial TV might come from a different parental subculture, with different values and attitudes toward the branded, material world of consumption compared with children who claim, either themselves or through parents, not to watch much commercial TV. Swedish culture might have a completely different set of values surrounding what's "good for" children as contrasted with U.K. kids, and that factor could mediate.

Chan (2000) looked at Chinese children's understanding and comprehension of television advertising in Hong Kong. A quota sample of 448 children—made up of 32 girls and 32 boys each from kindergarten and Grades 1 thru 6—were interviewed in May 1998. The results indicated that children in Grade 2 (aged 7 and 8 years) were beginning to understand what television advertising was and were aware of its persuasive intention. Over one third of older children from Grade 4 (aged 9 and 10 years) understood that television stations carry advertising in order to make money. Like children in the West, these children's main reason for liking and disliking commercials depended on their entertainment element. An understanding of television advertising, recall of brands from slogans, and comprehension of advertising content were consistently related to the cognitive development of children. Brand recognition from liked and disliked commercials was strong. Chan's study used interviews with a large sample of children without showing actual television commercials and yet, even under these conditions, 61% of children by 7 or 8 years of age were able to identify the persuasive and commercial function of advertising. It is interesting to note that this methodology—by which results are simply obtained by interview with no televisual props—still resulted in a majority of children understanding these crucial aspects of advertising by 8 years of age. Thirty years ago, the research of Ward and his associates, using a similar methodology, did not show such an understanding even by 11 or 12 years of age. In fact (Young, 1990), only a quarter of 11- to 12-year-olds in Ward's original studies were able to provide an explanation of why commercials were shown on TV that demonstrated an understanding of selling and profit motives. There is a strong case that children's understanding in this area, although influenced by cognitive development, will vary depending on the cultural availability of advertising. As advertising becomes more common, children become more sophisticated in their levels of awareness and comprehension. Chan's research has been extended to mainland China, and preliminary results with focus groups show an emerging understanding by 9- to 12-year-olds in Beijing (Chan & McNeal, 2002).

Jarlbro (2001) reviewed the literature and research on children and television advertising conducted during the last 6 years of the 20th century. This review complemented an earlier survey initiated by the Swedish Consumer Agency and conducted by Erling Bjurström, (Bjurström, 1994), which covered work done up to 1994. Jarlbro's study was far from comprehensive in its coverage of the research and it tended to focus on and criticize the research findings in the publications used by the advertising industry to defend television advertising to children. The study's aim was, therefore, explicitly polemical, and must be seen as a defense of the Swedish ban on television advertising directed to children (up to 12 years of age).

The polemical nature of the study seriously undermines its claims to scrutinize from a scientific viewpoint the research being done. This defect can be detected in Jarlbro's presumption that it is the funders of any research who determine the results of any research on television advertising and children. For example, she argued that the fact that research results do not agree on the age at which children can distinguish between ads and programs on TV could be explained by the use of different survey techniques, and that the choice of these techniques ultimately is "a consequence of who financed the survey" (p. 13). Although the use of different methods and techniques could—as one factor among others—explain why research results do not entirely coincide, there is no overall correspondence between the choice of methods and the funding of the research on TV advertising and children. The choice of methods and theoretical approaches varies among researchers funded by governmental authorities, consumer agencies, and consumer organizations as well as among those funded by the advertising industries or other groups with interests in TV ads to children. Supporters of advertising or opponents of advertising don't solely rely on research they have funded themselves, and can take into account any results in the public domain, with a preference for those that come through the peer review process. Jarlbro's unwarranted conclusion that the funding party, so to speak, "pays" for research results gave her report a flavor of anti-intellectualism, because it more or less explicitly denied that there is any independent and free research regarding how children are affected or influenced by TV advertising. Jarlbro's view was that the research on TV ads and children should be independent and free from nonscientific interests. However, for Jarlbro this view posed an intriguing paradox, because she so obviously spoke in the interest of the Swedish Consumer Agency, the group that funded her report.

Moore and Lutz (2000) were interested in how children of different ages related advertising of a product or brand to the experience of consuming or using it. Robertson and Rossiter (1974) had argued that discriminating between products as advertising and products as experienced was one of the skills that made up the ability of being able to understand the purpose of a television commercial. In addition, there are several theories of how adults integrate the commercial communications surrounding a product and the anticipated and actual experience. For example, a person who is literate with advertising will assume that the brand will be presented in the best possible light and will partially discount claims made in promotional material, thus forming lower-order expectations of the actual consumption experience.[3] Using a mixture of quantitative and qualitative techniques, they found that younger children, aged 7 and 8 years, had greater difficulty integrating the world within the ad with the product as experienced. This may be a result of the limitations of the information-processing capacities of the child at this age, or it could be that the younger children are less motivated to carefully reconcile the world of advertising (with its hyperbole and fantasy) with the world of trial purchase and consumption simply because they are less involved in the economic act of purchase and consumption, either as an individual or as a younger member of the family. Older children, aged 10 and 11 years, were more capable of integrating the information available in the brand as represented in the advertisement with the experience of consumption, in that exposure to the ad was able to "frame" the experience of the product. Thus, by the age of 10 or 11 years, children are capable of taking advertising into account by generating expectations of what the product might be like based on their knowledge of the promotional nature of advertising.

Perhaps the most important paper to emerge in the last few years was by John (1999). This review of the literature on consumer socialization of children over the last quarter of the 20th century constituted a landmark in the literature, and it must

---

[3]In other words, the consumer sees the marketing and responds, "Well—they would say that anyway" (discounting claims) and "I bet it's not as good as all that" (lowering expectations).

be looked at closely in the context of the child's knowledge about and understanding of advertising. John's model of child development, although recognizing the validity of much of Piaget's stage-developmental theories, assumes three stages in the processing of information. Children under 7 years of age are seen as limited processors. In the language of information processing, they have mediational deficiencies that make storage and retrieval difficult even when they are prompted and cued to do so. Children over 12 years of age, on the other hand, are able to use various strategies for storing, retrieving, and utilizing information, and this can be done in the absence of prompting and cuing. Between the ages of 7 and 11, however, although children might be able to deploy strategies to enhance information storage and retrieval that are similar to those used by older children, they need to be aided by explicit prompts and cues. How is this theory relevant to the debate about the child's understanding of advertising? As described earlier, it is generally accepted with a few exceptions that children under the age of 5 years only see advertising as entertainment and have a limited understanding, based on the perceptual qualities of spot advertising (they are short episodes between or within programs), of it. The evidence also points toward a growing understanding emerging between 5 and 8 years of age of the various functions and intents behind advertising—that it is promotional, informative, commercial, and persuasive. And yet, according to John, children still have a problem with advertising until 12 years of age. This problem relates to access and utilization of that knowledge. In a sense, although the understanding is there and can be used to critically cope with advertising, it may not necessarily be accessed and used in evaluating advertising messages.

John also made a case that there is a skill concerning the child's ability to take the perspective of other people (Selman, 1980) that develops from early childhood to adolescence, and that these developmental stages should be taken into account when considering the child's understanding of advertising. Children before the age of 6 years are unable to take the perspective of other people and view the world from their own point of view. Between 6 and 8 years of age, children realize that others have different opinions or motives, but believe that this comes from the other person having different information rather than adopting a different perspective on a situation. Between 8 and 10 years, children acquire an understanding that people with the same information can have different opinions or motives and can take this into account and consider another person's point of view. Development does not stop at 10 years of age, however, and being able to simultaneously consider the other person's point of view emerges from 10 to 12 years. This skill is vital in interpersonal negotiation and persuasion when people interact socially. Finally, the young adolescent can take the mature detached position of seeing another person's perspective as relating to social group membership or the social system within which they operate.

Both of these developmental sequences—information processing and perspective taking—are important when considering how literate children are when coping with advertising in all its multifunctional aspects. Being able to acquire and, importantly, utilize understandings about advertising and being able to understand the advertiser's point of view seem to be important elements of advertising literacy. Does this mean then that advertising to children under age 12 is unfair, and that this evidence should be used when regulating and controlling what, if any, advertising should be shown to children? Certainly the evidence should be considered, and it is not surprising that understanding such a complex genre like advertising has a developmental trajectory at least to adolescence. Bjurström (1994) was suggesting this when he concluded the relevant section of his report with the words "it is only around or after the age of 12 that we can be more certain that most children have developed a fuller understanding of the purpose or objective of advertising" (p. 42). This answer, in my opinion, is very different from the answer to the question "When do most children have an *adequate* or good-enough knowledge of the intent and purpose of advertising? Most of the evidence (in cultures with an experience of advertising) points to 8 years of age as the time when this emerges. It may be that children older than 8 years but younger than 12 apply this knowledge erratically, but that could apply to many people of different ages. The minimal requirements for understanding that advertising has an intent to persuade people to buy goods and services, that it informs and entertains but presents promotional material, are in place in most children by 8 years of age.

Martin (1997) conducted a meta-analysis of the child's understanding of the intent of advertising. A meta-analysis mines the various databases and archives in which results are reported in academic papers, and computes an effect size. It is then possible to amalgamate the results from several studies in order to draw general conclusions.[4] Although the author did not cite any single definitive age as the consensus when advertising is understood, two conclusions are worthy of note. One is that the data from 30 years of published work "suggests that younger children understand better the intent of advertising now than in previous years" (p. 214), which would suggest that kids are getting more sophisticated with advertising. The other, more sobering finding was that the samples were limited to predominantly White children and that when African-American children were sampled the lack of awareness of the purpose of advertising was considerably greater.[5]

AND IN CONCLUSION …?

In summary, by the time the child has reached about 5 or 6 years of age, he or she is beginning to acquire the rudiments of advertising literacy that are essential to the

---

[4]A problem with meta-analyses is that papers without significant results or those that don't show differences between groups in the expected direction stand a worse chance of being published in peer-reviewed journals, where the pressure to publish is extensive and growing, than do papers that provide significant results. Consequently, there is a bias in favor of the status quo or received wisdom at the time.

[5]It is always difficult to establish just why certain socioeconomic groups are unaware of the purpose of certain social arrangements such as advertising. I have argued before (Young, 1990) that awareness requires a certain critical detachment and recognition of process—where things come from and where things are going. Such an understanding is important only for those groups who are empowered to effect changes or else this knowledge is irrelevant to their daily lives and an existential recognition that "life's like that" is a more appropriate response. Certainly it would be patronizing and unacceptable to attribute a lack of awareness to a certain lack of savvy with these cultural forms. In addition, there are all sorts of problems with the testing or assessment situation to do with lack of interest, wariness of ulterior motives behind the questions, and so on.

cognitive awareness that advertising is a genre of communications with its own rules. These range from a simple promotional principle such as "you can't say bad things about the brand in an ad" through an understanding of the fact that advertising gives information to an awareness of why this information is promotional and persuasive. This last understanding of the role of advertising in the commercial world and its relationship to the production and consumption of goods and services is, according to some recent work, demonstrable in 8-year-olds. As more cross-cultural evidence emerges, however—and this area also has a history with evidence accumulating back to the early 1970s in the United States—it becomes clearer that norms of understanding are dependent on the sophistication with advertising, marketing, and promotional activity within that culture, and in that sense will depend on place and time.

REFERENCES

Acuff, D. S. (1997). *What kids buy and why.* New York: Free Press.

Atherton, M., & Wells, J. (1998, September/October). Business involvement in schools. *Consumer Policy Review,* pp.184–188.

Berger, A. A. (1974). Drug advertising and the pain, pill, pleasure model. *Journal of Drug Issues, 4,* 208–212.

Belk, R. W., Wallendorf, M., & Sherry, J. F., Jr. (1989). The sacred and the profane in consumer behavior: Theodicy on the odyssey. *Journal of Consumer Research, 16,* 1–38.

Berndt, T. J. (1997). *Child development* (2nd ed.). Madison, WI: Brown & Benchmark.

Bjurström, E. (1994). *Children and television advertising: A critical study of international research concerning the effects of TV-commercials on children.* Stockholm: The National Swedish Board for Consumer Policies.

Bulmer, S. (2001). *Children's perceptions of advertising.* Working paper series No. 01-05. Massey University at Albany, Auckland, New Zealand.

Chan, K. (2000). Hong Kong children's understanding of television advertising. *Journal of Marketing Communications, 6,* 37–52.

Chan, K., & McNeal, J. U. (2002). Children's perceptions of television advertising in urban China. *International Journal of Advertising and Marketing to Children, 3*(3), 69–79.

Clarke, J. (2002). The Internet according to kids. *International Journal of Advertising and Marketing to Children. 3*(2), 39–52.

Cook, D. T. (2000). The other "child study": Figuring children as consumers in market research, 1910s–1990s. *The Sociological Quarterly, 41*(3), 487–507.

Dammler, A., & Middelmann-Motz, A. V. (2002). I want one with Harry Potter on it. *International Journal of Advertising and Marketing to Children, 3*(2), 3–8.

Derscheid, L. E., Kwon, Y.-H., & Fang, S.-R. (1996). Preschoolers' socialization as consumers of clothing and recognition of symbolism. *Perceptual and Motor Skills, 82,* 1171–1181.

Donohue, T. R., Henke, L. L., & Donohue, W. A. (1980). Do kids know what TV commercials intend? *Journal of Advertising Research, 20*(5), 51–57.

Durkheim, E. (1915). *The elementary forms of the religious life.* London: Allen & Unwin.

Forceville, C. (1996). *Pictorial Metaphor in advertising.* London: Sage.

Gabriel, Y., & Lang, T. (1995). *The unmanageable consumer.* London: Sage.

Geuens, M., De Pelsmacker, P., & Mast, G. (2002). Attitudes of school directors towards in-school marketing: An exploratory study. *International Journal of Advertising and Marketing to Children, 3*(3), 57–67.

Gilbert, E. (1957). *Advertising and marketing to young people.* Pleasantville, NY: Printer's Ink Books.

Grumbine, E. E. (1938). *Reaching juvenile markets: How to advertise, sell, and merchandise through boys and girls.* New York: McGraw-Hill.

Henke, L. L. (1999). Children, advertising, and the Internet: An exploratory study. In D. W. Schumann & E. Thorson (Eds.), *Advertising and the World Wide Web* (pp. 73–80). Mahwah, NJ: Lawrence Erlbaum Associates.

Jarlbro, G. (2001). *Children and television advertising: The players, the arguments and the research during the period 1994–2000.* Stockholm: Swedish Consumer Agency.

Jhally, S. (1987). *The codes of advertising: Fetishism and the political economy of meaning in the consumer society.* London: Pinter.

John, D. R. (1999). Consumer socialization of children: A retrospective look at twenty-five years of research. *Journal of Consumer Research, 26*(3), 183–213.

Jones, A. (2002). Wireless marketing: The linking value of text messaging. *International Journal of Advertising and Marketing to Children, 3*(2), 39–44.

Kessen, W. (1979). The American child and other cultural inventions. *American Psychologist, 34*(10), 815–820.

Leiss, W., Kline, S., & Jhally, S. (1997). *Social communication in advertising* (2nd ed.). London: Routledge.

Lewis, M. K., & Hill, A. J. (1998). Food advertising on British children's television: A content analysis and experimental study with nine-year-olds. *International Journal of Obesity, 22,* 206–214.

Lakoff, G., & Johnson, M. (1980). *Metaphors we live by.* Chicago: University of Chicago Press.

Martin, M. C. (1997). Children's understanding of the intent of advertising: A meta-analysis. *Journal of Public Policy & Marketing, 16*(2), 205–216.

May, J. D. (1981). Practical reasoning: Extracting useful information from partial informants. *Journal of Pragmatics, 5,* 45–59.

McNeal, J. (1964). *Children as consumers.* Austin: Bureau of Business Research, University of Texas.

McNeal, J. (1987). *Children as consumers: Insights and implications.* Lexington, MA: Lexington Books.

Melody, W. H. (1973). *Children's television: The economics of exploitation.* New Haven, CT: Yale University Press.

Melody, W. H., & Ehrlich, W. (1974). Children's TV commercials: The vanishing policy options. *Journal of Communication, 24,* 113–125.

Moore, E. S., & Lutz, R. J. (2000). Children, advertising, and product experience: A multimethod enquiry. *Journal of Consumer Research, 27*(1), 31–48.

Packard, V. (1962). *The hidden persuaders.* London: Pelican.

Palmer, E. L., & McDowell, C. N. (1979). Program/commercial separators in children's television programming. *Journal of Communication, 29,* 197–201.

Pine, K., & Nash, A. (2001). Dear Santa: The effects of television advertising on young children. *International Journal of Behavioral Development, 26*(6), 529–539.

Pollay, R. W. (1986). The distorted mirror: Reflections on the unintended consequences of advertising. *Journal of Marketing, 50,* 18–36.

Powell, J., & Wicken, G. (2002). US kids and British children—identical or incomparable? *International Journal of Advertising and Marketing to Children, 3*(3), 33–40.

Procter, J., & Richards, M. (2002). Beyond pester power, into word-of-mouth marketing. *International Journal of Advertising and Marketing to Children, 3*(3), 3–11.

Robertson, T. S., & Rossiter, J. (1974). Children and commercial persuasion: An attributional theory analysis. *Journal of Consumer Research, 1,* 13–20.

Seiter, E. (1993). *Sold separately: Children and parents in consumer culture.* New Brunswick, NJ: Rutgers University Press.

Selman, R. L. (1980). *The growth of interpersonal understanding.* New York: Academic Press.

Simon, H. A. (1978). Information-processing theory of human problem solving. In W. K. Estes (Ed.), *Handbook of learning and cognitive processes* (vol. 5, pp. 271–195). Hillsdale NJ: Lawrence Erlbaum Associates.

Unnikrishnan, N., & Bajpai, S. (1996). *The impact of television advertising on children.* New Delhi: Sage.

Wells, W. (1965). Communicating with children. *Journal of Advertising Research, 5*(1), 1–12.

Young, B. M. (1990). *Television advertising and children.* Oxford, UK: Oxford University Press.

Young, B. M. (2000). The child's understanding of promotional communication. *International Journal of Advertising and Marketing to Children, 2*(3), 191–203.

Future Faces of Selling to Children

Sandra L. Calvert
Georgetown University

In an IBM television commercial, a middle-aged man is caught by a nun as he tries to fish coins from a fountain to purchase a drink from a machine. Meanwhile, a young woman pulls out her cell phone, points it at a vending machine, clicks a button, and a Coke immediately pops out into the slot below. She walks off with her product, and the company walks off with a record of who she is, where she is, and what she bought with her cell phone.

Television is big business, designed to sell products by delivering large audiences to commercial advertisers (Calvert, 1999). The content is the lure. In the information age, new media will continue this tradition of delivering people to advertisers, but the specific strategies will expand considerably. Technological developments will lead to new business practices—such as the e-commerce example just described—that can get customers to purchase their products. Technological tracking practices, built into devices like cell phones, will make it relatively easy for businesses to "know" in specific detail who their customers are, as well as their likes, dislikes, and buying patterns. Supermarkets already track their customers in such detail. It will be hip, cool, and a sign of status (particularly in youth cultures) to use your cell phone to get a drink from a machine. But there will be an additional cost for convenience and coolness—personal privacy. The kind of detailed information that can be obtained in the IBM wireless e-business commercial will allow businesses to tailor advertising practices to the individual, not just the group.

Young children before the age of about 8 years old do not understand that the intent of advertisements is to persuade them to buy a product (Calvert, 1999). In television advertisements, developmental skills at understanding the intent of advertisers guided policy decisions about how much and what kind of advertisements can be directed at a mass audience of children (Wartella & Ettema, 1974). These same problems in cognitive skills limit children's understanding of the intent of advertisements in our new and emerging interactive media, yet minimal safeguards are in place to meet children's cognitive limitations.

In this chapter, we examine children as a market, past and emerging advertising practices, the cognitive skills that children bring to understanding media advertisements, and policy issues and practices in the advertising arena.

CHILDREN AS A MARKET

Children influence purchasing power by buying or requesting products specifically designed for them as well as for their family (Siegel, Coffey, & Livingston, 2001). Over time, children have increasingly become an important group for generating advertising revenue. Children's buying power doubled from 1960 to 1980, and tripled during the 1990s (Montgomery, 2001). More specifically, in 1997 U.S. children aged 14 and under spent $24 billion dollars and influenced another $188 billion dollars in family purchases (McNeal, 1998). Adolescents, a group very familiar and comfortable with the Internet (Subramanyam, Greenfield, Kraut, & Gross, 2001), spent $141 billion dollars of their own money in the retail sector during 1998 (Russakoff, 1999).

The Internet, as well as television, has become a popular means for directing advertisements toward children. Overall, in 1998 the Internet generated $300 billion dollars in revenue in the United States (Montgomery, 2001) . Children and adolescents are part of that market. In September of 2001, 75% of 14- to 17-year-olds and 65% of 10- to 13-year-olds were Internet users in the United States (U.S. Department of Commerce, 2002). One of the popular online activities for adolescents is shopping (Subramanyam et al., 2001). Similarly, 46% of parents report that children request products that they encounter on the Internet, with CDs and tapes as top choices by kids (Cox, 1999). With such heavy use of the Internet by kids and teens, advertisers have a unique opportunity to brand their products and create loyalty for them (Nielsen/Net Ratings, 2002).

The products directed at children via television advertisements have remained remarkably consistent over time. These products focus on four primary categories: toys, cereals, candy, and fast food (Calvert, 1999). Seasonal variations in advertising strategies consistently lead to an increased number of toy advertisements appearing on airwaves during the Christmas buying season (Kunkel, 2001). These same kinds of products are directed at children online (Siegel et al., 2001), with television advertisements being able to send children to Web sites to purchase those products.

Although many of these same products are directed at children visiting online sites, the less regulated environment of the Internet leads to more types of products directed at children, particularly adolescents. On the Internet, Web sites promote products such as alcohol and tobacco, even though these products cannot be advertised to minors on television (Williams, Montgomery, & Pasnik, 1997). More specifically, although alcohol and tobacco are illegal products for minors, one cannot determine the age of those who visit online sites without violating every person's privacy. Moreover, young people associate products like alcohol and tobacco with coming of age, finding them desirable (Kunkel, 2001).

PAST AND EMERGING ADVERTISING PRACTICES

The strategies used to get children to buy commercial products involve two main directions: They must know the product name, and they must either be convinced to buy that product with their own money, or get their parents to purchase that product for them (Siegel et al., 2001). In the television area, children are exposed to more adult than children's programs, and hence advertisements are often directed at an age group other than their own. Children, however, recognize the products that are specifically directed at them, and pay more attention to and have more interest in those products (Kunkel, 2001).

With new interactive media, the concept of branding is common and is used to extend the scope of the advertiser (Montgomery, 2001). Branding is a concept designed to foster brand loyalty. Branding can involve a particular media company, a partnership among companies, or companies who create Web sites where the product is the content (Montgomery, 2001). For example, Web sites for children are often set up with favorite television characters traveling to new media. Popular characters can "talk" to children directly in online interactions, potentially making the experience more personal and realistic. This type of company branding can assist advertisers as they move fluidly across multimedia environments to target children. Companies can also loan their rights to license products—that is, their intellectual property—to other companies for a fee, thereby creating strategic alliances and partnerships (Montgomery, 2001; Tarpley, 2001a). For example, television properties like a popular animated character are often licensed to broadcasters for a fee; the broadcaster then puts that program online and also markets toys associated with that character. Or branding can involve specific toy companies who have Web sites designed to sell products to children. Children tend to be loyal customers, preferring one brand and, in dire circumstances, selecting one or two other brands (McNeal, 1998). This pattern makes children an ideal target for branded environments, and for practices that will foster brand recognition and loyalty in the future.

Sites for younger children often have a link for parents to buy products for their youngsters. With parental permission, sites can track individual children's preferences by following their mouse clicks. When Christmas or other special occasions arrive, the site can e-mail parents about what their child may want for a present.

These personal links are potentially a time saver for many busy parents, but they also create a privacy problem where users are always watched.

Web sites are also available for older children and adolescents who can shop by themselves with less parental supervision. Many children already know the sites where they can purchase their favorite products, such as the latest Pokemon character. Credit cards are often available for adolescents and, in the future, "money" will be available online for children and adolescents to use to purchase products. This "money" takes the form of digital wallets, in which parents can set up accounts for their children by putting a certain amount of "money" into a child's account via the parent's credit card (Montgomery, 2001). Icanbuy.com (www.icanbuy.com) and RocketCash.com (www.rocketcash.com) are two such services; the biggest obstacle to their use is parents' refusal to let their children use them (Montgomery, 2001). However, children can accumulate "capital" without their parents' knowledge or participation. For instance, bartering or "selling" information about oneself or one's parents to advertisers is another way to accumulate digital capital and products (Turow, 2001).

Other technologies, such as cell phones (which are already very popular with the adolescent age group), will be used to buy products in lieu of cash. The IBM commercial mentioned at the beginning of this chapter is but one example of how quickly products will be bought with new technologies. This ease of purchase will be accompanied by sophisticated marketing strategies directed at the individual that are based on his or her specific buying patterns. For example, messages can appear on an individual's cell phone targeting products to the owner that that individual will be likely to purchase.

With the advent of digital television (DTV) and the coming of convergence, in which previously distinct media platforms merge together, new opportunities will exist for children and adolescents to move immediately between a television program and a specific Web site where they can purchase a prized product. Viewers will be able to use Web-TV to click directly from the program to the Web site and buy products associated with the program. Emotional reactions created while viewing the program can then be used to cultivate impulsive buying patterns with less opportunity for viewers to reflect about whether the product is really needed or even wanted. For instance, *Dawson's Creek*, a popular adolescent television program, featured an intimate interaction between Dawson and Joey, his former girlfriend, in which he gives her a necklace. On the Web site for the program, visitors can purchase that very same necklace (Montgomery, 2000).

Embedding the advertisement within the program is yet another advertising technique that will become prominent with digital media (Tarpley, 2001a). Increasingly, remote controls allow viewers to skip to other television stations when a program moves to advertising segments. To address this problem, advertisers will increasingly pay to have their product appear within the program boundaries per se (Tarpley, 2001a). Thus, the candy or cereal or toy product will be an actual part of the program, not a separate entity. Products can even be inserted into already existing television programs. This type of approach can blur the line between the program sponsor and the program content, particularly for young children.

One of the most important changes in advertising practices involves the creation of personal relationships between the advertiser and individual children and adolescents, a practice that advertisers are quickly embracing (Calvert, 1999). Interactive environments allow them to do so seamlessly, through tracking devices. These relationships develop when a child or adolescent goes online and is later "remembered," or when e-mail is sent directly to that child about specific products of interest to him or her, based on previous activities and purchases. This technique allows advertisers to target and interact with specific users, rather than a mass audience. These kinds of relational marketing strategies are relatively inexpensive for advertisers and can establish a long-term relationship with potential customers (Montgomery, 2001).

T-technology involves one-click ordering on your television screen for products such as music CDs, other merchandise, travel, and food (Tarpley, 2001b). Although deployment has been slower than expected, t-technology is expected to generate $6 billion dollars in revenue over the next 5 years. Children and adolescents will both be part of this market.

Spam and mousetrapping are two additional techniques that are becoming more common in the online commercial marketplace (Calvert, 2000). Spam involves sending commercial or other kinds of material to users' e-mail addresses. These recipients often do not sign up for this "service"; instead, marketers obtain addresses by purchasing lists of e-mail addresses, sometimes created by using intelligent robots, to gather user e-mail addresses on chat rooms or other sites that are often frequented by adolescents (Calvert, 2000). This practice is particularly problematic when sexually explicit material is sent to minors, as there is no way to know the age of the person who has the e-mail account (Thornburgh & Lin, 2002). That means that the advertiser cannot be held legally accountable for sending sexually explicit material to underage minors.

Mousetrapping is a commercial practice in which the user cannot freely leave a site or a set of associated sites (Thornburgh & Lin, 2002). Each time the user tries to click out of a site, a new window is launched, sending them to another site. In essence, their "mouse" is "trapped." Often, these additional sites pay to have users sent to their sites. Typically, the only way to exit is to turn off the computer and then to start again.

Finally, some businesses use Web site addresses that mislead the user about where they are going online (Thornburgh & Lin, 2002). For example, www.whitehouse.com is a sexually explicit site, whereas www.whitehouse.gov is our nation's capital. Another tactic is to use slight misspellings of common words that take users to the "wrong" site. Children, who have comparatively worse keyboarding and spelling skills than do adults, may be more prone to such errors.

CHILDREN'S SKILLS AT UNDERSTANDING ADVERTISEMENTS

Although there will be increasing amounts of sophistication in directing advertisements to youth in the years ahead, children's processing of the advertiser's intent will remain limited by maturation-based cognitive skills. According to Piaget (1962), children advance through four stages of cognitive development: sensorimotor thought (ages 0 to 2 years, when thought is based in motor actions), preoperational thought (ages 2 to 7 years, when thought is intuitive and the belief in imaginary characters is particularly strong), concrete operational thought (ages 7 to 12 years, when thought is logical but bound to concrete examples), and formal operational thought (after age 12, when hypothetical thinking and abstract reasoning are possible).

Very young children in the sensorimotor and preoperational stages of development have a very limited understanding of what an advertisement is (Calvert, 1999; Wartella & Ettema, 1974). In fact, they often have difficulty discriminating the commercial from the program. Thus, the initial task of children is simply to discriminate the commercial from the program content; that discrimination takes place at about age 4 or 5 (Kunkel & Wilcox, 2001), during the preoperational stage of development. However, even once this fundamental discrimination is made, very young children initially think that commercials are there to give them information to assist them, rather than persuade them, when they buy products (Calvert, 1999).

The future advertising directed at these children will increasingly include animated characters that they view on television and then interact with online. Products will be integrated within the program, and branding will encourage young children to ask for the products of the imaginary characters they watch and interact with daily. Although young children generally know that animated characters are pretend, the line between what is real and what is pretend may become fuzzier when those animated characters interact with them. The increased links between television content and online media content will become a major avenue to target young audiences and build brand loyalty.

Take a child, Timmy, who is age 5. Timmy goes online with his mom. He likes to play games online, and his mom takes him to sites. However, his mom doesn't know too much about online Web sites. She relies on his favorite television characters to provide activities and Web sites for him. Because Timmy really likes cartoons that are broadcast on Cartoon Network, they spend most of their time on that site. Timmy doesn't understand the persuasive nature of advertisements yet. He does know that his favorite action figures can be purchased in the online shopping area of Cartoon Network. Because Timmy likes these products, his mom is responsive to his requests and she buys these toys for him. At age 5, Timmy is already cultivating brand loyalty to Cartoon Network.

By about age 7 or 8, children in concrete operations begin to understand the persuasive intent of commercial advertisements (Wartella & Ettema, 1974). At this age, children realize that advertisers are trying to get them to buy certain products. Even so, viewing repeated advertisements of the same product still causes this age group to request the advertised products (Ross et al., 1984). As children approach the end of concrete operational thought, they begin to understand that many claims made by advertisers are untrue. They remember buying certain products that didn't turn out to be what they had expected. At this point, they become somewhat cynical of advertiser claims (Boush, Friedstad, & Rose, 1994).

Advertisers increasingly refer to this age group as "tweens"—the 8- to 12-year-old preteen group that is on the verge of adolescence (Siegel et al., 2001).

One of the key targets for tweens is to pull them into the markets associated with adolescents. Gender differences are marked. Tween boys are a major market for video game makers who produce games of fast action and violent content. The tween market continues to be a target for branding by broadcasters, who attempt to keep tweens interested in their programs.

Tweens may well select products that will help them be a part of youth culture; their favorite products include food (particularly after-school snacks), music (particularly by young pop stars), fashion (such as Old Navy and Nike), and toys (e.g., Barbie and video games; Siegel et al., 2001). Older tweens are beginning to navigate the Internet without adult supervision, making it easy for advertisers to get them to be interested in selected products. For boys, computer and video games that can move seamlessly between the Internet and the home computing environment become an important avenue for activity, and they will visit sites to purchase new games with the latest bells and whistles. For girls, Barbie dolls and baby dolls are popular to age 10; thereafter, clothing, jewelry, and CDs take priority in their purchasing patterns (Siegel et al., 2001).

Take a tween, Mary, who is age 10. Unlike Timmy, she understands fantasy/reality distinctions and knows what an advertisement is. She still likes to play with Barbie and searches online for Barbie products. If she knows the right sites, she can make a purchase. But if she uses a search engine and puts in the words "Barbie dolls," she could end up with sites listed that contain sexually explicit content. If she goes to chat rooms to talk to other girls about her interests, her e-mail address may be harvested by robots and used to send her spam (Calvert, 2002). Unknown to Mary, every site that she visits is tracked by advertisers. They don't ask her for identifying, personal information, but they know her personal habits as well as the buying habits of other tween girls who, like her, come online.

The advent of formal operational thought allows youth to think abstractly. They can now understand the intent of advertisers, and they develop some cognitive safeguards to protect them from persuasive commercial practices. Even so, the material culture in which U.S. children develop often finds them wanting products that signal belonging to the group, bringing with it status and prestige (Siegel et al., 2001). Moreover, even adults can be tricked by smooth advertising techniques, believing that they can get something for nothing.

Teens are a major target of advertisers. Adolescents are often Internet users and they shop online. Music videos, online games, clothing, and all forms of status can be found and purchased online. Designer clothes are popular with teen girls (Siegel et al., 2001). Online forms of cash or credit card use enable the adolescent to purchase numerous products that can be delivered to their door. That means that products that are illegal for purchase—such as cigarettes, alcohol, and pornography—are potentially accessible to this age group. Spam and mousetrapping become ways for advertisers to influence adolescent purchasing activities.

Take Robert, a 16-year-old teen, who is very familiar with the Internet. Robert often plays video games, moving back and forth from his home console to online games. He also visits sports sites where he sees and then wants the latest in athletic gear. Being cool matters to him, so he purchases the right gear and clothes online. Homework is another way he spends his online time. Robert's parents rarely monitor his online activities because his computer is in his room. Robert sometimes wanders into online areas that arouse his curiosity, such as sexually explicit sites that are illegal for him to visit. He and his friends find ways to get into these sites. Robert and his friends also discover that they can buy tobacco online with his credit card. Online bartenders strike up conversations with Robert and ask him about his buying preferences, thereby creating a portfolio on him to create brand loyalty. Robert gets spammed on a regular basis by advertisers selling their products via his e-mail account. His e-mail account is fake, however, to prevent anyone from tracking him to his personal account. In some ways, he plays the advertiser game better than they do.

INTERVENTION STRATEGIES

Efforts to change children's knowledge of advertiser tactics mainly involve some type of media literacy training. In these educational interventions, children are taught about what the advertiser is trying to do. Some interventions work, but all remain limited by the child's cognitive level, which is associated with his or her age (Calvert, 1999). Put another way, age-based limitations prevent young children from understanding the basic underlying intent of commercials: to get a child to buy a particular product.

Based on the television literature, we can hypothesize that the same age-based limitations will apply in children's attempts to understand online advertisements. That is, children will not understand the persuasive intent of advertisements until age 7 or 8, when they achieve concrete operations. Even when the knowledge about commercial intent is available, the American tweens' and teens' desires to fit into the group may still be sufficient to get them to buy the "right" products. In Siegel et al.'s (2001) study, of tweens who went online the day before, 10% visited a commercial site. We also know that children click on ads more than adults do (Tarpley, 2001a). That means that youth may well be susceptible to online buying practices.

SOCIAL POLICY DIRECTIONS

Because of the cognitive limitations of young viewers, various policy initiatives have attempted to safeguard children from the influences of advertisements. The Federal Communications Commission (FCC) and the Federal Trade Commission (FTC) implement these policies.

The 1974 FCC guidelines to protect children from unfair or deceptive advertising practices included the separation principle, which was designed to help children discriminate the program from the commercial content. The separation principle consisted of three distinct components: host selling (i.e., hosts cannot sell products in segments adjacent to their programs), program-length commercials (i.e., products cannot appear within a program for advertising purposes), and bumpers (i.e., specific production techniques and content must be used to help children separate the commercial from the program content; Huston, Watkins, & Kunkel, 1989).

The separation principle—or, perhaps better said, the lack of the separation principle—is particularly important in understanding advertising in the new online media. Multimedia environments have been created in which popular children's television programs have moved to Web sites, but regulatory practices have not transferred from the television to the Internet arena. In particular, the separation principle is not implemented on the Internet. That means that hosts can sell products to children, there is no division between the commercial and the program content, and products can be integrated into the site in any place. In fact, the entire site can be an advertisement (Montgomery & Pasnik, 1996). Banners that flash advertised messages are common on children's Web sites, and there is no separation from other Web content. Moreover, children can stay on the advertised content for any length of time, a practice that is regulated for television content (Calvert, 1999).

Media convergence create new challenges for advertising practices directed at children. For instance, will a separation principle in television programs make any difference when a child who is watching Web-TV can click directly onto a Web site where those same principles are not required?

In the future, host selling will take on a new form. Intelligent, humanlike characters will be developed to create personal relationships with individual children and adolescents, thereby cultivating familiarity, affection, and trust (Hayes-Roth, 1999; Montgomery, 2001).

The one online area that has received legislative protection is children's right to privacy. In the early days of children's Internet use, advertisers often asked children information about who they were, gathered information about them and their families, and even sold this information to third parties (Allen, 2001). For instance, the superhero character Batman collected information for a city census. As residents and "good citizens" of Gotham City, children were asked to reveal personally identifying information about themselves (Montgomery & Pasnik, 1996).

The Center for Media Education was instrumental in documenting these invasive online advertising practices and in getting Congress to pass the Children's Online Privacy Protection Act (COPPA) in 1998. This law directed the FTC to restrict some of these data-collecting techniques by requiring advertisers to get parental permission before collecting personally identifying information for children age 13 and under. However, marketers now ask children to sign up for newsletters and then send children e-mails on a regular basis, a tactic that is also designed to sell their products (Center for Media Education et al., 1999).

Tracking information is a clear threat to privacy, yet little has yet been done to stop this practice. Cookies—electronic "tracks" of the mouse clicks and sites that individuals visit—were originally developed to provide the computer with a memory to enable online electronic commerce (e-commerce). Instead of having to fill in information every time a customer purchased products from an online site, a cookie allowed that customer to revisit the site and be remembered. Cookies facilitated e-commerce, but quickly became used to track user patterns. The default computer setting is for cookies to be enabled. Users have to turn cookies off and doing so requires some knowledge of how computer menus work. However, many applications won't work or run very slowly unless cookies are enabled. Such cookie-related information could be taught in computer literacy classes.

While people are sitting in the privacy of their homes, cookies now track almost every movement that they make online. Some cookies are rather innocuous. However, some are very invasive and violate privacy. Consider the following comment from an editorial: "Some cookies are fairly simple, saying, in effect, Bill Raspberry has just logged on to this particular Web site for the fourth time. Others are more complicated and a good deal more invasive: This guy is interested in guns, fast cars, and photography, so you might want to tailor your site's screen so that when he visits, he'll be hit with carefully targeted ads" (Raspberry, 2001, p. A15).

CONCLUSION

The new face of interactive media promises new ways of experiencing content, and new ways of being addressed by advertisers. Convergence, multimedia environments, and interactivity will allow personal marketing, personal relationships, and tracking of each child and adolescent's specific preferences and buying patterns. Privacy will be a commodity to be purchased rather than a right and a personal freedom.

The future promises a world of information and products at our children's fingertips. How well our children will use that information depends on how well we teach them to become educated consumers who understand advertising practices. It will also depend on the kinds of policies and laws that our society puts in place to protect children from deception and potential exploitation. Extending COPPA guidelines to older age groups, incorporating media literacy classes into K–12 education, and protecting a user's right to privacy are steps that the government can take to make the media landscape safer for children, tweens, and teens alike.

REFERENCES

Allen, J. C. (2001). The economic structure of the commercial electronic children's media industries. In D. Singer & J. Singer (Eds.), *Handbook of children and the media* (pp. 477–493). Thousand Oaks, CA: Sage.

Boush, D., Friedstad, M., & Rose, G. (1994). Adolescent scepticism toward TV advertising and knowledge of advertiser tactics. *Journal of Consumer Research, 21,* 165–175.

Calvert, S. L. (1999). *Children's journeys through the information age.* Boston: McGraw-Hill.

Calvert, S. L. (2000, August). *Is cyberspace for all girls?* Paper presented at the annual meeting of the American Psychological Association, Washington, DC.

Calvert, S. L. (2002). The social impact of virtual environments technology. In K. M. Stanney (Ed.), *Handbook of virtual environments technology* (pp. 663–680). Hillsdale, NJ: Lawrence Erlbaum Associates.

Center for Media Education, Consumer Federation of America, American Academy of Child and Adolescent Psychiatry, American Academy of Pediatrics, Junkbusters Corporation, national Alliance for Nonviolent Programming, National Association of Elementary Principals, National Consumers League, National Education Association, Privacy Times, and Public Advocacy for Kids. (1999, June). *Children's online privacy protection rule: Comment P994504* [Comments submitted to the Federal Trade Commission]. Washington, DC: Center for Media Education.

Cox, B. (1999, June). Parents deluged with Web buy requests from kids. *Ecommerce.* Retrieved February 10, 2002, from www.internetnews.com

Children's online privacy protection act. S. 2326, 105th Congress, 2nd Session. (1998).

Federal Communications Commission. (1974). Children's television programs: Report and policy statement. *Federal Register, 39,* 39396–39409.

Hayes-Roth, B. (1999, September). Automating one-to-one customer care with smart interactive toys. *Web Techniques,* pp. 59–65.

Huston, A., Watkins, B., & Kunkel, D. (1989). Public policy and children's television. *American Psychologist, 44,* 424–433.

Kunkel, D. (2001). Children and television advertising. In D. Singer & J. Singer (Eds.), *Handbook of children and the media* (pp. 375–393). Thousand Oaks, CA: Sage.

Kunkel, D., & Wilcox, B. (2001). Children and media policy. In D. Singer & J. Singer (Eds). *Handbook of children and the media* (pp. 589–604). Thousand Oaks, CA: Sage.

McNeal, J. (1998). Tapping the three kids' markets. *American Demographics, 20,* 37–41.

Montgomery, K. (2000, June). Presentation in plenary session "The Future of Children," the Annenberg Public Policy Center, Washington, DC.

Montgomery, K. (2001). Digital kids: The new on-line children's consumer culture. In D. Singer & J. Singer (Eds.), *Handbook of children and the media* (pp. 635–650). Thousand Oaks, CA: Sage.

Montgomery, K., & Pasnik, S. (1996). *Web of deception: Threats to children from online marketing.* Washington, DC: Center for Media Education.

Nielsen/NetRatings (2002, July). Nearly 20% of the active online population are kids and teens, creating opportunities for marketers, according to the Nielsen/NetRatings. Retrieved November 19, 2002, from Nielsen-NetRatings.com

Piaget, J. (1962). *Play, dreams, and imitation.* London: Routledge & Kegan Paul.

Raspberry, W. (2001, June 25). Privacy: The horse has left the barn. *The Washington Post,* p. A15.

Ross, R., Campbell, T., Wright, J., Huston, A., Rice, M., & Turk, P. (1984). When celebrities talk, children listen: An experimental analysis of children's responses to TV ads with celebrity endorsement. *Journal of Applied Developmental Psychology, 5,* 185–202.

Russakoff, D. (1999, April 19). Marketers follow youth trends to the bank. *The Washington Post,* p. A1.

Siegel, D., Coffey, T., & Livingston, G. (2001). *The great tween buying machine: Marketing to today's tweens.* Ithaca, NY: Paramount Market Publishing.

Subrahmanyam, K., Greenfield, P., Kraut, R., & Gross, E. (2001). The impact of computer use on children's and adolescents' development. *Journal of Applied Developmental Psychology, 22,* 7–30.

Tarpley, T. (2001a). Children, the Internet, and other new technologies. In D. Singer & J. Singer (Eds.), *Handbook of children and the media* (pp. 547–556). Thousand Oaks, CA: Sage.

Tarpley, T. (2001b, August). *New media technologies and their implications for children.* Paper presented at the annual meeting of the American Psychological Association, San Francisco.

Thornburgh, D., & Lin, H. S. (Eds.) and The Committee to Study Tools and Strategies for Protecting Kids From Pornography and Their Applicability to Other Internet Content. (2002). *Youth, pornography, and the Internet.* Washington, DC: National Academy Press.

Turow, J. (2001). Family boundaries, commercialism, and the Internet: A framework for research. *Journal of Applied Developmental Psychology, 22,* 73–86.

United States Department of Commerce (2002, February). A nation online: How Americans are expanding their use of the Internet. Retrieved November 19, 2002, from http://www.ntia.doc.gov/ntiahome/dn/html/anationonline2.htm

Wartella, E., & Ettema, J. (1974). A cognitive developmental study of children's attention to television commercials. *Communication Research, 1,* 46–69.

Williams, W., Montgomery, K., & Pasnik. S. (1997). *Alcohol and tobacco on the web: New threats to youth.* Washington, DC: Center for Media Education.

PART

V

At Closing Curtain

18

Realities and Challenges in the Rapidly Changing Televisual Media Landscape[1]

Edward L. Palmer
Davidson College

The dizzying pace of change in the televisual media landscape provides stark realities, significant challenges, and notable opportunities for children's growth, education, and socialization. How those realities, challenges, and opportunities will translate into the lives, bedrooms, and futures of young children will depend largely on how revolutionary new technologies are implemented, funded, distributed, and consumed. Tarpley (chap. 2) sketched the daily lives and experiences of two hypothetical families—the Smiths and the Joneses. Although both had the latest televisual technologies at their fingertips, their daily family experiences differed dramatically. The heart of the difference lay in the parental tone, guidelines, and values expressed within the family setting, and this difference—like an intricately woven quilt—permeated their respective households. Carefully monitored, informative use at the Smiths paralleled *laissez-faire,* unlimited use and access at the Joneses: one set of technologies, two families, and a world of difference in the lives and development of consuming children.

This difference points up the critical role of parenting within this televisual media landscape. With an unprecedented explosion in viewing options, video and subscription video on demand, personal video recorders, interactive TV/enhanced TV, interactive program guides, unfiltered Internet access, and new handheld/portable technologies emerging continuously, the media's realities, challenges, and op-

---

[1]Please note that all cites of specific chapters refer to chapters within this volume.

portunities form sharp and compelling contrasts. This chapter examines key aspects of these realities, challenges, and opportunities within each face of children's televisual media, exploring vital issues and implications for the future.

INSTRUCTIONAL/EDUCATIONAL TELEVISUAL MEDIA FACE

Realities

Programming

Availability.   As Crane and Chen (chap. 4) demonstrated in their description of American and European media, there is a broad and diverse range of children's programming available in a vastly expanded array of media platforms. Television and VCRs have been joined by the elaborate buffet of choices cited in the introduction to this section. From the computer to the Internet, CD-ROMs to DVDs, VOD to SVOD, palm pilots to personal video recorders, children quickly learn a technological alphabet that would be foreign for many of their elders.

Content and "Educational" Definition.   In the United States, the so-called "3-hour rule"—committing commercial networks to 3 hours a week of educational programming—has spawned various programming initiatives. The vast majority of these initiatives have been prosocial rather than cognitive in scope and content. In both commercial and public broadcasting spectrums, the net result has been a decrease in cognitive development programming initiatives (Asamen & Berry, chap. 6; Crane & Chen, chap. 4; Lee & Huston, chap. 5).

Underserved Tweens and Teens.   Most program production initiatives have focused on preschoolers. Older children, tweens, and teens have notably fewer program choices than their younger counterparts do (Crane & Chen, chap. 4).

Global Diversity in Structures, Funding, and Access.   The world is, indeed, a very diverse "global village," and within it the differences in public broadcasting systems, their structures, technical sophistication, and political/governing structures are enormously diverse. In a spectrum from the U.K.'s BBC established by Royal Charter and funded through annual television set licensing to Japan's publicly funded national broadcasting service (NHK), one sees the breadth of the range within developed countries. Add to this picture the reality that "public service" becomes a propaganda arm of the ruling regime in many undeveloped or developing nations, and the reality that publicly funded does not equal public service comes center stage. A child born anywhere in the world is not granted the privilege of equal access—or, in many countries, any access—to instructional or educational programming. This era of rapid technological change leaves behind not only the child in a remote village but also the child in the developed country's inner-city ghetto or rural, economically depressed community (Crane & Chen, chap. 4; Moss, chap. 3).

Corporate Change and Commercial Influence

Conglomerates and "Branding."   Where once instructional/educational broadcasting was the province of school systems and educational consortia, these entities have long since faded and given way to corporate conglomerates whose diverse families include network broadcasting, cable, film, and telephone companies. Emerging as significant educational/instructional entities, the cable channel members of these families have become "branded" addresses for children's programming. A child and his or her parents know what programming to expect simply by going to a given channel address. Duplicate and repeat programming is shared with the commercial broadcasting member of the media family, facilitating its ability to meet educational programming requirements without major funding commitments. This "all in the family" arrangement provides economies of production. It also limits or eliminates production opportunities by smaller corporate or startup entities (Crane & Chen, chap. 4).

Instructional/Educational or Commercial?   Conglomerates, branding, and the rise in Internet usage have left public broadcasting entities with funding shortfalls. In order to compete, public broadcasting and entities such as Sesame Workshop have had to seek commercial sponsorships, public/private partnerships, merchandise licensing contracts, and so on, and the child who views these programs produced under such arrangements now sees sponsorship messages that bear curious and striking resemblance to commercials (Crane & Chen, chap. 4; Moss, chap. 3).

Standards for Separation of Conglomerate Entities.   Mergers and creation of conglomerates have run well ahead of any regulatory standards for separating corporate entities. For example, as Crane and Chen (chap. 4) pointed out, there currently is no standard in place to prohibit AOL/Time Warner from featuring a star or stars on their cable channel and, de facto, promoting a forthcoming Warner Brothers movie. One media family member simply happens to lend a hand to another, and the child viewer, along with her or his siblings and primary caretakers, is oblivious to this "family goodwill and cooperation."

Group Perceptions and Role Models

Children's Televisual Worldview.   In developed countries, such as the United States, televisual programming continues a long-standing pattern of stereotypes in gender, ethnic, age, sexual orientation, and disability role depictions. Children see women, ethnic groups, the elderly, gays/lesbians, and those with disabilities in stereotypical roles or—in many instances—not at all. A Native American child, for example, will not find any role model, nor will the "privileged" child see the Native American child depicted. Spawned by producers who themselves have little or no knowledge of cross-cultural and role diversity, the program world becomes largely male dominated, consisting of people with middle- or upper-class socioeconomic status, and generally focused on beauty and youthful appearance. Although these groups are given role diversity and latitude, groups not fitting that mold become stereotyped or invisibly present within the script background (Asamen & Berry, chap. 6; Crane & Chen, chap. 4; Lee & Huston, chap. 5).

Social Interaction and Career Aspiration Role Modeling. Television programming provides the "laboratory" in which young children find tacitly endorsed social interaction and career aspiration role modeling. Young viewers see the "recommended" roles for sibling and friend, parent and child, male and female interaction. Repeated viewing of gender and ethnic associations with given roles creates both general societal expectations as well as personal role placement and level of self-esteem. The absence of a child's own ethnicity within role modeling sends its own message about individual self-respect, self-worth, and "appropriate" career aspiration goals (Asamen & Berry, chap. 6).

Developmental Effects

Factors Influencing Learning and Retention. Both *media platform* and *content* influence children's learning and retention. Educational/instructional television, for example, affects cognitive growth more than social behavior, whereas computer games enhance spatial and iconic skills. Compared with computers, the television and VCR influence prosocial behavior more effectively, and the degree of this influence weighs heavily on adult mediation and the lessons or activities following viewing. Lee and Huston (chap. 5) demonstrated the critical importance of matching media platform to content type and learning goal. Media context becomes an equally important consideration.

Myths of Media Platforms. There is a widespread perception that television is a "lean back" medium whereas the Internet is "lean in"—the former is relaxation, whereas the latter is more intense and engaged (Crane & Chen, chap. 4). Lee and Huston (chap. 5) demonstrate that—like most absolute perceptions and heuristics—this distinction is not nearly as clear-cut as the labels suggest. As Moss (chap. 3) pointed out when quoting Schramm, Lyle, and Parker (1969, p. 61), the critical question becomes not what television does to children, but "what children do with television." This insight from the past promises to serve us well as a guideline in moving forward. Several current media platforms provide opportunity for both "low-road" (more concrete) and "high-road" (more abstract) transfer, and the difference is moderated by elements such as the user approach (knowledge seeking, feature exploring, apathetic) and context such as coviewing or coplaying and adult mediation/involvement with the child (Lee & Huston, chap. 5).

Challenges

Many of the current and future challenges naturally stem from the realities cited. Each of the areas—programming, corporate/commercial influence, perceptions/role models, developmental effects—express issues to be addressed as we seek to educate our children effectively. One of the most basic issues is *programming content and access.* Taken in a global context, making instructional/educational programming equally available to the child in the remote rural village, the economically depressed farm community, and the inner-city ghetto will be an exercise in global commitment (government as well as private/personal). Critical and central to this commitment will be ensuring that content is, in Fisch's (chap. 7) terms, "broadly user-friendly." To "educationally Westernize" a remote village will do little to help these children and, likely, much to harm them. They must be met "where they are," in the culture and context in which they live.

There are several related challenges inherent to content and access. Stemming the receding tide, a *commitment to more cognitive development programming* will be vitally important. This commitment will require major funding initiatives and creative funding arrangements—among them, likely, public and corporate partnerships. A consistent funding source that is insulated from governing political "winds" will be essential to program development and long-range program planning. America—with its tradition of low taxation—has yet to develop this consistent support, but it can be done with minimal commitment on an individual-citizen basis. One could look on this in the parlance of national defense—knowledgeable and inquiring children are an effective defense against ignorance and narrow, parochial perspectives.

Part of this commitment entails a *broad spectrum of diverse role models.* Providing cultural pluralism—as well as a variety of gender, age, sexual orientation, and disability representations—will be important starting points, and the elements among them that may be emotionally charged (e.g., sexual orientation, Islamic characterizations) can be defused by the broad, natural child understanding that would come, over time, with exposure to such programming. Until this breadth and diversity is present among producers themselves, their challenge will be to move beyond convenient stereotypes to a deeper understanding of the diverse people and cultures they portray within their scripts.

Stemming the "digital divide"—both internally and globally—will be a continuing challenge. As wealth—both individual and national—acquires the latest technology, there comes the challenge of cultivating and developing partnership arrangements with the economically and culturally disadvantaged. Once again, it becomes an issue of sensitization and commitment.

Regulating child access to sites and information that are detrimental to them as individuals, to their healthful development, and to general societal welfare becomes a major challenge. Like so many aspects of fast-paced, technological change, the technologies themselves far outpace society's capability to catch up with them in the regulatory realm, and a democratic, open society lends additional complexity to this catch-up mode (see Huesmann & Skoric, chap. 11). At one level, it can be educational for a child to find out from the Internet how to make a bomb. There are scientific principles involved that can be instructive to the young, inquiring mind. At yet another level, the motivation for this educational quest and its knowledge becomes blatantly and—in too many instances—tragically apparent. There need to be safeguards in place that primary caretakers can implement and rely on to ensure that particular sites are not accessible by their children. As well, caretakers themselves need to be sensitized and educated to the effective use of these safeguards. In addition, sites that intentionally set out to confuse the child (e.g., the pornographic site whitehouse.com) need to be flagged and the names regulated.

The influence of conglomerate and corporate institutions has several dimensions and related challenges. Part of the challenge will require *regulatory separation of corporate entities within conglomerates* such that one corporate family member cannot lend a hand to pad the pocket of another. The issue resembles insider trading, and a regulatory separation of these entities is ethically essential to child and societal fairness. Another dimension of this challenge entails *media literacy education* among young children. Although the phrase has become overused, shopworn, and a bit hackneyed, understanding the media techniques through which televisual media seek to influence the child is essential to a child's preparation for wholesome participation in the televisual media environment.

Research Questions

Program Based

There are many exciting and challenging questions for the academic research community, and pursuit of those questions will carry major educational benefits. Crane and Chen's (chap. 4) "kidcentric" research seeks to understand the target audience, how these children think, and what they want and need. Effective instructional/educational program planning requires this "walking with" children approach rather than "programming to" them. Reaffirming a commitment to formative and summative research—what works, what doesn't, and how to effectively change—is equally essential to moving forward.

Technology Based

The design of effective technology platforms for children's learning is closely related to the program-based approach. Just as a handle needs to be shaped to one's natural grip, so too must technologies approach "the natural" in the child's world. Fisch (chap. 7) addressed this question compellingly as he advocated meeting child audience needs from the child's perspective first and foremost, rather than beginning with an existing technology and its limitations. In Fisch's view, the technology needs to be created to fit the child, and where such technological fit does not yet exist, the challenge becomes to create appropriate technology rather than to modify the child's natural behaviors.

Culturally Based

A remarkably similar approach was advocated by Asamen and Berry (chap. 6) in the cultural context. Because many areas of the cultural landscape remain unexplored, Asamen and Berry recognized the pitfalls in formulating research questions and designs that are exclusively quantitative. In their view, one needs to come to a basic level of cultural understanding before quantitative methods can have any meaning or relevance. To gain this level of understanding, one must begin by qualitatively "walking" and absorbing the cultural context and zeitgeist. Within this approach, one maximizes the likelihood of productively addressing questions such as why African American electronic media have not positively influenced African American self-concept, for example. What role the family and the peer environment serve as media filtering agents constitutes another research area that can benefit from creatively blended qualitative and quantitative research approaches.

Cognitively Based

Lee and Huston (chap. 5) point out the disconnect between cognitively effective learning approaches for young children and the predominance of prosocial programming. Although research has shown that the cognitive program format is most effective with young children, the majority of available programming, by contrast, is prosocial. In short, most of what children view—the prosocial and its narrative format—ranks among the least effective programming for their age group. Because cognitive programming requires extensive planning and resources, producers opt for the less rigorous, less strenuous route. As a result, the opportunity to foster children's cognitive growth through well-designed, creative programming is largely lost. To match effective programming type to the needs and readiness of children is a challenge and commitment that, for the most part, still remains ahead of us.

Other relevant cognitively based questions pertain to the role of cooperation, coplay, and interaction in learning effectiveness. There are early research signs that these elements in the computer and gaming contexts, for example, facilitate cognitive learning. Such questions—examined across the new technologies spectrum—will become especially timely.

ENTERTAINMENT TELEVISUAL MEDIA FACE

Realities

Program Content and Child Preference

Many of the realities that we have described as part of the instructional/educational face are equally prevalent within the entertainment face. With technology rapidly changing, Scharrer and Comstock (chap. 9) noted ironically how little has changed programmatically since the 1950s. The staple diet of program content and plot continues to be the consumption and juxtaposition of good and evil. Again, as in educational programming, White middle- and upper-class males predominate, and stereotypical depictions are the norm in the realms of gender, ethnicity, age, disability, and sexual orientation. Violent content continues to be popular with children of all ages, and the explosion in media platforms has magnified these available choices.

With Internet, cable, TV, and video widely wired to American children's bedrooms, they have easy and ready access to this content cornucopia. A steady stream of fantasy-violence and human-violence video games stock retail shelves to meet children's—most notably male children's—preferences. Long-standing program preference patterns continue, with young children opting for cartoons and animation and older children choosing sitcoms and action adventure.

A curious thematic paradox pervades programming. Family and family values are focused on and idealized, whereas unprotected, nonmarital sexual intimacy without risk or responsibility is prominently depicted. The most dominant theme in MTV casts women as sex objects and targets or victims of sexual aggression. Violence and aggression are plot staples (Huesmann & Skoric, chap. 11), and alcohol consumption is frequently depicted as a fun-loving, social activity (Scharrer & Comstock, chap. 9).

Child-Based Effects

Because children's emotions are immediate, amplified, and unfiltered by life experience, the likelihood of negative, detrimental effects runs high. Placed in the context of Van Evra's model, Bryant and Bryant (chap. 10) viewed the nature of these effects as being heavily dependent on the program input (e.g., content and formal features), mediating variables (e.g., cognitive maturity, context, and purpose of viewing), and the viewing activity itself (e.g., how much perceived realism and cognitive processing are involved). Concern about deleterious effects relates to areas such as stereotyping, fear and fright reactions, unhealthy sexual attitudes and behaviors, and socialization within a violent media world. In the words of Bryant and Bryant (chap. 10), "Children's televisual world is a very violent place." Our children go there often.

Huesmann and Skoric (chap. 11) demonstrated that the children who go there (i.e., the violent place of the televisual world) most often are the children most negatively affected, but the prevalent early assumptions that only those children predisposed to aggression were affected have now been empirically dispelled. Viewing media violence affects *all* children, and longitudinal research confirms the carry-through from early viewing to later behavior patterns. This 50-year body of research, including hundreds of empirical studies, has shown both the relationship between—and the cause-effect linkage of—children's viewing of media violence and their subsequent aggressive behavior. As televisual participants, children clearly are highly vulnerable and much more affected than adult viewers are (Huesmann & Skoric, chap. 11).

Entertainment and education have long been partners in programming, and young children are very familiar with the blend. In televisual media contexts, the entertainment aspect becomes a necessity with children, especially preschoolers, and shows such as *Sesame Street* owe part of their long-standing success and effectiveness to the delicate interweaving of formative and summative research, mutual respect, and independence among academicians/researchers and the creativity of writers/producers. Within this entertainment milieu, Bryant and Bryant (chap. 10) found fertile ground for communicating prosocial lessons such as generosity, talking through conflicts, and letting children's imagination flow. As we have seen within a variety of author contexts, these lessons are notably enhanced through adult coviewing.

Remembering again the underscored importance of "what children do with TV" (Schramm et al., 1961, as quoted in Moss, chap. 3), Bryant and Bryant (chap. 10) identified specific uses and gratifications that have beneficial effects. Televisual media use can reduce anxiety, provide opportunities for play, enable a person to escape unpleasant life experiences, and provide a pseudo-intimate social relationship with a media personality (e.g., "Mister Rogers says I'm special"). One can debate the therapeutic implications of thinking a media personality relates to and knows you personally, but the intimacy presumption is there with young children, and offers an oasis for some in a solitary or unpleasant milieu. In this era of changing family demographics, televisual media may have become pseudo-caregiving as well. Children also use televisual media for mood management—to provide comfort or to avoid discomfort (Bryant & Bryant, chap. 10; Vorderer & Ritterfeld, chap. 12). Given the prevalence of violent program content, the challenge to beneficial effects is a formidable one, but the potential and the opportunity exist to address that challenge.

Desire to Be Entertained

Vorderer and Ritterfeld (chap. 12) reminded us that a desire to learn is not our primal human motivation. A child wishes to be entertained, and producers and advertisers are quick to accommodate. Seeking to entertain as broadly as possible in a mass-audience context, producers extend the age range downward for a given program. A program perhaps initially produced and directed to tweens will now be broadened to include preschoolers and, in some instances, even toddlers in its audience. This creates what Vorderer and Ritterfeld termed "the continuous flow of fit and nonfit moments." It is this realm of downward-extended nonfits that can prove harmful to a child's well-being.

Nonfit comes in contexts such as watching, with older children or grownups, a program the child has not selected. Although the two viewers come to the same program, they come with very different cognitive-processing abilities and they see and experience things very differently. There is also the seductive appeal of electing to watch a nonfit program to prove one's "grownup" prowess to peers—an appeal that all too often leaves the child with a residue of fear and fright that can maintain a long-standing legacy.

Up to a point, children match adult preferences in entertainment programming. Both are attracted by action, entering the media reality, and repetitive behaviors (as in play). The child, like the adult, identifies with the hero or heroine and dislikes the villain. Child entertainment preferences branch off from the adult's in formal feature contexts, such as blends of music and narrative, special effects, and animation. These differences in preference readily surface in interactive entertainment venues.

For the televisual experience to be entertaining (i.e., pleasurable), the child must feel both self-efficacy and control of his or her immediate environment. One can pleasurably take on excitement from a secure personal/environmental base. Becoming detached from the secure moorings of such a base brings the specter of being overwhelmed.

Challenges and Research Questions

A Will to Respond

As Huesmann and Skoric (chap. 11) analyzed key aspects of the televisual violence history and policymaking, several glaring realities quickly surfaced. In the face of compelling effects-related research evidence, the landscape of violence available to children has not diminished on television and can now be found in many new televisual contexts. The evidence of effects is, and has been, in place for quite some time. From congressional subcommittees in the 1950s to the Surgeon General's Report in 1972, the 10-Year Follow-Up Report in 1982, and a continuing growth of empirical data, the effects of violent televisual media upon children have been known (Murray, Rubinstein, & Comstock, 1972; Pearl, Bouthilet, & Lazer, 1982). Thirty years ago, the Surgeon General found the data sufficient to justify action. Thirty years later, the profitability of televisual violence, its global marketability, and First Amendment arguments leave the landscape little changed. Huesmann and Skoric (chap. 11) viewed concerted will and effort on the part of all constituencies—parents, lawmakers, educators, writers, producers, and sponsors—as critical to productive change.

Noninteractive/Interactive

As the noninteractive meets the interactive within burgeoning new technology platforms, the range of exciting challenges and research questions mushrooms dramatically. What researchers know meets head on with what still is to be learned and discovered. Within the noninteractive, for example, successes and failures were "out there" among the program characters, with the child being solely an observer. The interactive, by contrast, places success and failure squarely in the hands of the child participant. What impact this has on the child's televisual experience, sense of self-efficacy, and self-worth remains an open question.

Time Investment and Learning Enhancement

Vorderer and Ritterfeld (chap. 12) noted the long-standing, educator-based assumption that children's involvement in televisual entertainment constituted a general waste of time and replaced activities that would be more productive and beneficial. Although admitting that the question remains open, Vorderer and Ritterfeld suggested that this investment of televisual entertainment time may prove to be enhancing to learning. Lee and Huston (chap. 5) found resonance with this view, and pointed out the various cognitive effect elements to be examined in the interactive televisual media context. Acknowledging that the prevalence of violent programming is no meager or insignificant challenge to prospects for enhancement, one can hope—along with Bryant and Bryant (chap. 10)—that "the best is yet to come."

ADVERTISING/SELLING TELEVISUAL MEDIA FACE

Realities

Ad Issue History and Societal Concerns

As early as 1931, Felix observed that "Advertising will be ready for the visual medium long before the visual medium is ready for advertising" (as quoted in Adler, 1980, p. 238). His comment was based on the knowledge that American television had been born, raised, and nurtured in a capitalistic society that had fine-tuned commercial radio broadcasting and promised to pursue young television as well. When American commercial television producers discovered children as a market, making advertising suitable and appropriate for the medium and devising marketing strategies emerged rapidly and comprehensively. Ad approaches encompassed all the formal features mentioned earlier as appealing to children. With appeals to happiness, fun, and popularity among one's peers, advertising quickly socialized children into the commercial ways of capitalism, materialism, and the marketplace.

Johnson and Young (chap. 13) highlighted many of the issues that accompanied child-targeted advertising, and the bumpy road of lurches and twists that greeted societal concerns along the way. If a young child could not cognitively discriminate programs from commercials, vulnerability was a given and grassroots efforts sought to make broadcasters ethically accountable and morally responsible. Encountering major industry lobbies who financially supported both Congress and U.S. presidents, the American situation has had a kid versus giant feel to it. Any steps in the interests of children would not be simple or easy … if, indeed, they were even possible. As Johnson and Young (chap. 13) documented that long road, they took us through issues and questions of whether children have been, can be, or will be considered a special audience that requires special attention and regulatory consideration. However, different constituencies have put different spins on that potential "yes," "perhaps," or "no," and the negative adherents have never wanted to appear disinterested or hurtful to children. The issues and initiatives gamut has run all the way from recommending banning advertising to young children to having youngsters run free in the open marketplace. Midrange initiatives have included requiring program/commercial separation, audio and visual ad disclaimers, banning host selling, targeting specific product types, prosocial/health-informative counterads, and the like.

The issue history has been one of going two steps forward, then taking one step back—sometimes taking two or perhaps more steps back. As part of the general, American political milieu, any progress has depended—and continues to depend—heavily on the political agenda of the party in power, the concerted reach and stridency of grassroots voices, and whether it appears politically beneficial to Congressional representatives or the president to listen and respond. Unlike a British system, for example, with more built-in governmental stability, the American system's prevailing winds readily can change in 2- or 4-year cycles. Money matters generally govern, profits generally prevail, and regulatory measures are generally voluntary. Indeed, it would be headline news if a major commercial broadcast station's license had not been renewed by the FCC because of noncompliance with children's advertising guidelines. It simply does not happen. Johnson and Young (chap. 13) recounted the many facets of this landscape: its issues, its challenges, and its intermittent small-step victories. Given the forces and the milieu, the presence of small-step victories such as the Children's Television Act of 1990 becomes enormously significant.

Ad Content and Children's Exposure

The late Senator Everett Dirksen made the well-known quote (paraphrased here) that "With a billion here and a billion there, pretty soon we're talking about real money." The children's market, which now generates revenues in the $24 billion range, has entered that "real money" realm; with children influencing $190 billion in family purchases, the realm has become all the more real and enticing. American children's annual exposure to commercials has tripled since 1970, and even the 1970 level formed the equivalent of watching nonstop commercials from 8 A.M. till 12 midnight continuously for 6 months. If one ever doubted that U.S. children comprised a commercial market, that doubt has long since evaporated. Kunkel and McIlrath (chap. 14) estimated that 25% of a U.S. child's television viewing hour is devoted to persuasive messages, with roughly 17% of that time being product commercials and the remainder being program promotions (often for adult programming) and public service announcements.

What children see in product commercials has remained relatively constant across the past 30 years—toys, cereals, candies, and fast-food restaurants. Toy commercials dominate in the Christmas season, whereas cereal and candy ads gain prominence throughout the rest of the year. Most of the advertised cereals are heavily sugared—some more than 50% sugar by weight—and candies, snacks, cookies, and sodas join the heavily sweetened lineup. This cadre of empty-calorie food products advertised to children has raised major health concerns among different constituencies, ranging from the Surgeon General to parents, educators, and professional organizations such as the American Academy of Pediatrics. Johnson and Young (chap. 13) outlined this series of product-related health concerns in detail.

Children's commercials constitute a veritable seminar or workshop on how to attract the attention of youthful eyeballs. From musical jingles to bright colors, animated star characters, fantasy, magic, zooms, closeups, and the like, a young child's attention is virtually ensured. Fun, happiness, and peer popularity are promised with product purchase; basic price, quality, or nutritional information is minimized or kept securely out of sight.

Disclosures and disclaimers are aired so momentarily that even an adult cued to watch and listen for them is unlikely to catch them. Any children who successfully see or hear are unlikely to understand these disclosures and disclaimers, because phrases like "partial assembly required" or "items sold separately" reach beyond their comprehension level.

Gender, Ethnicity, and Stereotyping

Unlike children's programming, the gender frequency of ad characters appears to be reaching equality. Gender appeals, however, differ: Boys' ads often feature high levels of action/aggression, whereas girls' ads are generally tranquil and passive. This difference extends a gender stereotype that has been prevalent throughout children's ad history. From the 1970s, when only one in four ads featured a non-Caucasian character, total ethnic character representation has gained in frequency, although ethnic minority roles within ads continue to be predominantly token (Kunkel & McIlrath, chap. 14).

Content-Related Policies

The terms *voluntary, network- or station-specific,* and *good faith* generally summarize industry's approach to children's ad content regulation. As with programming, there has never been an industry-based general policy implemented that applied uniformly to all children's advertising across all commercial networks, and when it appeared that the federal government was going to step in with a heavy hand, networks routinely sought to ward off regulation with measures such as the prosocial snippets and drop-ins that were created in the 1970s. Kunkel and McIlrath (chap. 14) outlined in detail the policies of the FCC relating to children's advertising, and one finds within their chapter the translation nuances that tend to occur between policy and practice. When host selling was banned, for example, program-length commercials emerged, as did commercials designed to look like PSAs. Although some products—such as alcohol, cigarettes, and vitamin pills—cannot be advertised during children's programming, a child's general ability to discriminate, to comprehend, and to understand is significantly challenged by ads for other adult products that can and do air during children's programs.

Content-Related Issues

Recent issues relate to where U.S. children's advertising should be permitted to go. Should it, like Mary's little lamb, "follow her to school one day"? It already has, and in many diverse venues, from athletic scoreboards to corporate-sponsored educational materials, from school-systemwide cola contracts to Channel One, from textbook covers to product samples, from hallways to lunchrooms, from school buses to computer labs. Many financially strapped school systems welcome these initiatives as ways to help cover their costs of operation. The overall effect of these diverse commercial entries on the education, health, and values of America's children remains an open question (Kunkel & McIlrath, chap. 14).

Effects

Ad Identification and Comprehension.   Smith and Atkin (chap. 15) provided an in-depth analysis of research relating to a child's ability to distinguish programs from commercials and the subsequent step of understanding persuasive intent. They concluded that 4- to 5-year-olds generally have discrimination ability, whereas persuasive-intent understanding comes in the 7- to 8-year-old time frame. As children understand intent, they develop mistrust and dislike for ads. Ad disclaimers require, at minimum, simple language and further research into audio/video effects and the roles of context and experience.

Intended.   Ad intent to create *brand recall* and *recognition* works well with children … very well, in fact. Even a 3-year-old can match brands to logos well above chance. Not surprisingly, recall and recognition increase with age, and are positively correlated with variables such as repetition and association. Ads prove equally effective in creating *product desire* and *purchase requests*. Research also correlates ad viewing with product category and specific brand *consumption*. *Persuasive appeals* such as *premium offers* rely heavily on variables such as premium type, product type, and target audience for their level of effectiveness. As well, celebrity endorsers have strong impact on children's desire for a product.

Unintended.   Children's purchase requests lead to *parent–child conflict*. Although the conflict itself may have been unintended on the part of the advertiser, the purchase request surely was intended and places parents in a very difficult position. Children who view ads also may perceive the setting of children's ads to be better than their own, resulting in unhappiness. Not surprisingly, the child whose purchase request is refused by the parent will be unhappy as well. Children's eating habits correlate closely with the extensiveness of their ad viewing. When sodas replace milk in children's diets and candy and highly sugared cereals are seen as nutritious, there is a problem. The implications of this problem are far reaching. More difficult is the question of whether ads cultivate *materialistic ideals* among viewing children. Correlational data suggest linkage, but these data, by definition, do not indicate directionality. Further experimental evidence will be needed to clarify the existence and nature of this effect. *Self-perception* effects are most pronounced among adolescent females, who are surrounded by media images of ideal beauty and thinness. The unattainable ideal torpedoes these girls' self-perception.
   One of the most prominent effects relates to America's legal drug—alcohol. Young viewers—as early as 10th grade—find both alcohol ads and their fun, sociability, gender, and adventure themes very appealing. Combined with distiller products such as "alcopops" targeting entry-level drinkers, these ad appeals are especially effective. Smith and Atkin (chap. 15) pointed out that parental mediation/discussion, prosocial alcohol ads, and critical viewing curricula can have an important moderating effect.

Issues/Politics

Young (chap. 16) introduced us to a wide range of central issues and questions. As he "shook the mix," so to speak, he forced us to think about global issues pertaining to advertising and our children. Noting that they are, indeed, *our* children and the decision of how best to raise and care for them is ours, we are not let "off the hook."

The explosion of media platforms and choices and their heavy presence in U.K. and U.S. homes and bedrooms have fostered newly acquired cyber skills while fanning anxieties about uses and effects. Young (chap. 16) found the roots of these anxieties in three broad categories: basic assumptions about advertising, marketing, and the nature of children; the technologies that carry these ads and marketing messages; and the context in which children access these messages.

Assumptions About Advertising, Marketing, and Children

Advertising and Marketing. Whether one perceives youngsters as "children" or as "kids," one must understand that these are two distinctly different images. Whereas *children* are perceived as potential victims of advertising and marketing, who therefore need protection, *kids* are perceived as streetwise, savvy, and quite ready for the ad-filled marketplace. With ads blending the factual, the rhetorical, and the promotional, there inevitably are ingredients in the ad formula for which young children are unprepared. Languagewise, however, we "kid" ourselves with that very term.

Technologies Carrying Ad Messages to Youngsters. The televisual media—once hailed as windows on the world, promoting family togetherness and tranquility—have now become threatening windows, promising family anxiety and strife. These promises look even more anxiety provoking when one considers the hundreds of channels available alongside cable, satellite, and the Internet, together with rapidly emerging technologies and in-school marketing.

Context in Which Children Access Televisual Messages. Quoting Durkeim and Belk, Young (chap. 16) observed that the once sacred has become secularized, and the once secular has become sacred. The newly sacred include shopping malls and department stores. Children access the messages of this newly sacred within their once-sacrosanct homes and schools. Citing extensive cross-cultural research, Young observed a convergence at age 8 as the time when children have an understanding of persuasive intent. He further noted that full information-processing and perspective-taking capacities do not emerge until age 12. The timeline for these capacities varies across cultures and ethnicities, depending in part on level of experience with televisual media. Young advocated adopting the cognitive-development paradigm of John as a meaningful extension of Piaget's earlier work, and he noted that a cognitively based decision on advertising to children would warrant protecting them up to age 12. Although he left the final decision door ajar a bit, it seems clear that Young took the perspective of viewing our young as children more so than as kids.

Future Perspectives

Calvert (chap. 17) provided both a vivid and a sobering view of the future of children's ads. Her approach to this future examined children as a market, past and emerging ad practices, cognitive skills that children bring to televisual media, and policy issues and practices.

Children as a Market and Ad Practices

Land of Market Opportunity.   With children, tweens, and teens spending $1.3 billion a year online, and their given receptivity to branding and brand loyalty, the world of commerce is quite willing to target and creatively market to this group. The combination of new and emerging televisual media provide fertile ground for marketing creativity. Where once one conceived of children's televisual advertising as being the ads broadcast during program breaks, that conception now literally has gone far "out of the box." Children now can have digital wallets (i.e., credit cards), be marketed to on their cell phones, and can click on a mouse to purchase a product that they've glimpsed within one of their favorite programs. These are but the tip of the "beyond." Relational cyber marketing will "remember" unique aspects of an individual child (via tracking and purchase patterns), and advertisers will develop a personal marketing relationship with such children. Ads will be embedded in programs to avoid the potential for ad zapping, and children will be up to their necks in a land of t-technology, cookies, spam, mouse trapping, and other cyber terms and practices. It's quite likely that children will travel smoothly through this brave new world, but whether they will be prepared to process it will be quite another matter.

Cognitive Skills and Regulatory Challenges

Although ad techniques are creatively blending with programming and platforms in new televisual media, children's cognitive skill levels have not and cannot keep pace. Their cognitive levels of understanding are relatively stable. One cannot rush the 5- or 6-year-old child into understanding persuasive intent or taking another individual's perspective. Meanwhile, the ad and marketing techniques are tracking these children and invading their daily cognitive worlds. Regulatory measures that, at their best, have had fits and starts in the television ad spectrum are totally useless in this new landscape where hosts can sell, ads can be embedded in programs, products can be integrated into any Web site anywhere, and program idols can model something that the child can immediately access and purchase. If a child, through tracking, receives a porn-site promotion, the vendor can say they didn't know the recipient was a child. All these aspects of the new landscape pose formidable—if not insurmountable—challenges for families and regulators. These challenges will sorely test both our political and technological will.

A Question of Privacy

The title of this heading is itself a bit of a misnomer, because we no longer have privacy. Slowly at first and, in the new landscape, now quite rapidly, it has eroded. How much the marketing world knows about us and our children is not an open question. Clearly, the information that the marketing world has already accumulated is enormous, and the sites in which it is stored and shared are equally vast; but, for our children in the new televisual landscape, this reservoir of data is growing rapidly. Is it a price we pay for technological "progress"? Is it a price we are willing to pay on behalf of our children? Calvert (chap. 17) concluded that within the future landscape, privacy will be a commodity to be purchased rather than a right or a freedom. The implications for us and for our children are, indeed, far reaching.

CONCLUDING THOUGHTS

All of the three faces of televisual media described in this book have enormous potential, but pose formidable challenges. In order to fully tap their potential, one must address these challenges. The picture that has emerged provides an ironic study in contrasts. Technologically, we have progressed and continue to progress at breakneck speed. At the same time, we have inherited the unresolved problems of our televisual past. The digital divide between the haves and the have-nots is still there. Stereotyping and flawed and faulty ethnic representations fill our media. There still seems to be an insatiable appetite for televisual violence, and marketers sell to our children without the children being able to fully understand and defend against these messages. For too long we have repeated the mantra that although other people's children might be affected by the content of this media flood, our children would be all right. We all need to turn our attention and our efforts to resolving these issues, for the sake of our children and their future. In the words of Huesmann and Skoric at the conclusion of their chapter: "The future of our children and society is too precious for us not to act."

REFERENCES

Adler, R. P. (1980). Children's television advertising: History of the issue. In E. L. Palmer & A. Dorr (Eds.), *Children and the faces of television: Teaching, violence, selling.* New York: Academic Press.

Murray, J. P., Rubinstein, E. A., & Comstock, G. A. (Eds.). (1972). *Television and social behavior, reports and papers.* Washington, DC: U.S. Government Printing Office.

Pearl, D., Bouthilet, L., & Lazar, J. (Eds.). (1982). *Television and behavior: Ten years of scientific progress and implications for the eighties.* Washington, DC: U.S. Government Printing Office.

Schramm, W. L., Lyle, J., & Parker, E. B. (1961). *Television in the lives of our children.* Stanford, CA: Stanford University Press.

Author Index

A

Abramsky, S., 166, *188*
Achenreiner, G. B., 274, *281*
Acsione, F. R., 100, *103*
Acuff, D. S., 336, *345*
Adams, M. S., 220, *239*
Adler, R. P., 173, *186*, 266, 267, 268, 269, 270, *281*,
     288, *298*, *323*, 371, *377*
Aitken, P. P., 277, *281*
Albiniak, P., 28, 39
Al-Deen, H, S, N., 168, *186*
Alexander, A., 56, *80*, 273, *285*, 288, *298*
Alexander, K. J., 131, *138*
Allen, J. C., 355, *356*
Allen, M., 166, *189*, 205, *215*
Allen, R. L., 111, 112, 119, *121*
Allred, E., 179, *187*
Andersen, R. E., 203, *214*
Anderson, B., 224, *237*
Anderson, C. A., 176, *186*, 220, 229, *237*, *238*
Anderson, D. R., 85, 90, 100, 101, *102*, *103*, 125,
     132, *137*, 168, *186*, *191*, 201, 212, *213*,
     214, 251, *257*
Anderson, J. A., 113, 118, *121*, *123*,
Anderson, J. D., 231, *238*
Andison, F. S., 220, *237*
Appleton, H., 92, *103*
Arend, R. A., *213*, *216*
Armstrong, G. M., 272, *282*
Asamen, J. K., 109, 110, 111, 120, *121*, *122*
Ascione, F. R., 100, *103*
Ashburn, L., 220, *239*
Atherton, M., 335, *345*
Atkin, C. K,146, *156*, *158*, 176, 180, *188*, 212, *215*,
     220, *239*, 291, 292, 293, 294, *298*, 305,
     308,309, 310, 311, 312, 313, 314, 316,
     318, 319, *320*, *321*, *324*
Atkin, D., 169, 170, *186*
Aust, C. F., 207, *217*
Austin, E. W., 172, *186*, 201, *213*, 319, *320*, *321*,
Austin, M. J., 278, 279, 280, *281*, *282*
Axelson, J. A., 110, *121*

B

Bachman, J. G., 146, *159*
Bacue, A., 165, 167, *192*, 205, *217*
Baggaley, J., 46, *54*
Bajpai, S., 332, *346*
Baker, R. K., 145, *156*, 226, *238*
Baldwin, T. F., 183, *186*
Ball, S. J., 92, 93, 101, *103*, 145, *156*, 226, *238*
Bandura, A., 11, *25*, 115, *121*, 144, 149, 153, *156*,
     165, 173, *186*, 205, 210, *213*, 220, 221,
     225, *238*, 245, 256, *257*, 306, 312, *321*
Banks, J. A., 118, *121*
Baptista-Fernandez, P., 169, 170, *188*
Baratz, D., 303, *323*
Barcus, F. E., 170, *186*, 205, *213*, 289, 290, 291, 292,
     294, *298*
Barner, M. B., 166, *186*
Baron, R. A., 149, *157*, *158*
Barr, R., 287, *298*
Barry, A. M., 274, *282*
Barry, T., 308, *321*
Bartlett, S. J., 203, *214*
Bartsch, R. A., 166, *186*
Baruth, L. G., 109, *121*
Barwise, T. P., 162, *186*
Bauer, R. A., 273, *282*
Baxter, R. L., 181, *186*
Beauvais, F., 319, *320*, *324*
Becker, H. J., *54*
Beentjes, J. W. J., 89, *103*, 203, *213*, 242, 243, 244,
     258
Belk, R. W., 335, 336, *345*,
Bell, R., 276, *282*
Bellamy, R. V., Jr., 242, 245, 254, *262*
Belson, W., 147, 148, *156*, 220, *238*
Bence, P. J., 271, *282*, 288, 289, 290, 291, *298*
Benjamin, L., 288, *298*
Bente, G., 247, *258*
Berg, C., 169, *186*
Bergemann, L., 305, 307, *323*
Berger, A. A., 339, *345*
Berger, S., 115, *121*

379

N

O

389

Subject Index